A PRACTICAL GUIDE TO
CORPORATE GOVERNANCE

A PRACTICAL GUIDE TO CORPORATE GOVERNANCE

Fourth edition

RICHARD SMERDON

SWEET & MAXWELL  **THOMSON REUTERS**

First edition 1998
Second edition 2004

Published in 2010 by Thomson Reuters (Legal) Limited
(Registered in England & Wales, Company No 1679046.
Registered Office and address for service:
100 Avenue Road, London, NW3 3PF) trading as
Sweet & Maxwell

For further information on our products and services, visit
www.sweetandmaxwell.co.uk

Typeset by Servis Filmsetting Ltd, Stockport, Cheshire
Printed and bound in Great Britain by CPI Anthony Rowe, Chippenham
and Eastbourne

No natural forests were destroyed to make this product;
only farmed timber was used and replanted

A CIP catalogue record for this book is available from the British Library

ISBN 978-0-414-04238-4

I dedicate this book to the All Party Parliamentary Corporate Governance Group and to the Genesis Initiative

Contents

Chapter 3
The Board and its Structure
Richard Smerdon

Chapter 4
Directors: Part 1—Duties and Liabilities with special reference to the Companies Act 2006
Richard Smerdon

Contents

Chapter 5
Directors: Part 2—The Non-Executive Director
Richard Smerdon

Chapter 6
Voices from the Boardroom
Dr Sharon Studer

Chapter 7
Board Evaluations
Dr David Ladipo

Chapter 8
The Chairman
Richard Smerdon

Chapter 9
The Company Secretary
Richard Smerdon

Contents

Chapter 20
Corporate Social Responsibility
Richard Smerdon

Chapter 21
Pension Funds
Paul Lee

Contents

Contents

Preface

As in previous editions, this book attempts to describe the current governance landscape in relation to UK "Premium" listed companies in straightforward and (save for some passages in this Preface) non-polemic terms. It is intended to be a reference work to help practitioners such as listed company secretaries, fund managers, lawyers, auditors and non-executive directors find the immediate answers to governance questions—even if more detailed work and advice is then required to produce a fuller answer. Even though the work deals almost entirely with listed companies, it is clear that the 2010 UK Corporate Governance Code, referred to in detail in this book, is an excellent "benchmark" of best practice which private companies and public bodies can use with advantage to work out their own governance regimes as seems best for them.

The first edition of this book published in 1998 was intended to reflect the just published Hampel Report on corporate governance and the newly designed Combined Code. That report and the Combined Code were built on the platform established by the magisterial 1992 Cadbury Report and Code on the financial aspects of corporate governance which itself was a response to the financial scandals in the early 1990s, such as Polly Peck and Maxwell.

The second edition published in 2004 reflected the Higgs Review on the role and effectiveness of non-executive directors, the Turnbull Guidance on internal control and the Smith Guidance for audit committees, and a new Combined Code on Corporate Governance, all of which was a response to the concerns arising out of the collapses of Enron and Worldcom in the United States and Marconi in the UK.

The third edition published in 2007 reflected primarily the passing of the Companies Act 2006 which, amongst a vast number of other provisions, codified, as well as introducing some new, directors' duties; codified and developed the law on derivative shareholder actions, and brought the internet firmly into the operation of shareholder communication.

This edition follows previous precedent as a response to major upheavals and the reactions of regulators: namely, the banking crises of 2007/2009 and the reactions of the Treasury, the Financial Services Authority and the Financial Reporting Council.

Depressingly, the governance features of the banking crisis repeated all the characteristics of earlier crises (i.e. arrogant, over-paid senior executives and ineffectual chairmen and non-executives) albeit this time in the financial sector—the non-financial sector seemingly having "got it" in relation to governance.

In the case of the Treasury the response was the "Walker" Review of corporate governance in UK banks and other financial industry entities, written by Sir David Walker, the final report of which was published in November 2009. Apart from anything else, the Review deserves to be read as an example, like the Cadbury Report itself, of beautifully written prose. Sir David made an urgent plea for boards and especially chairmen to concentrate more on the behavioural aspects of the conduct of boards, less "group think" and process, and more debate and challenge.

In the case of the FSA the "governance" response was the Consultation Paper 10/3 published in January 2010 and entitled *"Effective corporate governance"*. The FSA proposed changes in what it terms "significant influence controlled functions" and also outlined the future monitoring and enforcement measures it intended to take in order to support many of the Walker recommendations. As this book goes to press the final Policy Statement has not yet been published by the FSA.

In the case of the FRC the reaction is the 2010 UK Corporate Governance Code, formerly known as the Combined Code and published in June 2010, and the Stewardship Code (itself a recommendation of Walker) published in July 2010. In addition, the FRC has commissioned a review of the "Turnbull Guidance" on internal control, to be completed at some point in 2011, and a review by ICSA of the outstanding 2003 Review of the role and effectiveness of non-executive directors written by the late Sir Derek Higgs, expected later in 2010 but after this book has gone to press.

The FRC's UK Corporate Governance Code reflects both a long review and consultation during 2009 and also those aspects of the Walker Review recommendations not taken up by the FSA. Notably, new principles and provisions give more prominence to boardroom behaviour as urged by Walker, namely, the job of the chairman in creating the conditions for open debate and challenge and the role of non-executive directors in "challenging" the executive team and making the board as a whole responsible for defining the risk appetite of the company.

The Code also makes the board as a whole responsible for explaining in the annual report "the business model" of the company. This reflects a corresponding recommendation by Walker in an attempt to wrest some sense of listed corporate strategic direction and aspiration out of the nonsenses created by the accounting bodies both national and international, in conspiracy to some extent with CFOs, which have resulted in those exercises in encyclopaedic opacity known as "the report and accounts".

The new Code also requires all directors of FTSE 350 companies to offer themselves for re-election at each annual meeting. Early indications are that several prominent institutions are against this provision and will be supportive of reasoned explanations for non-compliance.

The new Code also requires, for the first time, that appointments to the board must be open as regards diversity and gender. It is a particular scandal in UK governance that still so few women are on FTSE 350 boards; and since the coalition Government has ruled out quotas and has not come forward with any new ideas it seems that the drag on performance of FTSE companies by drawing upon the current narrow talent pool of male, pale and ageing non-execs is set to continue.

The Stewardship Code is an attempt to bring to account the institutional owners of companies eloquently inveighed against after the banking collapses of 2007, amongst others, by Lord Myners as Treasury Minister with particular responsibility for City matters. Ever since his ground-breaking report in 1996 *"Developing a winning partnership"* Paul Myners, as he then was, has campaigned for a more meaningful relationship between institutional investors and their investee companies. It remains to be seen whether in fact the Stewardship Code brings about the sort of real engagement which Lord Myners has been calling for, or whether, as seems to be the feeling in some EU Commission circles, given the fragmented, transitory and global nature of modern "ownership" (hedge funds and the like) it is in fact impossible for domestic UK pension and life funds and their fund managers to make any real difference.

The book has been comprehensively revised since the third edition to incorporate all the changes in the 2010 UK Corporate Governance Code as well as reflecting the Walker Review on banking governance, the 2010 Stewardship Code for institutional investors and current best practice in the areas of remuneration for directors, financial reporting, audit and the audit committee, risk management and internal control. It also has updated chapters on the governance initiatives from the EU Commission and in the United States, and an updated chapter on the not-for profit sector. I also have written a short, new chapter on banking governance following the Walker Review.

As before I have been wonderfully assisted by a team of specialists in the areas of financial reporting and audit (Tim Copnell and Alex Owen from KPMG), risk management (Alex Ellison from SAP), directors' remuneration (Karen Cooper from Osborne Clarke), D&O insurance (Ed Smerdon from Sedgwick Detert Moran Arnold LLP), governance initiatives from the EU Commission (Dr David Doyle) and in the US (Alex Cohen from Latham & Watkins, Washington), activism and pension fund (Paul Lee from Hermes) and not-for-profit governance (Douglas Cracknell). I would like to express my deep thanks to my colleagues for yet again being prepared to give the time and their precious expertise in very busy lives to this work.

I have dedicated this book, firstly, to the All Party Parliamentary Corporate Governance Group of which I am honoured to be the Rapporteur, and in particular to the inspirational Facilitator of that Group, Jennifer Bryant-Pearson. Without her tireless work and enthusiasm the Group, now chaired by Lord Myners, would not be able to continue to be the force for policy-making good that it has become—and on the way to have also become about the best attended and vibrant Group of its kind in Parliament.

I have also dedicated the book to the Genesis Initiative, of which I am a board member. The Genesis Initiative is an organisation comprising a large number of SME trade organisations which promotes and develops policy in relation to SMEs. It also is closely supported by parliamentarians who believe in the vital importance of a thriving SME sector and I would like to pay tribute to the chief executive Alan Cleverly OBE who is the driving force and inspiration behind the organisation.

I should also like to thank Lesley Stephenson, editor of the *Non-Executive Director* and *Non-Exec.com*, who organises and gives me the chance to lecture to groups of potential non-executive directors in the *Financial Times* programme called *"So you want to be a non-executive director"*. It's been a great pleasure to work with her and to be able to address such especially able audiences.

Thanks are also publicly due to my wife Dr Caroline Bowden who despite her own demanding job running a research project at Queen Mary, University of London, presents me every other Christmas with a leather bound version of the latest edition of this book! I would like to record that I am deeply touched by and also grateful to her for her support and interest in my work.

One of the perks of writing a book is that it enables the author to write a preface containing the occasional piece of total self indulgence, and so I would just like to express my love and admiration for my children Ed, Helen and Jenny and my lovely grandchildren, Madeline, Sam, Joe, Isobel, Charlie, Anna and William.

Finally, my thanks to the editorial team at Sweet & Maxwell: Suzanna Wong, Katherine Milburn and especially to Claire Patient who as senior editor has with more patience and professionalism than is reasonable to ask brought the last three editions to publication.

Richard Smerdon
July 2010
London

Acknowledgements

Grateful acknowledgement is made for permission to reproduce material. I am especially thankful to: OPSI in respect of licences to reproduce extracts from the Companies Act 2006; The DTI/HM Treasury in reproducing and quoting from extracts from the January 2003, Higgs Review into the role and effectiveness of non-executive directors; The MIT Press, Cambridge, Mass. for permission from the 2004 edition of this book to quote from the article "Corporate Governance and Equity Prices" in the Quarterly Journal of Economics, Volume CXVIII, February 2003, issue 1; Mr Paul Myners (now Lord Myners CBE) for permission from the 1998 edition of this book to reproduce extracts from the 1996 report "Developing a Winning Partnership"; Oxford University Press for permission from the 2004 edition of this book to quote from "Corporate Governance and Chairmanship" by Sir Adrian Cadbury, 2002, OUP; "Strategy+business": The table at para.1.006 is reprinted with permission from the 2004 edition of this book from "strategy+business", the award winning management quarterly by Booz Allen Hamilton www.strategy-business.com; the Financial Services Authority in reproducing extracts from the Listing Rules, and the Model Code all of which is covered by the FSA copyright notice "© The Financial Services Authority"; and Unilever Plc from the 2007 edition of this book for permission to quote extracts from Unilever reports and accounts and governance policy. While every care has been taken to establish and acknowledge copyright and contact the copyright owners, the publishers tender their apologies for any accidental infringement and would be happy to come to a suitable arrangement with the rightful owners in each case.

About the Author

Richard Smerdon

Richard Smerdon was a company lawyer by training and profession, having retired in 2003 as a senior corporate partner of Osborne Clarke, the European law firm whose main offices are in London, Thames Valley, Bristol, Palo Alto California, Cologne and Munich.

He is a specialist in corporate governance and was acknowledged as such in relation to the UK in the foreword of the European Commission's 2003 report on governance codes written by Holly Gregory of the US law firm Weil, Gotschal & Manches LLP.

He is Rapporteur to the All Party Parliamentary Corporate Governance Group, and a lecturer on the *Financial Times* programme: "*So you want to be a non-executive director*".

He is also the editor of the Wolters Kluwer UK publication "Practical Governance" and of Gee's Practical Governance Handbook and is contributing editor to the European Corporate Governance Institute research newsletter and he is a member of the editorial board of the Wolters Kluwer UK Corporate Practice Service. He is a board member of the Genesis Initiative, an organisation of SME trade associations dedicated to promoting and developing policy initiatives for the SME sector.

Table of Cases

Table of Statutes

Table of Statutory Instruments

Table of Rules and Reports

Chapter 1

Definition, Background and Purpose of Corporate Governance, and does it matter anyway?

The structure of this chapter is as follows:

- Part 1—Definitions;
- Part 2—The development of corporate governance in the UK;
- Part 3—What is the theoretical basis of corporate governance?;
- Part 4—Does the Code and corporate governance work and does it matter?

Part 1: Definitions

Cadbury definition

On December 1, 1992, the Cadbury Report on the Financial Aspects of Corporate Governance was published.[1] It defined corporate governance as "the system by which companies are directed and controlled".[2] In January 1998 the Hampel Committee on Corporate Governance published its final report and adopted that definition. In January 2003 the Higgs Review of

1.001

---

[1] *http://www.ecgi.org/codes/code.php?code_id=132.*
[2] The definition goes on (and is worth quoting such is its classic elegance and timeless truth):

> "The shareholders role in governance is to appoint the directors and the auditors and to satisfy themselves that an appropriate governance structure is in place. The responsibilities of the board include setting the company's strategic aims, providing the leadership to put them into effect, supervising the management of the business and reporting to shareholders on their stewardship. The board's actions are subject to laws, regulations and the shareholders in general meeting".

the role and effectiveness of non-executive directors[3] also approved that definition.

The 2009/2010 Combined Code review by the Financial Reporting Council ("FRC") adopted that definition and in the preamble to the 2010 revised Code—now renamed "the UK Corporate Governance Code"—the FRC went on:

> "Corporate governance is therefore about what the board of a company does and how it sets the values of the company and is to be distinguished from the day to day operational management of the company by full time executives."

The Cadbury definition will therefore be used for the purposes of this book since it is the definition which has most successfully stood the test of time and is most widely adopted. However, examples of other definitions are given below.

Governance codes are about due process and structure

1.002 The use in the Cadbury definition of the word "system" is striking in that it emphasises that much of the activity of governance is about "structure" (make up of boards, numbers of and types of non-executive directors, board committees and the like) and "process" (provision of information, internal controls, financial reporting, terms of service agreements), as distinct from "values" or other behavioural matters or the societal or economic obligations of companies.

Indeed the "Preface" to the 2010 UK Corporate Governance Code published by the FRC in June 2010[4] states:

> "it (the Code) cannot guarantee effective board behaviour because the range of situations in which it is applicable is much too great for it to attempt to mandate behaviour more specifically than it does. Boards there-fore have a lot of room within the framework of the Code to decide for themselves how they should act."

This book concentrates primarily on "structure" and "process", since for practitioners these are the day by day manifestations of governance in most companies. However, as appropriate, for example, in the field of corporate social responsibility, the book will try to explain concisely how attention to certain broader values is an essential part of good governance.

---

[3] *http://www.bis.gov.uk/files/file23012.pdf.*
[4] See *http://www.frc.org.uk/corporate* and follow the prompts.

"Behaviour" matters however

Thus, although codes of corporate governance deal with process and struc-   **1.003**
ture, it is clear that codes will not work effectively unless boardroom behaviours fulfil the intentions behind the process and structure. The chairman is
crucial in delivering that behaviour.

The Walker Review of banking governance[5] put it as follows:

> "Boards and board behaviour cannot be regulated or managed through
> organisational structures and controls alone; rather behaviour is developed
> over time as a result of responding to existing and anticipated situations.
> It is the dynamic process through which behaviour evolves that underlines
> the responsibility of the chairman to ensure that his or her board takes time
> to purposefully evaluate its behaviour and the implications on the effective
> functioning of the board.
>
> Behaviour is learnable, changing and dependent upon situational
> demands such as strategic context, social influence and the dynamic of the
> group itself. A chairman will both influence and be influenced by his or her
> vision of the desired direction of the board and the organisation, by the
> existing and hoped-for strategy of the future and by existing and the actual
> and anticipated behaviours and demands of others on the board.
>
> Susceptibility to social influence is not a trait of those who lack
> willpower; it is hard-wired into all of us."

Other definitions and approaches to the meaning of corporate governance

Other definitions

Other definitions have attempted to embrace a broader definition which puts   **1.004**
the company into a context of a wider societal obligation. Indeed, in a speech
by Sir Adrian Cadbury in 2000, he said:

> "corporate governance is concerned with holding the balance between
> economic and social goals and between individual and communal goals.
> The corporate governance framework is there to encourage efficient use of
> resources and equally to require accountability for the stewardship of those
> resources. The aim is to align the interests of individuals, corporations and
> society."[6]

---

[5] November 26, 2009, Annex 4 p.139.
[6] Sir Adrian Cadbury, Global Corporate Governance Forum, World Bank, 2000.

A definition in 2002 which emphasised economic objectives as the proper business of governance, stated:

"Corporate governance is a field in economics that investigates how to secure or motivate efficient management of corporations by the use of incentive mechanisms, such as contracts, organizational designs and legislation. It is often limited to the question of improving financial performance, for example, how the corporate owners can secure or motivate that the corporate managers will deliver a competitive rate of return."[7]

The 1999 OECD definition of corporate governance is strikingly similar to that of Cadbury:

"corporate governance is the system by which business corporations are directed and controlled. The corporate governance structure specifies the distribution of rights and responsibilities among different participants in the corporation, such as the board, managers, shareholders and other stakeholders, and spells out the rules and procedures for making decisions on corporate affairs. By doing this, it also provides the structure through which the company objectives are set, and the means of obtaining those objectives and monitoring performance."[8]

In July, 2003 the late Mr Alastair Ross Goobey said at the annual meeting of the International Corporate Governance Network:

"corporate governance is only about reducing the cost of capital: if we can't establish that beyond peradventure then we are wasting our time. This is not a moral crusade."

Other approaches

1.005 *A business-focused objective for corporate governance*   Governance may be said to combine a "business objective" and a "practical objective" to deliver that business objective. The "business objective" could be expressed as follows:

(a)   the increase of shareholder value;

(b)   the taking into account of the legitimate interests of stakeholders such as creditors, employees, suppliers, customers and the environment;

---

[7] Mathiesen, 2002, *http://www.encycogov.com.*
[8] OECD, April 1999.

(c) controlling financial, business and operational risk;

(d) reducing the cost of capital.

The practical objective is to put in place a "system" (to use the Cadbury corporate governance definition) or structure of direction and control which stands the best chance of delivering the business objective.

As so often, the Cadbury Report still puts the matter best:

> "The country's economy depends on the drive and efficiency of its companies. Thus the effectiveness with which their boards discharge their responsibilities determines Britain's competitive position. They must be free to drive their companies forward, but exercise their freedom within a framework of effective accountability. This is the essence of any system of good corporate governance."

A values-based understanding of governance—"soft" governance However, **1.006**
also at the heart of the governance issue is the self-evident point that any process is only as good as the people operating it. If the chairman and CEO and board have the will to run their boards with the values of:

- honesty, trust and candour;

- integrity;

- openness;

- transparency;

- courage to dissent and ask awkward questions;

- willingness to debate;

then the chances are that the board will make sound and prudent business decisions. If boards are not run with these core values, then there must be a strong risk, regardless of whether all the governance boxes are ticked or not, that sooner or later bad decisions will be made and shareholder value destroyed.

Figure 1.1 illustrates the seven principles of what has been termed "soft" governance.

Figure 1:1 The seven principles of soft governance[9]

1. **Select the right people.** Recruit directors with the courage to challenge the CEO. Look for self-confident CEO-level candidates who can engage in real debate without dragging in their egos.
2. **Train, train, train.** Orient new directors by arranging face-to-face meetings with all the top executives. Provide briefing books, arrange site visits, and factor in time to build relationships. Remember ongoing education for all directors.
3. **Inform and communicate.** Deliver relevant information early and in multiple formats. Leave time on the agenda for open discussion. Don't skimp on site visits and retreats; they can yield give-and-take.
4. **Balance the CEO's power.** Make sure only independent directors recruit new directors, control the committees' chairmanships, hold meetings without the CEO, and control succession. Remember that committees can appropriate power.
5. **Establish new behaviours.** Hire CEOs who value teamwork and want full feedback. Establish a tone of collegiality and "constructive skepticism". CEOs and directors must nurture a culture of listening.
6. **Devote the time.** Board membership requires time to prepare, time to discuss, time to develop relationships. All directors must open their schedules to absorb information and make decisions.
7. **Evaluate and improve.** Establish a tradition of continual improvement. Directors should examine and refine practices as do other professional teams. Evaluate the CEO, evaluate the board as a whole, and evaluate individuals.

Perspectives on the nature of corporate governance from the non-corporate sector

1.007   Readers of the Higgs Review were struck by the favourable comparisons which Higgs made between the private corporate sector and the public and not-for-profit sectors in terms of open recruitment procedures and other matters. It is clear that the public and not-for-profit sectors have done a great deal of thinking about governance and it has to be said that these sectors are generally a good deal more open minded and willing to learn in their

---

[9] Reproduced from "strategy+business" Issue 30, Spring 2003, "Corporate Governance: Hard facts about soft behaviours", by kind permission of Booz Allen Hamilton. See "Acknowledgements" above.

approach to the subject. Not only are their recruitment procedures more transparent but also the pool of talent is drawn from a wider range and comprises many more women and people from ethnic groups than the commercial sector; the attention paid to post-appointment induction and training is also impressive. Public company boards and institutional shareholders have tended to approach all this from a rather condescending point of view, as if these sectors really have nothing to offer the commercial world—forgetting that large charities and public bodies are responsible for resources at least as large as many commercial companies and that they have human resource and stakeholder issues at least as complex as the commercial sector.

It is for this reason that this book contains chapters on the not-for-profit sector (Ch.22) by way of introduction to this topic, and also to the area of pension fund trusteeship (Ch.21) where until recently there have been some rather opaque aspects on which some light needs to be shone.

Part 2: The development of corporate governance in the United Kingdom

Cadbury—1992

The expression "corporate governance" started to appear in American **1.008** law journals in the 1970s and was imported from America into the UK. It took firm root when Sir Adrian Cadbury was asked in May 1991 to chair the Committee on the Financial Aspects of Corporate Governance by the Financial Reporting Council, the London Stock Exchange and the accounting profession. The Cadbury Committee was born out of the scandals (Maxwell, Polly Peck, Barings), which hit the City of London and the UK financial markets during the late 1980s.

The Cadbury Committee reported in December 1992 and took the view that governance was not a matter for legislation, a view then supported by the City and Government. The Cadbury Report produced a Code of Best Practice, comprising 19 Provisions and 14 Notes dealing with board and committee structures, remuneration and financial reporting, and describing the appropriate relationship with auditors. The London Stock Exchange (as it then was) then altered the Listing Rules so as to require listed companies to state in their annual reports either that they complied with the Cadbury Code or to explain any non-compliance—so was born the "comply or explain", rather British, principles-based approach to governance which has found increasing favour throughout the world, except for the United States, where detailed regulation, such as the SEC Rule book and the Sarbanes-Oxley Act, enforceable in the courts and buttressed by the sanction of substantial fines and/or (in the case of directors) imprisonment against the company and its directors, is preferred.

Directors' pay—the Greenbury Report—1995

1.009 Alongside the corporate sector scandals was the rise of the "fat cats"—senior executives of newly privatised utility monopolies paying themselves (or rather being rewarded by allegedly "independent" remuneration committees) remuneration packages which were judged excessive and non-transparent. It became ever more difficult to discern precisely how much was being paid in relation to pension contributions, the terms of share option schemes and other bonus arrangements.

As a result of the sense of increasing public unease, not only with the companies' boards themselves, but also with the institutional investors' generally flaccid approach, it began to be felt that unless legislation was brought in, there would continue to be a lack of accountability on the part of powerful boards of directors and chief executives. The Greenbury Committee on directors' remuneration was convened in January 1995, reporting in July 1995.

The Greenbury Committee was also against legislation and produced its own code in relation to directors' remuneration and this code was adopted into the Listing Rules on a "comply or explain" basis.

The Combined Code—1998[10]

1.010 In November 1995, following the recommendations of the Cadbury and the Greenbury Committees that a new committee should review the implementation of their findings, a Committee on Corporate Governance was established under the chairmanship of Sir Ronald Hampel, the then Chairman of ICI. The Hampel Committee's final report was issued in January 1998.

The criticisms of Cadbury and Greenbury preceding the establishment of the Hampel Committee, whilst acknowledging the considerable benefits that had arisen from their recommendations and codes, were that inadvertently they had resulted in a so-called "box ticking" mentality or approach to governance. In other words, if the letter of the codes had been observed and "ticked", the company was deemed to be in good condition. It was well known, however, that some companies, including the Maxwell companies, could tick every box of the codes and yet be fundamentally flawed. The common factor in the flawed governance of these companies was the presence of over powerful chief executives who often combined the role of chairman of boards many of whose directors were over cosily associated with or easily intimidated by the chief executive/chairman.

It was the Hampel Committee's view, therefore, that there should be a shift away from the box ticking approach into the application of a general set of

---

[10] Succeeded in 2010 by the UK Corporate Governance Code.

principles underpinned by a Code dealing with specific items. Companies should say in the new Code how they *applied* these "principles"—it was an attempt to make boards think about the issues. The London Stock Exchange therefore once again altered the Listing Rules so as to require that companies should state in their annual reports how they *applied* the 18 "Principles" drafted by the Hampel Committee and to state whether they *"complied"* with 42 Provisions which underpinned the Principles. To the extent of any non-compliance with the Provisions companies were required to explain such non-compliance. The combination of the two, Principles and Provisions, was called "The Combined Code" and was published in June 1998.

Turnbull—1999

In September 1999 the Institute of Chartered Accountants of England and **1.011** Wales published a report[11] on internal control in response to the then Principle D.2 and associated Provisions of the (then) Combined Code that companies should "maintain a sound system of internal control" and should conduct an annual review of "the effectiveness of the system of internal control" which should be reported to shareholders. The "Turnbull" Guidance on Internal Control, as it was called after the name of its chairman, Mr Nigel Turnbull, published in a short booklet, reproduced in full in App.6,[12] a number of lucid guidelines whereby companies could introduce and maintain effective internal controls and thereby manage risk better.

Institutional shareholder activism and the Stewardship Code

Parallel to these developments was the rise of the movement known as **1.012** "shareholder activism" whereby institutions, such as pension and other fund managers, Hermes Pension Fund Management and PIRC, began to introduce voting policies on issues such as independent non-executive directors, the separation of CEO and chairman and executive remuneration which were intended to remind boards that owners took their responsibilities and powers seriously. There was, even so, considerable criticism by Government of the institutions generally for failing to live up to their responsibilities by using their votes, as the dismal proxy return demonstrated. It appeared that most institutional investors were idle when it came to exercising their powers as owners. A report published by Dr Chris Mallin[13] of Warwick Business School in 1995 surveyed the FTSE 250 companies to ascertain the voting

---

[11] *http://www.icaew.co.uk.*
[12] The Turnbull Guidance on Internal Control as printed in App.6 contains the amendments proposed by the Turnbull review committee chaired by Mr Douglas Flint in September 2004.
[13] Now Professor Mallin of Birmingham University.

behaviour of each of the companies' institutional shareholders. The survey indicated that the normal number of votes cast on any given resolution was about 35 per cent of the total which could be cast.

Criticism also was made, and still continues, to the effect that there are structural conflicts of interest within institutional shareholders themselves in the sense that they are both trustees for the savings of millions of people who entrust their savings to them, but they and the fund managers which they appoint invest those savings in companies to which they also try to sell financial products and services and which in that sense are their clients.[14] Another criticism has been that fund managers appointed by the institutions have to adopt a short-term approach in order to get returns for their client institutions or face the sack. Activism, it is said,[15] in an attempt to achieve the performance required of fund managers, induces short-term thinking by the managers of the companies in which the fund managers invest. Finally, there is criticism of the governance of the institutions themselves: "We know of no systematic review of the internal governance of the institutional community. One is needed".[16]

In 2000 the Treasury commissioned Mr Paul Myners, then chairman of Gartmore Investment Management, to write a report on the broad issue of institutional investment. The report[17] was published in March 2001 in which, amongst many other recommendations affecting the investment industry generally, he urged that pension funds should give clear mandates to the fund managers managing their funds:

"The mandate should incorporate the principle of the US Department of Labor Interpretive Bulletin on activism. Managers should have an explicit strategy, elucidating the circumstances in which they will intervene in a company; the approach they will use in doing so; and how they measure the effectiveness of this strategy."

In fact it was not until October 2002 that the Institutional Shareholders' Committee agreed and published a clear statement of guidance on the subject of intervention[18] in the face of clear signs that the Government was prepared to legislate to force institutions to use their votes, explain their voting policies and intervene in companies where governance was sub-standard, if they did not show more energy in these matters.

---

[14] Company Law Review, Final Report, Vol.I, paras 3.52–3.54.
[15] "Investment Chains: Addressing corporate and investor short-termism". TUC, March 15, 2006. *Reforming company and takeover law in Europe*, Guido Ferrarini et al, Oxford 2004, p.200. See also Ch.18 (Institutional Shareholder Activism) of this book.
[16] "The New Agenda for ICGN" by Adrian Cadbury and Ira M Millstein, 2006: *http://www. icgn.org/publications/discussion-documents.*
[17] "Institutional Investment in the UK"—*http://www.hm-treasury.gov.uk/Documents/Financial_ Services/Securities_and_Investments/fin_sec_mynfinal.cfm.*
[18] *The Responsibilities of Institutional Shareholders and Agents* published by the Institutional Shareholders' Committee in October 2002.

Following the 2008/2009 banking crisis the institutions were singled out for particular criticism once more especially in relation to their failure to curb remuneration excesses in the banks. Lord Myners said in a debate in the House of Lords on December 2, 2009:

> "I share my noble friend's concern that there is precious little evidence that those at the top of our banks appreciate the concern about those extraordinary levels of income . . . The real responsibility must lie with the shareholders. Accordingly, I have written to the NAPF, the CBI and the TUC, urging them to use their influence to persuade trustees to ask their fund managers: 'What are you doing to stop these unreasonable and unjustifiable levels of remuneration?'"

The Walker Review of corporate governance in UK banks therefore proposed a new to be called the "stewardship code", which would set out the principles to be adopted by institutional shareholders in exercising good stewardship of the investments in British companies under their control. The FRC after consultation published the Stewardship Code in June 2010 and as a consequence what had previously been contained in s.2 of the Combined Code (institutional shareholders) is not intended to remain in the UK Corporate Governance Code.[19]

UK post-Enron initiatives

It has to be said that since the introduction of the 1998 Combined Code there appears to have been a low level of actual corporate wrongdoing (as distinct from (in the case of many financial companies) incompetence) by British companies.[20] However, during the economic downturn from 1997 to 2003 a number of well-publicised corporate collapses occurred (of which Marconi was perhaps the most notorious) in which shareholder value was destroyed on a huge scale. Common features were powerful executive teams ranged alongside respectable if over-respectful non-executive directors who may not in all cases have had sufficient knowledge of the business into which the company was trying to transform itself—who on the Marconi board knew enough about US technology companies as the company bet the shop on huge US technology company acquisitions during the 1990s? Concerns in the

1.013

---

[19] To be strictly accurate, the version of the UK Corporate Governance Code published in June 2010 contains a "Schedule C Engagement principles for institutional shareholders", with the footnote as follows: "This schedule will cease to apply when the Stewardship Code for institutional investors being developed by the FRC comes into effect".

[20] It might fairly be said that the misstatement of oil reserves by the Royal Dutch Shell Group in 2001 is the most obvious example in recent times of UK corporate wrongdoing at FTSE 100 level. The "restatement" of iSoft accounts for 2005 due, it was said, to "aggressive" revenue recognition might also be cited as another example.

UK were heightened by the scandals in corporate America exemplified by Enron, Worldcom and Tyco.

Common features of these American scandals were fraudulent accounting practices compounded by poor auditing by auditors for whom the value of non-auditing services vastly outweighed the auditing work; autocratic, unaccountable and outrageously overpaid CEOs; and non-executive directors who did not appear really to understand their businesses and whose independence in some cases was undermined by inappropriate remuneration and benefits and commercial side deals.

As a response to these disturbing features of US corporate life the Treasury and the Department of Trade and Industry commissioned three studies:

(a)   A review conducted by Sir Derek Higgs of the role and effectiveness of non-executive directors which reported in January 2003.[21]

(b)   A report on Combined Code Guidance for Audit Committees chaired by Sir Robert Smith under the auspices of the Financial Reporting Council and which also reported in January 2003.[22]

(c)   A report into the UK's arrangements for audit and accountancy regulation of the Co-ordinating Group on Audit and Accounting Issues which reported on January 29, 2003.[23]

More detailed analysis of these reports will appear in later chapters of this book.

The Higgs Review and the 2003 Combined Code

1.014   The 2003 Higgs Review "into the role and effectiveness of non-executive directors" turned out to be something of a surprise. Mr Higgs (as he then was) had been portrayed in the press as a middle-of-the-road investment banker with a traditional background in the City of London and on the boards of various public companies. In the event his Review contained strong criticism of the lack of true "independence" of many non-executives; the lack of rigour in the way in which non-executive directors were recruited, the narrowness of the pool and the lack of proper induction procedures, appraisal and further professional development. He drafted a completely new Combined Code which was taken forward by the FRC and turned into what became the 2003 Combined Code comprising Principles, Supporting Principles and Provisions. The Higgs review is still the most comprehensive analysis of the nature of the work of non-executive

---

[21]   *http://www.bis.gov.uk/files/file23012.pdf*, also set out in App.2 of this book.
[22]   *http://www.frc.org.uk/publications*, also in App.15 of this book.
[23]   *http://www.bis.gov.uk/files/file20380.pdf*.

directors, and the 2010 UK Corporate Governance Code is still in large part a reflection of the version of the Combined Code which he and the FRC produced in 2003.

UK Company Law Reform—2006

On November 8, 2006 the Companies Act 2006 ("the CA 2006") was granted **1.015** Royal Assent: the culmination of a process of consultation and review which started in March 1998. The body set up to review company law, the Company Law Review ("CLR") produced its final report on July 26, 2001. A year later on July 16, 2002, the Department of Trade and Industry in response produced an interim White Paper called "Modernising company law" (Cm.5553), and then in 2005 published the White Paper, "Company Law Reform" (Cm.6456) which was reflected in the Company Law Reform Bill introduced in the House of Lords in March 2006.

The Government "spin" about the Bill was that it was intended to "think small": in other words, the Act was intended to help the smaller company rather than the public company, in contrast to previous company legislation. It is true that there are simpler procedures for incorporation and reporting and a strong attempt has been made to simplify the language. However, the Act (the longest in history!) contains 1,300 sections and 16 schedules and the subject matter of large parts of the Act is complex.

To be fair, in broad terms, only approximately one third of the Act is "new" company law: of the remainder, approximately half comprises the "restatement" of the unrepealed parts of the Companies Act 1985 and subsequent legislation, and half comprises implementation of the EU Takeover, Modernisation and Transparency Directives. The eminent and sometimes mischievous company lawyer, Lord Wedderburn, described the new Act as a "huge but essentially modest statute".[24]

It has to be doubted whether the average company director of a small company will find the Act any more user friendly than earlier legislation, especially the provisions relating to the newly defined duties of directors.

The headline provisions of the CA 2006 relating to governance are:

- the purported "codification" of directors' duties[25];

- the introduction of statutory provisions giving restricted rights for shareholders to bring derivative actions against directors under Pt 11;

- more flexibility relating to shareholder resolutions and electronic voting;

---

[24] *Financial Times*, Letters, November 10, 2006.
[25] An analysis of CA 2006 Pt 10 Ch.2 is set out in Ch.4 (Directors—Duties and Liabilities).

- very significantly enhanced rights to the beneficial owners of shares whose shares are held by nominees enabling them to exercise virtually the same rights as if they were registered.

- enhanced shareholder rights in Pt 13 of the Act reflecting the Shareholder Rights Directive; and

- a requirement to include a "business review" in the annual report which, among other things, requires companies to disclose material contracts—thus including particulars of the suppliers who play a material part in the supply chain to or from the company.

The provisions relating to directors reflect to a great extent the CLR recommendations, and also reflect the so-called "enlightened shareholder value" view of directors' duties—a middle of the road approach, as distinct from the strictly capitalist "shareholder value" approach at one extreme, and at the other end of the spectrum, the "pluralist" approach.[26] The enlightened shareholder value approach requires that the directors must promote the success of the company for the benefit of its members—the shareholders—but that in doing so they must have regard to the interests of a wider view of the activity of the company comprising, for example, the environment or employees. A closer analysis of directors' duties and the provisions relating to the derivative action is contained in Ch.4 of this book (Directors, Part 1—Duties and Liabilities with special reference to the Companies Act 2006).

The 2007/2009 banking crisis and the Walker Review of banking governance[27]

1.016   As is by now well known, in the years 2007 to 2009 the US and British banking system suffered a collective nervous breakdown. In both countries banks had both financed and brought onto their balance sheets hundreds of billions worth of mortgages and derivatives based on so-called "sub-prime" borrowers and houses: that is to say, borrowers of uncertain earnings to whom the banks had lent large multiples of "self-certified" earnings in order to finance mortgages often over 100 per cent of the value of houses whose values had plunged overnight. These derivatives and other financial products based on sub-prime financing were quickly dubbed "toxic assets" because of their poisonous effects on the balance sheets of US and UK banks.

---

[26] See further paras 1.025 et seq. below, and also the Attorney-General's explanation of this approach in the debate at the Committee stage of the Bill extracts of which are repeated in Ch.4 (Directors—Duties and Liabilities) of this book, para.4.023.

[27] See also OECD: *The Corporate Governance Lessons from the Financial Crisis*, February 2009 (at *http://www.oecd.org/dataoecd/32/1/42229620.pdf*) and *Corporate Governance and the Financial Crisis: Key Findings and Main Messages*, June 2009 (at *http://www.oecd.org/dataoecd/3/10/43056196.pdf*).

In the UK the Northern Rock Bank was brought into public ownership in February 2008 in order to stop a full scale run on the bank.

In October 2008 the Government effectively took control of a number of large UK banks by injecting £37 billion of new equity capital into Royal Bank of Scotland Group Plc ("RBS"), Lloyds TSB and HBOS Plc, to avert then collapse of these banks. The Government stressed, however, that it was not "standard public ownership" and that the banks would return to private investors "at the right time"

The iconic "villain" of those times was Sir Fred Goodwin, chief executive of RBS, who was cast as the architect of the bank's downfall and required to resign shortly before the announcement by RBS in November 2008 of the then largest corporate loss in British history of £24.1 billion. Sir Fred's early retirement on an annual pension of £700,000 (subsequently reduced to £340,000 p.a.) caused a national outcry.

The crisis caused many to think that the governance of financial institutions had failed and that yet again destruction of shareholder value on a huge scale to say nothing of the disastrous impact on the UK economy had occurred as a result of over powerful chief executives and weak non-executive directors. In addition the "bonus culture" whereby employees of financial institutions were paid grotesque bonuses regardless of long-term performance which were rewards for unmeasured risk taking. It was also said that the chief regulatory body for the financial sector, the Financial Services Authority, had failed to spot the danger signs and rein in the financial institutions.

The Government therefore in February 2009 asked Sir David Walker to conduct a review into the corporate governance of UK Banks and other financial industry entities (using the unlovely mnemonic of "BOFIs") and the final recommendations of the review were published in November 2009.[28] At the same time the Financial Reporting Council announced a review of the Combined Code, and a new chairman and chief executive of the FSA, Lord Turner and Hector Sants were appointed with a brief to reform its approach to regulatory oversight.[29]

The Walker Review found that the necessary element of boardroom challenge to chief executives was absent in many BOFIs: it was a behavioural issue not something which could be dealt with by more prescription. Moreover, that the "bonus culture" had resulted in a complete lack of reference to the long term measurement of success.

There were also a series of interventions by the Treasury minister Lord Myners during 2009 ranging from boardroom reform (compulsory seminars, greater diversity, professional "devil's advocates" on boards and technical specialists to guide audit committees) to radical ideas to encourage greater shareholder activism including giving long-term shareholders double voting

---

[28] *A review of corporate governance in UK banks and other financial industry entities*, November 26, 2009, *http://www.hm-treasury.gov.uk/walker_review_information.htm.*
[29] See also Ch.25 (Governance of Banks and Other Financial Industry Entities) para.25.006.

rights; and the proposal that the Takeover Code should be extended to require the bidder company to set out the risks and rewards it expects its own shareholders to be affected by following a proposed takeover.

Other suggestions were that AGM votes approving the annual accounts and the appointment of directors should comprise an actual majority of the total votes able to be cast and not just those voting at the meeting: it being argued that this would really engage shareholders.

The 2010 UK Corporate Governance Code

1.017   In April 2010 as a considered response to the banking crisis of 2007/2009 and also the 2009 Walker Review of banking governance the FRC published the successor to the Combined Code—called "the UK Corporate Governance Code"—following an extensive consultation exercise during 2009.[30] A fuller analysis of the 2010 UK Corporate Governance Code ("the Code") is contained in Ch.2 (The Regulatory Regime), and in any event the Code will be referred to in detail throughout this book. In essence, the Code attempts to give listed companies[31] a large degree of latitude to set out in narrative form how they approach governance. The use of "Principles" and "Supporting Principles" set out in the Code requires (Premium listed) companies to say in a governance statement in their annual reports how they have *applied* the Principles and Supporting Principles in their annual reports, while in relation to Provisions, companies have to say whether they *comply*, and if not, why not—thus: "*comply or explain*".

The Code essentially continues the emphasis in the previous "Higgs" 2003 Combined Code on the "effective" board: a board where:

- the functions of chairman and CEO are fulfilled by separate people, (A.2.1) and the power of the CEO is dispersed through the appointment of "independent" non-executive directors (B.1) and committees of the board (e.g. audit and remuneration) comprising independent directors;

- appointments to the board must be made on merit "with due regard for the benefits of diversity, including gender" (B.2);

- directors of FTSE 350 companies must offer themselves for re-election every year (B.7.1);

---

[30] The UK Corporate Governance Code took effect for those listed companies to which it applied in respect of financial years commencing on or after June 29, 2010.

[31] To be strictly accurate, "Premium" listed companies alone are required by the FSA Listing Rules to include a UK Corporate Governance Code statement in their annual reports, as distinct from "Standard" or non-Premium listed companies which as from April 6, 2010 have the lesser burden of stating in their annual reports merely what code of governance (if any, but if not, why not) they apply and any material departures from that code, plus a statement on risk management and internal control. See also Ch.2 (The Regulatory Regime).

- the chairman is responsible for ensuring a culture of "openness and debate" (A.3);

- it is for the board to determine and justify "independence"; but a number of pointers are set out which may question independence, e.g. serving on a board for more than nine years (B.1.1);

- the independent non-executive directors are subject to contractual arrangements which set out the terms of the appointment, and to annual performance evaluations (B.2.3 and B.3.2);

- directors are required to update their skills (B.4);

- executive remuneration is tied closely to performance and risk management (Schedule A) and severance terms are kept to a maximum of one year's benefits (D.1.4);

- boards should be externally evaluated every three years and internally each year (B.6.and B.6.2);

- audit committee responsibilities are set out and reflect the Smith recommendations, including the requirement that at least one member of the audit committee should have recent and relevant experience and the requirement that the audit committee has prime responsibility for recommending the appointment of the auditor (Section C).

- the board as a whole must determine the level of risk it is willing to take (C.2);

- the board must in each annual report give an explanation of the basis on which the company generates or preserves value over the longer terms (the business model) and how it intends to achieve that aim (C.1.2).

Other 2010 governance initiatives

The Stewardship Code

The Stewardship Code was published in July 2010.   **1.018**

Turnbull Guidance review

The FRC's intention has been to begin consultation some time in the   **1.019**
second half of 2010 (maybe September/ October) and for the guidance to be
published early in 2011, but this is not fixed.

Higgs "Guidance"

1.020   The Higgs review in 2003 contained in appendices a number of useful guidance notes and precedents (e.g. a suggested contract for non-executive directors). Some of these appendices are set out in the appendices to this book. The FRC has been conducting during 2010 an update of the "Higgs guidance" and asked the ICSA to lead that. The plan was to consult on revised guidance in June 2010 with the guidance itself being published by the FRC before the end of 2010.[32]

The European Union and corporate governance

1.021   Chapter 23 (The EU) sets out a full description of the current position in the EU.

What follows is a brief outline of the development of EU interest in the issues of governance. In continental Europe corporate governance had not greatly occupied the minds of boards of European companies until the EU Commission started to take an interest from 2000. Many European countries[33] had by 2000 or shortly thereafter adopted codes of corporate governance, but enthusiasm for implementation at supervisory board level in the context of dual board structures as distinct from the Anglo-American unitary board model, and, indeed, at shareholder level, was muted. The reason was largely to be found in the history and structure of corporate ownership and control of continental companies.[34] Many companies were controlled by complex cross shareholding interests and by "blockholders", that is to say, entities which might be individuals or family companies or huge commercial conglomerates which had built up over many years, and at significant cost, controlling stakes, including in many of the largest European public companies.

In Germany, the historical development of post-war reconstruction corporate activity was through the country's banks which effectively controlled corporate Germany and in particular supervisory boards. Thus supervisory boards of companies in continental Europe were controlled by individuals representing the controlling interests—"control" being a different matter from "ownership" of the equity share capital.[35]

In continental Europe, also, the blockholding and cross-shareholding

---

[32] The revised guidance can be found on the FRC's and ICSA's websites.

[33] e.g. in France the "Vienot" recommendations; in Germany, the Berlin Initiative Group's "Cromme" Code of Corporate Governance; in Italy, the "Preda" report and code of conduct; and in the Netherlands, the "Tabaksblat" Code of Corporate Governance.

[34] *The Control of Corporate Europe*, Fabrizio Barca and Marco Becht (eds), OUP, 2001; *Reforming Company and Takeover Law in Europe*: Guido Ferrarini et al., Oxford, 2004.

[35] *The Control of Corporate Europe*, Fabrizio Barca and Marco Becht (eds), OUP, 2001; *Reforming Company and Takeover Law in Europe*: Guido Ferrarini et al., Oxford, 2004.

corporate structures which characterise the continent tended to result in a somewhat gridlocked aspect to boards and the interests which control them. Moreover, local national laws have inhibited shareholder rights and cross-border voting. Thus, as a generalisation, shareholder activism as understood in Anglo-American markets where shareholdings are much more fragmented has not been a feature of continental European governance.

However, as the availability of and increasing need for capital in Europe from global sources, and in particular, Anglo-American sources has grown, and the developing wish of European shareholders to achieve liquidity for their shareholdings has become apparent, so the providers of capital and the stock markets underpinning them have indicated that boards of continental European companies will have to get serious about standards of corporate governance, shareholder rights and company law reform if they are to be successful in accessing capital and providing liquidity for shareholders.[36]

Accordingly, the EU Commission, and in particular the Directorate General Internal Markets, took the view in the late 1990s that if continental Europe was going to be successful in opening up its capital markets to global capital there would need to be a programme of reform. The European Commission therefore commissioned two reports; a comparative study of corporate governance codes[37] and a report on company law reform, including corporate governance, from a "High Level Group of Company Law Experts" selected by the Commission.

The comparative study recommended in 2002[38] that energy should not be spent in attempting to consolidate corporate governance codes into a European code, but rather that measures should be put in hand to reform company law to amend the 4th and 7th Company Law Directives in a Company Law Directive[39] so as to remove inhibitions on trans-border shareholder rights and make boards more responsive to shareholders.

In May 2003 the company law reform report was published, called "The Final Report of the High Level Group of Company Law Experts" or more colloquially, "the Winter Report" named after the chairman, the distinguished Dutch lawyer, Jaap Winter. Immediately following the Winter

---

[36] In the interests of a balanced view by way of countering the impression which may have been given by the author that continental Europe was a barren area in terms of governance, it should be pointed out that by 2002 there were no less than 13 EU countries which had codes of governance best practice of one form or another and several of these countries (e.g. France, UK, Belgium) had more than one code of practice issued by different bodies within the State: See *Comparative Study of Corporate Governance Codes relevant to the European Union and its Member States*, Weil, Gotschal and Manges, January 2002. However, the same study concluded that the problem with governance in the EU was not the absence of Codes but the national laws and corporate structures which concentrated power in too few hands.

[37] See *Comparative Study of Corporate Governance Codes relevant to the European Union and its Member States*, Weil, Gotschal and Manges, January 2002.

[38] See *Comparative Study of Corporate Governance Codes relevant to the European Union and its Member States*, Weil, Gotschal and Manges, January 2002.

[39] 2006/46/EC which was published in the Official Journal on August 16 with an implementation date of September 5, 2008.

Report the European Commission through the DG Internal Market published an "Action Plan" setting out the Commission's objectives for the modernisation of company law and enhancement of corporate governance in the EU.[40] The Action Plan contains six groups of issues of which one is corporate governance. The general approach of the Action Plan in relation to corporate governance is not to legislate by Directives on matters of corporate governance but rather "Recommendations" or Regulations.[41]

So far, Recommendations[42] have been issued on reinforcing the role of non-executive directors, disclosure of directors' remuneration and shareholder approval of director share options. However, Directives will be required in order to modernise company law across the EU. The Shareholder Rights Directive which strengthened shareholder rights at meetings was implemented in the UK by the Companies (Shareholders' Rights) Regulations 2009 taking effect on August 3, 2009. The Commission is also working closely with the Organisation for Economic Co-Operation and Development which itself has produced a revised set of principles of corporate governance which are being applied in several eastern-European countries and in Asia.[43]

Chapter 23 deals more fully with the topic of governance and the European Union.

Contractual corporate governance

1.022   Contractual corporate governance refers to the ways and means by which individual companies can deviate from their national corporate governance standards by increasing (or reducing) the level of protection they offer to their shareholders and other stakeholders. Although this topic has not yet been widely addressed in academic literature, it is rapidly gaining importance, particularly in the context of increasing globalisation of capital and product markets. It also raises important policy questions for market regulators and finance practitioners.

The rise of the Financial Reporting Council

1.023   The Financial Reporting Council ("FRC") and its two main subsidiaries, the Accounting Standards Board and the Financial Reporting Review Panel, were formed in 1990 in order to promote best practice in financial reporting.

---

[40] *http://europa.eu.int/comm/internal_market/company/modern/index_en.htm.*
[41] Recommendations are intended to be persuasive; Regulations are binding on Member States and entities within those states; Directives are binding on Member States and enforceable by the Commission, but Member States are required to implement their provisions into state legislation which then become binding on the subjects of those states as between state and subject.
[42] See Ch.23 (The EU) for references.
[43] *http://www.OECD.org.*

It gained a significant increase in its reputation and powers, firstly, when in 1992 it co-sponsored the Cadbury Report and subsequent Cadbury Code, and then in 2002 when it took responsibility for drafting a broadly acceptable revised Combined Code in 2002/2003 following the Higgs review into the role and effectiveness of non-executive directors. Under the Companies (Audit, Investigations, and Community Enterprise) Act 2004, the FRC took control also of the Professional Oversight Board for Accountancy and the Accountancy Investigation and Discipline Board. It was the FRC which commissioned the Smith Report and Guidance on the role of audit committees, published in 2003[44] and whose principal recommendations found their way into the revised Combined Code of 2003. More recently it was the FRC which took responsibility in 2009 for the revision of the Combined Code, an exercise which has resulted in the 2010 UK Corporate Governance Code.

The stated aim of the FRC is to "promote confidence in corporate reporting and governance". In pursuit of this aim its five stated objectives are to promote:

- high quality corporate reporting;

- high quality auditing;

- high standards of corporate governance;

- the integrity, competence and transparency of the accountancy profession;

- its effectiveness as a unified independent regulator.

Although the FSA has since the banking crisis of 2007/2009 been developing governance regulation for the financial sector (see the FSA's January 2010 Consultation Paper 10/3 "effective corporate governance") it can fairly be said that the FRC is now the pre-eminent independent influence in the UK in the regulation of corporate governance.[45]

Part 3: What is the theoretical basis of corporate governance?

Two main theories of corporate governance have been promoted in recent years: the "shareholder value" theory, which was developed into the "enlightened shareholder value" concept outlined in the Company Law Review of 2001 and adopted by the Government in the Companies Act 2006; and the   **1.024**

---

[44] "Audit Committees—Combined Code Guidance", published by the FRC, January 2003.
[45] In an interview with the *Financial Times* published on May 28, 2010 following her appointment as Chairman of the FRC, Lady Hogg said: "My role and the challenge is to make the FRC more than the sum of its parts". In July 2010 the Government announced a consultation exercise on the proposal that the UK Listing Authority and the FRC should merge, with the FRC taking the overall supervisory role.

"stakeholder" or "pluralist" approach. Although the debate has moved on in favour of the "enlightened shareholder value" concept, it is still relevant to an understanding of the issues to say something about these two approaches.

"Shareholder value" and "enlightened shareholder value" versus "pluralist"[46]

1.025   In broad terms, the "shareholder value" theory requires boards to regard the enhancement of their owners' investments over time as the overriding objective.

The "stakeholder" or "pluralist" approach, in crude terms, says that the goal of shareholder value, whilst clearly having to bear in mind the needs of customers, suppliers and employees, etc. has failed:

> "The important issues of corporate governance lie deeper. What is the relationship between the structure of rules, laws and conventional practices within which companies operate and their style of management and the decisions which they make? There are increasingly widespread claims that the incentives, pressures and restraints on British managers lead to short-term decision-making, and to failures to invest in physical equipment, in people and in the development of businesses, and that these factors are ultimately profoundly damaging to Britain's economic performance."[47]

There are at least two problems, however, about the "stakeholder" or "pluralist" approach. The first is that in countries where the corporate model is supposed to allow for what one might call the "stakeholder" dimension, there has not exactly been a shortage of scandals of corporate failures—Germany, Italy and Japan being particularly prominent. The same failures of internal control appear to happen in such countries as they have happened in Britain and the United States. The second problem is to design the type of corporate model and a hierarchy which would in reality provide satisfactory accountability to the different and varying stakeholder groups.

A false antithesis?

1.026   In truth, it is misleading to suggest that there is a mutually exclusive polarisation of approaches as between "shareholder value" and "stakeholder" or "pluralist" protection.

---

[46] See fn 51 below and also *http://www.bis.gov.uk/files/file40139.pdf* for the explanation given by the Attorney-General in the Committee stage of the Company Law Reform Bill of these terms.
[47] Quoted by Professor John Kay in his illuminating chapter on corporate governance in *The Business of Economics* (1996, OUP) in collaboration with Aubrey Silberston.

Even the Hampel Report in 1998, which many saw as an unashamed endorsement of red-blooded "shareholder value" as the objective of governance recognised the larger dimension:

"A company must develop relationships relevant to its success. These will depend on the nature of the company's business, that they will include those with the employees, customers, suppliers, credit providers, local communities and government. It is management's responsibility to develop policies which address these matters; in doing so they must have regard to the overriding objective of preserving and enhancing the shareholders' investment over time. The Board's task is to approve appropriate policies and to monitor the performance of management in implementing them."

The "enlightened shareholder value" approach to governance

The Company Law Review[48] published in July 2002 articulated what has become known as the "enlightened shareholder value" view of the duties of directors as follows:

1.027

"The Review considered to whom directors should owe duties and consulted on this issue on several occasions. Its conclusion, with which the government agrees, was that the basic goal for directors should be the success of the company in the collective best interests of shareholders, but that directors should also recognise, as circumstances require, the company's need to foster relationships with its employees, customers and suppliers, its needed to maintain its business reputation, and its need to consider the company's impact on the community and the working environment."

That consensus view was also expressed in the "Hermes Principles" published in October 2002 by Hermes Pensions Management Ltd, the UK's largest pension fund management company and a long-time "activist fund"[49]:

"In summary, a company's primary consideration should be the generation of long-term shareholder value, and this should be based on appropriate financial disciplines, competitive advantage and within a framework which is economically, ethically and socially responsible and sustainable."

It is interesting to note the emphasis being placed by Hermes on a "framework which is economically, ethically and socially responsible and sustainable", and the added emphasis reflects a growing belief by investors that

---

[48] "Modernising Company Law", Cm.5553, July 2002.
[49] *http://www.hermes.co.uk/pdf/corporate_governance/hermes_principles.pdf.*

in achieving enhanced shareholder value, corporations should behave in a socially responsible manner which has regard to all who have a stake in the company.[50]

The "enlightened shareholder value" approach has been formalised into the Companies Act 2006 in the provisions dealing with directors duties,[51] and in particular in the new duty to "promote the success of the company" under s.172, for the benefit of shareholders as a whole but having "regard (amongst other things) to" a number of stakeholder interests including employees, customers and the environment.[52]

"Shareholder value"—what does it mean?

1.028 It is surprising that there is so little guidance as to the meaning of the expression "shareholder value" in view of the amount of reference to it, as if somehow it is self evident. Of course, the more obvious meaning is that year on year the value of the shares and/or the "yield" on the shares of the company concerned increases. However, in a prolonged bear market where market forces in relation to the share price of a particular company may be beyond the control of the board of an individual company no matter how well the underlying performance of the company, how is "shareholder value" judged in those circumstances?

At a conference in March 2006 sponsored by the London Stock Exchange one of the speakers[53] suggested that the objective of "long-term shareholder value" was a mix of increase in share price over time, a satisfactory return on investment and capital, organic growth and successful growth by acquisition.

A somewhat more systematic approach was suggested by Hermes Pension Fund Management. In its "Principles"[54] it states "in financial terms this [i.e.

---

[50] See further Ch.20 (Corporate Social Responsibility).

[51] In Grand Committee stage of the Companies Bill the Attorney-General put it as follows:

"The Company Law Review considered and consulted on two main options. The first was 'enlightened shareholder value' under which a director must first act in the way that he or she considers, in good faith, would be most likely to promote the success of the company for the benefit of its members. I shall come back to the question . . . about what is meant by 'success'. Secondly, in doing so, he or she must take account, where relevant and so far as reasonably practicable, of other factors such as the impact of the company's activities on the community and the environment . . . The alternative approach was the pluralist approach, which is strongly supported by some people. Under it, directors would be required to serve a range of wider interests—employees, suppliers, local communities and the environment—not subordinate to, but as a means of achieving, shareholder value. The Company Law Review came down firmly on the side of enlightened shareholder value. The Government agree that this is the right approach. It resolves any confusion in the minds of directors as to what the interests of the company are, and prevents any inclination to identify those interests with their own. It also prevents confusion between the interests of those who depend on the company and those of the members."

[52] See Ch.4 (Directors—Duties and Liabilities).

[53] Mr Jeremy Booker, VP corporate governance, BP.

[54] *http://www.hermes.co.uk/pdf/corporate_governance/Hermes_Principles.pdf.*

shareholder value] is best measured by the present value of the cash flows from investment discounted at an appropriate cost of capital". This Hermes defines as "WACC"—Weighted Average Cost of Capital, meaning the cost of funding taking into account the cost of debt and equity capital. The Hermes Principles go on to state:

"The best companies are demonstrably aware of the importance of WACC to all decision-making. WACC is an important number. If a company sets it too high, it will discount too heavily the value it creates, particularly over the long term. If it sets it too low, it will invest in a way which destroys value."

It remains to be seen whether the Hermes view of "WACC" will find approval generally.

Figure 1.2 provides an extract from the WACC principles.

Figure 1.2   Hermes WACC principles

A company will usually be funded by a mixture of equity and debt. WACC—the weighted cost of capital—is the cost of funding taking into account the cost of debt and equity capital.

WACC can be a difficult number to calculate precisely. It is important that investors know that companies understand their cost of capital, but very few companies state clearly in their annual report and accounts their WACC assumptions. Given that WACC underpins the financial goals of a company seen from an investor perspective this is somewhat surprising. One of the few companies that does make a clear statement on its WACC is Geest plc. It is also a good example of frank reporting to shareholders.

> Geest seeks to enhance shareholder value. The average post-tax return on invested capital including goodwill in 2000 was 16% (1999: 17%) versus a weighted cost of capital (WACC) of less than 10%. Geest has had an inefficient balance sheet entirely funded by shareholders, and as a result we have operated with a sub-optimal WACC. As borrowings increase to fund our growth, our WACC will decrease.
>
> (Geest plc annual report 2001)

As this document is written late in 2002, an average FTSE 100 company cost of debt might be around 6% (4% post-tax). A large FTSE company may have a cost of equity of between 7% and 9%. Therefore WACC for an average large FTSE company may be of the order of 7%–8%, and higher where risk perceived by investors increases the cost of both equity and debt capital.

As pension fund investors, our required return on equities is projected at 8%. The FSA assumed investment returns for assessing maturity targets of life policies are 6%–8%. The purpose of highlighting these numbers is not to set expectations for returns on investment, but to set them into context in a realistic way. Reasonable expectations are more likely to result in rational plans that will deliver reasonable outcomes.

Good companies make realistic assumptions. However some are tempted to make unrealistic assumptions about profitability and then discount at a high rate to counter the risk of their optimism. This has implications for the types of projects that will be invested in. With higher discount rates time distant returns count less in relative terms. An overly high discount rate discriminates against longer term projects and builds in unhelpful short-termism.

The debate about the meaning and relevance of "shareholder value" as a measure of board room performance re-started in the wake of the banking crisis of 2007/2009 and the FRC review of the then Combined Code. In a letter to the *Financial Times*[55] in 2010 the issue was summarised in these terms:

> "For a time, any manager with the power of chief executive-hood at a company that has previously built up tangible and intangible assets (reputation, goodwill, brands) can delight the market with quarterly earnings inflated by short-term cost cutting, rather than by building sustainable value. But focusing on shareholders to the exclusion of environmental and social impacts will exact a heavy long-term price . . . This is why Richard Lambert of the CBI is right to insist on a mixture of key performance indicators reflecting the triple bottom line of economic, social and environmental performance."

"Comply or explain", "apply or explain" and the curse of "box ticking"

1.029 As part of an excellent introductory passage to the 2010 UK Corporate Governance Code published by the FRC there is an aide memoire headed "comply or explain". It is worth quoting part of it here:

> "1. The 'comply or explain' approach is the trademark of corporate governance in the UK. It has been in operation since the Code's beginnings and is the foundation of the Code's flexibility. It is strongly supported by both companies and shareholders and has been widely admired and imitated internationally.
> 2. The Code is not a rigid set of rules. It consists of principles (main and supporting) and provisions. The Listing Rules require companies to apply the Main Principles and report to shareholders on how they have done

---

[55] April 16, 2010, from Mr David Grayson, Director, Doughty Centre for Corporate Responsibility, Cranfield School of Management.

so. The principles are the core of the Code and the way in which they are applied should be the central question for a board as it determines how it is to operate according to the Code.

3. It is recognised that an alternative to following a provision may be justified in particular circumstances if good governance can be achieved by other means. A condition of doing so is that the reasons for it should be explained clearly and carefully to shareholders, who may wish to discuss the position with the company and whose voting intentions may be influenced as a result. In providing an explanation, the company should aim to illustrate how its actual practices are both consistent with the principle to which the particular provision relates and contribute to good governance.

4. In their responses to explanations, shareholders should pay due regard to companies' individual circumstances and bear in mind, in particular, the size and complexity of the company and the nature of the risks and challenges it faces. Whilst shareholders have every right to challenge companies' explanations if they are unconvincing, they should not be evaluated in a mechanistic way and departures from the Code should not be automatically treated as breaches. Shareholders should be careful to respond to the statements from companies in a manner that supports the 'comply or explain' process and bearing in mind the purpose of good corporate governance. They should put their views to the company and both parties should be prepared to discuss the position."

At the time of publication of the Higgs Review in 2003, Mr Higgs pleaded with institutions and press to adopt a grown-up attitude to the "comply or explain" approach of the new and extended Combined Code. It would only work, he reasoned, if companies were to be judged on the quality of their explanation for aspects of the Code which were not complied with rather than being judged on the absence of a "tick in the box": "It could become, 'comply or get your trousers down in the press'". He also advised: "I would say to shareholders: 'Don't create a little hatched empire of corporate governance which has no connection to the substance of investment decisions'".

The "comply or explain" approach is no "cheap" system of regulation for companies or particularly for shareholders. The advantages are said to be:

- it retains flexibility rather than mandating rigid structural requirements;

- it requires [ideally] thoughtful application and disclosure by companies and thoughtful analysis by shareholders;

- it encourages companies to go further than traditionally legislators/ regulators have forced companies to go;

- it necessitates boards and shareholders to engage with each other.

As against that, it is said that companies/boards may be seen as unfettered and unaccountable if they adopt the "comply or explain" approach.

Moreover, occasionally, engagement by shareholders will lead to conflict: voting against board recommendations, removal of directors, etc.; and there is a danger that explanation (rather than compliance) is labelled as a failure. In the 2009 review of the then Combined Code by the FRC it was put to the FRC by a number of respondents that the approach should be rather one of "apply or explain" a concept adopted by the Dutch corporate governance regime: It being said that such an approach allowed more flexibility in departing from the Code provided that explanations were given. However, the FRC rejected that approach and in a specific "comply or explain" part of the preamble to the 2010 UK Corporate Governance Code it said:

> "Whilst shareholders have every right to challenge companies' explanations if they are unconvincing, they should not be evaluated in a mechanistic way and departures from the Code should not be automatically treated as breaches."

It is not yet clear whether the "comply or explain" approach will be successful in the sense that Higgs pleaded for. One reason for this is the organisations known by various names such as "proxy companies" or "voting agencies" or "rating agencies".[56] These organisations, which are appointed by funds to act as their proxies and have huge voting power and influence, are building databases of governance ratings of listed companies. The data is based essentially on "boxes" compiled by reviewing the annual reports. Points are given for boxes which are ticked and deducted for boxes which are not, regardless of the justifications given for the absence of a tick. The largest agencies have indicated that decisions not only on voting but also on placing investment funds will have regard to these ratings.

However, as a welcome contrast to this approach, in October 2005, Hermes Pension Fund Management, one of the largest and most activist funds in the UK, in its response to the review of the Combined Code by the FRC said[57]:

> "The one practical barrier to implementing the Code seems to be a tendency to regard its provisions as rules rather than guidelines, and therefore to avoid non-compliance at almost all costs. We have written to several companies which have disclosed an intention to make changes for reasons which appear to be related solely to the Code, to encourage them to do what is right for their business rather than simply to comply. At Hermes, we have sufficient staff and a deliberate commitment to seek to understand each of the companies in which our clients invest such that we have a proper basis for our decision as to whether to accept the explanations which we

---

[56] For example ISS—Institutional Shareholder Services: *http://www.riskmetrics.com/index.html*.
[57] *http://frc.org.uk/corporate/reviews.cfm*.

are given. We are committed to the principle of comply or explain. We would welcome more companies and particularly small companies having the confidence not to comply for its own sake but to explain their good reasons for non-compliance. We co-wrote the Quoted Companies Alliance guide to the Code to provide encouragement to smaller listed companies in this regard. One further point is that the improvements in the quality of disclosure mentioned above have been noteworthy with regards to some smaller companies where, previously, disclosure had been of limited value."

This approach is the approach adopted by the FRC and the two largest institutional shareholder groups in the UK, namely the National Association of Pension Funds ("NAPF") and the Association of British Insurers ("ABI").

However, the third largest group, PIRC, which represents a number of local authority pension funds, does seem, or at least is firmly so perceived by its investee companies, to insist that failure to comply is "failure" regardless of explanation. That approach seems also to be adopted by so-called "voting" or "proxy" agencies operating out of the US (e.g. ISS).

So, at this point, the jury is very much out as to which way the "box ticking/comply or explain" debate will go. There is still even after the Walker Review and the 2009 review of the Code by the FRC a chance that an unintended consequence of the Code will be a return to the situation which Higgs intended to avoid, namely, that companies will strive to tick every governance box even if (as in Maxwell and Enron, for example) the essential *values* which good governance is intended to promote may be absent—whilst other companies which may for good reason not wish to tick every box, but nevertheless essentially practice the values of good governance, will be downgraded.[58]

Part 4: Does the Code and corporate governance "work" and in any case does it matter?

The Code[59]—has it worked?

In the review carried out by the FRC in 2009 following the banking crisis the FRC found in general that companies were adopting the Code in spirit as well as letter.[60]   **1.030**

---

[58] para.7 of the Preface to the Code exhorts chairmen personally to draft the passages of the governance code dealing with Leadership and Effectiveness in the hopes of avoiding the "fungus of boiler plate".
[59] Formerly called *the Combined Code*, but now to be called *the UK Corporate Governance Code*.
[60] See *http://www.frc.org.uk/corporate*.

The main features of the feedback to the FRC can be summarised as:

"• The Combined Code and its predecessors had contributed to clear improvements in governance standards since the first code was introduced in 1992;

• While there were differing views about the extent to which the perceived shortcomings in governance in the banking sector were replicated in the listed sector as a whole, many considered at least some of them to be specific to that sector;

• There was a recognition that the quality of corporate governance ultimately depended on behaviour not process, with the result that there was a limit to the extent to which any regulatory framework could deliver good governance; and

• Market participants expressed a strong preference for retaining the current approach of 'soft law' underpinned by some regulation, rather than moving to one more reliant on legislation and regulation. It was seen as better able to react to developments in best practice, and because it could take account of the different circumstances in which companies operate it could set higher standards to which they were encouraged to aspire.

While the view of a large majority of respondents was that there was no need for a complete overhaul of the content of the Combined Code, there were a number of parts of the Code which needed further review and possibly revision.

Both companies and investors expressed reservations about the way in which 'comply or explain' works in practice, and it was clear that more needed to be done to encourage all parties to apply it in the intended manner.

The FRC shared the market's view that the flexible 'soft law' approach remained the most appropriate way of raising standards of corporate governance in listed companies, as did Sir David Walker in his banking governance review. But the continuing credibility of that approach depended on there being consensus that the contents of the Code were conducive to best practice, and on companies and investors acting in the spirit, not just the letter, of the Code and 'comply or explain'.

In particular it was of critical importance that there are sufficient institutional investors willing and able to engage actively with the companies in which they invest. 'This cannot be taken for granted—dispersed ownership, the declining market share of UK insurance companies and pension funds and resource constraints are all potential obstacles to achieving this objective. In their turn, companies must be willing to welcome communication with their shareholders as an opportunity to obtain an informed external perspective on their performance'."

Does corporate governance in general "work"? Three views

The "it's broke and we need to mend it" view

In a paper published in February 2010 by the doyen of governance gurus, **1.031**
Robert ("Bob") AG Monks, entitled "Corporate Governance past, present
& future".
He concluded as follows:

"This paper is based on two assumptions:

- A self-governing corporate structure is optimal *if* it can be made to
  work.
- The history of the last 30 years of supposed corporate 'self-restraint'
  coupled with the economic debacle of the last two years offers com-
  pelling evidence that current efforts at corporate governance are not
  working.

Who, then, will step into the breach? This time, three assumptions are at
play:

- Involved owners (i.e. shareholders) are the 'last best chance' for an
  internally governed corporate structure.
- Ownership as presently construed is so diffuse and often so transient
  that even the most committed owners have virtually no say in corporate governance and often must endure onerous expenses even to be
  actively ignored.
- Therefore, two classes of ownership are both desired and needed:
  passive shareholders, who choose not to exercise ownership rights,
  and stewardship shareholders, who already bear a fiduciary responsibility for funds under their management.
- Clearly, realizing this vision of empowered owner-stewards will
  entail federal action:

  - First, only the federal government can create a framework of
    legally enforceable responsibility.
  - Second, government enforcement will be central to creating an
    environment within which leaders of the fiduciary community
    can develop practices for selecting fiduciaries and for monitor-
    ing portfolio companies.
  - Third, enlightened governmental guidance can also assure
    that this new cadre of corporate stewards equally represents

(a) computer-selected shareholders – i.e., through index funds – with their wide perspective and (b) long-term owners of carefully chosen equities with their narrower focus on specific corporate performance.

- Fourth and finally, government action will be needed to create a mechanism for compensating these corporate owner-stewards – a practical recognition of the asymmetry of responsibility between their duties and the non-participation of the passive owners for whom this cadre will serve as proxy."

The sceptical but broadly supportive view

1.032   The banking crisis of 2007/2009 was described by many commentators as a failure in governance.[61] In January 2006 KPMG and the research consultancy Lintstock published research[62] from a number of top FTSE companies into attitudes among company secretaries, executive and non-executive directors towards contemporary governance requirements. The research seemed to show that there is still some way to go before those who have to execute governance at listed company level are convinced about its added value, and that institutional investors themselves are still not engaging as comprehensively as they might with their investee companies.

"So, despite the fact that most of our respondents felt that where and when it had occurred, the level and quality of engagement had improved all around, they were fairly unanimous in their belief that their spend on corporate governance compliance didn't represent much value for shareholders.

Our respondents indicated that success to the organisation was defined not only in financial terms but by some non-financial measures as well, which all pointed toward creating long-term value. They seemed to imply that good governance lay at the heart of sustainable long-term value but stopped short of saying that there is a definitive premium applied to their share price because of it. For them it was more conclusive to argue about the discount effect of bad governance than the other way around. This echoed the findings we reported on last year where fund managers' perceptions of the quality of governance had an asymmetric effect on their share valuations. In their view, where companies were considered to be above a minimum governance threshold, further movements towards

---

[61] "But serious deficiencies in prudential oversight and financial regulation in the period before the crisis were accompanied by major governance failures within banks. These contributed materially to excessive risk taking and to the breadth and depth of the crisis". Walker Review of the governance of banks, November 2009, p.9.
[62] KPMG/Lintstock.

better governance had little or no effect on the valuations. The valuations were only impacted where the standards fell below the minimum threshold."

In truth, judged solely in terms of corporate performance, there is very little evidence to show any convincing link between performance or valuation and good governance, at least as defined in terms of the former Combined Code, now the UK Corporate Governance Code.

The optimistic view

Judged in terms of issues such as: **1.033**

- support for share price;

- cost of and ability to raise capital;

- internal control and risk management;

- reputational standing;

- relationship of trust between shareholders and board;

there is a general belief that good governance does lead to greater resilience of share price, stronger internal controls and risk management and a better relationship with shareholders.

"We believe the code has had a marked impact on the quality of corporate governance in the UK ... disclosure overall has improved significantly. Disclosure adds value by reducing investor concern and uncertainty. By doing so it cuts the cost of capital and allows companies to generate excess return."[63]

Management consultants McKinsey published in 2002 the widely quoted Global Investor Opinion Survey[64] suggesting that companies with high corporate governance standards were worth significantly more to investors than those with loose governance standards—even if the comparison was between companies with identical business and financial profiles. For the purposes of the survey, well-governed companies were defined as those having:

(a) a significant amount of "independent" directors including financial specialists on the board;

---

[63] Hermes submission to the FRC Consultation on the review of the Combined Code, 2005: *http://www.frc.org.uk/corporate/combinedcode.cfm.*
[64] Search Google: "McKinsey Global Investor Opinion Survey 2002".

(b)   a culture of broad disclosure;

(c)   strong rights and equal treatment for shareholders.

McKinsey found that 78 per cent of European investors put a higher value on well-governed companies. The average premium specified was 12 per cent for UK companies and 18 per cent for US companies.

Research published in February 2003 by Harvard University found that:

> "corporate governance is strongly correlated with stock returns during the 1990s. An investment strategy that purchased shares in . . . 'Democracy' firms with strong shareholder rights and sold shares in . . . 'Dictatorship' firms with weak shareholder rights, earned abnormal returns of 8.5 per cent per year."[65]

The study commented that it was not possible to establish causality between governance and performance, but it was possible to establish the correlation.

Good governance is also said to provide a bulwark against the destruction of value:

> "Governance is a risk factor that needs to be better understood by investors, stakeholders and companies themselves. While researchers are still trying to build empirical evidence that good governance creates value, we have vivid and recent case studies in both developed and emerging markets that show how poor corporate governance can destroy value."[66]

The ISS 2006 Global Investor Study found that:

> "although almost seven in ten investors believe that corporate governance offers value, 81% said that they do not yet have metrics in place to assess the specific value of their corporate governance activities. As one U.S. investment manager put it, however, 'Just because corporate governance is hard to quantify doesn't mean it can't offer competitive advantage.' In fact, almost 30% of institutional investors indicated that corporate governance offers their firm a competitive advantage and a plurality of almost 40% said that the most significant advantage of corporate governance is enhanced shareholder returns."

---

[65] Gompers, Ishii and Metrick: the *Quarterly Journal of Economics*, Vol.CXVIII, February 2003, Issue 1, p.107 (MIT Press, Cambridge, Mass).
[66] George S Dallas, Managing Director and Global Practice Leader, Standard & Poor's (2005).

Conclusion

It seems that good governance matters, partly because it is a risk manage- **1.034**
ment and control process, a "good thing" in its own right, partly because
capital raising is believed to be cheaper, and partly simply because investors
believe it matters and are apparently prepared to pay a premium for it, or
at least to support management through bad or hostile times and give it the
benefit of the doubt. At least for the foreseeable future, governments and
institutions are going to insist on imposing governance regimes broadly, in
Europe, along UK Corporate Governance Code lines. At the same time, it
is to be expected that values-based and sustainability driven governance will
attract increasing attention.

Finally, it is worth repeating that "governance" should never be allowed
to obstruct honest commercial endeavour and enterprise: As the late and
much lamented Jonathan Charkham put it: "Even a megaton of governance
is no substitute for invention, entrepreneurial skill, originality, and sheer
managerial competence and integrity".[67]

---

[67] *Keeping Better Company*, J Charkham, Oxford, 2005.

Chapter 2

The Regulatory Regime

General regime for Premium listed companies[1]

Corporate governance in the UK in relation to Premium listed companies[2] is driven by six main influences: **2.001**

---

[1] This book deals with the rules applying to Premium listed companies (see fn 2 below) and thus the UK Corporate Governance Code, on the basis that non-Premium or Standard listed companies will adopt corporate governance codes which although possibly less comprehensive than the UK Corporate Governance Code will nevertheless cover the same ground as that Code thus making the UK Corporate Governance Code the benchmark of good practice. The Quoted Companies Alliance has been working on a suitable code and reference should be made to their website for the latest position: *http://www.quotedcompaniesalliance.co.uk*.

[2] On October 9, 2009 the FSA announced changes to the listing regime with effect from April 6, 2010. The changes are explained in an FSA paper which can be read online at *http://www.fsa.gov. uk/pages/Doing/UKLA/pdf/listing_regime_faqs.pdf*. There is also set out in App.1 to this book a copy of Sch.B to the UK Corporate Governance Code ("Disclosure of Corporate Governance arrangements") which contains an excellent description of the Premium and Standard governance disclosure regimes and the respective requirements of the Disclosure and Transparency Rules and the Listing Rules. The principal changes to the Listing Rules have been as follows:
- the creation of two listing standards—Premium and Standard;
- all Premium listed companies (including overseas companies) must comply with "super-equivalent" standards, including a requirement to "comply or explain" against the UK Corporate Governance Code;
- all Standard listed companies must comply with EU minimum listing standards including the requirement to provide a "corporate governance statement" together with a description of internal control and risk management systems. However, Standard Listed companies will not be included in any of the FTSE Indices. The Corporate Governance statement must be in accordance with the FSA's Disclosure and Transparency Rules DTR 7.2.1 and 7.2.2. In essence they require a statement on internal controls and risk management and a statement as to which code of corporate governance the company observes and an explanation as to significant departures from that code or (if the case) why the company has decided not to observe any code. The Quoted Companies Alliance is at the latest practicable date before publication of this book drafting a corporate governance code suitable for AIM and Standard listed companies;
- Standard listings will be available to UK companies and not just to overseas companies (as was the case prior to the Listing Rule changes); and
- the establishment of a simplified procedure allowing companies with an equity listing to transfer with shareholder consent from one segment to another without the need to cancel their listings but losing their FTSE quoted status if moving to Standard from Premium.

- the Financial Reporting Council[3] ("FRC") which as described in Ch.1[4] has taken on the responsibility for the drafting and keeping up to date of governance codes for Premium listed companies, and currently the UK Corporate Governance Code. In reality, because the FRC also controls all the audit and financial reporting standards and disciplinary bodies, the FRC is now the main guiding influence in the UK on corporate governance;

- the Financial Services Authority ("FSA") as the ultimate enforcer of the Listing Rules, which, in this context, includes the "Model Code" governing dealings in shares by directors, and Listing Rules 9.8.6R and 9.8.7R and 9.8.7AR requiring "Premium Listed" companies to include a statement in the annual report of the application of and compliance with the UK Corporate Governance Code.[5] It is also the "competent authority" under s.1269 of the Companies Act 2006 ("CA 2006") for making "corporate governance rules" (e.g. the Disclosure and Transparency Rules) for issuers arising out of EU legislation. Hence, arising out of the Walker Review of corporate governance in UK banks and other financial industry entities, the FSA issued a Consultation Paper in January 2010 (CP 10/3)[6] The objective was stated of producing final rules in a Policy Statement (PS) in the third quarter of 2010: too late for inclusion in this edition but which of course may be accessed on the FSA website: *http://fsa.gov.uk*;

- statutes, such as relevant parts of the CA 2006, and the common law applicable to the interpretation of those statutes, and regulations (e.g. Listing Rules and Disclosure and Transparency Rules) having the force of law;

- quasi-regulatory, namely, principles-based codes of best practice, and in particular the UK Corporate Governance Code, descriptions and explanations of which are required to be given by listed companies under the Listing Rules[7];

  - institutional voting policies and shareholder activism;
  - public and press pressure.

Arguably, *any* legislation which governs the duties and conduct of a company or its directors might be said to fall within the governance regulatory regime.

---

[3] *http://www.frc.org.uk*.
[4] See para.1.023, Ch.1 (Definition, Background and Purpose of Corporate Governance).
[5] Known as the Combined Code in respect of financial years ending before the financial year commencing on or after June 29, 2010.
[6] *http://www.fsa.gov.uk/pubs/cp/cp10_03.pdf*.
[7] Arguably, such codes may be said to be regulatory in the sense that the Listing Rules are regulatory, but the "best practice" set out in the UK Corporate Governance Code is not in itself enforceable as a law or regulation. However, the requirement under Listing Rule 9.8.6 to set out a governance statement or "statement of application and compliance" *is* sanctionable under the Listing Rules. See further this chapter.

However, if one accepts the definition of corporate governance submitted at the commencement of Ch.1,[8] then it might be appropriate simply to confine an examination of the regulatory regime to relevant aspects of the "system by which companies are directed and controlled", and hence confined to an examination of "structures" and "process". In these terms the purely regulatory regime is relatively light at least in terms of extent if not effect, since on the whole the UK has chosen up until the CA 2006 to deal with corporate governance by quasi-regulation and principles-based codes, especially the Combined Code (now the UK Corporate Governance Code).

However, and in particular following the CA 2006, there are laws and regulations which directly impact on governance in a broader sense of laws which directly affect boardroom conduct: for example, laws in relation to directors' duties and shareholder rights, and laws relating to the contents of company reports and auditing and financial reporting.

The regulatory regime with which this book will primarily be concerned comprises essentially:

- those parts of the CA 2006 dealing with the duties and liabilities of directors and directors' remuneration, the annual report, including the new "business review", the annual general meeting and board meetings, financial reporting, and shareholder rights;

- Chapter 7 Pt 10 of the CA 2006 which is concerned with director indemnities and D&O insurance;

- the Disclosure and Transparency Rules and Listing Rules 9.8.6R, 9.8.7R and 9.8.7AR dealing with reporting under the UK Corporate Governance Code[9]; and

- EU Directives and Recommendations which are governance focused and arise from the Company Law Action Plan.[10]

Chapter 24 also sets out a concise appraisal of the principal governance and securities laws of the United States, including the Sarbanes-Oxley Act 2002, which affect UK companies whose securities are traded in the United States.

There are also a number of other important but ancillary "governance related" laws governing the conduct of directors (for example, wrongful trading or under the Financial Services and Markets Act 2000).[11] The "quasi-regulatory" regime comprises the Model Code governing dealings by directors in shares (set out in full in App.17); and the UK Corporate

---

[8] i.e. the Cadbury definition: "The system by which companies are directed and controlled".
[9] See App.1 of this book which contains the excellent Sch.B to the Code and sets out in clear form the respective disclosure regimes required by the Disclosure and Transparency Rules and the Listing Rules.
[10] See Ch.23 (The EU).
[11] See also Ch.19 (Communicating and Engagement with Shareholders).

Governance Code published originally as the "Combined Code" in 1998 and thereafter revised several times, the current version published by the FRC in June 2010 as the UK Corporate Governance Code. The 2010 Code took effect in respect of Premium listed companies in respect of financial years commencing on or after June 29, 2010.

Institutional voting policy and "activism" by institutional shareholders, is discussed in detail in Ch.18 (Institutional Shareholder Activism).

Press and public pressure is not dealt with in this book, but is a highly significant if occasionally wayward force.

The Disclosure and Transparency Rules and the Listing Rules

2.002 As the UK's competent authority under the Financial Services and Markets Act 2000, the FSA is responsible for making and enforcing the Disclosure and Transparency Rules and the Listing Rules governing admission to listing.

The full text of Disclosure and Transparency Rules 7.1 and 7.2 and Listing Rules 9.8.6R, 9.8.7R, 9.8.7AR are contained in the relevant chapters of the FSA Handbook, which can be found at *http://fsahandbook.info/FSA/html/handbook.*[12]

The Disclosure and Transparency Rules sub-chapters 7.1 and 7.2 apply to issuers whose securities are admitted to trading on a regulated market (this includes all issuers with a Premium or Standard listing). The Listing Rules 9.8.6R, 9.8.7R and 9.8.7AR and UK Corporate Governance Code apply to issuers of Premium listed equity shares only. There is some overlap between the mandatory disclosures required under the Disclosure and Transparency Rules and those under the Listing Rules.[13] In respect of disclosures relating to the audit committee and the composition and operation of the board and its committees, compliance with the relevant provisions of the Code will result in compliance with the relevant Rules.

Statute

The Companies Act 2006

2.003 The CA 2006 received Royal Assent on November 8, 2006. The parts of the CA 2006 which are primarily the subject of this book, namely, Pt 10

---

[12] An excellent summary of the respective Rules and the relationship between the Disclosure and Transparency Rules and the Listing Rules is set out in Sch.B to the Code and is itself printed in App.1 to this book.

[13] Areas of overlap are summarised in the Appendix to Sch.B of the Code, the full text of which is set out in App.1 of this book.

(Directors, except the "conflict of interest duties" were implemented in October 2007), Pt 11 (Derivative claims), Pt 12 (company secretaries), and Pt 13 (Resolutions and meetings) were implemented by statutory instrument to take effect also as from October 2007 whilst Pt 15 (Accounts and reports) and Pt 16 (Audit) were implemented in April 2008.

It is a huge piece of legislation, the longest Act in British history. Part of the reason for its length was the need to implement parts of the EU Modernisation, Transparency and Takeover Directives, and to consolidate or "re-state" large parts of the Companies Act 1985 not repealed by the CA 2006. As a broad generalisation, however, the remainder of the Act covers the ground covered in previous Companies Acts. Thus, the familiar ground of the types of company, methods of incorporation, share capital, accounts, meetings, publication and filing of documents and the duties and powers of the Registrar of Companies appears in the CA 2006 but in a contemporary context and updated to take account of many of the recommendations of the Company Law Review.

A material part of the legislation deals with electronic communication. The legislation also takes account in various contexts of "small", "medium-sized", "quoted" and "traded" companies.

Any attempt in this initial view of the regulatory environment to identify particular aspects of the CA 2006 which impact on governance, as distinct from the whole range of company law, is bound to be selective and somewhat arbitrary. However, the following seem obvious and significant to mention at this stage, with more detailed treatment in the later chapters of this book.

Directors' duties and liabilities

The CA 2006 introduces a statutory statement of duties of directors to clarify   **2.004** their responsibilities and the law regulating directors' conflicts and declarations of interest, embedding in statute the concept of "enlightened shareholder value".[14] Under that concept, directors must promote the success of the company for the benefit of its shareholders, but must "have regard to" long-term and wider factors such as employees, the environment, suppliers and customers. The CA 2006 also codified the circumstances in which a shareholder can force a company to sue a director for breach of duty under what is known as a "derivative action".

A fuller analysis of these provisions is contained in Ch.4 (Directors—Duties and Liabilities).

---

[14] See further Ch.1 (Definition, Background and Purpose of Corporate Governance), para.1.025 and Ch.4 (Directors—Duties and Liabilities).

Director indemnities by companies and directors' and officers' insurance

2.005   Chapter 7 Pt 10 of the Act re-states the provisions of the Companies (Audit, Investigations and Community Enterprise) Act 2004 permitting companies, in terms, to indemnify directors against liabilities and insure them against third-party claims. This regime is described in detail in Ch.12 (D&O Insurance and Indemnification).

Narrative reporting

2.006   Section 417 of the CA 2006 has introduced a statutory requirement for a "business review" to be contained in the annual report. The business review is intended to encourage boards to be more open about their strategic aims and the extent to which they are succeeding in those aims. In response to concerns about liability for negligent misstatement in the annual report there is a welcome attempt to provide a "safe harbour" in the form of relief from liability, on terms, in s.463 (liability for false or misleading statements in reports).

A more detailed analysis of these provisions is in Chs 4 (Directors—Duties and Liabilities), 16 (The Annual Report) and 13 (Financial Reporting).

Directors' remuneration

2.007   The CA 2006 ss.420–422, make provision for regulations in relation to directors remuneration and the subject of directors' remuneration is fully dealt with in Ch.11 (Directors' Remuneration).

Shareholder power—enhanced rights of beneficial owners

2.008   Up until the CA 2006 it was not possible for the beneficial owners of shares whose shares were registered in the name of nominees (e.g. ISAs or PEPS or trusts) to require companies to send them, as distinct from the registered nominee, information about the company, including the annual report and accounts. Nor was it possible at law for the beneficial owner if not registered, to require companies to circulate statements or requisition meetings, or to speak or vote at meetings, or for that matter, do any of the things that a registered member could do.

The provisions of Pt 9 of the CA 2006 now completely reverse that position. In effect, the nominee holder can grant the beneficial owner, if requested, the same rights to vote, speak at, appoint proxies, receive information, receive the annual report and accounts, circulate shareholder resolutions and have all other rights as if (s)he were a registered member.

Although early indications are that these provisions are being largely ignored by beneficial owners, the implications of these provisions may over time be immense, and listed companies will need to gear up to meet the requirements of the beneficial owners who are not registered. If a significant number of individual beneficial owners start to exert their rights under the CA 2006 the result could be an interesting extension of activism as powerful if not more powerful than the institutions.

Political donations

Part 14 of the CA 2006 restates the regime for control of political dona- **2.009** tions and expenditure as inserted by the Political Parties, Elections and Referendums Act 2000 into Pt 10A of the Companies Act 1985. Breach of these provisions can impose on directors personal liability to reimburse the company.

Corporate governance rules

Section 1273 of the CA 2006 inserts into the Financial Services and Markets **2.010** Act 2000 provision for the FSA, as the "competent authority" as required by the EU Transparency Directive, to make rules under the heading of "corporate governance". This it has done in the "Disclosure and Transparency Rules"[15] ("DTR") in which DTR 7.1 deals with corporate governance rules for Standard listed companies.[16]

EU Directives and Recommendations

As part of the EU Company Law Action Plan a number of Recommendations **2.011** and Directives aimed at establishing common standards of governance throughout the European Union have been issued or are proposed. A fuller analysis is set out in Ch.23 (The EU).

Other relevant statutes

These are discussed in Ch.4 (Directors—Duties and Liabilities). **2.012**

---

[15] See the FSA Handbook: *http://fsahandbook.info/FSA/html/handbook/DTR.*
[16] See fns 1 and 2 above.

Quasi regulation

The UK Corporate Governance Code

Background

2.013   In the 1998 Hampel Report (2.1), the Hampel Committee drew a distinction between "principles" of corporate governance and more detailed "guidelines" like the Cadbury and Greenbury Codes:

> "With guidelines, one asks 'how far are they complied with?' with principles, the right question is: 'How far are they applied in practice?'. We recommend that companies should include in their annual report and accounts a narrative statement of how they apply the relevant principles to their particular circumstances. Given that the responsibility for good corporate governance rests with the board of directors, the written description of the way in which the board has applied the principles of corporate governance represents a key part of the process. We do not prescribe the form or context of the statement which could conveniently be linked with the compliance statement required by the Listing Rules."

That formula of "applying" principles and "complying" with or "explaining" in relation to provisions has since been adopted in all iterations of the UK corporate governance codes from the Combined Code to the current UK Corporate Governance Code.

The Combined Code/the UK Corporate Governance Code

2.014   The Higgs review in January 2003 (set out in full in App.2) suggested an extensive enlargement of the Combined Code which after review by the FRC was published in July 2003 as "the Combined Code on Corporate Governance" and adopted by the UK Listing Authority with effect from financial years commencing on or after November 1, 2003. The Combined Code was further revised by the FRC in 2006 and 2008 and revised and published in April 2010 under the new name of "the UK Corporate Governance Code".

    The 2010 edition of the UK Corporate Governance Code[17] applies to all Premium listed companies for financial years beginning on or after June 29,

---

[17] See the FRC website *http://www.frc.org.uk* for the full text.

2010.[18] It consists of 18 Main Principles, 28 Supporting Principles (together, "Principles") and 52 Provisions ("Provisions"). In addition, there are seven provisions set out in Schedule A to the Code on the design of performance related information, and in Schedule B is set out the disclosure requirements for corporate governance required by the Disclosure and Transparency Rules and the Listing Rules and the Code.[19] Schedule C has the "engagement principles for institutional investors", which are to fall away once the "Stewardship Code" compiled by the FRC in 2010 and published in June 2010 has come into force. The Code also refers to guidance from the "Turnbull" guidance on internal controls (see Ch.15 (Risk Management and Internal Control) and the Smith Guidance for audit committees (see Ch.14 (External Audit, Internal Audit and the Audit Committee)) both of which may be found in full on the FRC website.

The effect of these latter two sets of guidance[20] is that in respect of the Code disclosures required by Listing Rule 9.8.6R (for UK incorporated companies and 9.8.7R (for overseas companies) in the annual report on internal control and internal audit and audit committees, companies will need to test these against the Turnbull and Smith Guidance respectively. However, it is submitted that the making of any such disclosures should be subject to the overall flexibility of approach prescribed in the preamble wording to the UK Corporate Governance Code headed: "comply or explain" (see para.2.016 below).

Footnotes 13 and 15 of the Code make it clear that the two sets of guidelines "suggest" rather than "prescribe" ways of applying the relevant Code Principles and Provisions and of complying with the relevant Code Provisions, not to prescribe.

Further support for this approach in relation to internal audit and internal controls comes from the Preface to the Turnbull guidance on internal control (see the FRC website).

Model Code governing directors' dealings

The UK Listing Authority and the Annex 1 to UK Listing Rule 9 lay down rules in the form of a code ("The Model Code", a copy of which is in App.19) governing the dealing by directors and other insiders in the shares of companies of which they are directors.   **2.015**

---

[18] Since the great majority of listed companies' financial years run from January 1 to December 31 and although many listed companies undoubtedly will start to report against the revised UK Code in the April 2011 reporting season it is likely that the majority of annual reports reporting against the new Code will occur in the April 2012 season.

[19] See App.1 to this book for the full text of this useful Schedule.

[20] Which overlap the FSA DTR Rules 7.2.5, 7.1.1 and 7.1.3.

Enforcement of the UK Corporate Governance Code and the Listing Rules

2.016 Enforcement of the Code is shared between the FSA as guardian of the Listing Rules and the FRC as the promoter of the Code.[21] The sanctionable breach which arises is breach of the Listing Rules, hence the FSA's role, not breach of the UK Corporate Governance Code. The Listing Rules require that companies to which the Code applies shall apply the Main Principles of the Code and report to shareholders that they have done so. If such a company fails to insert a disclosure statement in its annual report which complies with the Listing Rules then the sanctions which apply are those which would apply for breach of any other Listing Rule, ranging from censure to fines to de-listing.

However, experience has shown that on the whole, public censure from the FRC, shareholder pressure and press comments have also been powerful engines to ensure compliance.

However, within that backstop regulatory framework a good deal of latitude is given to board to design governance strategy.

The general approach is set out in the introductory wording to the 2010 UK Corporate Governance Code under the headings "governance and the code" and "comply or explain" and also in the Preface to the Code. These comprise a highly important context for the Code and should be carefully studied when working out how to approach the Code.[22]

The preamble to the Code describing the approach to the "comply or explain" principle makes it clear that it is for boards to determine how the Code operates.

"2.The Code is not a rigid set of rules. It consists of principles (main and supporting) and provisions. The Listing Rules require companies to apply the main Principles and report to shareholders on how they have done so. The principles are the core of the Code and the way in which they are applied should be the central question for a board as it determines how it is to operate according to the Code.

3. It is recognised that an alternative to following a provision may be justified in particular circumstances if good governance can be achieved by other means. A condition of doing so is that the reasons for it should be explained clearly and carefully to shareholders,[23] who may wish to discuss the position with the company and whose voting intentions may be influenced as a result. In providing an explanation, the company should aim

---

[21] However, in July 2010 the Government announced that it would start a consultation exercise on the proposal that the UK Listing Authority and the FRC should merge, with the FRC taking the overall supervision of the Listing Rules.

[22] See the FRC website *http://www.frc.org.uk*>UK Corporate Governance Code.

[23] References to shareholders also apply to intermediaries and agents employed to assist shareholders in scrutinising governance arrangements.

to illustrate how its actual practices are consistent with the principle to which the particular provision relates and contribute to good governance.

4. In their responses to explanations, shareholders should pay due regard to companies' individual circumstances and bear in mind in particular the size and complexity of the company and the nature of the risks and challenges it faces. Whilst shareholders have every right to challenge companies' explanations if they are unconvincing, they should not be evaluated in a mechanistic way and departures from the Code should not be automatically treated as breaches. Shareholders should be careful to respond to the statements from companies in a manner that supports the 'comply or explain' process and bearing in mind the purpose of good corporate governance. They should put their views to the company and both parties should be prepared to discuss the position.

5. Smaller listed companies, in particular those new to listing, may judge that some of the provisions are disproportionate or less relevant in their case. Some of the provisions do not apply to companies below the FTSE 350. Such companies may nonetheless consider that it would be appropriate to adopt the approach in the Code and they are encouraged to do so. Externally managed investment companies typically have a different board structure which may affect the relevance of particular provisions; the Association of Investment Companies' Corporate Governance Code and Guide can assist them in meeting their obligations under the Code.

6. Satisfactory engagement between company boards and investors is crucial to the health of the UK's corporate governance regime. Companies and shareholders both have responsibility for ensuring that "comply or explain" remains an effective alternative to a rules-based system. There are practical and administrative obstacles to improved interaction between boards and shareholders. But certainly there is also scope for an increase in trust which could generate a virtuous upward spiral in attitudes to the Code and in its constructive use."

Sanctions for breach of the Listing Rules

In the highly unlikely event that a listed company did decide not to include a **2.017** statement of application and compliance in accordance with Rule 9.8.6R et al. then the FSA has powers to impose disciplinary measures.

The FSA Handbook [24] sets out the enforcement approach of the Authority [25] in relation to a breach of the Listing Rules as follows:

"Disciplinary measures are one of the regulatory tools available to the FSA. They are not the only tool, and it may be appropriate to address

---

[24] See *http://fsa.gov.uk/pages/handbook*.
[25] See *http://fsa.gov.uk/pages/handbook*.

many instances of non-compliance without recourse to disciplinary action. However, the effective and proportionate use of the FSA's powers to enforce the requirements of the Act,[26] the rules and the Statements of Principle[27] will play an important role in buttressing the FSA's pursuit of its regulatory objectives. The imposition of disciplinary measures (that is, financial penalties, public censures and public statements) shows that regulatory standards are being upheld and helps to maintain market confidence, promote public awareness of regulatory standards and deter financial crime. An increased public awareness of regulatory standards also contributes to the protection of consumers."

The disciplinary measures available to the FSA under Pt V (Performance of Regulated Activities) and Pt XIV (Disciplinary Measures) of the Act are:

"(1) public statements and public censures (described in ENF 12); and
(2) financial penalties (described in ENF 13).

ENF 11 Annex 1 and ENF 11 Annex 2 contain diagrams describing how these disciplinary measures may apply to firms and approved persons respectively.

Other measures are available to the FSA where it considers it is necessary to take protective or remedial action, (rather than disciplinary action) or where a firm's continuing ability to meet the threshold conditions or where an approved person's fitness and propriety to perform the controlled functions to which his or her approval relates, is called into question. These include:

(1) the variation or cancellation of permission and the withdrawal of a firm's authorisation (described in ENF 3 and ENF 5);
(2) the withdrawal of an individual's status as an approved person (described in ENF 7); and
(3) the prohibition of an individual from performing a specified function in relation to a regulated activity (described in ENF 8).

Additional considerations apply in determining whether to take enforcement action for market abuse cases (section 123 of the Act (Power to impose penalties in cases of market abuse)). These are described in ENF 14 (Sanctions for market abuse). The Act also gives the FSA criminal prosecution powers in relation to insider dealing and misleading statements and practices offences. These are described in ENF 15 (Prosecution of criminal offences)."

---

[26] Financial Services and Markets Act 2000.
[27] The Statements of Principle issued by the FSA under s.64(1) of the Financial Services and Markets Act (Conduct: Statements and codes) with respect to the conduct of approved persons and set out in that part of the FSA Handbook as "High Level Standards" has the titles "Statements of Principle" and "Code of Practice for Approved Persons".

Smaller listed companies

The Hampel and Higgs views

There were (see Higgs Review at para.2.014) as at January 2003, 1,847 listed **2.018** companies outside the FTSE 350 whose capitalisations ranged from a few hundred thousand pounds to hundreds of millions of pounds. The average size of the boards of such companies was six, with two non-executive directors, three executive directors, and a chairman. Eighty-five per cent of smaller listed companies had audit and remuneration committees but less than 29 per cent have a nomination committee.

In principle, however, there is no distinction in terms of governance standards for listed companies by reason of size.[28] The Hampel Report (1.10) said:

"For the most part, the larger listed companies have implemented both Codes (i.e. Cadbury and Greenbury) fully. Smaller companies have also implemented most provisions, but there are some aspects with which they find it harder to comply. We considered carefully whether we should distinguish between the governance standards expected of larger and smaller companies. We concluded that this would be a mistake. Any distinction by size would be arbitrary; more importantly, we consider that high standards of governance are as important for smaller listed companies as for larger. But we would urge those considering the governance arrangements of smaller listed companies to do so with flexibility and a proper regard to individual circumstances."

The Higgs Review recommended that apart from the recommendation that no one individual should sit on all three committees of the board (which did not ultimately find its way into the revised UK Corporate Governance Code) there should be no differentiation in the Code's provisions for larger and smaller companies:

"I recognise, however, that it may take more time for smaller listed companies to comply and that some of the Code's provisions may be less relevant for management of smaller companies."

---

[28] It is appreciated that the introduction by the FSA in April 2010 of revised rules for Premium and Standard listed companies (see fns 1 and 2 above) which enable Standard listed companies to adopt a code of governance other than the UK Corporate Governance Code appears on the face of it to make a distinction in governance standards between first and second tier companies. However, within the Premium listed sector there are wide variations in size, but no distinction is made on grounds of size save for the minimum number of non-executive directors for sub-FTSE 350 companies, i.e. at least two independent non-executive directors.

In line with this approach, the "comply or explain" preface to the 2010 UK Corporate Governance Code states:

> "Smaller listed companies, in particular those new to listing, may judge that some of the provisions are disproportionate or less relevant in their case. Some of the provisions do not apply to companies below the FTSE 350. Such companies may nonetheless consider that it would be appropriate to adopt the approach in the Code and they are encouraged to do so."

Accordingly, Code Provision B.1.2 which requires that at least half the board, excluding the chairman, should comprise non-executive directors "determined by the board to be independent" is mitigated in relation to "smaller companies" to require at least two such directors. "Smaller companies" are defined as those below the FTSE 350 throughout the year immediately prior to the reporting year.

Code Provision D.2.1 provides that in relation to the remuneration committee, a minimum of two members comprising independent non-executive directors for smaller companies as against three for FTSE 350 companies is permitted.

Code Provision C.3.1 has the same mitigating provision in relation to the audit committee which would otherwise require a minimum of three independent non-executive directors.

The greatest practical difficulty for smaller companies is the finding of suitable non-executive directors. Hampel (3.10) acknowledged that:

> "This is a real difficulty, but the need for a robust independent voice on the board is as strong in smaller companies as in large ones. In many smaller companies, the executives are also major shareholders and the level of external scrutiny by other shareholders and the market is low. Non-executive directors do a vital job in safeguarding minority interests and ensuring good governance."

The Higgs Review (paras 10.15 et seq.) suggested however that it was time to widen the pool from which non-executives were chosen by considering suitable people (and in particular more women and people from ethnic minority groups with suitable qualifications) drawn from private companies, larger charities and local government and public bodies such as Health Care trusts.

AIM companies

2.019 As at November 2009 over 3,000 companies were listed on the Alternative Investment Market of the London Stock Exchange. The Higgs review (16.9) stated: "My recommendations are directed at listed companies, but I hope and expect that many of them will also be of relevance to non-listed companies".

The Rules of the London Stock Exchange relating to AIM companies contain no provisions relating to governance save for AR 2 of the Third Schedule to the Nominated Adviser Rules which puts the onus on the nominated adviser to: "consider, with the directors of an applicant, the adoption of appropriate corporate governance measures".[29]

In practice, however, the agreements between "nominated advisers" of AIM listed companies and the companies themselves require AIM companies to adopt governance standards in relation to the separation of the roles of chairman and CEO, the appointment of remuneration, audit and nomination committees, and the appointment of non-executive (including independent) directors and restrictions on actions which may not be done by a company without the consent of the nominated adviser. In practice, any AIM company hoping to attract institutional investors will have to show that its governance procedures match those of smaller listed companies (see para.2.018 above).

In addition the QCA[30] has published a guidance booklet for AIM companies called "Corporate Governance Guidelines for AIM Companies" (February 2007).[31] This most useful booklet sets out a practical regime of governance principles and provisions for AIM companies which selects those parts of the UK Corporate Governance Code to which AIM companies should aspire.

The Quoted Companies Alliance ("QCA")

The QCA is a well established not-for-profit organisation that was formed   **2.020**
solely to represent the interests of smaller quoted companies on the Main List (i.e. sub-FTSE 350), AIM companies and "PLUS".[32]

Its stated objective is to "promote the interests of the small and mid-cap quoted company sector" by:

- **Lobbying** Government, Brussels and other regulators to reduce what it says is the costly and time consuming burden of regulation, which falls disproportionately on the small and mid-cap quoted community. This work is done primarily by its technical committees.

- **Promoting** the small and mid-cap quoted company sector, and taking steps to increase investor interest and improve shareholder liquidity. This is done by its technical committees and press contacts.

---

[29] London Stock Exchange AIM Rules for nominated advisers, Sch.3 (Nominated Adviser Responsibilities), Rule AR 2: *http://www.londonstockexchange.com/companies-and-advisors/aim/advisers/aim-notices/aim-rules-for-nominated-advisers.pdf.*
[30] See para.2.020 below.
[31] See *http://www.quotedcompaniesalliance.co.uk/guidance_booklets.asp.*
[32] Previously OFEX: *http://www.plusmarketsgroup.com.*

- **Educating** companies in the sector about best practice in areas such as corporate governance and investor relations. This is facilitated through its events and publications.

- **Providing a forum** for small and mid-cap quoted company directors to network and discuss solutions to topical issues with their peers, sector professionals and influential City figures via its events programmes.

Governance standards suggested by the QCA

2.021   The QCA website, *http://www.quotedcompaniesalliance.co.uk*, gives details of its governance publications on its publications page including a booklet called "Corporate Governance Guidelines for AIM Companies" (February 2007). At the time of printing of this book the QCA was working on a revised set of Guidelines which amongst other things would be appropriate for Standard listed companies.[33]

Private/family companies

2.022   There is no regulatory regime for governance which is specific to private or family companies other than those provisions of the CA 2006 which enable private companies, for example, to dispense with the Annual General Meeting and (in the case of "small" companies) to prepare annual accounts which are exempt from the full accounting regime and from audit.[34]

Indeed many private companies regard arrangements relating to governance as unwonted interference and needless bureaucracy.

However, attitudes have changed greatly in recent years and will continue to change as private companies continue to seek equity capital from sources other than the pockets of the founders.

There are good reasons why private companies, sometimes known as SME's (small and medium enterprises) should look at governance arrangements:

- in many cases SMEs are largely financed by their founder owners either by personal borrowings secured on their personal assets (for example their houses) or by bank debt secured by personal guarantees again secured on personal assets. The stakes are very high. Putting some basic governance structure and processes in place can help manage the risk of management taking undue risks and so avoid personal vulnerability to the owner managers;

---

[33] See fns 1 and 2 above.
[34] See generally CA 2006 Pt 15.

- the working capital of most SMEs has (despite the credit crunch) to be financed by bank borrowing. Banks take governance strongly into account in their assessment of risk;

- where there are several owner/founder investors, the existence of solid governance can create a great sense of mutual confidence and trust;

- as an SME grows and needs fresh equity capital from "outside" investors, their willingness to invest will be significantly enhanced if they feel that in addition to commercial ability and flair there is good governance in place;

- in any event, any equity investment will be made under an investment agreement which will require governance structures and processes;

- many SMEs are "family" companies: there is a need to ensure that as family management retires or dies out or becomes unable to manage the challenges of a growing company so replacements of suitable calibre can be found and brought in. Thus, the presence on the board of one or more trusted non-family non-executive directors who can speak candidly and identify suitable candidates for succession can make the difference to the company declining or flourishing.

Many providers of development capital to small companies believe governance procedures are an aid to sound management. Accordingly, some capital providers, including business angels, commonly require specific provisions for corporate governance to be built into the contractual relationship governing the terms upon which they introduce capital to private companies. These include:

- the right to appoint an independent non-executive director or directors;

- a requirement that board meetings should be held at least every other month;

- a requirement that paperwork for meetings should be comprehensive and formal (agendas, board papers and minutes);

- monthly management accounts comprising a profit and loss account, balance sheet and cash flow forecast;

- a requirement that there be an audit committee under the chairmanship of a non-executive director;

- sometimes, changes in auditors and solicitors.

In addition, investors clearly have a legitimate interest in the size of salaries and other payments made to the directors and senior staff. This may not justify the appointment of a remuneration committee, but the principle of accountability to shareholders is the same.

The presence of non-executive directors on the boards of private companies requires a particularly sensitive approach. There may be a mismatch of expectations that can be alleviated by setting out terms of the appointment in a simple letter, with detailed preliminary discussions between the director concerned and senior staff.

Private family-owned companies are beginning to recognise that a strong system of appropriate governance may be beneficial to the long-term health of a company—a non-executive outside director who is trusted by the family may be able tactfully to guide the family shareholders and directors towards succession planning or in coping, for instance, with the sudden death or illness of a principal director/shareholder.

Again, the successful family company may well wish to seek a listing whether on the full board or AIM or PLUS[35] or Share Exchange. Listing Authority regulations, AIM practice and the requirements of nominated advisers and institutional shareholders all combine to require governance procedures to be in place. Too often, at the moment of float, the outside directors are newly appointed and are strangers to the rest of the board, and the procedures of the audit committee and the remuneration committee are untried. It is only sensible to start putting these into place a year, say, before a float.

---

[35] Formerly OFEX, see fn 32 above.

Chapter 3

The Board and its Structure

Introduction

"If the board is not taking the company purposefully into the future, who is?"[1]   **3.001**

"It is board leadership which generates the drive on which the growth of individual companies and of the economy as a whole depends."[2]

David Jackson as company secretary of BP, expressed the role of the board as follows:

"The role of the board is to govern the company on behalf of the share-holders. The board should focus on those tasks which are within its unique capability and ensure that management tasks are clearly delegated to the executive. The goals of the company should be properly articulated by the board as should the strategy for achieving those goals. Both should be understood by both management and shareholders. The board should ensure that the assets of the company are only deployed for the purpose of achieving the goals. The board must monitor the implementation of the strategy and the judgments the executive management takes in that respect.

In all of this clarity is key: clarity in respect of the role of the board and the nature of the delegation to the executive; clarity in a monitoring role of the committees; clarity above all in the purpose of the company and its communication to shareholders."[3]

In an ideal world all boards of directors would comprise a diverse group of experienced and talented individuals, all of whom would espouse and practice the characteristics and values of good commercial sense, courage, openness and integrity. The aim of the Higgs Review on the role and effectiveness of

[1] Sir John Harvey Jones, *Building Better Boards*, the then DTI, December 2004.
[2] Sir Adrian Cadbury, *Building Better Boards*, the then DTI, December 2004.
[3] *Building Better Boards*, the then DTI, December 2004.

non-executive directors,[4] the Smith Guidance for audit committees,[5] the Combined Code, the Walker Review of corporate governance in UK banks[6] and since June 2010, the UK Corporate Governance Code, has been to provide benchmarks and guidance as to *structure, process* and *behaviour* so as to enable boards to achieve as near to the ideal as is practicable in the real world. The objective of this chapter is to describe these different benchmarks and guidance. It should never be forgotten, however, that: "even a megaton of governance is no substitute for invention, entrepreneurial skill, originality, and sheer managerial competence and integrity".[7]

The role of the board

3.002   Main Principle A.1 (the role of the board) of the UK Corporate Governance Code (under the heading "Leadership") states as follows:

> "Every company should be headed by an effective board, which is collectively responsible for the long term success of the company."

The Supporting Principle sets out the following guidance:

> "The board's role is to provide entrepreneurial leadership of the company within a framework of prudent and effective controls which enables risk to be assessed and managed. The board should set the company's strategic aims, ensure that the necessary financial and human resources are in place for the company to meet its objectives and review management performance. The board should set the company's values and standards and ensure that its obligations to its shareholders and others are understood and met.
>
> All directors must act in what they consider to be in the best interests of the company, consistent with their statutory duties."[8]

Does power reside in the board? Directors and senior managers below main board level—executive committees

3.003   In the wake of the 2007/2009 financial crisis, the All Party Parliamentary Corporate Governance Group ("APPCGG") published in 2009 a comprehensive study of the locus of power, responsibility and accountability within the UK's largest and most successful companies. The study entitled "Who Manages UK plc?" was conducted by corporate advisory firm Lintstock on

---

[4] See App.2.
[5] See App.15 and Ch.14 (External Audit, Internal Audit and the Audit Committee).
[6] November 26, 2009; HM Treasury.
[7] Jonathan Charkham: *Building Better Boards*, Oxford, 2005.
[8] For directors of UK incorporated companies, these duties are set out in the ss.170 to 177 of the Companies Act 2006.

behalf of the APPCGG. Participants in the study included 117 companies within the FTSE 350.

The study noted that in most debates about the corporate governance of listed UK companies, attention naturally focuses on the role and effectiveness of board members. However, over the past 10 years, the proportion of the board which is composed of hands-on, executive, directors has declined to the point where they now account for less than a third of all board members in the FTSE 350. Thus, in many respects, "the senior executives who slip below the governance radar are now the people who really run UK plc".

More specifically, the results of the study show that, on average, 45 per cent of the senior managers who constitute the executive committees of Britain's largest and most successful companies are not represented at board level. For example, whilst HR directors (the majority of whom are women) are present in just 6 per cent of all FTSE 350 boardrooms, they are present in nearly 50 per cent of all executive committees. These executive committees also possess a good deal of delegated authority. For example, the median company within the FTSE 350 allows its executive committee to make acquisitions up to a value of £10 million without recourse to board approval; and in some instances this level of delegated authority rises to well above £100 million.

As the authority and influence of the executive committee has grown, many companies are now making determined efforts to increase the exposure of their non-executive directors not just to the executive committee but to the "high potentials" in the layer below. And, in most instances, these efforts are taking place in the context of a drive to strengthen the board's oversight of risk and internal control, by providing more opportunities for non-executive directors to obtain a "gut feel" for the strengths and weaknesses inherent in their businesses.

Commenting on this development, David Ladipo, a Lintstock Partner, noted that:

> "This drive to strengthen the human, face-to-face, interaction between board members and operational management comes in the wake of a credit crunch whose origin seems, in part, to have been occasioned by an over-reliance on hard, mechanical, systems of risk measurement and an under-reliance on more intersubjective and visceral systems of risk identification."

Board composition[9]

General configuration

A board which is composed strictly in compliance with the UK Corporate **3.004** Governance Code would have the following features:

---

[9] See also Ch.6 (Voices from the Boardroom).

- a chairman (Main Principle A.3) who would have declared significant commitments before appointment and in the annual report and also changes in commitments and their impact (Code Provision B.3.1);

- a chief executive as a separate individual from the chairman (Code Provision A.2.1);

- "an appropriate combination of executive and non-executive directors (and, in particular, independent non-executive directors)" (Supporting Principle B.1), and a board appointed "on merit, against objective criteria and with due regard for the benefits of diversity on the board, including gender". None of the executive directors would have taken on more than one non-executive directorship in a FTSE 100 company nor the chairmanship of such a company (Code Provision B.3.3);

- at least half the board, (Code Provision B.1.2) excluding the chairman, would comprise non-executive directors determined by the board to be independent (defined in Code Provision B.1.1). However, a smaller company (sub-FTSE 350) would have at least two independent non-executive directors (Code Provision B.1.2);

- the number of independent non-executive directors would be at least three (except in the case of smaller companies—sub FTSE 350—when two is the minimum) in order to comply with Code Provision D.2.1 which requires that the remuneration committee has at least three independent non-executive directors, and Code Provision C.3.1 which has the same requirement for the audit committee;

- at least one member of the audit committee would have "recent and relevant financial experience" (Code Provision C.3.1);

- a senior independent director from among the independent non-executive directors (Code Provision A.4.1).

Size

3.005   Among the supporting principles to Main Principle B.1 (composition of the board) of the UK Corporate Governance Code is the supporting principle that the board "should be of sufficient size that the requirements of the business can be met and that changes to the board's composition and that of its committees can be managed without undue disruption, and should be not so large as to be unwieldy".

Research conducted by Grant Thornton for the FRC released in December 2009 showed that the average FTSE 350 board has 5.2 non-executive directors compared to 3.3 executive directors, which is broadly similar to 2008.

However, the composition of the board continues to be an area of change with 80 companies not having at least half the board made up of independent NEDs for the entire year. This is the single most common area where companies have had to resort to explaining their compliance. With the exception of some unexpected events, the majority appear to have arisen through ineffective succession planning. Outside the FTSE 100, companies had just 4.5 NEDs. This is reflected in the Grant Thornton finding that the Mid 250 find it harder to comply with the provision on board composition: the percentage of FTSE 100 companies choosing to explain their board structure in 2009 was 15.2 per cent, compared to 32.5 per cent in the Mid 250. There are clearly a number of companies which have only the minimum number of NEDs required in order to be compliant, but if one resigns due to unforeseen circumstances, they become non-compliant while they look for a replacement.

The Grant Thornton research for the FRC reviewed the amount of direct sector experience brought by NEDs on the board. They found that although the average size of the board had fallen over the last five years, the number of NEDs with direct sector experience increased from 23 per cent to 30 per cent, perhaps suggesting that greater consideration is being given to the experience an NED can bring.

Turning to other specific experience required to comply with the Code, 31 companies, including eight in the FTSE 100, did not in 2009 disclose who on the audit committee had "recent and relevant financial experience".

The Higgs Review felt that size is an important factor. Currently, the average size of the board of a UK-listed company is seven, comprising three executive and three non-executive directors and a chairman. The average FTSE 100 board is generally bigger with an average of 12 members, of whom six are non-executive directors, five are executive directors and one is chairman. Nearly half FTSE 100 boards have 12 or more members. However, the Review found a welcome trend towards smaller boards.[10] Some commentators have suggested that the ideal decision-making body is between eight and 10 members. To some extent, however, size will also be constrained by the requirement is of the UK Corporate Governance Code as to the numbers of independent non-executive directors and as to the composition of the various board committees (see above—para.3.004).

The 2009 Walker *Review of corporate governance in UK Banks and other financial industry entities* (paras 3.2, 3.6 and 3.7) suggested that boards of BOFIs (Banks and Other Financial Industry entities) were being constrained from appointing from within the organisation non-executives of financial experience on the grounds that they were not "independent" within the meaning of the Code. Thus, if appointed it would require an enlargement of the board so as to get the Code-required number of "independents". The Review felt that this was an undesirable side effect of the "independent" director rules.

---

[10] But query whether in fact any reduction on board size is being compensated for by an increase in the "Executive Committee": See above.

Balance

3.006   Main Principle B.1 of the UK Corporate Governance states:

> "The board and its committees should consist of directors with the appropriate balance of skills, experience, independence and knowledge of the company to enable them to discharge their respective duties and responsibilities effectively."

The Supporting Principles include the guidance:

> "The board should be of sufficient size ... that changes to the board's composition and that of its committees can be managed without undue disruption, and should not be so large as to be unwieldy."

> "The board should include an appropriate combination of executive and non-executive directors (and in particular independent non-executive directors) such that no individual or small group of individuals can dominate the board's decision taking."

Chairman and chief executive

3.007   The chairman and chief executive should be separate individuals. UK Corporate Governance Code Provision A.2.1 states:

> "The roles of chairman and chief executive should not be exercised by the same individual. The division of responsibilities between a chairman and chief executive of should be clearly established, set out in writing and agreed by the board."

Moreover, Code Provision A.3.1 states that the chairman should be independent as defined in Provision B.1.1 of the UK Corporate Governance Code, as at the date of appointment, and that the chief executive should not go on to be chairman of the same company except in exceptional circumstances and after consultation with major shareholders accompanied by reasons to shareholders at the time of the appointment and in the next annual report. The role of the chairman is described in more detail in Ch.8 (The Chairman).

There is no doubt that institutional shareholders feel strongly about the undesirability of the chief executive going on to become the chairman, simply because it is perceived to be difficult for a chief executive to make the transition without hanging on to behaviour and attitudes needed for the role of chief executive, but not of chairman.

However, in recent times there have been examples of companies which have elevated chief executives to the role of chairman, amongst which are Barclays Bank and HSBC, where Mr Matt Barrett and Mr Stephen Green, respectively, were appointed chairman, having each been chief executive. In line with the then Combined Code, both groups had to explain their decision to appoint from inside. Indeed, Barclays was the first to produce a "comply or explain" letter in 2003 to shareholders worried about Mr Barrett's appointment. Moreover, it is striking that HSBC and Barclays were outstanding as banks which did not in the 2007 banking crisis require to be bailed out by Government help; and some commentators drew the conclusion that the elevation of experienced bankers to chairmanship, as distinct from those banks (e.g. RBOS) which got people from non-banking backgrounds was one of the reasons why these banks survived the crisis in relatively good order.

The ITV saga

Of much greater controversy is the combination of chair and chief executive. In November 2006 the then chairman of the BBC, Mr Michael Grade, left to become executive chairman of a languishing ITV. One institutional shareholder was quoted at the time as saying: **3.008**

> "If the appointment of an executive chairman is what it takes so be it. But we will look for checks and balances and good independent directors."

In the event and with the benefit of hindsight the combination of roles has proved unfortunate for ITV. In April 2009 Mr Grade announced that he wished to relinquish his chief executive role and to become non-executive chairman. However, it became clear that potential chief executives were being put off by the presence of a chairman who had been also CEO, and so Mr Grade made it clear that he would also stand down as chairman. At the point the board was left with the problem of filling two posts and decided to start with the CEO role whilst looking out for a chairman at the same time. By October 2009 the posts had not been filled, as candidates sought to negotiate terms, including chairmen or CEOs they did not favour which the board declined, with the shortlist of candidates for both posts getting smaller as names withdrew. It was described as a mess which could have been mitigated if the roles had always been kept separate. In November 2009 it was announced that Mr Archie Norman would be appointed chairman.

The Marks & Spencer saga

Sir Stuart Rose was appointed chief executive of Marks & Spencer in 2004 under the chairmanship of the then Mr Paul Myners. In March 2008 he was appointed executive chairman with effect from June 2008 when the then **3.009** chair retired, but on the basis that he would relinquish the CEO role in June 2010 and would become non-executive chairman with a view to his retiring in 2011. Again the appointment gave rise to misgivings among investors but it was felt that rather than risk Sir Stuart Rose leaving it would be better to accommodate his wishes. It proved difficult to fill the role of chief executive as 2010 approached, but in November 2009 it was announced that Mr Mark Bolland would be appointed from the supermarkets Morrisons as chief executive.

Numbers of independent non-executive directors

3.010   Code Provision B.1.2 states that:

"Except for smaller companies [defined as below the FTSE 350 throughout the year immediately prior to the reporting year] at least half the board, excluding the chairman, should comprise non-executive directors determined by the board to be independent. A smaller company should have at least two independent non-executive directors."

In addition, since the Code requires that the audit committee and the remuneration committee should, except in the case of smaller companies, comprise at least three independent non-executive directors the exact numbers will vary between three and more than three if that larger number is required to ensure compliance with Provision B.1.2.

Definition of independence

3.011   UK Corporate Governance Code Provision B.1.1 requires the board to state in the annual report each director[11] it considers to be independent and in particular why it considers that directors are independent notwithstanding the existence of relationships or circumstances which may appear relevant to its determination:

"including if the director:

- has been an employee of the company or group within the last five years;
- has or has had within the last three years a material business relationship with the company either directly, or as a partner, shareholder,

---

[11] Provision A.3.1 states that the chairman should, on appointment, meet the independence criteria set out in this provision, but thereafter the test of independence is not appropriate in relation to the chairman.

director or senior employee of a body that has such a relationship with the company;

- has received or receives additional remuneration from the company apart from a director's fee, participates in the company's share option or performance related pay scheme, or is a member of the company's pension scheme;
- has close family ties with any of the company's advisers, directors or senior employees;
- holds cross-directorships or has significant links with other directors through involvement in other companies or bodies;
- represents a significant shareholder; or
- has served on the board for more than nine years from the date of their first election."

The role of the non-executive director including a broader discussion of the meaning of "independence" is contained in greater detail in Ch.5 (Directors—The Non-Executive Director).

The senior independent director

UK Corporate Governance Code Provision A.4.1 states: **3.012**

"The board should appoint one of the independent non-executive directors to be the senior independent director to provide a sounding board for the chairman and to serve as an intermediary for the other directors when necessary. The senior independent director should be available to shareholders if they have concerns which contact through the normal channels of chairman, chief executive or other executive directors has failed to resolve or for which such contact is inappropriate."

The Higgs Review stated that it saw the "role of the senior independent director as important in the relationship between shareholders and the board".

The Supporting Principle to Main Principle E.1 (dialogue with shareholders) states that: "whilst recognising that most shareholder contact is with the chief executive and finance director, the chairman should ensure that all directors understand their major shareholders issues and concerns."

UK Corporate Governance Provision E.1.1 states:

"The senior independent director should attend sufficient meetings with a range of a major shareholders to listen to their views in order to help develop a balanced understanding of the issues and concerns of major shareholders."

It is clear that the primary channel of communication should be the chairman, but that non-executive directors, and in particular the senior independent director, must be given an opportunity to attend "scheduled" (as distinct from meetings specially "set up" for the purpose of meeting non-executive directors) meetings with major shareholders and should expect to attend meetings if requested by major shareholders.

The role of the senior independent director as described by Unilever plc[12]

3.013   "The role of the Senior Independent Director is:–

- to preside at meetings of the Independent Non-Executive Directors convened at least once per year to consider agenda items set by them;
- to participate with the Chairman in the process of setting the agenda for Board meetings and establishing the schedules for meetings;
- to participate in the process of dealing with any conflict of interest between the Company and the Chairman . . .;
- to participate in the process of Directors Induction and Training . . .;
- to participate in the Board evaluation process . . .; and
- to attend meetings with a range of major shareholders in order to help develop a balanced understanding of their issues and concerns."

Recruitment and appointment and diversity

3.014   Main Principle B.2 (Appointments to the board) states: "There should be a formal, rigorous and transparent procedure for the appointment of new directors to the board".

The Supporting Principle to B.2 of the Code states that:

"the search for board candidates should be conducted, and appointments made on merit and against objective criteria and with due regard for the benefits of diversity of diversity on the board, including gender."

Care should be taken that appointees have the time available to devote to the job.[13] In addition, (Supporting Principle B.2) the board should satisfy itself that plans are in place for the:

"orderly succession for appointments to the board and senior management, so as to maintain an appropriate balance of skills and experience

---

[12] Unilever Plc Corporate Governance manual—*"The Governance of Unilever"* March 2009.
[13] Main Principle B.3.

within the company and on the board and to ensure progressive refreshing of the board."

Code Provision B.2.1 requires that there should be a nomination committee which should lead the process for board appointments and make recommendations to the board (see below at para.3.018).

Paragraph 10.1 of the Higgs Review states:

"Ensuring that the board as a whole has an appropriate mix of skills and experience is essential for it to be an effective decision-making body. There is no "standard" board or "standard" non-executive director, nor can there be. It is the range of skills and attributes of skills acquired through a diversity of experiences and backgrounds that combine to create a cohesive and effective board. The balance of skills and experience required inevitably changes to reflect the changing needs of the business. Identifying individuals of suitable quality and background is essential for a high performing board. The nominations and appointment process is crucial to strong corporate performance as well as effective accountability."

Higgs commented on the "high level of informality in the process of appointing non-executive directors". Almost half of the non-executive directors surveyed for the Review were recruited to their role through personal contacts or friendships. Only 4 per cent had had a formal interview, and 1 per cent had obtained their job by answering an advertisement. The situation was widely criticised and he accepted that it led to an overly familiar atmosphere in the boardroom. Higgs stated that he believed that a "rigorous, fair and open appointments process is essential to promote meritocracy in the boardroom" and that best practice for nominating and appointing directors should be universally adopted.

The Higgs Review also referred to the assumption that business experience is important for a non-executive director:

"I believe, however, that the qualities necessary for an effective contribution to the board can also be acquired from a variety of backgrounds. The interplay of varied and complementary perspectives from members of the board can significantly benefit board performance."

Higgs pointed out that it is truly in the interests of a company to ensure that the best people are recruited to direct and supervise it. It is also important that boards recognise their responsibility and appoint on merit. However, the Review research showed that non-executives are typically white males nearing retirement age with previous public company director experience. There were less than 20 non-executive directors on FTSE 100 boards under the age of 45. Only 7 per cent of non-executive directors were found to be non-British, and 1 per cent was from black and ethnic minority groups. The Review pointed out that the very low number of female non-executive directors is striking in comparison with other professions and with the population of managers in UK companies overall. Across the corporate sector as a whole, around 30 per cent of managers overall are female. Women held only 6 per cent of non-executive posts, and there were two female chairmen in the FTSE 350.[14] The diversity and mix of public sector appointees is significantly broader. Higgs therefore invited chairman of listed companies to encourage and facilitate their executive directors as suitable senior management just below board level to take one non-executive director position in a non-competitor board. He also hoped that in future boards would draw more actively from groups under represented, even if the appointees are not yet at board level.[15]

The UK Code in Supporting Principle B.2 speaks of the benefits of diversity, including gender. The gender reference was introduced following the 2009 consultation process on the UK Code and reflects the growing impatience with the lack of progress in including more women on listed company boards. The Tyson Report on the recruitment and development of non-executive directors, published in 2003, felt that there was merit in diversity in the overall approach to recruiting a suitable board:

"Diversity in the backgrounds, skills and experiences of NED's enhances board effectiveness by bringing a wider range of perspectives and knowledge to their honest use of company performance, a strategy at risk. Diversity can also send a positive and motivating signal to customers, shareholders and employees, and can contribute to a better understanding by the company's leadership of the diverse constituencies that affect its success."

A pragmatic approach by Vodafone was quoted in the 2004 DTI publication *Building Better Boards*:

---

[14] Research published in November 2009 from Cranfield University School of Management showed that less than 7% of non-executive directors across all British-quoted companies are women. In the FTSE 100, 12% of non-executive directors are female, while in the FTSE 250 9% of the non-executive directors are—and 62% of these companies have no women non-executives at all. However, the research also found that "there are now 2,281 women (up from 1,877 last year) on the corporate boards and executive committees/senior teams of all the FTSE listings. The report identified 100 women who are currently on the executive committees of the FTSE 100 or 250 companies that should be seriously considered for boardroom appointments. These women were selected from the largest organisations, but there are an additional 2,181 women in the huge and growing pipeline of female talent available to the FTSE 100 boards. Professor Susan Vinnicombe OBE, co-author of the report said: "This year's report demonstrates unequivocally that we have a huge and growing pipeline of female talent to FTSE 100 corporate boards. We support the proposal made earlier this year of a voluntary quota of 30% women on corporate boards over the next ten years".
[15] See also the Tyson Report on the Recruitment and Development of Non-Executive Directors, June 2003, *http://www.london.edu/facultyandresearch/research/docs/TysonReport.pdf*. The report supported the notion that suitable people from backgrounds other than mainstream commercial business could be effective non-executive directors, but that there would be a need for companies to provide training.

"Checklist for new board appointments

- What's the business requirement going forward?
- What skills, knowledge, experience are we looking for or feel we are missing?
- What's the overall balance of the board in terms of age, profile, gender and geographical spread?
- How does any new appointment relate to longer term succession planning?
- What's the availability of people with the skill sets, experience and market credibility we need?
- Select the best available candidate."

Committees of the board

As a preliminary point, the authority to establish committees of the board should be included in the articles of association which will need to be inspected to ensure that adequate authority is there. **3.015**

The audit committee

A full discussion of the composition and role of the audit committee is set out in Ch.14 (External Audit, Internal Audit and the Audit Committee). UK Corporate Governance Code Provision C.3.1 requires that the board should establish an audit committee of at least three, or in the case of smaller companies two, members, who should all be independent non-executive directors. The board should satisfy itself that at least one member of the audit committee has "recent and relevant" financial experience.[16] **3.016**

Provision C.3.3 requires that the terms of reference of the audit committee, including its role and the authority delegated to it by the board, should be "made available", which the Code indicates[17] can be satisfied by publication on the company's website.

The remuneration committee

A full discussion of the composition and role of the remuneration committee is set out in Ch.11 (Directors' Remuneration). **3.017**

Code Provision D.2.1 requires that the board should establish a remuneration committee of at least three, or in the case of smaller (sub-FTSE

---

[16] See also Ch.14 (External Audit, Internal Audit and the Audit Committee).
[17] Note 4. See also *http://www.icsa.org.uk* for suggested terms of reference.

350) companies, two, members, who should all be independent non-executive directors, but may now include the chairman provided that (s)he was independent at the time of appointment and provided that (s)he does not chair the committee.[18] Suggested duties for the remuneration committee[19] are set out in App.16.

The nomination committee

3.018 Code Provision B.2.1 requires that there should be a nomination committee which should "lead the process for board appointments and make recommendations to the board". A majority of members of the nomination committee should be independent non-executive directors. The chairman or an independent non-executive director should chair the committee, but the chairman should not be chair of the nomination committee when dealing with the appointment of a successor to the chairmanship.

Code Provision B.2.2 requires that the nomination committee should evaluate the balance of skills, experience, independence and knowledge on the board and, in the light of this evaluation, prepare a description of the role and capabilities required for a particular appointment.

For the appointment of the chairman, the nomination committee should prepare a job specification, including an assessment of the time commitment expected, recognising the need for availability in the event of crisis. Other significant commitments should be disclosed both before appointment and included in the annual report. Changes to such commitment should be reported to the board, and included in the next annual report.

The nomination committee should ensure that the terms and conditions of appointment of non-executive directors are made available for inspection at the company's registered office during normal business hours and can be inspected at the AGM (for 15 minutes prior to the meeting and during the meeting).[20]

Code Provision B.2.4 requires that a separate section of the annual report should describe the work of the nomination committee,[21] including the process it has used in relation to board appointments. An explanation should be given if neither an external research consultancy nor open advertising has been used in the appointment of a chairman or a non-executive director.

---

[18] Under Code Provision D.2.1 the chairman of the board may also be a member of, but not chair, the remuneration committee if (s)he was considered independent at the time of appointment as chairman.

[19] The terms of reference of the remuneration committee must be "made available", and publication on the company's website will satisfy that requirement. See also *http://www.icsa.org.uk* for suggested terms of reference.

[20] Footnote 9 in the Code.

[21] This Provision overlaps with FSA Rule DTR 7.2.7R (see Sch.B to the Code reproduced in App.1 of this book).

Suggested duties are out in App.16 and terms of reference can be accessed at *http://www.icsa.org.uk.*

Effectiveness and "challenge"[22]

A new Section B has been included in the 2010 UK Corporate Governance **3.019** Code headed "Effectiveness". Under this heading, apart from two new Main Principles dealing with "composition" and "commitment" the section repeats largely wording from the earlier Combined Code but groups under this new heading the earlier material dealing with "composition", "appointments", "commitment", "development", "information and support", "evaluation" and "re-election".

The Higgs Review on the role and effectiveness of non-executive directors identified a number of key characteristics of an effective unitary board. First, a chairman who has a strong, complementary relationship with the chief executive and the members of the board is a central element of an effective board. The Review pointed out that a culture of openness and constructive dialogue in an environment of trust and mutual respect is also a prerequisite for an effective board: "The chairman has a central role to play in fostering these conditions through their own actions and through engagement with the members of the board".

Research commissioned by the Higgs Review found that confidence in executive conduct is not achieved once and for all, but rather through continuous active engagement of the non-executive directors with the executives in all aspects of the board's work:

"There is a potential for a virtuous dynamic in which executive perceptions of the value of non-executive directors' experience and contribution encourages greater executive openness that, in turn, allows for greater non-executive engagement."[23]

Higgs pointed out that inappropriate or ill-informed non-executive contributions can quickly break this virtuous dynamic, by leading to executive frustration or defensiveness and attempts to minimise the role of the non-executive directors. Of course, in turn, this feeds the non-executive directors' suspicion of executive directors.

The 2009 Walker Review[24] speaking of banks and other financial industry entities (BOFIs) put the issues of "challenge" at the heart of the relationship:

---

[22] See also *Review of corporate governance in UK banks and other financial industry entities* (the Walker Review) November 26, 2009 *http://www.hm-treasury.gov.uk*; and the DTI publication *Building Better Boards: http://www.bis.gov.uk/files/file19615.pdf.*

[23] para.8.2, Higgs Review on the role and effectiveness of non-executive directors 2003.

[24] p.8. See fn 15 above.

". . . principal deficiencies in BOFI boards related much more to patterns of behaviour than to organisation. The right sequence in board discussion on major issues should be presentation by the executive, a disciplined process of challenge, decision on the policy or strategy to be adopted, and then full empowerment of the executive to implement. The essential challenge step in the sequence was missed in some board situations and must be unequivocally embedded in future. The most critical need is for an environment in which effective challenge of the executive is expected and achieved in the boardroom before decisions are taken on major risk and strategic issues."

The London Stock Exchange in association with RSM Robson Rhodes published in 2004 a guide called "corporate governance—a practical guide". It lists the key questions facing a board which wishes to be effective:

- Does the board have clear objectives and monitor its performance against them?

- Is the board focusing on the correct areas for its decision-making?

- Is the chairman leading the board effectively?

- Does the board provide a challenging yet supportive environment for the executive directors? Is there a full discussion of all major decisions are taken? Is the board meeting schedule suitable for the needs of business? Does the board receive effective board papers of the right length and quality? Are they provided in a timely manner?

- How have key board decisions turned out? How could the decision-making process be strengthened for the future?

- Is there a thorough boardroom appraisal process with a follow-up action plan?

The American based National Association of Corporate Directors[25] also identified a number of characteristics of an effective board:

"An effective board:

  (a)   knows and understands the company's business and competition;
  (b)   focuses on strategic issues;
  (c)   provides intelligent 'capital' including performance enhancing ideas, networking and strong support of corporate best practices;

---

[25] *http://www.nacdonline.org*>NACD BRC on Board Evaluation—2005 Edition.

(d)   demands high, but realistic standards of performance;

(e)   enhances decision making with rigorous analyses;

(f)   energises management by empowering management and holding them accountable;

(g)   tracks and retains a top leadership team and has a strategy for the orderly succession and replacement both of the leadership team and of the board itself;

(h)   links executive compensation to shareholder value."

Evaluation[26]

Main Principle B.6 of the UK Corporate Governance states: **3.020**

"The board should undertake a formal and rigorous annual evaluation of its performance and that of its committees and individual directors."

The Supporting Principle states:

"The chairman should act upon the results of the performance evaluation by recognising the strengths and addressing the weaknesses of the board and, where appropriate, proposing new members be appointed to the board or seeking the resignation of directors.

Individual evaluation should aim to show what each director continues to contribute effectively and to demonstrate commitment to the role (including commitment of time for board and committee meetings and any other duties)."

Provision B.6.1 states:

"The board should state in the Annual Report how performance evaluation of the board, its committees and its individual directors has been conducted."[27]

A new Provision B.6.2 has been inserted requiring external evaluation of the boards of FTSE 350 companies as follows:

"B.6.2. Evaluation of the board of FTSE 350 companies should be externally facilitated at least every three years. A statement should be

---

[26] See also Chs 6 (Voices from the Boardroom) and 7 (Board Evaluations) for a fuller discussion of director evaluation and appraisal.

[27] Code Provision B.6.3 states in relation to the chairman: "The non-executive directors, led by the senior independent director, should be responsible for performance evaluation of the chairman, taking into account the views of executive directors".

made available [*including the company's website*] of whether an external facilitator has any other connection with the company."[28]

The Higgs Review suggested that every board should continually examine ways to improve its effectiveness. The Review research showed that over a third of boards never formally evaluate their own performance, and three-quarters of non-executive directors and one half of chairmen never have a formal personal performance review. Higgs felt that a board performance appraisal gives the chairman the information and confidence to manage to board more effectively. It helps a chairman to identify and address the strengths and weaknesses of the board and consider whether the board has the right balance of skills for the future. The chairman should seek the resignation of under-performing directors and make new appointments to the board.

Sometimes it will become clear either to the board and its chairman or to the director concerned that a new appointment is not working, and the appraisal system will quickly provide a forum for the issue to be dealt with: "In cases where a new appointment is not working an early 'blame free' resignation is preferable to continuing an unsatisfactory role".[29]

The chairman has a key role in arranging the evaluation process for boards and for individual non-executive directors. Conduct of the evaluation by an external third party can bring objectivity to the process and its value should be recognised by a chairman. Higgs advised that while the results of board evaluation as a whole should be shared with the board, the result of individual assessments should remain confidential between the chairman and the non-executive director concerned.

The Unilever 2009 Annual Governance statement describes its evaluation process as follows:

"**Background:** It is important that the Board and Board Committees evaluate the effectiveness of their performance in a rigorous and structured way so that Unilever may confirm to its shareholders that it has high corporate governance standards. The Chairman is responsible for ensuring that such evaluation exercises take place and the Group Secretary is responsible for their organisation. The Chairman in conjunction with the Senior Independent Director leads the process whereby the Board assesses its own performance.

The Board
The evaluation process of our Boards will consist of an internal three-year cycle with an independent third party evaluation carried out if the Boards

---

[28] Both Sir David Walker and the FRC proposed an external evaluation of the board every three years: "Our findings show that only 14% of the FTSE 350 (FTSE 100: 21%, Mid 250: 11%) undertook such an evaluation in the current year. Only 16 companies provided detailed disclosure on the process used to evaluate the performance of the chairman" [Walker Review July interim report 2009].

[29] Higgs Review, para.11.23.

consider appropriate. The Group Secretary will perform the evaluations. Following each evaluation a report will be prepared based on appropriate interviews and responses to questionnaires. The report shall be reviewed and discussed by the Board following its submission to the Board by the Chairman. Thereafter the Chairman implements the actions that the Board decide are appropriate.

Individual Directors

The Chairman in conjunction with the Senior Independent Director conducts the process of evaluating the performance of individual Directors in their role as a member of the Board. The Senior Independent Director conducts the process whereby the Board evaluates the performance of the Chairman. He consults the Executive Directors and his fellow Non-Executive Directors. The Senior Independent Director shares the resulting assessment with the Chairman. These individual assessments are taken into account in the evaluation of the performance of the Board as a whole.

Board Committees

Each Chairman of a Board Committee leads the process of evaluating the performance of that committee. This includes taking the views of the Board on the performance of that committee. The Chairman of the Committee reports on the results of the process to the Board.

Timing

The evaluations are carried out on an annual basis. All evaluations are designed to be completed before the Nomination and Remuneration Committees meet in late October/early November to discuss remuneration packages and the nominations for candidates for election as Directors of NV and PLC at the Annual General Meetings in the following year.

Processes

The Group Secretary provides guidance on how to carry out evaluation processes and the criteria to be used. The Group Secretary updates this guidance each year in the light of internal experience and external best practice.

Reporting

An annual report to shareholders is made in the Corporate Governance statement within the Annual Report and Accounts which confirm that the evaluation processes have been carried out and describes the processes that were used."

Suggested guidelines for carrying out performance appraisal for both the board as a whole and for non-executive directors individually as suggested by the Higgs Review are set out in App.12,[30] but companies will need to tailor the suggestions to meet their own needs.

---

[30] See also *http://www.fsa.gov.uk/pubs/ukla/lr_comcode2003.pdf* for online version.

Commitment

3.021   A new Principle B.3 was inserted in 2010 into the UK Corporate Governance Code as follows:

> "All directors must be able to allocate sufficient time to the company to discharge their responsibilities effectively."

This new Principle is followed by the three Code provisions which repeat the earlier Combined Code Provisions A.4.3, A.4.4 and A.4.5.

Matters reserved to the board and delegation of decision making

3.022   As far back as the Cadbury Report in 1992 concerns had been expressed that boards had allowed decisions of a fundamental kind to be taken by executive management without reference to the board.

Accordingly, UK Corporate Governance Code Provision A.1.1 requires as follows:

> "The Annual Report should include a statement of how the board operates, including a high level statement of which types of decisions are to be taken by the board and which are to be delegated to management."[31]

The Unilever 2009 corporate governance statement indicated that the following matters were reserved to the board:

> "The Board business includes considering and deciding upon the following:–
>
> - the strategies for the shaping of the portfolio and direction of the Group and priorities in corporate resource allocation;
> - the Corporate Annual Plan;
> - the Operating Framework
> - the quarterly business performance reports;
> - nominations for Board appointments, including board succession planning;
> - the Board Remuneration Policy and the individual remuneration packages of Directors, in accordance with the respective rules and obligations for NV and PLC;
> - any alteration in the capital of NV or PLC including without limitation the purchase, disposal, allotment, re-issue or cancellation of

---

[31] App.13 contains a suggested list of matters which should be reserved for the exclusive decision of the board.

share capital whether issued or not subject to the authorities of the general meetings of shareholders of NV and PLC;

- the convening of a meeting of the shareholders of either NV or PLC and the setting of the agenda thereof and generally ensuring that a satisfactory dialogue with shareholders takes place;
- the financial policy and the dividend policy for the Group;
- the determination of retained profit reserves of NV and declaration or recommendation of a dividend of either NV or PLC;
- the appointment or removal of the Group Secretary of Unilever;
- any proposal to the general meeting of shareholders of NV and PLC to amend its Articles of Association and its Memorandum and Articles of Association respectively;
- the review of the functioning of the Board and its committees;
- any proposal to alter or terminate the Equalisation Agreement;
- the alteration or termination of the Deed of Mutual Covenants, the Agreement for Mutual Guarantees of Borrowings and the Governance of Unilever;
- the Annual Report and Accounts for adoption by the shareholders;
- the quarterly and annual results announcements;
- any merger, acquisition, joint venture or disposal where the value of consideration paid or received, or of the assets contributed by Unilever or contributed by other parties, exceeds €500 million;
- any capital expenditure project or the acquisition of a single brand which is not within the Corporate Annual Plan and which has a value exceeding €250 million;
- any contract or agreement for goods or services which is not within the Corporate Annual Plan and which has a value exceeding €250 million;
- the initiation or settlement of any litigation or claim with a value in excess of €100 million;
- any single long-term borrowing, outside the Corporate Annual Plan, where the value exceeds €750 million;
- cost of hedging net investment exposures in excess of €60 million per annum;
- either hedging or leaving unhedged net equity balance sheet exposures in excess of €5 billion per currency;
- the endorsement or amendment of the following Unilever Policies namely, the Code of Business Principles, the Code of Ethics for Senior Financial Officers, the Compliance Manual for Listing and Disclosure Rules (including the Unilever Share Dealing Code), the Risk Management Policy, the Corporate Pensions Policy, the Accounting and Reporting Policy and such other policies as the Board decides;
- the remits and membership of committees of the Board and deciding upon any issues arising from its receipt and review of reports from the same;

- conflicts of interest involving Directors or significant (holders of 10 per cent or more) shareholders;
- compliance with all relevant legislation and regulations; and
- all other matters of a non-operational nature not specifically delegated to the Chief Executive Officer;
- Intra-Group transfers provided that the third party costs associated therewith e.g. tax, stamp duty and fees, are €250 million or more;
- Unilever's entry by means of direct investment to or exit from any country (Indirect investment requires to be noted by the Board).

Development and induction[32]

Development

3.023   Main Principle B.4 of the UK Corporate Governance Code states:

"All directors should receive induction on joining the board and should regularly update and refresh their skills and knowledge."

The Supporting Principles suggest that:

"The chairman should ensure that the directors continually update their skills and the knowledge and familiarity with the company required to fulfil their role of those on the board and on board committees. The company should provide the necessary resources for developing and updating its directors knowledge and capabilities.

To function effectively all directors need appropriate knowledge of the company and access to its operations and staff."[33]

Code Provision B.4.1 states:

"The chairman should ensure that new directors receive a full, formal and tailored induction on joining the board. As part of this directors should avail themselves of opportunities to meet major shareholders."

Code Provision B.4.2 (newly inserted in 2010) states:

"The chairman should agree and regularly review with each director, their training and development needs."

---

[32] See also Ch.5 (Directors—The Non-Executive Director) and Chs 6 (Voices from the Boardroom) and 7 (Board Evaluation) for a more detailed analysis.
[33] A Principle newly inserted in 2010.

To be effective, newly-appointed non-executive directors quickly need to build their knowledge of the organisation to the point where they can use the skills and experience they have gained elsewhere for the benefit of the company. The research for the Higgs Review showed that less than one-quarter of non-executive directors received a formal briefing or induction after appointment. Often it is left to new non-executive directors to take the initiative in seeking an induction programme and to ask the right questions in order to receive the right information. "This is not acceptable".[34]

Non-executive directors interviewed for the Review reported that visiting company locations and attending company events, together with the informal contact with board and management that this brings, is significant in the development of their knowledge of the business and its people. Opportunities should also be provided to ensure that non-executive directors see regularly, and at first hand, the performance of the senior management team.

Appendix 10 contains a copy of a suggested induction programme, and para.5.017 below further discusses this topic.

As regards professional development, on their appointment, non-executive directors should already have relevant skills, knowledge, experience and abilities. Nevertheless, a non-executive director's credibility and effectiveness in the boardroom will depend "not just on their existing capability but on the ability to extend and refresh their knowledge and skills".

Higgs' research revealed that two-thirds of non-executive directors and chairmen had not received any training or development. Of those who considered that they had, the training was often in the form of experience of being a member of a board, rather than any structured process: "It is questionable the extent to which the experience alone is sufficient to maintain up-to-date knowledge".

There is a low demand for formal training. There is also a relatively limited supply of training specifically aimed at non-executive directors by business schools.[35] The Higgs Review suggested that a case study based approach using dynamic, real corporate life situations may be more useful than a lecture based approach to professional development:

---

[34] Higgs Review, para.11.3.

[35] The Judge Business School, Cambridge and the CBI (*http://www.cbi.org.uk*) provides such courses; the London Stock Exchange also runs a series of programmes on corporate governance, as do conference organisers such as Informa and Hawkpoint.
Providers of Board Development Programmes: (Source, DTI, *Building Better Boards* 2004); Ashridge Management College *http://www.ashridge.org.uk*; Cranfield School of Management *http://www.cranfield.ac.uk*; Durham University Business School; *http://www.dur.ac.uk/dubs*; Henley Management College *http://www.henley.reading.ac.uk*; Manchester Business School *http://www.mbs.ac.uk*; Institute of Chartered Secretaries and Administrators *http://www.icsa. org.uk*; Institute of Directors *http://www.iod.com*; Leeds Metropolitan University *http://www. leedsmet.ac.uk/fbl*; London Business School *http://www.london.edu*; Loughborough University *http://www.lboro.ac.uk/departments/bs*; Oxford University/Templeton *http://www.gtc.ox.ac. uk*; Sunley Management Centre *http://www.sunley-northampton.co.uk/index.php*; University of Bristol *http://www.bris.ac.uk/index/faculties*; University of Salford *http://www.business.salford. ac.uk*; 3i *http://www.3i.com*.

"It is my belief that there should be a step change in training and development provision so that it is suited to the needs of boards."

The UK Corporate Governance Code places the prime responsibility for professional development on the chairman,[36] but in practice, the responsibility is vested in the company secretary to organise and arrange suitable professional development.[37]

Induction

3.024   ICI described its induction process (DTI *Building Better Boards* 2004, p.18) as follows:

"We arrange for all new directors to meet as many people in the company as they can, across HR, Finance, Strategic Planning, for example, as well as out in the field. They are advised at the outset that they are going to have to travel to get to know the business and that they will continue to do that throughout their time on the board. That's very important if they're to keep up to speed. Each new director has a formal induction session led by the Company Secretary, augmented by the Assistant Secretary and someone at a senior level with a good deal of company experience, explaining the issues for ICI. They cover aspects such as Risk, Regulation and Practice, including fiduciary duties, duties of care and diligence, how the board is managed, what makes an effective board, the UK Corporate Governance Code and regulations. This way, new directors become more effective contributors more quickly."

The response from new directors is valuable. Peter Ellwood (Chairman) mentions a recently appointed female non-executive director:

"She began by meeting a large number of people in Head Office, followed by several days at production sites and research laboratories to see what the business is really about. I then had a dinner meeting with her so that we could capture and subsequently use the feedback she gave—I'll discuss that information with the CEO. It's not just a one-way flow—her fresh pair of eyes is invaluable to us."

Peter Ellwood, chairman, is in no doubt of the benefits to the business:

"It's bottom line common sense to give new directors a thorough induction. It's not rocket science, it's good practice, because it means that the people

---

[36] Supporting Principle B.4.
[37] See fn 15.

joining the board will be more effective. It's adding value and enabling these people to contribute much more quickly, making the most of their talent for the benefit of the business and its shareholders right from the start."

In BP's 2008 corporate governance report dealing with induction and training it stated:

"Induction
The induction of new board members is the responsibility of the chairman, who is assisted by the company secretary in this task. All new directors receive a full induction programme, including a 'core' element covering the principles and the legal and regulatory duties of directors. Non-executive directors receive further induction content devised according to their own interests and needs, together with the requirements of the committees on which they will serve. This would include meetings and briefings on the operations and activities of the group, the strategy and the annual plan and the company's financial performance. The induction programme is targeted for completion within the first nine to 12 months of non-executive directors taking office, while the executive director programme is arranged in the course of their business activities.

Training and site visits
Directors and committee members receive briefings on BP's business, its markets, operating environment and other key issues during their tenure as directors to ensure they have the necessary skill and knowledge to perform their duties effectively. Board members are also kept updated on legal and regulatory developments that may impact their duties and obligations as directors of a listed company.
In the past two years, the board and its committees have sought greater opportunity to meet at BP's operating sites. This has enabled board members to see a selection of BP's businesses e.g. the Texas City refinery, gas production in Colorado, exploration and production activities in Azerbaijan and the alternative energy solar facility in Maryland. These site visits have given directors the opportunity to meet both operational staff and government and community leaders in the parts of the world where BP operates. All non-executive directors are required to participate in at least one site visit per year."

Unilever's 2009 annual governance statement described board induction and training as follows:

"Background
The provision of an appropriate induction programme for new Directors and ongoing training for existing Directors is a major contributor to the maintenance of high corporate governance standards in Unilever.

The Chairman is responsible for ensuring that such induction pro-grammes and training are provided and the Group Secretary actually provides them.

Ultimately, however, it is the individual Director's responsibility to iden-tify his needs and take steps to ensure that he is adequately informed about Unilever and his responsibilities as a director.

Induction Programme

The Group Secretary provides new Directors, both Executive and Non-Executive, with a briefing on their legal and regulatory responsibilities as Directors of NV and PLC. This includes provision of a Directors' Manual containing all key Unilever documents relevant to their roles and respon-sibilities. The Group Secretary also provides documents setting out the current structure and performance of Unilever's business.

The induction briefing may include briefings from internal and outside legal counsel, the Auditors, other senior corporate officers and others as the Group Secretary judges appropriate. This is weighted to cover any particular areas of responsibility that the Director is taking on.

The Group Secretary provides new Non-Executive Directors with brief-ings on the business of Unilever. This programme comprises initial docu-mentation, presentations from relevant executives and opportunities to visit business operations.

The induction process is designed to:–

- build an understanding of the nature of Unilever, its businesses and the markets and regulatory environments in which it operates;
- provide an appreciation of the responsibilities of a Non-Executive Director of Unilever;
- build links to Unilever's people; and
- build an understanding of Unilever's main relationships.

Ongoing Education

The Group Secretary keeps the Board briefed on legal and regulatory developments relevant to the responsibilities of the Directors.

The Group Secretary ensures that the programme to familiarise the Non-Executive Directors with the business is maintained over time and kept relevant to the needs of the individuals involved. The Group Secretary confers with the Chairman and Senior Independent Director to ensure that this is the case.

Reporting

A report annually to the Board and to shareholders is included in the Corporate Governance statement within the Annual Report & Accounts on the induction and training activities arranged during the year."

Information and support

It is obvious that the quality of decision making by a board will reflect the **3.025** information given to it. The UK Corporate Governance Code recognises the issue. Main Principle B.5 (information and support) states:

> "Boards should be supplied in a timely manner with information in a form and of a quality appropriate to enable it to discharge its duties."

Among the Supporting Principles it is stated:

> "The chairman is responsible for ensuring that the directors receive accurate, timely and clear information. Management has an obligation to provide such information but directors should seek clarification or amplification where necessary.
>
> Under the direction of the Chairman, the company secretary's responsibilities include ensuring good information flows within the board and its committees and between senior management and non-executive directors as well as facilitating induction and assisting with professional development as required."

Information must be provided sufficiently in advance of meetings to enable non-executive directors to give issues thorough consideration and must be relevant, significant and clear. However, Higgs Review research reported that 21 per cent of the FTSE 100 non-executive directors interviewed said they received too much information. It is therefore important that non-executive directors give constructive feedback on the value of material provided and guidance on what is required. Where information is not appropriate this should be clearly signalled to the chairman. Indeed, Higgs felt that it should be part of the annual evaluation of the board's performance to examine whether the information provided to the board meets directors' expectations and requirements.

Meetings of non-executive directors

Code Provision A.4.2 states: **3.026**

> "The chairman should hold meetings with the non-executive directors without the executives present. Led by the senior independent director, the non-executive directors should meet without the chairman present at least annually to appraise the chairman's performance and on such other occasions as are deemed appropriate."

In para.8.7 of the Higgs Review, he drew attention to a number of submissions that the non-executives should meet on their own to increase their effectiveness and to allow for more organised discussion of issues of governance and overall performance:

"I agree that it is helpful for non-executives to have such meetings without executive directors present, and on occasion without the chairman present. Such discussions are informal and do not replace other discussions between the board as a whole. They should not be seen to signal a problem. They can allow concerns to be raised and shared on matters such as the provision of information or succession planning."

Legal advice and insurance

3.027   Chapter 4 (Directors: Part 1—Duties and Liabilities with special reference to the Companies Act 2006) contains a full discussion of the possible liabilities of directors and a risk management strategy, part of which is D&O insurance. Chapter 12 discusses D&O insurance.

UK Corporate Governance Code Provision B.5.1 states:

"The board should ensure that directors, especially non-executive directors, have access to independent professional advice at the company's expense where they judge it necessary to discharge their responsibilities as directors. Committees should be provided with sufficient resources to undertake their duties."

It is sometimes difficult to assess situations where directors legitimately believe that they need independent advice in order to work out an issue in the best interests of the company, on the one hand, and, on the other hand, a situation where a director finds himself in conflict with the board as an individual on an issue which is not concerned with the company but rather his or her individual position. The former case is a suitable subject for legal advice to be taken at the expense of the company, whereas the latter is not.

In relation to insurance cover, UK Corporate Governance Code Provision A.1.3 states: "The company should arrange appropriate insurance in respect of legal action against its directors".

Chapter 12 sets out in detail a description of directors' and officers' insurance cover and its limitations.

Re-election, succession, resignation and retirement

3.028   UK Corporate Governance Code Main Principle B.7 (re-election) states: "All directors should be submitted for re-election at regular intervals, subject to continued satisfactory performance".

In 2010 the FRC introduced a new and controversial Provision[38] which spelled out exactly what "regular" means: UK Corporate Governance Code Provision B.7.1 states:

"All directors of FTSE 350 companies should be subject to *annual* [author's italics] election by shareholders. All other directors should be subject to election at the first annual general meeting after their appointment, and to re-election thereafter at intervals of no more than three years. Non-executive directors who have served longer than nine years should be subject to annual re-election. The names of directors submitted for election or re-election should be accompanied by sufficient biographical details and any other relevant information to enable shareholders to take an informed decision on their election."

UK Corporate Governance Code Provision B.2.3 states:

"Non-executive directors should be appointed for specified terms subject to re-election and to statutory provisions relating to the removal of a director. Any term beyond six years for a non-executive director should be subject to particularly rigorous review, and should take into account the need for progressive refreshing of the board."

The Higgs Review itself felt that it should be exceptional for a non-executive director to serve for more than six years but subsequent representations by industry pointed out that many non-executive directors are extremely effective performers after six years and the matter was therefore left to shareholders to determine by re-election in accordance with the UK Corporate Governance Code.

The Code emphasises the need for succession planning in a supporting principle to Main Principle B.2:

"The board should satisfy itself that plans are in place for orderly succession for appointments to the board and to senior management, so as to maintain an appropriate balance of skills and experience within the company and on the board and to ensure progressive refreshing of the board."

As regards resignation, the commonly held view is that a director should only resign from a board on a matter of board policy (as distinct from illness or other personal circumstances) as a last resort. Higgs put it (para.12.31):

---

[38] There were indications in July 2010 that institutional investors did not regard this provision as useful and would sympathetically review explanations for non-compliance. See *Financial Times*, July 19, 2010, letters.

"I believe that resignation should be regarded very much as a last resort once other efforts to resolve problems have failed. Indeed, non-executive directors may be constrained from resigning by their fiduciary duty to act in the company's best interests."

There may be occasions when a director is in strong disagreement with his or her fellow directors about policy, but it is his or her duty to stay and argue the case unless and until his or her position becomes intolerable. In such a case UK Corporate Governance Code Provision A.4.3 provides that concerns must be reflected in the minutes but that: "on resignation, a non-executive director should provide a written statement to the chairman, for circulation to the board, if they have any such concerns".

How should the matter be reported to shareholders? The 1998 Hampel Report put it this way:

"There are many reasons for a director's resignation which need not concern shareholders—health, family commitments, increased work commitments; in these cases the privacy of the individual should be respected. But it has been suggested to us that shareholders are entitled to know if a resignation results from a policy disagreement or a personality clash. This may be helpful in appropriate cases; there are likely to be rumours, and open disclosure may be in shareholders' interests."

As regards retirement on grounds of age, the UK Corporate Governance Code contains no guidance, but clearly age will be one of the considerations which will be taken into account by the chairman in the evaluation and appraisal of the director concerned which may or may not justify recommendation by the chairman for re-election.

The Hampel Report drew back from making any recommendations as to the appointment or reappointment of directors over the age of 70:

"Some have proposed that companies should not disapply the statutory age limit for directors at 70; or alternatively that directors over the age of 70 should submit themselves for re-election annually . . . This assumes that the effectiveness and objectivity of the director will decline with increasing age and length of service. There is a risk that this could happen, and boards, and the individuals themselves, should be vigilant against it. But a reasonably long period on the board can give directors a deeper understanding of the company's businesses and enable them to make a more effective contribution. Individuals' capacities, and their enthusiasm for the task, vary widely, and a recommendation would be inappropriate."

Conclusion

Effective boards are not only about structure, even though the benchmarks **3.029** and guidance described above have become an essential part in determining board structures and behaviours. At the heart of every effective board should be a system of values based on openness, integrity and accountability. As the Cadbury Report in 1992 put it:

> "They [openness, integrity and accountability] go together. Openness on the part of companies, within the limits set by their competitive position, is the basis for the confidence which needs to exist between business and all those who have a stake in its success. An open approach to the disclosure of information contributes to the efficient working of the market economy, prompts boards to take effective action and allow shareholders and others at scrutinise companies more thoroughly. Integrity means both straightforward dealing and completeness."

A board which follows the benchmarks and guidance described above, and also which possesses these values is likely to be both sustainable and highly effective.

Chapter 4

Directors: Part 1—Duties and Liabilities with special reference to the Companies Act 2006

Since, as a matter of law, no distinction is made between the duties owed to a company by a non-executive director and a full-time executive director (a principle implicitly embraced in the "duties of directors" provisions in Pt 10 of the Companies Act 2006 ("the CA 2006") which came into effect in October 2007, it is important for all directors to have an understanding of their duties and liabilities: In particular the "general duties" newly codified and introduced in the CA 2006—as well as duties arising from other relevant parts of the CA 2006, such as the parts dealing with financial reporting: that will be the ground with which this chapter is mainly concerned.[1]

4.001

In addition, because responsibility for good governance increasingly, if incorrectly, is falling exclusively on the shoulders of non-executive directors, a separate chapter (Ch.5 (Directors—The Non-Executive Director)) will deal with the particular position of non-executive directors.

Chapter 6 (Voices from the Boardroom) describes the actual experiences of independent non-executive directors in dealing with specific issues, and Ch.7 (Board Evaluations) deals with the problematic subject of board evaluation.

The scheme of this chapter

- a glossary of definitions;

4.002

- an overview of the post-CA 2006 regulatory regime governing directors duties in the context of corporate governance;

---

[1] For an outline of the position of directors pre-October 2007 see, e.g. the 3rd edition of this book.

- the "general duties" of directors under the CA 2006:
    - background and summary;
    - detailed analysis;
    - a review of some of the common law cases relevant to the general duties;

- the duty to declare an interest in existing transaction or arrangement;

- transactions between directors and the company which require shareholder approval;

- directors' duties and liabilities in relation to financial reporting under the CA 2006, including the "Business Review";

- derivative actions against directors under the CA 2006;

- ratification;

- relief granted by the courts for breaches of duty;

- the right for a director of a listed company to take legal advice at company's expense;

- ceasing to be a director;

- D&O insurance;

- a personal risk strategy.

A glossary of definitions

Director

4.003   A director "includes any person occupying the position of director by whatever name called" (CA 2006 s.250). It should be noted that a person can be a director as a matter of law without bearing that title. In the case of many companies limited by guarantee, for example, the directors may be known as "council members" or "trustees" or "governors". However, there may be people in a company who are called "directors" but are simply paid officials given the title as a matter of status and who are not directors as a matter of law.[2]

Section 155 also recognises that a corporate body can be a director provided that the company also has at least one natural person acting as a director.

---

[2] See also fn 3 below for case references in the context of "de facto" directors where the definition of "director" has been discussed.

Non-executive or independent directors

The law makes no distinction between executive and non-executive directors. **4.004**
Non-executive directors are "directors" for all purposes of the legislation.

Shadow directors

A "shadow director" is defined (CA 2006 s.251) as "a person in accordance **4.005**
with whose directions or instructions the directors of the company are accustomed to act" and is treated as a matter of law as a director, and will therefore
be subject to the full regime of duties set out in CA 2006 ss.171 to 182.

A person is not deemed a shadow director "by reason only that the
directors act on advice given by him in a professional capacity".

The CA 2006 addresses the question of whether a holding company can be
regarded as a shadow director. Section 251(3) provides that a body corporate
is not to be regarded as a shadow director of any of its subsidiary companies for the purposes of general duties of directors, transactions requiring
members of approval or a contract with a sole member who is also a director,
"by reason only that the directors of the subsidiary are accustomed to act
in accordance with its directions or instructions". Clearly, therefore, it is an
open question depending on the circumstances of the case as to whether a
holding company, or for that matter, an individual controlling shareholder
can be regarded as a "shadow director".

It is arguable, but probably the case, that banks and other commercial
organisations that offer management advice to companies with which they
have dealings, as an adjunct to buttressing a commercial relationship,
can be said to be acting in a professional capacity and not as a shadow
director.

In many cases, it will be clear whether or not a person is a shadow director.
Sometimes, someone for whom the named directors are mere puppets will
obviously be a shadow director. On the other hand, the company solicitor
will not, provided (s)he does no more than give the company legal advice and
renders such other services as form a normal part of a solicitor's practice.

Alternate directors

The articles of association of some companies allow directors to nominate **4.006**
alternate directors to attend and vote at board meetings if they are unable to
do so themselves. The CA 2006 does not contain any provisions relating to
alternate directors as such but they are regarded as "directors" in the fullest
sense as a matter of law in relation to decisions taken at board meetings at
which they were present.

All the circumstances and implications should be considered carefully by the individual concerned before nomination as an alternate director is accepted.

Associate directors

4.007 Some companies appoint "associate directors" who are not board members, but who are nevertheless acknowledged to hold very senior positions within the company. It is possible that associate directors will be deemed to be full directors if they participate in the company's policy decisions other than as experts or advisers to the full directors.

De facto director

4.008 A de facto director is a person who acts as a director without having been duly appointed as such, or continues so to act after his or her formal appointment has been terminated or expired. There is no definition of a de facto director in the CA 2006 but the Court of Appeal has stated3 that the crucial issue in determining de facto directorship was whether the individual in question had assumed the status and functions of a company director so as to make him or herself responsible as if (s)he had been formally appointed as a director. It is submitted, however, that the definition of "director" in CA 2006 s.250 (see above) is wide enough to incorporate a de facto director.

Nominee director

4.009 The term "nominee director" generally means a director appointed by a third party such as a shareholder or lender, to represent the interests of his or her appointor and report to the appointor. However, as a matter of law

---

[3] See *Re Kaytech International Plc, Secretary of State v Kaczer* [1998] All E.R. (D) 655; see also *Secretary of State for Trade and Industry v Hall* [2006] EWHC 1995 (Ch); *The Times*, August 2, 2006; Millett J. in *Re Hydrocarbon (Corby) Ltd* [1993] B.C.C. 161; *Secretary of State for Trade and Industry v Hollier* [2007] B.C.C. 11; and *Re Paycheck Services Ltd: HMRC v Holland* [2008] B.C.L.C. 613; [2008] B.C.C. 37; [2009] Bus.L.R. 1. In that case HMRC acted against a husband and wife who were said to be de facto directors of 42 composite companies (all in liquidation and whose directors were all "corporate") and who, as part of a tax avoidance scheme, were said to have paid millions of pounds in unlawful dividends without providing for the companies' potential liability to higher rate corporation tax. Although the Court of Appeal in reversing the first instance decision, held that on the facts the husband and wife were not to be regarded as de facto directors, the first instance judgment is an authority on de facto directorship, the test for lawful dividends, whether there is strict liability on directors for paying unlawful dividends, the availability of Companies Act 1985 s.727 and the width of discretion under Insolvency Act 1986 s.212. CA 2006 s.105 now requires that every company must have at least one "natural" director.

(s)he must primarily observe his or her duties as a director of the company in the best interests of the company, and must not act exclusively in the best interests of his or her appointor—to do so will be a breach of duty. In the event of a conflict of interest between the interests of the company and the interests of the appointor, that conflict must be declared and, if necessary, authorised by the board (see further paras 4.035 and 4.036 below). Otherwise (s)he runs the risk of being in breach of s.175 (duty to avoid conflicts of interest) and s.177 (duty to declare interest). In addition, (s)he owes to the company the duty of confidentiality as part of the overall duty under s.172 to promote the success of the company, and therefore will have to get permission from the board to disclose confidential information to his or her appointor.

Persons "connected" with a director

Section 251 sets out the definition of "connected person" which is used in many **4.010** of the sections of CA 2006 Pt 10 in relation to the regulation of directors. The persons who are "connected" for this purpose with a director include:

- certain family members (see s.253);

- certain companies with which the director is connected (see s.254);

- trustees of a trust under which the director or a relative mentioned in s.253 or a company with which the director is connected is a beneficiary (but not if the trust exists for the purposes of an employees' share scheme as defined in s.1166 or a pension scheme);

- certain partners; and

- certain firms with legal personality (such as a Scottish firm in which the director is a partner).

This section, together with ss.253 to 255, replaces Companies Act 1985 ("CA 1985") s.346.

Members of a director's "family"

Section 253 sets out those members of a "director's family" who fall within **4.011** the definition of persons connected with the director. The list includes all those family members falling within the definition of connected person in CA 1985 s.346, and in addition it covers:

- the director's parents;

- children or step-children of the director who are over 18 years old (those under 18 were already included under CA 1985 s.346);

- persons with whom the director lives as partner in an enduring family relationship; and

- children or step-children of the director's unmarried partner if they live with the director and are under 18 years of age.

Director "connected with" a body corporate

4.012   Section 254 determines whether a company or other body corporate is a person "connected" with a director. Broadly speaking, the director, together with any other person connected with him or her, must be interested in 20 per cent of the equity share capital, or control (directly or indirectly through another body corporate controlled by them) more than 20 per cent of the voting power exercisable at any general meeting.

Schedule 1 to CA 2006 contains the rules for determining whether a person is "interested in shares" for this purpose.

Director "controlling" a body corporate

4.013   Section 255 defines the circumstances in which a director is deemed to control a body corporate for the purposes of s.254. These circumstances involve two cumulative hurdles. First, the director or any other person connected with him or her must be interested in the equity share capital or be entitled to control some part of the voting power exercisable at any general meeting. Secondly, the director, fellow directors and other persons connected with him or her must be interested in more than 50 per cent of the equity share capital or be entitled to control more than 50 per cent of the voting power exercisable at any general meeting.

An overview of the post-Companies Act 2006 regulatory regime governing directors' duties and liabilities in the context of corporate governance

4.014   The regulatory regime governing duties and liabilities of directors in the context of corporate governance falls broadly under the following categories[4]:

---

[4] It is appreciated that there are many more statutory duties which may give rise to personal liability on directors other than those referred to in this chapter; of which among the more significant, for example and to run the risk of being accused of being selective, might be regarded as s.37 of the Health and Safety at Work, etc. Act 1974 and s.157 of the Environmental

- the eight "general duties" set out in CA 2006 ss.171 to 177, and which are analysed in this chapter;

- transactions between the company and directors which require shareholder approval under the CA 2006: these are outlined in this chapter;

- duties and liabilities in relation to financial reporting arising mainly under the CA 2006: these are also outlined in this chapter and dealt with in more detail in Ch.13 (Financial Reporting);

- "continuing obligations" under the Listing Rules[5] and the Model Code[6] governing dealings by directors in shares in listed companies;

Protection Act 1990, both of which impose personal liability on directors where the offence under that legislation has been committed "with the consent or connivance of, or to have been attributable to any neglect on the part of, any director, manager, secretary or other similar officer of the body corporate". Directors and others may also face criminal liability under the Enterprise Act 2002 for operating trade cartels; directors of companies doing business in the United States may find themselves extradited under the Extradition Act 2003 to answer US criminal charges, e.g. under anti-trust laws; directors of pension funds which become insolvent might find themselves liable to contribute to the fund the deficit under the Pensions Act 2004. However, it is beyond the scope of this book to identify all personal statutory liabilities, and references have been confined to the statutory duties considered most closely connected with governance issues.

[5] The directors are responsible for ensuring that the company complies with its obligations under the Listing Rules at all times. The FSA has power under s.91 of the FSMA to fine and/or censure directors of listed companies who are "knowingly concerned" in a contravention of the Listing Rules. The director has to have had knowledge of the relevant facts and some involvement in the breach.

[6] The Model Code, Annex 1 to Ch.9 of the Listing Rules, is a set of guidelines regarded by the FSA as setting a minimum standard of good practice and with which the company must comply as part of its continuing obligations. The Model Code covers occasions where, even though not expressly prohibited by the statutory provisions, it would be undesirable for a director to buy or sell his or her company's securities.
The main prohibitions on dealings under the Model Code are as follows:
- a director must not deal in his or her company's securities at any time when (s)he is in possession of unpublished "insider" information of a price sensitive nature in relation to them;
- a director must not deal in his or her company's securities on considerations of a short term nature;
- the director must not deal in his or her company's securities during any "close period", which is the period of two months immediately preceding the preliminary announcement of the company's annual results, and the same period before the announcement of half-yearly results, or, if shorter, the period from the relevant financial period end up to and including the time of the announcement;
- in any case, a director must not deal in securities of his or her company unless (s)he has first received clearance from his or her chairman or another director designated for the purpose. If there exists any unpublished information which is likely to require an announcement, then clearance must be refused even if the relevant director was not him or herself aware of the information.

- statutory duties and liabilities in relation to insider dealing under the Criminal Justice Act 1993 ("CJA")[7]; and market abuse[8] and other offences under the Financial Services and Markets Act 2000[9] ("FSMA 2000");

- duties arising or sanctions imposed under the Insolvency Act 1986 ("IA 1986")[10] and the Company Directors Disqualification Act 1986 ("CDDA 1986")[11];

---

[7] It is a criminal offence under the CJA 1993 for an individual who has unpublished price sensitive information, which (s)he knows is "inside" information from an inside source, to deal on a regulated market in securities whose price would be likely to be significantly affected if that information is made public. An individual becomes an insider if (s)he has unpublished price sensitive information either because (s)he or his or her source is a director, employee or shareholder of an insider or is someone who has this information through his or her job or office whether or not (s)he or that other person occupies a confidential position in relation to the issuer of the relevant securities. "Inside information" is information which relates to particular securities or to a particular issuer of securities. It must be specific or precise and must not have been made public; and if it were made public it must be likely to be price sensitive information. There are exceptions to these widely drawn rules: for example, an individual is not prohibited from acting where (s)he did not expect the dealing to result in a profit attributable to the inside information and an individual may deal or encourage another to deal if (s)he reasonably believed that the inside information had been widely disseminated.

[8] The FSMA 2000 Pt VIII makes it a criminal offence for a person to engage in "market abuse". There are three requirements for a finding of market abuse. First, the conduct must occur in relation to "qualifying investments" traded on a specified market. Secondly, the abuse must take one or more forms, the central characteristic of which is that it is likely to give a regular user of the market a force or misleading impression as to the supply of, or demand for, or as to the price or value of, investments of that kind. Thirdly, the behaviour must amount to a failure to observe the standards of behaviour reasonably expected of him or her by regular market users. The Act also identifies three types of behaviour as market abuse. These are:
- the misuse of information;
- behaviour which is likely to mislead market participants as to the price or value of investments; and
- conduct likely to distort the market.
Each of these aspects is further defined or developed in the Act.

[9] For example, FSMA 2000 provides that it is an offence for a person to induce a person to deal in investments by deliberately or recklessly making misleading, false or deceptive statements, promises or forecasts or dishonestly concealing material facts.

[10] IA 1986 s.214 empowers the court, on the application of a liquidator of a company, to order any director or shadow director of a company to make a personal contribution to its assets if:
- the company has gone into insolvent liquidation; and
- at some time before the commencement of the liquidation, that director or shadow director knew or ought to have concluded that there was no reasonable prospect of avoiding such a liquidation.

[11] The Department of Business, Innovation and Skills has powers under the CDDA 1986 to apply to the court to make a disqualification order of between two and 15 years against a person who is found to be "an unfit director" of an insolvent company. Disqualification can apply to offences under the Companies Acts as well as insolvency, and it is often those offences, on a relatively technical nature, (e.g. failure to file annual returns, accounts, etc.) which will be used as background evidence to mount a successful application for disqualification. In relation to insolvency, every liquidator and receiver is empowered to supply the Insolvency Service with a report relating to the circumstances of the insolvency and in certain cases the liquidator or receiver must submit a supplementary report, known as a D notice identifying facts and matters which may give rise to consideration of whether disqualification proceedings should be brought. Registers of disqualified directors are kept by credit risk companies.

- EU Directives and Recommendations relating to company law and corporate governance[12];

- "corporate obligations"—that is to say, the overall responsibility of the board to procure that the company complies with the law.

Who can sue directors?

Under English law[13] only the company itself can sue its directors, present or past, for breach of duty. Commonly, however, it is the board which is the successor board to the board on which the director concerned sat which takes action, as, for example, in the case of the *Equitable Life Assurance Society*[14] (as to which see further Ch.5 (Directors—The Non-Executive Director)). That successor board will often occur after a takeover, of course. In addition, the liquidator and/or administrator of a company may take action in the name of the company.   **4.015**

Powers are given to the court to permit an individual shareholder to make a claim against a director for breach of duty in the name of and on behalf of the company under the "derivative action" procedure. The procedure is permitted where the director concerned in effect controls the company and wrongfully uses that position to stop any action. However, the point is that the derivative action is in essence still an action by the company.

The "general duties" of directors under the Companies Act 2006

The CA 2006 substituted as from October 2007 the former equitable and common law principles with its own statement of eight "general duties".[15] However, the CA 2006 requires that the interpretation of those duties be made in accordance with the rules of equity and common law. Paragraphs 4.048 to 4.054 below contain a discussion of some of the leading cases which will still be relevant in approaching the interpretation of the general duties.   **4.016**

This part of the chapter describes the background to the provisions of the CA 2006 dealing with directors' general duties.

In June 2007 the then DTI, now called the Department of Business Innovation and Skills (BIS), published extracts from ministerial statements in a paper called: "Companies Act 2006, Duties of directors, Ministerial

---

[12] Described in Ch.23 (The EU).
[13] *Foss v Harbottle* (1843) 2 Hare 461, 67 E.R. 189.
[14] *Equitable Life Assurance Society v Bowley* [2003] EWHC 2263 (Comm).
[15] The author takes the view that the "duty to act within powers" heading to s.171 is in reality two distinct duties, as set out in s.171, namely (a) the duty to act in accordance with the constitution; and (b) the duty to only exercise powers for the purposes for which they are conferred.

statements". In the preamble to that paper guidelines to the duties were summarised in a table as follows[16]:

Guidance for company directors–

1) Act in the company's best interests, taking everything you think relevant into account

2) Obey the company's constitution and decisions taken under it

3) Be honest, and remember that the company's property belongs to it and not to you or to its shareholders

4) Be diligent, careful and well informed about the company's affairs. If you have any special skills or experience, use them

5) Make sure the company keeps records of your decisions

6) Remember that you remain responsible for the work you give to others.

7) Avoid situations where your interests conflict with those of the company. When in doubt disclose potential conflicts quickly

8) Seek external advice where necessary, particularly if the company is in financial difficulty

The scheme of this section

4.017   For ease of reference, para.4.018 of this section of the chapter will give the background to the eight "general duties" as set out in CA 2006 ss.171 to 177. Paragraphs 4.020 and 4.047 both summarise and then deal with the "general duties" in more detail; and paras 4.048 to 4.054 contain a review of some of the case law governing existing common law/equitable principles as they relate to directors' duties by reference to the new general duties.

Background

4.018   The eight "general duties"[17] of directors are set out in CA 2006 ss.171 to 177. These duties were said by the Government during the progress of the Company Law Reform Bill (as it was then called) to form a code of conduct "which sets out how directors are expected to behave; it does not tell them

---

[16] *http://www.berr.gov.uk/files/file40139.pdf* (as at November 2009).
[17] See fn 15.

in terms what to do".[18] The statutory duties are said to have derived from the existing equitable and common law rules. The Law Commission and the Scottish Law Commission recommended that there should be a statutory statement of a director's main fiduciary duties and his or her duty of care and skill in their joint report: "*Company directors: regulating conflicts of interests and formulating a statement of duties*". The Company Law Review's ("CLR") main recommendations in respect of general duties were summarised in Ch.3 of the final report of the Review. The CLR recommended that there should be a statutory statement of directors' general duties,[19] and that this should, with two exceptions, amount to a codification of the then current law.

In particular the CLR wanted:

- to provide greater clarity on what is expected of directors and make the law "more accessible". The Review sought to address the key question "in whose interests should companies be run?"[20] in a way "which reflects modern business needs and wider expectations of responsible business behaviour";

- to make development of the law in this area more predictable;

- to correct what the CLR saw as defects in the then current duties relating to conflicts of interest.

The Government accepted these recommendations and they were incorporated into CA 2006 Ch.2 of Pt 10 under the heading: "General Duties of Directors".

The general duties—summary and more detailed analysis

The eight general duties of directors are: **4.019**

- the duty to act in accordance with the company's constitution[21];

- the duty to only exercise their powers for the purposes for which they are conferred[22];

- the duty to promote the success of the company[23];

- the duty to exercise independent judgment[24];

---

[18] DTI Explanatory Notes [Bill 190-EN] issued on May 24, 2006, para.280.
[19] p.40, para.3.7.
[20] p.40, para.3.7.
[21] CA 2006 s.171(a) and see fn 39 below for the definition of "constitution".
[22] CA 2006 s.171(b).
[23] CA 2006 s.172.
[24] CA 2006 s.173.

- the duty to exercise reasonable care, skill and diligence[25];

- the duty to avoid conflicts of interest[26];

- the duty not to accept benefits from third parties[27];

- the duty to declare their interest in a proposed transaction or arrangement.[28]

The general duties are owed to the *company*,[29] not to individual shareholders or stakeholders. Accordingly, even where permission is given by the court to an individual shareholder to bring a derivative action under CA 2006 Pt 11, only the company can enforce a finding against a director arising out of such an action.

However, and save where the company is insolvent,[30] the new duty "to promote the success of the company" under s.172 has to be exercised for the benefit of its "members as a whole". That expression means all the members of a company, majority and minority, present and future.

In arriving at the decision as to whether a particular course of action undertaken in the course of promoting the success of the company pursuant to s.172 is for the benefit of "members as a whole", directors must also "have regard (amongst other matters) to" six factors, such as the interests of employees or the effect on the community and the environment, etc. as set out in s.172(1) and these factors are described in more detail below in paras 4.023 et seq.

The general duties replace the former equitable/common-law fiduciary duty and duty of skill and care[31] and are to be "interpreted and applied in the same way as common law rules or equitable principles, and regard shall be had to the corresponding common law rules and equitable principles in interpreting and applying the general duties".[32]

The consequences of a breach of the general duties and the enforcement of those duties (except for the duty under s.174 to exercise reasonable care, skill and diligence) are to be determined and done "in the same way as any other fiduciary duty owed to a company by its directors".[33]

---

[25] CA 2006 s.174.
[26] CA 2006 s.175.
[27] CA 2006 s.176.
[28] CA 2006 s.177.
[29] CA 2006 s.170.
[30] CA 2006 s.172(3) makes it clear that the duties under s.172 are subject to the rules requiring directors, in certain circumstances (i.e. companies on the verge of insolvency) to consider or act in the interests of creditors.
[31] CA 2006 s.170(3).
[32] CA 2006 s.170(4).
[33] CA 2006 s.178(2).

A more detailed analysis of the general duties

The duties are owed to the company

Section 170 of the CA 2006 codifies the then existing law in stating that the general duties in ss.171 to 177 are owed by directors to and enforceable by the *company*, not to shareholders individually nor other third parties.[34] Moreover a person who ceases to be a director continues to be subject to the duty to avoid conflicts of interest as regards the exploitation of any property, etc. of which (s)he became aware of the time when (s)he was a director, and to the duty not to accept benefits from third parties as regards things done or omitted by him or her before (s)he ceased to be a director.[35] **4.020**

This is not to say that a director can never be liable to a shareholder. If a sufficient relationship or nexus is established between the director and the shareholder, for example, in the context of a statement on which it was reasonable to suppose that a shareholder or proposed shareholder would rely, then the director may well be liable for negligent misstatement or misrepresentation to the shareholder concerned.[36]

General duties replace equity and common law duties but are to be interpreted in accordance with principles of equity and common law

Section 170(3) states that the general duties are based on "certain common law rules and equitable principles as they apply in relation to directors *and have effect in place of those rules and principles* (author's emphasis) as regards the duties owed to a company by a director". The general duties are under s.170(4) to be interpreted and applied in the same way as common law rules or equitable principles, "and regard shall be had to the corresponding common law rules and equitable principles in interpreting and applying the general duties". **4.021**

The courts are therefore given primary responsibility to interpret and develop the general duties in a way, it is said, which reflects the nature of the rules and principles they replace. "Thus developments in the law of trusts and agency should be reflected in the interpretation and application of the

---

[34] This is in effect a codification of the long established rule in *Foss v Harbottle*. The rights given to a shareholder to commence a derivative action against a director under CA 2006 Pt 11 are exercisable in relation to a breach or intended breach of a director's duties to the *company*, not the shareholder.

[35] CA 2006 s.170(2).

[36] *Platt v Platt* [1999] 2 B.C.L.C. 745; *Re Chez Nico (Restaurants) Ltd* [1992] B.C.L.C. 192; *Coleman v Myers* [1997] 2 N.Z.L.R. 225; *Peskin v Anderson* [2001] 1 B.C.L.C. 372; *Caparo Industries Plc v Dickman* [1990] 2 A.C. 605.

duties".[37] Paragraphs 4.048 to 4.054 below look at some of the case law in relation to these common law rules/equitable principles.

The eight general duties[38]

Duty to act within powers (section 171)

4.022   Section 171 of the CA 2006 imposes two general duties under which a director must:

(a)   act in accordance with the company's "constitution"[39];

(b)   only exercise powers for the purposes for which they are conferred.

It is therefore of fundamental importance that directors should make themselves familiar with the memorandum of association during any transitional period whilst CA 2006 ss.17, 28 and 29 come into force, and with the articles of association, in particular, as well as any other parts of the "constitution" which are relevant[40] and comply with and ensure that the company complies with the obligations and limitations contained in the "constitution". Despite the fact that CA 2006 s.31(1) provides that in future companies will be deemed to have unrestricted objects, until companies change their constitution so as to get rid of existing objects clauses (deemed by CA 2006 s.28 to have become part of the articles of association of a company) it will be important to ensure the directors do not act ultra vires their powers, and as the *Equitable Life* case showed,[41] if directors interpret the articles of association allegedly incorrectly, they can be sued for breach of fiduciary duty. Getting specialist outside advice is essential in the event of doubt.

The duty to exercise powers for the purposes for which they are conferred

---

[37] CLR Bill Explanatory Notes [Bill 190—EN] May 24, 2006.

[38] See fn 15 above.

[39] CA 2006 s.17 "defines" this expression as including: (a) the company's articles of association (which by reason of s.28 treats the provisions of the memorandum of association as provisions of the articles); and (b) any resolutions and agreements to which Ch.3 of Pt 3 applies (see s.29). This section is a new provision. It sets out this definition which applies throughout the Act, and the other "Companies Acts" (defined in s.2), unless the context requires a wider or more restricted meaning (see for example s.257, which expands the definition of a company's constitution for the purposes of Pt 10). The concepts of a company's constitution and the rights and obligations arising under it are used both in Pt 3 and elsewhere in the Act. The definition is expressed to be non-exhaustive. In addition to the provisions of a company's articles and the resolutions and agreements to which Ch.3 of Pt 3 applies (described in s.29), the contents of certain other documents are clearly of constitutional relevance for certain purposes. For example the certificate of incorporation summarises key information pertaining to the company such as whether it is public or private limited—see s.15.

[40] See fn 39.

[41] See further Ch.5 (Directors—The Non-Executive Director).

means that they must not exercise these powers for their own personal interests or the special interests of a third party, but must exercise them solely for the benefit and best interests of the company. In para.4.050 below there is an analysis of the leading case on this issue.[42]

Duty to promote the success of the company and the six factors (section 172)

This is the duty at the heart of the general duties and which is likely to cause most concern to directors anxious to ensure that they are acting lawfully. **4.023**

Under CA 2006 s.172 a director of a company must act in the way (s)he considers, in good faith, would be most likely to promote the success of the company for the benefit of its members as a whole. Thus the primary and overriding duty is to members.

However, s.172(1) provides that in fulfilling that duty a director must "have regard (amongst other matters)" to six factors, namely:

(a)   the likely consequences of any decision in the long-term;

(b)   the interests of the company's employees;

(c)   the need to foster the company's business relationships with suppliers, customers and others;

(d)   the impact of the company's operations on the community and the environment;

(e)   the desirability of the company maintaining a reputation for high standards of business conduct; and

(f)   the need to act fairly as between members of the company.

The foregoing duty is subject to any enactment or rule of law requiring directors, in certain circumstances, to consider or act in the interests of creditors of the company (subs.(3)), thus preserving the regime applicable where the company is or may become insolvent.

Section 172 is a new duty and in the debates in Parliament which discussed this clause at the committee stage considerable concern was expressed that the clause in reality creates a new duty which gives rise to uncertainty for directors as to exactly what such a duty involves and to whom it is owed and how it is to be discharged. It was said that such a clause at the very least would require a significant "paper trail" in order to demonstrate that directors had taken decisions which had regard, where relevant, to the six factors

---

[42] *Howard Smith v Ampol Petroleum* [1974] A.C. 821 at 835. See also *Hogg v Cramphorn Ltd* [1967] Ch. 254.

set out in the section, thus diverting them from their central task of running a successful business.

The government's view at the time rather reinforced that concern:

"We do not, however, claim that the interests of the company and of its employees will always be identical; regrettably, it will sometimes be necessary, for example, to lay off staff. The drafting . . . must therefore clearly point directors towards their overarching objective. We have made it clear that [the clause] will make a difference, and a very important difference. The words 'have regard to' mean 'think about'; they are absolutely not about just ticking boxes. If 'thinking about' leads to the conclusion, as we believe it will in many cases, that the proper course is to act positively to achieve the objectives in the clause, that will be what the director's duty is. In other words 'have regard to' means 'give proper consideration to'. . . . Consideration of the factors will be an integral part of the duty to promote the success of the company for the benefit of its members as a whole. The clause makes it clear that a director is to have regard to the factors in fulfilling that duty. The decisions taken by a director and the weight given to the factors will continue to be a matter for his good faith judgment."[43]

4.024   *What does "success" mean?* The Attorney-General at the time of the Committee Stage of the Company Law Reform Bill (as then entitled) in the House of Lords, Lord Goldsmith, went to some lengths to explain the purpose and thinking behind what is now s.172, and in view of the rule in *Pepper v Hart*[44] it may be of interest to quote an extract from his statement:

"... the starting point is for the director to act in a way that he considers in good faith to be most likely to promote the success of the company for the benefit of its members ...

... what is success? The starting point is that it is essentially for the members of the company to define the objectives that they wish to achieve. Success means what the members collectively want the company to achieve. For a commercial company, success will usually mean long-term

---

[43] Margaret Hodge, *Hansard*, Commons Report, col.(789) October 17, 2006.

[44] Following the decision in *Pepper v Hart* ([1993] A.C. 1993), if primary legislation is ambiguous or obscure the courts may in certain circumstances take account of statements made in Parliament by Ministers or other promoters of a Bill in construing that legislation. The DTI published in June 2007 the verbatim statements of Ministers during the passage of the Bill: see *http://www.berr.gov.uk/files/file40139.pdf*. Reference should also be made to the DTI Explanatory Notes *http://www.opsi.gov.uk/acts/en2006/ukpgaen_20060046_en.pdf* which, it is submitted, might also be taken into account by the courts in interpreting the will of Parliament when construing the CA 2006. A warning note as to the scope of using *Pepper v Hart* thinking was contained in the judgment of Lord Sumner in *Bristol Guardians v Bristol Waterworks Co* [1914] A.C. 379 at 396–397 when he said: "... it is said that the clause is ambiguous ... the answer is that it is not ambiguous. Two constructions are arguable and one is right: that is all." The author is indebted to Mr Christopher Liddle for this reference.

increase in value. For certain companies, such as charities and community interest companies, it will mean the attainment of the objectives for which the company has been established. But one can be more refined than that. A company's constitution and the decisions that a company makes can also go on to be more specific about what is the appropriate success model for the company. I have indicated that usually for a company it will be a long-term increase in value, but I can imagine commercial companies that would have a different objective as to their success.

Success can ultimately be determined only on a company-by-company basis, and it is impossible that it may change over time. The noble Lord asked, pertinently, who decides in those circumstances whether the success is taking place. We go back to the basic duty that it is for the directors, by reference to those things that we are talking about—the objectives of the company—to judge and to form a good faith judgment about what is to be regarded as success for the benefit of the members as a whole. It will be for the directors to determine; it is their good faith judgment that will matter, and they will need to look to the company's constitution, shareholder decisions and anything else that they consider relevant in helping them to reach that judgment."

What is meant by "members as a whole"? [continuing the quoted extract **4.025** from the Attorney-General's statement]

"The duty is to promote the success for the benefit of the members as a whole—that is, for the members as a collective body—not only to benefit the majority shareholders, or any particular shareholder or section of shareholders, still less the interests of directors who might happen to be shareholders themselves. That is an important statement of the way in which the directors need to look at this judgment that they have to make."

What does "having regard (amongst other matters) to" the six factors **4.026** *mean?* At the time of the debate about s.172 and the six factors, it was said that no hierarchy is given to the various potentially conflicting interests comprising the six factors that must be taken into account: for example, should a company purchase environmentally sustainable materials which are more expensive than non-sustainable materials, or vice versa—which is more likely to promote the success of a company?

The problem is exacerbated by the law existing prior to the implementation of the CA 2006 which, in terms, prohibited directors from preferring other stakeholders in favour of shareholders; apart, that is, from CA 1985 s.309 which required directors to have regard to the interests of employees as well as members, or in an insolvency situation when regard had to be given to the paramount interests of creditors. Accordingly, there is limited "law" currently available to which directors or their advisers can have access in order to work out exactly what weight should be attached to the six factors as between themselves and as between them and shareholders.

It is also not clear what the individual six factors mean as a matter of law.[45]

Finally, it is not clear what "amongst other matters" means: what "other matters" is meant by this phrase? Is it simply the normal commercial or legal considerations which a board assesses in making decisions, or is it a reference to any residual common law or equitable principles which are not included in the Act—in which case that rather makes a nonsense of ss.170, 178 and 179 which in terms say that the general duties are to be substituted for all previous common law duties and equitable principles.

The Attorney-General offered no help in relation to the "other matters" issues but tried to throw light on the six factors in the debate in the House of Lords Grand Committee stage:

"The noble Lord, Lord Hodgson, asked how a company that tends to expand takes into account the different factors referred to in Clause [172] (1). If, for example, the directors need to consider what the interests or needs of its future 'business relationship with . . . suppliers' will be.

If the company can see only dimly what the nature of its future business relationship with its suppliers will be, it will be rather hard for the directors to take it into account. They must do so only so far as is reasonably practicable. But having said that . . . I should have thought that the directors would say, 'We aim to be this sort of company and the consequence of that is that we are likely to have this sort of relationship with a number of suppliers. We can't identify specifically what they are, so when we are making our decisions, it is something to which we need to have regard.' It

---

[45] There is some law in relation to the subject of giving benefits to employees, and there is some law in relation to the duty to behave fairly as between shareholders. In relation to employees, CA 1985 s.309(1) allowed directors to have regard to the interests of the company's employees in general, as well as the interests of its members, and that was taken to mean the reversal of the decision in *Parke v Daily News* [1962] Ch. 927, in which the court held that ex-gratia payments to employees on the closing down of the company were contrary to the director's fiduciary duties, as the shareholders had no continuing interest in maintaining good relations with employees. *Hutton v West Cork Railway Co* [1883] 23 Ch. D. 654 at 673 was authority for the proposition that directors could pay benefits to employees if they regarded that as being in the best interests of the company as a whole.

In relation to the duty to behave fairly as between shareholders, it is said that this is not a requirement to give equal treatment to all shareholders, only that the treatment should be fair. The duty was explained in *Mutual Life Insurance v Rank Organisation Ltd* [1985] B.C.L.C. 11 where US shareholders of Rank brought an action on the grounds that the directors had excluded them from participating in a rights issue. The directors justified the exclusion on the grounds of the cost and effort which would be incurred in meeting US registration requirements if the offer had been extended to all shareholders. The action was unsuccessful it being held that the directors had exercised their powers in good faith in the interests of the company and that they had in fact exercised them fairly as between the different shareholders. See also *Re BSB Holdings Ltd (No.2)* [1996] 1 B.C.L.C. 155.

Paragraphs 4.048 to 4.054 below analyses some more cases which may have a bearing on the interpretation of s.172.

is not and cannot be an absolute duty . . . but that is not a reason for not including it as part of the enlightened shareholder value approach."

Another problem is that by identifying certain factors which directors must take into account, the burden of proof is imposed upon directors to establish that they have duly considered the six factors, or that they were irrelevant. To quote the explanatory notes issued by the then DTI[46]:

"It will not be sufficient to pay lip service to the [six] factors. In many cases the directors will need to take action to comply with this aspect of the duty."

This would suggest that merely reciting in board minutes that the directors have considered the factors is not, of itself, going to suffice. The explanatory notes go on to say that, however, the duty does not require a director:

"to do more than good faith and the duty to exercise reasonable care, skill and diligence would require, nor would it be possible for a director acting in good faith to be held liable for a process failure which would not have affected his decision as to which course of action would best promote of the success of the company".

Paragraphs 4.048 to 4.054 below contains an analysis of some common law cases which may have some bearing on the interpretation of s.172, including the difficulty of decision-making where there is no apparent hierarchy between the factors which directors have been required to take into account.

The "paper trail" and delegation of powers In order to help stave off possible **4.027** subsequent claims of breach of duty under s.172 either by a successor board or by a liquidator or by an aggrieved shareholder under the new "derivative" claim provisions of Pt 11, directors will need to consider not only monitoring the basis for their deliberations, decisions and actions, but also establishing appropriate processes where they have delegated their powers. They will need to consider the terms of any delegation, such as its scope, reporting obligations and provisions for monitoring.

Board meetings may have to be extended to allow time to produce evidence of the way in which the directors have addressed their decision in the light of the six factors so as to ensure that decisions are "lawyer-proofed" against challenge.

Company secretaries will need to ensure that in board papers relating to material decisions and corresponding minutes of board and committee meetings attention is paid to tracking the wording of the section so as to show that the various factors have been taken into account.

---

[46] para.325. See: *http://www.publications.parliament.uk/pa/ld200506/ldbills/034/en/06034x–.htm* or the OPSI website: *http://www.opsi.gov.uk*.

The risk for directors is that a successor board (as in the *Equitable Life* case[47]) or a liquidator or an aggrieved shareholder in pursuance of a claim against the previous board for an alleged breach of the "duty to promote the success of the company" will draw attention to any apparent failure to take into account the six factors as evidence of a general lack of attention to the correct performance of duties. That is why careful records will be important.

Duty to exercise independent judgment (section 173)

4.028   Section 173 of the CA 2006 requires a director to exercise independent judgment, but that duty is not infringed by his or her acting either in accordance with an agreement binding on the company which restricts the future exercise of discretion by its directors, or in a way authorised by the company's constitution.

This duty has been described as a duty on the director not to agree to restrict his or her power to exercise an independent judgment. It is also described as a duty on a director not to "fetter" his or her discretion. Thus a director may not bind him or herself to vote on board resolutions (or to fulfil other functions as a director) in a particular way—(s)he must consider all the circumstances at the time and decide on what is in the best interests of the company. This duty must be borne particularly in mind by directors who have been appointed by a shareholder or other third party to "look after my interests".

However, it is often the case that the company will enter into a contract and the directors undertake to exercise their powers in such a way as to ensure the proper execution of the contract, having come to the good-faith view that it is in the best interests of the company to enter into such a contract. Such an undertaking is not in breach of the duty to exercise independent judgment.[48] It seems from the cases that the key to understanding the principle is that directors should not give undertakings in advance to recommend a course of action to shareholders in case at the time of the recommendation, the directors are no longer of the view that the proposed course of action is in the best interests of the company. Nor should directors give an unqualified undertaking to make statements to shareholders in the future. Directors should make it clear if asked that their obligations are subject always to the proper fulfilment of their duties to the company and to its shareholders at the relevant time, and therefore advance commitments must be severely conditional on that principle.

---

[47] See paras 4.054 and 5.002 below.
[48] *Fulham Football Club Ltd v Cabra Estates Plc* [1994] 1 B.C.L.C. 363 at 392. See also *Rackham v Peek Foods Ltd* [1990] B.C.L.C. 895; and *John Crowther Group Plc v Carpets International Plc* [1990] B.C.L.C. 460.

Duty to exercise reasonable care, skill and diligence (section 174)[49]

Section 174 of the CA 2006 requires a director to exercise reasonable care, skill and diligence. The section defines this as meaning the care, skill and diligence that would be exercised by a reasonably diligent person with: **4.029**

   (a)   the general knowledge, skill and experience that may reasonably be expected of a person carrying out the functions carried out by the director in relation to the company, and

   (b)   the general knowledge, skill and experience that the director has.

The first leg of the test is generally described as the "objective" test, and the second as the "subjective" test. The objective test is the basic benchmark of care, skill and diligence, but the subjective test recognises that some directors may have special knowledge, skill and experience, in which event they will be required to conform to that standard.[50]

A director must observe the "higher" of these tests.

Components of the duty of care

   •   What does a director need to know? **4.030**

   •   What standard does a director need to reach?[51]

Knowledge   The following are suggested[52] expectations of the level of knowledge and effort (diligence) reasonably required of a director: **4.031**

---

[49] See also the summary of the common law view of "duty of care" in paras 4.030 et seq. below.
[50] See *Re D'Jan of London Ltd* [1993] B.C.L.C. 646 where Hoffmann L.J. approved and applied this test in determining a director's duty of care, a test then expressed in the context of insolvency only in IA 1986 s.214. The *Re D'Jan* test in the context of directors duties as a whole has now been codified by CA 2006 s.174. See also *Gregson v HAE Trustees Ltd* [2008] EWHC 1006 (Ch) [2008] 2 B.C.L.C. 542; and *Lexi Holdings Plc v Luqman* [2009] EWCA Civ 117.
[51] In certain states in the United States (e.g. Delaware) the courts have developed a doctrine known as the "business judgement rule" which broadly means that the courts will not question decisions made by directors in good faith in what they believe to be in the best interests of the company. The UK does not have such an articulated rule, but in practice judges in the UK are reluctant to second guess decisions demonstrated as having been made in good faith in the best interests of the company. Australia codified a "business judgement" rule in 2001 and the rule was exhaustively considered in *ASIC v Rich* [2009] N.S.W.S.C. 1229. Austin J. considered the business judgment rule in the context of the collapse of One.Tel, a listed telecommunications company, in May 2001. ASIC's claim was that each of the four defendant directors had committed multiple breaches of the statutory duty of care and diligence under s.180(1) of the Corporations Act 2001. The business judgment rule, is set out in s.180(2) and (3) of the (Australian) Corporations Act 2001 (Cth) and immediately follows the statutory duty of care and diligence. Accordingly the case may be instructive in any analysis of the nature of the duty of care.
[52] See *AWA Ltd v Daniels* (1995) 37 N.S.W.L.R. 438 CA; 13 A.C.L.C. 614, an Australian case which has received approval in the English courts and which contains a detailed analysis of the duty of care of which the list is a summary extracted by the author.

- become familiar with the business of the company;

- guide and monitor the management of the company;

- ensure regular board meetings;

- get outside specialist advice on issues of substantial importance;

- ask searching questions of managers;

- understand the regulatory environment in which the company operates and measures taken to comply with that environment;

- do not "shut eyes" to corporate misconduct;

- remember that there is an affirmative duty to seek out knowledge—as discussed in Ch.5 in relation to non-executive directors, there is a duty to challenge information provided by executive officers.

Standard

4.032

- The benchmark is the "objective" and "subjective" tests set out under s.174 (see above).

- Persons with a degree of specialist knowledge who are appointed to the board by reason of that specialist knowledge will be expected to display a higher standard of due diligence in relation to the use of that specialist knowledge.

In *Re Continental Assurance Company of London Plc (In Liquidation) (No.1)*[53] a senior executive of a bank was appointed a non-executive director of the company and its subsidiary. In breach of the financial assistance provisions of the CA 1985, the subsidiary made a loan to the holding company. When the subsidiary became insolvent, the director was disqualified—his ignorance about the purpose of the loan was held not to be a defence, but was evidence of his failure to exercise the appropriate degree of competence, especially in the light of his experience as a banker and his ability to understand the accounts of the holding company.

In *Re Barings Plc (No.5)*[54] the executive chairman of the bank faced disqualification proceedings following the insolvency of the bank caused by unauthorised securities trading of an individual employee. He was unsuccessful in defending himself in arguing that his expertise was in the corporate finance side of the business, that he had very little understanding of the activities in which the trader was involved and that he relied on the internal audit department and external auditors. The judge said that "directors have,

[53] [1997] 1 B.C.L.C. 48.
[54] [1999] 1 B.C.L.C. 433.

both collectively and individually, a continuing duty to acquire and maintain a sufficient knowledge and understanding of the company's business to enable them properly to discharge their duties as directors". (See Ch.5 for a further account of this case in the context of the duties of non-executive directors.)

It also has to be remembered that the duty of care may well be construed in the light of other contemporary statements relating to the duties of directors, and in particular non-executive directors; for example, the 2003 Higgs Review into the role and effectiveness of non-executive directors.[55] Many of the recommendations of the Higgs Review have found their a way into the Combined Code and subsequently in June 2010 into the UK Corporate Governance Code.

Does the modern law of duty of care imply for directors of listed companies observance of the UK Corporate Governance Code, Higgs and Walker?

It is submitted that non-observance or breach of the UK Corporate Governance Code and a disregard or ignorance of the modern view of the duties of a director recommended by the 2003 Higgs *Review of the role and effectiveness of non-executive directors* and the 2009 Walker *Review of corporate governance in UK banks and other financial industry entities* would be regarded by a judge as a breach of the duty of care.   **4.033**

However, on the basis of the benchmarks suggested above, if directors make good faith, business judgments and decisions in the best interests of the company as they in good faith believe them to be then the courts would be reluctant to second-guess those judgments and decisions.[56]

Duty to avoid conflicts of interest (section 175)[57]

Under s.175 a director "must avoid a situation in which (s)he has, or can have, a direct or indirect interest that conflicts, or may conflict, with the interests of the company".   **4.034**

---

[55] See App.2.
[56] See fn 50 above and paras 4.048 to 4.054 below for some more common law cases on this subject.
[57] The author is indebted to the explanatory notes published by the then DTI for illumination of these provisions: see the OPSI website: *http://www.opsi.gov.uk*. These provisions were implemented in October 2008. For an excellent article reviewing current law on this topic see Sweet & Maxwell Company Law Newsletter issue number 268, February 2010, written by Stephen Griffin, Professor of Law at the University of Wolverhampton. See also guidance papers from General Council 100 Group: January 2008 guidance on the new statutory duty: *http://www.corporate.practicallaw.com/6-382-9093/4and5*.

4.035   *What is a "conflict of interest"?*[58]   A conflict of interest arises if directors place themselves in a position where their personal interests or duties to other persons are liable to conflict with their duties to the company, unless the company gives its consent. A conflict of interest may, in particular, arise when a director makes personal use of information, property or opportunities belonging to the company or when a director enters into a contract with his or her company. Conflicts of interest may also arise whenever a director makes a profit in the course of being a director, in the matter of his or her directorship, without the knowledge and consent of his or her company.

The duty to avoid conflicts of interest covers all conflicts, actual and potential, between the interests of the director and the interests of the company. This includes conflicts relating to the exploitation of the company's property, information or opportunity for personal purposes. The only conflicts not covered by this duty, are those relating to transactions or arrangements with the company (interests in transactions or arrangements with the company must be declared under s.177 in the case at a proposed transactions or under s.182 in the case of existing transactions unless an exception applies under those sections).

Section 180(4) preserves any current ability of the members of a company to authorise conflicts that would otherwise be a breach of this duty by virtue of (a) any rule of law; or (b) where the company's articles contain provisions for dealing with conflicts of interest.

4.036   *Where the duty is not infringed?*   Under s.175(4) to (6) the duty is not infringed if:

- in the case of private companies, unless the constitution prevents this, authorisation has been given by directors who are genuinely independent in the sense that they have no direct or indirect interest in the transaction;

- in the case of a public company, but only if its constitution expressly permits this, authorisation has been given by the independent directors; or

- "if the situation cannot reasonably regarded as likely to give rise to a conflict of interest".

Board authorisation is effective only if the meeting is quorate *without* counting the director in question or any other interested director, and if the matter was agreed to without their voting or would have been agreed to if their votes had not been counted (s.175(6)). The conflicted directors may not be counted towards a quorum.

---

[58] For a recent examination of the issues in construing the meaning of this expression in the Court of Appeal see *O'Donnell v Shanagan* [2009] EWCA Civ 751.

Board authorisation of conflicts of interest will therefore be the "default" position for private companies, but public companies will need to make provision in their constitution to permit board authorisation; or get the approval of members in general meeting by ordinary resolution.

Examples of conflict cases In the case of *JJ Harrison (Properties) Ltd v*   **4.037**
Harrison[59] a director of a company acquired some land from the company at a price which reflected the fact that planning permission had been refused to develop the land. At the time of the acquisition, however, the director was aware that the prospect of planning permission being granted had improved. That awareness was not disclosed to the board at the meeting to approve the transaction. The court found that the director was in breach of his fiduciary duties to the company and held the property upon trust for the company. Accordingly he was liable to account for the profits he made from the subsequent sale by him of the land. If that case were held today it is probable that the same result would arise, the director being held to be in breach of s.175.

In *Scottish Co-operative Wholesale Society Ltd v Meyer*[60] the directors of a partly-owned subsidiary agreed to a policy of its holding company to withhold from the subsidiary business contracts which were diverted to the parent company. The minority shareholders in the subsidiary sued the directors of the subsidiary who were "appointees" of the holding company (and also directors of the holding company) they were held to be in breach of their duties to the subsidiary by their inaction in failing to protect the company from the loss of business, and therefore were liable to account for that loss. Again, it is submitted that the same result would happen today.

It has been said that s.175 may create problems of multiple directorships. Should a director refuse to take on a directorship in another company in the same business as the company on which (s)he already sits as a director, on the grounds that (s)he is under a duty "to avoid conflicts of interest". Many non-executive directors are invited to join boards for the reason that they are experienced in the same line of business, and it is completely accepted by the companies concerned as a sensible situation provided that the director is alert to possible conflicts and obtains informed consent before a conflict arises.

Bell v Lever Bros Ltd[61] provides some assistance in the approach of the courts to multiple directorships of companies which on the face of it might be regarded as competitors or in the same line of business. The usual problem is that such directors may become aware of opportunities and be faced with the challenge of trying to work out to whom those opportunities should be directed. Up until s.175 the diversion of business opportunities without informed shareholder consent would have been regarded as in breach of fiduciary duty. Accordingly, in view of the wording of this section it will be

---

[59] [2002] 1 B.C.L.C. 162.
[60] [1959] A.C. 324.
[61] [1932] A.C. 161.

imperative for directors to get the informed consent and authorisation of the board (provided the articles, in the case of a public company, so permit) to other directorships under the provisions of s.175(4)(b) or (5).

The circumstances may also amount to a transaction falling within CA 2006 Pt 10 Ch.4 (transactions requiring approval of members—see further below), so that if members do give approval then by reason of s.180(2) it is not necessary also to comply with s.175.

Duty not to accept benefits from third parties (section 176)

4.038   A director of a company must not accept a benefit from a third party conferred by reason of either his or her being a director or, (s)he doing (or not doing) anything as director.

"Third party" means a person other than the company, and an associated body corporate or a person acting on behalf of the company or an associated body corporate.

Benefits received by a director from a person by whom his or her services (as a director or otherwise) are provided to the company are not regarded as conferred by a third party.

The duty is not infringed if the benefit cannot reasonably regarded as likely to give rise to a conflict of interest.

It would appear from the wording that it is not possible for directors to give approval, as under s.175, but it may be that the circumstances will fall within CA 2006 Pt 10 Ch.4 (transactions requiring approval of members—see further below) in which case by reason of s.180(2) it is not necessary also to comply with s.176.

Ratification under s.239 will also possible (see further below), but otherwise the duty under s.176 is strict.

It is assumed that the interpretation of this section will refer to the well-established cases concerning the principle that a director may not benefit from his or her office, since (s)he is a "fiduciary".

Perhaps the best known of these cases is *Regal (Hastings) Ltd v Gulliver*.[62] In that case Regal ran the Regal Cinema in Hastings. Regal formed a subsidiary to acquire the leases of two other cinemas with a view to disposing of the whole by selling the shares of Regal. The landlord required the subsidiary to have a capital of £5,000. However Regal could only afford to subscribe for £3,000. The directors of Regal held a majority of the shares in the subsidiary and it was agreed that the directors would find subscribers for 3,000 shares at one pound each. Four other directors took 500 shares and the chairman persuaded two companies in which he was interested to take 200 shares each, the secretary took 100 shares and the solicitor to Regal, at the request of the

---

[62] [1967] 2 A.C. 134.

board, took 500 shares. The share capital of Regal and the subsidiary were sold at a profit of £2.00 per share. No ratification of the transaction by shareholders took place. The new board of Regal after the sale won its case against the four directors and lost against the chairman and the solicitor. It was held, perhaps harshly, that the directors had received a benefit from a third party in their capacity as directors without ratification by members and should therefore account to Regal for that benefit.

If the *Regal* case were to be tried today, the directors would no doubt be accused of being in breach of s.175 (duty to avoid conflicts of interest) and s.176 (duty not to accept benefits from third parties). Accordingly the result would be the same, it is submitted. However, today it would be open to the directors to try to get authorisation by the board under s.175(5), but there might not be a quorum of non-interested directors, or to declare an interest under s.177, or to try to get ratification from members under s.239 provided that no interested director nor any person connected with him voted on the relevant resolution.[63]

Duty to declare interest in proposed transaction (section 177)

If a director has any direct or indirect interest in any *proposed* transaction or **4.039** arrangement with the company, (s)he has a duty to declare both the nature and extent of that interest to the other directors. Directors are required to update declarations of interests in proposed transactions or arrangements that become inaccurate or incomplete before the company enters into the transaction or arrangement. There is no materiality threshold. A small change in a director's shareholding, for example, in a company specified in a general notice of declaration will trigger the obligation to update.

A director need not declare an interest if it cannot reasonably be regarded as likely to give rise to a conflict of interest; or if, or to the extent that, the other directors are already aware of it (and for this purpose the other directors are treated as aware of anything of which they ought reasonably to be aware); or if it concerns the terms of his or her service contract that have been or are to be considered by the directors.

When does the declaration have to be made?   The declaration must be made **4.040** before the company enters into the transaction or arrangement.

How is the declaration to be made?   The declaration may be made at a **4.041** meeting of the directors or by notice in writing to the directors under s.184 or s.185 (general notice).

---

[63] See also *North West Transportation Co v Beatty* (1887) 12 App. Cas. 589; and *Imperial Credit Association v Coleman* (1873) L.R. 6 H.L. 189.

4.042   *What is a general notice?*   A general notice under s.185 is notice given to the directors to the effect that the director has an interest (as member, officer, employee or otherwise) in a company or firm and is to be regarded as interested in any transaction or arrangement that may, after the date of the notice, be made with that company or firm; or is "connected"[64] with a specified person and is to be regarded as interested in any transaction, etc. that may, after the date of the notice, be made with that person.

The notice must state the nature and extent of the director's interest in the company or firm or the nature of his or her connection with the person, and the notice is not effective unless it is given at a meeting of the directors, or the director takes reasonable steps to secure that is brought up and read at the next meeting of the directors after it is given.

Clearly, therefore, a general notice is a good "default" position for directors to implement in cases, the example, of multiple directorships. Such a notice does not, of course, substitute for the need to avoid conflicts of interest under s.175. However, as has been explained (paras 4.034 et seq.), a conflict situation can be authorised by the directors in the circumstances permitted under s.175(5).

Consequences of a breach of the general duties

4.043   Under s.178 the consequences are said to be the same as would apply if the "corresponding common law rule or equitable principle applied". The duties (with the exception of the duty to exercise reasonable care, skill and diligence under s.174) are enforceable in the same way "as any other fiduciary duty owed to a company by its directors".

Thus, it would appear that the traditional remedies still apply, namely:

- damages or compensation where the company has suffered loss;

- restoration of the company's property;

- an account of profits made by the director;

- rescission of a contract where the director failed to disclose an interest[65];

- injunction.

Overriding effect of articles of association

4.044   Section 180(4)(b) makes it clear that if the articles contain provisions for dealing with conflict of interest, then the general duties are not infringed by

---

[64] See glossary of definitions at the beginning of this chapter.
[65] See also para.4.054 below (*Damages*). Note also that the court may grant relief under CA 2006 s.1157. See para.4.076 below.

anything done (or omitted) by the directors in accordance with those provisions. Most articles of association of public companies require that conflicts of interest must be declared and permit the board to authorise, provided that the director concerned plays no part in the proceedings. As experience of the general duties develops it will be interesting to see if articles of association are amended so as to permit a range of activities otherwise forbidden by the general duties.

Duty to declare interest in existing transaction—criminal sanction (section 182)

This duty is not one of the eight "general duties", nor is it a new duty, but **4.045** rather an amplification and tightening up of the duty previously contained in CA 1985 s.317.

Under s.182 a director will commit a *criminal* offence if (s)he:

- fails to declare a direct or indirect interest in an *existing* transaction or arrangement with the company to the other directors (unless that has already been declared before the transaction was entered into by the company);

- fails to update a declaration of interest; and

- fails to comply with the requirements as to the form and content of the director's declaration or updates.

The duty does not apply to the extent that the interest has been declared under s.177 (duty to declare interest in *proposed* transaction).

A declaration need not be made if the director is not aware of the proposed arrangement or transaction but the director is nevertheless treated as being aware of matters of which (s)he "ought reasonably to be aware" (s.182(5)).

A director need not declare an interest if it cannot reasonably be regarded as likely to give rise to a conflict of interest, or to the extent that the other directors are already aware of it, and for this purpose the other directors are treated as aware of anything of which the "ought reasonably to be aware". The duty is also not breached if the matter concerns terms of service that have been or are to be considered by a meeting of the directors or by a committee of the directors appointed for the purpose under the company's constitution. This would appear to mean that if a service contract is not going to be so considered by the directors, then the declaration has to be made.

When is the declaration to be made? The declaration must be made "as soon **4.046** as is reasonably practicable", but failure to comply with that timetable does not affect the underlying duty to make the declaration. A fresh declaration is required if the circumstances change.

4.047   *How and in what form is the declaration made?*   The declaration must be made either at a meeting of the directors, or by notice in writing (in accordance with the provisions of s.184), or by general notice (under the provisions of s.185).

Section 184 sets out the requirements for the form of the notice of declaration and the manner of service. Section 185 sets out the procedure for a general notice, and is described above in para.4.042.

A review of some more cases illustrating the equitable/common law approach to directors' duties

4.048   Under CA 2006 s.170(3), the new general duties are based on common law rules and equitable principles as they apply in relation to directors and have effect in place of those rules and principles. Under s.170(4) these general duties are to be interpreted and applied in the same way as common law rules and equitable principles, and "regard shall be had to the corresponding common law rules and equitable principles in interpreting and applying the general duties". It is therefore a question as to how case law will be applied in interpreting the codified duties. In dealing with the general duties described in paras 4.022 and 4.044 above references were made to a number of cases which may be relevant. Paragraphs 4.048 to 4.054 are intended to analyse some more cases to help show how the existing common law and equitable principles might be applied in relation to the codified provisions.

The "business judgment rule"[66]

4.049   So called following many decisions[67] to the effect that the courts will not try to second guess the bona fide business judgment of directors unless the business view was so extreme that no reasonable director would hold it, either by taking into account factors that they should not have considered, or failed to take into account factors that they should have considered or if, having considered all the right factors, they have come to a conclusion so unreasonable that no reasonable person could have come to it.[68] A business judgment albeit a mistaken business judgment by a director in deciding in good faith and after exercising due care on whether or not a course of action is a sensible one for the company to take will not of itself result in liability. It is submitted that, even after the passing of the general duties legislation, the courts are

---

[66] See also fn 51 above.

[67] e.g. *Howard Smith v Ampol Petroleum Ltd* [1974] A.C. 821 at 835: "In doing so (the court) will necessarily give credit to the bona fide opinion of the directors, if such is found to exist, and will respect their judgment as to matters of management".

[68] *Associated Provincial Picture Houses Ltd v Wednesbury Corp* [1948] 1 K.B. 223.

likely to continue to refrain from applying their own business judgment[69] to a question raised by s.172 (duty to promote the success of the company) as to business judgments made in good faith and intended to promote the success of the company for the benefit of its members, having regard to the six factors described above, or those that are relevant. The courts will only intervene to question or set aside the business judgment if the director was negligent at arriving at that conclusion or did so in breach of any other general duty, e.g. duty to avoid a conflict of interest (s.175) or duty not to accept benefits from third parties (s.175).[70]

Powers to be exercised for a proper purpose and in the best interests of the company as a whole

The codified statutory duties under s.171(b) only to exercise powers for the purposes for which they are conferred and to exercise those powers "in the way he considers, in good faith, would be most likely to promote the success of the company"[71] are likely to continue to be interpreted in accordance with established cases such as *Re Smith & Fawcett Ltd.*[72] In that case the issued share capital of the company was held as to 50 per cent each by its two directors. One director died, and his executor applied to have his shares registered in his name. The remaining director refused, but offered to register half the shares and to buy the remainder at a fixed price. The executor sought rectification of the register of members alleging breach of fiduciary duty in refusing to register the shares of the deceased director. It was alleged that the surviving director was motivated by a collateral purpose, namely the desire to acquire half of the deceased directors shares at an undervalue. The articles provided that "the directors may at any time in their absolute and uncontrolled discretion refuse to register any transfer of shares". Despite such a wide power, the court held that the director was still subject to fiduciary duties which required him to exercise his powers "bona fide in the interests of the company". The court held that this meant "bona fide in what the director considered—not what a court may consider—is in the best interests of the company, and not for any collateral purpose". However, based on the evidence, the court was not satisfied that the surviving director was *not* acting in what he considered to be the interests of the company, and so the application to rectify the register by the executor failed. It is submitted that the case would be decided in the same way even after the CA 2006 if the judge found the same facts as to the state of mind of the surviving director on the basis of the evidence in court. However, were the case to be held after the coming into effect of the CA 2006,

4.050

---

[69] *Associated Provincial Picture Houses Ltd v Wednesbury Corp* [1948] 1 K.B. 223.
[70] *Regal (Hastings) Ltd v Gulliver* [1967] 2 A.C. 134. See further para.4.038 above.
[71] CA 2006 s.172(1).
[72] [1942] Ch. 304.

the surviving director would have been cross-examined as to the extent to which he had observed s.172, and in particular subs.(1)(f) in relation to the need to act fairly as between members of the company.

In *Howard Smith Ltd v Ampol Petroleum Ltd*[73] the trial judge found that the primary purpose of an allotment of shares by the directors was to dilute and remove the blocking stake of two other shareholders who had refused to accept an offer to buy the share capital of the company, an offer which the minority shareholders and a majority of the directors wished to accept. The judge held that the directors had not exercised their powers for a "proper purpose" (general duty under s.171(b)) since the aim, on the basis of the evidence, was to remove the blocking stake and not to act in the best interests of the company. Again, it is submitted that the result of the case would have been the same if tried after the CA 2006 for breach of s.171(b).

Duty to promote the success of the company and reconciling that duty with the six section 172 factors

4.051   It is not clear yet how the courts will accept arguments where directors have used s.172 (duty to promote the success of the company) to justify "poison pill" activity or refusal to accept the offer on non-financial grounds: for example, albeit an extreme example, where a bidder intends to demolish company offices, sack the workforce and build petrol stations, thus adversely impacting the community and the environment under subpara.(d) of s.172(1). Will the directors be entitled to argue that having due regard to such non-financial factors in compliance with s.172 means that they are entitled to reject a takeover offer at a price which, for the sake of argument, is at a substantial premium to the market price? The problem is that as observed in paras 4.026 to 4.027 above s.172 does not set out a hierarchy of considerations to which the directors must have regard.

The preamble to the six factors clearly states that a director "must act . . . to promote the success of the company for the benefit of its members as a whole", and taken on its face value that would seem to require the directors to serve the interests of members by accepting a good offer, having, however, first considered the impact of the six factors of s.172. The counter argument is that on these particular facts a board of directors which is required to "have regard . . . to" the community and environmental implications of the offer could not properly go forward with recommending the offer without running the risk of breaching s.172(1)(d). In the case of *Re BSB Holdings (No.2)*[74] where the directors were trying to reconcile the interests of different groups of shareholders, the court held that the directors *must* give priority to the best interests of the *company* as a whole and must not try to distinguish between

[73] [1974] A.C. 821.
[74] [1996] 1 B.C.L.C. 155.

groups of members. A similar line was taken in *Dawson International Plc v Coats Patons Plc*[75] which emphasised that directors duties are to the *company* and not current shareholders unlike the judgments in *Heron International Ltd v Grade*[76] where the court indicated that the interests of the target company in a takeover situation where there are competing bids are to be judged by reference to the interests of the current shareholders and that the duty of the directors is to obtain the best price. The position is far from clear, therefore, and advisers are going to be challenged to give clear advice in what is a wholly undeveloped area of law.

Conflict of interest and ratification of breaches of duty[77]

In *North West Transportation Co v Beatty*[78] the director, Beatty, sold a ship   **4.052**
for $125,000 to the company. There was a vote of shareholders to authorise the sale by the adoption of a new article. The resolution was passed only by reason of the votes of Beatty. Beatty was sued for breach of fiduciary duty because he had a conflict of interest and had profited personally from his position and should not have voted on the resolution. Beatty in fact won because the law as it then stood did not require an interested director who was a shareholder to refrain from voting. Accordingly the transaction was validly ratified by shareholders. Today, Beatty would be in breach of s.175 (duty to avoid conflicts of interest) unless the articles under s.182(4)(b) permit self-dealing; and an attempt to ratify that breach of duty under s.239(4) will be ineffective if the votes of the director concerned and "persons connected with him" carry the vote—under s.239 Beatty is not permitted to vote, nor any person" "connected" with him—ss.252 and 253 have a wide definition of "connected person".[79] Thus today, Beatty might well have lost his case. Of course, today, the transaction would also be regarded as a "substantial property transaction," under CA 2006 s.190, which under s.190 would require members' approval.

Duty to exercise reasonable care, skill and judgment

The leading modern case is *Re D'Jan of London Ltd* [1993] B.C.C. 646   **4.053**
where Hoffmann L.J. laid down the modern construction of this duty, now codified in CA 2006 s.174, and explained more fully in paras 4.029 et seq. above. *Re Barings Plc (No.5)*[80] is another modern case examining this

---

[75] [1991] B.C.C. 276.
[76] [1983] B.C.L.C. 244.
[77] See also a recent Court of Appeal analysis in *O'Donnell v Shanahan* [2009] EWCA Civ 751.
[78] [1887] 12 App. Cas. 589.
[79] See fn 88.
[80] [2000] 1 B.C.L.C. 523. See also para.4.032 above.

issue.[81] In the course of his judgment Morritt L.J. said that directors have, amongst other things, both collectively and individually, the continuing duty to acquire and maintain a sufficient knowledge and understanding of the company's business to enable them properly to discharge their duties as directors.[82]

Damages

4.054   If there is a breach of duty, damages will be assessed in accordance with the normal rules applicable to negligence or breach of fiduciary duty. A detailed analysis of these matters was set out in the judgment in *Queens Moat Houses v Bairstow*.[83] That case concerned the payment of dividends unlawfully out of non-existent reserves, and the directors were ordered to repay the unlawful dividends.[84]

In *Equitable Life Assurance Society v Bowley*, a claim for approximately £5 billion was made in 2002 by the Society against all the former directors who had allegedly been in breach of duty in relation to the Society's failure to honour a particular annuity commitment. The claim was withdrawn after a very lengthy court hearing at the end of 2005 without any payment being made by the directors, and all their costs were paid.

It was alleged that the directors, both executive and non-executive, of the Society had been in breach of their fiduciary duty in their misinterpretation of the articles of association,[85] and in breach of their duties of skill and care[86] in failing to make adequate provision for the annuities in question, failing to take independent advice at the appropriate time,[87] and failing to find a buyer for the Society when it became clear that the Society would be in financial difficulties in honouring the particular annuities. Many commentators felt that quite apart from the difficulties in proving breach of duty, there were extreme difficulties in proving a causative link between the alleged breach and the damages claimed.

---

[81] See also fn 50 above.

[82] See also *Associated Picture Houses Ltd v Wednesbury Corp* [1948] 1 K.B. 223; *Prudential Assurance Co Ltd v Newman Industries (No.2)* [1982] Ch. 204 and *Peskin v Andersen* [2001] 1 B.C.L.C. 372 for other illustrations of and judicial opinions about breach of duty and their consequences.

[83] [2000] 1 B.C.L.C. 549.

[84] Although relief was granted in part pursuant to CA 1985 s.727, now CA 2006 s.1157.

[85] Under the CA 2006, a breach of s.171(a).

[86] A breach of CA 2006 s.174.

[87] See also *Re Duomatic* [1969] 2 Ch. 365 where in addition to confirming the principle of a company being bound by the agreement of all the incorporators it was held that it was negligent not to obtain independent professional advice.

Non-executive directors

In relation to non-executive directors there have been recent judicial opinions on their particular responsibilities and these are discussed in Ch.5. **4.055**

Transactions between directors and the company which require shareholder approval

Long term service contracts

Section 188 requires, in terms, that a service contract which is longer than two years must be approved by members. Section 189 provides that a contract which contravenes s.188 is void to the extent of the contravention and is deemed to contain a term entitling the company to terminate it at any time by the giving of reasonable notice. **4.056**

Substantial property transactions

Under s.190 where a director buys from, or sells to the company, a non-cash asset worth in excess of £100,000 or 10 per cent of the company's asset value (subject in the latter case to a minimum of £5,000) the transaction must generally be approved by the shareholders. If it is not, the director who was party to the arrangement and any person "connected"[88] with that director and any director who authorised it are liable to account for any gain made as a result of the arrangement and to indemnify the company for any resulting loss. **4.057**

Loans to directors

Sections 197 to 214 contain provisions dealing with loans to directors. A company may not make a loan or quasi loan or "credit transaction" or enter **4.058**

---

[88] CA 2006 ss.252 to 254 and Sch.1 contain extended definitions of persons "connected with" a director. Members of a director's family are connected persons. For this purpose members of the family are a director's spouse or civil partner; any other person whether of a different sex or the same sex with whom the director lives as part of an enduring family relationship (except grandparents or grand children, brothers or sisters, aunts or uncles, or nephews or nieces); a director's children or stepchildren; any children or stepchildren of a person with whom the director lives and have not attained the age of 18; the director's parents. Connected persons also include a body corporate with which the director is connected, a firm in which the director is a partner, or a partner who is a connected person; or a person acting in his or her capacity as trustee of a trust the beneficiaries of which include the director or a connected person. It will be necessary to refer to in CA 2006 ss.252 to 254 and Sch.1 for detailed guidance.

into "related arrangements" to or with a director or a person connected with the director unless it has been approved by shareholder resolution. There are exceptions, for example, in relation to expenditure on company business, defending proceedings and minor business transactions not exceeding £10,000 in aggregate or £15,000 in the case of a credit transaction. Transactions in contravention render the director and any others who authorised the transaction liable to indemnify the company.

Payments for loss of office

4.059   Under s.215, payments for loss of office must be approved by shareholders. Such payments include retirement payments, or payments in connection with the transfer of all or part of the property of the company, or in connection with a transfer of shares in the company. Section 220 makes an exception where the payments concerned are made in discharge of a legal obligation or by way of damages for breach of such an obligation or by way of settlement or by way of pension in respect of past services. Payments made in contravention are to be held by the recipient on trust for the company and any director who authorised the payment is jointly and severally liable with the recipient to indemnify the company.

Directors' duties and liabilities in relation to financial reporting under the Companies Act 2006 including the "business review"

4.060   The general subject of financial reporting is dealt with in Ch.13. This section is concerned with the specific responsibilities of the directors in relation to the annual statutory accounts and directors' report including the new requirements for an annual business review. It examines the issue of negligent misstatement in relation to statements contained in the directors' report and business review.

Annual reports and accounts

Accounts to give a true and fair view

4.061   CA 2006 s.393(1) provides that the directors of a company:

> "must not approve accounts for the purposes of this chapter unless they are satisfied that they give a true and fair view of the assets, liabilities, financial position and profit or loss"

of the company or, in the case of a group, the group position.

Duty to prepare accounts

CA 2006 s.394 states that "the directors of every company must prepare **4.062** accounts for the company for each of its financial years".

Approval and signing of accounts

Section 414(1) of CA 2006 states that "a company's annual accounts must be **4.063** approved by the board of directors and signed on behalf of the board by a director of the company".

Section 414(4) states that if annual accounts are approved that do not comply with the requirements of the Act (and, where applicable, of art.4 of the IAS Regulations[89]):

> "every director of the company who (a) knew that they did not comply, or was reckless as to whether they complied, and (b) failed to take reasonable steps to secure compliance with those requirements, or as the case may be, to prevent the accounts from being approved, commits an offence."

Duty to prepare directors' report

Section 415(1) provides that the directors of a company must prepare a **4.064** directors' report for each financial year of the company. Again:

> "in the case of a failure to comply with the requirement to prepare a directors' report, an offence is committed by every person who (a) was a director of the company immediately before the end of the period for filing accounts and reports for the financial year in question, and (b) failed to take all reasonable steps with securing compliance with that requirement."[90]

Statement as to disclosure to auditors

The directors' report must under s.418 contain a statement to the effect that, **4.065** in the case of each of the persons who are directors at the time the report is approved:

(a)   so far as the director is aware, there is no relevant audit information of which the company's auditor is unaware, and

---

[89] Defined in s.474(1) as EC Regulation 1606/2002 of the European Parliament and of the Council of 19 July 2002 on the application of international accounting standards.
[90] CA 2006 s.415(4).

(b)   (s)he has taken all the steps that (s)he ought to have taken as a director in order to make him or herself aware of any relevant audit information and to establish that the company's auditor is aware of that information.

"Relevant audit information" means information needed by the company's auditor in connection with preparing his or her report.

A director is regarded as having taken all the steps that (s)he ought to have taken as a director if (s)he has:

(a)   made such enquiries of his or her fellow directors and the company's auditors to that purpose, and

(b)   taken such other steps (if any) for that purpose,

as are required by his or her duty as a director of the company to exercise reasonable care, skill and diligence.

If that statement is shown to be false every director who either knew the statement was false or was "reckless" as to whether it was false, and who failed to take reasonable steps to prevent the report from being approved, commits an offence.

Approval and signing of directors' report

4.066   Under s.419 the directors' report must be approved by the board of directors and signed on behalf of the board by a director or the secretary of the company. If the directors' report is approved and the report does not comply with the requirements of the CA 2006 every director of the company who knew that it did not comply, or was reckless as to whether it complied, and who failed to take reasonable steps to secure compliance or to prevent the report from being approved, commits an offence.[91]

Directors' remuneration report

4.067   CA 2006 s.420 states that the directors of a quoted company must prepare a directors' remuneration report for each financial year of the company. In the case of failure to comply with that requirement every person who was a director of the company immediately before the end of the period for filing accounts and reports for the financial year in question and who failed to take all reasonable steps in securing compliance with that requirement, commits an offence.

---

[91] CA 2006 s.419(3).

Under s.428 the directors' remuneration report must be approved by the board of directors and signed on the half of the board by a director or the secretary of the company.

If the remuneration report is approved but does not comply with the CA 2006 every director of the company who knew that it did not comply, or who was reckless as to whether it complied and who failed to take reasonable steps to secure compliance or to prevent the report from being approved, commits an offence.

Duty to circulate copies of annual accounts and reports

Section 423 of CA 2006 requires that every company must send a copy of its annual accounts and reports for each financial year, amongst others, to every member of the company, and s.424 sets out the time scale within which these documents must be sent out. Failure to comply is an offence not only by the company but "every officer of the company who is in default".   **4.068**

The annual business review

Section 417 of the CA 2006 requires that every company which is not subject to the "small companies' regime"[92] must include a "business review" in the annual directors' report.   **4.069**

The background to the business review, and, in particular, its development out of the original concept of an operating and financial review ("OFR") is explained in Chs 13 (Financial Reporting) and 20 (Corporate Social Responsibility). Essentially the business review is intended to implement the EU Accounts Modernisation Directive.[93]

Section 417(2) says that the purpose of the business review is "to inform members of the company and help them assess how the directors have performed their duty under s.172 (duty to promote the success of the company).

The business review must contain:

(a)   a "fair review" of the company's business, and

(b)   a description of the principal risks and uncertainties facing the company.

The review is also required to be a "balanced and comprehensive" analysis of:

---

[92] Defined in CA 2006 s.382.
[93] More specifically, Directive 2003/51/EC of the European Parliament and of the Council of 18 June 2003 concerning the modernisation of the 4th and 7th Directives on the annual and consolidated accounts of companies (Directives 78/660/EEC and 83/349/EEC respectively).

(a)   the development and performance of the company's business during the financial year, and

(b)   the position of the company's business of the end of the year, consistent with the size and complexity of the business.

In the case of a "quoted company"[94] the business review must "to the extent necessary for an understanding of the development, performance or position of the company's business, include:

(a)   the main trends and factors likely to affect the future development, performance and position of the company's business; and

(b)   information about:

    (i)   environmental matters (including the impact of the company's business on the environment),

    (ii)   the company's employees, and

    (iii)   social and community issues, including information about any policies of the company in relation to those matters and the effectiveness of those policies; and

    (iv)   information about persons with whom the company has contractual or other arrangements which are essential to the business of the company.[95]

If the review does not contain information of each kind mentioned above "it must state which of those kinds of information it does not contain".

The review must, "to the extent necessary for an understanding of the development, performance or position of the company's business, include:

(a)   analysis using financial key performance indicators, and

(b)   where appropriate, analysis using other key performance indicators, including information relating to environmental matters and employee matters.

---

[94] Defined in CA 2006 s.385(2) and s.531: essentially a company listed on the London Stock Exchange.

[95] This provision was introduced at a very late stage in the passage of the Bill, without consultation, and was said by commentators to be intended to force quoted companies to disclose details of suppliers essential to the company's business following intense lobbying over the way supermarket chains treat their suppliers. However, clearly its scope will extend far beyond that of suppliers to supermarkets and will include disclosure of not only suppliers but also any third party (e.g. customer) doing business with the company which is regarded (a) as "essential" to the business of the company and (b) "necessary for an understanding", etc. of the company's business.

"Key performance indicators" ("KPIs") means factors by reference to which the development, performance or position of the company's business can be measured effectively".[96]

Liability for false or misleading statements in reports—"Safe harbour"

Section 463 of CA 2006 provides that a director of a company is liable to compensate the *company* for any loss suffered by the company as a result of: **4.070**

(a)   any untrue or misleading statement in the directors' report or the directors' remuneration report; or

(b)   the omission from such a report of anything required to be included in it.

However, (s)he is so liable only if:

(a)   (s)he knew the statement to be untrue or misleading or was reckless as to whether it was untrue or misleading; or

(b)   (s)he knew the omission to be a dishonest concealment of a material fact.

The section makes it clear also that no person shall be subject to any liability to a person *other* than the company resulting from reliance, by that person or another, on information in a report.

There is no Reporting Standard suggested by the Accounting Standards Board for business reviews, and in January 2007 the Accounting Standards Board issued a report which recommended that no new Standard be issued.[97] The Accounting Standards Board issued in January 2006 a Reporting Statement (as distinct from a Reporting Standard) in relation to the OFR following the decision by the Government to withdraw a statutory OFR, and it is understood[98] that many of the larger listed companies intend to follow that Statement. It is further understood[99] that the "safe harbour" wording of s.463 will apply to statements made in an OFR which otherwise complies with the business review provisions of the Act.

---

[96] See Ch.13 (Financial Reporting) for an outline of relevant KPIs.
[97] January 7 Statement: Review of Narrative Reporting, *http://www.frc.org.uk/publications/pubs.cfm.*
[98] Brian Bannister, Director of Public Policy PwC, September 20, 2006.
[99] Brian Bannister, Director of Public Policy PwC, September 20, 2006.

Negligent misstatement generally in relation to statements made by directors

4.071   One of the major fears in relation to the proposals for a statutory OFR was that directors who made "forward looking" statements could find themselves liable to be sued by third parties who had allegedly relied on such statements for the tort of "negligent misstatement".

It would appear that in the absence of knowledge of, or recklessness about, any misstatement in a directors' report the "safe harbour" wording of s.463(4) precludes such action.[100]

The tort of negligent misstatement by a director may arise in circumstances where a director owes a duty of care to a third-party and makes a statement negligently as a result of which that third party suffers loss. The House of Lords has held[101] that for the imposition of a duty of care there must be foreseeability of damage, sufficient proximity of relationship, and it must be fair, just and reasonable for the duty to be imposed.

Directors must be careful, therefore, firstly, to ensure in any event that all public statements are prepared carefully with appropriate words of qualification, and, secondly, not to establish a relationship of proximity with a third-party to whom it may be found that (s)he owes a duty of care.[102]

Derivative claims by shareholders against directors

4.072   Prior to the CA 2006 it was possible at common law for an individual shareholder to apply to the court for leave to commence proceedings in the name

---

[100] See para.4.070 above. Statements which directors are required to make under the UK Corporate Governance Code may come within the ambit of the law of negligent misstatement. The relevant statements are those required by the following paragraphs of the UK Corporate Governance Code:
  • C.1.1 (*responsibility statement*)—"the directors should explain in the annual report their responsibility for preparing the annual report and accounts and there should be a statement by the auditors about their reporting responsibilities";
  • C.2.1 (*internal controls*)—"the directors should conduct a review of the effectiveness of the group's system of internal controls and should report to shareholders that they have done so. The review should cover all material controls, including financial, operational and compliance controls and risk management systems";
  • C.1.3 (*going concern*)—"the directors should report in annual and half yearly financial statements that the business is a going concern, with supporting assumptions or qualifications as necessary".
However, again, it would seem that since such statements are required by the Listing Rules to be included in the annual directors' report, they are also protected under the safe harbour wording of s.463.
[101] *Caparo v Dickman* [1990] 1 A.C. 831 analysed in App.20. See also an opinion letter dated July 7, 2005, written by Allen & Overy for CIMA on the subject of forward looking statements in the context of an operating and financial review but which contains an analysis of negligent misstatement:*http://www.cimaglobal.com/cps/rde/xchg/SID-0AAAC564-89D7FC76/live/root.xsl/12790_9445.htm.*
[102] See also *Possfund Custodian Trustee Ltd v Diamond* [1996] 1 W.L.R. 1351 and *Williams v Natural Life Health Foods Ltd and Mistlin* [1997] 1 B.C.L.C. 131.

of and on behalf of the company (a "derivative claim") against a director who had allegedly been in breach of duty, where it appeared that the wrong-doer director was him or herself improperly preventing the company from pursuing an action against him or her.[103]

A derivative action was prior to the CA 2006 something of a rarity since most actions for breach of duty against directors (or more commonly, former directors) are brought either by the board itself or by the liquidator or administrator following the commencement of liquidation or administration.

Nevertheless, the Law Commission[104] recommended the codification of the derivative action, but CA 2006 Pt 11 (ss.260 to 264), not only codifies but extends the ability of a member (provided that the court gives permission to do so) to bring a derivative claim in respect of a cause of action arising from an actual or proposed act or omission involving negligence, default, breach of duty or breach of trust by a director, even where the director has not benefited personally, and even if the director concerned does not control the majority of the company's shares.

In order to bring a claim under Pt 11 a number of considerations must be satisfied:

- it must be a "derivative" claim, that is to say the action must be brought by a member of the company; the cause of action must be vested in the company; and relief is sought on the company's behalf. A "member" is defined in s.112 and includes a person who is not a member but to whom shares in the company have been transferred or transmitted by operation of law, for example where a trustee in bankruptcy or personal representative of a deceased members estate acquires an interest in a share. The "member" does not have to have been a member at the time of the alleged wrongdoing;

- the claim can only be brought in pursuance of a court order under Pt 11 or under a court order in accordance with CA 2006 s.994 (unfair prejudice);

- in order to get permission from the court the applicant is required under s.261(2) to establish a prima facie case for a grant of permission, and the court will consider the issue on the basis of the claimant's evidence alone without requiring evidence to be filed by the defendant.

    The court must dismiss the application at this stage if what is filed does not show a prima facie case. If the application is not dismissed, the court may direct the company to provide evidence and, on hearing the application, may grant permission, refuse permission and dismiss the

[103] e.g. *Mubarak v Mubarak, The Times,* November 30, 2000; *Prudential Assurance v Newman Industries (No.2)* [1982] Ch. 204 and *Peskin v Anderson* [2001] 1 B.C.L.C. 372.
[104] *Shareholder Remedies*, para.6.15.

claim, or adjourn the proceedings and give such directions as it thinks fit. It was said by the then DTI that this initial procedure will enable the courts "to dismiss unmeritorious claims at an early stage without involving the defendants or the company";

- the applicant must if successful under s.262(2) *then* apply for permission to *continue* a derivative action, and the court must under s.262(3) refuse leave to continue the action if it is satisfied that:

    - a person acting in accordance with the general duty of directors to promote the success of the company (s.172—duty to promote the success of the company) would not seek to continue the action; or
    - the act or omission giving rise to the cause of action has, in terms, been authorised or ratified by the company, provided that in the case of ratification, the decision to ratify it is taken by members without reliance on the votes in favour by the director concerned or any connected person[105];
    - the court must also take into account a number of factors in considering whether to give permission to proceed (s.263(3)). For example, whether the claimant is acting in good faith, the importance that a person acting in accordance with s.172 (duty to promote the success of the company) would attach to continuing the claim; where, in the case of a future act, it is likely to be authorised or ratified; or in the case of something which has already occurred; whether the act or omission could be or is likely to be ratified; or whether the company has decided not to pursue the claim; and whether the act or omission could have been remedied by the member in own right rather than on behalf of the company. In addition, the court can have regard to any evidence before it as to the views of members of the company who have no personal interest in the matter.[106]

---

[105] See fn 88 above for definition of "connected".

[106] The relevant case on the subject of independent shareholders in relation to a derivative action is the case of *Smith v Croft (No.2)* [1988] Ch. 114. In that case the minority shareholders holding 12% of the share capital brought a derivative action complaining about the excessive remuneration paid to the executive directors who held 62% of the share capital. It was alleged that the remuneration payments were ultra vires and also were paid purely for personal benefit and without regard to the company's interests and as to some of the payments were unlawful financial assistance. Claim struck out because prima facie the company did not have a cause of action and also not a "fraud on the minority" exception to *Foss v Harbottle* (1843) 2 Hare 361. The judge took evidence from an independent shareholder holding 20% who did not wish for the action to proceed and the judge was persuasively influenced by that factor. It is submitted that under the new codified derivative action clauses in the CA 2006 the result would be the same, not only because of the views of independent shareholders (s.263(4)) but because ratification would probably have taken place under s.239(4) without using the votes of the directors concerned and persons "connected with him".

Concerns overdone?

In the debates in Parliament on this section, fears were expressed that the **4.073** mere codification of what had hitherto been a common law right would of itself give rise to speculative and opportunistic litigation against directors along the lines of US-style class actions. In fact in the short time since the coming into force of Pt 11 it appears that the courts are acting as a filtering mechanism and in many cases the judiciary have concluded that the shareholder grievances are best resolved through the use of the "unfair prejudice" petition procedure under CA 2006 s.994.[107]

The Secretary of State has power under s.263(5) to change the criteria governing permission both with regard to the absolute bar and the discretionary jurisdiction.

Other concerns which have been expressed[108] about the purported codification of derivative claims:

- claims may be brought in respect of any actual or proposed act or omission involving negligence, default, breach of duty or breach of trust on the part of a director. This is an extension of the existing law which has suggested that in addition to the breach of duty there has to be an additional element such as personal profit[109];

- the procedure allows a claim to be brought by any member even if they were not a member at the time the actions complained of took place;

- there is no need for a particular number of members: nor a percentage threshold of shareholding, to launch a claim. This would make it easy for the aggrieved stakeholders or campaigners, it is said, to purchase a single share and launch an action;

- there is no need to demonstrate any actual loss suffered by the company, or any benefit gained by the director, before commencing a claim;

- claims may be brought against not only directors but "other persons". This might, for example, include other parties to a transaction which (s) he is alleged to involve, or result from, the negligence or breach of duty of the directors;

- although a claim may only be pursued with the permission of the court, the court may not be able to conclude that the claim should not be

---

[107] See e.g. *Mission Capital Plc v Sinclair* [2008] EWHC 1339 (Ch); [2008] B.C.C. 866 and *Franbar Holdings Ltd v Patel* [2008] EWHC 1534 (Ch); [2008] B.C.C. 885). The author is indebted to the Sweet & Maxwell Company Law Newsletter issue 260, September 2009 for these references.
[108] "*War for talent? Attracting and retaining NEDs*", Linklaters, March 2006, p.9.
[109] *Daniels v Daniels* [1978] Ch. 406.

allowed without a substantive consideration of the issues.[110] The test the court has to consider is an objective one and there appears to be no scope to rely, as a defence, only on the good faith business judgment of directors[111];

- until the section is better understood, judges may be reluctant to refuse to grant permission to continue derivative claims based on its breach;

- elimination of the risk of litigation by ensuring their actions are authorised or ratified by shareholders will rarely be practical for listed companies.

Comment[112]

4.074　"It is to be hoped that the courts will be robust in refusing permission for claims by pressure groups or others seeking to gain publicity or impose their views on the company. Unless and until this becomes the established practice of the courts, companies will be exposed to claims which will at least require a defence at the hearing for permission to pursue the claim. While it would be an abuse of the court process for a shareholder to seek to pursue a claim for his own personal benefit, it may be difficult to prove that such an individual is pursuing his own interests rather than acting for the benefit of the company. Decisions taken by the courts in relation to the awarding of costs will also have an important bearing on the likelihood of litigation. It is worth bearing in mind that the courts have in the past been willing to order a defendant company to pay the costs of even an unsuccessful derivative claimant, provided that it was reasonable for the shareholder to bring the claim.[113]

. . . combined with the expansion of the scope of directors duties: the derivative claims procedure creates a real danger for UK companies, and some may come to the view that the UK is no longer an attractive location for business, particularly for publicly quoted companies."[114]

Ratification of acts or omissions by directors

4.075　Although not strictly speaking "ratification" nevertheless, the general duty to avoid conflicts of interest (s.175) can be complied with by authorisation by

---

[110] *Equitable Life Assurance Society v Bowley* [2003] EWHC 2263 (Comm).
[111] But query whether the courts would then under the "relief" provisions of s.759 (see below) relieve the director from liability if the judge were satisfied as to the good faith, honesty and reasonableness, etc. of the director concerned.
[112] "*War for talent? Attracting and retaining NEDs*", Linklaters, March 2006, p.9.
[113] *Wallersteiner v Moir (No.2)* [1975] Q.B. 373; *Jones v Jones* [2003] B.C.C. 226 at 229.
[114] "*War for talent? Attracting and retaining NEDs*", Linklaters, March 2006, p.9.

the directors; the general duty to declare an interest in a proposed transaction (s.177) can be complied with by satisfying the provisions relating to declarations of interest in CA 2006 s.177(2).[115] The duty to declare an interest in an existing transaction under s.182 can also be "cured" by notices under ss.184 and 185.

Breaches of duty or trust, or acts of negligence or default, can, subject to the exceptions described below, be ratified by an ordinary (bare majority) resolution of members under CA 2006 s.239. However, s.239(4) requires that the votes of any director member and any member "connected with him" (see fn 88 above) must be disregarded[116] if they are cast in favour of the resolution. It is for this reason that ratification will be difficult for many closely held private companies and, in practical terms, for listed companies also.

Breaches of duty that cannot be ratified include:

(a)   a breach involving dishonesty on the director's part;

(b)   a breach which results in the company performing an act which it cannot lawfully do;

(c)   a breach bearing directly on the "personal rights" of individual shareholders, for example, a refusal to register the transfer of shares for an improper purpose;

(d)   a breach involving "a fraud on the minority", that is, whereby the majority of the shareholders succeed in expropriating at the expense of the minority the assets of the company.

Relief from liability by the courts

Section 1157 of CA 2006 reproduces CA 1985 s.727. In terms it permits a court to grant relief from liability of a director if in proceedings for negligence, default, breach of duty or breach of trust it appears to the court that the director is or may be liable but that (s)he acted honestly and reasonably and that "having regard to all the circumstances of the case he ought fairly to be excused".   **4.076**

Thus, in *Bairstow v Queens Moat Houses*[117] and *Commissioners of Inland Revenue v Richmond*[118] both of which dealt with the unlawful payment of dividends, and applications to the court to order that the directors pay to the company the unlawfully declared dividends, relief was denied in two instances of unlawful payment but granted in a third instance.

---

[115] See para.4.034 et seq. above.
[116] But the director can attend, be counted in the quorum and take part in the meeting (CA 2006 s.239(4)).
[117] [2000] 1 B.C.L.C. 549.
[118] [2003] EWCA 999 (Ch).

Ceasing to be a director

4.077   There are a number of ways in which a person may cease to be a director:

- voluntary resignation (but care is needed in case that amounts to a breach of a contract of service);

- retirement by rotation. The articles of association may well contain provisions requiring that one third of the board should retire at each annual general meeting at the eligible for re-election. Principle B.7 of the UK Corporate Governance Code requires all directors to submit themselves for re-election at regular intervals. Provision B.7.1 spells out exactly what "regular" means and states that all directors of FTSE 350 companies should be subject to annual election by shareholders. All other directors should be subject to election by shareholders at the first annual general meeting after their appointment, and to re-election thereafter at intervals of no more than three years;

- there is no age limit under the CA 2006 but the company's articles may contain an age limit—query whether such a provision is now in breach of the Employment Equality (Age) Regulations 2006;

- almost invariably there will be other provisions in the articles of association which will deem the director to have vacated his or her office, for example, if (s)he is disqualified from being a director or fails to attend board meetings for more than a given period of time. The service agreement may also contain provisions deeming the director to have resigned as a director if his or her status as employee is terminated;

- removal by shareholders under CA 2006 s.168. Notwithstanding any provision in the company's articles or any agreement between the company and the director, a company may under s.168 by ordinary resolution remove a director before the expiration of his or her period of office. Such a removal will not preclude the right to compensation for wrongful dismissal. Special notice under s.312 is required, and the resolution to remove is not effective unless notice of intention to table it has been given to the company at least 28 days before the meeting at which it is to be considered and the company has given its members notice of any such resolution at the same time and at the same manner as it gives notice of the meeting. If that is not practicable, the company must give members notice, either by advertisement in a newspaper having an appropriate circulation or by any other method allowed by the articles, at least 14 days before the meeting at which the resolution is to be considered. If, after notice of intention to table such a resolution has been given to the company, the meeting is called for a date 28 days or less after the notice has been given to the company, the notice is deemed properly given, even though the notice was not actually given within the time required.

On receipt of the notice of an intended resolution to remove a director, the company must, at once, send a copy of the notice to the director concerned, and the director is under s.169 entitled to be heard on the resolution at the meeting at which it is put. The director is also entitled to make written representations to the company and to request that they be notified to members. The company must then in any notice of the resolution given to members stating the fact that the representations have been made, and send a copy of the representations to every member of the company to notice is sent. There are provisions which stop an abuse of this process.

If the notice of intended resolution to remove is given by members, as distinct from the board itself, then the members concerned will also need in all probability to accompany that notice with notice under s.303 requisitioning the directors to call a general meeting, signed by members holding at least 10 per cent of the paid-up voting capital, containing the resolution for removal.

Directors' and officers' insurance and company indemnities

A full treatment of this topic is given in Ch.12 (D&O Insurance and **4.078** Indemnification). It is important that directors should require companies on whose boards they serve to take out D&O insurance, as part of the overall risk management strategy (see para.4.080 below).

Code Provision A.1.5 states that "the company should arrange appropriate insurance cover in respect of legal action against its directors".

Section 232 of CA 2006 provides the general principle that:

"any provision that purports to exempt a director of a company (to any extent) from any liability that would otherwise attach to him in connection with any negligence, default, breach of duty or breach of trust in relation to the company is void."

Section 233 however, makes it clear that s.232 does not prevent a company from taking out *insurance* against liability for negligence, default, breach of duty or breach of trust.

In addition, s.234 permits a company to give a director an *indemnity* provided it falls within the definition of a "qualifying third party indemnity provision". The particulars of any indemnity must be disclosed in the annual directors' report.

Directors' rights to take independent legal advice at the company's expense

4.079 Under Provision B.5.1 the board must ensure that directors, especially non-executive directors, have access to independent professional advice at the company's expense where they judge it necessary to discharge their responsibilities as directors. Under Code Provision A.1.5 the company should arrange appropriate insurance cover in respect of legal action against its directors.[119]

   The intent of the Code is that a procedure should be adopted, and that any advice given in this manner should be reasonable, and the principles of common sense should prevail. "Independent legal advice" in this context must be the purposes of discharging the director's duties as a director, and should not conflict with nor be confused with, situations where the board as a whole takes a matter under advice.

   Should an individual director wish to take advice, (s)he should notify the chairman of the board, in writing, of his or her intention to do so, or in the case of the chairman, the senior independent non-executive director. The company secretary should also be sent a copy of the written notice at the same time. Any request to take legal advice should be reported to the board at the next available opportunity.[120]

Some suggestions for personal risk management

4.080 As the unfortunate *Equitable Life* case showed[121] there are significant difficulties to be faced by a director who is accused of wrongdoing. These include the risk to his or her health in terms of worry and the stress of lengthy legal proceedings, the loss of personal wealth as a result of any fine or award of damages, the risk to his or her reputation and hence to his or her long term career, and the risk of overwhelming legal costs.

   A director cannot remove risk entirely, and indeed most directors recognise and embrace the need to move the business forward which may necessitate taking risks, but not personal risks.

   The following suggestions may be found helpful:

---

[119] See Ch.12 (D&O Insurance and Indemnification) for details of how this is effected.

[120] Unilever's governance statement *"The Governance of Unilever"* contains the following:

> "Directors, both as a group and individually, are entitled to take independent professional advice, at the expense of Unilever, on matters relating to the proper discharge of their office. This does not extend to issues regarding their personal interests. The Joint Secretaries will arrange for advice to be obtained."

[121] See Ch.5 (Directors—The Non-Executive Director) for a fuller discussion.

A compliance strategy

Directors will need to determine which of the risk areas of a company's **4.081**
activities require a formal compliance programme, usually under the main
headings of people, product and financial. This risk evaluation should itself
be reviewed on a regular basis to ensure that any changes in the business are
properly reflected. The review might cover the following issues:

- evaluation of exposure in different areas of the business;

- identify the requirement for areas of the business which are particularly
  affected to have their own procedures for compliance;

- management responsibility for compliance: any policies must be
  "owned" by the parts of the business to which they apply, and specifically by the managers of those parts. Management of risk should not
  be seen as a requirement from the corporate centre or head office to
  which lip service is paid. The question "who is accountable?" must be
  answered;

- compliance is an integral part of the delegation of authority by directors. However although directors can delegate accountability, they
  cannot delegate responsibility;

- regular reporting on compliance to the board is a crucial part of the
  procedure. This complements and is in addition to the need to report
  immediately where major breaches occur;

- the opportunity for independent audit of compliance must be reserved.
  An internal audit can fulfil a vital function in checking on compliance
  and the reporting to, say, the company's audit committee[122];

- training and support for management's effort is in compliance is vital.
  The existence and requirements of the company's policy must be
  drawn to employees attention at appropriate times. Employees must
  understand the role that they have to play;

- insisting that the company take out D&O policies and indemnify
  directors.[123]

---

[122] See Ch.15 (Risk Management and Internal Audit).
[123] See Ch.12 (D&O Insurance and Indemnification).

Sensible governance procedures

4.082   Directors can significantly reduce risk by paying attention to "good govern-ance". That is the purpose of this book. As explored in Ch.1, claims are made for the benefits of governance which are impossible to verify. However, it is broadly accepted that as part of overall risk management and, certainly, per-sonal risk management, governance best practice will contribute materially to reduction in risk, and the potential for loss of shareholder value reduced.

The benchmark for assessing "good governance" is the UK Corporate Governance Code and non-executive directors of listed companies have a special responsibility for vigilant oversight of the observance of the UK Corporate Governance Code by their boards. For non-listed companies "good governance" can still comprise a range of options from insistence on regular board meetings with a proper agenda and supporting papers including of course financial reports through to selected aspects of the UK Corporate Governance Code as determined by the board to be useful for the company.

General conclusions

4.083   If this chapter has emphasised the personal risks run by directors, that is only because there is undoubtedly a greater trend at common law and now under the CA 2006 to impose personal liability on directors. Chapter 6 (Voices from the Boardroom) reveals a growing sense of personal exposure. Nevertheless, it would be unfortunate if businessmen and women refused to become directors because of an overdeveloped sense of anxiety about their personal liability. In the real world, the vast majority of directors try consci-entiously to carry out their duties to the best of their ability; they try to run companies which do not have, for example, risky health and safety conditions for workers and which do not pollute the environment; and they try to take reasonable care when arriving at decisions, including getting outside advice. Moreover they particularly try to run companies which will not become insolvent and thereby incur the risk of personal liability.

It is that generally reasonable level of care exercised by most directors in good faith which makes it unwise to embark on actions against directors without the strongest evidence of breach of duty, and if there is anything good which has come out of the *Equitable Life* case in proceedings which were fruitless, destroyed the professional careers of the directors concerned and hugely costly to the Society, it is that the difficulties of mounting a suc-cessful case for breach of duty except in the clearest of circumstances are formidable. The commercial health of the United Kingdom depends on pro-ducing a sustainable resource of able people willing to become directors, and fear of litigation should not be allowed to dissuade them.

Chapter 5

Directors: Part 2—The Non-Executive Director

Introduction

In Ch.4, the general law and practice relating to the duties and liabilities of **5.001** directors with particular reference to the CA 2006 were examined. It is vital that a person who becomes a non-executive director of a company should read and understand the duties and liabilities set out in Ch.4, including the need to work out a personal risk management strategy as suggested in Ch.4. There is no distinction between the status at law of a full-time executive director and a non-executive director.

The purpose of this chapter, however, is to look at the particular and unique position of the non-executive director in the light of the increasing responsibilities placed on the shoulders of non-executive directors for the governance of companies, and to look at the characteristics required of a non-executive director and the role which they can play.

Chapter 6 (Voices from the Boardroom) contains an analysis of interviews with listed company non-executive directors talking about the reality of the experience of independent non-executive directors, and Ch.7 deals with the issue of board evaluations.

Watchdog or bloodhound? A legal analysis of the role of the non-executive director

On March 15, 2004 Mr Peter Martin wrote to the *Financial Times*. He **5.002** explained that he had been a non-executive director of the Equitable Life Assurance Society, and was now being "brutally sued for upwards of £5 billion". He was one of nine former non-executive directors of Equitable Life who were being sued for breach of duty by the Society acting through its then current board of directors. Mr Martin further explained that he could no longer afford to employ lawyers and so would represent himself in person.[1]

Earlier in his letter he raised the question as to whether a non-executive director is a:

"watchdog or a bloodhound? If he asks and gets an answer, like a reliable but unaggressive watchdog getting a reassuring pat from a familiar and trusted hand, must he then probe and probe further thus implying a serious lack of trust which may seriously demotivate honest executives if taken too far?"

This is a key question which non-executive directors in one form or another constantly ask themselves. Putting it another way: how far do the general duties discussed in Ch.4 (Directors—Duties and Liabilities) and set out in ss.171 to 177 of the CA 2006, and especially ss.172 (duty to promote the success of the company) and 174 (duty to exercise reasonable care, skill and diligence),[2] require a non-executive director to probe the actions and decisions of the executive directors.

Trust until reason to distrust

5.003   There is judicial authority for the proposition that "men in responsible positions must be trusted . . . until there is reason to distrust them". In the case of *Re Continental Assurance Company of London Plc*[3] the judge said, in terms, that although a modern non-executive is expected to monitor the actions of the executives, it would be unrealistic to expect them to overrule the specialist directors, like the finance director.

However, the modern approach is getting tougher on non-executives

5.004   There is a surprising lack of judicial authority on the subject of how far non-executive directors should go in monitoring executive directors. However, in the Australian case of *AWA Ltd v Daniels*[4] which has been cited with approval in England, the New South Wales Court of Appeal stated: "In our opinion the responsibilities of directors require that they take reasonable steps to place themselves in a position to guide and monitor the management of the company". Sections 172 (duty to promote the success of the company)

---

[1] Equitable Life in late 2005 withdrew its claim against all directors and the former auditors, Ernst & Young, and paid all costs, estimated to amount to over £50 million.
[2] See Ch.4 (Directors—Duties and Liabilities) for full discussion of these duties.
[3] [2001] B.P.I.R. 733.
[4] (1995) 37 N.S.W.L.R. 438.

and 174 (duty to exercise reasonable care, skill and diligence) of CA 2006 reinforce that approach.

All this would suggest that non-executives must play a proactive role in gathering and testing information supplied by management—relying on information supplied by management would not appear to be enough. That approach was in fact supported by the Hampel Report in 1998:

> "The effectiveness of a board (including in particular the role played by the non-executive directors) is dependent to a substantial extent on the form, timing and quality of the information which it receives. Reliance purely on what is volunteered by management is unlikely to be enough in all circumstances, and further enquiries may be necessary if the particular director is to fulfil his or her duties properly."

However, interestingly, in the Higgs Review in 2003 into the role and effectiveness of non-executive directors he appeared to draw back from that somewhat sceptical approach and placed the emphasis on the supply of information by the chairman and company secretary, rather than a proactive approach by the non-executives. Main Principle B.5 of the UK Corporate Governance states: "the board should be supplied in a timely manner with information in a form and of a quality appropriate to enable it to discharge its duties".

Nevertheless, the better view, it is submitted, is that the courts would support the Hampel "pro-active" approach which itself corresponds to the Australian courts approach in the *AWA* case.

That view seems to be supported in the judgment of Morritt L.J. in *Re Barings Plc (No.5)*[5] where the Court of Appeal approved the summary of the law given by Jonathan Parker J. at first instance in these terms:

"(i) Directors have, both collectively and individually, a continuing duty to acquire and maintain a sufficient knowledge and understanding of the company's business to enable them properly to discharge their duties as directors;

(ii) Whilst directors are entitled (subject to the articles of association of the company) to delegate particular functions to those below them in the management chain, and to trust their competence and integrity to a reasonable extent, the exercise of the power of delegation does not absolve a director from the duty to supervise the discharge of the delegated functions;

(iii) No rule of universal application can be formulated as to the duty referred to above. The extent of the duty, and the question whether it

---

[5] [2000] 1 B.C.L.C. 523 at 535.

has been discharged, must depend on the facts of each particular case, including the director's role in the management of the company."

In the *Equitable Life* case[6] referred to at the beginning of this part of the chapter the former non-executive directors, together with the former executive directors, had been made defendants in proceedings commenced by the Society through its then current board in a claim for breach of duty and damages of over £5 billion. The former non-executives applied to Mr Justice Langley in 2003 in an interim application, asking him in effect to strike out the action against them on the grounds, inter alia, that there was no case to answer because they were entitled to rely on the executive directors, and in any case ought to be relieved from liability under the relieving provisions of what is now s.1123 (power of court to grant relief) because they had acted honestly and reasonably throughout. The judge refused to grant the application and said:

> "I do not think this statement [i.e. that directors are entitled to trust the full-time executives for information] does represent the modern law, at least, if (as the applicants were inclined to submit) it means unquestioning reliance upon others to do their job. It is well known that the role of non-executive directors in corporate governance has been the subject of some debate in recent years. For present purposes . . . it . . . suffices to say that the extent to which a non-executive director may reasonably rely on the executive directors and other professionals to perform their duties is one in which the law can fairly be said to be developing, and is plainly "fact sensitive". It is plainly arguable, I think, that a company may reasonably at least look to non-executive directors for independence of judgment and supervision of the executive management."

The *Equitable Life* case never went to judgment and the claims were in effect withdrawn. It has to be said that the law is still therefore unclear on many aspects of non-executive director duties in relation to the supervision of executives.

However, there seems to be little doubt that the day of the watchdog is over and the day, if not of the bloodhound, then perhaps the terrier is at hand. It seems inescapable that non-executive directors do, under the modern approach, and especially in the light of the statutory duties in ss.171 to 177 need to be alert to the extent to which they do not know what they do not know. They need to share that concern with great vigour with the executive

---

[6] See the judgment on October 17, 2003 of Langley J. in *Equitable Life Assurance Society v Bowley* [2003] EWHC 2263 (Comm) where nine former non-executive directors argued that there were no reasonable grounds for the claim against them in proceedings brought by the Society against the entire board for negligence and breach of fiduciary duty. A copy of the judgment may (as at August 2010) also be accessed at *http://www.equitablelifemembers.org.uk*. See also *Re Barings Plc (No.5)* (2000) 1 B.C.L.C. 523 at 525.

directors, not with a view to being bombarded with paper but rather to get executive directors into a proper mind-set of self examination and openness. Non-executives need to get executive directors to the point of being willing on occasions to test their recommendations against independent specialist scrutiny. Failure to do so may amount to breach of duty.

The role of the non-executive director as prescribed in corporate governance reports and the UK Corporate Governance Code

It is important for non-executives to understand what the UK Corporate **5.005** Governance Code is saying about the duties of a non-executive because Code rules will surely be regarded as the baseline from which to assess the statutory duty under CA 2006 s.174 to exercise reasonable care, skill and diligence.

Cadbury

The 1992 Cadbury Report and Code stated that non-executive directors **5.006** should bring "an independent judgement to bear on issues of strategy, performance, resources, including key appointments and standards of conduct".

Hampel

The 1998 Hampel Report (3.8) stated that: **5.007**

"Non-executive directors are normally appointed to the Board primarily for their contribution to the development of the company's strategy. This is clearly right. We have found general acceptance that non-executive directors should have both a strategic and a monitoring function. In addition, and particularly in smaller companies, non-executive directors may contribute valuable expertise not otherwise available to management; or they may act as mentors to relatively inexperienced executives. What matters in every case is that the non-executive directors should command the respect of the executives and should be able to work with them in a cohesive team to further the company's interest."

Later in the Hampel Report (3.15), Hampel pointed out that:

"Most non-executive directors are executives or former executives of other companies. This experience qualifies them both in constructive policy making and in the monitoring role. Non-executive directors from other backgrounds are often appointed for their technical knowledge, their knowledge of overseas markets or their political contacts. It was put to us that companies should recruit directors from a greater diversity of backgrounds. We do not favour diversity for its own sake, to give a politically correct appearance to the list of board members or to represent stakeholders. But we believe, given the diversity of business and size of listed companies, that there are people from other fields who can make a real contribution on the board."

Higgs

5.008   The 2003 Higgs Review into the role and effectiveness of non-executive directors (extracts of which are set out in App.2) stated that role as follows[7]:

> "**Strategy**: non-executive directors should constructively challenge and contribute to the development of strategies on the following issues:
>
> > *Performance*: non-executive directors should scrutinise the performance of management in meeting agreed goals and objectives and monitor the reporting of performance.
> > *Risk*: non-executive directors should satisfy themselves that financial information is accurate and that financial controls and systems of risk management are robust and defensible.
> > *People*: non-executive directors are responsible for determining appropriate levels of remuneration of executive directors and have a prime role in appointing, and where necessary removing, senior management and in succession planning."

Higgs pointed out[8] that there is a dual role both of monitoring executive activity (see also paras 5.002 to 5.004 above) and contributing to the development strategy:

> "An over emphasis upon monitoring and control risks non-executive directors seeing themselves, and being seen, as an alien policing influence detached from the rest of the board. An over emphasis on strategy risks non-executive directors becoming too close to executive management, undermining shareholder confidence in the effectiveness of board governance."

Higgs went on to say[9] that: "the key to non-executive director effectiveness lies as much in behaviours and relationships as structures and processes".

---

[7] Annex C, Higgs Review into the role and effectiveness of non-executive directors: *http://www. dti.gov.uk/bbf/corp-governance/higgs-tyson/page23342.html.*
[8] Review, para.6.2.
[9] Review, para.6.3.

Walker

In the Walker *Review of corporate governance in UK banks and other finan-* **5.009**
cial industry entities[10] in which Sir David Walker introduced the mnemonic
"BOFI" to signify banks and other financial industry entities he defined the
role of a non-executive director as follows:

> "In broad terms, the role of the NED, under the leadership of the chair-
> man, is: to ensure that there is an effective executive team in place; to
> participate actively in the decision-taking process of the board; and to
> exercise appropriate oversight over execution of the agreed strategy by the
> executive team."

Walker went on to describe the "challenge" role in terms of a spectrum:

> "NEDs and the boards of which they are members need to find the right
> point on the spectrum which ranges from relatively unquestioning support
> of the executive at one end to persistent and ultimately unconstructive
> challenge at the other. The importance of challenge will be greater the
> greater the entrenchment of the chief executive, especially if he or she is
> believed to face or tolerate little challenge from within the executive team
> and unreceptive or inaccessible to critical input from any other source. In
> an ideal situation, appropriate balance should be neither unduly acquies-
> cent nor unduly intrusive. But the balance actually struck before the recent
> crisis phase was much too close to the acquiescent or supportive end of the
> spectrum in several important cases."

The UK Corporate Governance Code

Main Principle A.4 (non-executive directors) of the UK Corporate **5.010**
Governance Code states:

> "As part of their role as members of a unitary board, non-executive
> directors should constructively challenge and help develop proposals on
> strategy."

The corresponding Supporting Principle states;

> "Non-executive directors should scrutinise the performance of manage-
> ment in meeting agreed goals and objectives and monitor the reporting of
> performance. They should satisfy themselves on the integrity of financial

---

[10] November 2009, *http://www.hm-treasury.gov.uk/walker_review_information.htm.*

information and that financial controls and systems of risk management are robust and defensible. They are responsible for determining appropriate levels of remuneration of executive directors and have a prime role in appointing, and where necessary removing, executive directors, and in succession planning."

The role of non-executive directors as described by Unilever[11]

Role and responsibility

5.011   In the Unilever annual report and accounts 2008 the key elements of the role and responsibilities of the non-executive directors were described as follows:

> "The Non-Executive Directors share responsibility for the execution of the Boards' duties, taking into account their specific responsibilities, which are essentially supervisory. In particular, they comprise the principal external presence in the governance of Unilever, and provide a strong independent element.
>
> The key elements of the role and responsibilities of our Non-Executive Directors are:
>
> - supervision of and advice to the Chief Executive Officer;
> - developing strategy with the Chief Executive Officer;
> - scrutiny of performance of the business and Chief Executive Officer;
> - oversight of risks and controls;
> - reporting of performance;
> - remuneration of and succession planning for Executive Directors; and
> - governance and compliance.
>
> Our Non-Executive Directors are chosen for their broad and relevant experience and international outlook, as well as their independence. They form the Audit Committee, the Nomination Committee, the Remuneration Committee and the Corporate Responsibility and Reputation Committee."

The qualities of a non-executive director

5.012   (a)   *Integrity and high ethical standards.* "First and foremost, integrity, probity and high ethical standards are a prerequisite for all directors" (Higgs Review, para.6.13).

---

[11] 2008 Annual Report.

(b)   *Sound judgment.* Non-executive directors need to have sound judgment.

(c)   *Challenge.* This was a leading issue emerging from the Walker Review into banking governance.[12] Recommendation 6 of the Review stated: "As part of their role as members of the unitary board of a BOFI, NEDs should be ready, able and encouraged to challenge and test proposals on strategy put forward by the executive" and that such a requirement should be drafted into any letter of appointment of a non-executive director.

(d)   *Listen.* Non-executive directors should listen to the views of others, inside and outside the board.

(e)   *Expertise and knowledge.* Non-executive directors must acquire the expertise and knowledge to discharge their responsibilities. They must be well-informed about the business, the environment in which it operates and the issues it faces. This also requires a knowledge of the markets in which the company operates.

(f)   *Strong interpersonal skills.* Higgs points out that much of the effectiveness of non-executive directors depends on exercising influence rather than giving orders and requires an establishment of high levels of trust.

(g)   *Independence.* Paragraph 9.1 of the Higgs Review stated:

"A major contribution of the non-executive director is to bring wider experience and a fresh perspective to the boardroom. Although they need to establish close relationships with executives and be well informed, all non-executive directors need to be independent of mind and willing and able to challenge, question and speak up. All non-executive directors, and indeed executive directors, need to be independent in this sense."

The topic of independence is dealt with later in this chapter (para.5.018).

---

[12] "Apart from the inadequacy of relevant financial experience in some (but not all) failed boards, it is clear that serious shortcomings of other kinds were also relevant, above all the failure of individuals or of NEDs as a group to challenge the executive on substantive issues as distinct from a conventional relatively box-ticking focus on process. In some cases this will have reflected the diffidence of a NED in probing complex matters where even the forming of an appropriate question is itself a challenge. But beyond and separately from this, the pressure for conformity on boards can be strong, generating corresponding difficulty for an individual board member who wishes to challenge group thinking. Such challenge on substantive policy issues can be seen as disruptive, non-collegial and even as disloyal. Yet, without it, there can be an illusion of unanimity in a board, with silence assumed to be acquiescence. The potential tensions here are likely to be greater the larger the board size, so that an individual who wishes to question or challenge is at greater risk of feeling and, indeed, of being isolated." (Ch.4.3 of Walker Review into banking governance.)

(h) *Courage*. There will be times when a non-executive director will feel that (s)he has to speak up against the wishes of the chief executive, the chairman or the majority view. That requires courage.

Time commitment

5.013 Code Provision B.3.2 states:

"The letter of appointment should set out the expected time commitment. Non-executive directors should undertake that they will have sufficient time to meet what is expected of them. Their other significant commitments should be disclosed to the board before appointment, with a broad indication of the time involved and the board should be informed of subsequent changes."

The Unilever (2009) terms of appointment of non-executive directors provide as follows:

"Time commitment
We anticipate that your appointment will require a time commitment of at least two days per month. This will include attendance at scheduled Board meetings and the Annual General Meetings of Unilever NV or Unilever PLC. Other Board meetings and conferences are held as needed. You should also try and attend any meeting called by the Senior Independent Director and/or the Chairman and any other meetings of Unilever's Non-Executive Directors.

There will be at least one such meeting each year, with others held as needed. You may also be appointed as a member of a Board Committee in accordance with paragraph [   ] below.

Typically, each Committee meets four or five times per year. The Boards of Unilever NV and Unilever PLC reserve the right to change your membership of a Committee at any time.

Please endeavour, wherever possible, to avoid your other commitments from clashing with the timing of your Unilever commitments (which Unilever NV and Unilever PLC will consult you on."

Research conducted for the Higgs Review suggested that a non-executive director role usually involves a time commitment of between 15 and 30 days a year and the Walker Review recommended that non-executive directors of major bank boards should work for between 30 and 36 days per annum. Higgs said that the chairman and non-executive directors should have sufficient time to make themselves available at short notice to deal with major issues when they arise: "At such times, a non-executive director, particularly a chairman, may need to commit substantially more time".

Higgs was concerned that many non-executive directors held too many posts to enable them to give the necessary time commitment. However he pointed out that the variety of different appointments and individual circumstances meant that in his view it was "arbitrary and unrealistic to set a prescriptive limit for the number of non-executive directorships any individual not in full-time employment may hold".

The Walker Review recommended for major banks a minimum of 30 to 36 days commitment; "a greater time commitment than has been normal in the past."

Recruitment and appointment

Main Principle B.2 (appointments to the board) states: "there should be **5.014** a fair, rigorous and transparent procedure for the appointment of new directors to the board".

The Supporting Principles state:

"the search for board candidates should be conducted, and appointments made, on merit, against objective criteria and with due regard for the benefits of diversity on the board, including gender.

The board should satisfy itself that plans are in place for orderly succession for appointments to the board and to senior management, so as to maintain an appropriate balance of skills and experience within the company and on the board and to ensure progressive refreshing of the board."

The corresponding Code Provision B.2.1 places the responsibility for recruitment and appointment on the nomination committee. Under Code Provision B.2.2 the nomination committee is required to:

"evaluate the balance of skills, experience, independence and knowledge on the board and, in the light of this evaluation, prepare a description of the role and capabilities required for a particular appointment".

The Higgs Review felt that a "high level of informality" surrounds the process of appointing non-executive directors. Almost half of the non-executive directors surveyed for the Review were recruited through personal contacts or friendships. Only 4 per cent had had a formal interview, and 1 per cent had obtained their job through answering an advertisement.

Higgs was favourably impressed by the open and transparent procedures in the public sector, where there is a clear requirement to appoint on merit as set out in the Nolan Principles. He also spoke favourably of the procedures adopted by charitable and other voluntary groups.

Additional Higgs Review research also showed that non-executives "are typically white males nearing retirement age with previous Plc director experience". A very low number of female non-executive directors was also apparent and "striking in comparison with other professions and with the population of managers in UK companies overall". The research found that across the corporate sector as a whole, around 30 per cent of managers overall are female but only 6 per cent of non-executive posts are held by women. Again, the public-sector compared favourably in terms of boardroom diversity and mix.

Higgs pointed out those using personal contacts as main sources of candidates:

> "will tend to favour those with similar backgrounds to incumbent directors. A rigorous appointments process is important to offset this natural bias. The various criteria used for selection may also implicitly discriminate against women, such as requiring wider senior executive or plc board experience."[13]

Clearly, therefore, the message from Higgs is that boards first need to assess the mix of skills and qualities which are required to enable them to work most effectively. Boards, or rather chairmen of boards, need to ask if there is a need, for example, for more marketing experience, access to "the City", financial expertise, international experience or consumer experience?

When the criteria have been established and a job description prepared it will then be possible to brief search consultants and, in appropriate cases, to advertise.

Inevitably, personal contacts will also play a part in finding appropriate people, but such candidates must submit to the same rigorous appointments procedure as any other candidate. Search consultants should be encouraged to look outside the usual groups for possible candidates. Higgs pointed out that there are many excellent directors of Plc group subsidiary companies and successful private companies. Members of the boards of large charities and public bodies also have impressive experience in financial and resource management, and members of the professions are used to working in an advisory capacity to business and can bring a set of skills that are useful to the board.

As regards the appointment of a chairman Higgs suggested that three critical elements should be observed when a board appoints a new chairman:

(a) the lead independent director or deputy chairman, if independent, should normally lead the appointment process;

---

[13] For further research and comment on the issue of widening the pool see the Tyson Report on the recruitment and development of non-executive directors, June 2003. To view a copy, search on the internet under "Tyson Report". See also Ch.6 (Voices from the Boardroom).

(b)   a systematic approach should be taken to identify the skills of and expertise required for the role and a job specification prepared;

(c)   a shortlist of good candidates should be considered, rather than possible individuals being considered in turn. The process will almost certainly benefit from external advice.

Terms of appointment and annual re-election for FTSE 350 directors

There is set out in App.9 a basic letter of appointment[14] for a non-executive **5.015** director as suggested by the Higgs Review. The letter is set out under the following headings:

(a)   *Appointment* (meaning length of term). The letter sets out an initial term of three years and that continuation of the contract is contingent upon satisfactory performance and re-election at annual general meetings. Higgs suggests that non-executive directors are expected to serve two three-year terms, although the board may invite a director to serve for an additional period.

Code Provision B.2.3 states:

"Non-executive directors should be appointed for specified terms subject to re-election and to statutory provisions relating to the removal of a director. Any term beyond six years for a non-executive director should be subject to particularly rigorous review, and should take into account the need for progressive refreshing of the board."

(b)   *Re-election.* In a controversial move arising out of the 2009 review of the Combined Code and the Walker Review of banking governance the FRC introduced in June 2010 a provision into the Code which requires FTSE 350 directors to submit to annual re-election at the AGM.[15]

Code Provision B.7.1 states:

"All directors of FTSE 350 companies should be subject to annual election by shareholders. All other directors should be subject to election by shareholders at the first annual general meeting after

---

[14] In January 2010 it was announced by the FRC that the Institute of Chartered Secretaries and Administrators ("ICSA") would be undertaking a review of the precedents set out in the Higgs Appendices, but the results of that review will not be available until late in 2010. Reference should be made to the ICSA or FRC website for the up-to-date position.

[15] In the consultation draft of the Code the FRC had suggested the alternatives of annual re-election of the chairman or annual re-election of the whole board.

their appointment, and to re-election thereafter at intervals of no more than three years."

Code Provision B7.2 states:

"The board should set out to shareholders in the papers accompanying a resolution to elect a non-executive director why they believe an individual should be elected. The chairman should confirm to shareholders when proposing re-election that, following formal performance evaluation, the individual's performance continues to be effective and to demonstrate commitment to the role."

The 2008 Unilever annual report and accounts states that the non-executive directors submit themselves for re-election each year:

"The nomination for re-election is subject to continued good performance which is evaluated by the board, based on the recommendations of the Nomination Committee. The Nomination Committee carefully considers each nomination for reappointment. The non-executive directors normally serve for a maximum of nine years."

(c)　*Time commitment.* (See para.5.013 above.)

(d)　*Role.* Here set out the intended role which the company expects of the director. It should be agreed of course with the director and be as specific as possible. The Walker Review recommended that in the case of BOFI appointments there should in the letter of appointment be an emphasis on the need to intervene and challenge:

"Given the importance of clarify in this respect, the proposal here is that this key ingredient in the job specification of a NED in a BOFI board should be stated as a recommendation, with the expectation and, indeed, requirement in this respect to be incorporated in the letter of appointment and to serve as guidance in the FSA (controlled function) authorisation process."

That view was reflected in Recommendation 6 of the Walker Review and it is to be hoped that wording can be formulated in any letter of appointment of any non-executive which reflects the recommendation, whether or not a BOFI appointment:

"Recommendation 6
As part of their role as members of the unitary board of a BOFI, NEDs should be ready, able and encouraged to challenge and test proposals on strategy put forward by the executive. They should satisfy themselves that board discussion and decision-taking on risk matters is based on accurate and appropriately comprehensive

information and draws, as far as they believe it to be relevant or necessary, on external analysis and input."

See also para.5.005 above for further discussion on this point.

(e) *Fees.* It is interesting that the suggested clause in App.9 provides for the payment of cash plus a number of ordinary shares. Higgs Review research showed that average remuneration for non-executive directors of a company below the FTSE 350 is £23,000 per annum.[16] For chairmen it is £78,000 per annum.

Research conducted by Deloitte in 2006[17] indicated median total fee levels (£) by size of company as follows:

Market capitalisation (£m)	Non-executive chairman	Non-executive deputy chairman	Senior independent	Non-executive director
300–600	106,500	58,900	37,700	34,400
1,000–2,500	167,400	64,000	47,700	43,000
10,000–25,000	384,000	104,500	77,500	66,500

Under Code Provision D.1.3 options should not be granted, but the direct purchase of shares (for example by taking part of the fee in shares) is strongly encouraged. If, exceptionally, options are granted then shareholder approval must be obtained in advance and shares so acquired held for one year after leaving the board.

(f) *Outside interests.* (A declaration as to outside interests (and see Ch.4 for new rules introduced under the CA 2006) relating to declarations of interest and avoidance of conflict of interest.)

(g) *Confidentiality.* (See the sample agreement for standard wording requiring the director to keep confidential information which is confidential to the company.)

(h) *Induction.* (See para.5.017 below.)

(i) *Review process.* (Annual evaluation—see para.5.020 and Ch.7 (Board Evaluations) below.)

(j) *Insurance cover.* (The company will maintain directors' and officers' liability insurance (see Ch.12 (D&O Insurance and Indemnification)).)

---

[16] It was reported in the *Financial Times* of October 24, 2006 that a joint study by the Institute of Directors and Croner had found that non-executive directors of companies valued at between £50 million and £500 million had risen to £31,000 p.a. on average.
[17] Research carried out by the Reward Technology Forum found that in 2007/2008 the average pay for non-executives was £85,576 and in 2008/2009 was £81,930.

(k) *Independent professional advice.* (In accordance with the UK Corporate Governance Code Provision B.5.1. This clause provides for a director to take independent professional advice in accordance with company procedure.)

(l) *Committees.* (A requirement to serve on one or more board committees.)

Code Provision B.3.2 requires that the terms and conditions of appointment of non-executive directors are made available for inspection at the company's registered office during normal business hours and at the Annual General Meeting (for 15 minutes prior to the meeting and during the meeting).

Pre-appointment due diligence

5.016   It is imperative that directors should carry out pre-appointment due diligence on companies on whose boards they have been invited to serve. It is no good finding out about the company at the first board meeting, particularly if it is in financial difficulties or has other problems. If the appointment process itself has been thorough and rigorous it can be expected that the prospective director will have considerable information by the time the invitation to join is made.

There is set out in App.7 a suggested checklist for all new board members drafted by the Higgs Review. The questions are not intended to be exhaustive and they should in any event be tailored to the company itself. In addition, there will be available on the internet a surprising amount of information. A prospective director should aim to be familiar with the company and any problems before (s)he is appointed. It also important, of course, for the prospective director to talk to the chairman, the chief executive and the finance director and also the lead independent director.

Induction[18]

5.017   Main Principle B.4 (Development) states: "all directors should receive induction on joining the board . . .". Code Provision B.4.1 states:

"the chairman should ensure that new directors receive a full, formal and tailored induction on joining the board. As part of this, directors should avail themselves of opportunities to meet major shareholders."

---

[18] Ch.3 (The Board and its Structure) para.3.024 contains examples from ICI Unilever and BP of their induction processes.

All too often new directors receive no induction or an induction "pack" without having the opportunity to meet the management or visit the company locations.

The Unilever 2008 corporate governance report stated in relation to induction as follows:

"Board induction and training

Upon election, Directors receive a comprehensive Directors' Manual and are briefed thoroughly on their responsibilities and our business. Updates on corporate governance developments and investor relations matters are frequent agenda items at Board meetings. Ongoing training is provided for Directors by way of site visits, presentations, circulated updates, teach-ins at Board or Board committee meetings on, among other things, Unilever's business, environmental, social and corporate governance, regulatory developments and investor relations matters. In 2008, Board meetings were held at the offices of Hindustan Unilever in Mumbai which included a visit to local retail outlets and the Bangalore Research and Development Centre and in Unilever's operations in New York which included trade visits and a visit to the New Jersey Customer Insight and Innovation Centre."

There is set out in App.10 an induction checklist suggested by the Higgs Review. The Higgs Review found that non-executive directors who visited company locations and attended company events, together with the informal contact with board and management brought to the table significant knowledge of the business and its people. In addition, "opportunities should also be provided to ensure that non-executive directors see regularly, and at first hand, the performance of the senior management team".

Independence

A feature both of the Higgs Review in 2003, the Walker Bank governance review in 2009 and of the 2010 UK Corporate Governance Code is the attention paid to the independence of non-executive directors, and the importance of the board itself being the ultimate determiner of the independence of a director. **5.018**

Code[19] Provision B.1.1 states:

"The board should identify in the annual report each non-executive director it considers to be independent. The board should determine whether a

---

[19] Provision A.3.1 states that the chairman should, on appointment, meet the independence criteria set out in this provision, but thereafter the test of independence is not appropriate in relation to the chairman.

director is independent in character and judgement and whether there are relationships or circumstances which are likely to affect, or could appear to affect, the director's judgement. The board should state its reasons if it determines that a director is independent notwithstanding the existence of relationships or circumstances which may appear relevant to its determination, including if the director:

- has been an employee of the company or group within the last five years;
- has, or has had within the last three years, a material business relationship with the company either directly, or as a partner, shareholder, director or senior employee of a body that has such a relationship with the company;
- has received or receives additional remuneration from the company apart from a director's fee, participates in the company's share option or a performance-related pay scheme, or is a member of the company's pension scheme;
- has close family ties with any of the company's advisers, directors or senior employees;
- holds cross-directorships or has significant links with other directors through involvement in the other companies or bodies;
- represents a significant shareholder; or
- has served on the board for more than nine years from the date of the first election."

The significance of the emphasis on independence lies partly in the recommendation of the Higgs Review which was reflected in Code Provision B.1.2 that except for companies below the FTSE 350 (throughout the year immediately prior to the reporting year) at least half the board, excluding the chairman, should comprise non-executive directors "determined by the board to be independent". A smaller company (i.e. sub-FTSE 350) should have at least two non-executive directors. However a more important aspect of the characteristic of independence both as defined above and in terms of personal character is the point made by Higgs that "a major contribution of the non-executive director is to bring wider experience and a fresh perspective to the boardroom".

The reason for the rigorous definition of independence is that there is a natural potential for conflict between the interests of executive management and shareholders in the case of, for example, director remuneration, or audit (where decisions on the financial results can have a negative impact on remuneration), or indeed in a range of other instances.

As Higgs points out (para.9.3):

"Although there is a legal duty on all directors to act in the best interests of the company, it has long been recognised that in itself this is insufficient to give full assurance that these potential conflicts will not impair objective board decision-making."

He therefore concluded that a board is strengthened significantly by having a strong group of non-executive directors with no other connection with the company: "These individuals bring a dispassionate objectivity that directors with a closer relationship to the company cannot provide".

However, Higgs did not intend to be taken as meaning that non-executive directors who have a recent or existing connection of some kind with the company had no place on the board: "They may indeed be valuable, but they should be additional to the requisite proportion of independent non-executive directors". It should be noted that the emphasis in the UK Corporate Governance Code is on the *board's* responsibility to determine whether or not a person is "independent". It is for the board to determine that factor, but clearly a determination which flew in the face of the definition of independence contained in the Code would require considerable justification in the eyes of shareholders.

A corrective approach to the question of independence was outlined in the 2009 Walker Review, pointing out that a rigid construing of the independence rules had limited the choice of experienced but independent-minded people from within the organisation. The point made has general application and is worth making here:

"The substance as distinct from the form of independence relates to the quality of independence of mind and spirit, of character and judgement, and a NED who brings both independence of approach in this sense together with relevant industry experience is most likely to be able to bring effective and constructive challenge to the board's decision-taking process.

This has particular relevance to the recruitment as NEDs of former executives – which is inhibited by the independence criterion under the Code where the individual served as an employee of the company within the previous five years. This restriction was introduced on the basis of concern that NEDs with a close past association with the company could not be expected to bring sufficient objectivity to their role. But it cannot be regarded as a satisfactory outcome that the experience of many BOFI executives, including CEOs, is effectively excluded from the industry because they are unable to serve on the boards of the entities from which they retire, may in practice, and understandably be unwilling to serve on boards of entities with which they were in keen competition in their former executive roles. It is also noteworthy that bank boards where the previous CEO became chairman appear to have performed relatively well both over a longer period and in the recent crisis phase."

It may be necessary, therefore, sometimes, for the board, or more aptly the chairman, to be prepared to take a firm view in the interests of getting the right person on board, and to "explain" robustly to shareholders why he thinks it is necessary.

Information, performance evaluation and development

Information

5.019   Main Principle B.5 (information and support) of the UK Corporate Governance Code states:

> "The board should be supplied in a timely manner with information in a form and of a quality appropriate to enable it to discharge its duties."

The corresponding Supporting Principles state:

> "The chairman is responsible for ensuring that the directors receive accurate, timely and clear information. Management has an obligation to provide such information but directors should seek clarification or amplification where necessary.
>
>   Under the direction of the chairman, the company secretary's responsibilities include ensuring good information flows within the board and its committees and between senior management and non-executive directors, as well as facilitating induction and assisting with professional development as required.
>
>   The company secretary should be responsible for advising the board through the chairman on all governance matters."

Higgs stated that in order for a non-executive director to be effective, adequate information of the right kind "is vital". Information must be provided sufficiently in advance of meetings to enable non-executive directors to give issues thorough consideration "and must be relevant, significant and clear". There is a danger of too much information, and it is the responsibility of the secretary and chairman to collate and rationalise the flow of information so that it is meaningful and digestible. Good non-executive directors also satisfy themselves that they have appropriate information of sufficient quality to make sound judgments and non-executive directors should not hesitate in seeking clarification or amplification where necessary, and should also give constructive feedback on the value of material provided and guidance on what is required. If information is not appropriate then the chairman should be told. Indeed, it should be part of the annual evaluation of the board's performance to examine whether the information provided to the board had met directors' expectations and requirements.

  In a telling passage in the Review, Higgs states:

"Where a board is working effectively there will be a culture of openness. The non-executive directors' contributions will be valued and trusted and the manipulation of information should not be an issue. The emphasis of information flows should be on clarity and transparency."

Performance evaluation[20]

Main Principle B.6 (evaluation) of the UK Corporate Governance Code states: "The board should undertake a formal and rigorous annual evaluation of its own performance and that of its committees and individual directors".   **5.020**

The corresponding supporting Principle states:

"The chairman should act on the results of the performance evaluation by recognising the strengths and addressing the weaknesses of the board and, where appropriate, proposing new members be appointed to the board or seeking the resignation of directors.

Individual evaluation should aim to show whether each director continues to contribute effectively and to demonstrate commitment to the role (including commitment of time for board and committee meetings and any other duties)."

Although the Principles indicate annual evaluations, external reviews can take place less frequently and Provision B.6.2 states that:

"Evaluation of the board should be externally facilitated at least every three years. Where consultants are used a statement should be made available of whether they have any other connection with the company."

The corresponding Code Provisions B.6.1 and B.6.3 state:

"B.6.1 The board should state in the Annual Report how performance evaluation of the board, its committees and its individual directors has been conducted.
B.6.3 The non-executive directors, led by the senior independent director, should be responsible for performance evaluation of the chairman, taking into account the views of executive directors."

It will also be recalled that Code Provision B.2.3 provides, among other things, that if a non-executive director serves a term beyond six years (s)he should be subject to "particularly rigorous review".

---

[20] See also Ch.7 (Board Evaluations) for a sceptical look at methods of evaluation.

The 2008 Unilever corporate governance report stated in relation to performance evaluation as follows:

"Board evaluation
The evaluation process of our Boards consists of an internal three year cycle with an independent third-party evaluation carried out if the Boards consider appropriate. The last time an independent third-party evaluation was carried out was in 2006. In 2007 and 2008 the Chairman, in conjunction with the Senior Independent Director, conducted the internal evaluation process. An extensive questionnaire for all Board members formed part of the evaluation process. In addition, the Chairman conducted a process of evaluating the performance of each individual Board member, including an interview with each. The evaluation of the performance of the Chairman was led by the Senior Independent Director. Committees of the Boards evaluate themselves under supervision of their respective chairmen taking into account the views of respective committee members and the Boards. The results of the various evaluations were discussed by the Boards and changes were made in respect of Board practices and processes where considered necessary."

In relation to *performance evaluation*, Chs 6 (Voices from the Boardroom) and 7 (Board Evaluations) contain an analysis of the approach to evaluation by companies and directors. The Higgs Review research showed that over one-third of boards never formally evaluate their own performance, while over three-quarters of non-executive directors and over half of chairmen never have a formal personal performance review.[21]

Higgs felt that a board performance appraisal gives the chairman the information and confidence to manage the board more effectively:

"It helps a chairman to identify and address both strengths and weaknesses of the board and consider whether the board has the right balance of skills for the future. If not, the chairman should seek the resignation of under-performing directors and make new appointments to the board."

Higgs suggests that the chairman has a key role in arranging the evaluation process for the whole board and for individual non-executive directors. Conduct of the evaluation by an external third party can bring objectivity to the process and its value should be recognised by chairmen. Higgs recommended that when the chairman's own performance is reviewed, an external third party or the senior independent director should act as facilitator.

The result of the board evaluation as a whole should be shared with the

---

[21] Since the Higgs Review and the provisions for appraisal and evaluation in the Combined Code, now the UK Corporate Governance Code the position has improved significantly.

board, but the results of individual assessments should remain confidential between the chairman and the non-executive director concerned.

There is set out in App.12 suggested guidance drafted by the Higgs Review for carrying out performance appraisal, for both the board as a whole and for non-executive directors individually.

Development

Main Principle B.4 (development) states "All directors . . . should regularly   **5.021**
update and refresh their skills and knowledge".

The Supporting Principles state:

"The Chairman should ensure that the directors continually update their skills and the knowledge and familiarity with the company required to fulfil their role both on the board and on board committees. The company should provide the necessary resources for developing and updating and updating its directors knowledge and capabilities.

To function effectively all directors need appropriate knowledge of the company and access to its operations and staff."[22]

Code Provision B.4.2 states:

"B.4.2 The Chairman should regularly review and agree with each director their training and development needs."

Research conducted for the Higgs Review (para.11.7) revealed that two-thirds of non-executive directors and chairmen had not received any training or development. Of those who said that they had, the training was often in the form of experience of business or being a member of a board, rather than any structured provision. "It is questionable the extent to which this experience alone is sufficient to maintain up-to-date knowledge".

Higgs characterised the process of training or development as "professional development tailored to the individual". Potential directors need to understand the role of the board, obligations and entitlements of directors of listed companies and the behaviours needed for effective board performance. For existing directors, knowledge of such things as strategy, management of human and financial resources, audit and remuneration can often be usefully updated or expanded. Updates on legal, regulatory and other obligations are also useful.

It was pointed out in the Review that demand for formal training is "very low". There is a relatively limited supply of training specifically aimed at

---

[22] Author's italics: new Principle in the UK Corporate Governance Code.

non-executive directors by business schools.[23] Accordingly, many companies organise their own in-house training.

The 2005 BP governance "board performance report" described "Training" as follows:

"Our directors are updated on BP's business, the environment in which it operates and other matters throughout their period in office. Our directors are advised on their appointment of the legal and other duties and obligations they have as directors of a listed company. The board regularly considers the implications of these duties under the board governance policies. Our non-executive directors also receive training specific to the tasks of the particular board committees on which they serve."

Relationships with shareholders

5.022   Main Principle E.1 (dialogue with institutional shareholders) states:

"There should be a dialogue with shareholders based on the mutual understanding of objectives. The board as a whole has responsibility for ensuring that there is a satisfactory dialogue with shareholders takes place."

The corresponding Supporting Principles state:

"Whilst recognising that most shareholder contact is with the chief executive and finance director, the chairman should ensure that all directors understand their major shareholders' issues and concerns.

The board should keep in touch with shareholder opinion in whatever ways are most practical and efficient."

The corresponding Code Provisions E.1.1 and E.1.2 state as follows:

"The chairman should ensure that the views of shareholders are communicated to the board as a whole. The chairman should discuss governance and strategy with major shareholders. Non-executive directors should be offered the opportunity to attend *scheduled*[24] meetings with major shareholders and should expect to attend meeting*s* if requested by major shareholders. The senior independent director should attend sufficient meetings with a range of major shareholders to listen to their views in order to help develop a balanced understanding of the issues and concerns of major shareholders.

---

[23] See fn 24 Ch.3 (The Board and its Structure) for a list of institutions which offer courses.
[24] Author's italics: introduced into the 2010 Code so as to make it clear that non-executive directors should not need to meet shareholders at specially arranged meetings.

The board should state in the annual report the steps they have taken to ensure that the members of the board, and in particular the non-executive directors, develop an understanding of the views of major shareholders about the company, for example through direct face to face contact, analysts' or brokers' briefings and surveys of shareholder opinion."

Until the Higgs Review it was generally assumed that non-executive directors should not have direct contact with shareholders. That was a matter for the chief executive and sometimes for the chairman. The Higgs research indicated that the majority of non-executive directors never discussed company business with their investors. Interviews with investors revealed that rarely do they speak directly with non-executive directors, and only then when there is a serious problem: "Even in these circumstances, discussion has often centred on director remuneration rather than on wider strategy or governance issues".[25]

Interviews with non-executive directors conducted by the Higgs Review revealed that investors are distant and disengaged in their view. Executive directors were found to have reservations about more direct contact between non-executive directors and shareholders on the grounds that non-executive directors would not have enough detail available to them to present an accurate picture of company performance.

Higgs did not accept the argument however that the annual general meeting should be the main or indeed only mechanism through which major shareholders and non-executive directors have direct contact. Instead, it seemed that the preferable approach would be for non-executive directors to attend some of the regular meetings that executive directors and the chairman hold with larger investors. Higgs further recommended that in cases where investors have complained of difficulties in making contact with non-executive directors the company secretary should act as a conduit for contacts from major shareholders to non-executive directors.

The senior independent director

See Ch.3 (The Board and its Structure) para.3.012 for a discussion of this role.   **5.023**

Meetings of non-executive directors

Code Provision A.4.2 states that: **5.024**

"The chairman should hold meetings with the non-executive directors without the executives present. Led by the senior independent director, the non-executive directors should meet without the chairman present at least

---

[25] Higgs Review research back-up.

annually to appraise the chairman's performance and on such occasions as are deemed appropriate."

In 2008 the non-executive directors of Unilever met five times as a group:

"Meetings
The Non-Executive Directors meet as a group, without the Executive Directors present, under the leadership of the Chairman. In 2008 they met five times. In addition, the Non-Executive Directors (including the Chairman) usually meet before each Board meeting with the Chief Executive Officer, the Chief Financial Officer, other senior executives and the Group Secretary."

Resignation and retirement

5.025   See Ch.3 (The Board and its Structure) para.3.028 for a discussion of retirement and also the circumstances in which resignation is appropriate; also Ch.4 (Directors—Duties and Liabilities) para.4.077 for the circumstances in which directors can cease to hold office, including removal by shareholders. On resignation, a non-executive director should provide a written statement to the chairman, for circulation to the board, if they have concerns which are unresolved about the running of the company or a proposed action. In any event, even if they do not resign, unresolved concerns should be recorded in the board minutes.[26]

Succession planning

5.026   The chairman will be primarily responsible for ensuring orderly succession planning of the non-executive directors. Unilever keeps a schedule showing the expected dates of retirement of the non-executive directors which it publishes publicly on its website.[27]
          The Walker Review felt that more emphasis should be placed on succession planning:

"The Code should emphasise succession planning more clearly, perhaps through a provision that encourages chairmen to report annually on the process being followed and progress made."

Accordingly, a supporting principle to Main Principle B.2 (appointments to the board) states:

---

[26] Code Provision A.1.4.
[27] *http://www.unilever.com/investorcentre/corpgovernance.*

"The board should satisfy itself that plans are in place for orderly succession for appointments to the board and to senior management, so as to maintain an appropriate balance of skills and experience within the company and on the board *and to ensure progressive refreshing of the board.*"[28]

Liabilities and risks for non-executive directors and directors' and officers' insurance

In Ch.4 (Directors—Duties and Liabilities) the current position relating to liabilities attaching to the office of director is described, together with suggestions for a personal risk strategy, of which D&O insurance cover is undoubtedly an important part.   **5.027**

Code Provision A.1.3 requires that the company should arrange appropriate insurance cover in respect of legal action against its directors. In Ch.12 there is therefore a full treatment of the topic of D&O insurance.

The non-executive director in the family-controlled company

Private companies

In June 1997, a survey commissioned by the accountants Kingston Smith called *The Survivors—Private Companies' Progress Since the Recession*, written by Gill and Roger Hussey of the Bristol Business School, surveyed 100 private companies with turnovers of between £500,000 and £10,000,000.   **5.028**

The survey found that a majority of the companies interviewed had brought in non-executive directors because they offered specific skills, such as legal or financial knowledge. Another important advantage of appointing an independent non-executive director was related to decision making and the management of change and the sensitive issue of succession. In the words of one interviewee, "a non-executive director can take a non-emotional view—in a family business, the executive directors may be too close to the company".

The survey found that another interviewee commented that his non-executive director, who was a retired chief executive, was a great asset to the company. In the early days, when the company was formed following a management buyout, the director concerned "had brought formality and discipline to the board meetings which otherwise would have been lacking".

Similarly, a number of owners of family-run businesses commented on the advantages of impartiality and fresh prospective brought by non-executive

---

[28] Words in italics inserted in the 2010 UK Corporate Governance Code.

directors. It also has to be said that the presence of an experienced non-executive director can often be a bridge for the company at a time of crisis, for example, the sudden death of the chief executive or a major shareholder, the wish by a major shareholder to sell, or a family bust up.

The survey also appeared to find that companies with non-executive directors were more likely to have a planned strategy than companies without non-executive directors, and that such a plan was more likely to become long term.

Listed companies

5.029 On the other hand, being a non-executive director of a listed family-controlled company can be difficult, involving sometimes the need to stand up to the family, represented often on the board by the chairman. Examples of this in recent times are the supermarket chain Wm Morrison, where the institutional investors insisted in 2004 that the board should be strengthened by the appointment of independent non-executive directors after a set of disastrously inaccurate profit warnings following a massive acquisition; and the clothing retailer Matalan, where the non-executives had to insist that the founding chairman took a back seat while they evaluated and negotiated with his advisers on the price offered by him in 2006 to buy out the minority share not owned by the family. It was reported by the *Financial Times* on October 24, 2006, that a non-executive director said that there had been:

> "tense negotiations when non-executives stood up to the chairman, publicly disclosing his intention to take the company private and insisting that he stand back from the day to day running of the business".

Eventually a price was agreed which the independent directors felt able to recommend.

Conclusion

5.030 Both now and even more so in the future the job has to be more professional and structured than in the past. The debate has rightly often been about independence, but other real issues are personal integrity, access to adequate information and commitment of time. As Higgs put it, non-executive directors "are the custodians of the governance process".

Chapter 6

Voices from the Boardroom

Dr Sharon Studer[1]

The corporate governance changes introduced in 2003 (Higgs, Smith, the Combined Code—now the UK Corporate Governance Code) were met in some quarters with angst and wringing of hands. Although some reacted positively to the new rigour, in others there was a distinct unease that the UK was overreacting to what some thought to be a US problem. One survey reported that up to three quarters of large company directors were against the changes.[2] Chairmen were heard to threaten de-listing rather than comply with the Code.   **6.001**

Given the passage of time, it seemed useful to reflect on the impact the changes had. Interviews were conducted with 10 chairman and non-executive directors (NEDs), as well as with three firms who specialise in recruiting non-executive directors. The interviews explored the response to governance changes, seeking an understanding of how NEDs are reacting to the new requirements.

Respondents were asked to speak of issues important to them, as well as to respond to a broad set of questions around the governance changes. The sample included FTSE 100 and 250 chairman and non-executive directors from a balance of finance, media, and technology companies. Everyone interviewed held at least two non-executive positions, and most had experience of three to five.

---

[1] Sharon Studer is a Non-Executive Director of Simmons & Simmons, a leading international law firm. She was a member of the Oxford University Audit Committee until 2009 and until 2008 a Non-Executive Director for TNS, a worldwide market research company, where she chaired the Remuneration Committee. She is a Fellow of the British Computer Society, and was recently appointed to the BCS Strategic Panel for Women. Sharon is a certified Executive Coach, working with board members and director level managers. She has spent 25 plus years in senior management positions within technology and media industries. She was a UK KPMG partner responsible for their technology business strategy group. She holds a PhD with an emphasis in psychology and statistics from the University of Minnesota. This chapter was written for the 2007 edition of this book but references to the UK Corporate Governance Code are as at July 2010.

[2] *Daily Telegraph*, October 26, 2004.

Overview

6.002   Prosaic as it may be, the most consistent view of the recent governance changes was positive. Comments included "the guidelines raised the game", the "broad structure works", and "things had improved for the better". When non-executive directors had experience of both US and European boards, all thought that the UK had broadly got the balance right.

Perceived beneficial effects included boards dealing with issues with greater rigour and in a more substantive way. The separation of the chairman and CEO role, and the fact that CEOs cannot readily move into the chairman role, were seen as further positive outcomes, providing greater independence and accountability.

There were caveats of course. Some indicated their concern that governance was usurping time that could be better spent on strategy, and others highlighted the significant increase in time that was now required as a non-executive. A number of respondents expressed concern over the risk-reward ratio of being a NED.

In the balance of this chapter, I will review the major themes that came up in the interviews.

Role of non-executives

6.003   Non-executives saw corporate governance, succession planning, and contributing to company strategy all as critical components of their role. The role was seen as representing the wider interests of the company stakeholders, but with a priority focus on shareholders. Choosing senior people was seen as particularly critical, on the principle that if the right people were in place this would result in an appropriate strategy and results. As one respondent noted, "If there is a well-chosen executive in place, there is a much more limited role for the non-executives".

There was some nuance regarding the role of strategy, with a "horses for courses" perspective. A technology company board member noted that in cases of highly complex issues, it is unreasonable to assume the board would play a central role in all the key technical issues. That said, the most typical view was that the board should be populated with people whose expertise can be drawn on in developing as well as challenging strategy.

Succession planning is seen as key, with non-executives having a fundamental role in choosing the chief executive, chief financial officer, and chairman. The shortening tenure of chief executives has been an issue; a Booz Allen Hamilton survey indicates the European CEO turnover rate is 16.8 per cent, a figure 425 per cent higher than 1995 when they first conducted the survey. Given the increasing pressure on chief executive performance, it was also viewed as critical that attention be paid to the quality of direct reports.

This was important not only to ensure quality and an appropriate skills mix on the top team, but also to have visibility of candidates for succession planning. This was seen as so important that one respondent indicated they spent nearly as much time as a board reviewing top talent and succession as they did on company strategy.

The role of choosing the chair was seen as particularly critical, in that the chair plays a central role across all key board functions. As the UK Corporate Governance Code notes:

> "The chairman is responsible for setting the board's agenda and ensuring that adequate time is available for discussion on strategic issues. The chairman should also promote a culture of openness and debate by facilitating the effective contribution of non-executive directors in particular and ensuring constructive relations between executive and non-executive directors."[3]

This was a theme cutting across a number of discussions, in that if there was frustration that something was not being achieved in a board setting, the underlying reason was usually that the chair wasn't willing to take on the subject.

Given that the chair sets the board agenda, unless (s)he was disposed to take on an issue, it never became a topic of discussion. This was seen as particularly true regarding strategy discussions, with a strong conviction expressed that strategy reviews need to be meaningful, forward looking business discussions. As one person noted, "It's really key that the chair drives the agenda. If he doesn't, it won't happen", and in the words of another, "Our chair is willing to challenge decisions, including ones he supported historically, which sends out the right message to everyone".

Governance v strategy

Chairmen and non-executives expressed concern about the increasing time spent on governance issues. As one said, "There is an increasing sense of the policeman about the non-exec these days". As noted above, some felt that the energy spent on governance deflected time from business strategy. This was seen as particularly true in the US, but was also raised as a concern in the UK. Representatives from the finance sector in particular noted that statutory and regulatory issues took a significant amount of board time.

Again, the chairman played a key role in finding the right balance between governance and strategy. Although a number of studies have documented frustration with the increasing time spent on governance to the detriment

6.004

---

[3] Supporting Principle A.3.

of strategy,[4] the respondents in this survey were reasonably sanguine on the subject. They felt the balance was broadly right, and that the Combined Code—now the UK Corporate Governance Code overall "provided a vehicle for implementing best practice".

Given that the people interviewed were from companies with a market capitalisation of a billion pounds sterling or more, most of the issues raised related to medium to large companies. These companies have a relatively sophisticated infrastructure to deal with corporate governance, and a range of advisors to assist them in the process. A number of people mentioned that this is clearly different for smaller companies, where the governance changes may well be seen as more burdensome.

Recruitment process

6.005   As a result of governance changes, recruitment was now a much more professional process, with searches always done through executive search firms. A respondent noted that "the day of the chairman appointing his mates" was past. If a chairman or director suggested a candidate, they would always be put through the recruitment process and be interviewed by the relevant nomination committee people.

There was a view by some that even with the rigour introduced in the past few years, some decisions are still made outside the formal process. One respondent noted, "By the time the formal Nomination Committee was held, the decision had pretty much been made". This wasn't seen necessarily as a bad thing, assuming due process was followed. As one person noted, "It simply reflects the reality that decisions often take place through an extended series of informal emails and phone calls around these key events".

Board composition

6.006   The greater emphasis on diversity was seen as one of the changing features of boards. People commented on the need for diversity not only in the sense of gender or ethnic background, but for a generally broader balance. This included people with different geographical experience, and a desire to get genuinely independent views from people with different industry backgrounds. Search criteria now included looking for more functional skills, such as strategy, human resource, or IT skills. It was noted that historically non-executives were brought on in part to introduce new business or facilitate contacts; this still occurred in some cases where people were recruited who had a deep understanding of a particular business segment. This had

---

[4] Russell Reynolds, *The Chairman's Report; Corporate Governance, for Good or Ill?*, 2005.

implications not only for helping understand how buying decisions are made, but to also help understand upcoming product requirements in a particular industry segment.

The "door opening" function was seen as something that was more likely to be requested in small companies. Even in these cases, it was viewed as something that was likely to be strategic, such as bringing in someone who had directly relevant company experience in building or expanding market opportunities.

All respondents indicated they put a fair amount of thought into getting a well balanced board, seeking industry and market segment skills as well as an increasing emphasis on a broad array of functional skills. Respondents generally reacted positively to the requirement that half of the board (excluding the chairman) be independent, and as one respondent noted:

"We deliberately sought someone who would help us challenge our thinking. It's one of the things we try to assess in our interviews; will they ask the tough questions, and hold their own in a discussion."

Speaking to people responsible for recruiting non-executives, they indicate that there is a stronger push for a diversified field of candidates. Successful executive women are much sought after, as are people with strong international experience. In the US, they note, there has been a very strong push for a broader ethnic mix, although that hasn't filtered through to the UK to the same extent.

In the pursuit of diversity, both NED and search firm respondents indicated that a company's initial criteria may be relaxed. Normally companies seek candidates that have successful operational experience in a comparable role and company. Respondents acknowledged this criteria is often loosened to broaden the candidate pool.

The Cranfield[5] report that publishes an annual account on women executives in FTSE 100 companies notes, "The new female directors are more likely to be international, have board experience and have much richer, more varied backgrounds than the men". The challenge of how to embed diversity continues to be a key issue. As one search person said, "Boards need to be more creative. They are still quite conservative in what they are looking for".

The pool needs to be broadened not only for reasons of diversity, but also because it is more difficult to attract the traditional FTSE 100 candidate to non-executive positions. Post Higgs, FTSE 100 chairs can only chair one FTSE 100 company. Audit committee chairman now need to have recent relevant financial experience. The rise of private equity has also meant that people who formerly might have been attracted to board positions now have an attractive alternative. Private equity was seen to have the advantages of

[5] Female FTSE Index 2005.

greater potential financial reward, a real opportunity to influence performance, and less public scrutiny.

Search firms also note that candidates are being much more selective. They
are taking on fewer NED positions, and do more background checks before
agreeing to join. As one noted, "They are much more thorough about their
due diligence. They will talk to both a company's auditors and brokers before
they go ahead". (PricewaterhouseCoopers LLP, for example, has developed a
due diligence tool called The Test to assist NEDs in evaluating any new NED
position they might consider.)

Higgs and others have argued that boards benefit from greater diversity,
and encouraged broadening the search criteria for candidates. Laura Tyson's
report,[6] commissioned by the DTI, looked specifically at how to expand the
number of available applicants for NED positions. These initiatives have had
some effect, with female FTSE 100 NEDs going up from 60 in 2000 to 107
in 2005.[7]

These initiatives have had a cumulative effect of raising interest levels, and
as one search person said, they get at least three or four curriculum vitae
every day from people who are unlikely to meet most companies' criteria.
Another search firm partner noted, though, "There is a real dichotomy out
there. There is this enormous pool that want to be on boards, but they don't
match what clients are looking for".

Board working practices

6.007   The topic of board working practices generated a great deal of discussion,
and was an area where chairman and non-executive directors had put a fair
amount of thought. Respondents noted that to be an effective board member
requires a different skill set than that of an operator, and not everyone is able
to make the transition. Whereas an executive director has a position within
a corporate hierarchy that enables one to get things done, this control disap-
pears as a non-executive and one is dependent on one's ability to persuade
and influence other board members.

A search firm partner noted, "This is a typical problem for a new NED.
They come in all enthusiastic and keen, and are in real danger of getting in the
way . . . After about the first year, they figure out the right balance". Some
respondents said they had struggled in making the transition themselves.
One interviewee who was both a non-executive director and a chief executive
noted, "They [non-executives] think their role is to make decisions, but it is
only to make quite selected ones. It can be a tough discipline to learn".

Particularly as a new NED, there is no real vehicle that addresses how to
manage this transition. As one search firm respondent said, "This clarity

---

[6] *Recruitment and Development of Non-Executive Directors*, Laura Tyson, 2003.
[7] Female FTSE Index 2005, Executive Summary.

around role is a big issue that emerges from board appraisals . . . This really falls to the chairman to address". This can be challenging, however, in that chairmen are not likely to want to discourage active participation, and it is not clear as to where the line is to be drawn.

The UK Corporate Governance Code indicates the non-executive should both constructively challenge and help develop the strategy, as well as scrutinise the performance of management.[8] Respondents were clear that they didn't see their role "as second-guessing management" but where the boundary lay between challenge and letting them get on with the job was unclear. No-one indicated they had figured out how to deal with it at board level. As one respondent said, "It should probably be dealt with in the induction process, but we are still finding our way on this one".

A whole new branch of consulting has emerged to deal with board behaviour, ranging from training and induction for new NEDs to the board appraisal process. One respondent noted that the better training vehicles introduced post Higgs actively address this issue, and provide role playing to help new NEDs think through how to handle various board scenarios. Another commented that the use of a professional coach had been used to address issues that had come up in the boardroom.

Although there are challenges as a new NED, some also commented on issues that developed as an established board member. One respondent thought his effectiveness had diminished after only two terms, indicating the CEO "learned how to manage me over time". Another NED who had faced a challenge in getting something accepted noted, "Sometimes you need to step back and think again about how to approach something . . . you will not always gain support from your first attempt at raising an issue".

While persuasive skills are one clear criterion for being an effective board member, another key skill was being an effective team player. All of the respondents stressed the importance of working together, and indicated there was a big incentive to collaborate. This held true for recruiting new board members as well, where positive consideration was given to candidates seen as team players.

When consensus was not achieved, this often led to significant board problems. It was viewed as a damaging process to take a vote and get voted down, so every effort was made to manage decisions to consensus. As one person noted in discussing a remuneration level disagreement, the after effect "poisoned the atmosphere for months". Another said, "Overt disagreement on a board is a disaster". A couple of respondents spoke of non-executives on occasion leaving the board because they had not adjusted either as a board member in general, or simply were not a team player. As one respondent pointed out, "You simply don't renew their appointment when it comes up after two years".

---

[8] Main and Supporting Principle A.4.

Looking at it from a slightly different perspective, one respondent indicated he was "amazed at how non-collaborative board work is". With executives, there are many opportunities for informal discussion on key topics, whereas informal networking opportunities don't exist to the same extent for non-executives. Some commented that emails proved to be a useful tool to raise items outside of board meetings; they are quick and informal and thoughts and ideas could be tested without requiring a full discussion. Compared to holding an executive position, much of the work of non-executives takes place in the actual board meeting.

When sensitive issues do come up, the ability to have an informal dialogue was seen as important. One person noted he had been in a position where it "was considered almost disloyal to have separate meetings", and over time they created a climate where this has now became an accepted practice. Another noted that corporate governance is forcing companies to evolve, "and that the changes have forced a healthy debate around the issues".

The role of chairman is again key in creating this space for conversation. The Higgs report comments specifically on this issue, noting that the chairman should, "manage the board to ensure that sufficient time is allowed for discussion of complex or contentious issues, where appropriate arranging for informal meetings beforehand to enable thorough preparation for the board discussion".[9] Although many boards hold an informal board dinner two to three times a year where these types of discussions took place, these usually happen at set times in the year which may not necessarily correspond to when issues arise.

Non-executives noted the need to have sufficient time for important topics. As one respondent commented:

> "Sometimes you need two or three runs at a topic before you feel comfortable with it as a board. It is important to signpost early when you feel more time will be required for discussion."

Challenging the status quo was seen as a particularly difficult issue, when NEDs wanted to raise issues against the prevailing way of doing things. One chairman had provided guidance to one of his non-executives, noting the NEDs would be more effective if they "hunted as a pack". The Higgs' requirement that half of the board be independent goes some way to addressing this issue, and it then becomes incumbent on the chair and the NEDs to ensure they work together as a team to achieve the desired changes.

---

[9] Higgs Review, para.5.12, see App.2 of this book.

Board assessment

Board assessment has moved on considerably in the last few years, and a **6.008** number of boards are now using quite sophisticated processes. One chairman walked me through a complex performance diagram for each of his board members, illustrating their strengths and weaknesses relative to the other board members on 12 pre-agreed criteria. Another spoke of a web-based application that provided each member an assessment of themselves, including information on where they stood relative to the high and low scores in the group, as well as feedback from his peers on his performance.

There was some scepticism expressed of board evaluations, with a view that "one cannot really expect 10 to 12 people to say they are behaving inappropriately". In this view, board performance was only likely to be improved marginally from this process. A more positive view was held by one respondent, who noted that board appraisals were a good opportunity for reflective one-on-one discussions between the chair and an individual NED. As one noted, "It provided a good opportunity not just to talk about my performance, but to have an open discussion about how to improve some of the board activities".

One of the developments in this area is 360 degree board feedback, where one goes beyond feedback from other board members, and reaches out to the full range of stakeholders for feedback, including that of major shareholders. One respondent who had done this felt it had been a very positive experience, and was looking at expanding it to other boards. At a minimum, this sort of discussion would provide an ongoing dialogue with key audiences about company and board performance.

Although there was some scepticism, the broad view was that board appraisals were beneficial, and over time would contribute to improving board's working practices.

Role of senior independent directors

The role of the senior independent director was seen as an ambiguous one, **6.009** with some respondents unclear on the role's merits. As the UK Corporate Governance Code notes, the major shareholder contact is with the chief executive and the finance director, noting that the chairman should ensure that all directors "are made aware of their major shareholders' issues and concerns".[10]

Most respondents indicated it would be cumbersome and repetitive to have too many layers of conversations going on with shareholders. The

---

[10] Supporting Principle E.1.

general view was in a well-run company with a good chair, there was no real requirement for this role, but that it could be effectively used as an "emergency safety valve".

Particularly in the situation where a chairman is being changed, the role of the senior independent was seen as critical. (S)he would provide the leadership during this transition, not only to facilitate the transfer but also in chairing the board should that be necessary. Also, the senior independent was seen as the person who would appraise the chairman.

Role of the company secretary

6.010   The management of governance issues was most typically administered by the company secretary. One person noted that through working on a US board, he had come to appreciate the role a very strong company secretary can play. The company secretary reminded them of their legal duties and limits, and reduced their requirement for outside legal advice. As with other board roles, personal style played a key role. He notes, "It is an extremely useful role . . . you have to be a very strong personality without showing it".

Committee structure

6.011   Much of the increased workload resulting from corporate governance changes have come in the committee structure. Both the audit and remuneration Committee had major changes as a result of the 2003 Combined Code, and while respondents recognised the value of these changes, indicated it had considerably increased the workload of these committees. In some cases, for example, the audit role was so significant, that risk management had now been spun off as a sub-committee.

Respondents noted that recruiting remuneration committee chair positions was particularly difficult; it was described by one interviewee as "the poisoned chalice". There was not only the pressure that comes from heightened visibility, but there was a significantly higher workload coming from the shareholder consultation that was required. Concern was expressed about the more limited flexibility in the current environment, and that everything "needed to be done by the rule book".

The audit committee chair was also called out as an increasingly onerous role, with significant time commitments required. Search firms indicated it was also a difficult position to recruit, in that existing chief financial officers often felt they had enough on their plate without taking on an NED role as well.

The changes that allowed the chairman to sit on the remuneration committee and chair the nomination committee were welcomed by the respondents, who felt this was a natural extension of the chairman's role. This was particularly true in the case of the nomination committee, in that the chair's role here was seen as vital to perform his own role effectively.

Risk/reward

There has been a fair amount of press on the risk/reward ratio felt by NEDs, **6.012** particularly following the *Equitable Life* case,[11] and these concerns were expressed in the interviews.

One respondent said, "The risk reward is totally out of kilter; I'd be very reluctant to take on another one (NED role)". Another person noted that the bureaucracy around the role had grown considerably. Given these pressures, they indicated "the balance is not as good as it used to be; this is not an issue that is fixable with money".

Most people felt that the demands on time had gone up considerably, and the pay had not matched the growth in risk and accountability. A number of people made the comparison to management consultants, indicating that the hourly rate for non-executive directors worked out at quite a bit less than comparable consultants. With FTSE 100 and 250 companies, there were often two overseas board meetings a year, which further exacerbated the time issue.

Even though the pay has gone up smartly, with some firms now paying in the £80–£100k range, this wasn't seen as sufficient to match the increased risks associated with the role. A couple of people spoke favourably of the US system, which allows the payment of non-executives to be made in company shares. Another indicated that equity-based payment would be inappropriate in that it was akin to "golden handcuffs", and that independence would suffer.

Non-financial rewards, such as the status and cache of being on a FTSE 100 board, were seen as another form of reward that came with being a non-executive director. As one search firm person said, "For some people, they've achieved their financial objectives, and becoming an NED of a FTSE 100 company is the path to titles and glory". The recognition that comes with a title in the UK is still seen by some as a strong pull, and providing a public good such as serving as an independent director was one way to enhance one's chances of achieving such an award.

Comparisons to other countries

A number of contributors also held positions on either continental or US **6.013** boards. When compared to what were viewed as the excessive requirements

---

[11] See Chs 1 (Definition, Background and Purpose of Corporate Governance), 4 (Directors—Duties and Liabilities) and 5 (Directors—The Non-Executive Director) for a fuller discussion of this case.

of Sarbanes-Oxley, there was a strong view that the UK had broadly got it right. Sarbanes-Oxley was seen as very burdensome, and some respondents indicated it would deter them from seeking a US listing.

Some people made comparisons to the two-tier board structure of a number of European countries, and indicated that the unitary board structure of the UK was more appropriate. A number noted that some European countries had some way to go to meet the rigours of the UK, and that given the benefits, felt they too would move in the same general governance direction.

Summary

6.014   This chapter explored the various dimensions of how NEDs perceive their roles. The reactions to the corporate governance changes themselves were largely positive. Respondents felt corporate governance was working, and were largely becoming embedded as a part of overall company processes. One person likened corporate governance to risk management; as she noted, "it is most effective when it is embedded in the system". When done well, it was felt a climate was created where there was a higher quality of debate.

Key points include:

- The NED role is reasonably well defined, with corporate governance, succession, and strategy all listed as a key part of the role. Within this, some disquiet was expressed that corporate governance was usurping time that would be better spent on company strategy.

- A key area of Higgs, and the subsequent Tyson report, was in expanding the candidate pool for NEDs. Women and people with international experience are two key areas where there has been higher demand from firms. Search firms who specialise in recruitment of NEDs note that boards are still reasonably conservative, and not surprisingly there is a higher comfort level with recruiting NEDs from traditional backgrounds.

- All three of the search partners interviewed indicated it is becoming increasingly difficult to identify and attract NEDs, despite rising compensation. Respondents indicated the risk/reward ratio has worsened, with private equity providing an attractive alternative for potential NEDs. The risk of serving on a board has risen, and respondents felt the time requirements had gone up considerably.

- Working as a team is seen as a key success component of effective boards. Ability to work with others, and persuade people to your point of view, is key to a well functioning team.

- The skills that got one to the board room may be different than those that make for a successful board member, and there may be a period of adjustment.

- There is often a learning process where new board members become skilled at contributing to board discussions without getting too actively involved in the executive function. More effective training and induction are seen as two vehicles to assist in this process, but it was also noted the chairman may need to become more involved in addressing this. Some noted that there may be a role for mentoring or coaching to facilitate new board members in particular. Board appraisals were seen as another positive vehicle to encourage more effective boards.

- The senior independent role was viewed as a necessary component in certain circumstances, particularly when a chairman was being replaced or in the case of providing an appraisal of the chair. Regarding the interface to the city, the senior independent role was viewed as an area with high potential for overlap and confusion, and hence unlikely to be a standard communication route.

Judging from the small sample of people interviewed, the recent corporate governance changes have been broadly accepted. Some of the goals of Higgs and others, such as developing a more diverse gene pool in the board room, have not yet been fully realised. The current pressures within the system, with NEDS taking on fewer roles and doing more due diligence on those they do take, is forcing firms to broaden the candidate shortlist. These changes were always going to take some time to filter through the system, and it will be interesting to watch the trends in this area. Given that most of the governance changes have been broadly achieved, it would seem to provide a general endorsement of how well judged the changes were.

Chapter 7

Board Evaluations

Dr David Ladipo[1]

Introduction

This chapter examines the growing prevalence of board evaluations in the **7.001**
UK.[2] It argues that the readiness with which companies have embraced this
new "best practice" norm reflects the fact that most of the "low hanging"
corporate governance fruit has already been picked. In the UK, for example—
unlike the situation in the US and in other countries—there are few (readily
measurable) corporate governance structures than can be clearly linked to
financial performance. Moreover most UK companies have now made the
bulk of the changes to their board structure and composition that are necessary to ensure "full compliance" with the revised UK Corporate Governance
Code. The result is that further changes in their corporate governance structures are likely to generate diminishing financial and/or regulatory "returns".

It is hardly surprising therefore, that UK boards are placing more emphasis on governance *practices* rather than governance *structures*. In turn, this
switch of emphasis has led to a greater focus on the need to improve the performance of individual persons and of the information and decision-making
systems that link these persons together. The expectation amongst a growing

---

[1] David Ladipo is a partner and co-founder of the corporate advisory firm Lintstock where he
has primary responsibility for the firm's board effectiveness and stakeholder engagement services. He is also in charge of the firm's ongoing research initiatives. He read Philosophy, Politics
and Economics at Balliol College Oxford before moving to Girton College Cambridge where he
attained an MPhil in International Relations and a PhD in Social & Political Sciences. He was
made a Research Fellow of Churchill College Cambridge in 1997 and in the same year joined
the University's Centre for Business Research. He moved to Nottingham University in 1999
where he lectured in the School of Sociology and Social Policy. In 2002 he founded Lintstock.
This chapter was written for the 2007 edition of this book but references to the UK Corporate
Governance Code are as at July 2010.
[2] The 2010 edition of the UK Corporate Governance Code requires in Principle B.6 that the
board should undertake a formal and rigorous annual evaluation of its own performance and
that of its committees and individual directors, and, in Provision B.6.2, that the evaluation
should be externally facilitated at least every three years.

number of companies is that board evaluations will provide a powerful and effective way to further both objectives. But this chapter questions whether performance appraisals of individual directors are a helpful way to achieve the first objective and suggests that board chairmen should spend more time evaluating the *systems of information and decision making* that link board members to the company's senior management.

The UK Corporate Governance Code

7.002   Following the banking crisis of 2007/2009 the FRC carried out a review of the then Combined Code and in June 2010 published the UK Corporate Governance Code.

Evaluation is dealt with in Main Principle B.6 and subsequent Supporting Principles and Provisions.

These state as follows:

"Main Principle
The board should undertake a formal and rigorous annual evaluation of its own performance and that of its committees and individual directors.

Supporting Principles
The chairman should act on the results of the performance evaluation by recognising the strengths and addressing the weaknesses of the board and, where appropriate, proposing new members be appointed to the board or seeking the resignation of directors. Individual evaluation should aim to show whether each director continues to contribute effectively and to demonstrate commitment to the role (including commitment of time for board and committee meetings and any other duties).

Code Provisions
B.6.1 The board should state in the annual report how performance evaluation of the board, its committees and its individual directors has been conducted.
B.6.2 Evaluation of the board of FTSE 350 companies should be externally facilitated at least every three years. A statement should be made available of whether the external facilitator has any other connection with the company.
B.6.3 The non-executive directors, led by the senior independent director, should be responsible for performance evaluation of the chairman, taking into account the views of executive directors."

Supporting Principle B.7 states:

"The chairman should confirm to shareholders when proposing re-election that, following formal performance evaluation, the individual's performance continues to be effective and to demonstrate commitment to the role."

The emergence of a new "best practice" norm

Over the past five years, governments, financial regulators, and institutional investors have been busily concocting new codes of corporate governance "best practice". And with few exceptions, most of these new codes encourage the boards of listed companies to subject themselves to periodic evaluation of their performance. In some cases, the codes content themselves with the suggestion that the evaluation should be performed on a "periodic" or "regular" basis (see Table 7.1 below). But many codes, including the UK Code on Corporate Governance, recommend that the evaluation be undertaken on an annual basis[3] with an external evaluation every three years for boards of FTSE 350 companies.[4]

In most cases, the codes also stress that the evaluation must examine the performance not just of the board (and its committees) "as a whole" but of individual directors as well. In fact, of the codes listed in Table 7.1, the only two that do not explicitly advocate the exercise of individual performance evaluations are those of Japan and Sweden.

7.003

Table 7.1   Suggested Frequency of Board Evaluations

Country	Code/Report	Date	Frequency
Denmark	Norby Commission Report	2001	Annually
Japan	Governance Forum Principles	2001	Annually
Netherlands	Corporate Governance Code	2003	Annually
South Africa	King II Report & Code	2002	Annually
Spain	Olivencia Report	1998	Annually
Sweden	Asbrink Group Code	2005	Annually
UK	UK Corporate Governance Code	2010	Annually
US	Business Round Table Principles	2002	Annually
France	Bouton Report	2002	At least every three years
Italy	Corporate Governance Code	2003	Periodically
Australia	ASX Principles & Recommendations	2003	Regularly
Belgium	Code on Corporate Governance	2004	Regularly
Canada	Saucier Report	2001	Regularly
China	CSRC Code	2002	Regularly
US	NACD Report	2001	Regularly

[3] Main Principle B.6.
[4] Provision B.6.2.

As for who should conduct the evaluations, some suggest that the job is best left to the board chairman, others suggest that it should be the work of the nomination committee, and a handful recommend the use of external facilitators (viz. the codes of Belgium, France and Denmark).

The growing prevalence of board evaluations in the FTSE 100

7.004   Boards of UK-listed companies are not under a legal obligation to undertake a periodic evaluation of their performance. But, if a company decides not to undertake the evaluations suggested by Provision B.6.2 of the UK Corporate Governance Code, it is obligated under the Listing Rules of the Financial Services Authority, to explain its decision. And, on the evidence of the last three years, it looks as if most companies in the FTSE 100 have chosen to "comply" rather than explain.

As shown in Figure 7.1, in 2002, less than half the FTSE 100 were in the habit of conducting "formal and rigorous" board evaluations. By 2005, all but two companies claimed to have undergone this exercise (with the two exceptions excusing themselves on the grounds that it was too early to conduct such an exercise given the substantial changes in board composition that they had recently experienced).

In most cases, the evaluations were conducted by the board chairman. But between 2003 and 2005 there was a modest increase in the number of evaluations facilitated by external advisors (see Figure 7.2).

Figure 7.1 Percentage of FTSE 100 companies undertaking a formal board evaluation

Figure 7.2 Percentage of FTSE 100 companies where external advisors were used to facilitate the evaluation

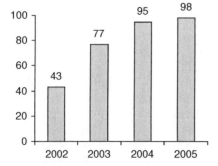

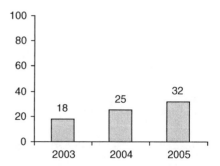

Sources: Spencer Stuart, *2004 UK Board Index*; Independent Audit, *Board Reporting 2005*; Robson Rhodes, *Board Evaluations: Results of a [2005] survey of FTSE 350 companies.*

Why did the conduct of board evaluations become a "best practice" norm in the UK?

On its own, the fact that UK companies have been quick to adopt the latest **7.005** "best practice" norm of corporate governance is neither puzzling nor particularly interesting. But the factors that underlie the sudden popularity of this norm are far from clear and could, potentially, be rather interesting. My own, preferred, explanation of this phenomenon is that it is yet another manifestation of the ancient law by which "nature abhors a vacuum". More specifically, there are two "vacuums" that are filled by the embrace of the board evaluation norm. The first is a researchers' vacuum and the second is a practitioners' vacuum.

The research vacuum

Until relatively recently, there was plenty of space for ambitious young **7.006** academics who wished to make their name by demonstrating a causal link between certain "measurable" aspects of corporate governance (e.g. board composition or the rights afforded to shareholders) and firms' financial performance. But this space is now much more crowded than it was before and the resulting empirical evidence suggests that many of these easily observable, "structural", corporate governance differences do not lead to significant differences in financial performance.

For example, in their oft-cited review of "Corporate Governance and Equity Prices", Gompers et al.[5] admit that, in all the literature examining the valuation and long-run performance implications of board membership and structure: "there is a weak or nonexistent link with firm value or performance". Dalton and Dalton[6] arrive at the same conclusion after analysing hundreds of studies undertaken over the past half century.

For example, in their analysis of 159 studies on the relationship between board composition and firm financial performance, Dalton and Dalton found no evidence of a systematic relationship between the two. Not only was firm performance uncorrelated with the proportion of non-executive directors on the board, there was no correlation between firm performance and the presence of independent directors.

Likewise, in their examination of 69 studies on the relationship between firm financial performance and the roles of chairman and CEO, Dalton and Dalton found that firms where the positions of chairman and CEO were

---

[5] Gompers, Ishii, and Metrick (2001) "Corporate Governance and Equity Prices", July 2001, Working Paper, Harvard Business School and NBER.
[6] Dalton, GM and Dalton, DR (2005) "Boards of Directors: Utilising Empirical Evidence in Developing Practical Prescriptions", *British Journal of Management*, Vol.16, S91–S97.

separated did not outperform firms where these positions were combined. The rather obvious conclusion which they draw from this is that:

"There is no empirical support to warrant the guidelines and/or legislation mandating independent board structures, as captured by independent director representation and the separate board leadership structure. In sum, structural independence does not equal performance advantage."

But what about that other article of corporate governance faith, viz. that greater levels of director equity holdings will more perfectly align their interests with those of shareholders, resulting in higher firm performance? Once again, the evidence, as analysed by Dalton and Dalton suggests that this claim lacks any empirical support. They analysed 229 studies over a 70-year time period and found no evidence of a relationship between CEO, executive or board member equity holdings and financial performance.

So are there *any* (readily measurable) corporate governance structures that have been correlated with firm performance? Yes, but the evidence from recent years suggests that the corporate governance provisions that can be clearly correlated with firm performance are mostly related to so-called "entrenchment provisions", i.e. constitutional limitations on shareholders' voting power or anti-takeover defences. For example, when studying the performance of 1,500 large US firms during the 1990s, Gompers et al.[7] found that an investment strategy that bought the 150 firms with the weakest entrenchment provisions and sold the 150 firms with strongest entrenchment provisions would have earned abnormal returns of 8.5 per cent per year during that decade.

To arrive at their calculations, Gompers et al. used a broad index of 24 entrenchment provisions. But when Bebchuk et al.[8] revisited the same data set, they found that the correlation with firm performance was driven by just a handful of provisions (with no evidence that the remaining provisions were negatively correlated with either firm value or stock returns). The provisions that they identified were as follows:

- staggered boards;
- limits on the ability of shareholders to amend charters and bylaws;
- supermajority requirements for mergers;
- poison pills;
- golden parachutes.

---

[7] Gompers, Ishii and Metrick (2003) "Corporate Governance and Equity Prices", *Quarterly Journal of Economics*, 118(1), February 2003, 107–155.
[8] Bebchuk, Cohen and Ferrell (2005) "What Matters in Corporate Governance", Discussion Paper No.491, March 2005, John M Olin Center for Law, Economics and Business, Harvard University.

But, as described below, the prevalence of such provisions and their potential for entrenchment is much lower in the UK than in the US.

Staggered boards

In staggered boards, directors are divided into classes, typically three, with **7.007** only one class of director coming up for election each year. In the US, this normally means that shareholders cannot replace a majority of the directors in any given year, no matter how widespread the support for such a change of control. And the result, as shown in earlier work conducted by Bebchuk et al.[9] is that, in the US, staggered boards help to insulate directors from the market for corporate control by providing a powerful defence against removal in either a proxy fight or proxy contests.

But the situation in the UK is very different because the Companies Act provides that investors in UK companies are entitled to requisition an extraordinary general meeting (if the shareholders calling for this meeting represent 10 per cent or more of the voting share capital) and put forward resolutions to appoint and/or remove directors. In other words, even though most directors in the UK are only put up for election once every three years, a would-be acquiring company—provided it has sufficient shareholder support—can oust the management of a UK-listed company in a relatively short space of time.

Limits on the ability of shareholders to amend charters and bylaws

In the sample examined by Bebchuk et al.[10] these limitations usually took the **7.008** form of supermajority requirements that made it difficult for shareholders to pass a charter or bylaw amendment opposed by management. In the US, the result usually makes it extremely difficult for non-management sharehold-ers to remove any defensive provisions that management had previously inserted into the charter or bylaws. Once again, the situation in the UK is very different.

As explained in Bebchuk,[11] under the law of Delaware (the most important corporate jurisdiction, which serves as domicile to a majority of US public companies) and the Model Business Corporation Act (which is followed by the corporate codes of 24 US states), charter amendments must be initiated

---

[9] Bebchuk, Coates and Subramanian (2002) "The Powerful Antitakeover Force of Staggered Boards: Theory, Evidence & Policy", *Stanford Law Review*, 54, 887–951. See also Bebchuk, Coates and Subramanian (2003) "The Power of Takeover Defenses", Working Paper, Harvard Law School and NBER.

[10] Op. cit. (2005).

[11] Bebchuk (2005) "The Case for Increasing Shareholder Power", *Harvard Law Review*, 833, January 2005, 844–865.

and brought to a shareholder vote of approval by the board. Regardless of how many shareholders want a given charter amendment and of how long they have supported the amendment, shareholders may not vote on it unless the board first elects to have such a vote.

By contrast, in the UK, although changes in the memorandum or the articles of association also require a supermajority approval of 75 per cent of the votes cast at a shareholder meeting, management does not have a privileged position with respect to initiating such changes. Instead, shareholders in the UK have a right to propose special resolutions to amend the memorandum or articles of association at the annual shareholder meeting (provided that proper notice is given). Furthermore, notwithstanding anything in the company's memorandum or articles of association, shareholders holding 10 per cent or more of the company's shares have the power to call an extraordinary general meeting and can bring a proposal to amend the memorandum or articles of association to a vote in such a meeting.

Supermajority requirements for mergers

7.009   In the US, some companies also have supermajority requirements for merger approvals which may block a bidder implementing a merger even when the bidder controls the target's board of directors (since stockholder approval may remain below the specified percentage). Not surprisingly, these requirements can discourage outsiders from seeking to gain control of the board through a hostile bid or a proxy contest. In the UK, a supermajority approval of 75 per cent of the votes cast at a shareholder meeting is also required to effectively implement a merger. But these are statutory requirements which apply to all listed companies in the UK and the approval threshold cannot, therefore, be revised downwards by an "enlightened" board seeking to subject itself to greater takeover discipline.

Poison pills

7.010   These "pills" (otherwise known as shareholder rights plans) are rights that, once issued by the company, serve to deter hostile bidders from buying shares as long as the incumbents remain in office and refuse to redeem the pill. For example, the pill might allow the target to issue a large number of new securities, often preferred stock, to existing shareholders with rights to convert the security into a large number of common shares if a takeover occurs. This immediately dilutes the percentage of the target owned by the acquirer, and makes it more expensive for the bidder to gain control of the target's stock. The use of such pills is remarkably widespread in the US. During the 1990/2003 period examined by Bebchuk et al.,[12] the proportion of large US companies with one or more poison pills ranged from 54 per cent to 59 per cent.

In the UK, by contrast, it is extremely difficult for managers to employ such defensive tactics. As described in Armour et al.,[13] takeovers of public companies are regulated by the City Code on Takeovers and Mergers. Rule 21 of the Code provides that from the point in time at which the incumbents believe that an offer might be imminent, the board of directors may not issue shares, options, or convertible securities, agree to sell, dispose of or acquire assets of a material amount, or enter into any contract otherwise than in the ordinary course of business. Admittedly, the Code does not apply to actions when there is no threat of a bid. But the structure of shareholder rights in the UK (more particularly, the fact that new share issues always require the consent of a majority of shareholders) makes it hard for any board to unobtrusively commit itself to a poison pill.

Golden parachutes

These so-called "parachutes" are terms in executive compensation agree-   **7.011**
ments that provide executives with pre-determined payouts in the event of a change of control. According to Bebchuk et al.,[14] lawyers in the US typically recommend such parachutes to any incumbents who believe there is a significant likelihood of their company being acquired. In theory, the relationship between golden parachutes and firm performance should be ambivalent. On the one hand, they might serve the interests of shareholders by making incumbents more willing to accept an acquisition. On the other hand, they reduce the extent to which directors are subject to the pecuniary discipline exerted by the market for corporate control. But whatever the net motivational impact of such provisions, the empirical results show they have a negative correlation with firm financial performance.

Yet, once again, this finding is now of relatively limited interest to boards in the UK. It is true that during the 1990s, the merits of "liquidated damages" (whereby the compensation paid to departing directors is made according to a pre-determined formula which guarantees a certain proportion of salary and other entitlements rather than resulting from a negotiated process of "mitigation") were the subject of considerable contention amongst institutional investors and corporate governance policy makers.[15] But there is

---

[12] Op. cit. (2005).
[13] Armour, Deakin and Konzelmann (2003) "Shareholder Primacy and the Trajectory of UK Corporate Governance", June 2003, Working Paper No.266, ESRC Centre for Business Research, University of Cambridge.
[14] Op. cit. (2005).
[15] Compare, for example, the different stances advocated by the Greenbury and Hampel Committees. Whereas the Greenbury Committee emphasised the need for companies to reduce compensation "to reflect departing directors' obligations to mitigate damages by earning money

Figure 7.3 Percentage of hostile takeover bids that succeeded during the period 1988–1998

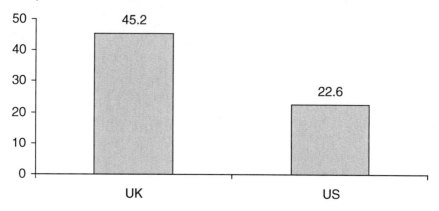

Source: Schneper & Guillén (2004)

now a fairly widespread consensus amongst investors (as articulated by the National Association of Pension Funds and the Association of British Insurers) that such provisions are no longer desirable.[16] This consensus is reflected in the compensation contracts of most directors in the FTSE 350.

In fact, not only are UK companies relatively free of the constitutional provisions which entrench the power of US incumbent directors, but they are also subject to a regulatory regime that is much more "permissive" of takeovers. Not surprisingly (as shown in Figure 7.3 above), hostile bids[17] are twice as likely to succeed in the UK than in the US.

The practitioners' vacuum

7.012   The fact that, in the UK, there are few (readily measurable) governance *structures* than can be clearly linked to firm performance has prompted many corporate advisors to emphasise the importance of (hard to measure) governance *practices*. But the academic "research vacuum" is a slow-burning catalyst and there are other, more proximate explanations, for the growing

elsewhere", the Hampel Committee advocated the use of liquidated damages as a way to avoid the "problems of mitigation and inevitably subjective arguments about performance". But, in the end, the tide of investor opinion swung away from Hampel and back to Greenbury.

[16] The Association of British Insurers and the National Association of Pension Funds, "Best Practice on Executive Contracts and Severance—A Joint Statement", December 2003.

[17] Schneper and Guillén report that during the period 1988–1998, the SDC Platinum database of M&A transactions shows 219 hostile bids in the UK, of which 99 were successful, compared with 429 in the US, of which only 97 were successful (Schneper and Guillén, "Stakeholder Rights and Corporate Governance: A Cross-National Study of Hostile Takeovers", Working Paper, April 2004, The Wharton School, University of Pennsylvania).

desire to examine how—in specific industries and at specific points in a company's development—a particular set of practices can help or hinder board effectiveness. These include the fact that most companies in the UK have made most, if not all, the changes to their board structure and composition that are necessary to ensure "full compliance" with the revised 2003 Combined Code on Corporate Governance.

Take for example, two of the more contentious elements in the revised 2003 Combined Code (and now the UK Corporate Governance Code) and its accompanying guidance notes, viz. that:

- non-executive directors who have served on a board for more than nine years should be subject to annual re-election (because tenure in excess of this limit may have adverse implications for a director's independence); and

- the letter of appointment sent to non-executive directors should set out the expected time commitment, and that non-executive directors should undertake that they will have "sufficient time" to meet what is expected of them (the implication being that they should not hold several directorships at the same time).

In the seven years since the publication of the revised 2003 Combined Code, many of the UK's large listed companies have substantially "refreshed" the composition of their boards to ensure that they meet both the spirit and the letter of the Code's provisions. Thus, by June 2006, there were only three companies in the FTSE 100 where the average tenure of the non-executive directors was in excess of nine years (see Figure 7.4 below) and more than a third of companies were devoid of any non-executive directors with more than nine years tenure.[18]

Likewise, amongst the pool of directors in the FTSE 100, very few individuals held more than one other directorship in a major (i.e. FTSE 350) UK listed company. In fact—as shown in Figure 7.5 (below)—there were only 13 companies in the FTSE 100 where the average number of additional directorships (in other FTSE 350 companies) held by non-executive directors amounted to more than one.

Thus after three years of board "renewal" and "recomposition"—and with most of the Higgsian boxes now "ticked"—the senior corporate governance officers within these firms—from board chairmen to company secretaries—are more able (and willing) to get to grips with the "knottier" governance issues which tend to emerge during the course of a board evaluation.

---

[18] For many observers (the author included) the insistence on culling long-toothed directors represents a retrograde step for British companies. The learning curve for a non-executive director can be quite lengthy and seasoned directors (e.g. those who have served on the board for more than three terms) often provide the board with a wealth of experience and "organisational memory".

Figure 7.4 Average tenure of non-executive directors amongst the FTSE 100

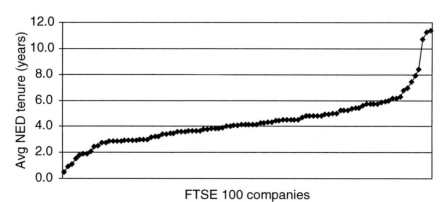

Source: Lintstock's corporate practice database

Figure 7.5 Average number of additional directorships (in other FTSE 350 companies) held by non-executive directors in the FTSE 100

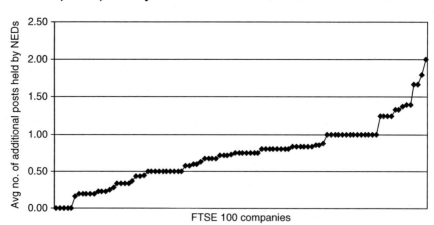

Source: Lintstock's corporate practice database

What should be evaluated? Persons or systems?

7.013   In light of the observations above, it would appear that most UK companies have exhausted whatever small opportunities they might have had to effect *structural* changes in their governance regimes that would yield a financial return. It is hardly surprising, therefore, to find researchers and practitioners alike placing more emphasis on the need to improve:

Figure 7.6 Percentage of Company Secretaries who believe that over time, performance evaluations within their company will improve directors' individual contributions and/or board performance generally

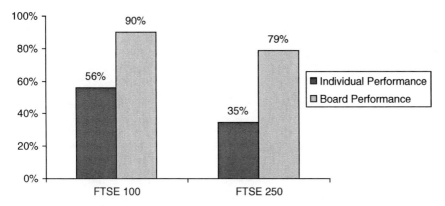

Source: Edis-Bates Associates, "Evaluating the Code: Is Board Performance Evaluation Working", October 2005.

(a)   the performance of *individual persons;* and

(b)   the *information and decision making systems* that link these persons together.

What is more puzzling, however, is the growing belief (particularly amongst larger companies) that board evaluations can be a powerful and effective way to further *both* objectives. A recent survey of UK company secretaries shows that while only a third of company secretaries in the FTSE 250 believe that performance evaluations will improve directors' individual contributions (see Figure 7.6 above), the same is true of more than half the company secretaries in the FTSE 100.

What is interesting about this belief is that it runs counter to a long line of argument and empirical research that considers individual performance appraisals to be nothing short of "fatal" for any organisation committed to "real" business effectiveness. Take, for example, the writings of William Edwards Deming, the acknowledged "Godfather" of the "total quality management" movement, whose "seven deadly diseases" provide an uncannily good diagnosis of many of the so-called "governance" failures of the past six years (from Enron to Parmalat).

These seven diseases[19] consist of the following:

---

[19] See Walton (1986) *The Deming Management Method*, New York: Dodd, Mead.

(1)   lack of constancy of purpose;

(2)   emphasis on short-term profits;

(3)   evaluation by performance, merit rating, or annual review of performance;

(4)   mobility of management;

(5)   running a company on visible figures alone;

(6)   excessive medical costs;

(7)   excessive costs of warranty, fuelled by lawyers who work for contingency fees.

The pathology of the third disease is described by Deming as follows:

"(The annual review) nourishes short-term performance, annihilates long-term planning, builds fear, demolishes teamwork, nourishes rivalry and politics ... It leaves people bitter, crushed, bruised, battered, desolate, despondent, dejected, feeling inferior, some even depressed, unfit for work for weeks after receipt of rating, unable to comprehend why they are inferior. It is unfair, as it ascribes to the people in a group differences that may be caused totally by the system that they work in."[20]

Deming, of course, is not alone in believing that improvements to systems, rather than individual efforts, are the most effective way to secure organisational effectiveness. As described by Coens and Jenkins,[21] the same is true of a whole of host of "revered business visionaries" including Russell Ackoff, Joseph Juran and Peter Senge.

The vogue for individual performance evaluations also runs counter to the disdain in which such evaluations are held by most of those who are subjected to them. As described by Peter Block,[22] if we had any respect for the appraisal process would we consider using it in our personal lives?

"Would we say to our spouse, significant other, or intimate friend: 'Dear it is time for your annual performance appraisal. For the sake of our relationship and the well-being of the family unit, I want you to prepare for a discussion of your strengths and weaknesses and the ways you have fallen short of your goals for the year. Also, honey, I would like for you to define some stretch goals for the coming year.' We might try this at home, but most likely only once."

---

[20] Deming (1986) *Out of the Crisis*. Cambridge, Mass: MIT, p.102.
[21] Coens and Jenkins (2000) *Abolishing Performance Appraisals*, San Francisco, CA: Brett-Koehler.
[22] See the foreword to Coens and Jenkins (*Abolishing Performance Appraisals*, p.xiv).

But perhaps the call for board directors to be subjected to individual performance appraisals should be seen as consistent (rather in conflict) with the general dislike and disdain in which such appraisals are held. There is, after all, a degree of schadenfreude to be had from knowing that board members are finally getting a dose of the same infantilising medicine that the rest of the workforce is made to swallow on an annual basis.

Nevertheless, however enjoyable it might be for middle management to know that board members are not exempt from individual performance appraisals, the chairman of the board needs to think very carefully about the way in which such assessments are performed and the impact thereof. This is because much of the research evidence suggests that although the various forms of individual appraisal are packaged as tools for "accountability" their real function is that of "control". As described by Coens and Jenkins:

> "We are comfortable with accountability, but not control—only monsters seek control. Our comfort with accountability is not misplaced. It's a worthy goal, at least to the extent that it means people should take responsibility for their work. The problem lies not in desiring accountability, but in the means of ensuring accountability. Rather than promoting accountability as a value, we try to force people to be responsible. We impose measurement and formal judgement to make sure that people are held accountable. This is precisely what appraisal does. With good intentions, we adorn appraisal with upbeat and friendly terminology, but the features of control are undeniably present and felt by every employee who undergoes the process."[23]

From a shareholders' perspective, a net advantage may accrue from subjecting *employees* to such forms of control—depending on the nature of the industry in which the company operates and the kind of activities engaged in by its workforce—even if control is won at the cost of genuine accountability. But with regard to board members, performance appraisals that are designed to secure employee control are unlikely to foster the emergence of good governors viz. those who are not subject to executive control, who exercise independent judgment, and who feel a genuine sense of accountability.

This is not to say that board chairmen should not assess, in the normal course of their activities, the contributions made by individual directors. Nor does it imply that they should desist from chastising or encouraging their colleagues. But it does mean that they should consider, very carefully, whether either of these actions should take place in the context of a "formal" annual performance evaluation. More generally, it suggests that board chairmen

---

[23] *Abolishing Performance Appraisals*, p.82.

should spend less time examining individual performance and more time evaluating the systems of information and decision making that link board members to the company's senior management.

How should the systems evaluation be conducted?

7.014   Once a company decides to undertake a "systems" evaluation of its board and its board committees, it faces a number of questions about how best to conduct this evaluation. Over the past few years, the experience we have gained in helping boards to conduct these "systems" evaluations suggests that there are two key prerequisites to a successful evaluation. Firstly, one must win the trust of all the persons who participate in the evaluation. Secondly, one must ensure that the evaluation is focused on "discovering and learning" rather than "measuring".

Securing trust

7.015   When it comes to securing the trust of board members and senior managers, there are four practices that always help. In the first instance, it helps if the evaluation is conducted by an "independent" facilitator. This need not involve the use of external consultants but it does require someone outside of the board and top-level management. Secondly, the independent facilitators should make it clear to their interlocutors that the evaluation is a systems evaluation and not an evaluation of their individual performance or that of their colleagues. Thirdly, the independent facilitators should make their interlocutors aware that any *ad hominem* remarks they make will be "de-personalised" before they are worked into the final report and that all quotes or observations will be fully anonymised and non-attributable. Finally, it helps if the facilitators' report is shared with all board members (not just the chairman) and if board members know this in advance.

Focus on discovery and learning rather than measurement

7.016   For some people, the "safest" way to conduct a systems evaluation of the board is to design a set of standardised questionnaires which can be applied to all board members and which are designed to produce easily comparable answers. For example, board members might be asked to "rate", on a sliding scale, the board's knowledge and understanding of the company's business risks. Or they might be asked to rate the board's contribution to the development of the company's strategy against the same scale. There is nothing inherently wrong with such an approach. On the contrary, this "rating" or "ranking" type question can often be a useful heuristic device provided it is used sparingly and provided it is asked via the medium of a face-to-face interview rather than a written "self-completion" questionnaire.

But when the evaluation consists largely or wholly of such questions, the exercise soon becomes a "chore" for those participating in it. A focus on standardised questions and responses also makes it more difficult for the facilitator to listen to the issues that are of real concern to his or her interlocutors. At the end of the exercise, the facilitator might be able to produce plenty of impressive charts showing the degree of consensus or disagreement on a long list of questions. But if the key issues that the board needs to address do not fall neatly into any of the facilitator's pre-determined questions, they may not come to the surface.

But let's assume the facilitator avoids the use of "self-completion" questionnaires and holds face-to-face interviews instead. Let's also assume that they make sparing use of "rating" or "ranking" type questions and, instead, devise a semi-structured interview schedule with lots of open-ended questions. This will give them much more freedom to probe and listen and gauge. But this freedom will not, of itself, be valuable unless they make use of it. And, to make use of this freedom requires that they be willing to deviate from (or, in some cases, entirely abandon) the interview script if they hit upon a new and unexpectedly fruitful line of enquiry.

The need to learn and discover (rather than measure) also requires that the facilitator employ an iterative approach to his or her interviews. In other words, they have to be willing to change the focus of each successive interview in response to information already received.

Last, but not least, the facilitators need to make sure that their interviews are not restricted to board members. In our experience, most of the really useful insights to be derived from board evaluations relate to the board's information system (and its link to the management information system) and to the systems by which decisions are delegated to senior managers (or are pushed back up to the board). To grasp these insights, the facilitator needs to interview not just the CEO and the other executives on the main board but a good selection of other senior managers as well.

When does the evaluation start to yield benefits?

How soon will the evaluation begin to yield some tangible benefits? For most **7.017** companies, our answer to this question is "sooner than you think but not necessarily in the way you might expect". Often, when my colleagues and I complete a board evaluation and are about to write up our final report, we will get a call or an email from the chairman saying two things. The first thing they will usually say is that they have spoken to the other board members and the response has been very positive ("they found the sessions really useful", etc.). The second thing they normally say is that they are really looking forward to a set of clear recommendations or "action points".

What is interesting about the latter observation is the way in which it reflects a habitual expectation that the value of an exercise must, ultimately, be demonstrable through a set of "corrections" and "improvements". In other words, the board members may well have found the discussions with the independent facilitator "really useful" but, in the absence of any concrete action point, there is no easy way for the company to gauge or even label this usefulness.

My colleagues and I sympathise with this viewpoint and we always conclude our evaluation reports by recommending specific steps that the board can take to "improve" its effectiveness. But at the end of the day, we are always left with the slightly melancholy feeling that the real value of our work has been realised before we have even put our fingers to the keyboard. This is because the directors we interview find the very act of sitting down with a neutral interlocutor—to discuss the areas in which the board can improve its performance and, in particular, its interaction with the company's senior management—a cathartic and refreshing exercise. And in many cases the issues that first surfaced during our interviews were already being fed into the board's discussions on strategy, risk management or internal control *before* we had delivered our final report.

Chapter 8

The Chairman

Introduction

In the preface to his defining book *Corporate Governance and Chairmanship*,[1] Sir Adrian Cadbury says:

8.001

"[Corporate governance] and chairmanship are inextricably linked, because corporate governance is concerned with the system by which companies are directed and controlled, which is clearly the responsibility of their boards of directors. Equally clearly, it is chairmen who are responsible for the working of the boards. Thus, the way in which corporate governance principles are put into practice is primarily a matter for board chairmen."

It is therefore appropriate to examine the office and role of chairman.

The job specification[2]

Sir John Harvey Jones once said "it is imperative that the company takes its drumbeat from the chairman". The significance of that statement is that ultimately it is the chairman who has the job of initiating, instilling and overseeing high standards of corporate governance but within the overall obligation to ensure an "effective board" to drive the organisation to successful performance.

8.002

In an attempt to translate that generalisation into a meaningful, but it is to be hoped, not overly simplistic, proposition, the job of chairman might be described as follows[3]:

---

[1] OUP, 2002.
[2] See App.11 (Higgs Guidance on the role of the chairman).
[3] The Unilever Plc 2005 corporate governance manual "*The Governance of Unilever*" contains a section on the responsibilities of the chairman as follows:

(a) to manage the board of directors with the objective of optimum commercial success and enhanced shareholder value;

(b) to develop a robust and constructive relationship with the chief executive in which the CEO understands that (s)he reports to the chairman as well as to the wider board;

(c) to be the guardian and enforcer of the values of the board in relation to stakeholders;

(d) to be the guardian and enforcer of the UK Corporate Governance Code;

"the chairman's general and specific responsibilities cover:
- conducting shareholders' meetings; . . .
- managing the board to ensure that it operates effectively;
- ensuring that the members of the board received accurate, timely and clear information, in particular about the company's performance, to enable the board to take sound decisions, monitor effectively and provide advice to promote the success of the company; encouraging active engagement by all the members of the board;
- in consultation with the senior independent director, setting and approving the board agenda to take full account of the issues and the concerns of all directors;
- promoting effective relationships and open communication, both inside and outside the boardroom, between non-executive directors and the executive directors;
- together with the senior independent director, building an effective and complementary board, initiating change and planning succession in board appointments, subject to board and shareholders' approval;
- monitoring effective implementation of board decisions;
- ensuring clear structure for and the effective running of board committees;
- together with the senior independent director and facilitated by the joint secretaries, maintaining effective communication with major shareholders so as to ensure the board develops an understanding of their views;
- in conjunction with the joint secretaries, taking the lead in providing a properly constructed induction programme for new directors that is comprehensive, formal and tailored;
- together with the senior independent director, taking the lead in identifying and meeting the development needs of individual directors;
- addressing the development needs of the board as a whole with a view to enhancing its overall effectiveness as a team;
- in conjunction with the senior independent director, ensuring that the performance of individuals and of the board as a whole and its committees is evaluated at least once a year;
- establishing a close relationship of trust with the group chief executive, by providing support and advice while respecting executive responsibility;
- convening and chairing semi annual corporate strategy review meetings in preparation for the board strategy conference;
- evaluating and monitoring compliance with corporate policies and governance processes;
- acting where appropriate as Unilever representative on corporate aims and policies including environmental and corporate social responsibility matters;
- guarding the corporate reputation including relations with major shareholders, government, academia and other relevant stakeholders and commentators;
- being a member of the nomination committee;
- providing advice and being available to assist the remuneration committee; [Note: the UK Corporate Governance Code permits the chairman to sit on the remuneration committee]; and
- receiving direct reports of the joint secretaries."

(e)   to establish with the board their relationship of confidence with and from shareholders and to be the primary person with whom shareholders share concerns.

Legal status

It is striking that under statute the role of chairman has recognition but no statutory status save in relation to the process of meetings.[4] The CA 2006 draft model memoranda and articles of association for public companies[5] describes the chairman's function largely in procedural terms.   **8.003**

In those articles the chairman is referred to solely in the context of the conduct of meetings of the board and shareholders.[6] The articles of association of public and private companies contain numerous references to the role of the chairman but again, only in the context of meetings and board meetings. Case law also is concerned only with the powers and duties of chairman in relation to the conduct of shareholders' meetings (see, for example, *Byng v London Life Association Ltd*[7]).

Behaviour—the Walker recommendations

Although the 2009 Walker Review of corporate governance in UK banks was directed at banks and other financial entities it contains in its analysis of the job of chairman outstanding observations into the behaviour of a chairman which are of general application and which bear repeating here[8]:   **8.004**

"1. Requisite behaviour of a board chairman
To be an effective chairman, his or her behaviour must cover:
1. **Integrating the board's collective thinking**. This is possible when a chairman excels at seeking and sharing information; building ideas into concepts; analysing and considering multiple perspectives and different alternatives; and can subvert his or her individual needs for commitment to a common goal.
2. **Empathy and promoting openness in board members.** The ability to listen at multiple levels is critical to successful chairmanship and team dynamics. Listening to what is not being said is as critical as listening to the words that are spoken. Only with this ability can a chairman engender deep trust and respect.

---

[4] See, e.g. CA 2006 ss.249, 319, 320, 321, 328, 329, 330, 356.
[5] Companies (Model Articles) Regulations 2008 implemented on October 1, 2009. Details can be accessed on the stationery office website at *http://www.opsi.gov.uk/si/si2008/uksi_20083229_en_1#sch1*.
[6] e.g. arts 11, 13, 35, 37.
[7] [1990] Ch. 170.
[8] Walker Review of corporate governance in UK banks and other financial industry entities, November 2009: Annex 4.

3. **Facilitating interaction.** This requires that a chairman's behaviour move seamlessly depending upon who needs to be in the conversation, rather than 'managing' the process. It requires that skills and expertise (authority) are valued and respected regardless of hierarchy or power dynamics.

4. **Developing others.** Undertaking active coaching, mentoring and development of talent within the board, in particular with new board members.

5. **Communicating complex messages succinctly.** Effective communication, through written and spoken means, reduces the cognitive load on the board freeing more time for analysis, exploration and learning.

6. **Collaborating across boundaries.** The ability to identify boundaries and successfully navigate across and within them is critical to creating a culture of collaboration and efficiency.

7. **Continuous improvement.** Good behavioural objectives include continuous evaluation against internal and external benchmarks. The continual focus on improvement is as much a mindset, as a behaviour. The behavioural capabilities (learnable components) and traits (intrinsic and innate components) of the high-performing chairman are extensive. Behaviours will include facilitation, empathy (consideration of and relating to others, followers and leaders) and coaching; strategic thinking behaviours such as concept formation and information search; inspirational behaviours such as influence, building confidence and communication and performance-focussed behaviours such as proactivity and continuous improvement. Traits might include physical vitality, stamina, eagerness to accept responsibility, need for achievement, courage, self-confidence, assertiveness, and openness to new ideas."

The demand for these behaviours and traits will vary depending upon the mix and maturity of the business and the mix and maturity of other board members. But leadership research from as far back as the 1950s has shown that traits do not influence leadership ability as much as a person's ability to learn rapidly from and facilitate behavioural development in others. Behaviour is the clue to performance because it is learnable and therefore can evolve with the demands of the context. A chairman's behaviour must operate at number of levels—task, group and systemic. It is both the source and the result of an ability to mobilise others to share a vision of an anticipated future state of affairs, and a willingness to collaborate to bring it about (i.e. taking the long view), while being clearly mindful of immediate next steps.

The UK Corporate Governance Code—the contemporary role of the chairman defined

8.005   As a result of the work of the Cadbury and Hampel committees, the Higgs and Walker Reviews, and the FRC review in 2009 of the then Combined

Code, a more substantive role for the chairman is recognised in the UK Corporate Governance Code. Thus, for example:

Leadership

The UK Corporate Governance Code sets out the job of chairman in these terms:　　**8.006**

> "Main Principle A.3
> The chairman is responsible for leadership of the board and ensuring its effectiveness on all aspects of its role.
>
> Supporting Principle
> The chairman is responsible for setting the board's agenda and ensuring that adequate time is available for discussion of all agenda items, in particular strategic issues. The chairman should also promote a culture of openness and debate by facilitating the effective contribution of non-executive directors in particular and ensuring constructive relations between executive and non-executive directors."

Possibly the most important function of the chairman apart from the building of an effective board is the function of ensuring that in its deliberations at and outside board meetings the views of all directors are heard—especially the views of non-executive directors in challenging (constructively) the executive team, and especially ensuring that more reticent non-executive directors are challenged and encouraged to express their views. The most striking and depressing aspect of the banking failures of 2008/2009 was the way in which over powerful senior executives were able to dominate the board. Only the chairman in reality can orchestrate an atmosphere in the boardroom so that challenging views are freely aired and a real debate conducted. If (s)he fails to do that it must be questioned whether (s)he is up to the job.

The 2009 Walker Review expressed the role thus in respect of banks and other financial industry entities ("BOFIs"):

> "A key necessary element in the chairman's role will be to ensure that board agendas allow sufficient time and priority for issues of substance, with documentation and presentation designed to promote discussion of alternative approaches or outcomes as distinct from what may often be an undue pre-emption of board time on process matters. These have their priority, but must not be allowed by the chairman to crowd out board discussion and decision-taking on substance. NEDs should also have more opportunity to discuss matters without the presence of the executives, so that they can share their thinking and develop alternative views. This probably calls for more meetings before and after main board meetings. But this in turn

calls also for sensitive balance between the need for constructive challenge and the need for the whole board to work co-operatively in arriving at and endorsing the strategy for the company that is ultimately agreed."

Separation from role of CEO

8.007   Provision A.2.1 makes it clear that:

"the roles of chairman and chief executive should not be exercised by the same individual. The division of responsibilities should be set out in writing and agreed by the board."

Independence

8.008   Code Provision A.3.1 states: "The chairman should *on appointment* [author's emphasis] meet the independence criteria in B.1.1 below".

In a footnote to this provision it is stated that: "compliance or otherwise with this provision need only be reported for the year in which the appointment is made". The implication of this is that the chairman may at some point become non-independent within the meaning of the criteria and that adjustments may need to be made to the board and to any committees on which the chairman may sit which require "independence".

Chairman should not have been CEO

8.009   Code Provision A.3.1 also states that:

"a chief executive should not go on to be chairman of the same company. If exceptionally a board decides that a chief executive should become chairman, the board should consult major shareholders in advance and should set out its reasons to shareholders at the time of the appointment and in the next report."

The reason for this is that there have been instances where the chief executive has gone on to become chairman but has not been able to adapt to the role. Instead (s)he has dominated the new CEO with the result that the company loses a sense of direction.

However, in recent times there have been examples of companies which have (successfully it is submitted) elevated chief executives to the role of chairman, amongst which are Barclays Bank and HSBC, where Mr Matt Barrett and Mr Stephen Green, respectively, were appointed chairman, having each been chief executive. In line with the Code, both groups had to explain their decision to appoint from inside. Indeed, Barclays was the first to produce a "comply or explain" letter in 2003 to shareholders worried about Mr Barrett's appointment. It is perhaps significant that neither of these banks had to be rescued with public money in the 2007/2009 banking crisis.

Other commitments

Code Provision B.3.2 provides: **8.010**

"The terms and conditions of appointment of non-executive directors should be made available for inspection. The letter of appointment should set out the expected time commitment. Non-executive directors should undertake that they will have sufficient time to meet what is expected of them. Their other significant commitments should be disclosed to the board before appointment, with a broad indication of the time involved and the board should be informed of subsequent changes."

Information provider

Supporting Principle A.3 requires that: **8.011**

"the chairman is responsible for ensuring that the directors receive accurate, timely and clear information. The chairman should ensure effective communication with shareholders."

This responsibility is further developed in Supporting Principle B.5:

"Under the direction of the chairman, the company secretary's responsibilities include ensuring good information flows within the board and its committees and between senior management and non-executive directors, as well as facilitating induction and assisting with professional development as required."

Development and induction responsibilities

The chairman is made responsible under Supporting Principle B.4 to: **8.012**

"ensure that the directors continually update their skills and the knowledge and familiarity with the company required to fulfill their role both on the board and on board committees."

Code Provision B.4.2 requires that the chairman should regularly review and agree with each director their training and development needs.

In relation to induction, under Code Provision B.4.1:

> "the chairman should ensure that new directors receive a full, formal and tailored induction on joining the board. As part of this, directors should avail themselves of opportunities to meet major shareholders."

Evaluation and evaluation follow up action

8.013 The Higgs Review (11.24) stated:

> "The chairman has a key role in arranging the evaluation process for the board and with individual non-executive directors. Conduct of the evaluation by an external third party can bring objectivity to the process and its value should be recognised by a chairman. When the chairman's own performance is reviewed, an external third party or the senior independent director should act as facilitator."

The Code places responsibility for follow up after evaluation on the chairman.

Supporting Principle B.6 requires that:

> "The chairman should act on the results of the performance evaluation by recognising the weaknesses of the board and, where appropriate, proposing new members be appointed to the board or seeking the resignation of directors."

Consultation role with shareholders on directors' pay

8.014 One of the Supporting Principles to Main Principle D.2 states:

> "The chairman of the board should ensure that the company maintains contact as required with its principal shareholders about remuneration."

In recent times the controversy about executive directors' pay has involved a disproportionate amount of time being spent by chairmen in negotiations with larger investors in an attempt to head off an adverse vote on the remuneration report at the next AGM.[9] Nevertheless, it is recognised that it is for the chairman to do this job.

---

[9] See Ch.11 (Directors' Remuneration).

Chief intermediary between shareholders and directors

Principle E.1 (dialogue with shareholders) of the UK Corporate Governance   **8.015**
Code says:

> "There should be a dialogue with shareholders, based on mutual under-
> standing of objectives. The board as a whole has responsibility for ensuring
> that a satisfactory dialogue with shareholders takes place".

Among the supporting principles is stated the chairman's role in ensuring an
effective link with shareholders:

> "Whilst recognising that most shareholder contact is with the chief execu-
> tive and finance director, the chairman should ensure that all directors
> understand their major shareholders' issues and concerns."

Drafting role in the annual corporate governance statement

Paragraph 7 of the Preface to the UK Code exhorts chairmen to take per-   **8.016**
sonal responsibility for drafting the Leadership and Effectiveness passages of
the annual corporate governance statement. The language is striking:

> "Chairmen are encouraged to report personally in their annual statements
> how the principles relating to the role and effectiveness of the board (in
> Sections A and B of the new Code) have been applied. Not only will this
> give investors a clearer picture of the steps taken by boards to operate
> effectively but also, by providing fuller context, it may make investors
> more willing to accept explanations when a company chooses to explain
> rather than to comply with one or more provisions. Above all, the per-
> sonal reporting on governance by chairmen as the leaders of boards might
> be a turning point in attacking the fungus of 'boiler-plate' which is so
> often the preferred and easy option in sensitive areas but which is dead
> communication."

The conduct of meetings[10]

Although the modern role for a public company chairman is far wider than   **8.017**
simply the chairmanship of meetings, nevertheless, command of process
is important: "The effort made by a chairman to ensure that meetings are

---

[10] See also *Shackleton on the Law and Practice of Meetings*, Sweet and Maxwell, 2006, and Ch.17
(The Annual General Meeting).

properly conducted may well be the most valuable contribution he makes to the good of his company" (Stanley Dixon). This is perhaps an overstatement, but it does underline the importance of getting process right. In general terms, the constitutional documents of companies and case law make the chairman responsible for the conduct of meetings of *shareholders* and give him wide powers, but within a framework of rules about fairness and even-handedness as between shareholders.

Thus, for example, in the Model Articles of Association for Public Companies introduced alongside the CA 2006,[11] art.43 states:

"Errors and disputes

(1)   No objection may be raised to the qualification of any person voting at a general meeting except at the meeting or adjourned meeting at which the vote objected to is tendered, and every vote not disallowed at the meeting is valid.

(2)   Any such objection shall be referred to the chairman of the meeting whose decision shall be final and binding."

In relation to *board* meetings, although the ability of a board to elect a chairman of meetings is invariably contained in articles of association, neither articles nor, indeed, case law, lay down any rules or responsibilities governing the chairman's conduct of board meetings. The paradox, of course, is that contemporary corporate governance places the chairman at the heart of the *board*, not the shareholders.

More about board building and shareholder relationships—the wider contemporary role[12]

8.018   In the context of contemporary corporate governance, the role of chairman has become crucial to the governance of a company even if that role is unsupported by law and depends entirely on usage and consent and best practice.

Building a board

8.019   In Sir Adrian Cadbury's book *Corporate Governance and Chairmanship*[13] he says:

"Next comes the chairman's responsibility for the composition of the board and the way in which it operates. Directing an enterprise through a

---

[11] See fn 5 above.
[12] See also the Unilever job description set out in fn 3 above.
[13] OUP, 2002, p.109.

board is a more difficult form of governance than is commonly supposed. It is a fundamental error to regard committees of any kind as natural forms of governance or to believe that if you sit competent people of goodwill around the boardroom table, they will function as an effective board. Boards have to be pieced together and then made to work. Building an effective board takes time and patience on the part of board members, but especially on the part of their chairman. It is the chairman's task to turn a group of capable individuals into an effective board team."

The composition of the board

As described in Ch.3 (The Board and its Structure), the UK Corporate **8.020** Governance Code imposes a number of basic constraints on the composition of the board which infers a basic, minimal configuration as follows:

(a)   chairman (independent (on appointment), non-executive);

(b)   chief executive;

(c)   except for sub-FTSE 350 companies at least half the board excluding the chairman, should comprise non-executive directors, "determined by the board" to be independent (Provision B.1.2).

Add to that the requirements that the audit committee must have at least one independent non-executive with "recent and relevant financial experience", and that one of the independent non-executive directors should be the "lead independent director", and these requisites shape the overall size and composition of the board.

However, these constraints imposed by the Code are only a part of the story. In reality, a skilful chairman and CEO will be looking to build a board which stands the best chance of delivering commercial success and enhance shareholder value; and have values with which the chairman as guardian of corporate values feels comfortable. Clearly, size is a relevant factor. Sir Adrian Cadbury cites with approval research suggesting that eight–ten members "will allow for effective debate and it is the job of chairman to restrain the verbosity of the few and encourage the participation of the majority".

Diversity is another factor not for its own sake, but rather to ensure that corporate policy is tested against informed views of well-qualified people from diverse backgrounds. Gender has to be an issue in that context and the current indefensible imbalance on boards of white males must surely lead to regulation to cure unless chairmen take early radical action to improve the diversity of boards.[14]

---

[14] Supporting Principle B.2 of the UK Code requires that appointments must recognise the value of diversity "including gender". See also paras 10.15 et seq. of the Higgs Report (App.2 of this

Perhaps the essential quality which a chairman should look for is independence of mind, coupled with the courage to test executive thinking in a rigorous, fair and open-minded way.

The chairman will also, of course, need to have at the board table a range of skills at executive and non-executive levels which (s)he and the CEO will regard as important to the development of the company.[15] It would be inconceivable for a UK company not to have a finance director as a full board member. Subject to overall suitability, a technology company will also have on the board its director of technology; a manufacturing company will have its director of production as a member; a company which is seeking to grow by (that most dangerous route) acquisition, must have on board experienced directors who understand the dangers and benefits of acquisitions, and the skills and experience to enable the board to be satisfied that the post-acquisition execution delivers the benefits claimed by management for the acquisitions.

Higgs also attached great importance to the need to ensure that non-executive directors have the time and commitment necessary to fulfil the job (see Ch.5 (Directors—The Non-Executive Director)).

Relationship with the CEO

8.021   In research conducted for the Higgs Review undertaken by Dr Terry McNulty of the University of Leeds and Dr John Roberts and Dr Philip Styles of the Judge Institute of Management, University of Cambridge[16] (including interviews with 40 directors of FTSE 350 boards), they commented as follows on the relationship between the chairman and the chief executive:

> "There is a rather minimalist version of the relationship that seems to be quite widespread, where a non-executive chairman spends little time in the office and places the onus of responsibility on the chief executive to contact him if 'big issues' arise. We believe that such a minimalist view of the role can effectively undermine the potential contribution of the non-executives. Other chairmen, however, take a much more proactive and engaged view of their role and relationship with the chief executive. An important part of this more developed relationship is very strong communication between

book) for particulars of his diversity research and also the Tyson Report on the recruitment and development of non-executive directors, June 2003.

[15] In a research paper published by Lintstock in December 2009 commissioned by the All Party Parliamentary Corporate Governance Group entitled "*Board oversight in difficult times*" it was clear that more emphasis after the financial crisis would, be place on sectoral expertise in the appointment of new non-executive directors (31 out of 50 respondents; financial expertise being the most sought after expertise: 43 out of 50 respondents).

[16] "*Creating accountability within the board: The work of the effective non-executive director*" *http://www.dti.gov.uk/cld/non_exec_review/pdfs/stilesreport.pdf.*

the two to ensure that as one chairman put it, 'the chairman and chief executive should be as one'.

> 'I have disciplined myself (with my chief executive) to have sessions, to actually put it in the diary—you know we will meet on this day every month to review all the major issues that are currently extant. It doesn't mean to say we only meet once a month because we just walk down a passage maybe once a day, but we meet formally to ensure that nothing is dropped in the communications. It's like a marriage in a curious way, I mean both parties have got to be sensitive to the characteristics of the other.'

In the most developed relationships there is often daily contact between the two and this allows for much greater reciprocal understanding. It is not just the fact of meeting very regularly but also the quality of communication that matters. It is essential that the chief executive has complete confidence that the chairman is not seeking to be a surrogate chief executive.

> 'I think the relationship has worked well and really what you need is a supporter so that you do not want someone who wants to do your job. I think that is a really critical thing in a business; you need one leader.'

Given that many chairmen have recently been active executives then this particular boundary often needs to be reinforced.

Where the relationship between the two seems to work best is where there is a valuable mix of different skills and experiences such that, when combined, the two complement each other's strengths and weaknesses. One particular area where the chairman can be particularly helpful to the chief executive is in relation to issues that concern the executive team. In the most developed relationship, the chairman meets not only with the chief executive but also spends time with all the senior executives. There is a danger in these relationships that there will be some blurring of executive and non-executive responsibilities, so here, again, the conduct of the chairman is vital in ensuring that such contact does not threaten the chief executive's responsibilities or damage trust between them.

> 'I suppose I would describe my relationship with the CEO as that of coach and athlete. That is the way I see it. It is my job to get the best performance out of him and out of the other executive directors. It is not my job to instruct, tell, do, whatever. I'm looking for them to run the company but for me to help them.'

What does a chairman get from the relationship? Several of those we interviewed argued that as chairman it was important not to crave the limelight and to be able 'to take pleasure in the executives' achievements'. For the chairman a developed relationship is vital not only as a way of supporting the performance of the chief executive and executives, but also as a source of knowledge and information about what is happening in the company.

Compared with other non-executives, the chairman should have a much stronger exposure and understanding of the company and its senior executives."

The 2009 Walker Review expressed the relationship in these terms (para.4.15):

"In all this, the relationship between chairman and CEO will be of critical importance. In a normal and healthy board situation, the chairman/CEO relationship should be based on mutual understanding and respect, and should be mutually supportive. But if the relationship is uncritically close, there is the risk of separation from and a degree of isolation of the NEDs; whereas a situation of persistent tension or disagreement between chairman and CEO may mean that, ultimately, one or both should leave the board. The CEO will need to establish and maintain his authority in the company – and failure to do so may mean that he is not up to the job. But if the embedding of authority, perhaps based on some early success or reputation, makes the CEO become effectively unchallengeable (and possibly a control freak), the CEO will themself be a major source of risk and will probably need to be removed. Albeit with the support of the board, this would be a matter ultimately for the chairman."

Relationship with the lead independent non-executive director

8.022   Code Provision A.4.1 states:

"The board should appoint one of the independent non-executive directors to be the senior independent director to provide a sounding board for the chairman and to serve as an intermediary for the other directors when necessary. The senior independent director should be available to shareholders if they have concerns which contact through the normal channels of chairman, chief executive or other executive directors has failed to resolve or for which such contact is inappropriate."

When the Higgs Review came out he gave a role to the senior independent director which was of concern to many as undermining the position of the chairman. However, the version of the then Combined Code published in July 2003 made it clear that the senior independent director should only be available to shareholders if contact through the "normal channels" of the chairman, etc. had failed to resolve concerns (former Provision A.3.3). It may be helpful in understanding the role, perhaps, to think of the lead independent director as deputy chairman. Clearly it is important that the chairman should be able to regard the lead independent non-executive director as a colleague and not as a threat.

Relationships with shareholders

Sir Adrian Cadbury states in his book[17]:   **8.023**

"Representing the company to the shareholders is a good illustration of the need to define the audience. Shareholders can be divided into two distinct groups from the outset—private individuals and institutions ... There are two other shareholder audiences, which chairmen also need to keep in mind. Employee shareholders are one, and they are becoming an increasingly important group in most companies. They are interested along with the shareholders in the profitability of the business as a whole, but they also have a particular interest in the activities on the part of the company to which they belong. In meeting their special interests, care has to be taken that they do not receive significantly more information internally, than is generally made available to shareholders externally.

The second audience is that of potential shareholders. Companies benefit from having as wide a spread of shareholders as possible, both geographically and as between types of shareholder."

Sir Adrian goes on to describe relationships with the financial institutions and, specifically, the three main groups which comprise financial institutions, namely, financial analysts, institutional shareholders, and sources of finance.

"The relationship between chairman and the chief executives and their company's largest shareholders is one which needs to be fostered on a continuing basis. Relationships cannot be established instantly, when the need arises from a company's point of view. The contacts which encompass this and the larger institutional investors will far as possible be direct and personal, involving chairmen and their senior colleagues."

Conclusion

In App.11 to this book there is set out the "Guidance for the Chairman" sug-   **8.024**
gested in the Higgs Review.[18] In it he summarises the role as follows:

"The chairman is pivotal in creating the conditions for overall board and individual director effectiveness, both inside and outside the board room."

---

[17] *Corporate Governance and Chairmanship.* OUP, 2002, p.132.
[18] ICSA was at the time of preparing this book for publication revising the Higgs precedents and so reference should be made to the ICSA and FRC websites for the up-to-date position.

Chapter 9

The Company Secretary

Introduction

The Cadbury Report stated that the company secretary "has a key role to **9.001** play in ensuring that board procedures are both followed and regularly reviewed". It pointed out that the chairman of the board looked to the company secretary for guidance on what his or her responsibilities are under the rules and regulations to which (s)he is subject, and on how those responsibilities should be discharged.

In view of the position which the secretary occupies in governance, this chapter summarises the key features of the role and responsibilities of the company secretary.

The company secretary and governance

The ideal

A Supporting Principle to Main Principle B.5 of the UK Corporate **9.002** Governance Code states:

"The company secretary should be responsible for advising the board through the chairman on all governance matters."

In para.11.29 of the Higgs Review he says:

"The role of company secretary is important . . . in supporting the executive performance of non-executive directors. The value of a good company secretary was a recurring theme amongst consultees. Ultimately the value of a company secretary's contribution will be determined by the calibre of the individual concerned."

It is crucial to safeguard the integrity of the position, so that their impartiality is not compromised. All the board also need a clear understanding of the role of the company secretary.

Higgs goes on to point out that in some companies, particularly smaller ones, the roles of company secretary and finance director are combined. Higgs reported that around 40 per cent of companies outside the FTSE 350 combine the roles:

> "There are obvious tensions in this in the context of impartiality and information provision. It is therefore desirable for larger companies, who are able, to separate the roles and for smaller companies with limited resources to recognise the potential for conflict of interest and to build 'Chinese walls' between the roles, by ensuring that information received in one capacity is not used for other purposes."

A specimen job description for the corporate governance role of the company secretary has been suggested by ICSA.[1]

The UK Corporate Governance Code

The role and appointment and removal

9.003 Provision B.5.2 of the UK Corporate Governance Code states:

> "All directors should have access to the advice and services of the company secretary, who is responsible to the board for ensuring that board procedures are complied with. Both the appointment and removal of the company secretary should be a matter for the board as a whole."

Observance of the UK Corporate Governance Code and governance generally

9.004 A supporting Principle to Main Principle B.5 (information and support) states:

> "The company secretary should be responsible for advising the board through the chairman on all governance matters."

Although the primary responsibility for ensuring the observance of the UK Corporate Governance Code and other rules of corporate governance must

---

[1] *http://www.icsa.org.uk*>Guidance.

vest in the board and in particular in the chairman, in practice it will be the company secretary who organises the process.

Paragraphs 11.31 and 11.32 of the Higgs Review state:

"The effectiveness of the company secretary will hinge on the nature of their working relationship with the chairman. The company secretary should be accountable to the board through the chairman on all governance matters. Though there may be certain matters on which the company secretary reports to the chief executive, this should not undermine their overall responsibility to the board on all matters of corporate governance.

It is crucial to safeguard the integrity of the position so that their impartiality is not compromised. All the board need a clear understanding of the role of the company secretary."

Information flow, induction procedures and professional development

A Supporting Principle to Main Principle B.5 of the Code (information and support) states: **9.005**

"Under the direction of the chairman, the company secretary's responsibilities include ensuring good information flows within the board and its committees and between senior management and non-executive directors, as well as facilitating induction and assisting with professional development as required."

Chapter 11 of the Higgs Review ("the well-informed non-executive director" and see App.2 of this book) devotes paras 11.25 to 11.34 under the heading "Information and the company secretary". In para.11.29 he says:

"The role of the company secretary is important in the provision of information and more widely in supporting the effective performance of non-executive directors. The value of a good company secretary was a recurring theme amongst consultees . . . At their best, as a provider of independent impartial guidance and advice, a good company secretary is uniquely well placed to assist a non-executive director and to support the chairman in ensuring good use is made of the non-executive directors.

The company secretary has a wide range of responsibilities . . . the facilitation of good information flows, provision of impartial information and guidance on board procedures, legal requirements and corporate governance, together with best practice developments. They can also play a key part in facilitating induction and professional development for board members. To ensure good communication within the board and its committees, it is good practice for the company secretary, or their designee, to be secretary to all board committees."

Need for a secretary

9.006   Under s.271 CA 2006, "a public company must have a secretary", but under CA 2006 s.270 a private company is not required to have a company secretary.

Under CA 2006 s.280, in the case of a public company, a provision (e.g. the articles of association) requiring or authorising a thing to be done by or to a director *and* the secretary is not satisfied by its being done by or to the same person acting both as director and as, or in place of, the secretary.

Qualifications of secretaries of public companies

9.007   Under CA 2006 s.273 the directors of a public company must "take all reasonable steps" to secure that the secretary of the company:

- is a person who appears to them to have the requisite knowledge and experience to discharge the functions of secretary;

- has one or more of the following qualifications:

    - has been a secretary of a public company for at least three of the five years immediately preceding his or her appointment;
    - is a member of any one of seven professional bodies (for example, the Institute of Chartered Secretaries and Administrators);
    - is a qualified barrister or solicitor (or advocate in Scotland);
    - is a person who by reason of having held any other position or being a member of any other body "appears to the directors to be capable of discharging the functions of secretary of the company".

Legal status

9.008   Although the legal status of the company secretary is nowhere stated in legislation, it is generally accepted that the secretary is the chief administrative officer of the company and therefore has, as regards matters concerned with the administration of the company, ostensible authority to enter into contracts on behalf of the company. The extent of those contracts relate to the employment of staff and the ordering of office machinery and stationery, and similar matters.

The Court of Appeal has held[2] that even where authority is not expressly conferred nor conferred by implication, the secretary is nevertheless the

---

[2] *Panorama Developments v Fidelis Furnishing* [1971] 2 Q.B. 711.

company's chief administrative officer and has ostensible authority in day to-day administrative matters. Thus, in that case, the company was bound by the secretary's act of ordering hire cars. Lord Denning said that the secretary:

> "is an officer of the company with extensive duties and responsibilities ... he is no longer merely a clerk. He regularly makes representations on behalf of the company and enters into contracts on its behalf which come within the day-to-day running of the company's business, so much so he may be regarded or held out as having authority to do such things on behalf of the company. He is certainly entitled to sign contracts connected with the administrative side of a company's affairs such as employing staff and ordering cars and so forth. All such matters now come within the ostensible authority of a company secretary."

As an "officer" of the company the company secretary is therefore included within the meaning of "officer" where it appears in the Companies Acts, and therefore particular care should be taken in relation to those parts of the Companies Acts where "officers" are liable to be prosecuted.

Key qualities

The ideal company secretary should possess at least the following qualities. **9.009**

Technical competence

The requirement of CA 2006 as to the qualifications for the company secre- **9.010** tary of a public company emphasises that (s)he will need to have knowledge and experience of company legislation, the requirements of the UK Corporate Governance Code, the Listing Rules and the Takeover Code, knowledge of the various Guidelines (directors' remuneration, corporate social responsibility, share dilution, voting, etc.) from institutional shareholders and institutional bodies such as the ABI and the NAPF, and a working familiarity (if (s) he is not also finance director) of accounting standards and principles.

Strength of personality

The company secretary is sometimes called "the conscience of the company". **9.011** That is to say, (s)he is expected to try to put forward the view of what the company "ought" to do over a wide range of ethical issues, including corporate governance. The putting forward of those views frequently requires great courage, because of overwhelming commercial pressures or a chief executive with a forceful personality. It is not reasonable to expect the company secretary to put his or her livelihood on the line, so boards of directors should encourage and support the expression of the "ethical" view, by the company secretary.

An ability to achieve good communication with and between the board

9.012   Clearly, if the company secretary is to have influence, (s)he must be able to communicate with and be heard by the board.

Good communication with outside advisers

9.013   Very often, the company secretary is the crucial link between the company and its merchant bank, accountants and solicitors. It is essential that (s)he is able to assess their competence, to co-ordinate their activities and to instil a sense of confidence in the advisers so that they feel free to discuss the affairs of the company with him or her.

Troubleshooting

9.014   The secretary must be unafraid to warn and advise the board and to act as a troubleshooter.

Integrity

9.015   The secretary must have the qualities of openness and integrity. (S)he must be trusted by everyone.

Management of key relationships

9.016   The company secretary stands at the centre of a web of relationships (some external and some internal), and it is the job of the company secretary to manage those relationships in a way that facilitates the business of the company. The particular relationships are with the following:

    (a)   chairman;

    (b)   chief executive and other executive directors;

    (c)   non-executive directors;

    (d)   the press;

    (e)   investment bankers and bankers;

(f)   lawyers;

(g)   auditors;

(h)   Companies House;

(i)   UK Listing Authority.

Key duties

There is no exhaustive definition which defines the secretary's duties. The **9.017**
Cadbury Schweppes 2005 report and accounts describes the duties of the
group company secretary as follows:

> "The group secretary is responsible for advising the board on all corpo-
> rate governance matters, ensuring that all board procedures are followed,
> ensuring good information flow, facilitating induction programmes for
> directors and assisting with directors continuing professional develop-
> ment. All directors have direct access to the advice and services of the
> group secretary and the appointment of [   ] as group secretary on
> [   ], following the retirement of [   ] was subject to the approval of the
> board as a whole. Any questions share owners may have on corporate gov-
> ernance matters, policies or procedures should be addressed to the group
> secretary at our registered office."

The Institute of Chartered Secretaries and Administrators ("ICSA") includes
the following in its list of core duties.

Board meetings

The secretary is responsible for co-ordinating, convening, running and minut- **9.018**
ing board meetings, and for being generally aware of the implementation or
otherwise of board decisions. (S)he must produce agendas with the help of
the chairman or chief executive, (s)he must attend and minute board meetings
and s(he) must maintain the records of resolutions and meetings of directors
which are required by CA 2006 s.248 and of resolutions and meetings of the
company which are required to be kept by CA 2006 ss.355 and 359.

General meetings

The secretary must assist in the settlement and co-ordination of documen- **9.019**
tation for circulation to shareholders, ensuring that the correct procedures
under the CA 2006 are followed and that meetings are minuted.

The annual report and accounts and annual general meeting

9.020 It is the job of the company secretary to assist the chairman in the preparation of the annual report, including, in particular, the governance disclosure statement under Listing Rule 9.8.6R (see Ch.2 (The Regulatory Regime)), to work with the board in the preparation of the annual report and to work with the auditors and the finance director of the company in the preparation of the annual accounts. The objective is to draw these together in the annual report and financial statements to be sent, with the notice of the annual general meeting, to shareholders each year. Since the London Stock Exchange requires that a "calendar" of company dates is supplied to the Stock Exchange for publication in advance of each financial year comprising the date of the announcement of the interim results, the payment of the interim dividend, the announcement of the annual results, the date of the annual general meeting and the preliminary date of the payment of the final dividend, it is a serious embarrassment if, due to inefficiencies in the company secretary's office, these dates are not observed. In the case of the annual report and accounts, together with the preliminary announcement, these need to be drawn together, under a process which starts at the end of the preceding financial year, for approval by the board. These are then dispatched to shareholders, so that they receive at least 21 clear days' notice (in practice, 24 days). See now Provision E.2.4 of the UK Corporate Governance, which requires 20 *working days'* [author's emphasis] notice of the annual general meeting. That process requires a great deal of co-ordination and planning.

The company secretary is the person primarily responsible for the organisational aspects of the annual general meeting. For a detailed discussion of the annual general meeting, see Ch.17.

Dividends

9.021 The secretary will also be responsible for the supervision of the registrars for the payment of dividends.

Constitution[3]

9.022 The company secretary must ensure that the company complies with the constitution of the company as amended from time to time, and must ensure that the memorandum and articles are kept up to date.

---

[3] See fn 39, Ch.4 (Directors—Duties and Liabilities) for definition.

General compliance

The secretary is, overall, responsible for ensuring compliance by the company **9.023** with its legal obligations. This does not mean, of course, that every single contract has to be reviewed by the company secretary and its compliance monitored, but rather that the directors and managers are aware of legislation which affects the company (for example, environmental protection legislation, health and safety legislation, product liability legislation, etc.) and must devise procedures for ensuring as far as practicable that the company's legal obligations are fulfilled.

Stock Exchange requirements

The secretary must supervise compliance with FSA Listing Rules the require- **9.024** ments of the Panel on Takeovers and Mergers,[4] oversee the release of authorised information to the public and the London Stock Exchange, and ensure the security of unreleased price-sensitive information.[5]

Statutory registers

The secretary must maintain the registers, amongst other registers, of members **9.025** and debenture holders (CA 2006 ss.113 and 743), charges (Companies Act 1985 ss.288–290), the register of directors and information relating to directors (CA 2006 ss.162–167), the register of interests in shares and debentures under CA 2006 s.808; (s)he must keep copies of directors' service contracts (CA 2006 ss.228 and 229).

Statutory returns

The secretary must file information with the Registrar of Companies to **9.026** report changes regarding the company or to comply with requirements for periodic filing; his or her duties also include the preparation and submission of annual returns, and the registration of charges.

Reports and accounts

The secretary must co-ordinate the publication and distribution of the com- **9.027** pany's annual report and accounts in conjunction with internal and external advisers.

---

[4] Now given statutory authority and powers under CA 2006 Pt 22.
[5] See paras 19.011 et seq. in Ch.19 (Communicating and Engagement with Shareholders).

Share registration

9.028   The secretary must deal with transfers and shareholders' queries, and issuing share and debenture certificates.

Shareholder monitoring

9.029   The secretary should monitor movements on the register of members, enquire of members as to beneficial ownership of holdings and keep a register of material share interests (CA 2006 Pt 22).

Share and capital issues

9.030   The secretary should supervise the implementation of changes in the company's shares and loan capital structure.

Acquisitions and disposals

9.031   The secretary should assist with corporate acquisitions and disposals, including the instruction of professional advisers, and ensure the effectiveness of all documentation and due diligence disclosures.

Non-executive directors

9.032   The secretary should make information available to non-executive directors and facilitate communication with other members of the board and organise the induction process. (See Ch.5 (Directors—The Non-Executive Director)).

Company seal

9.033   The secretary must ensure custody and proper use of the company seal.

Registered office

9.034   The secretary must administer and deal with correspondence at the registered office.

Subsidiary companies

The secretary must maintain a record of the group's structure and ensure that all subsidiaries comply with legal and procedural requirements.   **9.035**

General additional duties

It is common for the company secretary to be involved to a greater or lesser degree in the following responsibilities: **9.036**

(a)   the in-house legal function and liaison and instruction of outside legal advice;

(b)   the accounting function;

(c)   internal audit;

(d)   personnel;

(e)   Financial Services and Markets Act 2000 compliance (possibly as compliance officer);

(f)   insurance;

(g)   office and premises administration.

Liabilities

As an officer of the company, the secretary may be liable, with the directors, to default fines and other penalties where the Companies Acts refer to "officers". The Insolvency Act 1986, for example, gives the court sweeping powers in the course of the winding-up of a company, to award damages against every officer of a company (including the secretary) in respect of any misfeasance or breach of trust in relation to the company.   **9.037**

As an officer the company secretary can apply to the court for relief under CA 2006 s.1157 in relation to any liability in respect of negligence, default, breach of duty or breach of trust, although the secretary will not normally be liable for breach of trust or misfeasance if committed by the directors, even if this is committed with his or her knowledge. There has to be a process of actual involvement in the commission of the breach of duty.

Conclusion

The scope of the modern company secretary's role imposes very heavy responsibilities. The governance "debate" can only add to these responsibilities,   **9.038** and it is a real question for listed company boards to determine the level of resources that should go into investment in staffing and training of company secretaries and support staff. Failure adequately to invest in the company secretary function may result in a shortfall of standards of compliance generally, and governance in particular.

Chapter 10

Board Meetings—The Basic Rules

Introduction

This chapter in mainly concerned to outline the more important of the basic **10.001** rules and procedures relating to board meetings on the basis that board meetings are at the heart both of good governance and good commercial decisions; and "due process" provides the platform for effective board meetings. However, before doing so it is important to step outside the procedural context and talk about the function and character of effective board meetings.

Following the failures of governance in the banking sector leading to the crises of 2007/2009 the Institute of Chartered Secretaries and Administrators ("ICSA") produced a report in 2009 on boardroom behaviours[1] in which it stated:

> "... appropriate boardroom behaviours are an essential component of best practice corporate governance; and ... the absence of guidance on appropriate boardroom behaviours represents a structural weakness in our current system ..."

The function of board meetings

There are two principal functions: **10.002**

- to be the formal occasion recognised and regulated by company law for the valid making of decisions which bind the company;

- to be the forum in which the directors on equal terms can debate, determine and drive forward the long-term strategy for the company; and listen to, constructively challenge and hold to account the

---

[1] *Boardroom behaviours: A report prepared for Sir David Walker by the Institute of Chartered Secretaries and Administrators* see *http://www.icsa.org.uk* search boardroom behaviours.

executive directors, and in particular, the chief executive whether in terms of the long term strategy or short term "events" which need rapid decisions at board level.

The characteristics of effective board meetings[2]

10.003   It is suggested that the following features characterise successful board meetings:

- above all, a chairman[3] who;
    - sets a relevant agenda for the meeting;
    - takes time to discuss the agenda in advance with the chief executive, the company secretary and relevant non-executive directors;
    - controls the meeting effectively in terms of time management and allocation whilst ensuring that all voices are heard;
    - ensures that decisions are arrived at which can be clearly understood by those who have to execute them;

- informative and relevant board papers which include assessment of risks are circulated at least seven days in advance of the meeting if at all practicable. This is primarily the job of the chairman, chief executive and company secretary each of whom has a role to play in ensuring that all members of the board are adequately briefed so as to take informed decisions, but are not so overwhelmed with paperwork that it is difficult to see the wood for the trees;

- board meetings are held regularly between eight and eleven times each year;

- a high attendance record by directors;

- thorough preparation by the directors for each meeting: "the worst sound a chairman hears at the start of a board meeting is the sound of envelopes being torn open".[4]

- whilst the chairman, chief executive and other executive directors will inevitably play a large part in the proceedings it is essential that all directors are encouraged by the chairman to speak and in particular those non-executive directors who have some relevant expertise or particular responsibility at committee level;

---

[2] ICSA published in October 2009 a Guidance Note (ref 090928) called "specimen board meeting etiquette". See *http://www.icsa.org.uk*.
[3] For a fuller treatment of the role of the chairman see Ch.8 (The Chairman).
[4] Baroness Hogg, 2003.

- there should be a spirit of openness and candour so that constructive criticism and robust debate can take place. It may not be possible to agree every issue, and there should not be a policy of reaching agreement at any price.[5] A good chairman will be willing to have a "second bite" at an issue at the next board meeting if further consideration or information is needed. However, the board has a responsibility guided by firm chairmanship to try to reach a consensus which enables the executive team to implement clear policies;

- draft minutes are prepared by the company secretary, agreed with the chairman and circulated within 48 hours of the end of the meeting if at all possible, before recollections fade and to enable decisions to be implemented which accurately reflect board decisions.

Basic rules

Delegated authority for the board to run the company

Most companies have articles with wording similar to art.3 of the Model Articles of Association for Public Companies published under the CA 2006[6] as follows **10.004**

"3. Directors' general authority
Subject to the articles, the directors are responsible for the management of the company's business, for which purpose they may exercise all the powers of the company."

The board can delegate to committees

Other articles provide for the delegation of directors' powers to committees in the terms similar to the following[7]: **10.005**

"5.—(1) Subject to the articles, the directors may delegate any of the powers which are conferred on them under the articles—
(a) to such person or committee;
(b) by such means (including by power of attorney);
(c) to such an extent;

---

[5] UK Corporate Governance Code Provision A.4.3 says that "where directors have concerns which cannot be resolved about the running of the company or a proposed action, they should ensure that their concerns are recorded in the board minutes".
[6] Companies (Model Articles) Regulations 2008.
[7] Companies (Model Articles) Regulations 2008.

(d) in relation to such matters or territories; and
(e) on such terms and conditions;
as they think fit."

"Committees[8]
6.—(1) Committees to which the directors delegate any of their powers must follow procedures which are based as far as they are applicable on those provisions of the articles which govern the taking of decisions by directors.
(2) The directors may make rules of procedure for all or any committees, which prevail over rules derived from the articles if they are not consistent with them."

It is pursuant to powers such as these that the committees required by the UK Corporate Governance Code, namely, the audit committee, the remuneration committee and the nomination committee are established.

Frequency of board meetings

10.006   UK Corporate Governance Code Provision A.1.1 states: "The board should meet sufficiently regularly to discharge its duties effectively".

UK Corporate Governance Code Provision A.1.2 includes the requirement that the annual report should set out the number of meetings of the board and committees of the board and individual attendance by directors.

It would be usual for board meetings of most listed companies to be held 10 times a year at roughly four-week intervals.

Notice of meetings

10.007   The Cadbury Report (para.4.23) stated that:

"the basic procedural requirements are that the board should meet regularly, with due notice of the issues to be discussed supported by the necessary paperwork, and should record its conclusion."

Unless a company's articles provide otherwise, every member of a board is entitled to be given notice of a board meeting. Failure to give notice to all directors will invalidate decisions taken at the meeting. See also para.10.009 below ("Paper meetings") on this topic in relation to the 2009 Inspectors' report into the affairs of MG Rover. The question sometimes arises as to

---

[8] Companies (Model Articles) Regulations 2008.

whether, on the subject of, for example, the dismissal of the chief executive, which is a matter which ought normally to be dealt with by way of resolution of the board, there is any need for the chief executive (her/himself also a director) to be given notice of the meeting. The answer is that (s)he must be given notice and failure to give notice will result in an invalid board meeting.

As the valid exercise of directors' powers can only take place at a board meeting of which due notice has been given and at which a quorum is present[9] it is important that "due notice" is given.

Model art.8[10] provides as follows:

"8. Calling a directors' meeting

(1) Any director may call a directors' meeting.

(2) The company secretary must call a directors' meeting if a director so requests.

(3) A directors' meeting is called by giving notice of the meeting to the directors.

(4) Notice of any directors' meeting must indicate—
    (a) its proposed date and time;
    (b) where it is to take place; and
    (c) if it is anticipated that directors participating in the meeting will not be in the same place, how it is proposed that they should communicate with each other during the meeting.

(5) Notice of a directors' meeting must be given to each director, but need not be in writing.

(6) Notice of a directors' meeting need not be given to directors who waive their entitlement to notice of that meeting, by giving notice to that effect to the company not more than 7 days after the date on which the meeting is held. Where such notice is given after the meeting has been held, that does not affect the validity of the meeting, or of any business conducted at it."

Agenda and board papers

In practice, well-run companies take trouble in the drawing up of an agenda prior to a board meeting, and "best practice" would indicate that in the larger companies, the chairman and the secretary will take responsibility for drawing up the agenda after consulting the chief executive and relevant non-executive directors. Supporting board papers should also be attached, in accordance with Main Principle B.5 of the UK Corporate Governance Code and Supporting Principles, so that directors can come to a board meeting informed of the issues. (See also Ch.3 (The Board and its Structure), **10.008**

---

[9] *Re Haycraft Gold Reduction and Mining Co* [1900] 2 Ch. 230.
[10] See the Companies (Model Articles) Regulations 2008.

para.3.025 for further comment on the quality of the information which should be supplied to the board.)

Where the business of the meeting comprises a formal legal exercise, such as the acquisition of another company or the approval of a prospectus, then the company's advisors will prepare draft minutes in advance by way of a formal agenda.

"Paper meetings"—The Phoenix/Rover saga

10.009 This is the expression sometimes given to describe alleged board meetings where the paperwork suggests that a meeting has taken place (minutes and even the signature of a chairman) but in reality no such meeting has taken place. There is no such thing as a valid "paper meeting" in that sense. Any purported resolutions are ineffective. The articles of association may, however, allow valid resolutions of the board if signed by all directors[11] or for the valid passing of resolutions by electronic means or on the telephone.

There are also occasions when draft minutes are prepared in advance of the meeting in order to make sure that the correct resolutions are passed and the correct business conducted, usually in the context of the carrying out of a formal exercise, such as a prospectus or capital raising exercise. It is sometimes tempting to "take the minutes as read". However, this is an incorrect procedure. The minutes should be read in full and the resolutions passed correctly, usually by majority vote of those present and voting.

Perhaps the "low point" in recent times in relation to board meeting procedure was the insolvent group known popularly as "MG Rover" the parent company of which was called "Phoenix Venture Holdings Limited". In the 2009 Inspectors' report into the affairs of the group commissioned by the then Department of Trade and Industry[12] attention was drawn to the fact that on many occasions notice of board meetings of companies within the group was given to some only of the directors, whilst minutes recorded directors as present some of whom were out of the country![13]

---

[11] See, for example, Model arts 17 and 18.

[12] *http://www.bis.gov.uk/files/file52783.pdf*, Ch.XXII.

[13] The following extract from Ch.XXII of the Inspectors' report will give the flavour:

> "Mr Edwards told us that he was not familiar with the idea that all the directors of a company needed to be given notice of a board meeting. When giving evidence about Project Platinum, Mr Stephenson suggested: 'In a transaction of this type, if a company is doing it and a number of board directors are doing it, and there is a requirement, for example, for a quick impromptu board meeting to rubber stamp it, my experience in other companies would be the board members delegated to do it would call that meeting and actually they would not invite all the other board members. You just have to have a quorum of members present'. 5. Mr Beddow said that he did not think all directors needed to be given notice of all meetings; he explained that he would not have expected to be invited to meetings 'which just require perhaps a couple of people there to endorse documents or bank mandates or whatever' or 'even necessarily if there were items that didn't directly impinge on [him] or the business as a whole that may have been specific to some function or activity; engineering, for example'."

Quorum and what constitutes a "meeting"

Most articles of association provide that the quorum for the transaction **10.010** of business of directors may be fixed by the directors and unless so fixed at any other number shall be two. Some articles provide that a quorum can be one. Clearly in the case of the single director company, that is sensible, but it would be generally speaking undesirable, for obvious reasons, for that provision to be inserted in the case of companies where the boards are larger than one, unless there is also provision built into the articles for waiver of the quorum provisions in writing by all the directors (which may include facsimile or email authority).

The question is sometimes raised as to what constitutes a "meeting"—is it necessary for two or more people to be physically in the same place at the same time in order to constitute a "meeting"? The Court of Appeal has held[14] that a shareholders' meeting would be properly constituted where there were fully functional mutual audio-visual links between the members of a company, in other words, where everyone can be seen and heard and can speak, and it is thought that a similar approach would be taken in relation to board meetings.[15]

However, it is common for articles to make provision for board meetings to be held by telephone communication, including a telephone conference call and a video conferencing facility.

In practical terms, it is desirable for at least two directors to be in a single location at the same time, connected to other directors by way of conference call or video. Facilities should be such so as to enable contributions to be made by all persons present in the conference call.

Votes on a resolution would be counted by asking each of the directors to indicate orally whether (s)he is voting in favour or against a particular resolution or by show of hands—that is a matter for the chairman.

Can a director deliberately frustrate the quorum procedure provisions in order to ensure that no valid board decision is taken? If a director deliberately frustrates the quorum provisions of articles, there are three possible solutions.

Many articles of association provide that if a quorum is not present at a particular board meeting, then the board meeting can be automatically adjourned for a fixed period of days and reconvened at the same time and place, say, seven days later, when the quorum *then* present will constitute a valid quorum.[16]

Application may be made by a director or a member to the court under CA 2006 s.306 (power of court to order a meeting) or if one of the directors

---

[14] *Byng v London Life Association Ltd* [1990] Ch. 170.
[15] See also Model arts 8 to 10.
[16] Model art.11 of the Model public company articles has wording to resolve the issue.

is a member of the company, then it may be open to that director to make an application to the court under CA 2006 Pt 30 s.994 (unfair prejudice) for an order that the business of the company be not so frustrated, either by amending the quorum provisions or by permitting the decision which is required to be taken. The applicant will have to show that "the company's affairs are being ... conducted in a manner that is unfairly prejudicial to the interests of members generally (including at least himself) or ... that any actual or proposed act or omission of the company ... is or would be so prejudicial".

It is also open, of course, for the company to pass a special resolution changing the articles so as to alter the quorum provisions, but in that event the directors will have to take care that such a procedure is not itself treated by the minority director (if (s)he is also a member) as giving grounds for an application by that minority director under CA 2006 s.994.

In calculating whether or not a quorum is present, it is also necessary to have regard to regulations in the articles of association, such as: "A director shall not be counted in the quorum present at a meeting in relation to a resolution on which he is not entitled to vote" (see below in relation to conflict of interest). It may be necessary, therefore, to split the items of business so that those items where the director can be included in the quorum can be dealt with, and if no quorum is present in relation to the items on which a director is interested, then the meeting will have to be adjourned until such time as a proper quorum is present.

Failing all that, a shareholders' meeting will need to be convened in order (subject to s.994 and to the articles) to authorise the directors to carry into effect a particular action. If the director concerned, or his or her associates, proceeds to frustrate the quorum provisions for meetings of shareholders, then as an alternative to the s.994 procedure, the CA 2006 s.306 procedure can be applied and the court can order the meeting to take place in any manner the court thinks appropriate.

Matters which should always be reserved to the board for decision

10.011   Provision A.1.1 of the UK Corporate Governance Code states:

> "... There should be a formal schedule of matters specifically reserved for its decision. The annual report should include ... a statement of how the board operates including a high level statement of which types of decisions are to be taken by the board and which are to be delegated to management."

No matter how effective a board of directors may be it is not possible for the directors to have hands on involvement in every area of the company's business. An effective board controls the business but delegates day-to-day responsibility to the company management. That said, there are a number of matters which should in the interests of the company only be decided by the board of directors as a whole. It is incumbent upon the board to make it clear what these matters reserved for the board are.

In App.13 there are set out a suggested list of matters reserved for the board. The size and contents of those reserved matters will vary according to the size and nature of the company's business. For example, all companies will have a different view on the establishment of the financial limits as to transactions which should be referred to the board.

Certain of the matters included in the reserved matters list should, under the recommendations of the UK Corporate Governance Code, be the responsibility of the audit, nomination or remuneration committee. However, it is important that these committees recognise which final decisions should be taken by the board as a whole, and suggestions for these are set out in App.13.

In drawing up the reserved matters list it is important to establish procedures for dealing with matters which have to be dealt with urgently, often between board meetings. It is recommended that, where practical and permitted by the articles of association, the approval of all directors should be obtained by means of a written resolution. In all cases, however, the procedures should balance the need for urgency with the overriding principle that each director should be given as much information as possible and have an opportunity to requisition an emergency meeting of the board to discuss the matter prior to the commitment of the company.

Proceedings at board meetings[17]

Flexibility of proceedings

Most articles of association have wording similar to this,[18] namely: "Subject to the articles, the directors may make any rule which they think fit about how they take decisions". Accordingly, it is open to the directors, but subject to the provisions of the articles (which can, of course, be altered by special resolution to as to create the flexibility required), to organise their proceedings with some flexibility.   **10.012**

Binding nature of board decisions

A director is bound by valid decisions of the board at meetings at which (s) he is not present. If, however, decisions taken at such a board meeting are   **10.013**

---

[17] ICSA has published a Guidance Note (ref 09028) called "Specimen board meeting etiquette".
[18] Public company Model art.19

in breach of the directors' duties, then under CA 2006 s.1157 the court can limit the scope of a director's liability for breach of duty if (s)he himself acted honestly and reasonably, and was not a party to that breach.

Chairman

10.014   See also Ch.8 for a discussion on the role of the chairman.

Articles commonly provide that the directors can appoint a director to be the chairman of the board[19] and can remove him or her from office at any time. The chairman should preside at every meeting at which (s)he is present, but if (s)he is not present at the meeting, the directors who are actually present can appoint another director to be chairman of that meeting. Where the chairman is elected for an unspecified period, (s)he is entitled to remain chairman until the directors decide otherwise.[20]

The articles may also provide that, in the case of an equality of votes, the chairman shall have a second or casting vote,[21] but in the absence of such a provision, the chairman does not have a casting vote.

Conflicts of interest

10.015   The provisions of the CA 2006 dealing with conflicts of interest and notifications of interest are dealt with more fully in Ch.4 (Directors—Duties and Liabilities). In summary, however, CA 2006 s.175 requires directors to avoid a situation in which they have, or can have, a direct or indirect interest that conflicts, or possibly may conflict, with the interests of the company. If such a situation arises authorisation may be given by the independent directors if, in the case of a public company, its constitution includes a provision enabling the independent directors to authorise the matter.[22] Authorisation must be given at a duly convened meeting which is quorate without counting the director who is interested and where the vote does not include the vote of the director concerned.[23]

Directors should under CA 2006 s.177 give notice[24] of any conflict of interest in a *proposed* transaction to the board via the secretary before the relevant business is discussed or any relevant resolution is put. If notice is not given, or if the transaction is not subsequently approved by resolution of members,

---

[19] Public company Model art.12.

[20] *Foster v Foster* [1916] 1 Ch. 532.

[21] Model art.14.

[22] For example, Model art.16(2) which spells out the circumstances in which a conflicted director can participate in the meeting and vote on a matter in which (s)he has an interest actual or proposed.

[23] For example, Model art.12(3).

[24] See CA 2006 ss.184 and 185 for methods of giving notice.

then under CA 2006 s.178, the director concerned risks being in breach of his or her fiduciary duty and the other general duties provisions of CA 2006 ss.171 to 177, and the transaction is liable to be set aside.

If a director fails to declare an interest in an *existing* transaction[25] then the director in addition risks criminal sanctions under CA 2006 s.183.

In the case of *Guinness Plc v Saunders*[26] it was held that the declaration of an interest must be made at a full board meeting as distinct from a committee meeting.

Voting at, minutes of and resolutions of meetings of directors

Most articles of association provide that all questions shall be decided by simple majority,[27] each director having one vote—if an alternate director is also a director, (s)he will have two votes at a meeting at which his or her appointor is absent. **10.016**

It is not necessary for a resolution to be proposed and seconded; what is required, however, is that the wording of the resolution is clear, and therefore it is always best practice for the chairman to state the resolution being put to the meeting in clear terms.

Minutes

CA 2006 s.248 requires that every company must cause minutes of all proceedings at meetings of directors "to be recorded".[28] CA 2006 s.249 provides that minutes that have been signed by the chairman of that or the next meeting of the board are evidence (but it is not stated as "conclusive evidence"), of the proceedings. It may sometimes be necessary to take statements from other directors or, preferably, the company secretary, if there is confusion as to the proceedings or the resolution actually passed.[29] **10.017**

UK Corporate Governance Code Provision A.4.3 provides that unresolved concerns should be recorded in the minutes:

---

[25] CA 2006 ss.182–187.

[26] [1990] 2 A.C. 663.

[27] Model art.13(1).

[28] Note that it is left open as to how they should be recorded: electronic recording would appear to be permitted.

[29] Ch.XXII of the 2009 MG Rover Inspectors' report contains the following extract from a witness:

> "When we asked [ ] how often board minutes were produced retrospectively, [the witness] said: '*Sometimes. I mean, hopefully not very often, but from time to time, it would happen that something which, you know, for the sake of good practice should probably have been minuted, for one reason or another it slipped through and didn't get done; you would then seek to try and, if it wasn't too late, to try and, you know, document what should have happened'.*"

"Where directors have concerns which cannot be resolved about the running of the company or a proposed action, they should ensure that their concerns are recorded in the board minutes."

CA 2006 s.40(1) states that:

"In favour of a person dealing with a company in good faith, the power of the directors to bind the company, or authorise others to do so, he is deemed to be free of any limitation under the company's constitution".

Section 40(2)(b)(ii) states that the third party "is presumed to have acted in good faith unless the contrary is proved". Of course, however, a decision of the directors which is taken beyond their powers could result in the directors being sued for breach of fiduciary duty by the company itself.[30]

Conclusion

10.018 Regular, well-conducted board meetings are at the heart of corporate governance. The chairman has primary responsibility for ensuring that they take place, that they are properly constituted and well conducted and that their decisions are correctly minuted. If these factors are attended to, effective governance will be made much easier.

[30] CA 2006 s.170.

Chapter 11

Directors' Remuneration

Karen Cooper[1]

Background

The subject of executive remuneration continues to raise much controversy **11.001** in the context of good corporate governance. For many years, escalating rewards for executives have frequently out paced the returns afforded to shareholding investors, and have significantly exceeded average salary rises for employees. However, the global banking crisis has prompted fresh criticism of executive pay in the UK, particularly in failing financial institutions. Many organisations have responded to this and tough economic conditions by freezing or reducing pay increases. A survey by PricewaterhouseCooper revealed that during 2009, FTSE 100 executives received average basic pay increases of 1 per cent while around 60 per cent of FTSE 250 executives received no pay increase. By comparison, in 2008, FTSE 350 pay increases averaged 6 per cent as against 3.7 per cent in the wider market. However, it remains to be seen whether this trend will continue or is simply a short-term reaction to the global recession.[2]

Undoubtedly there will be continued pressures to retain and attract the best talent. Companies will need to provide remuneration strategies to do so, but

---

[1] Karen Cooper graduated from St Anne's College Oxford in 1991, and is the partner who heads up the employee benefits practice at Osborne Clarke. Her experience spanning more than 15 years in this field encompasses the design, implementation and communication of a broad range of employee incentives both on a national and international level, including tax approved and "all employee" schemes as well as "executive only" arrangements.

Karen advises a broad range of Osborne Clarke's clients including both privately-owned business and companies whose shares are listed in the UK or on foreign markets. The incentives team works closely with the corporate finance practice, advising on the employee benefits aspects of mergers and acquisitions, corporate restructurings and flotations. Karen is an active member of the Share Plan Lawyers Organisation; she writes and lectures on incentives issues and has a particular interest in corporate governance matters.

[2] Executive Compensation Review of the Year 2009 published by PricewaterhouseCoopers 2010.

the pressure to avoid rewards for mediocre or poor performance and structures which potentially promulgate risk is becoming stronger. This chapter looks at how good governance has developed over time, who is responsible for ensuring suitable remuneration policies are in place, and the requirements for companies in relation to disclosure of executive pay packages.

The historical perspective

11.002   The successive findings of Cadbury, Greenbury, Hampel, Turnbull and Higgs have mapped the requirements for companies adhering to good corporate governance in the context of executive pay. Whilst Cadbury recommended the full and clear disclosure of directors' total emoluments, and for remuneration committees to be made up wholly or mainly of non-executive directors, it was not until Hampel (which was set up to review the effectiveness of the Cadbury and Greenbury recommendations), that broad principles for remuneration packages, procedure and disclosure were more formally enshrined into the Combined Code.[3]

In April 2002, the Secretary of State and the Chancellor appointed Derek Higgs to review the effectiveness and the role of the non-executive director. His report noted that "too often the governance discussion has been shrill and narrowly focused on executive pay with insufficient attention to the real drivers of corporate success". His review led to a number of recommendations, including a widening of the role of the remuneration committee and its terms of reference, along with a clear mandate for committees to set the remuneration packages for the chief executive, chairman and executive managers.

However, despite this focus, the extent to which successive governments have been prepared to intervene in questions of determining levels of executive pay has been somewhat limited.

The DTI consultation on directors' remuneration concluded that remuneration was a matter for shareholders to determine, but recognised that the legal framework could be improved. As a result, the Directors' Remuneration Report Regulations 2002 introduced requirements for more meaningful disclosure for remuneration for listed companies and for shareholders to vote at the AGM on the remuneration report.

Following the introduction of the Companies Act 2006 ("CA 2006"), the disclosure requirements for directors' remuneration are now to be found in CA 2006 s.420 and the Large and Medium-sized Companies and Groups (Accounts and Reports) Regulations 2008 Sch.8. Further details are set out in para.11.013.

---

[3] Following Hampel, the Financial Reporting Council ("FRC") issued a revised code in July 2003 applied to financial years beginning on or after November 1, 2003. The FRC issued a further revised Combined Code on June 27, 2006 and consulted on further changes in the early part of 2010 following the publication of the Walker Review.

What we are therefore left with is a series of interlocking and overlapping rules, principles and guidelines, with very little legislation. This contrasts starkly with the approach in the US where governments have reacted to the corporate scandals of recent years and provided wide powers of intervention for the Securities and Exchange Commission ("SEC"). The Sarbanes-Oxley Act has targeted the role and responsibilities of officers of companies, in terms of financial reporting and internal control processes, but it has also aimed to tackle the whole notion of executives acting in their own interests, particularly their financial interests.

The role of the financial crisis

The global financial crisis prompted a series of reviews and reports on the extent to which remuneration policies and poor governance encouraged risk-taking in the financial services sector. Although the majority of these reviews were primarily aimed at financial institutions, some are likely to have wider impact. **11.003**

From January 1, 2010, 26 of the biggest banks and building societies in the UK have been subject to the Financial Service Authority's ("FSA") Code of Practice on Remuneration Policies. This takes the form of remuneration principles and requires bonus structures to promote effective risk management, achieved primarily through deferral and the use of risk-adjusted performance measures. The role of the FSA in policing remuneration policies has also been enhanced. During the course of 2010, the FSA will consult on further proposals to widen significantly the scope of the Code and the number of entities subject to it. The proposals include provisions to render void an employment contract if it is in breach of the Code.

The Walker Review[4] also advocated remuneration policies that promote effective risk management, called for enhanced disclosure of remuneration arrangements (including for those below board level, if their remuneration exceeded £1 million per annum) and a significantly increased role for the remuneration committee.

Following the publication of the Walker Review, the FRC decided to bring forward the Combined Code review planned for later in 2010 so that corporate governance in listed companies could be assessed at the same. This review and subsequent consultation resulted in the publication of the amended Combined Code, now known as the UK Corporate Governance Code, on May 28, 2010, which applies to accounting periods beginning on or after June 29, 2010.[5]

In addition, draft regulations have been published under the Financial

---

[4] A review of corporate governance in UK banks and other financial industry entities—final recommendations published November 26, 2009.
[5] The UK Corporate Governance Code published by the FRC June 2010.

Services Act 2010 that would require enhanced disclosure on remuneration by the largest UK and overseas banks operating in the UK.[6] As the proposals currently stand, banks would be required to publish information on the number of people (including "high end" employees) that have total annual remuneration packages falling within bands of £500,000, starting from £500,000 and going up to £6 million, and in bands of £1 million thereafter (a lower starting point and smaller steps than originally suggested by the Walker Review). A public consultation will take place on the proposals during the course of 2010.

The remuneration committee

The role and constitution of the remuneration committee

Role

11.004   The primary role of the remuneration committee is to set both the remuneration policy and the level of remuneration for all executive directors and the chairman. This not only covers salary and benefits, but bonus and pension entitlements and participation in share incentive arrangements.

> "The committee should also recommend and monitor the level and structure of remuneration for senior management. The definition of senior management for this purpose should be determined by the board but should normally include the first layer of management below board level."

The committee is also responsible for ensuring that disclosure of directors' remuneration is made in accordance with, the Large and Medium-sized Companies and Groups (Accounts and Reports) Regulations 2008 Sch.8 and CA 2006 Pt 15 Ch.6.

The ABI also emphasise that part of the committee's role is to bring independent thought and scrutiny to the development and review process together with an understanding of the business which contribute to shareholder value.[7]

Constitution

11.005   The UK Corporate Governance Code provides how the committee should be constituted. Provision D.2.1 states "the Board should establish a

---

[6] Executives' Remuneration Reports Regulations 2010.
[7] ABI Guidelines on Executive Remuneration, December 2009.

remuneration committee of at least three, or in the case of smaller companies[8] two members who should all be independent non-executive directors. The remuneration committee should make available its terms of reference,[9] explaining its role and the authority delegated to it by the board. The terms of reference should be available both on the company's website and by request, along with the terms and conditions of appointment of non-executive directors. Where remuneration consultants are appointed, a statement should also be made available in the year in which the appointment is made as to whether they have any other connection with the company.

There is no restriction on the company chairman serving on the remuneration committee, in circumstances where he or she is considered to be independent at the time of their appointment (as chairman). However, Provision D.2.1 recommends that the individual should not also chair the remuneration committee.

The Higgs report recommended that only independent directors should sit on the remuneration committee and that the committee should be responsible for appointing remuneration consultants. This was largely in response to the criticism that advisers were often too close to the executive. Annex E of the Higgs Review contained a summary of the principle duties of remuneration committees which was contained in the Related Guidance and Good Practice Suggestions of the Combined Code.[10] The FRC has commissioned the Institute of Chartered Secretaries and Administrators ("ICSA") to work with others on its behalf to update these materials, and to consider whether additional guidance is required on related issues raised in Sections A (Leadership) and B (Effectiveness) of the new UK Corporate Governance Code. ICSA's draft guidance makes a number of changes to the original Higgs Guidance, as it places a greater emphasis on the role of the chairman in creating an effective board and the board's role in establishing a culture of high-performance. The completed guidance is expected to be issued to the FRC in October 2010.

Meetings

The frequency with which the remuneration committee will need to meet will **11.006** be dependent upon the size and nature of the company involved. The committee will need to approve the disclosure in relation to the directors' remuneration report, but will also need to deal with such issues as the adoption of a new equity scheme, the appointment or termination of an executive or a change to the overall strategy in relation to employee reward.

---

[8] Smaller companies are defined as those below the FTSE 350 during the year prior to the reporting year.
[9] The principal duties of the remuneration committee are set out in App.16.
[10] The principal duties of the remuneration committee can be found in App.16.

In order to assist the remuneration committee and to address the increasingly complex regulatory, fiscal and accounting environment, it will of course need to consult specialist remuneration consultants, lawyers and accountants.

Setting directors' remuneration policy

11.007   It is the duty of the committee to devise the overall policy on directors' remuneration. The starting point for any working remuneration committee is the guidance in the UK Corporate Governance Code. Principle D.1 "The Level and Components of Remuneration" states that:

> "Levels of remuneration should be sufficient to attract, retain and motivate directors of the quality required to run the company successfully, but a company should avoid paying more than is necessary for this purpose. A significant proportion of an executive director's remuneration should be structured so as to link rewards to corporate and individual performance."

A new "Supporting Principle" has been introduced stating that:

> "the performance-related elements of executive directors' remuneration should be stretching and designed to promote the long-term success of the company."

It further requires the remuneration committee to judge where to position their company relative to other companies. But they should use such comparisons with caution, in view of the risk of an upward ratchet of remuneration levels with no corresponding improvement in performance, and should be sensitive to pay and employment conditions elsewhere in the group, especially when determining annual salary. This is a clear warning that the rewards for directors should not routinely outstrip those of other staff without proper justification.

It is recognised that remuneration consultants may be required to provide advice to the committee. The Walker Review noted that there needed to be "greater confidence in the integrity and professionalism of external consultants".[11] There has been much media comment on the role remuneration consultants have played in escalating remuneration packages during better times, particularly those in the financial services sector. Provision D.2.1 seeks to address the question of independence, stating that:

> "Where remuneration consultants are appointed, a statement should be made available of whether they have any other connection with the company."

---

[11] Walker Review, para.7.53.

The changes introduced in the 2010 revision of the UK Corporate Governance Code are intended to emphasise that a significant proportion of the total remuneration package of executive directors should align their interests with those of shareholders. This is especially important in the context of share-based remuneration which is addressed in more detail in para.11.024. Schedule A to the UK Corporate Governance Code provides more specific guidance in relation to the design of performance related remuneration.[12] Committees are advised to consider whether directors are to be eligible for bonuses and if so, performance conditions should be relevant, stretching and designed to enhance shareholder value and to promote the long-term success of the company. Upper limits should be set and disclosed. Schedule A further notes that there may be a case for part payment in shares to be held for a significant period.

The guidance advises committees to consider the appropriate use of long-term incentive schemes. It notes that traditional share option schemes should be weighed against other long term incentive arrangements, and that executive share options should not be offered at a discount save as permitted by the Listing Rules. Shares or other forms of deferred remuneration should not vest prior to a period of three years, with directors being encouraged to hold their shares for a further period following vesting, subject to the need to finance any costs or tax liabilities.

When awarding long term incentives, committees are encouraged to consider challenging performance criteria that reflect the company's objectives including non-financial performance metrics "where appropriate". In addition, remuneration incentives should be compatible with risk policies and systems, although the revised Schedule A has stepped back from suggesting that bonuses should be risk adjusted.

The UK Corporate Governance Code is clear that remuneration committees should consult the chairman and/or chief executive about their proposals for other executive pay, although warns against potential conflicts of interest where executive directors or senior management are involved in advising or supporting the committee.[13] The UK Corporate Governance Code emphasises the role of the chairman of the board in maintaining contact with key shareholders about remuneration matters.

Procedure

Principle D.2 (Procedure) of the UK Corporate Governance Code states **11.008** that there should be a formal and transparent procedure for developing policy on executive remuneration and for fixing the remuneration packages

---

[12] Sch.A to the UK Corporate Governance Code is contained in App.1.
[13] See comments regarding constitution of the remuneration committee and chairman in para.11.005 et seq.

of individual directors. No director should be involved in deciding his own remuneration.

The Supporting Principle specifies that the committee should consult the chairman and/or chief executive about their proposals relating to the remuneration of other executive directors.

In looking to formulate and keep under review a meaningful remuneration policy the committee may want to consider the following steps:

(i) *External market practice*
    The committee should be aware of the overall context for setting their policy, both in terms of the economic environment and current best practice. The committee will usually need to appoint remuneration advisers to supply market data and to provide guidance and advice.

(ii) *Consultation*
    The committee should consult with the key individuals within the business—the chief executive, finance and HR directors. However, where executive directors or senior management are involved in advising or supporting the committee, care should be taken to recognise and avoid conflicts of interest.

(iii) *Shareholder views*
    The committee should consult with a number of key shareholders in setting the remuneration policy to have an understanding of their views. The chairman of the board should ensure that the company maintains contact as required with its principal shareholders about remuneration.

Institutional shareholder groups such as the Association of British Insurers ("ABI") and the National Association of Pension Funds ("NAPF") advise remuneration committees to maintain a constructive and timely dialogue with their major institutional shareholders and the ABI on all matters relating to remuneration (both in terms of policy setting and in its practical implementation). They recommend any proposed departure from the stated remuneration policy should be subject to prior approval by shareholders. They emphasise the need for a full and clear explanation of the policy, establishing a clear link between reward and performance to be detailed in the remuneration report.

Interaction of the Listing Rules and the UK Corporate Governance Code

11.009 Paragraph 9.8.6(5) and (6) of the Listing Rules require companies with a Premium listing to provide an explanation in their annual report of how they have applied the Code. The form and content are not prescribed, but sufficient information should be given to enable shareholders to evaluate how the principles have been applied. This requirement will also apply to an overseas company with a Premium listing in the UK.

Whilst there is no breach of the Listing Rules if a company has not complied, provided it has explained its reasons for doing so, the disapprobation of shareholders and the consequences of this are seen as sufficient. In Higgs' view, this "comply or explain approach established by Sir Adrian Cadbury has worked well" and the FRC has not seen any need to change this approach in recent years.

Disclosure

The disclosure requirements in the context of executive remuneration are found in a set of overlapping provisions throughout the CA 2006 s.421, the Large and Medium-sized Companies and Groups (Accounts and Reports) Regulations 2008 Sch.8 and the Listing Rules. It is hoped that now the CA 2006 is in force, some attention will be paid to codifying the disclosure requirements. This section looks at requirements as they stand now in more detail. **11.010**

The UK Corporate Governance Code

The UK Corporate Governance Code no longer includes a principle in relation to the disclosure of directors' remuneration as this has been superseded by the requirements of the Large and Medium sized Companies and Groups (Accounts and Reports) Regulations 2008. **11.011**

Company Law Requirements

CA 2006 s.420 obliges the directors of a quoted company to prepare a directors' remuneration report for each financial year of the company. This obligation rests with all directors, not just those of the remuneration committee. Section 421 gives the Secretary of State power to make regulation as to the requirements for the contents of the remuneration report. Non-compliance in preparing the report and putting it to shareholders is a criminal offence. **11.012**

The remuneration report must be approved by the board and sent to shareholders with the accounts and delivered to the Registrar of Companies.[14] An ordinary resolution to approve the remuneration report must be put to shareholders at each AGM under CA 2006 s.439. However, no individual entitlement is to be conditional upon the resolution being passed.

---

[14] CA 2006 s.423.

The Large and Medium-sized Companies and Groups (Accounts and Reports) Regulations 2008[15]

11.013 The regulations came into force on April 6, 2008 and apply to all companies which are formed and registered under the UK Companies Act and whose shares are listed on the Official List, the New York Stock Exchange, Nasdaq and certain EU exchanges. They do not apply to companies with shares traded on the Alternative Investment Market (although the AIM Listing Rules now require disclosure of directors' remuneration for financial years ending March 31, 2010 onwards).

When the regulations in their original form (the Directors' Remuneration Report Regulations 2002) were introduced, one of the most significant changes was the requirement to hold a compulsory annual shareholders' vote on directors' remuneration packages. As mentioned previously, that requirement is now contained in CA 2006 s.439. Some have criticised the measure for lack of "teeth", as no remuneration would become repayable in the event that the resolution failed to be approved by a majority of shareholders. However, recent high profile votes against the remuneration report have illustrated the power of shareholders to rise against the tide of ever increasing pay-outs for underperforming executives.

During the course of 2009, shareholders voted against remuneration reports at the annual general meetings of Cable & Wireless, Royal Dutch Shell and Bellway Homes. The votes against the reports were registered primarily in protest at new incentive arrangements for executives which were perceived as potentially excessive, particularly in the case of Bellway where corporate performance had been badly affected by the general economic climate.

The Walker Review recommended that where a remuneration report attracted support from less than 75 per cent of the votes cast, the chairman of the remuneration committee should stand for re-election in the following year, regardless of the term of their appointment. This proposal was not included in the final version of the UK Corporate Governance Code, although, in future, all directors of FTSE 350 companies should be subject to annual election by shareholders in any event.

The requirements of the regulations are as follows: the company must publish an annual remuneration report on directors' remuneration forming part of the annual report sent to shareholders along with the notice of the AGM approved by the board and signed on its behalf by a director or secretary. The report must disclose full details of the individual packages for directors, the role and composition of the committee, the board's policy in respect of remuneration and certain information about performance. The requirement to put an annual resolution to shareholders is also included.

---

[15] SI 2008/410.

Most companies discharge their obligation by setting out the report in two parts. The first part explains the policy elements and the second contains the detailed breakdown of each directors' total remuneration which is audited by the company's accountants.

First part—non-audited

For the purposes of the regulations, references to directors include any persons who serves as such at anytime in the period beginning with the end of the relevant financial year and ending on the date the report is laid before the company in general meeting.[16]   **11.014**

Policy statement

The policy statement[17] will usually explain how the supporting principle of UK Corporate Governance Code D.1 described in para.11.007 has been achieved. Typically the policy will state it is designed to attract retain and motivate executives, and to provide them with remuneration which aligns their interests with shareholders at a level which is in line with the market place.   **11.015**

Performance conditions   The policy statement must also include for each director a summary of the performance conditions relating to share options or awards under long-term incentive plans, including why the conditions were chosen. There also needs to be an explanation of how the conditions are monitored and if they are compared with external factors or performance of other companies, how this comparison is made or measured. Any significant changes to the entitlement of directors to share options or long-term incentives during the year should also be made.[18] Where any entitlement of a director to share options or long-term incentives is not subject to performance conditions, an explanation should be provided.   **11.016**

Contractual requirements   The company must explain its policy on the duration of contracts with directors, notice period and termination payments.[19]   **11.017**

---

[16] Large and Medium-sized Companies and Groups (Accounts and Reports) Regulations 2008 Sch.8 para.3(5).
[17] Large and Medium-sized Companies and Groups (Accounts and Reports) Regulations 2008 Sch.8 para.3(1).
[18] Large and Medium-sized Companies and Groups (Accounts and Reports) Regulations 2008 Sch.8 para.3(2).
[19] Large and Medium-sized Companies and Groups (Accounts and Reports) Regulations 2008 Sch.8 para.3(4).

Performance graph

11.018   This section of the report must contain a line graph showing the total share-holder return performance of a holding of shares in the company, and a hypothetical holding of shares of the same kind and number as those by reference to which a broad equity market index is calculated over the five preceding financial years, and an explanation of the reasons for the choice.[20] This is a requirement irrespective of whether TSR is a performance measure for share-based remuneration. TSR should be calculated using a "fair method" as set out in the regulations and the report should show the name of the index used and the reason for selecting it. The rationale for this comparison is to provide some objectivity as to whether the remuneration policy has aligned the interests of executives with those of shareholders.

Constitution of the committee

11.019   The report must name each director on the committee and any person who provided advice or services to the committee, including the nature of the services and whether they were appointed by the committee.[21]

Service contracts

11.020   The report must include the details of the dates of all directors' service contracts, the unexpired term, notice periods, details of any compensation provisions on termination and any other details to enable shareholders to estimate the liability of the company in the event of early termination of the contract. The report must also give an explanation for any significant compensatory award paid to former directors.[22]

Statement of consideration of conditions elsewhere in the company and group

11.021   The report must contain a statement as to how the pay and employment of employees in the group were taken into account when determining directors' remuneration for the relevant financial year.[23]

[20] Large and Medium-sized Companies and Groups (Accounts and Reports) Regulations 2008 Sch.8 para.5.
[21] Large and Medium-sized Companies and Groups (Accounts and Reports) Regulations 2008 Sch.8 para.2.
[22] Large and Medium-sized Companies and Groups (Accounts and Reports) Regulations 2008 Sch.8 para.6.
[23] Large and Medium-sized Companies and Groups (Accounts and Reports) Regulations 2008 Sch.8 para.4.

Second part—audited

The information to be provided in the second part of the report must contain detailed information on the following: **11.022**

Schedule 8 Paragraph	Details
7 Emoluments and compensation	For each director the total amount of salary, fees, bonus paid or receivable, sums paid by way of expenses which are chargeable to UK income tax, compensation or other payments for loss of office, estimated value of any non-cash benefits received must be included. These figures must be shown for the current and previous financial year in tabular form.
8–9 Share Options	For each director, the number of shares under option at the beginning of the year or the date of appointment, and at the end of the financial year, or earlier cession of employment must be included. Details of those options granted, exercised and which have lapsed during the year and those which have been amended or varied should also be included. For all outstanding options, details of the price paid (if any), the exercise price, the date from which they can be exercised and the date provided for lapse—this information must be supplied in tabular form. For each option which has been exercised during the relevant financial year, the market price of the shares under option at exercise, and for all outstanding options, the market price at the end of the year and the highest and lowest price of the share during the year must be provided. A summary of the performance conditions and any changes made to them during the year must also be included along with the market value of the shares at the time of exercise.[24]

---

[24] If such disclosure would be excessive in length it is permissible to aggregate options with the same terms and conditions and instead of disclosing prices for each share option, disclose on the basis of weighted average prices (Large and Medium-sized Companies and Groups (Accounts and Reports) Regulations 2008 Sch.8 para.10). However, the information in relation to "underwater options" cannot be aggregated with those "in the money" and full disclosure must be provided in respect of options awarded, exercised or amended during the relevant year.

11–12 Long term incentive schemes	This section covers similar disclosure requirements as for options, but in relation to equity interest which are structured differently.
	For each director details of the "scheme interest"— (usually called awards) held at the beginning of the year or the date of appointment (if later), those held at the end of the financial year, the vesting period and any variations made during the year must be included. Details of awards made (including the market price of the shares and any performance conditions) and those vested in the financial year (including details of shares or assets received on vesting) must also be shown. A "long term incentive scheme" has a special definition for the purposes of the disclosure of information for these regulations[25] with the result that a deferred bonus arrangement (increasingly common among FTSE companies) will need to be disclosed in this section.
13 Pensions	Where the director has rights in respect of a defined benefit scheme, details of accrued benefits and any changes made during the year, and the transfer value for that year and the previous year (less the director's contributions) should be shown. Where the director had defined contribution pension rights under a money purchase scheme, the amount of contributions paid by the company must be disclosed.
14 Excess retirement benefits	For each director and any former director, a statement of benefits paid during the year in excess of normal entitlements (e.g. benefit improvements/ augmentations).

[25] Large and Medium-sized Companies and Groups (Accounts and Reports) Regulations 2008 Sch.8 para.11(5) provides that "long term incentive scheme" means any agreement or arrangement under which money or other assets may become receivable by a person and which includes one or more qualifying conditions with respect to service or performance that cannot be fulfilled within a single financial year, and for this purpose the following must be disregarded, namely:

(a) any bonus the amount of which falls to be determined by reference to service or performance within a single financial year;
(b) compensation in respect of loss of office, payments for breach of contract and other termination payments; and
(c) retirement benefits.

15 Compensation for past directors	The report must contain details of any significant award made in the year to any person who was not a director of the company at the time the award was made but who had previously been a director, including compensation for loss of office and pensions. Although "significant award" is not defined, it is expected that items such as continuing share options and long term incentive awards that result from an exercise of a discretion by the remuneration committee should be disclosed, as should any consultancy arrangements or continued employment following cessation as a director.
16 Sums paid to third parties	For each director a statement of the aggregate amount of consideration paid to or receivable by third parties for the director's services.

Some have criticised the regulations for failing to require a total figure for remuneration paid in the year. Whilst there is a requirement to show total salary, annual bonus and benefits, there is no need to aggregate this with the value of share awards and pensions, which are shown separately although as discussed in para.11.023 below, the Listing Rules refer to disclosure being made of "the total remuneration" for each director.

It is also often difficult when looking at the remuneration report to assess the full level of individual directors' remuneration packages. A Government consultation is taking place in 2010 to consider narrative reporting in corporate accounts generally and this will also address information about directors' remuneration and whether the current disclosure requirements provide clear and usable information about the total remuneration paid to directors.[26]

Listing Rules

Listing Rule 9.8.4 sets out the information which must be included in the annual report and accounts. Some of these will relate to remuneration. LR 9.8.4(4) requires disclosure of any long-term incentive schemes approved by shareholders, and LR 9.8.4(5) details of any emoluments waived by directors. LR 9.8.6 requires a statement setting out the equity interest of directors in respect of notifiable transactions.   **11.023**

---

[26] "Corporate law and governance. The Future of Narrative Reporting" issued by BIS, August 2, 2010.

LR 9.8.8 sets out the information which the report to the shareholders of a company with a Premium listing[27] by the board on directors' remuneration must contain. These include:

Statement of the company's policy on executive remuneration.[28]	
Information in tabular form together with explanatory notes on each element of the remuneration package.[29]	This information must show the amount of each element in the remuneration package for the period under review of each director, by name, including but not restricted to, basic salary and fees, the estimated money value of benefits in kind, annual bonuses, deferred bonuses, compensation for loss of office and payments for breach of contract or other termination payments
The total remuneration for each director.[30]	This must be shown for the period under review and the preceding period.
Any significant payments made to former directors.[31]	This information must be shown for the period under review.
Share options.[32]	Details must be shown of all share options, including Save As You Earn options, held by each director by name.
Long term incentive schemes.[33]	Details are required of the interests of each director at the start and end of the period under review, together with information about any awards that have been granted during the period and when they crystallise. Details must be shown of the monetary value and number of shares, cash payments or other benefits received by each director under any long-term incentive scheme during the period.

[27] Amendments to the Listing Rules to introduce two levels of listing—Premium and Standard, took effect from April 6, 2010.
[28] LR 9.8.8(1).
[29] LR 9.8.8(2)(a).
[30] LR 9.8.8(2)(b).
[31] LR 9.8.8(2)(c).
[32] LR 9.8.8(2)(d).
[33] LR 9.8.8(3)–(4).

The auditors of the company must review the disclosures made under LR 9.8.8R(2), (amount of each element in the remuneration package and information on share options) LR 9.8.8R(3), (4) and (5) (details of long-term incentive schemes for directors), LR 9.8.8R(11) money purchase pension schemes, and LR 9.8.8R(12) (defined benefit pension schemes). If as a result of this review the auditors are of the opinion that there is non-compliance, the auditor's report must provide full details.

There is some overlap between those requirements and the Large and Medium-sized Companies and Groups (Accounts and Reports) Regulations 2008 Sch.8 but some differences do exist, particularly with regard to how defined pension benefit transfer values are shown and what constitutes a long-term incentive scheme for the purposes of the required disclosures.

Introducing share incentive schemes

Designing performance related remuneration

Perhaps one of the most contentious elements of the remuneration package is **11.024** the level and form of equity incentives for executives. Whilst Principle D.1 of the UK Corporate Governance Code warns against paying executives more than is necessary, it is the variable element of bonus and incentive schemes which have contributed most to the "ratcheting-up" of overall remuneration in recent years. The value of awards made under long-term incentive plans have increased as a percentage of salary and even following the global recession, it is not uncommon to see maximum potential pay-outs in excess of 100 per cent of base salary where executives hit all of their targets.

What is becoming apparent is the potential blurring of the distinction between short-term awards, such as annual bonuses and longer-term awards. This is primarily due to the global trend, fuelled in the UK by the Walker Review and other policy statements following the financial crisis, that performance-related awards should be subject to some form of deferral and forfeiture, in the event that the company's performance is not sustained. This is evident in Schedule A of the UK Corporate Governance Code which makes the general point that the remuneration committee should consider whether directors *should* be eligible for annual bonuses and, if so, performance conditions should be relevant, stretching and designed to enhance shareholder value and promote the long-term success of the company.

In terms of designing equity awards, there is an incredibly wide variety of schemes in operation in the market place today which to a certain extent have overtaken the basic executive share option scheme which was predominant in the 80s and 90s. Schemes are now devised, not only with executive reward in mind, but to achieve the most from the increasingly complex tax and accounting environment. Appendix 18 summarises the main "all-employee" and executive schemes which companies may adopt and a description of their broad tax effects.

One of the biggest challenges facing the remuneration committee is to design schemes within a best practice framework. What best practice constitutes is set out in Schedule A of the UK Corporate Governance Code, but the guidelines of institutional shareholder bodies such as the ABI and NAPF have equally become the benchmark for good governance in this area. What is clear is that regular dialogue with shareholders prior to the adoption of any new scheme or the amendment to existing arrangements is highly recommended.

Schedule A of the UK Corporate Governance Code provides the following guidance:

- traditional share option schemes should be weighed against other kinds of long-term incentive scheme;

- executive share options should not be offered at a discount except as provided for in the Listing Rules;

- benefits under these types of arrangement should not be payable for a minimum period of three years;

- directors should be encouraged to hold their shares for a further period after vesting or exercise (subject to the need to finance the costs of acquisition and associated tax liabilities);

- any new long-term incentive schemes (as defined in the Listing Rules) and significant changes to existing schemes should be approved by shareholders. New schemes should preferably replace existing schemes or at least form part of a well considered overall plan incorporating existing schemes. Total potential rewards should not be excessive;

- incentives should be compatible with risk policies and systems;

- challenging performance criteria reflecting the company's objectives, including non-financial performance metrics where appropriate, should be central to the rewards provided; and

- grants under executive share option schemes or other long-term schemes should normally be phased rather than awarded in one block.

Listing rules—shareholder approvals for equity plans

11.025 LR 9 governs the specific requirements for shareholder approval in respect of executive share schemes for a company with a Premium listing and those of its subsidiaries. LR 9.4.1 provides that following types of scheme must be approved by an ordinary resolution of the shareholders of the listed company in general meeting prior to adoption:

(a)   employees' share schemes which involve or may involve the issue of new shares or the transfer of treasury shares; and

(b)   long-term incentive plans in which any director of the listed company can participate.

LR 9.4.2 contains two exemptions from the shareholder approval requirement for the following long-term incentive plans as follows:

*   arrangements where participation is offered on similar terms to all or substantially all eligible employees (provided that all or substantially all eligible employees are not directors of the listed company); and

*   arrangements where the only participant is a director of the listed company (or an individual whose appointment as a director is contemplated) and the arrangement is specifically to facilitate in unusual circumstances the recruitment or retention of the relevant individual.

In the second case there are fairly extensive disclosure requirements in relation to the arrangement which must be included in the first annual report published by the company after the date on which the individual is eligible to participate in the arrangement. This is essentially the information set out below which would be necessary had prior approval been sought in normal circumstances. The use of this exemption is noted with caution and committees should consider reliance on this only in exceptional circumstances which justify the approach.

An employees' share scheme has the same meaning as CA 2006 s.1166 and is essentially a scheme for encouraging or facilitating the holding of shares by or for the benefit of employees or former employees of a group.

A long-term incentive scheme is defined as an arrangement, (other than a retirement benefit plan, a deferred bonus or any other arrangement that is an element of an executive directors' remuneration package) which may involve the receipt of any asset (including cash or any security) by a director or employee of the group which includes one or more conditions in respect of service and/or performance to be satisfied over more than one financial year and pursuant to which the group may incur a liability (other than set up and administration costs). In reality, most executive share option schemes and performance share plans do therefore require the consent of shareholders in advance. It should be noted that the definition of long-term incentive plan is wide enough to cover not just share schemes but those where benefits are provided in the form of cash.

LR 13.8.11 requires the circular to shareholders to either include the full text of the scheme or a description of its principal terms. It must also provide if directors of the listed company are to act as trustees, details of that trustee-ship or interest.

The circular must also state the provisions (if any) relating to the following:

- individuals who are eligible to participate;

- limits on the numbers of securities or cash subject to the scheme;

- the maximum entitlement for any participant;

- the basis of determining participants' entitlement to and terms of securities/cash/benefits and any adjustment to them which cannot be altered to the advantage of participants without the prior approval of shareholders in general meeting (other than minor amendments to benefit administration of the scheme, or to account for legislative changes, etc.); and

- whether benefits are pensionable.

The resolution can authorise the directors to establish further schemes based on the scheme approved by shareholders but modified to take account of local tax, exchange control or securities laws in overseas countries, provided that any shares made available under a further scheme count towards the dilution limits of the main scheme.

Where the scheme rules are not circulated, the circular should provide a statement that they will be available for inspection from the date of posting the circular at a place in or near the City of London or at such other place as the FSA may determine, and at the place of the meeting for at least 15 minutes before and during the meeting.

ABI guidelines

11.026   The ABI guidelines (set out in App.17) have long been seen as the industry standard on good corporate governance. Their guidance, which was reissued on December 15, 2009, *Principles and Guidelines on Remuneration* is designed to provide a practical framework and reference point for shareholders in reaching voting decisions and for companies in deciding upon their remuneration policy. They also published a position paper in January 2010 to help remuneration committees understand how shareholders expect the guidelines to be implemented in the current challenging economic climate. The ABI actively monitor the remuneration reports of all FTSE 100 companies and will "rate" them according to how new schemes comply with their best practice guidelines.

The main principles in relation to share-based remuneration are as follows:

- share incentive schemes should align the interests of executive directors with those of shareholders and link reward to performance over the long term;

- shareholders should approve all new share-based incentives or any substantial changes to existing schemes by means of a separate and binding resolution. The operation rationale and cost should be fully explained so that shareholders can make an informed decision;

- it is desirable to align the interests of chairmen and independent directors with those of shareholders, for example through payment in shares bought at market prices. However, it is inappropriate for chairmen and independent directors to receive incentive awards geared to the share price or corporate performance that would impair their ability to provide impartial oversight and advice;

- shareholders encourage companies to require executive directors and senior executives to build up meaningful shareholdings in the companies for which they work;

- the dilutive effect of share incentives should not exceed 10 per cent in 10 years, with a further limitation of 5 per cent in 10 years in respect of discretionary schemes; and

- the mix of incentives should reflect the company's needs, establish an appropriate balance between fixed and variable remuneration, and be based on targets that are appropriately stretching, verifiable and relevant which take account of risk.

The 2009 guidelines recognise the issues that arose from unchecked remuneration policies in the financial services sector and note that remuneration committees should also pay particular attention to arrangements for senior executives who are not board members but have a significant influence over the company's ability to meet its strategic objectives. Remuneration committees should have oversight of all associated risks arising as a result of remuneration.

Structuring a share incentive scheme

Committees will need to seek advice on the complex legal, tax and regulatory framework, not only from remuneration specialists but lawyers and accountants and of course maintain an open dialogue with institutions and shareholder representative bodies such as the ABI. However, the following features will be particularly key to the remuneration committee's deliberations: **11.027**

Overall structure

Most schemes today are either designed as traditional share options or performance share plans. Option schemes will usually involve the executive   **11.028** receiving the right to acquire shares at a set price at some point in the future (providing certain performance conditions have been met). The exercise price should be set at the current market price of the shares and should not incorporate any discount.

Performance share plans usually involve the provision of "free shares" at the end of the appropriate performance period. The number of shares received will usually be linked to performance. Performance share plans have grown in popularity over recent years, as they are less significantly affected by share price movements and can have a less significant impact on the profit and loss account (see para.11.037). As the shares are provided at no cost to the executive, fewer shares are required than any equivalent market value option. To this end they can reduce dilution.

In the light of a new top rate of income tax of 50 per cent for those with income above £150,000, and proposed increases to national insurance contributions in 2011, there has been some interest in alternative forms of share incentive schemes that tax gains more favourably as capital.[34] However, the ABI, in a Position Paper in January 2010 warned against remuneration structures that "seek to increase tax efficiency" if they would result in additional costs to the company or an increase in its own tax bill and should not as a matter of principle compensate directors for higher tax rates. In particular, remuneration committees should be aware of the potential damage that could be done to a company's and shareholders' reputations as a result of implementing such schemes, and any latent income tax liabilities which may exist should more tax aggressive forms of remuneration be challenged by HMRC.

Vesting

11.029   The ABI consider that performance conditions should be measured over a period of three or more years, and "strong encouragement" is given to the use of longer periods and deferred vesting schedules "in order to motivate the achievement of sustained improvements in financial performance". Where restricted shares are granted, the ABI are of the view that better alignment of interest with shareholders is achieved if dividends payable to shareholders accrue in relation to vested awards. However, dividend expectations should be taken into account in assessing the size of grants to be made.

Performance conditions

11.030   The ABI guidelines look for challenging performance conditions to govern the vesting of awards or the exercise of options. They should relate to overall

---

[34] See App.18 for more details on these and other common types of employees' share schemes.

corporate performance, be demanding in the context of the prospects of the company and the prevailing economic environment, be measured relative to an appropriate peer group and be clearly disclosed and transparent. The reasons for selecting the performance conditions together with the overall policy for granting share awards should be fully explained to shareholders.

Where awards are made with a high potential value shareholders expect commensurately higher levels of performance: "full vesting should be dependent upon achievement of significantly greater value creation than applicable to threshold vesting". Threshold vesting amounts should not be significant by comparison to annual base salary, and cliff-edge vesting is considered inappropriate.

The ABI favour total shareholder return relative to an index or peer group, but emphasise that the committee should satisfy themselves prior to vesting that this is a genuine reflection of the company's underlying performance. In some sectors or niche industries committees may have challenges in actually formulating a meaningful "relevant and representative" comparator group, and earnings per share measures may still be relevant as a performance measure, particularly for share option plans. However, the general trend is towards using a combination of measures. A survey carried out by KPMG on Directors' Compensation in 2009 shows that while 32 per cent of FTSE 100 performance share plans used TSR alone as a performance measure, 48 per cent used a combination of TSR and ESP or another measure.

Re-testing

The ABI are firmly of the view that retesting of performance conditions is unnecessary and unjustified, particularly in light of their recommendation that awards should be made on an annual phased basis. This grant policy is encouraged to reduce the risk of unanticipated outcomes as a result of share price volatility or cyclical factors.   **11.031**

Change of control provisions

Scheme rules should not provide for automatic vesting on a change of control event, and/or on the early termination of a participant's employment. The ABI note that shareholders expect that the underlying financial performance of a company that is subject to change of control should be a key determinant of what share-based awards if any, should vest for participants. Where awards vest early, the committee should be satisfied that the performance measures are robust over any shorter time period and explain their reasoning in the remuneration report. Any vesting on a change of control should be on a time pro-rata basis, taking into account the amount of the vesting period that has elapsed at the time of change of control.   **11.032**

Dilution limits

11.033 The ABI guidelines on the acceptable level of shareholder dilution in connection with employee share plans has become market practice in the industry. Where awards are to be satisfied from the issue of new shares or the use of treasury shares, the commitment in respect of all arrangements should not exceed 10 per cent in 10 years. The ABI also recommend that commitments should not exceed 5 per cent in 10 years in respect of executive schemes (but recognise that this may be exceed where vesting is dependent upon superior levels of performance—with full vesting at top quartile). There are some companies where higher limits are approved by shareholders, but generally only specific commercial reasons have justified such an approach. For smaller companies, up to 10 per cent of the ordinary share capital may be used for discretionary, executive schemes, provided that the total market value of the share capital used for the scheme at the time of grant does not exceed £1 million.

Cost

11.034 Shareholders bear the overall costs of share arrangements—either through dilution of their holdings, or in cash terms where shares are funded by market purchase. The ABI guidelines require the cost of schemes to be disclosed at the time shareholder approval is sought to enable shareholders to assess the benefits. The potential and expected value of awards should be included. Some guidance is provided in the Appendix to the guidelines, but in the light of fast changing accountancy practice, this continues to be a difficult area for committees to get right.

Life of awards/schemes

11.035 It is best practice to limit the life of a scheme to 10 years and limit the ability for awards to vest to no more than 10 years from their date of grant. The ABI recommend that awards should not vest where employees leave voluntarily, or are dismissed for cause. The guidelines recognise that where individuals cannot complete service periods it is to be expected that a portion of awards vest but in accordance with the period completed and the achievement of appropriate performance criteria.

Shareholding requirements

11.036 The ABI guidelines note that institutional shareholders encourage companies to require their senior executives to build up meaningful shareholdings in companies for which they work. Consistent with this approach consideration should be given to incorporating provisions in incentive schemes to require retention of a proportion of shares to which participants become entitled until such times as shareholding guidelines are met. This approach does seem to be gradually influencing the design of schemes, but the number of companies that set shareholding requirements is not, at present widespread.

Accounting

The emergence of International Financial Reporting Standard 2 and the **11.037** UK Financial Reporting Standard 20 requiring companies to recognise the cost of share-based remuneration in their report and accounts is having a significant impact on both the design and structure of remuneration packages.[35] The fair value of equity awards must be calculated at the time of grant and recognised as an expense. The source of shares used in the plan (whether newly issued, existing shares held in an employee benefit trust or treasury shares) does not have an impact on the expense charge. There are a number of methods of establishing "fair value". A traditional model for option valuation is the Black Scholes method and whilst has its limitations is fairly simple to use and freely available on many financial organisation websites. It takes account of factors such as expected volatility dividends and the life of the options. Other methods of valuation include the bi-nominal and Monte Carlo methods. These are more sophisticated but tend to work better in the context of performance-based awards. They produce a value based on an assumption about exercise behaviours.

Whilst there is a general consensus that accounting treatment should not drive the structure of remuneration schemes, there is now a focus on performance share plans, stock appreciation rights (settled in cash or shares) and other non-option based schemes which may have a better effect on the profit and loss account. Committees must have a clear understanding of the financial impact of the schemes they are devising and seek appropriate accounting advice as part of this process.

Directors' service agreements

The length and structure of directors' service agreements has increasingly **11.038** come into the debate on good corporate governance over recent years and the ABI/NAPF best practice statement on executive contracts and severance had become a clear benchmark in this area.

---

[35] IFRS 2 applies to all listed companies preparing consolidated accounts for the period after January 1, 2005. FRS 20 applies to UK companies from January 1, 2005 (if listed) and from January 1, 2006 for AIM and unlisted companies.

The UK Corporate Governance Code

11.039   Provision D.1.5 of the UK Corporate Governance Code provides that notice periods and service contracts should be set at one year or less. If it is necessary to offer longer notice or contract periods to new directors, these should reduce to one year or less after the initial period. It is apparent that whilst compliance with this principle is improving, there is some way to go before many companies reach this target.

Company law requirements

11.040   CA 2006 s.229 introduced a right for shareholders to request a copy of any director's service agreement and introduced more stringent requirements for shareholder approval of long-term directors' service contracts.

CA 2006 s.227 defines what is meant by a director's service contract and encompasses both contracts for services and letters of appointment. The Act requires that all directors' service contracts (or a précis of their terms where not in writing) are held at the company's registered office or the location where its register of members is kept, during the term of office and for a minimum period of one year from the date of termination or expiry of the contract.[36]

Shareholders are entitled, on payment of a fee to request a copy of the contract or précis. This must be supplied within seven days of the request.[37] The requirement for shareholder approval of directors' service contracts in excess of five years (formerly in CA 1985 s.319) has been reduced to two years or more under CA 2006 s.188. All provisions relating to a guaranteed term of a director's employment with a company or with a subsidiary or holding company in excess of two years must be approved by shareholders in advance.

Compensation payments

11.041   The whole issue of rewards for executive failure continues to grab headlines and despite rigid guidelines from shareholder bodies continues to be a problem.

The ABI/NAPF statement is emphatic in its tone:

"It is unacceptable that failure which detracts from the value of an enterprise and which can threaten the livelihood of employees can result in

---

[36]   CA 2006 s.228(3).
[37]   Clause 229(1) provides members with a right of inspection of service contracts free of charge.

large payments to its departing leaders. Executives whose remuneration is already at a level which allows for the risk interest in their role, should show leadership in aligning their financial interest with those of their shareholders."

They recommend that at the outset a clear idea of the potential cost of termination in monetary terms should be established. Remuneration committees often face difficult decisions, particularly where high profile or public terminations are involved. Executives are of course under a duty to mitigate their loss, although the poorer performing directors will perhaps have more difficulty in finding alternative roles that those who have a better performance record.

Liquidated damages clauses in contracts are becoming more common. These effectively set the level of severance payment at the outset. However, they rarely take into account any duty to mitigate loss and as they are contractual, they cannot usually be negotiated on termination if for example the executive is terminated for poor performance. Benefits under such clauses are taxable in the hands of the director (incurring a national insurance contribution on the company at 12.8 per cent[38]) whereas compensation payments are not always taxable. Where a director is removed for poor performance, his or her ability to find alternative positions will of course be less strong than those who can mitigate their loss by finding new roles quickly. The ABI/NAPF comment that "shareholders do not believe the liquidated damages approach is generally desirable. Boards which adopt this approach should justify their decision".

The ABI welcome the use of phased payments to exiting directors, whereby the remaining contractual payments are made on the usual monthly basis. In the event that the departing executive secures new employment, the payments cease.

CA 2006 ss.215 to 222 have introduced a number of changes in relation to payments for loss of office from the 1985 regime. The new provisions extend to compensation payments not only for loss of office, but to compensation in connection with the management of a company's affairs or those of any subsidiary company. Shareholder approval is required for payment of compensation to directors on retirement or loss of office unless they are damages for breach of contract or pension for past services in accordance with the director's service contract. The Act makes clear that compensation includes benefits payable other than in cash and cover payments made to any person connected with the director or to any person at his or her direction.

Such compensation payments must be approved by shareholders in advance. If a company is to make a compensatory payment for loss of office to a director of its holding company, the proposal must be approved by a

---

[38] Rates as at April 6, 2010. Employers' NIC rates will increase to 13.8% with effect from April 6, 2011.

resolution of the company itself and the holding company. A resolution approving compensation of this nature is not effective unless a memorandum setting out the particulars of the proposed payment (including its amount) is made available to the members whose approval is sought. If this is done by written resolution, the memorandum must be sent to each member, or if the resolution is to be considered at a meeting, the memorandum must be made available for members' inspection at the company's registered office for 15 days prior to the meeting and at the meeting itself.

CA 2006 s.218 also requires shareholder approval in relation to a payment for loss of office to a director in connection with the transfer of the whole or any part of the undertaking of the company or in connection with the a share transfer relating to shares in the company or a subsidiary resulting from a takeover bid.

Remuneration of non-executive directors

11.042   The remuneration of non-executive directors has not raised particular controversy over the years and most receive their fees in the form of cash or shares.

UK Corporate Governance Code Provision D.1.3 states that levels of remuneration for non-executive directors should reflect the time commitment and responsibilities of the role. It specifically states that remuneration for non-executive directors should not include share options or other performance-related elements, but if exceptional circumstances justify such grants, shareholder approval should be sought in advance and any shares acquired on the exercise of options should be held until at least one year after the non-executive leaves the board. There is little published guidance as to what exceptional circumstances would justify the holding of share options, but the UK Corporate Governance Code does warn that this may be relevant to the director's independence.

UK Corporate Governance Code Provision D.2.3 states that:

> "The Board itself, or where required by the Articles of Association, the shareholders should determine the remuneration of non-executive directors within the limits set in the Articles of Association. Where permitted by the Articles, the board may however delegate this responsibility to a committee who might include the chief executive."

The ABI guidelines provide that:

> "the chairman and non-executive directors should be appropriately remunerated either in cash or in shares bought or allocated at market price. The grant of incentives linked to share price or performance is not appropriate as could impair the ability of chairmen and independent non-executives to provide impartial oversight and advice."

ABI guidelines go on to recommend that where in exceptional circumstances specific reasons arise for wishing to include the chairman in share incentive arrangements, these should be fully discussed and approved by shareholders in advance. The ABI recommend that participants are expected to hold all shares awarded under such schemes for the duration of their term in office.

The allocation of shares to non-executive directors should be handled with care to ensure compliance with company law requirements.

Pensions

Pensions are probably the most challenging area of remuneration for the **11.043** committee to negotiate. The wholesale reform of UK pensions legislation, which came into force on April 6, 2006—commonly referred to as "A-day" will clearly have a significant impact on executives' pension arrangements. In addition, far-reaching restrictions on tax relief for pensions contributions, including anti-forestalling measures aimed at higher earners, announced in 2009 and subject to further consultation during 2010/2011, will also have an effect on the perceived value of pensions. The ABI guidelines warn however that companies are not responsible for compensating individuals for changes in personal tax liabilities such as those resulting from changes to pensions taxation and add that companies "may wish to consider whether there may be ways of delivering remuneration that are more cost-effective than a pension fund and more aligned with shareholder value creation" in light of A-day changes.

The guidance in Schedule A of the UK Corporate Governance Code requires committees to consider the pension consequences and associated pension costs to the company of basic salary increases and any other changes in pensionable remuneration, especially for directors close to retirement. Committees should also be aware of the financial commitment that defined benefit (or final salary) schemes involve.

The ABI guidelines state that shareholders recognise that pension entitlements accruing to directors represent a significant and potentially costly item of remuneration which is not directly linked to the performance of the company. It is of the view that there should be informative disclosure identifying incremental value accruing to pension scheme participation and any other superannuation arrangements and related contingent commitments arising from service during the year in question. Changes to transfer values should be fully explained. Where there are discretionary increases in pension entitlement, significant changes in actuarial and other relevant assumptions, or ex-gratia awards or contributions, these should be fully explained and justified. Companies should recognise the risks of changes to future mortality rates and investment returns and how to limit the potential liability created by pension commitments.

Model Code and regulatory issues

11.044   The committee need to be aware of the Model Code under the Listing Rules[39] to ensure that awards are made within the appropriate period. Scheme rules are usually designed so that awards are granted within the period of 42 days following the announcement of a company's annual or half year results to ensure this is the case. Awards can be made at other times provided the committee believes exceptional circumstances exist. Equally directors are responsible for compliance with the Model Code in relation to the decisions they make to exercise an option or sell the underlying shares acquired.

Directors and individuals who discharge managerial responsibility are also obliged to notify the company in respect of transactions in shares both under the CA 2006 and the disclosure requirements under the Listing Rules. With effect from March 6, 2009, persons who discharge managerial responsibility are permitted to enter into trading plans to give them more flexibility to deal in shares without breaching the terms of the Model Code or placing themselves under suspicion of dealing on the basis of inside information.

Europe

EU Recommendations on remuneration

11.045   The UK is not alone when it comes to negative publicity in relation to executive pay. As part of its Action Plan on company law and corporate governance (Modernising Company Law and Enhancing Corporate Governance in the EU),[40] the EU[41] Commission issued a Recommendation on December 14, 2004 intended to foster an appropriate regime for the remuneration of directors of listed companies. The Recommendation acknowledged the diversity in corporate governance systems across the community, but emphasised the need to disclosure of accurate and timely information and transparency in company dealings with investors. Two further Recommendations on remuneration were made on April 29, 2009, one of which related to remuneration in the financial services sector, the other which related generally to remuneration of directors of listed companies. This second Recommendation complements the earlier Recommendation and provides further guidance on the design of an appropriate remuneration policy. The European Parliament

---

[39] Annex 1 to LR 9 and set out in full in App.19.
[40] See Ch.23 (The EU) for more detail.
[41] Recommendations are just that: they have no binding effect, and in the case of the directors' remuneration Recommendation the UK already has rules which are more rigorous than the recommendation as a result of the various disclosure obligations described above.

in May 2010 called on the Commission to introduce further legislation on remuneration and corporate governance, noting that the Recommendations had not been substantially put into practice by Member States. However, the Recommendation provisions are already covered in the Large and Medium-sized Companies and Groups (Accounts and Reports) Regulations 2008, the UK corporate Governance Code and UK institutional best practice, and therefore their impact has not been noticeable in the UK.

Further developments at the European level are expected in relation to remuneration in the financial services sector. Prescriptive rules on the form of banking bonuses are likely to be introduced in January 2011 under the Capital Requirements Directive.

The Transparency Directive

A further development out of the EU is the Transparency Directive which **11.046** deals with the ongoing obligations for issuers whose securities are traded on an EU market. The purpose of this Directive is to improve the information available to investors. Under the Directive issuers will need to provide annual financial reports within four months after the end of the financial year and detailed half-yearly financial reports not later than two months after the end of the relevant period. Interim statements will be required between reports to provide explanations of material events and transactions and a general description of the financial position and performance of the issuer and its undertakings.

The Listing Rules and the Disclosure Rules incorporate the Transparency Directive in the form of the Disclosure and Transparency Rules. The Financial Services and Markets Act 2000 was also changed and CA 2006 Pt 43 is enacted so as to implement the Transparency Directive.

Chapter 12

D&O Insurance and Indemnification

Edward Smerdon[1]

What is D&O insurance?

Directors' and officers' liability ("D&O") insurance has grown in prominence **12.001**
in the UK in the last five years, beginning with its inclusion in the Higgs Review
and subsequent Combined Code and in 2010 the UK Corporate Governance
Code and ICSA Guidance, followed by the new laws on indemnification, and
recently the heightened interest in executive protection arising out of some
notorious extradition cases. It is an insurance policy bought by companies
for the benefit of their directors and officers, insuring them in respect of their
potential liabilities as directors and officers. Some policies also reimburse the
companies themselves to the extent they have lawfully indemnified the directors and officers, and may provide separate cover to the company in respect of
securities claims that are also brought against their directors.

In London, D&O insurance is provided by commercial insurance companies and the Lloyd's market, usually via insurance brokers, either as a
bespoke product or as part of a wider insurance programme. Its availability,
scope and price is ultimately dictated by supply and demand. This has led
to periods when the cover has been cheap to buy and broad in coverage, for
instance the insurance market was soft between 1996 and 2002. In 2003/2004,
following heavy losses suffered by insurers during that soft market, when
claims exceeded premiums particularly as a result of D&O claims in the US,

---

[1] Edward Smerdon is the managing partner of the London office of the US law firm, Sedgwick
Detert Moran and Arnold LLP. He is recognised as a leading lawyer in insurance and reinsur-
ance, including coverage disputes, non-contentious product development and transactional
work. His particular emphasis is on liability insurance/reinsurance, where he has developed a
market leading role in the field of directors' and officers' liability, professional liability, other
financial lines insurance, and property and casualty insurance. Nearly all of his work is international related, involving coverage problems in five continents. Mr Smerdon mainly acts for
London and Bermuda insurance markets, but also for some major international companies who
need advice on their insurance programmes. He has become a leading authority on the interaction between D&O insurance and indemnification.

the market for D&O hardened, which meant there were fewer insurance companies providing the cover and at increased cost. This however soon changed again (as a rule of thumb for every year of hard market there are at least two soft years) and by 2005 the product was becoming cheaper again and broader in scope, with increasing levels of cover available. In 2007 the market was very soft with high levels of competition and the D&O product had become relatively inexpensive to buy and broader in scope than ever before. On top of this, the recent change in the law on companies' indemnification of their directors has focused attention on complimentary insurance products that fitted around the indemnification, or step in should it fail for some reason. The "credit crunch" which started in 2007/2008 has led to a hardening of the D&O market in respect of financial services companies, banks and finds, but for other companies has remained as soft as ever.

Whilst D&O cover is not compulsory, the UK Corporate Governance Code[2] anticipates that all publicly quoted companies should buy and provide it for their directors in order to persuade them to take up positions which involve more responsibility and potential exposure than in the past.

A brief history of D&O insurance

12.002   D&O insurance has been available in the UK for over 20 years, however, it was rarely offered or bought until s.310 of the Companies Act 1985 ("CA 1985") was amended by the Companies Act 1989 ("CA 1989"), now s.233 of the Companies Act 2006 ("CA 2006"), so as to expressly allow companies to purchase D&O insurance for their directors. Even then, take up was slow and the products available extremely restrictive in their scope of coverage, with low limits of the amount of indemnity available.

This was partly because they were based upon the US D&O product, by then mature, which suited the US risks well but did not necessarily cope effectively with UK liabilities. It was also because in the early 1990s the long-established law governing directors' duties was such that they were to be judged according to very subjective criteria which meant that liability to the company would be extremely rare. This relatively benign climate changed following the spectacular corporate collapses of the early/mid 1990s with the introduction of codes of best practice and various cases in which courts began to take a tougher view of directors' duties. By the end of the 1990s the accepted test for a director's standard of care was that contained in the Insolvency Act 1986 s.214(4)[3] which effectively provides there is a minimum standard of care required to be met.

---

[2] Code Provision A.1.3 states: "The company should arrange appropriate insurance cover in respect of legal action against its directors".
[3] That of: "A reasonably diligent person having both—(a) the general knowledge, skill and experience that may reasonably be expected of a person carrying out the same functions as are carried out by that Director in relation to the company and (b) the general knowledge, skill and experience that that Director has".

With the soft insurance market of the late 1990s and increased demand, D&O insurance became more popular and, with increasing amounts of regulation and its position in the UK Corporate Governance Code, it is now fully established.

Types of cover available—who is covered?

Standard form D&O policies all follow a similar format in the basic cover provided. There are two heads of cover routinely provided and a third which is provided in addition to public companies. A number of further options exist. A brief description of each is set out below.

12.003

Side A cover—the directors and officers

All policies provide cover to the directors and officers in respect of their personal liabilities (this head is often referred to as "Side A cover"). In the UK this is the most widely used cover.

12.004

"Directors and officers" are normally defined in the policy by reference to their statutory definitions which rely primarily on their de facto roles. The definition of director will therefore embrace not only those registered as directors at Companies House, but also any individual who in fact performs the role of director. As regards officers, these will typically include the company secretary and senior managers but again the emphasis is upon the role actually performed. In both cases the cover is for "natural persons" and therefore "corporate directors" are not covered.

The cover provided for the directors and officers is typically broad so long as four basic elements are in place: there must be a "*Loss*" suffered as a result of "*Claims*" made against the directors and officers in respect of a "*Wrongful Act*" committed "*in their capacity as Directors & Officers*".

The Side A cover of the policy will only be triggered where all four elements exist. Some examples as to how this works in practice, by reference to different types of problem, appear later in the chapter in the section "What is covered?".

The D&O policy is what is known as a "claims made" policy and so the final requirement for cover in all cases is that the claims are made during the policy period (typically one year from the inception date). Frequently a situation arises where a claim is anticipated in the policy period but not made until afterwards. In this event, if the directors have notified the insurer of the potential claim during the policy period any subsequent claim will be deemed to have been made within the policy period.

Side A only products have become more prevalent with the new laws on indemnification, as they are tailored to fit around the indemnification provided by the company and step in should it fail. This topic is addressed later in this chapter.

Side B cover—company reimbursement

12.005   Claims that are made against the company are not covered under a D&O policy unless additional "entity" coverage has been provided by the insurers (see below for instance "Side C cover"). However, the company may be covered if and to the extent it has lawfully indemnified the directors and officers in respect of *their* liability. This head of cover is often referred to as "Side B cover".

Company reimbursement cover used to be more commonly triggered in the US, where companies have routinely indemnified their directors, but not in the UK, due primarily to the provisions of CA 1985 s.310, which in relation to directors were replaced by CA 1985 ss.309A and B and when implemented in October 2007 are embodied in CA 2006 s.232 and s.234. Section 310 was a much criticised section, both for its ambiguity and for its effectively prohibiting companies from indemnifying their directors in circumstances where they are now exposed to much greater threats from, for instance, US shareholders. The provisions in ss.309A and 309B, now CA 2006 s.232 and s.234, are examined in more detail later in this chapter but the basic position is that UK companies are now permitted to indemnify their directors in certain situations. Where they do so, for example by advancing defence costs, Side B cover is potentially available, although it is often subject to an excess.

Side C cover—securities entity cover

12.006   This head of cover, only needed by public companies, covers the company in respect of claims made against it under s.90 of the Financial Services and Markets Act 2000 ("FSMA 2000") or otherwise, for misleading particulars in any public offering of shares, where the directors are also sued. Such claims have in the past been rare but in principle can be brought against both the directors and the company at the same time, for the same losses. In addition, UK companies with US listings will be exposed to lawsuits from ADR holders under US securities laws, for which this cover is also provided. Whilst under Side A the directors may be covered under the D&O policy, the company would not, and so this cover is given to enable the directors and company to share the responsibility for defending the claims, using the same defence team. Whilst this is convenient, it may not ultimately be in the directors' best interests as costs incurred by the company in respect of its exposures may reduce the amount of cover available to the directors personally.

Investigation costs cover

Under the FSMA 2000, the Financial Services Authority ("FSA") has **12.007** sweeping powers to investigate the affairs of public companies. There have been numerous other pieces of legislation within the last decade that have produced enhanced powers for regulators, the Office of Fair Trading and the Data Protection Commissioner being other examples. Investigations by regulators are therefore part of the day-to-day life of any company, particularly public and financial services companies, and are costly where legal representation is necessary.

An investigation by a regulator will usually start out as an investigation of the company, not of the directors, and without any allegation of wrongdoing on the part of the directors. The costs of attending an investigation would therefore not be covered elsewhere in the policy because the investigation, or at least its preliminary stages, is unlikely to meet the four elements identified above that are required for Side A (and Side B) to be triggered (there being no "claim" for instance). However, insurers recognise the benefit of directors (either personally or more commonly on behalf of the company) being legally represented in such proceedings as a claim may follow later. Cover is therefore now given for such legal representation costs, often without regard to whether the costs are being incurred on behalf of the company or the directors. As an example of the difference a soft market can make to the product, this head of cover used to be subject to a lower limit (a "sub-limit") than the other heads because it would be more likely to be used; it is currently being given without any lower limit.

Outside board cover

This used to be an optional or very restricted cover but is now standard. It **12.008** covers employees of the company who, at the direction of the company, sit on the boards of other companies, in respect of their potential liability as directors of those companies. Such cover is popular with venture capital companies who routinely place nominee directors on the boards of companies in which they have invested. It is a more risky cover for the insurers to give because they cannot easily assess these risks. Rather than insist on the details of every such company, insurers usually impose restrictions so that it is not automatically given for certain types of company (such as those with listings or US domicile), and that the cover only operates over and above (a) any D&O insurance bought by the outside company, and (b) any indemnification available from the outside company.

Other optional covers

12.009 The fundamental heads of cover have now been dealt with but it is possible to secure additional cover via extensions to the basic policy wording. This is commonly done either by extensions offered within the policy document or by way of "endorsements" to the policy, which are added on. Below are some examples of additional heads of cover:

Employment practices liability ("EPL") insurance

12.010 EPL covers a company in respect of employment claims made against it that arise out of working practices adopted by the company or its employees. Examples might include unfair dismissal, discriminatory conduct or sexual harassment. Such claims would seldom otherwise be covered under a D&O policy as they are generally against the company as employer (although see paras 12.013 et seq. below). The insurance provides defence costs cover for the company in defending such claims. There is an argument that as an entity coverage it can erode the amount of cover available for the directors personally and should therefore be bought separately.

Prosecution costs cover

12.011 Production costs covers the costs of a director taking *new* proceedings to appeal or overturn or challenge a judicial or governmental order against them. Side A cover will include the costs of bringing/defending appeals of claims but in certain exceptional circumstances the only right of appeal lies in taking a new and different type of proceeding to the one in which the claim against them was brought. An example is in the context of extradition where, once the magistrates' court has decided in favour of extradition it is the Home Secretary who decides to allow the extradition and signs the order for extradition. The only appeal of that lies by taking a new proceeding in the High Court, against the Government. This does not fit happily within the traditional policy structure but conceptually should be covered as part of the protection afforded to directors, and so today it has become relatively routinely provided.

Non-executive directors' additional limit[4]

12.012 Non-executive directors' additional limit is a special additional amount of cover (sometimes expressed as a percentage of the policy limit of indemnity)

---

[4] A typical example of this clause states: "In the event of payments in respect of LOSS arising from all CLAIMS on behalf of any INSUREDS exhausting the Limit of Liability . . . then the

provided on top of the usual limit of cover which is available to the non-executive directors only, once the policy limit has been fully exhausted by claims (involving executive and/or non-executive directors and/or the company). The theory behind this is that the policy is more likely to become exhausted by attritional claims against the executive directors, leaving less cover available for the non-executives to defend themselves on the less frequent occasion of their being sued. Also, it is in recognition of the heightened interest of non-executives in D&O insurance following the Higgs Report.

What is covered?

The nature of the liability risks facing directors has changed over the last 15 years and so has the cover provided by the D&O policy. In practice claims have been brought against directors in the UK relatively infrequently. This may have been for a variety of reasons, including, as mentioned above, the more relaxed standards of conduct that for so long existed, the limited groups of people that under English law could bring claims with any prospects of success, and the relatively benign claims culture in the UK, by comparison to the US. Whilst the UK legal regime has some considerable way to go before it exposes directors to the liability risks imposed on their US counterparts, a gradual increase in potential exposure has heightened interest in the D&O policy, and what it in practice covers. **12.013**

As mentioned above, the amount of cover provided may change with time, according to insurance market conditions. If in doubt about the amount of cover provided under a policy, it is advisable to ask the company's insurance brokers to comment.

The policy—general

When a problem that needs to be notified to the insurers arises it is for the directors to show that it falls within the cover in the first instance. This is done by reference to the heads of cover available (see above). The reader is reminded that Side A cover, which is provided for the directors and officers in respect of their potential liabilities, requires four basic elements to be in place: there must be a *"Loss"* suffered as a result of *"Claims"* made against the directors and officers in respect of a *"Wrongful Act"* committed *"in their capacity as Directors & Officers"*. **12.014**

The definition of *"Directors & Officers"* has already been discussed above.

Limit of Liability of this Policy Shall be increased by the sum set forth in the [Schedule] in the aggregate in respect of [Side A and Side B coverage] for the benefit only of NON-EXECUTIVE DIRECTORS at the date of the WRONGFUL ACT" (Source: Axis Specialty D&O Policy 2006).

The policy definition of "*Loss*" will usually be sufficient to embrace compensatory damages awarded against the directors, settlement payments, defence costs, and the claimant's costs where the claim has been successful. Defence costs are usually payable "as incurred" which means they are paid by the insurers as they fall due, rather than reimbursed at the end, however, to be absolutely certain of this the policy should contain an express "advancement of costs" provision (relevant to the conduct exclusions, below). The policy definition of "*Claims*" will usually include pre-action protocol or other letters threatening proceedings, civil proceedings, regulatory proceedings and criminal prosecutions. Finally, the policy definition of "*Wrongful Act*" will typically be broad, embracing all types of actual and alleged misfeasance; the crucial element is that there be allegations of wrongdoing.

Importantly, there is no coverage limitation on where claims can be brought, unless claims in certain territories are expressly excluded. Directors of companies with US listings, parent companies or subsidiaries stand a higher chance of being sued and so a "US exclusion" would be unacceptable to them.

Below, we look at the most common areas of exposure for directors in the UK and comment upon how Side A of a typical policy might respond.

Civil claims brought by the company

12.015   Claims by the company are in theory the main source of liability claims for directors, as it is to the company that directors primarily owe their duties, although in practice such claims are infrequently brought. The situation most commonly occurs after the constitution of the board changes significantly and the new board recommends to the company that it brings proceedings against the retired directors for mismanagement.

Such claims are for, inter alia, civil damages and will usually make allegations concerning the management of the company. In this event, the four elements needed for there to be cover will usually be present. Where the claim contains a restitutionary element, for instance where the directors are required to repay sums they allegedly should never have received, this aspect will not usually be included within the cover.

Derivative claims

12.016   Generally the principle of "majority rule" applies to companies. However, minority shareholders have always had a theoretical common law right to bring an action against the directors in the name of and on behalf of the company where the directors have also been majority shareholders and have allegedly been guilty of egregious conduct that is manifestly against the company's interests (known as committing a "fraud on the minority"). Practically speaking however this right is very rarely exercised given uncertainty over its application and the perceived legal hurdles to overcome. CA 2006 ss.260 to 264 contain provisions designed to make the circumstances in which such claims may be brought, and the machinery for bringing them, clearer. Commentators have expressed fears that an unwanted side effect may be to open the doors to more frequent claims because the current legal hurdles will be replaced by more discretionary considerations, even though the court will provide an early "filter" to weed out the hopeless or nuisance claims of disgruntled shareholders. Such claims will otherwise closely resemble claims by the company as described above and for that reason are likely to be covered.

Since the law changed there have been a number of "low profile" derivative actions commenced under the new machinery, but to the best of the author's knowledge, none proceeded past the court filtering system.

Claims by shareholders

It is established law that directors do not generally owe a duty to individual **12.017** shareholders. This has not prevented minority shareholders from trying to bring claims against directors from time to time. Such claims ought to fail, however, the directors will need to incur costs defending the proceedings, at least to the point where they may be struck out. The four necessary elements for the cover to be triggered are likely to be present, except for example where a director, who is also a shareholder, is sued in his or her capacity as a shareholder (such as in a shareholder dispute). Claims under CA 2006 s.994 for unfair prejudice may fall into this category, depending upon the particular allegations.

Claims by third parties

Generally in their dealings with third parties, the directors are representa- **12.018** tives of the company and therefore it is the company that ought to be liable where the directors have caused others loss and damage. However, where the company has subsequently ceased to exist, particularly where the director in question was also the main shareholder and driving force behind the company, a third party may allege that the director is liable on the basis that they assumed a personal responsibility for their actions, beyond that assumed by the company.

The four necessary elements for cover may be present, as it is likely there would be a civil claim for damages alleging a wrongful act. However, it is arguable that if the claimant succeeds in establishing that the director assumed personal responsibility, (s)he could not have been acting in their capacity as a director. On the other hand, the crucial factor may be that the director could not have been in a position to assume personal responsibility had they not been a director at that time. Coverage may ultimately depend on the precise language used in the policy.

Claims arising out of public offerings

12.019   As mentioned above, claims may be brought against the directors (and the company) for misleading particulars following a public offering of shares. The liability imposed by FSMA 2000 s.90 is at first sight strict, however, the effect of the statutory defence contained in FSMA 2000 Sch.10 means that the directors are only likely to liable where they did not act reasonably, thus introducing the requirement of fault. In practice few claims under this provision have been brought reflecting a benign claims culture and lack of recent significant corporate failures, but FSMA 2000 s.90 is likely to be used more frequently in future. UK companies with level 2 and 3 ADR programmes will face equivalent claims under US securities laws. The claims are civil in nature and for compensatory damages, therefore are again likely to trigger the cover because all four necessary elements are present.

Employment practice liability ("EPL") claims

12.020   Usually employees with a complaint bring proceedings against the company employer, which is not covered under the D&O policy. In cases of discrimination or harassment, a claimant may also join the employee most directly responsible for the matter complained of. This employee may coincidentally also be a director, however, the position of director is unlikely to be crucial to the establishment of the wrongful act alleged, and therefore it could not be said to have been committed in the capacity as a director. Companies with specific concerns as to their exposure to employment claims should seek to address them through EPL insurance.

Insolvency Act claims

12.021   A major source of potential claims against directors is after the company has entered insolvent liquidation, under the Insolvency Act 1986. Liquidators have broad powers to bring claims against directors for misfeasance on behalf of the company (under s.212), for fraudulent trading (under s.213) and for wrongful trading (under s.214).

     Coverage of misfeasance claims is likely to be subject to similar considerations as for claims by the company (see above). Claims for fraudulent trading are likely to present additional considerations for the cover (see "What is excluded?" below). In respect of wrongful trading, the directors may have to contribute to the assets of a company if they continued trading in circumstances where they knew or ought to have known there was no reasonable prospect that the company would avoid going into insolvent liquidation. The claim is civil in nature and involves an actual or alleged wrongful act. A possible doubt is over whether a "loss" has been suffered: a requirement "to contribute to the assets of the company" sounds restitutionary in nature, however, the remedy is likely in effect to be compensatory.

Disqualification claims

Under the Company Directors Disqualification Act 1986 s.6, directors of **12.022**
a company which has become insolvent will be disqualified if their conduct makes them unfit to manage a company.

Liquidators complete a confidential "D Report" to the Insolvency Service on the directors' conduct, and thereafter the Insolvency Service may bring proceedings for disqualification. There is no other recourse available under the Act. This procedure has been used against directors in increasing numbers in recent years.

In practice the directors incur substantial costs defending these proceedings, and so there is a "loss" notwithstanding the absence of any award of damages. Similarly, disqualification proceedings usually fall within the definition of "claim" even though this is not a civil claim for damages. An allegation of a "wrongful act in the capacity of a director" is obviously involved as the right to disqualify is based upon the director's conduct.

Criminal proceedings

There are many criminal offences for which directors may be charged in their **12.023**
capacity as directors. Directors will then incur potentially substantial costs defending themselves to a criminal trial, so a "loss" is thereby suffered. Any criminal fine imposed can not be covered due to public policy, and in any event would fall outside the normal definitions of "loss". Criminal proceedings will normally constitute a "claim" and obviously involve an allegation of a "wrongful act in the capacity of a director" and so the cover is likely to be triggered. Due to uncertainty whether extradition proceedings, and in particular, the appeal of an order of the Home Secretary, are covered as a "claim", policies are generally giving express cover for the process to ensure the protection is there.

FSMA 2000 proceedings, fines and restitution orders

Directors incurring costs in co-operating with the FSA in an investigation **12.024**
of the directors' conduct will be covered for such costs if the circumstances

amount to a claim (i.e. where there are allegations of a wrongful act). In the absence of a claim the investigation costs cover (above) is likely to apply. Once the FSA issues its findings and makes an order, the directors can appeal by taking a new proceeding to a Financial Services and Markets Tribunal. The taking of such an appeal proceeding may be subject to the same coverage doubts as the extradition appeal process and therefore some policies are giving broader "prosecution costs" cover than simply for extradition.

However, whether the remedies are covered by the D&O policy is more open to question. Under FSMA 2000 s.91, the directors may be fined by the FSA for breaches of FSMA 2000 for "such amount as it considers appropriate". This is a relatively new phenomenon. The fines are not "criminal" in nature and therefore in theory are capable of coverage under insurance. However, the FSA outlawed the possible coverage of such fines under insurance policies from January 1, 2004 on the basis insurance removes the incentive for compliance. In any event, it is doubtful whether a "loss" has been incurred: typical definitions do not embrace fines of any nature.

Under FSMA 2000 s.382, the FSA may impose restitution orders upon the directors. Another new area of exposure for directors, a restitution order may attract cover depending on which type of restitution order it is. An order for repayment of any profits that have been earned by the directors as a result of, for example, a breach of the Listing Rules, is unlikely to be embraced by "loss". However, an order requiring payment by the directors of a sum equivalent to the loss or other adverse effect of the breach that has been caused to others, such as shareholders, could be a "loss" because it is essentially compensatory in nature.

Conclusions

12.025　From the above, it can be seen that in respect of the major areas of potential claims that can be brought against directors in the UK, the losses incurred by those directors are covered under the D&O policy. This is not, however, the only consideration, as coverage is also subject to the other terms, conditions and exclusions of the policy (see below).

What is excluded?

12.026　Assuming the problem notified to the insurers by the directors has satisfied the four tests for cover outlined above, the losses will be presumed covered under the policy unless otherwise excluded. At this point if the insurers assert the loss is excluded, then it is their responsibility in law to demonstrate that a relevant exclusion applies, not the directors' responsibility to demonstrate an exclusion does not apply.

When the D&O policy was in its infancy, mainly because the nature of the exposures was not fully understood and insurance capacity was scarce, it contained a long list of exclusions. Now, the product has matured and insurers are using more targeted exclusions for specific matters not intended to be covered. This has effectively reduced the number and breadth of the standard exclusions used. However additional exclusions may be added on a bespoke basis by way of endorsement.

In this section, there is brief consideration of the standard exclusions.

Dishonesty, unlawful gain, deliberate breach of rules

These are known as "conduct" exclusions as they relate to the directors' **12.027** behaviour. Losses arising from dishonest acts are always excluded, indeed the policy is unable to cover those guilty of dishonest acts as a matter of public policy. Losses arising from unlawful gain, such as the receipt of remuneration to which the director was not entitled, and losses as a result of a deliberate breach of rules are also excluded. However, importantly, the exclusion is usually severable, which means that it should be considered separately for each director and applied only to a director guilty of the relevant misconduct. The effect of this, for example, is that directors who may be the subject of a claim which involves the dishonesty of another director will be covered so long as they were not dishonest themselves.

As to how the exclusion is applied, the usual requirement is that conduct be "actual" and, practically speaking, that means the exclusion only bites if a court finds that a director was a guilty of the relevant excluded conduct. For instance, an allegation of dishonesty will be insufficient to trigger the exclusion. The effect of this is that the exclusion will not actually apply unless or until there is a finding of dishonesty at the conclusion of the claim (or an admission, but this is rare). Because the directors' defence costs are normally covered "as incurred", the insurers should pay them regardless of whether there is a question mark over the directors' behaviour, particularly if there is an express advancement of costs provision in the policy.

In the event of an ultimate finding of excluded conduct, any damages awarded against the guilty directors would be excluded and the insurers may be entitled to claim reimbursement of their outlay for defence costs from them.

Claims arising out of public offerings

As mentioned in the last section, claims under FSMA 2000 s.90 against the **12.028** directors are generally covered by the terms of Side A cover. UK companies with level 2 and 3 ADR programmes will be exposed to equivalent claims under US securities laws. However, public offerings are considered by insurers to bring an increased risk of claims (despite, as mentioned above, the low incidence of such claims in the UK historically). In the early days of the D&O policy, claims against directors arising out of them were likely to be routinely excluded across the board.

However, in 2007, whilst policies generally exclude claims arising from public offerings, they provide that the exclusion will not be applied in the event the directors disclose any imminent public offering during the policy period, for which cover is sought, and an appropriate additional premium is paid to the insurers. This is an example of how insurers are providing cover that matches the actual exposure, and pricing it appropriately, rather than simply excluding cover.

Separate bespoke cover for the directors and the company in respect of public offerings is also available (often known as "Public Offering of Securities Insurance"). The companies brokers should be asked to advise on the best approach.

Civil claims brought by the company

12.029 As mentioned above, claims by the company are generally covered within the terms of Side A cover. However, the way the cover has been structured in theory left insurers vulnerable to attempts by directors to recover first party losses of the companies they managed from insurers under the policy when there had in reality been no claim against them at all.

This concern gave rise to what is known in the industry as the "Assured v Assured" exclusion. In the early days in its most basic form (now relatively rare), the exclusion prevented there being coverage of any claims brought by the company.

Despite the insurers' legitimate concern, the clause was seen as a blunt tool in circumstances where the company, under English law, is the primary source of claims against directors. Consequently, over the years, the clause has been refined in an attempt to allow "arm's length" claims that are brought by the company. Common examples of arm's length claims that are now commonly covered are claims brought by an administrator or liquidator of a company, claims brought by the company at the recommendation of a new board of directors against former directors (*Equitable Life* being an example), derivative actions and claims sanctioned by the shareholders in a vote.

In a further dilution of the detrimental effect of the clause for directors, the exclusion frequently does not now affect the coverage of the directors' defence costs, therefore, even if the claim itself falls foul of the exclusion, the directors would have their defence costs paid. This removes the incentive for the artificial formulation of a claim.

In many recent policies the exclusion for non-US claims has been removed altogether but with the insurers retaining the right to take over and control the defence of such claims rather than leave the directors to do so (the latter being the usual position—see below). This seems to be the most effective way to remove the risk of "abusive" claims and ensure the cover is given for legitimate claims.

Personal injuries, physical damage, pollution, professional liability and other insurance

Claims brought directly for personal injury, physical damage, pollution **12.030** and the provision of professional services are routinely excluded as they are considered to be more appropriately covered under other types of insurance purchased by the company. This dovetails with another routine exclusion/ limitation, for losses that are covered by other insurance policies taken out by the company (the norm is to state that the D&O policy is to sit in excess of more specifically relevant insurance). In practice this does not mean any significant gap in cover for the directors because such claims should be covered by EL/PL, property and professional liability insurance also purchased by the company.

However, claims against directors that arise *indirectly* from personal injury, physical damage, pollution and professional liability are normally covered. Consequently, for example, a claim for losses based on mismanagement brought by the company because its business was adversely affected by environmental proceedings, or for loss of business as a result of a high profile class action of personal injury claims, will usually be covered.

Pre-existing claims

It is routine for claims arising from (1) matters notified under a previ- **12.031** ous D&O policy and (2) litigation that existed before the policy period to be excluded. The reason for this is that previous D&O policies should be applicable to such matters, and so the current policy should not also apply.

Pension trustee liability

Directors may also be trustees of the company's pension fund. The D&O **12.032** policy will exclude liabilities incurred in their capacity as pension trustees. This is because it is essentially a different kind of risk to directors' liability, to be assessed separately, and a bespoke policy purchased for it (a "pension trustee liability policy").

Events that affect the cover

12.033   There are some important additional clauses in the policy which dictate how it reacts to certain events that take place during and at the end of the policy period.

Acquisitions/new subsidiaries

12.034   Directors of companies acquired by the insured company during the policy period may be covered automatically under the insured company's D&O policy for claims arising from matters post-dating the acquisition, so long as the acquired company is not listed, nor domiciled in the US, nor has total assets over a certain percentage of the newly consolidated assets of the insured company. If any of these provisos are not met then there will be no automatic coverage and the insurers will have to be approached to agree to cover the acquired company's directors on terms to be negotiated. Importantly, and in any event, the cover only applies to claims arising from facts and matters occurring *after* the date of acquisition.

Takeovers/mergers

12.035   Where the insured company is itself taken over or merges into another entity where the other entity is the survivor then the policy will cease providing ongoing cover, and from the transaction date until policy expiry will only cover claims in respect of facts and matters occurring *prior* to that date (this situation is usually referred to as the policy going into "run-off"). The company should be included within the acquirer's D&O policy for claims arising out of post-transaction facts and matters.

Non-renewal

12.036   In the unlikely event that the D&O policy is not renewed due to either the insurer or the company deciding not to continue the D&O programme for a further year, and the policy is not replaced with another D&O policy with a different insurer, then usually, upon payment of an additional premium, an "extended reporting period" will be applied. This allows the directors to report, up to 12 months after the policy has expired, claims which arise out of facts and matters which occurred prior to policy expiry, and coverage will be provided subject to the policy's terms and conditions.

Buying a policy

Finding the right cover

A D&O policy can be purchased through the company's insurance brokers **12.037** either as a bespoke cover or as part of the company's wider insurance programme. If the latter it may be possible to achieve savings in overall premium paid but there may be sacrifices made in terms of the policy's "fit" with the directors' precise needs.

Given the relatively complex nature of the cover, and the potential expense involved, it is important to seek advice from the brokers on the most suitable product for the directors' particular circumstances. There is arguably a conflict of interest between what the directors want cover for, and what the company is prepared to buy, but as the company pays the premium this issue is rarely explored.

The brokers will then need the directors to provide accurate information about the company's business in order to obtain quotations from the various insurers approached by them. It is possible the insurers' underwriters will invite the directors to meet with them to answer any additional questions they may have. Where there are legitimate concerns over disclosure of sensitive information the underwriters are usually prepared to sign a confidentiality undertaking. This also provides an opportunity for the directors to ask the underwriters any questions they have about the policy they may be buying.

Ultimately, the main buying criteria for the directors will be price, the amount of coverage provided, and the quality of the security.

Policy limits

An important issue to consider with the insurance brokers is the amount **12.038** of cover to purchase. A standard level of cover for small/medium-sized companies is up to £10 million but for large public companies limits of say, £200 million or more can be bought. Such limits are usually expressed to be "in the aggregate", which means that once payments by the insurers in respect of claims notified in that policy period have reached that sum, the cover is exhausted. Put another way, the policy limit will be eroded by every payment made under the policy, regardless of on whose behalf it has been paid. This can mean that the cover is severely depleted by one claim against a director, leaving the others exposed. This may be of particular concern to non-executive directors who are less exposed to claims than their executive counterparts but will be concerned of their position in the event of corporate collapse, by which time the limit of cover might have been considerably eroded by costs incurred by the executives in respect of other matters (hence the possible provision of extra non-executive director cover as mentioned above).

Much comes down to the nature of the risk, the size of the company and the number of directors intended to be covered. The cover available is not going to be sufficient to cover directors of large companies for losses equivalent to their market capital, therefore, one approach is to essentially treat the cover as a defence fund so as to provide each director in the company with sufficient resources to defend themselves against a significant claim. It is important to remember that as all subsidiary companies are usually included within the policy, the number of directors needing protection can be very large. A possible starting point in the analysis is to allow £1 million of cover for every director in the group (so if there are 50 directors in all an amount in the region of £50 million cover should be considered). It is also important not to purchase too much cover—whilst a high level of cover provides more protection, it may also encourage the bringing of "deep pocket" claims. Ultimately advice should be sought from the company's insurance brokers.

Excesses

12.039   Side A cover (for the directors themselves) is seldom subject to an excess, but Side B cover (company reimbursement) usually is, although the amount is small compared to the policy limit. Policies frequently contain "presumptive indemnity" language which provides that if the company is permitted to indemnify the directors it shall be presumed to be doing so and therefore the Side B excess shall be applied irrespective of whether the company in fact is indemnifying the directors. Since UK companies have been permitted to indemnify their directors in certain situations since April 6, 2005 this clause potentially creates a gap in cover for the directors for the amount of the Side B excess where their companies do not in fact indemnify them. The clause has as a result been modified so that if the company does not indemnify the excess shall not apply to the directors, and the insurers shall be entitled to claim the excess from the company instead (see also below "How do D&O insurance and indemnification interact?").

Formation of the insurance contract

12.040   There are special legal considerations for the formation of insurance contracts of any nature and D&O is no different. The directors and officers owe a duty of utmost good faith to the insurers, which involves the disclosure of all facts that are material to the insurers' assessment of the risk, and to ensure the information provided is accurate. In the event of a material non-disclosure or misrepresentation by the directors, the insurers may be entitled to avoid the contract "ab initio" which means that no claims under it are payable, and the premium is returned, as if the contract never existed. The consequences of this for the directors could be catastrophic in the event of a significant claim.

The D&O policy is widely accepted, however, to be "composite" in nature, which means that each director has a separate and distinct duty of disclosure of facts and matters within his or her knowledge. Whilst at first sight this appears onerous, one important effect of this is that one director will not be presumed to have the same knowledge as another director and so a misrepresentation or non-disclosure by one will not necessarily place the cover in jeopardy for the others. An example of this might be in the case of a director who has dishonestly concealed the true nature of the company's financial position from the company's auditors and his or her co-directors. That director is unlikely to disclose this to the insurers, and so, if discovered, this would entitle the insurers to avoid his or her cover, but probably not that of the others.

Since the soft market of 2007 insurers have gone a stage further and expressly waived rights to avoid the policy except where a misrepresentation/non-disclosure to insurers was committed dishonestly.

How is information disclosed to the insurers? It is obviously in the insurers' interests to elicit the most accurate information possible about the state of a company's health before deciding whether to offer cover, and at what price. There are various ways in which this is done but the primary sources of information remain the proposal form and the company's most recent annual report and accounts, usually submitted with the proposal form.

The proposal form and basis of contract

This is a form similar in nature to that which is completed prior to taking out any insurance. In the case of D&O insurance it will request factual information that is not readily ascertainable from the annual report and accounts. It will usually conclude by asking whether the directors are aware of any circumstances that could reasonably be expected to give rise to a claim. This requires some enquiry by the directors before they answer. If in doubt about disclosing information, they should consult their insurance brokers, given the possible consequences of material non-disclosure or misrepresentation. **12.041**

Whilst each director is responsible for disclosing all material facts actually known to them, they are not all obliged to complete a separate proposal form. The usual practice is for the company secretary to complete the form on behalf of the directors, having consulted them as to the information to be disclosed. (S)he then signs on behalf of the board. In doing so, the company secretary is acting as the directors' and officers' agent.

Some policies state that the information in the proposal form shall be the "basis of the contract". This elevates the status of the answers to fundamental terms of the contract so that even an immaterial fact that is misstated potentially allows the insurers to discharge the contract against all directors.

Since the soft market of 2007 such clauses have largely been removed from policies, however, the language of the policy should be carefully checked to confirm this.

The annual report and accounts

12.042   The annual report and accounts is the other document that should be produced to the insurers. They are entitled to assume it is accurate, however, the latest version may have been released a number of months before the proposal form is completed. In this event, the proposal form may contain a question about material changes to the company during that period. As these documents form part of the presentation to insurers, and are relied upon, there may be consequences where the company later issues a restatement. One line of argument may be that the financial position of the company was misstated and therefore the policy can be avoided against all directors. Whilst this is a possible outcome it is not the most likely: the court is more likely to take the view that the accounts themselves did not constitute a misstatement but that any director aware at policy inception that they were incorrect was guilty of not disclosing that fact to insurers so the policy is simply voidable against those directors (and not against anyone who was unaware they were wrong).

Notification and handling of claims

12.043   A typical D&O policy contains, in addition to clauses that define the amount of cover, a number of additional terms and conditions that are required to be complied with by the directors and the insurers in order for the policy to operate properly. Misunderstandings as to how these clauses work can lead to problems in the event of claims.

The policy will contain "claims conditions" that govern when and how claims should be advised to the insurers. It is important that the directors and/or company secretary are familiar with these provisions as it can make the difference between a claim being covered, partially covered, or not covered at all.

Notification and claims handling issues are dealt with briefly in this section.

Notification of claims and/or circumstances

12.044   In order to attract coverage, a claim must be notified to the insurers. Most notification provisions require that the directors notify claims or circumstances that may give rise to claims to the insurers "as soon as reasonably practicable". If in doubt as to whether a situation requires notification, directors should err on the safe side and consult the brokers (through whom such notifications are normally made).

The consequences of a failure to comply depend on the status of the clause, from non-coverage altogether (if the clause is stated to be a "condition precedent" to insurers' liability, or if the policy period has expired by the time the insurer receives notice) to a possible reduction in the amount of cover equivalent to any tangible prejudice caused by delay that can be established by the insurers.

Reasonable co-operation

It is usually a requirement that the directors provide such assistance to the insurers in their assessment of a claim as they may "reasonably require". Problems may arise here due to the sensitive nature of the underlying circumstances that have given rise to the notification. The directors have a legitimate interest in maintaining confidentiality, but the insurers also have a legitimate (but competing) interest in investigating the claim so that they can ascertain their exposure. The problem is resolvable by way of a confidentiality undertaking provided by the insurers. **12.045**

An unreasonable refusal to assist will at the very least result in delays in the confirmation of indemnity for a claim by the insurers, which could lead to cash flow problems for the directors.

Admissions of liability, settlements or payments without prior approval

The policy is likely to contain a provision preventing the directors from admitting liability, settling or making payments without the prior approval of the insurers, which is not to be unreasonably withheld. Where an early and desirable settlement is available, the directors should provide the fullest information possible to the insurers in support of the proposed settlement, in order that approval may be considered. This is important because insurers are required to satisfy their reinsurers that payments made under the policy are in recognition of an ascertained legal liability exposure. **12.046**

Settlement without requesting approval first may again lead to cash flow problems where the director is obliged to make a payment but is not immediately reimbursed for it, and could reduce the amount of cover ultimately provided.

Claim control

Most policies allow the directors to determine, within reason, the manner in which claims are defended, and they may appoint the legal team of their **12.047** choice (subject to the costs being reasonable—see below). In the event of a difference of opinion as to the appropriate defence strategy, then usually a clause in the policy will provide that the issue will be referable to a Queen's Counsel for determination (this is known as a "QC clause"). An exception to the general position that directors control their own defences is where the claim is brought by the company outside the US. Instead of such claims being subject to an "Assured v Assured" exclusion (see above) the insurers reserve the right to control the directors' defence in order to guard against any abuse of the policy that could result from the directors and their company agreeing the claim should be brought in order to access the policy proceeds.

Reasonable costs

12.048   The policy covers the directors for their "reasonable and necessary" defence costs. What may be "reasonable and necessary" will be assessed by the insurers according to the severity/complexity of the claim, the proposed lawyers' rates and the amount of work involved.

One issue that frequently arises is the appointment of a different law firm by each director in respect of a claim made that has been made against all of them. This inevitably duplicates the work done and so the cost may not be strictly necessary. Frequently policies now provide that if and to the extent there is no conflict of interest between the directors, the insurers will not regard the appointment of more than one law firm as "reasonable" and they must all use the same defence firm.

Disclosure of the policy to third parties

12.049   It is likely to be a requirement that the existence and terms of the policy are not disclosed by the directors to any third party. This is so as not to encourage claims to be brought.

Indemnification of directors

12.050   On April 6, 2005 the CA 1985 was amended, by new ss.309A and 309B, to permit companies to indemnify their directors in certain situations and such rights are now contained in CA 2006 s.234.

Until April 6, 2005 UK law[5] governing indemnification rights largely prohibited indemnification except to the extent a director had successfully defeated a claim and had unrecovered costs and expenses. The original

---

[5] CA 1985 s.310.

reasoning behind the prohibition was that indemnification could undermine directors' incentive to perform their role with due care and skill and thereby compromise their duties to the company. Given that today directors are subjected to claims more routinely by reason of their position, such a concern seems misplaced and without indemnification directors of UK companies are at a significant disadvantage to their US counterparts.

Framework for indemnification

In order to fully understand indemnification rights and obligations it is necessary to be aware of the way they are set out in law and in agreements. **12.051**

General law

The overriding source of indemnification rights comes from CA 1985 ss.309A **12.052** and 309B, which when implemented in October 2007 are restated in CA 2006 s.234. The law now permits indemnification in certain situations (see below). Any indemnification provision that is broader than what is permitted by the Act is void in its entirety (not merely to the extent it is broader) under CA 2006 s.232. The Act is permissive in that it does not oblige companies to indemnify their directors.

Articles of association

Notwithstanding the general law now permits indemnification of directors, **12.053** a company is not permitted to indemnify its directors unless the shareholders have granted such permission, in line with the law. This is provided via the articles of association ("Articles"), which is one of the constitutional agreements of the company. It is an agreement between the shareholders themselves and with the company, but not the directors (in their capacity as directors). The Articles therefore dictate whether the company has the power to indemnify, and to what extent, so long as it is no broader than is provided by the law. It is therefore possible the power to indemnify created by the Articles may be more restrictive than is permitted under the law.

Some companies' Articles set out the further provisions of CA 1985 s.310 (as it was) in order to grant the power to indemnify to the extent provided by that very restrictive provision. Those companies, if they intended to give broader indemnification under the new law have needed to revise the relevant Article in order to set out the more permissive terms of CA 1985 ss.309A and 309B which on implementation in October 2007 are restated in CA 2006 s.234, otherwise they will not be permitted to indemnify their directors to any significant extent. Other companies' Articles have simply contained a statement that the company may (a "permissive right") or will (a "mandatory right") indemnify to the extent permitted by the law or such other applicable law. Such Articles should not require amendment to give effect to the indemnification provisions and were automatically broadened on April 6, 2005 to the extent allowed under CA 1985 ss.309A and 309B and when implemented CA 2006 s.234.

Indemnification agreements

12.054 The directors, who are the beneficiaries of the indemnity, but who are not party to the Articles, have no direct enforceable right to be indemnified to the extent permitted by the Articles, even if the Articles state that the company *will* indemnify the directors. The Contracts (Rights of Third Parties) Act 1999 allows some third party beneficiaries under a contract to enforce its terms but s.6 expressly precludes the application of such rights to companies' Articles. Therefore, without a separate indemnification agreement between the company and the directors conveying the indemnity the company may have the power to indemnify but is not obliged to do so and therefore indemnification is entirely discretionary (which is obviously unsatisfactory from the directors' point of view).

The indemnification agreements can take different forms but are usually designed to operate separately from the directors' service contracts, in order that they survive the retirement of the directors and remain enduringly enforceable. Often the indemnity is conveyed formally in a "deed of indemnity", or if the Articles contain a mandatory right of indemnification, by a letter confirming that such mandatory right is directly enforceable by the director. This would take the form of a statement in a letter along the lines of:

> "The Company hereby agrees and confirms that the provisions of Article XX of the Company's Articles (as the same may from time to time be amended or modified) ("the Indemnity") shall be enforceable by you against the Company. By countersigning this letter you undertake that you will promptly give the Company written notice of any matter or circumstance which may give rise to a claim by you under the Indemnity . . . The provisions of this letter shall continue to apply after you cease to be a director of the Company . . . This letter is governed by, and shall be construed in accordance with, English law."

As with the Articles, any indemnification agreements existing at April 6, 2005 should be reviewed to see if they require amendment to ensure that, if desired, they are as broad as permitted by the law.

The law does not prohibit companies from agreeing to indemnify directors in respect of matters that arose before the law was changed in April 2005 (known or unknown at the time of agreement). However, directors who had already retired, and did not have a indemnification agreements already, are at a potential disadvantage at least until the relevant limitation period of any claims that could be brought against them has expired. There is nothing to stop such directors requesting indemnification retrospectively—but the companies are not obliged to provide such indemnity and may refuse to do so.

Extent of permitted indemnification

CA 2006 s.232 (formerly CA 1985 s.309A) which will be implemented in October 2007 provides that any agreement exempting a director from liability to the company is void, and unless a company's indemnification arrangements fall within the scope of a "Qualifying Third Party Indemnification Provision" ("QTPIP") they are also void. The provisions apply equally where a company agrees to indemnify its own directors or where a group/parent company agrees to indemnify the directors of another group (or the parent) company. CA 2006 s.234 sets out the criteria for indemnification arrangements to be a QTPIP. They comprise a list of categories of claims for which a company may agree to indemnify its directors, on certain terms. These are set out as follows. **12.055**

Claims by the company

As stated above, claims by the company are theoretically the most likely under English law as it is to the company that directors primarily owe their duties. Such claims are brought intermittently against former directors and are significant in size. Further, CA 2006 will cement the right of minority shareholders to bring derivative actions against directors, in the name of the company. The law (obviously) does not permit a liability to the company to be indemnified—so any payment made by a director to the company by way of a judgment or settlement (including damages and claimants' costs) is not indemnifiable. **12.056**

The company is permitted to advance defence costs to directors it is suing so they may defend themselves effectively, however, where a final judgment (after appeals) is given against the director, those costs must be repaid. Such a "claw back" does not appear to apply to settlements where the director agrees to make a payment to the company.

Criminal proceedings

Criminal fines cannot be indemnified. The costs of defending criminal proceedings are indemnifiable and may be advanced by the company. However, **12.057** if the director is finally convicted (after appeals), the costs must be repaid, no matter the precise nature of the offence.

Regulatory proceedings

12.058   Regulatory fines or penalties cannot be indemnified. The costs of dealing with regulatory proceedings are indemnifiable and may be advanced. Unlike the position with criminal proceedings, there is no automatic claw back of costs if the director is found liable (unless the director is found to have acted dishonestly).

Claims by third parties

12.059   As stated above, claims by parties outside the company are quite rare because of the protection given to directors by the corporate veil which courts are reluctant to go behind: in dealings with third parties the directors are acting as officers of the company and so it is against the company that most causes of action lie. However, and very importantly, third parties for the purposes of this definition include shareholders or any person or company who purchased the company based upon misleading information. In particular, claims by shareholders based on misleading offering documentation could be more prevalent in future, with UK pension funds taking a more robust stance on corporate failure than they have in the past. In addition, directors of US subsidiaries of UK companies and directors of UK companies with US listings are vulnerable to US shareholder lawsuits and indemnification is vital in such situations.

The law does not impose any restrictions on indemnification of such claims (assuming no dishonesty on the part of the directors), and so damages are indemnifiable and there is no claw back of advanced defence costs in the event the director settles or is found liable to the third party.

Advancement of costs and claw back mechanisms

12.060   As mentioned above, the company may advance defence costs to a director as they are incurred in all cases but in respect of claims by the company and criminal proceedings those costs must be repaid on a final judgment (after appeals) against the director, and in another claims where the court finds the director acted dishonestly. The advancement of costs by the company is therefore regarded as a loan to the director, to be repaid in the event of such outcomes. Loans by the company to the directors are prohibited by CA 1985 s.330 (CA 2006 s.197); however, an express exception to that rule was created when the law changed so as to permit the advancement of defence costs, now under CA 2006 s.205. This states that the advancement provisions in a QTPIP do not contravene CA 1985 s.330 (CA 2006 s.197) so long as they require the advanced costs to be repaid in the event of an adverse final judgment in a criminal or other proceedings. Here there is arguably an inconsistency with the provisions of CA 1985 s.309A (CA 2006 s.234) which only require the claw back in respect of criminal and *civil proceedings brought by the company*. There is consequently some uncertainty over the interaction of the two provisions—for instance, where an indemnity agreement only provides for claw back in the event of a final judgment against the director in criminal or civil proceedings by the company, it complies with s.309B (CA 2006 s.234(3)), but arguably does not comply with s.337A (CA 2006 s.205) in order to exempt the agreement to advance from the general prohibition of directors' loans. The author's view is that this should not restrict the scope of the indemnity or advancement allowed under CA 2006 s.234 so long as the indemnity agreements mirror its provisions.

How do D&O insurance and indemnification interact?

Directors should seek as broad an indemnity from their companies as the companies are permitted to provide pursuant to the Act. However, directors will be without protection in the following instances: **12.061**

- Where the company is insolvent or otherwise financially unable to pay the indemnification; claims by a company's liquidators are obviously non-indemnifiable for this reason and liquidators represent a potent source of claims for small/medium-sized companies (and, occasionally, large companies).

- Where the law does not permit the company to indemnify. The most obvious gap in the indemnification protection is where the director is liable to the company (see above).

- In instances where the claw back machinery applies following an adverse final judgment.

- Where the company otherwise refuses to indemnify. This may be because the relevant indemnification agreement is more restrictive than the law permits, or because for some other reason the company does not honour its obligations under the indemnification agreement.

These potentially significant gaps can be filled by D&O insurance, either via the traditional D&O policy, or via a cheaper Side A only D&O policy which is specifically designed to fit around the indemnification and plug gaps. The Side A policy will also pay where the company is able (and required) to pay but does not, however, the D&O insurer may be able to subrogate against the company in respect of the director's right to be indemnified in this situation; or in the case of a traditional D&O policy the cover shall be provided under Side A but treated as being under Side B (company reimbursement) and the relevant Side B excess will be charged to the company.

The interaction of indemnification agreements and D&O insurance in a given case needs careful consideration in order to provide a cost effective solution with seamless protection provided by complementary commitments from the company and the D&O insurer. Whilst the company's insurance brokers are responsible for fitting the D&O policy to the risk, lawyers may be needed to interpret indemnification agreements to ensure the desired protection is given, and anticipate possible problems in their interaction with the D&O coverage. In this respect, the directors and the D&O insurers have the same interests—to maximise the indemnification available from the company.

Chapter 13

Financial Reporting

Alex Owen[1]

Introduction

The purpose of this chapter is to provide company directors and non-financial advisors with a description of the general principles and issues set out in Section C of the UK Corporate Governance Code in relation to financial reporting.

13.001

What the UK Corporate Governance Code recommends

Section C of the UK Corporate Governance Code looks at three aspects of accountability and audit: financial and business reporting; risk management and internal control; and the audit committee and its auditors.

13.002

The Main Principle C.1 relating to financial reporting sets out the board's reporting responsibilities: "The board should present a balanced and understandable assessment of the company's position and prospects". The related Supporting Principle goes on to state that this responsibility extends to interim and other price-sensitive public reports and reports to regulators, as well as to information required to be presented by statutory requirements.

The corresponding Provisions state:

- The directors should explain in the annual report their responsibility for preparing the accounts, and there should be a statement by the auditors about their reporting responsibilities (C.1.1).

- The directors should include in the annual report an explanation of the basis on which the company generates or preserves value over the

[1] Alex Owen is a senior manager at KPMG. Alex joined KPMG in 1999 after qualifying at a smaller firm of accountants, and worked in KPMG's audit practice until 2004 when he joined the Department of Professional Practice.

longer term (the business model) and the strategy for delivering the objectives of the company (C.1.2).[2]

- The directors should report in the annual and half-yearly financial statements that the business is a going concern, with supporting assumptions or qualifications as necessary (C.1.3).[3]

The Code is clear on what the responsibilities of directors are but what it does not do is explain what constitutes a "balanced and understandable assessment" and how this can be achieved—this is the role of company law and the UK's independent regulator for corporate reporting and governance, the Financial Reporting Council ("FRC") and its operating bodies.

The problem[4]

13.003   The Cadbury Report[5] pointed out that a basic weakness in the then current system of financial reporting is the possibility of different accounting treatments being applied to what are essentially similar facts, with the consequence that results or financial positions could be reported differently, each apparently complying with the overriding requirement to show a true and fair view. This poses a fundamental problem for the users of accounts—how do they know that the accounts they are reading provide a reasonable assessment of the company's activities? Shareholders, and other users of the accounts, require a company's annual report and accounts to present a balanced and meaningful picture of the company's performance and prospects in order to make informed decisions.

The answer to the problem voiced by Cadbury is in part resolved by a generally accepted set of standards which (a) limit the scope for uncertainty and manipulation and (b) make the accounts understandable to the reader. In the UK this is provided by the law in the shape of the Companies Act 2006 ("CA 2006") and financial reporting standards as developed by the Accounting Standards Board ("ASB") which is an operating body of the FRC. The law and financial reporting standards are discussed in further detail later in this chapter.

---

[2] Fn 12 to the UK Corporate Governance Code states that it would be desirable if the explanation were located in the same part of the annual report as the business review required by CA 2006 s.417. Guidance as to the matters that should be considered in an explanation of a business model is provided in paras 30 to 32 of the Accounting Standard Board's Reporting Statement: Operating and Financial Review.

[3] Fn 13 to the UK Corporate Governance Code states that "Going Concern and Liquidity Risk: Guidance for Directors of UK Companies 2009" suggests means of applying this part of the Code.

[4] For a clear exposition of how to spot accounting manipulation read Sherman et al. *Profits You Can Trust* FT Prentice Hall, 2003.

[5] Report of the Committee on the Financial Aspects of Corporate Governance: The Code of Best Practice (1992), Cadbury Committee on the Financial Aspects of Corporate Governance.

In recent years the view expressed by Cadbury has been taken one step further and the need for comparing the activities and results of companies has been extended beyond national boundaries. The growth of global businesses has made the use of a global set of accounting standards desirable and has led to the development of International Financial Reporting Standards ("IFRSs"), which have been adopted by the EU as well as other jurisdictions (see below). As a consequence, EU-adopted IFRSs are now the required standards for the consolidated accounts of UK companies listed on the main market of the London Stock Exchange and other EU regulated markets,[6] and AIM.[7]

The benefits of this comparability are succinctly set out in the Cadbury report:

"The lifeblood of markets is information and barriers to the flow of relevant information represent imperfections in the market. The need to sift and correct the information put out by companies adds cost and uncertainty to the market's pricing function. The more the activities of companies are transparent, the more accurately will their securities be valued." (Cadbury Report para.4.48).

The remainder of this chapter will look at the current rules and principles that surround financial reporting to ensure that the activities of companies are reported in a clear and meaningful manner.

What the law requires

The CA 2006 received royal asset on November 8, 2006 and is the realisation **13.004** of the Company Law Review, which began in 1997 and was the first thorough review of company law for many years. It replaces almost all the provisions of the Companies Act 1985 ("CA 1985")[8]. The remainder of this chapter relates to CA 2006 and refers to the post implementation position of the Act.

CA 2006 Pt 15 Ch.4 sets out the law regarding the preparation of annual accounts. It covers the "true and fair view", which is a principle that underpins the whole of financial reporting in the UK; the preparation of accounts; further information to be included in the accounts; and procedures for the approval and signing of accounts.

CA 2006 Pt 15 is not a radical departure from the relevant section of the CA 1985. In the main it has been re-ordered and simplified. The key changes in this section of the Act relate to the "true and fair view" and the implementation of a "think small first" basis which aims to make the law more accessible for small companies.

The full text of Pt 15 Ch.4 is set out in App.4.

---

[6] For financial periods beginning on or after January 1, 2005.
[7] For financial periods beginning on or after January 1, 2007.
[8] The 1985 Act's provisions regarding company investigations has been retained.

True and fair view (section 393)

13.005   The true and fair view is the standard to which all accounts have to be prepared, and directors must not approve any statutory accounts that do not give a true and fair view. CA 2006 requires that all statutory accounts, regardless of whether they are complied under UK GAAP or IFRS should present a true and fair view.

The concept of "true and fair" is set out later in this chapter.

Preparation of individual accounts (sections 394 to 397)

13.006   The directors of every company must prepare accounts for the company for each of its financial years. Those accounts are referred to as the company's "individual accounts" (s.394) and must be prepared in accordance with s.396 ("Companies Act individual accounts") or in accordance with international accounting standards ("IAS individual accounts").

Companies Act individual accounts (section 396)

13.007   Companies Act individual accounts ("CAIA") must comprise:

- a balance sheet as at the last day of the financial year which gives a true and fair view of the state of affairs of the company as at the end of the financial year; and

- a profit and loss account which gives a true and fair view of the profit and loss of the company for the financial year.

IAS individual accounts (section 397)

13.008   Where the directors of a company prepare IAS individual accounts, they must state in the notes to the accounts that the accounts have been prepared in accordance with international accounting standards.

Preparation of group accounts (sections 398 to 408)

13.009   This area of Pt 15 Ch.4 best illustrates the "think small first" basis. CA 1985 set out the law for large companies and then provided exemptions for small and medium-sized companies. CA 2006 sets out the law for small companies first and the provisions for other companies are given as additional requirements, hence the "think small first".

This arrangement has, to a certain degree, been upset by recent changes, which create a new category: companies subject to the small companies regime. These are companies that would otherwise qualify for the small companies regime save for their being members of an ineligible group. An ineligible group is defined in s.384(2) and includes any group which contains a public company. Companies taking advantage of the small companies exemption will typically be "small" subsidiaries of public companies, although the scope of the exemption is a little wider. If a company takes advantage of the exemption, it can omit certain information from the directors report,[9] and choose not to file the directors' report and profit and loss account with Companies House.

A key change in CA 2006 relates to the size of companies which are required to prepare group accounts. Previously, CA 1985 exempted small and medium companies, subject to certain conditions. However, owing to the decision to raise the medium-sized thresholds to the EU maximum, the Government decided that too many groups were able to apply this exemption. As a consequence, the CA 2006 allows only those parent companies in small companies regime the choice of not preparing group accounts. Parent companies that are not in the small companies regime *are required to* prepare group accounts, although there are a number of important exemptions for these companies, which are mentioned below.

Sections 399 to 408 set out the additional provisions for companies that are not small companies and includes exemptions from preparing group accounts for a:

- company that is included in EEA group accounts of a larger group (s.400);

- company that is included in non-EEA group accounts of a larger group (s.401);

- company where none of whose subsidiary undertakings need be included in the consolidation (s.402).[10]

Section 403 sets out the circumstances in which group accounts should be prepared in accordance with international accounting standards ("IAS group accounts") or in accordance with CA 2006 s.386 ("Companies Act group accounts"). Section 404 defines what is deemed to comprise Companies Act group accounts and s.405 states in what circumstances a subsidiary can be excluded from consolidation.

---

[9] In particular, these companies are exempt from the s.417 requirement to provide a business review.

[10] Please also refer to FRS 2, *Accounting for subsidiary undertakings*, which states that a subsidiary should be excluded from consolidation where: (a) there are severe long term restrictions; or (b) the interest in the subsidiary undertaking is held exclusively with a view to subsequent sale.

Now that there are two reporting frameworks, i.e. Companies Act and IAS, s.407 makes clear that the directors of a parent company must secure that the individual accounts of the parent company and each of its subsidiary undertakings are all prepared using the same financial reporting framework. This is discussed further at para.13.012.

Information to be given in notes to the accounts (sections 409 to 413)

13.010   The Secretary of State has made separate provision by regulations requiring information about related undertakings to be given in notes to a company's accounts, with certain exemptions (s.409).

Parts of CA 2006 that outline the specific disclosure requirements regarding employees and directors benefits (ss.411–413) are different to CA 1985. Further to s.412, the Secretary of State has made regulations that make provision for the disclosure of directors' remuneration. These are broadly the same as the requirements in CA 1985.[11] However, the requirements relating to the disclosure of directors' loans (s.413, and called advances, credit and guarantees in the CA 2006) are less detailed than its predecessor, although users should bear in mind that accounting standards also have their own requirements regarding the disclosure of related party transactions.[12]

Approval and signing of accounts (section 414)

13.011   This section of CA 2006 requires that a company's annual accounts should be approved by the board and signed on behalf of the board by a director of the company. It also sets out the consequences of approving annual accounts that do not comply with the requirements of the Act or of art.4 of the IAS Regulation. The full text of s.414 is set out in App.4.

Financial reporting regimes

13.012   In June 2002 the EU adopted a Regulation that requires all listed[13] companies in the EU (including banks and insurance companies) to prepare their

---

[11] One notable difference, which applies to accounting periods beginning on or after April 6, 2009, is that the directors' remuneration report must contain a statement of how pay and employment conditions of employees of the company and of other group undertakings with the same group as the company were taken into account when determining directors' remuneration for the year.
[12] For UK GAAP, FRS 8 *Related party disclosures*; for IFRS, IAS 24 *Related party disclosures*.
[13] Listed companies in the context of the EU 2005 Regulation means any companies that at the balance sheet date have securities, including debt, admitted to trading on a regulated market of any Member State.

consolidated financial statements under IFRS for financial years beginning on or after January 1, 2005.

The aim of the Regulation was to develop comparable financial reporting across Europe leading to increased transparency and lower costs of capital for companies. Many countries have chosen to adopt IFRS, others such as Japan, Canada and China plan to converge with IFRS in the future, or are currently in the process of either converging with IFRS or permitting IFRS to be used in their territories. The worldwide adoption of, or convergence with, IFRS is viewed by many as the beginning of a single global set of financial reporting standards, with easier access to global capital markets.

Although the EU Regulation did not apply to the individual accounts of parent and subsidiary companies (nor the group accounts of parent companies that do not have securities traded on an EU regulated market—for example, AIM[14] companies and private groups) a statutory instrument ("SI") was issued in November 2004 which modified CA 1985 to, amongst other things, permit companies to choose to use IFRS rather than domestic accounting requirements. This revision is effective for financial years starting on or after January 1, 2005.

UK companies currently have a choice of two financial reporting regimes: UK GAAP or EU adopted IFRS. The UK Accounting Standards Board ("ASB") has been considering its plans for convergence with IFRS for some time, and in August 2009 it issued a consultation on the subject: Policy Proposal: *The Future of UK GAAP*. The ASB's proposal is to create three financial reporting tiers:

- Tier 1: listed and other publicly accountable companies would have to use "full" IFRS.

- Tier 2: those companies that are not in Tier 1 (but are outside the small companies regime) would be permitted to adopt the IASB's *IFRS for SMEs*, which is a simplified version of IFRSs with fewer disclosure requirements. However, they would be permitted to move to Tier 1 if they desire.

- Tier 3: those companies that qualify for the small companies regime would be permitted to use the Financial Reporting Standard for Smaller Entities, which is a simplified version of UK GAAP. Likewise, they would be permitted to move to Tiers 2 or 1 if they wished.

Over 150 parties responded to the consultation and, at the time of writing, the ASB is considering those responses. Depending on the results of the consultation, the ASB's intention has proposed to apply the new regime to financial

---

[14] Although AIM has mandated IFRS for the group accounts of AIM companies for financial years commencing on or after January 1, 2007 (see AIM r.19).

years beginning on or after January 1, 2010, although it remains to be seen if this goal is achieved.

In the case where companies are in a position to choose which regime it follows, once a company has moved to IFRS, it may not return to IFRS unless there is a "relevant change of circumstances" (s.395, s.403), i.e.:

- the company becomes a subsidiary of another company that does not prepare IFRS individual accounts;

- the company ceases to be a subsidiary undertaking; or

- the company's or a parent's securities are no longer admitted to trading on an EU regulated market.

The decision to switch to IFRS therefore requires very careful consideration—especially as there are realised profit and taxation considerations to take into account.

UK GAAP

13.013 Accounts prepared under Generally Accepted Accounting Principles in the UK should be prepared in accordance with the following mandatory elements:

- the law, i.e. the CA 2006;

- accounting standards, that is Statements of Standard Accounting Practice ("SSAPs") and Financial Reporting Standards ("FRSs") issued by the ASB since 1990;

- Abstracts issued by the ASB's Urgent Issues Task Force ("UITF");

- for listed companies, the Listing Rules (or AIM rules, as appropriate).

Furthermore, certain sectors and industries issue Statements of Recommend Practice (SORPs), which supplement accounting guidance. Although SORPs do not have the same status as accounting standards, the bodies that issue them are recognised by the ASB and compliance with the requirements with SORPs is highly recommended. If a company does not comply with a relevant industry SORP, accounting standards require that fact and the reasons why the company has departed from the requirements of the SORP to be disclosed in the accounts.

We have very briefly covered the elements of the law which relate to financial reporting earlier in this chapter. It is worth however covering in brief the standards and concepts which direct how the law is applied, i.e. accounting standards, the "true and fair view" and accounting principles.

Accounting standards

CA 1985 requires directors to state whether the company's accounts have **13.014**
been prepared in accordance with applicable accounting standards, to disclose particulars of any material departure from those standards and the
reasons for the departure. For the purposes of UK company law applicable
accounting standards constitute FRSs and SSAPs. Accounting standards are
issued by the ASB and apply to all accounts that are required to show a true
and fair view of the profit or loss for the financial year and of the state of
affairs of an entity at its balance sheet date.

The ASB's UITF responds to urgent matters as they arise and issues an
Abstract when it has reached its consensus. A UITF Abstract has the same
authority as an accounting standard.

The Financial Reporting Review Panel ("FRRP") was established in 1990
and seeks to ensure that the provision of financial information by public and
large private companies complies with relevant accounting requirements.
The FRRP select a number of accounts for review which are drawn from
the range of companies within the Panel's remit, accounts are also selected
for review on the basis of company specific factors such as poor corporate
governance.

True and fair view

CA 2006 s.393 states that directors of a company must not approve accounts **13.015**
unless they are satisfied that they give a true and fair view of the assets, liabilities, financial position and profit or loss of the company. The concept of a
true and fair view lies at the heart of financial reporting in the UK. It is undefined in legislation or elsewhere and is essentially a matter of professional
judgment. It is a dynamic concept because its content evolves in response to
changes in accounting and business practice.[15]

The ASB's Statement of Principles which the ASB uses as a general
framework to help shape and develop new standards provides the following
description of the true and fair view:

"It is inherent in the nature of the true and fair view concept that financial statements will not give a true and fair view unless the information
they contain is sufficient in quantity and quality to satisfy the reasonable
expectations of the readers to whom they are addressed."

---

[15] The status of the true and fair requirement and its continuing importance to financial reporting (both UK GAAP and IFRS) was reaffirmed by Martin Moore QC in an opinion he wrote
on behalf of the FRC. His opinion can be found at the FRC's website at *http://www.frc.org.uk/
about/trueandfair.cfm.*

Accounting principles

13.016 In addition to the "true and fair view" there are six key principles which underlie the preparation of financial statements under UK GAAP. These principles are: going concern, accruals, relevance, reliability, comparability and understandability which are the core qualities of financial information set out in the Statement of Principles.

Detailed guidance of their practical application can be found in the ASB's *Statement of Principles for Financial Reporting*, and FRS 18 *Accounting Policies*.

IFRS

13.017 From 2005, for those companies applying IFRS, GAAP in the UK will be:

- the CA 2006, insofar that it applies[16];

- accounting standards that have been adopted by the EU. These will include IAS, IFRS;

- interpretations that have been adopted by the EU;

- reporting Standards issued by the ASB that are applicable to UK companies reporting under IFRS;

- for listed companies, the Listing Rules.

Accounting standards and interpretations

13.018 The International Accounting Standards Board ("IASB") develops ("IFRS"). Like the ASB, the IASB has a separate committee, the International Financial Reporting Issues Committee ("IFRIC") that looks at emerging issues which require immediate attention.

For companies incorporated within the EU standards issued by the IASB must be endorsed by the EU before they can be applied by a company—this is known as the endorsement mechanism. Companies may not adopt standards that conflict with existing IFRSs until they have been endorsed. Where an IFRS is adopted before endorsement, companies should note that transitional provisions will not be available.

---

[16] Companies that use EU-adopted IFRS will prepare their financial statements in accordance with the requirements of IFRS rather than accounting requirements of the Companies Act. However some requirements of the Act will continue to apply.

IASB's conceptual framework

The overriding requirement of financial statements prepared under IFRS, **13.019** like those prepared under UK GAAP, is for them to give a fair presentation, i.e. a true and fair view.[17] In addition to this, the IASB has a conceptual framework.

The IASB Framework provides a broad discussion of the accounting principles that underlie the preparation of financial statements under IFRS. One of the aims of the framework is to assist preparers of financial statements in applying IFRS and for other parties such as auditors and users of the accounts. It discusses many of the topics covered in the ASB's Statement of Principles such as relevance and reliability and discusses assets, liabilities, income and expenses, providing definitions and recognition criteria. The Framework discusses the measurement of assets and liabilities in broad terms and the concepts of capital and capital maintenance.

The IASB uses the Framework as an aid to drafting new or revised IFRS. The Framework also provides a point of reference for preparers of financial statements in the absence of any specific standards on a particular subject.

In July 2006, the IASB and the US Financial Accounting Standards Board ("FASB") announced that they are undertaking a joint project to develop a common conceptual framework that both Boards can use to develop new and revised accounting standards. The stated aim of the IASB and FASB is to develop one set of financial reporting rules globally. This is a project that will take some 10 to 15 years.

Narrative reporting: operating and financial review and the business review

The Cadbury Committee also recognised the advantage to users of reports **13.020** and accounts of some explanation of the factors likely to influence a company's future progress. The inclusion of an essentially forward-looking business review in a company's annual report is likely to address this.

There has been much debate over narrative reporting and it has had a rather chequered history. In March 2005 legislation came into force for all companies (except small companies) to expand their directors' report to include a business review, and separate legislation was put in place for UK-quoted companies to prepare an operating and financial review ("OFR"). However, the OFR was repealed in early 2006 after a volte-face by the Government. This caused some consternation and another consultation took place regarding the OFR and its place in financial reporting. As a consequence, the OFR

---

[17] Martin Moore, in his opinion which is referred to in fn 15, opined that the fair presentation requirement of IFRS is equivalent to a true and fair view.

was effectively reintroduced through the business review requirements of the CA 2006.

The detailed requirements of both the business review and the voluntary OFR are dealt with in Chs 16 (Reporting to Shareholders—The Directors'/ Annual Report) and 20 (Corporate Social Responsibility). In this section we will look at one requirement which is common to both and is closely aligned with financial reporting: key performance indicators ("KPIs").

KPIs are defined by the ASB's Reporting Statement: Operating and Financial Review (RS1) as follows:

> "KPIs are factors by reference to which the development, performance or position of the business of the entity can be measured effectively. They are quantified measurements that reflect the critical success factors of an entity and disclose progress towards achieving a particular objective or objectives."

KPIs are often used by the board and management to measure their progress against the businesses financial and non-financial performance objectives at regular intervals throughout the financial year.

The business review requires directors to give a balanced and comprehensive review of the performance and development of the business and to include where necessary financial and non-financial KPIs (the voluntary OFR has the same requirement). KPIs are an effective way for directors to illustrate their narrative reporting.

Guidance on what should be included in a business review can be found in the ASB's Reporting Statement: Operating and Financial Review. Although this is a voluntary reporting statement of best practice, it offers guidance on many requirements of the business review and the ASB has produced a schedule mapping the guidance in the reporting statement to the legal requirements.[18] The statement specifically addresses KPIs, and recommends the following:

- The KPIs disclosed should be those that the directors judge are effective in measuring the delivery of their strategies and managing their business. Regular measurement using KPIs should enable an entity to set and communicate its performance targets and to measure whether its achieving them.

- Comparability will be enhanced if the KPIs disclosed are accepted and widely used, either within the industry sector or more generally.

- An entity should provide information that enables members to understand each KPI disclosed in the OFR.

[18] The guidance can be found at the ASB's website: *http://www.frc.org.uk/asb/press/pub1480. html.*

- For each KPI disclosed in the OFR:

  - the definition and its calculation method should be explained;
  - its purpose should be explained;
  - the source of the underlying data should be disclosed and, where relevant, assumptions explained;
  - quantification or commentary on future targets should be provided;
  - where information from the financial statements has been adjusted for inclusion in the OFR, that fact should be highlighted and a reconciliation should be provided;
  - where available, corresponding amount for the financial year immediately preceding the current year's should be disclosed;
  - any changes to KPIs should be disclosed and the calculation method used compared to previous financial years, including significant changes the underlying accounting policies adopted in the financial statements, should be identified and explained.

Directors may find it difficult to decide on how many KPIs to include in their business review. Directors should focus on the KPIs best able to measure the performance of the business, usually those they already monitor at board level, rather than disclose KPIs which do not actually inform the directors in the running of the business.

Additionally directors may find that although they are using KPIs in common with other companies in the same industry they may calculate them differently. The ASB deals with this issue by recommending that companies disclose the calculation method used and source of underlying data and assumptions used. Over time it is likely that the KPIs used by companies operating within the same sector will be calculated on the same basis.

UK Corporate Governance Code

The recently introduced UK Corporate Governance Code (June 2010) rec-   **13.021**
ommends that directors include in the annual report an explanation of the basis on which the company generates or preserves value over the longer term (the business model) and the strategy for delivering the objectives of the company (C.1.2). This provision appears to have been introduced in response to common failings in business reviews identified by the FRRP—including a lack of clarity about the business model adopted and the specific risks and uncertainties, and the use of boilerplate descriptions.[19]

A footnote to the UK Corporate Governance Code suggests that it would

---

[19] Review of the effectiveness of the Combined Code, Progress Report and Second Consultation, FRC, July 2009.

be desirable if the explanation referred to above were located in the same part of the annual report as the business review required by CA 2006 s.417. Furthermore, guidance as to the matters that should be considered in an explanation of a business model is provided in paras 30 to 32 of the ASB's Reporting Statement: Operating and Financial Review. These paragraphs set out that:

- the OFR should include a description of the business and the external environment in which it operates as context for the directors' discussion and analysis of performance and financial position;

- a description of the business is recommended in order to provide members with an understanding of the industry or industries in which the entity operates, its main products, services, customers, business processes and distribution methods, the structure of the business, and its economic model, including an overview of the main operating facilities and their location;

- every entity is affected by its external environment. Depending on the nature of the business, the OFR should include discussion of matters such as the entity's major markets and competitive position within those markets and the significant features of the legal, regulatory, macro-economic and social environment that influence the business. For example, an entity may disclose the fact that it has significant operations in a number of different countries, which could have an impact on the future development and performance of the business.

Conclusion

13.022   One aim of those that "regulate" and legislate the financial community is to ensure that financial and non-financial information presented in company communications is understandable and comparable, and that its activities are transparent. The current rules and principles that surround financial reporting aim to ensure that this is the case. However, the application of these rules and principles, as set out in financial reporting standards, in either IFRS or UK GAAP, can be complex. The key for company directors is to remember that the board is remitted by the UK Corporate Governance Code to "present a balanced and understandable assessment of the company's position and prospects". If company directors are presented with information from management which is not clear and meaningful then they should challenge the authors.

Chapter 14

External Audit, Internal Audit and the Audit Committee

Tim Copnell[1]

External audit

Introduction and background

"The purpose of the statutory audit is to provide an independent opinion **14.001**
to the shareholders on the truth and fairness of the financial statements, whether they have been properly prepared in accordance with the
Companies Act and to report by exception to the shareholders on the other
requirements of company law such as where, in the auditors' opinion,
proper accounting records have not been kept."

ICAEW, July 2006

Audits serve a fundamental purpose in helping to enforce accountability
and promote confidence in financial reporting. Relationships between prin-
cipals (shareholders) and their agents (directors) are of particular importance in understanding how audits have evolved and continue to develop.
Shareholders delegate the responsibility for managing the affairs of a

[1] Timothy Copnell is the Associate Partner in charge of the KPMG sponsored UK Audit
Committee Institute, founded by Timothy to communicate with audit committee members
and help enhance their awareness, commitment, and ability to implement effective audit committee processes. In 2004/2005 Timothy was awarded the Accountancy Age "Accountant of
the Year" for his work with audit committees. Timothy qualified as a chartered accountant
in 1989 and joined KPMG's Department of Professional Practice in 1993 where he took
responsibility for corporate governance matters. His role includes advising on private sector
corporate governance and responding to major UK corporate governance developments.
Timothy is the Author of the *Audit Committee Guide* (ICSA, 2004) and KPMG's series of
practical guides to corporate governance developments. He also writes regular articles for
various publications.

company to the directors and the financial statements are a key mechanism by which shareholders hold the directors to account.

Potential conflicts of interest arise as a result of the separation of ownership from control. The statutory audit is a mechanism for shareholders to help ensure that the directors are acting in the company's best interests and it therefore plays a fundamental stewardship role.

Statutory and quasi-statutory duties

The Companies Act 2006

14.002 In relation to a company's annual accounts, the basic statutory duty set out in s.495 of the Companies Act 2006 ("CA 2006") is that the auditor must report clearly whether in their opinion, the annual accounts give a true and fair view:

  (a) in the case of an individual balance sheet, of the state of affairs of the company as at the end of the financial year,

  (b) in the case of an individual profit and loss account, of the profit or loss of the company for the financial year,

  (c) in the case of group accounts, of the state of affairs as at the end of the financial year and of the profit or loss for the financial year of the undertakings included in the consolidation as a whole, so far as concerns members of the company.

Furthermore, the auditor's opinion must state whether the annual accounts have been properly prepared in accordance with the relevant financial reporting framework; and in accordance with the requirements of CA 2006 (and, where applicable, art.4 of the IAS Regulation).

The auditor's report must be either unqualified or qualified; and must include a reference to any matters to which the auditor wishes to draw attention by way of emphasis without qualifying the report.

With respect to the directors' report, s.496 requires that the auditor state in their report on the company's annual accounts whether in their opinion the information given in the directors' report for the financial year for which the accounts are prepared is consistent with those accounts.

If the company is a quoted company, s.497 requires that the auditor, in their report on the company's annual accounts for the financial year, report to the company's members on the auditable part of the directors' remuneration report; and state whether that part of the directors' remuneration report has been properly prepared in accordance with the Act.

A company's auditor, in preparing their report, must carry out such investigations as will enable them to form an opinion as to:

(a)   whether adequate accounting records have been kept by the company and returns adequate for their audit have been received from branches not visited by him, and

(b)   whether the company's individual accounts are in agreement with the accounting records and returns, and

(c)   in the case of a quoted company, whether the auditable part of the company's directors' remuneration report is in agreement with the accounting records and returns.

Where the auditor can not opine positively on (a) to (c) above; or the auditor fails to obtain all the information and explanations which, to the best of their knowledge and belief, are necessary for the purposes of the audit; they must state that fact in their report.

If the requirements of s.412 (disclosure of directors' benefits: remuneration, pensions and compensation for loss of office) or, in the case of a quoted company, the requirements of s.421 (information forming the auditable part of the directors' remuneration report) are not complied with, the auditor must include in their report, so far as they are reasonably able to do so, a statement giving the required particulars.

It should be noted that the duty to prepare the accounts themselves is the responsibility of the directors. It is the company which has a duty to keep adequate accounting records (s.386) and it is the directors who have a duty to prepare, for each financial year of the company, accounts which give a true and fair view of the state of the affairs of the company and its profit or loss for the financial year (s.394, s.396).

The Financial Services and Markets Act 2000 ("FSMA")

Auditors of a person authorised under the Financial Services Authority ("FSA") may also be under a positive duty to communicate matters to the FSA, for example, where the auditors reasonably believe that there may have been a breach of any of the statutory requirements applicable to the authorised person or where the auditors reasonably believe that the company may cease to be a going concern.   **14.003**

If it appears to the FSA that the auditors of an authorised person have failed to comply with a duty imposed on them under the FSMA, it may disqualify them from being the auditors of the relevant body or person.

Listing Rules

Listing Rule 9.8.10R requires that before publication of the annual report, a listed company must ensure that the auditors review: **14.004**

(a) the statement made by the directors pursuant to Listing Rule 9.8.6R(3)—that is to say the directors' statement to the effect that the business is a going concern, together with supporting assumptions or qualifications as necessary, that has been prepared in accordance with "Going Concern and Liquidity Risk: Guidance for Directors of UK Companies 2009", published by the Financial Reporting Council ("FRC") in October 2009. The Listing Rules do not provide for sanctions against the auditors in the event that the review or the statement is incorrect.

(b) the statement made by the directors pursuant to Listing Rule 9.8.6R(6) only insofar as it relates to the objectively verifiable elements of Section C (Audit Committees and Auditors) of the UK Corporate Governance Code. This is the statement setting out the company's compliance (or reasons for non-compliance if appropriate) with the provisions of the UK Corporate Governance Code relating to the:

- directors' responsibility statement (C.1.1);
- directors' review of the effectiveness of internal control and risk management systems (C.2.1);
- constitution of the audit committee and the independence and experience of audit committee members (C.3.1);
- roles and responsibilities of the audit committee and written terms of reference (C.3.2);
- publication of the audit committee's terms of reference and disclosure of the manner in which the audit committee has discharged its duties (C.3.3);
- audit committee's review of whistle blowing arrangements (C.3.4);
- audit committee's review of the effectiveness of internal audit activities (C.3.5);
- audit committee's role in recommending the appointment, reappointment and removal of the external auditor (C.3.6);
- explanation of how auditor objectivity and independence is safeguarded (C.3.7).

Furthermore, a listed company must ensure that the auditors review the disclosures made pursuant to Listing Rule 9.8.8R(2) (amount of each element in the remuneration package and information on share options); Listing Rule 9.8.8R(3), (4) and (5) (details of long term incentive schemes for directors); Listing Rule 9.8.8R(11) (money purchase schemes); and Listing Rule 9.8.8R(12) (defined benefit schemes). If, in the opinion of the auditors the listed company has not complied with any of the requirements set out in these paragraphs, the listed company must ensure that the auditors' report includes, to the extent possible, a statement giving details of the non-compliance.

Common law duties

The letter of engagement appointing the auditors will set out the terms **14.005** and conditions of engagement and the limitations on liability sought to be imposed by the auditors. Common law undoubtedly imposes on auditors a duty to exercise reasonable skill and care and fiduciary duties not to profit from the position and not to place themselves in a conflict of interest, breach of any of which will render the auditors liable in damages in tort and/or breach of contract. In relation to the statutory audit, the purpose of the relevant statutory provisions is to provide shareholders at general meetings with information on the financial position of the company which may assist that meeting, and not to provide shareholders or other third parties with information on which they might base the decisions on whether or not to invest in the company. There is set out in App.20 a note on the leading case in this matter, *Caparo Industries Plc v Dickman*[2] where the auditors were held not liable to third parties even where the auditing process was carried out negligently. This is not to say, however, that an auditor would not be liable to third parties where the necessary relationship of "proximity" imposed a clear duty of care by the auditors to that third party.

Auditing standards

The Auditing Practices Board ("APB"), a constituent body of the FRC, **14.006** has issued International Standards on Auditing ("ISA") (UK and Ireland), which provide standards and guidance on the objectives and general principles governing an audit of financial statements. The ISA (UK and Ireland) are the standards as issued by the International Audit and Assurance Board ("IAASB"), supplemented, where necessary, by standards and guidance from the UK auditing standards previously in issue.

Auditing standards and guidance

Auditing standards provide the basic principles and essential procedures with **14.007** which auditors are required to comply when carrying out:

- statutory audits of companies in accordance with the Companies Acts;

---

[2] [1990] 2 W.L.R. 358.

- audits of financial statements for entities established in accordance with other UK or Irish legislation, for example building societies, credit unions, friendly societies, pension funds, charities and registered social landlords;

- public sector audits in the UK, including those carried out either on behalf of the national audit agencies or under contract to those agencies;

- other audits performed by audit firms registered with the members of the Consultative Committee of Accountancy Bodies ("CCAB") unless the nature of the engagement requires the use of other recognised auditing standards; and

- other audits where audit firms not registered with members of the CCAB elect, or are required by contract, to perform the work in accordance with UK or Irish auditing standards.

The APB also issues guidance to auditors of financial statements in the form of Practice Notes and Bulletins. Practice Notes and Bulletins are persuasive rather than prescriptive and are indicative of good practice. Practice Notes assist auditors in applying auditing standards to particular circumstances and industries and Bulletins provide timely guidance on new or emerging issues.

Ethical standards

14.008   ISAs require compliance with the APB's ethical standards and relevant ethical pronouncements relating to the work of auditors issued.

APB ethical standards apply to the audit of financial statements in both the private and public sectors. However, auditors in the public sector are subject to more complex ethical requirements than their private sector counterparts. This includes compliance with legislation such as the Prevention of Corruption Act 1916, concerning gifts and hospitality, and Cabinet Office guidance.

Auditor's Code

14.009   The Auditors' Code, published by the APB, provides a framework of fundamental principles which encapsulate the concepts that govern the conduct of audits and underlie the ethical and auditing standards. A copy of the Auditor's Code is set out below.

"The Auditors' Code

Accountability

Auditors act in the interests of primary stakeholders, whilst having regard to the wider public interest. The identity of primary stakeholders is determined by reference to the statute or agreement requiring an audit: in the case of companies, the primary stakeholder is the general body of shareholders.

Integrity

Auditors act with integrity, fulfilling their responsibilities with honesty, fairness, candour, courage and confidentiality. Confidential information obtained in the course of the audit is disclosed only when required in the public interest, or by operation of law.

Objectivity and independence

Auditors are objective and provide impartial opinions unaffected by bias, prejudice, compromise and conflicts of interest. Auditors are also independent, this requires them to be free from situations and relationships which would make it probable that a reasonable and informed third party would conclude that the auditors' objectivity either is impaired or could be impaired.

Competence

Auditors act with professional skill, derived from their qualification, training and practical experience. This demands an understanding of financial reporting and business issues, together with an expertise in accumulating and assessing the evidence necessary to form an opinion.

Rigour

Auditors approach their work with thoroughness and with an attitude of professional scepticism. They assess critically the information and explanations obtained in the course of their work and such additional evidence as they consider necessary for the purposes of their audit.

Judgment

Auditors apply professional judgment taking account of materiality in the context of the matter on which they are reporting.

Clear, complete and effective communication

Auditors' reports contain clear expressions of opinion and set out information necessary for a proper understanding of the opinion. Auditors communicate audit matters of governance interest arising from the audit of financial statements with those charged with governance of an entity.

Association

Auditors allow their reports to be included in documents containing other information only if they consider that the additional information is not in conflict with the matters covered by their report and they have no cause to believe it to be misleading.

Providing value

Auditors add to the reliability and quality of financial reporting; they provide to directors and officers constructive observations arising from the audit process; and thereby contribute to the effective operation of business capital markets and the public sector."

Internal audit

Introduction and background

14.010 "Internal auditing is an independent, objective assurance and consulting activity designed to add value and improve an organisation's operations. It helps an organisation accomplish its objectives by bringing a systematic, disciplined approach to evaluate and improve the effectiveness of risk management, control and governance processes."

Institute of Internal Auditors[3]

The role of internal audit is very different to that of external audit. While the role of the external auditor largely stems from the legal requirement that an independent auditor should report to shareholders their opinion on the truth and fairness of the financial statements, internal audit focuses primarily on the company's system of internal control—looking at reputational, operational or strategic risks. They also give an independent opinion on whether internal controls—such as policies and procedures—put in place to manage such risks are fit for purpose and working as intended.

Generally the work of internal audit encompasses checking that the assets of the organisation are being appropriately safeguarded; that operations are conducted effectively, efficiently and economically in accordance with the

---

[3] Code of Ethics and International Standards for the Professional Practice of Internal Auditing, Institute of Internal Auditors, March 2004, *http://www.iia.org.uk*.

organisation's policies; that laws and regulations are complied with; and that records and reports are accurate and reliable.

Professional standards

The Institute of Internal Auditors ("IIA") is the leading voice and recognised **14.011** authority on internal auditing. They promote best practice throughout the internal audit profession and develop the profession for the benefit of their members.

The International Standards for the Professional Practice of Internal Auditing (Standards),[4] published by the IIA, provide guidance for the conduct of internal auditing at both the organisation and individual auditor levels.

The Standards comprise "Attribute" and "Performance Standards". Attribute standards focus on the purpose, authority, responsibility, independence, objectivity, proficiency, due professional care, and quality assurance and improvement of the audit activities. Performance standards provide guidance on the nature of audit work and planning, conducting, managing, communicating, and reporting throughout the audit activity. These standards also address areas such as resource and risk management, policies and procedures, control, and governance.

Compliance with the IIA's standards is considered essential for internal auditors discharging their duties.

UK Corporate Governance Code

The UK Corporate Governance Code[5] does not require, or even recommend **14.012** the formation of internal audit functions per se. However it does set out that role and responsibilities of the audit committee should include monitoring and reviewing the effectiveness of the company's internal audit function. The Code goes on to recommend that where there is no internal audit function, the audit committee should consider annually whether there is a need for an internal audit function and make a recommendation to the board, and that the reasons for the absence of such a function should be explained in the relevant section of the annual report.

Clearly, the need for an internal audit function will vary depending on many factors including the scale, diversity and complexity of the company's activities and the number of employees, as well as cost/benefit considerations.

---

[4] See fn 3.
[5] The UK Corporate Governance Code (June 2010) sets out standards of good practice in relation to issues such as board composition and development, remuneration, accountability and audit and relations with shareholders, *http://www.frc.org.uk/corporate/ukcgcode.cfm.*

An adequately resourced internal audit function, however, can make a strong contribution to the assurance on risk and control required by management and the board. If an internal audit function does not exist, management would need to apply other monitoring processes in order to assure itself, the audit committee and the board that the system of internal control is functioning as intended.

The FRC's Guidance for Audit Committees,[6] annexed to the UK Corporate Governance Code, provides further guidance on the factors for audit committees to consider when undertaking an assessment of the need for an internal audit function. The guidance states that the audit committee should also consider whether there are any:

> "trends or current factors relevant to the company's activities, markets or other aspects of its external environment that have increased, or are expected to increase, the risks faced by the company. Such an increase in risk may also arise from internal factors such as organisational restructuring or from changes in reporting processes or underlying information systems".

Where an internal audit function does exist, the FRC's Guidance for Audit Committees goes on to state that the audit committee should review and approve the internal audit function's remit; ensure that the function has the necessary resources and access to information to enable it to fulfil its mandate; and ensure that it is equipped to perform in accordance with appropriate professional standards for internal auditors.

With regard to monitoring and reviewing the effectiveness of the company's internal audit function, the FRC's Guidance for Audit Committees recommends that the audit committee should:

(a) ensure that the internal auditor has direct access to the board chairman and to the audit committee and is accountable to the audit committee;

(b) review and assess the annual internal audit work plan;

(c) receive a report on the results of the internal auditors' work on a periodic basis;

(d) review and monitor management's responsiveness to the internal auditor's findings and recommendations;

(e) meet with the head of internal audit at least once a year without the presence of management; and

---

[6] The FRC's Guidance for Audit Committees is designed to assist company boards in making suitable arrangements for their audit committees, and to assist directors serving on audit committees in carrying out their role, *http://www.frc.org.uk/corporate/ukcgcode.cfm*.

(f)   monitor and assess the role and effectiveness of the internal audit function in the overall context of the company's risk management system.

Independence and objectivity

Independence is a fundamental attribute of internal audit. For independence   **14.013**
to be achieved, the head of internal audit would normally have direct access to any member of the executive board and to the chairman of the audit committee and should be accountable to the audit committee. They should also have ample opportunity to meet with the audit committee in private session, without the presence of management.

The IIA's professional standards, set out that the key condition for achieving independence is freedom from interference in relation to "determining the scope of internal auditing, performing work and communicating results". Nevertheless, internal audit independence can be difficult to achieve; sound organisational safeguards need to be in place. Notwithstanding the audit functions accountability to the audit committee, it is in some way also accountable to management—at least as regards "pay and rations".

Issues around the internal audit function's independence are particularly acute in smaller organisations. In such situations, the audit committee should be aware of this issue and should ensure that it is comfortable with the degree of independent assurance it receives.

Internal audit objectivity is also vital to ensure that their work is of practical value to an organisation and can be acted upon. Audit committees who use or rely on the work of the internal audit function need to be confident that it has been prepared by someone whose only interest is to provide a fair and impartial assessment.

The IIA's Code of Ethics[7] defines objectivity as follows:

"Internal auditors:

(a)   Shall not participate in any activity or relationship that may impair or be presumed to impair their unbiased assessment. This participation includes those activities or relationships that may be in conflict with the interests of the organisation.

(b)   Shall not accept anything that may impair or be presumed to impair their professional judgement.

(c)   Shall disclose all material facts known to them that, if not disclosed, may distort the reporting of activities under review."

---

[7] See fn 3.

The Code of Ethics goes on to state that objectivity relates to having the ability to make unbiased judgments and avoid situations in which the internal auditor's judgment may be compromised. For example, if an internal auditor performed a review of an activity for which they had authority or responsibility could, or could be perceived to, damage their objectivity.

Internal audit mandate

14.014   Whilst the audit committee generally determines internal audit's mandate and powers, the role of internal audit normally includes:

(a)   the control environment as a whole, i.e. how executive management directs and controls the business.

(b)   the processes by which risks are identified analysed and managed;

(c)   controls over key operational and functional processes;

(d)   processes that deliver change and systems development initiatives;

(e)   the reliability and integrity of corporate management information;

(f)   the safeguarding of assets;

(g)   compliance with relevant legislation.

The reports from internal audit will be used by the board (via the audit committee) along with those from management and compliance functions, to provide evidence on which the board can base its corporate governance disclosures in the annual report and accounts.

Interaction with external audit

14.015   To ensure that there is not an unnecessary duplication of work carried out by the internal and external auditors; the audit committee should ensure that efforts are co-ordinated. The head of internal audit would normally liaise with the external auditor and may in some cases agree a joint programme of work.

Forming an internal audit function

14.016   It is good practice to develop a formal internal audit charter, which is agreed with the audit committee. This will define the scope of the internal audit function's work, its reporting lines and its right of access to people, properties, records and information. This should be circulated to the organisation's managers to make sure that they are aware of the role of the internal audit function and their obligations to provide access to information and records to enable their internal auditors to carry out their role.

The head of internal audit should determine the function's programme of work and this should be approved by the audit committee. The head of internal audit should then ensure that their department carries out that work in accordance with the *Standards for the Professional Practice of Internal Auditing* in accordance with the IIA's International Standards (see above).

Once the nature and extent of the resources committed to internal audit are determined, the head of internal audit should develop an audit plan based on the risks inherent in the organisation. This will inform the scope and priority of audit assignments.

A new head of internal audit will need to determine the organisation's business objectives and whether adequate processes are in place for identifying, assessing and managing the risks that impact on the achievement of such objectives. If the head of internal audit considers that the risk management processes are adequate and embedded, they may rely, where possible, on the organisation's own view of the assessment of risks in terms of their probability and impact to determine the audit work to be carried out. If the head of internal audit considers that management's views cannot be relied on, they should determine where further work is required. For example, they may need to work with management to determine the key risks or to reassess management's evaluation of the adequacy of the organisation's response to risks.

Where the head of internal audit feels that the organisation's risk management processes are "fit for purpose", their focus will turn to how management gets assurance that its risk management activities are actually "operating as intended".

The head of internal audit may choose to audit complete systems or processes, specific business units or particular risks. In all cases, the internal audit function will need to review business objectives and risk management processes within each auditable area.

In determining the resources required to deliver the plan of audit assignments, the head of internal audit may decide to recruit an in-house team of suitable auditors to meet all audit assignment requirements. They may also use external providers to either supplement the in-house team with staff who have specific skills (co-sourcing) or to run the function for the company under an outsource arrangement.

The knowledge, skills and attributes of a good head of internal audit will differ from organisation to organisation. Nevertheless, the IIA recommend a combination of the following:

(a)   Excellent communication skills. The ability to constructively challenge management, clearly explain and identify findings and persuade management to take action.

(b) Good interpersonal skills. The ability to work confidently with board members and management; and to command their respect.

(c) Sound judgment and commercial awareness.

(d) An understanding of the principles and application of good corporate governance, risk management and control processes and procedures.

(e) The ability to act independently and with an objective frame of mind.

(f) The ability to lead, motivate, manage and develop teams.

(g) The ability to motivate change programmes and act as a catalyst for organisational change.

(h) Practical experience of working in internal audit.

(i) An appropriate professional qualification, such as the IIA's MIIA Qualification.

The audit committee

Introduction and background

14.017 The primary role of an audit committee is to oversee the potential conflicts of interest that can arise during the preparation, publication and audit of financial statements.

Audit committees have evolved from ad hoc committees with few defined responsibilities to what they are today: critical committees with growing responsibilities that are accountable to the board of directors, and ultimately to shareholders.

Brought to prominence in the UK through Sir Adrian Cadbury's *Report on the Financial Aspects of Corporate Governance*[8] in 1992, the duties of audit committees have grown with successive corporate governance reports. These culminated in the Financial Reporting Council's UK Corporate Governance Code[9] and the related Guidance for Audit Committees.[10]

The UK Corporate Governance Code contains the basic best practice recommendations relating to audit committees. The Guidance for Audit Committees goes further in providing direction on how companies might apply and comply with the UK Corporate Governance Code provisions and principles relating to audit committees. A copy of the Guidance for Audit Committees as annexed to the UK Corporate Governance Code is set out in App.15.

---

[8] *The Financial Aspects of Corporate Governance* was produce in 1992 by a committee (the Cadbury Committee) set up by the London Stock Exchange and the accountancy profession.
[9] See fn 5.
[10] See fn 6.

EU requirements

Until recently, specific practices were not mandated. However, the EU's **14.018** Eighth Company Law Directive (the Statutory Audit Directive)[11] mandated some audit committee related requirements which have been implemented via the FSA's Disclosure and Transparency Rules ("DTR").[12] The new requirements, however, have long been part of the UK Corporate Governance Code and as such, the FSA assert that companies complying with the relevant Code provisions are deemed as having fulfilled the DTR requirements.

The DTR requirements are as follows:

- DTR 7.1.1R states that an issuer must have a body which is responsible for performing the functions set out in DTR 7.1.3R (see below), and that at least one member of that body must be independent and at least one member must have competence in accounting and/or auditing.

- DTR 7.1.2 states that the requirements for independence and competence in accounting and/or auditing may be satisfied by the same member or by different members of the relevant body.

- DTR 7.1.3 R states that an issuer must ensure that, as a minimum, the relevant body must:
    - monitor the financial reporting process;
    - monitor the effectiveness of the issuer's internal control, internal audit where applicable, and risk management systems;
    - monitor the statutory audit of the annual and consolidated accounts;
    - review and monitor the independence of the statutory auditor, and in particular the provision of additional services to the issuer.

Further DTR rules set out what disclosure is required and what information should be included in the corporate governance statement.

Membership, meetings and resources

Main Principle C.3 (audit committee and auditors) of the UK Corporate **14.019** Governance Code states:

"The board should establish formal and transparent arrangements for considering how they should apply the corporate reporting and risk

---

[11] Directive 2006/43/EC of the European Parliament and of the Council of 17 May 2006 on statutory audits of annual accounts and consolidated accounts, amending Council Directives 78/660/EEC and 83/349/EEC and repealing Council Directive 84/253/EEC.
[12] FSA's DTR Ch.7.1 Audit Committees.

management and internal control principles and for maintaining an appropriate relationship with the company's auditor."

Code Provision C.3.1 states:

"The board should establish an audit committee of at least three, or in the case of smaller companies [i.e. sub-FTSE 350] two, independent non-executive directors. In smaller companies the company chairman may be a member of, but not chair, the committee in addition to the independent non-executive directors, provided he or she was considered independent on appointment as chairman. The board should satisfy itself that at least one member of the audit committee has recent and relevant financial experience."

Notwithstanding the UK Corporate Governance Code recommendation, the size of an audit committee should vary depending upon the needs and culture of the company and the extent of delegated responsibilities to the committee. The objective is to allow the committee to function efficiently, all members to participate, and an appropriate level of diversity of experience and knowledge. Committees of three to six individuals are generally most appropriate to achieve those objectives.

Appointments to the audit committee should be made by the board on the recommendation of the nomination committee (where there is one), in consultation with the audit committee chairman. Terms of three years, with staggered expiration dates to ensure continuity, are common though most companies have no set policies for rotating committee members. In the absence of a rotation policy, it is important for the board of directors to evaluate an audit committee member's performance to see that it meets both the board's and committee's expectations.

Independence

14.020   Audit committee independence is the cornerstone of the committee's effectiveness, particularly when overseeing a company's financial reporting integrity and evaluation of areas where judgments and decisions are significant. Audit committee members must be adept at communicating with management and the auditors and ready to ask key, probing questions about the company's financial risks and accounting and financial reporting.

It is up to the board to assess the integrity and independence of an audit committee candidate, so every member's appointment is an occasion for careful deliberation. The board should have a strong understanding of the relevant definitions of independence and how a lack of independence occurs and is interpreted in practice. Independence issues are most prevalent with respect to business relations. The board should also be cognisant and mindful of situations in which the definition of independence is met; yet perceived conflicts of interest may still arise.

Financial expertise and other skills

Like any non-executive director, audit committee members should (at least **14.021** as a group) possess a wide range of knowledge, skills and personal attributes: sound judgment; integrity and high ethical standards; strong interpersonal skills; and the ability and willingness to challenge and probe. Specifically, audit committee members must have expertise, or access to expertise, that goes beyond mere familiarity with financial statements. They must be able to understand the rules and, more importantly, the principles that underpin the preparation of financial statements. They must be prepared to invest the time necessary to understand why critical accounting policies are chosen, how they are applied, and satisfy themselves that the end result fairly reflects their understanding.

The UK Corporate Governance Code states that the board should satisfy itself that at least one member of the audit committee has recent and relevant financial experience. It is sensible that the other members are, at least, financially literate.

Recent and relevant financial experience is deliberately undefined—each board should determine its own criteria. However, it is clear that it must go beyond a basic familiarity with financial statements and perhaps comprise past employment experience, or a qualification, in finance or accounting or related service that may include experience as a CEO, with financial reporting oversight responsibilities, or finance director.

Generally the audit committee member with the highest level of financial expertise also chairs the committee, but this need not necessarily be the case. The member who is designated as having "financial experience" should be aware of his or her role, but it is not necessary for them to be identified in the annual report and accounts under UK regulations. For companies who have or will raise capital in foreign jurisdictions involving additional financial reporting obligations, audit committees should consider having at least one member of the audit committee with accounting or financial management expertise in that foreign country.

Members should have experience in areas pertinent to the business. A committee's effectiveness in performing its mission is certainly enhanced by, and is often dependent upon, the members' experience, knowledge and competence in business matters, financial reporting, internal controls and auditing.

All members should seek periodic continuing professional education both inside and outside the boardroom. Management, internal and external auditors, and the company secretary are sources of background information and training for audit committee members. Periodic briefings, reports and presentations by management, external auditors and internal auditors for audit committee members should cover operational and financial issues specific to the company and the industry, and updates on new accounting and auditing standards. Companies should offer, and committees should insist on, the kind of training that will enhance their financial literacy and make it possible for them to fulfil their fiduciary responsibilities. This is especially true of new members, who should receive a complete orientation that allows them to function effectively from the very beginning.

Audit committee meetings

14.022   A detailed agenda is vital for keeping the committee focused. Effective agendas are set with input from the CEO, finance director and the internal and external auditors. The audit committee chairman, however, should maintain accountability for the agenda and not delegate it to management.

There should be as many meetings as the audit committee's role and responsibilities require. The FRC's Guidance for Audit Committees recommends that there should be no fewer than three meetings during the year, held to coincide with key dates within the financial reporting and audit cycle. However, audit committee chairmen may wish to call more frequent meetings. There should be sufficient time permitted to cover all agenda items and allow time for all parties to ask questions or provide input. There should also be sufficient time for the committee members only to have a private session at each meeting.

Furthermore, an appropriate interval should be allowed between audit committee meetings and main board meetings to allow any work arising from the audit committee meeting to be carried out and reported to the board. This is all very much common sense but serious problems may arise if questions of substance are raised for the first time at the final audit committee meeting and are answered in a way different from that in which might be expected. If the final audit committee meeting is to be conducted effectively, then the chairman should be entering into communication with both the finance director and internal and external auditors some time in advance of the audit committee meeting and bringing matters of concern to the attention of the audit committee members. The relationship with the auditor should be such that any serious concerns are brought to the audit committee's attention promptly, though in a non-adversarial way.

The FRC's Guidance for Audit Committees sets out that no one other than the audit committee members should be entitled to attend any meeting of the audit committee. It is the audit committee itself that should decide who should attend any particular meeting (or part of a meeting). Nevertheless, it is to be expected that the external audit lead partner, head of internal audit and the finance director will regularly be invited to attend meetings as well as perhaps the CEO or group chairman. The CEO often has vital insights to share; however, the audit committee chairman should ensure that the CEO does not inhibit open discussion at the meeting.

Management should be expected to discuss key accounting estimates and subjective adjustments for each interim period. External auditors should periodically discuss the appropriateness of accounting, including accounting alternatives and choices made by management. Private executive sessions should be held with the external auditors at least once a year. Leading practice would also suggest private sessions with the head of internal audit.

Formal meetings of the audit committee are at the heart of its work. However, they will rarely be sufficient. Audit committee chairman, and to a lesser extent the other members, may need to keep in touch with the board chairman, the chief executive, the finance director, the external audit lead partner and the head of internal audit on a continuing basis.

Formal minutes should be prepared, circulated to external and internal auditors as appropriate, approved by the audit committee and then reviewed by the full board of directors. Important documents related to the meeting should be attached to the minutes, including the agenda.

Audit committee resources

The audit committee should be provided with sufficient resources to under-   **14.023**
take its duties. It should have access to the services of the company secretary on all audit committee matters including: assisting the chairman in planning the audit committee's work, drawing up meeting agendas, maintenance of minutes, drafting of material about its activities for the annual report, collection and distribution of information and provision of any necessary practical support. The company secretary should ensure that the audit committee receives information and papers in a timely manner to enable full and proper consideration to be given to the issues.

The board should make funds available to the audit committee to enable it to take independent legal, accounting or other advice when the audit committee reasonably believes it necessary to do so.

Responsibilities

UK Corporate Governance Code Provision C.3.2 states: **14.024**

"The main role and responsibilities of the audit committee should be set out in written terms of reference and should include:

- to monitor the integrity of the financial statements of the company and any formal announcements relating to the company's financial performance, reviewing significant financial reporting judgments contained in them;

- to review the company's internal financial controls and, unless expressly addressed by a separate board risk committee composed of independent directors, or by the board itself, to review the company's internal control and risk management systems;
- to monitor and review the effectiveness of the company's internal audit function;
- to make recommendations to the board, for it to put to the shareholders for their approval in general meeting, in relation to the appointment, reappointment and removal of the external auditor and to approve the remuneration and terms of engagement of the external auditor;
- to review and monitor the external auditor's independence and objectivity and the effectiveness of the audit process, taking into consideration relevant UK professional and regulatory requirements;
- to develop and implement policy on the engagement of the external auditor to supply non-audit services, taking into account relevant and ethical guidance regarding the provision of non-audit services by the external audit firm; and to report to the board, identifying any matters in respect of which it considers that action or improvement is needed and making recommendations as to the steps up to be taken."

Overseeing financial reporting

14.025   The audit committee should monitor the financial integrity of the financial statements and any formal announcements relating to the company's financial performance. As part of this review, the audit committee should ensure they are made aware of accounting policy or disclosure issues and that this information is communicated to them early enough to enable appropriate action to be taken as needed. The audit committee should inquire of management and/or the auditors regarding recommended audit adjustments and disclosure changes, those made by management and those not made by management; the accounting principles and critical accounting policies adopted by management; unusual transactions; and accounting provisions and estimates included in the financial statements. A thorough understanding of all of these factors is integral to the committee's ability to meet its oversight responsibilities.

The FRC's Guidance for Audit Committees recommends that the audit committee's oversight role be extended beyond the financial statements and related information (e.g. the operating and financial review, and corporate governance statements relating to the audit and to risk management), to include, where practicable, the review of other statements containing financial information and requiring board approval (e.g. significant financial returns to regulators, release of price sensitive information and summary financial statements). Often it will not be practicable for an audit committee to review such statements before board approval. Where this is the case, the audit committee should satisfy itself that adequate control processes are in place.

It is management's, not the audit committee's nor the auditors', responsibility to prepare complete and accurate financial statements and disclosures in accordance with financial reporting standards and applicable rules and regulations. However, the audit committee needs to assure itself that the external auditors are satisfied that the accounting estimates and judgments made by management, and management's selection of accounting principles, reflect an appropriate application of Generally Accepted Accounting Practice ("GAAP"). The appropriateness, including the degree to which management bias, if any, is evident, of the company's accounting principles and underlying estimates and the transparency of the financial disclosures in reflecting financial performance would be at the core of discussions between the audit committee and external auditor. The committee should be interested in discussing and understanding the auditors' views on accounting issues, and should actively seek to develop a relationship with the external auditor that allows a full, frank and timely discussion of all material issues.

Overseeing the system of internal controls

Risk management involves identifying risks that may prevent a company **14.026** from achieving its objectives, analysing those risks, avoiding certain risks, and managing the risks that remain. The board of directors is ultimately responsible for the risk management system and for reviewing its effectiveness. The company's management is responsible for the identification, assessment, management and monitoring of risk, for developing, operating and monitoring the system of internal control and for providing assurance to the board that it has done so.

The process related to identifying and managing the company's risks, as a part of the company's overall control environment, influences the identification and management of financial risks that can affect the company's financial reporting—a matter of critical importance to the audit committee.

The audit committee, as a committee appointed by the board of directors, is responsible for assisting the board in fulfilling its oversight responsibilities. In particular, the audit committee's primary duties and responsibilities are to monitor the management of the principal risks that could impact the financial reporting process of the company, monitor the integrity of the system of internal controls regarding financial reporting and accounting compliance, and oversee the internal and external audit process.

In addition to their direct oversight responsibilities for risks relating to financial reporting, audit committees are sometimes asked by the board to examine objectively the degree to which management has assumed "ownership" for overall risk management, the appropriateness of the risk management strategy and process adopted in addressing this responsibility, and the adequacy and effectiveness of systems to support the process.

The FRC's Guidance for Audit Committees specifically addresses the issue of non-financial risk in recommending that the audit committee should review the wider aspects of internal control and risk management systems unless expressly addressed by the board or a separate risk committee comprised of independent directors. Furthermore, except to the extent that this is expressly dealt with by the board or risk committee, the audit committee should review and approve any statements included in the annual report in relation to internal control and the management of risk.

There is a tension here between the role of the audit committee as articulated in the FRC's Guidance for Audit Committees and the FRC guidance *Internal Control: Guidance for directors on the Combined Code* (the Turnbull Report) which expressly states that "reviewing the effectiveness of internal control is an essential part of the board's responsibilities" and that "the board takes responsibility for the disclosures on internal control in the annual report and accounts". Turnbull does not preclude the audit committee from carrying aspects of the boards review work, however, the results of the committees' work should be reported to, and considered by, the board prior to the board reaching its own conclusions.

Turnbull's report goes on to clarify the role of board committees in the review process. It states that the role of such committees:

"including the audit committee, "is for the board to decide and will depend upon factors such as the size and composition of the board; the scale, diversity and complexity of the company's operations; and the nature of the significant risks that the company faces."

It is imperative that audit committees ensure they understand any responsibilities they have for internal controls beyond those related to financial reporting.

Management is responsible for designing and implementing an effective system of internal control. The audit committee must determine that management has implemented policies that ensure the company's risks around financial reporting (and, where applicable, the wider sphere of business risk) are identified and that controls are adequate, in place, and functioning properly. As part of its assessment, the audit committee should consider requesting from management an overview of the risks, policies, procedures, and controls surrounding the integrity of financial reporting. However, the committee should strive to ensure that the information it receives is manageable—it should not be so voluminous as to deter a proper understanding of the key risks. It is more important that the audit committee gains meaningful insight into the key sources of risk and how such risks are managed, and responds with pertinent challenge than be presented with a substantial, albeit complete, register of all the risks facing the business.

The role of the audit committee with regard to risk management is further complicated by Sir David Walker's recommendation[13] that the boards of FTSE 100-listed banks and life insurance companies should establish a board risk committee separately from the audit committee. The review goes on to suggest that such board risk committees should have responsibility for oversight and advice to the board on the current risk exposures of the entity and future risk strategy, including strategy for capital and liquidity management, and the embedding and maintenance throughout the entity of a supportive culture in relation to the management of risk alongside established prescriptive rules and procedures.

Unlike many of Sir David Walker's recommendations, the recommendation to establish a risk committee was not embraced by the FRC when re-drafting the UK Corporate Governance Code. As a consequence, there are no recommendations (or expectations) that would steer a non-financial services company towards establishing a risk committee. However, this does not mean that it would be inappropriate to establish a risk committee if it were in the best interests of the company.

It should be noted that the risk committees conceived by Sir David Walker will almost certainly include some executive representation which is quite different from the wholly "independent" risk committees referred to in the UK Corporate Governance Code. Furthermore, the raison d'être appears to be different too. The risk committees referred to in the UK Corporate Governance Code are concerned with ensuring internal control and risk management systems are fit for purpose and working as intended. By contrast, the risk committees envisaged by Walker are focused upon the oversight of current risk exposures and future risk strategy.

Whatever the role of the risk committee, audit committees (and the board as a whole) should be careful to ensure that (i) the full board does not devolve total responsibility to either risk or audit committee; (ii) both committees (should a risk committee be established) are fully aware of their role and responsibilities; and (iii) communication between each committee is full and transparent.

Overseeing internal audit

While UK Corporate Governance Code Provision C.3.2 sets out that the role of the audit committee should include monitoring and reviewing the effectiveness of the company's internal audit function, Code Provision C.3.5 goes further: **14.027**

"The audit committee should monitor and review the effectiveness of the internal audit activities. Where there is no internal audit function, the audit

---

[13] A Review of Corporate Governance in UK Banks and other Financial Industry Entities, Sir David Walker, November 2009.

committee should consider annually whether there is a need for an internal audit function and make a recommendation to the board, and the reasons for the absence of such a function should be explained in the relevant section of the annual report."

The FRC's Guidance for Audit Committees provides additional guidance for audit committees and in particular the committee's role in reviewing the work of the internal audit function. This is discussed in more detail in the section on internal audit above.

It is good practice for the audit committee to be involved in developing and approving the internal audit department's mandate, goals and mission to be certain of its proper role in the oversight function. A collaborative effort with both management and internal audit in the development of the internal audit mandate often helps ensure a proper balance between the assessment of internal controls related to financial reporting and other special projects, operational efficiency and risk management responsibilities.

The audit committee should also be satisfied that the internal audit function has adequate resources. The committee should stay up to date on the scope and results of the department's operations and management's responses to the department's recommendations on internal controls and compliance.

The objectivity and independence of the internal audit function should be periodically evaluated. The committee should monitor and assess internal audit effectiveness in the overall context of the company's risk management system and, in particular, ensure that the internal audit department's involvement in the financial reporting process is appropriate. Self-assessment by the head of internal audit is an effective assessment tool, but it should not be the sole means by which the effectiveness of the internal audit function is reviewed. The committee should draw its own conclusions based on its experience of and contact with the internal audit function.

In monitoring the work of the internal audit function, the audit committee should review and assess the annual internal audit work plan; receive a report on the results of the internal auditors' work on a periodic basis; and review and monitor management's responsiveness to the internal auditor's findings and recommendations.

Overseeing external audit

14.028   First and foremost, the external auditor and audit committee should have a strong and candid relationship—anything less may limit the committee's effectiveness in achieving its oversight responsibilities. The audit committee should ensure that the external auditors are accountable to the audit committee—and through them, to the board of directors and ultimately the company's members. The audit committee should ensure its actions and communications with the external auditor are consistent with this accountability. The audit committee should also ensure that they communicate their expectations to the external auditor, and that both parties understand and have agreed to those expectations.

UK Corporate Governance Code Provision C.3.2 sets out that the role of the audit committee should include, inter alia:

(a)   making recommendations to the board in relation to the appointment, reappointment and removal of the external auditor and to approve the remuneration and terms of engagement of the external auditor;

(b)   reviewing and monitoring the external auditor's independence and objectivity and the effectiveness of the audit process, taking into consideration relevant UK professional and regulatory requirements; and

(c)   developing and implementing a policy on the engagement of the external auditor to supply non-audit services.

UK Corporate Governance Code C.3.6 goes further in stating:

"The audit committee should have primary responsibility for making a recommendation on the appointment, reappointment and removal of the external auditors. If the board does not accept the audit committee's recommendation, it should include in the annual report, and in any papers recommending appointment or reappointment, a statement from the audit committee explaining the recommendation and should set out reasons why the board has taken a different position."

Making recommendations to the board on the appointment, reappointment and removal of the external auditors is an important audit committee responsibility. The audit committee's recommendation to the board should be based on its assessment of the qualification, expertise and resources, and independence of the external auditors and the effectiveness of the audit process. The assessment should cover all aspects of the audit service provided by the audit firm, and include obtaining a report on the audit firm's own internal quality control procedures. If the audit committee recommends considering the selection of possible new appointees as external auditors, it should oversee the selection process.

The audit committee should approve the terms of engagement and recommend the remuneration to be paid to the external auditor in respect of audit services provided. In doing so, it should satisfy itself that the level of fee payable in respect of the external audit is appropriate and that an effective audit can be conducted for such a fee.

In the unlikely event that the board does not accept the audit committee's recommendation regarding the appointment/reappointment of the auditor, compliance with the UK Corporate Governance Code requires the company to include in the annual report, and in any papers recommending the appointment or reappointment of the auditor, a statement from the audit committee explaining its recommendation and the reasons why the board has taken a different position.

If the external auditor resigns, the audit committee should investigate the issues giving rise to such resignation and consider whether any action is required.

Independence

14.029 The audit committee should consider the auditor's independence and annually carry out procedures to ensure the independence and objectivity of the external auditor, taking into consideration relevant UK professional and regulatory requirements. For their part, all auditing firms should have internal policies and procedures in place and properly monitored to ensure that the audit firm and its individual members are independent from the company.

In considering matters that may bear on the auditor's independence, both the auditor and the audit committee should consider whether conflicts exist, such as the auditor holding a financial interest, either directly or indirectly, in the company; personal and business relationships of the auditors' immediate family, close relatives and partners with the company; economic dependence by the auditor through its the relationship with the company; and the nature and extent of services provided by the auditor in addition to the audit engagement. Each year the audit committee should seek from the audit firm, information about policies and processes for maintaining independence and monitoring compliance with relevant requirements, including current requirements regarding the rotation of audit partners and staff.

To ensure that non-audit services provided by the auditor do not impair, or appear to impair, the auditor's independence or objectivity, the audit committee should develop, and recommend to the board, a policy in relation to the provision of non-audit services. In determining the policy, the audit committee should consider the skills and experience of the audit firm; the potential threats to the auditor's independence and objectivity; and any controls put in place by the auditor to mitigate such threats.

In principle, the audit committee should not agree to the auditor providing a service if the result is that:

(a) the auditor has a financial or other interest which might cause them to be reluctant to take actions that would be adverse to the interests of the audit firm (**self interest**);

(b) the results of the non audit service performed by the auditor may be included in the accounts, and thus not subject to proper review (**self review**);

(c)   the auditor undertakes work that involves making judgments and taking decisions which are the responsibility of management (**management**);

(d)   the auditor undertakes work that involves acting as advocate for the company (**advocacy**);

(e)   the auditor is predisposed to accept or not sufficiently question the company's point of view (**familiarity**);

(f)   the auditors' conduct may be influenced by fear or threats (**intimidation**).

The policy devised by the audit committee should generally specify the types of non-audit work from which the external auditors should be excluded; the type of work for which the external auditors can be engaged without referral to the audit committee; and the type of work for which a case-by-case decision is necessary. Where non-audit services require approval on a case by case basis, it may be appropriate for the policy to allow "pre-approval" for certain types for work, subject to a fee limit determined by the audit committee. The subsequent provision of any service by the auditor would then be ratified at the next meeting of the audit committee. More generally, a de minimis fee limit might apply.

Understanding the audit cycle

The committee needs to understand the scope of the audit and how it is to **14.030** be approached. An open discussion with the auditor can throw up quite a number of areas where the audit committee assumes work is done where it isn't and where audit effort is directed and the audit committee has absolutely no appreciation of it. Audit committees should have an interest in the areas of detailed substantive testing which the auditors intend to carry out and on the other hand those where they intend to rely on internal control and the means by which they justify that reliance. The committee should also be concerned that there is adequate coverage of (say) divisions or subsidiaries, particularly those that are remote either geographically or culturally.

The committee should also ensure that an appropriate audit plan is in place. A proper dialogue needs to take place as to whether the business risks identified by the auditor are the only business risks or whether there are other risks that should be taken account of in view of the audit committee's own knowledge of the company's risk environment. This applies both at a strategic level, those risks which are fundamental to the achievement of the company's strategy and at the more detailed operational level, those risks which impact the day to day operations, the recognition of revenue and cost, the custody and value of assets and completeness of recognition of liabilities.

Moving to the end of the audit cycle, the audit committee should oversee the audit findings, including any changes in audit approach or any modification to the standard auditors' report. The issues to be discussed will depend on individual company and audit circumstances. Nevertheless, the audit committee should:

(a) discuss with the external auditor major issues that arose during the course of the audit and have subsequently been resolved and those issues that have been left unresolved;

(b) review key accounting and audit judgments; and

(c) review levels of errors identified during the audit, obtaining explanations from management and, where necessary the external auditors, as to why certain errors might remain unadjusted.

Sufficient time should be allowed to enable the audit committee to complete its review and engage in an appropriate dialogue with the external auditor. An appropriate timetable should be agreed with the board, finance director and the auditor.

Where the auditors identify material weaknesses in either accounting or internal control systems during their audit report, they report these to the company in a "management letter". As part of the ongoing monitoring process, the audit committee should review the management letter and also review and monitor management's responsiveness to the external auditor's findings and recommendations.

During an audit many representations are made to the auditors, either unsolicited or in response to specific enquiries. In addition, CA 2006 now requires that the directors' report must contain a statement to the effect that, so far as each director is aware, there is no relevant audit information of which the company's auditors are unaware; and that each director has taken all the steps that (s)he ought to have taken in order to make him or herself aware of any relevant audit information and to establish that the company's auditors are aware of the information.

The audit committee should review such representations before signature by management and consider whether appropriate systems are in place to ensure the information provided to auditors is complete and appropriate.

Assessment of the external auditor

14.031 The audit committee has primary responsibility for selecting, evaluating, and, if need be, replacing the auditor. The committee's evaluation should consider the auditor's competence, the quality and efficiency of the audit, and whether the audit fee is appropriate in relation to the size, complexity, and risk and control profile of the company to ensure that the company's audit is not compromised.

The UK Corporate Governance Code recommends that the audit committee should review and monitor the external auditor's independence and objectivity and the effectiveness of the audit process, taking into consideration relevant UK professional and regulatory requirements. The FRC's Guidance for Audit Committees builds on this recommendation by further recommending that the audit committee assess the effectiveness of the audit process, and in doing so:

(a) review whether the auditor has met the agreed audit plan and understand the reasons for any changes, including changes in perceived audit risks and the work undertaken by the external auditors to address those risks;

(b) consider the robustness and perceptiveness of the auditors in their handling of the key accounting and audit judgments identified and in responding to questions from the audit committees, and in their commentary where appropriate on the systems of internal control;

(c) obtain feedback about the conduct of the audit from key people involved, e.g. the finance director and the head of internal audit; and

(d) review and monitor the content of the external auditor's management letter, in order to assess whether it is based on a good understanding of the company's business and establish whether recommendations have been acted upon and, if not, the reasons why they have not been acted upon.

Relationship with the board

UK Corporate Governance Code Provision C.3.3 states that: **14.032**

"The terms of reference of the audit committee, including its role and the authority delegated to it by the board, should be made available. A separate section of the annual report should describe the work of the committee in discharging those responsibilities."

In essence, the focus of the audit committee terms of reference should define the scope of the committee's oversight responsibilities and how these are to be discharged. The role of the audit committee is for the board to decide and it should tailor its terms of reference to the company's specific needs and clearly outline the committee's duties and responsibilities, including structure, process and membership requirements. The terms of reference should ideally describe the background and experience requirements for committee members and set guidelines for the committee's relationship with management, the internal and external auditors, and others.

An audit committee's terms of reference and responsibilities should be co-ordinated with other committee responsibilities—some companies have a risk committee, others have committees focused on a particular business risk (e.g. investment committee, environmental committee, etc.). Care should be taken to define clearly the roles and responsibilities of each.

The terms of reference should serve as a guide in establishing the audit committee work plan and meeting agendas. The work plan would specifically set out how the audit committee intends to fulfil each of its responsibilities as disclosed in the terms of reference. Terms of reference prepared by the audit committee should be approved by the board.

It is very important that the audit committee take into consideration the responsibilities laid out in the terms of reference and related work plan as each meeting's agenda is set, and that all responsibilities are reviewed on at least an annual basis.

Once established, the audit committee terms of reference should be updated annually. The annual assessment of the committee's terms of reference should be a robust process reflecting changes to the company's circumstances and any new regulations that may impact the audit committee's responsibilities.

The UK Corporate Governance Code recommends that audit committee terms of reference be disclosed to shareholders through inclusion on company websites—most listed companies now do this.

Whistleblowing

14.033   UK Corporate Governance Code Provision C.3.4 states:

> "The audit committee should review arrangements by which staff of the company may, in confidence, raise concerns about possible improprieties in matters of financial reporting or other matters. The audit committee's objective should be to ensure that arrangements are in place for the proportionate and independent investigation of such matters and for appropriate follow-up action."

The nature of fraud risk is expanding. The globalisation of business means that management may find it is doing business with people it doesn't know in countries it has never visited, employing cultural standards it doesn't understand. As well, technological advances have changed the speed and ways business transactions are recorded; these advances have enhanced opportunities for fraud and have greatly increased the potential quantum of losses arising from fraud.

The audit committee is not involved in day-to-day management, and therefore not closely involved with the detail on matters related to fraud and unethical activities. However, it can usefully focus attention on the need for proper policies and procedures to help prevent fraud and unethical activities. The committee should question whether appropriate policies have been issued and whether they are user friendly and adopted by all relevant business units. Polices which might be considered include a fraud response plan and a whistleblowing policy (see below). The committee should consider not just whether these are appropriate but whether they are effective and how the business units have confirmed this. The audit committee's objective should be to ensure that arrangements are in place for the proportionate and independent investigation of such matters and for appropriate follow-up action—therefore an oversight role.

Communication with shareholders

UK Corporate Governance Code C.3.7 states: **14.034**

"The annual report should explain to shareholders how, if the auditor provides non-audit services, auditor objectivity and independence is safeguarded."

The FRC's Guidance for Audit Committees goes further in recommending that the directors' report should contain a separate section that describes the role and responsibilities of the audit committee and the actions taken by the audit committee to discharge those responsibilities.

The audit committee section should include, among other things:

(a) a summary of the role of the audit committee;

(b) the names and qualifications of all members of the audit committee during the period;

(c) the number of audit committee meetings and attendance by each member;

(d) a report on the way the audit committee has discharged its responsibilities;

(e) an explanation of how the committee reached its recommendation to the board on the appointment, reappointment or removal of the external auditors. This explanation should normally include supporting information on tendering frequency, the tenure of the incumbent auditor, and any contractual obligations that acted to restrict the audit committee's choice of external auditors;

(f)   an explanation of how, if the auditor provides non-audit services, auditor objectivity and independence is safeguarded.

The chairman of the audit committee should be present at the AGM to answer questions, through the chairman of the board, on the report of audit committee's activities and matters within the scope of audit committee's responsibilities.

The UK Corporate Governance Code and the status of the FRC's Guidance for Audit Committees

14.035   Both the Schedule B to the UK Corporate Governance Code (Disclosure of Corporate Governance Arrangements) and fn 16 to Main Principle C.3 (Audit Committee and Auditors) of the Code suggest that the FRC's Guidance for Audit Committees, is there for guidance and is not prescriptive. Schedule B to the Code states:

> ". . . the Turnbull Guidance and FRC Guidance on Audit Committees contain further suggestions as to information that might usefully be disclosed in the internal control statement and the report of the audit committee respectively."

Footnote 16 says: "the FRC Guidance on Audit Committees suggests means of applying this part of the Code".

Nevertheless, most companies will find the guidance very persuasive and helpful in guiding audit committees along the right lines.

Audit committees—A question of information, debate and judgment

14.036   If audit committees are to provide meaningful protection for investors, they must be in a position to challenge the executive management and draw sufficient to dubious practices—even in apparently successful companies. They must be proactive, not merely reactive, in seeking to ensure the quality and integrity of financial statements and accompanying reports. To do this, committee members must be dedicated, independent, and able to challenge the views to management and relevant experience.

Audit committees fulfil an important role that requires considerable commitment on behalf of its members. It is no longer appropriate for audit committees meet twice a year to rubber stamp the interim and annual financial statements. To be fully effective, audit committee members must be prepared to invest the time necessary to understand why critical accounting principles were chosen, how they were applied, and why the end result fairly presents their company's actual status. In essence this means that audit committee

members need to understand their business, the substance of complex transactions such as off-balance sheet structures and the use of derivatives, and
ensure that the accounts fairly reflect their understanding. In an increasingly
demanding corporate environment this may mean non-executive directors
need to devote a greater amount of time to their role and this may mean
accepting fewer non-executive appointments.

It is not unreasonable to suggest that financial ties may threaten the independence of non-executive directors and therefore their ability to actively
challenge management. However, adherence to some checklist of criteria may
not be the real solution. It is imperative that all audit committee members are
able, both in theory and in practice, to express views to the board that are different to those of the chief executive officer and be confident that, provided
this is done in a considered way, they will not suffer.

Even those audit committee members who are vigorously independent,
diligent and knowledgeable, will prove ineffective unless they have both
access to, and a understanding of, all the relevant information. Audit committees are only as good as the information they received and are usually
reliant on the finance director and both internal and external auditors. Trust
has an important role to play. Audit committee members fulfil an oversight
function; they do not have a hands-on role. Consequently, they must put a
great deal of trust in their executive colleagues and auditors to tell them what
they need to know. Nevertheless, if they experience surprises (e.g. material
effects of a change in accounting policy come to light just before they are
due to approve the financial statements), they need to start questioning their
relationship with management and consider how they can ensure they get relevant and timely information. Useful questions to ask the auditor before recommending the approval of the financial statements might include questions
posed by Warren E Buffet, in the chairman's letter accompanying Berkshire
Hathaway Inc's 2002 annual report:

(a) If the auditor were solely responsible for preparation of the compa-
     ny's financial statements, would they have in any way been prepared
     differently from the manner selected by management? This ques-
     tion should cover both material and non-material differences. If the
     auditor would have done something differently, both management's
     argument and the auditor's response should be disclosed. The audit
     committee should then evaluate the facts.

(b) If the auditor were an investor, would (s)he have received—in plain
     English—the information essential to his or her understanding the
     company's financial performance during the reporting period?

(c) Is the company following the same internal audit procedure that
     would be followed if the auditor himself were CEO? If not, what are
     the differences and why?

(d)   Is the auditor aware of any actions—either accounting or operational—that have had the purpose and effect of moving revenues or expenses from one reporting period to another?

If an audit committee asks tough questions like these, then structural and procedural issues such as the audit committee's constitution becomes of less importance.

Such questions should be asked at least a week before the company's results are released to the public in order to allow differences between the auditors and management to be aired with the committee and resolved. If the timing is tighter—(say) if the preliminary announcement is imminent when the audit committee meets with the auditors—it will be difficult for the audit committee to exercise effective oversight.

Chapter 15

Risk Management and Internal Control

Alexandra Ellison[1]

Introduction

What a difference a few years makes!

Risk management is the systematic addressing of the dangers associated with   **15.001**
achieving an advantageous balance of risk and reward. In some cases risks
can be managed through the application of internal controls.

Risk is inherent in business, indeed it is acknowledged that we are in business to take risks; a company takes risks to pursue opportunities to earn returns for its owners. Striking a balance between risk and return is the key to maximising shareholder value. Risk when it is well managed is a good thing.

The financial crisis of 2008/2009 brought risk management into sharp and critical focus. When the financial crisis hit, seemingly unimaginable risk was everywhere, and the utterly unbelievable happened, such as the demise of Lehman Brothers and others, and the breakup or restructuring of major financial institutions in the UK, US and well beyond. As we all know, the whole world reeled.

[1] Alexandra Ellison is a Director, GRC Risk Management EMEA, Customer Collaboration Unit, at SAP, the global business software solutions group, where she advises customers on how to gain the most from SAP's Governance, Risk and Compliance solution. Her roles in SAP have included responsibility for operational risk management and internal controls in Europe, Middle East and Africa. Alex worked with the project team which defined and set up enterprise risk management in SAP in 2003, and was a member of SAP's award winning European Enterprise Risk Management team in 2004. Prior to joining SAP, Alex was a Senior Manager with PricewaterhouseCoopers in their Global Risk Management Consulting practice where she specialized in financial risk management systems. Previous to PwC, Alex had a role managing delivery of consulting, educational and support services for a global corporate treasury systems provider, and had held other management and commercial roles within UK and international businesses. At City University, London, Alex gained a BSc in Systems and Management, and she has an MA in International Relations from The University of Kent at Canterbury. Alex is a regular speaker at conferences on the practical application of risk management in business.

It is a totally reasonable question to ask—where was risk management in all of this? What went wrong and why, and if financial institutions—whose risk management practices were significantly advanced in maturity and sophistication—got it wrong; what hope is there for mainstream corporate companies?

Could better risk management or improved internal controls have helped alleviate the crisis? In fact the reflections went much deeper. Was the crisis a failure to do risk management properly or was it a failure of risk management as a business technique to deliver what it is supposed to do?

So there are broadly two schools of thought: one that claims it is a failure of risk management as a business technique. The Value @ Risk model in particular has been criticised. So basically algorithms and mathematical models are blamed. The other school of thought postulates that it was a failure to do risk management properly or even a failure of executive management to properly discharge its governance responsibilities—a failure, in fact, of executives and management to practice good corporate governance.

It is people who use risk management modelling techniques, it is management who present the risk results to the board, it is executive boards that have a duty to use judgement on the information provided and make decisions. It is the Chairman and Chief Executive who are accountable to shareholders and stakeholders about the stewardship of the company, not the equations on pieces of paper or computer printouts.

It should therefore not come as a surprise that in the recent review of the UK Corporate Governance Code that the code has been strengthened in respect of risk management requirements. The crux of the issue is that even if the mathematical model is flawed, it is how and to what extent it is used that matters.

The link between risks at a business level and the practice of risk management as a technique has been disjointed. Risk management might have been taking place, but it was not fully integrated in the way the business was being managed.

Additionally, it is acknowledged that strategic risk management has been neglected. Or put another way, there has been too much focus on risks that can be addressed by the application of controls at the expense of other categories of risk. The financial crisis didn't occur because of an internal controls failure (like previous crises such as Barings bank demise). The financial crisis is a strategic risk management failure, compounded into a systemic risk management catastrophe.

All this leads to the fact that UK companies, large and small, can and should improve the way they undertake risk management to better safeguard the interests of their shareholders. This belief and expectation is reflected in the changes in the UK Corporate Governance Code. The section of the code that explicitly addresses risk management has been enhanced as follows:

UK Corporate Governance Code—effective 2010	The Combined Code on Corporate Governance—effective 2007
SECTION C: Accountability	Accountability and Audit
C.2. Risk Management and Internal Control	C.2. Internal Control
Main Principle The board is responsible for determining the nature and extent of the significant risks it is willing to take in achieving its strategic objectives.	(no previous equivalent)
The board should maintain sound risk management and internal control systems.	The board should maintain a sound system of internal control to safeguard shareholders' investment and the company's assets.
Code Provision The board should, at least annually, conduct a review of the effectiveness of the company's risk management and internal control systems and should report to shareholders that they have done so. The review should cover all material controls, including financial, operational and compliance controls.	The board should, at least annually, conduct a review of the effectiveness of the company's system of internal controls and should report to shareholders that they have done so. The review should cover all material controls, including financial, operational and compliance controls and risk management systems.

Risk management and internal control are the cornerstones of good corporate governance. A lot of attention in previous legislation and guidance has been given to internal control; and while risk management is mentioned in the same context it has been cited as an adjunct. The new UK Corporate Governance Code redresses this balance and places risk management firmly in the driving seat with respect to internal controls.

Risk management is an antecedent to internal control and internal control is or should operate within a coherent risk management framework. Risks can be dealt with or treated in two distinct ways:

(1)   through the application of risk mitigation measures, and/or

(2)   through the application of internal controls.

Risk mitigations are often one-off actions or a discrete set of steps. Internal controls are usually repeatable steps or actions embedded in a process or they could themselves be process steps.

Therefore internal control is one particular type of risk treatment. But it is important to note that not all risks, and in particular strategic risks, can be treated by the application of controls.

In Part 1 of this chapter we deal with risk management and in Part 2 we deal with internal control.

The UK Corporate Governance Code—main changes

15.002   Main Principle C.2 states:

> "The board is responsible for determining the nature and extent of the significant risks it is willing to take in achieving its strategic objectives. The board should maintain sound risk management and internal control systems."

Code Provision C.2.1 states:

> "The board should, at least annually, conduct a review of the effectiveness of the company's risk management and internal control systems and should report to shareholders that they have done so. The review should cover all material controls, including financial, operational and compliance controls."

The most significant change in the code with respect to risk management is the addition of the first sentence of the Main Principle C.2—"the board is responsible for determining the nature and extent of the significant risks it is willing to take in achieving its strategic objectives". What exactly does this mean and what should the board do to make sure this happens?

In risk management jargon this means determining risk appetite and setting risk tolerance.

Risk appetite

15.003   Risk appetite is the amount of risk a company wants to "take on" or "pursue". What is the overall risk profile of my company? What type of business am I in? It can be broad statements or key concepts. It is a strategic rather than a tactical discussion, it's a top down discussion and it is usually helpful to enable the discussion with concrete examples in relation to shareholder expectations. Low risk businesses usually have modest, reliable, predictable returns. High risk businesses have volatility, possible high returns, possible zero returns. Low risk businesses are in industries such as utilities, food products, healthcare, they are typically defensive stocks. Higher risk businesses are those that are fast moving and innovative such as telecoms or technology. New ventures in new products, in volatile markets and geographies would typically indicate a higher risk appetite. What regulators are looking for is corporate behaviour that matches the stated risk appetite. The key words here are clarity and predictability. So the UK regulators are looking for a clearer articulation of the risk appetite of the company and this would be along the key dimensions on which the business is being measured, such as: customer satisfaction, revenue growth, employee diversity, profitability. This clear statement of intent should be predictably reflected in actual behaviour and actions.

A company could define risk appetite levels such as:

- "the executive board is not willing to accept risks under any circumstances"—that would be zero risk; or

- "the executive board is willing to accept risks in certain circumstances that may result in unprofitable revenue growth, inability to attract and retain top talent"—that might be moderate risk appetite level.

Examples of risk appetite statements could be:

- "high acceptance that XYZ venture may fail" or

- "zero acceptance of regulatory non-compliance" or

- "low acceptance of serious injury or fatalities in the working environment".

For instance, a mining company, sending people underground in potentially dangerous situations will want to take all reasonable steps to avoid danger to employees—low risk appetite, but for a Security firm, say, providing protection to people or property in high risk countries or regions, there is a philosophical acceptance of the risk of casualties—high risk appetite.

Risk tolerance

Risk tolerance is about nailing it down. If risk appetite is strategic, risk tol- **15.004**
erance is tactical. With respect to the example above "high acceptance that
XYZ venture may fail" the risk tolerance is where you make it clear the point

at which you pull out. With respect to, say, your customer satisfaction target of 90 per cent, you might define your tolerance range as 85–95 per cent. Risk tolerances will usually be ranges or values relevant to key performance indicators ("KPIs").

The definition of risk tolerance is a bottom up exercise, it's tactical, and it is really important because it forms the basis on which risk monitoring can take place. PwC was recently quoted as saying "Risk is good if it's understood". Defining risk appetite and risk tolerance clearly is about getting risk understood. And this understanding applies when communicating with external stakeholders as well as employees going about their daily duties.

So, in summary, by defining risk appetite, the scene is set for the company to view its significant risks in the context of the strategy it is pursuing. By defining risk tolerances the degree to which those risks can be accepted or carried is also articulated. This enables risks to be understood in the context of the monitoring of the performance of the business. Thus risk management is linked to the strategic and operational performance.

It is generally accepted that determining risk appetite and setting risk tolerance is not an easy exercise. This is especially the case with respect to determining risk appetite, in large part because the output can appear rather vague. However, the very fact that the board will have to go through the exercise, is the value itself. It is possible that the process will highlight shortcomings or gaps in the risk management process which will need to be addressed. Later in this chapter are some useful information sources that are worth reviewing to help boards work on this aspect of the code requirements.

Sound risk management system

15.005   C.2 Main Principle ". . . The board should maintain sound risk management and internal control systems".

The key here is that there needs to be system in place for risk management (as well as internal control—which was already covered in the previous version of the Code). "System" means systematic treatment of risk management. So it is something structured, with a routine and using a method, technique or procedure. It is not "back of an envelope" once a year type exercise, but a process, explicit and repeatable. What is needed is a process and tools for risk management that stand up to audit scrutiny. They need to be thorough, sensible and reliable. There will need to be evidence that the process is in place and that it works.

Annual review of risk management

15.006   The Code Provision C.2.1 has also been slightly reworded to increase the importance of risk management:

"The board should, at least annually, conduct a review of the effectiveness of the company's risk management and internal control systems and should report to shareholders that they have done so. The review should cover all material controls, including financial, operational and compliance controls.

Risk management is now right at the heart of the provision rather than as an add-on at the end of the sentence as was previously the case. Previously the board had only to conduct an annual review of the effectiveness of the company's internal controls and report it to shareholders, now it must conduct an annual review of the *effectiveness* of the company's risk management as well.

What is an effective risk management system? And how do you prove it?

We have only to look at the endeavours of the ratings agency Standard & Poors ("S&P") to see it is quite problematic to evaluate effective risk management. S&P has stated it is, starting in 2010, to include evaluation of a company's enterprise risk management ("ERM") as part of its credit-rating decisions. In fact they have been including ERM discussions in meetings with companies that they rate since 2008. Two areas are of particular interest to S&P; that of risk management culture and strategic risk management. AAA-rated financial institutions crashed spectacularly, and S&P has been evaluating the effectiveness of their risk management for some time. This suggests that distilling effective risk management is a "work in progress" for S&P.

15.007

Below are the questions S&P has stated it includes in its effective risk management "discussion" with companies:

"1. What are the company's top risks, how big are they, and how often are they likely to occur? How often is the list of top risks updated?

2. What is management doing about top risks?

3. What size quarterly operating or cash loss has management and the board agreed is tolerable?

4. Describe the staff responsible for risk management programs and their place in the organization chart. How do you measure the success of risk management activities?

5. How would a loss from a key risk affect incentive compensation of top management and planning/budgeting?

6. What discussions about risk management have taken place at the board level or among top management when strategic decisions were made in the past?

7. Give an example of how your company responded to a recent "surprise" in your industry. How did the surprise end up affecting your company differently than others?"

Boards should be prepared to explain and defend the way they conduct risk management in their company to external stakeholders, such as S&P, external auditors and UK regulators. This means that the board must really understand how risk is being managed in the business rather than, as has sometimes been the case in past, just blindly "signing off" what is being done in their name.

Of course, the perspective of a rating agency will not necessarily be exactly the same as the authors of the new UK Corporate Governance Code. The former's focus is on liquidity and credit worthiness, where as the latter's focus is on the company as a well governed going concern. However, in the absence of updated Turnbull guidance to clarify risk management guidelines further (in the way that the guidance already does for internal control management), the S&P checklist is a reasonable starting point for boards.

The role of the audit committee

15.008   Other minor changes to the code reinforce the enhanced emphasis on risk management.

UK Corporate Governance Code—effective 2010	The Combined Code on Corporate Governance—effective 2007
SECTION C: Accountability	Accountability and Audit
C.3. Audit Committee and Auditors	C.3. Audit Committee and Auditors
Main Principle The board should establish formal and transparent arrangements for considering how they should apply the corporate reporting and <u>risk management</u>* and internal control principles and for maintaining an appropriate relationship with the company's auditors.	The board should establish formal and transparent arrangements for considering how they should apply the financial reporting and internal control principles and for maintaining an appropriate relationship with the company's auditor.
Code Provision C.3.2 ". . . to review the company's internal financial controls and, unless expressly addressed by a separate board risk committee composed of independent directors, or by the board itself, to review the company's internal control and risk management systems."	Code Provision C.3.2 ". . . to review the company's internal financial controls and, unless expressly addressed by a separate board risk committee composed of independent directors, or by the board itself, to review the company's internal control and risk management systems."

*Authors underlining to highlight the change.

Main Principle C3 has been amended to include "risk management" to have equal importance alongside corporate reporting and internal control:

> "The board should establish formal and transparent arrangements for considering how they should apply the corporate reporting and <u>risk management</u> and internal control principles and for maintaining an appropriate relationship with the company's auditors." (Authors underling to highlight the change.)

Code Provision C.3.2 remains unchanged and states that the audit committee has a particular role and responsibility (among others) as follows:

> "to review the company's internal financial controls and, unless expressly addressed by a separate board risk committee composed of independent directors, or by the board itself, to review the company's internal control and risk management systems".

The Turnbull Guidance

In relation to risk management and internal control there was an annex **15.009** to the Combined Code specifically addressing the application of risk and control principles and provisions, which is commonly known as the Turnbull Guidance on Internal Control.[2]

The Turnbull Guidance is not a manual, it is a more detailed exploration of the responsibilities of the board and management around internal control and risk management. In this context the board can exercise sound business judgment to apply the guidelines appropriate to its own company's particular circumstances.

It is quite clear from the Code that Internal Control and Risk Management Systems are the direct concerns of the board and its committees. It is the board's responsibility to protect the interest of shareholders and the assets of the company through its risk management and internal control. Not only must the board do this, but the process must be "formal and transparent", and has to be reviewed and assessed at least annually and the existence of this reported to shareholders. If an audit committee exists its remit is the review of the company's internal control and risk management systems.

It is worth noting that the Turnbull Guidance has **not** been updated during the 2009 review and does not reflect the changed emphasis on risk management that is present in the 2010 new UK Corporate Governance Code.

---

[2] The full title, following minor revision in October 2005 is "*Internal Control—Revised Guidance for Directors on the Combined Code*". The Guidance is published by the FRC. The Guidance will be referred to in this chapter by its commonly known name: "the Turnbull Guidance on Internal Control". The Guidance is being reviewed in 2010 and reference should be made to *http://www.frc.org.uk* for the up-to-date position.

However, in all other respect the Turnbull Guidance is sound. A review and update to bring it entirely in line with the new Code will be completed during 2010.[3]

What skills and time are needed to discharge risk management responsibilities?

15.010　Two other Code additions are relevant in the area of risk management. The first is the new Main Principle, in Section B: Effectiveness:

"The board and its committees should have the appropriate balance of skills, experience, independence and knowledge of the company to enable them to discharge their respective duties and responsibilities effectively."

The second new Main Principle in Section B: Effectiveness:

"All directors should be able to allocate sufficient time to the company to discharge their responsibilities effectively."

These two new Main Principles relate in general to all the duties and responsibilities of the board members. It is evident that the FRC require boards to take a much more direct and active role in the management of the risks their organisation faces. So it is therefore vital that among board members there is sufficient subject matter expertise in risk management to enable this to take place and that furthermore time is allocated to a robust and insightful evaluation of the risks. Risk management needs to be more than an item on the board meeting, risk or audit subcommittee agenda, which gets a rushed five minutes air time at the tail end of a meeting once a year. When the Turnbull Guidance is updated the FRC's specific expectations may become clearer.

Part 1: The concepts of risk and risk management

15.011　The concept of risk has a long history, which is comprehensively charted and explained, for those interested in the historical perspective, in *Against The Gods—The Remarkable Story of Risk,* by Peter Bernstein.[4] However, it is only relatively recently that risk management has emerged as a discipline in its own right and found favour in the business community.

In a modern corporate context, risk, and risk management have many

---

[3] Refer to *http://www.frc.org.uk.*
[4] Bernstein, *Against the Gods: The Remarkable Story of Risk*, 1996, John Wiley & Sons, Inc.

facets. There is a particular resonance depending on the industry, business activities, geographic span and complexity of an organisation:

- environmental protection;

- health and safety;

- IT and security;

- quality assurance of processes and products;

- business continuity and disaster recovery;

- crisis management;

- risk transfer via insurance products;

- identification of issues by internal audit;

- opinion of external auditors as part of the general audit;

- corporate treasury department's management of financial risk;

- internal control department;

- the compliance officer.

The list could go on and on. It is likely that in many, or even most organisations, the various departments or units (such as those listed above) dealing with risk and control matters operate fairly autonomously, or possibly even in complete ignorance of the remit and responsibilities of each other. Important in getting risk management right is bringing these activities together in a unified or co-ordinated manner.

A business definition of risk

Risk is an overused word and because risk is ubiquitous and, we as individuals in our personal lives encounter and have to deal with it, it is important therefore to clearly define what risk and therefore risk management means in a business context. Of course, it is never that simple; there is not one single agreed definition of risk or risk management which is general or specific to business. However, in a business context a definition sometimes used is: **15.012**

> "Risks are uncertain future events that could influence the achievement of the organisations objectives including strategic, financial and operational or threaten its core survival."

There are five key words relevant for any definition of risk: future, uncertain, outcomes, positive, negative.

- **Future**—risk is, above all, forward looking—risk management aims to do the seemingly impossible—manage the future.

- **Conditional**—uncertain—events may happen or they may not; there is always a probability of less than 100 per cent attached to a risk.

- **Outcomes**—there are multiple scenarios—risk management is about informed decision making toward the outcome most desired.

- **Positive**—some (but not all) risk has an upside—risk management aims to maximise beneficial outcomes.

- **Negative**—all risk has a downside—risk management aims to minimise or eliminate undesirable outcomes.

Risks in a business context are often categorised, although there is no single agreed definition as to what the categories are and to which sub-categories they belong.

Three broad categories are:

- **Strategic risk**—sometimes referred to as business risk; the risks associated with strategic decisions such as where to invest: new markets, new product lines, new territories, new factories, etc.

- **Financial risk**—the remit of the finance and corporate treasury department; usually including credit risk, market risk and cash management.

- **Operational risk**—risks associated with the tactical, day-to-day activities of doing business, and with processes, systems and people; included here would be business continuity risks, as well as legal and regulatory risks.

Brand or reputational risk could be fitted into the strategic or operational risk category. Regulatory risk is often a category in its own right, rather than being grouped as an operational risk. What is important for a business is to define a taxonomy appropriate to the particular circumstances of the business which adds clarity to coverage of the topic and allows everyone to talk the same language.

The Turnbull Guidance on Internal Control makes it clear that it is a responsibility of the board of directors to ensure that they have a system of internal control that is effective in managing risks in the manner which it has approved. It is stated in para.16:

"In determining its policies with regard to internal control, and thereby assessing what constitutes a sound system of internal control in the particular circumstances of the company, the board's deliberations should include consideration of the following factors:

The nature and extent of the risks facing the company;

The extent and categories of risks which it regards as acceptable for the company to bear;

The likelihood of the risks concerned materialising;

The company's ability to reduce the incidence and impact on the business of risks that do materialise; and

The costs of operating particular controls relative to the benefit thereby obtained in managing the related risks."

The enterprise risk management "gold standard"

The gold standard in risk management in the business world is the holistic or **15.013** systemic management of risk known as ERM. In ERM the company's risk appetite and tolerance is made explicit in a risk policy. Risks are identified, analysed, managed and monitored in a common framework applicable to all parts of the corporation. This includes determination of the likelihood of risks occurring and, if they do occur, the impact they would have set against the cost of taking action including the consideration of compensating factors. It is important that risks are not viewed in isolation of each other or their relationship to company goals but instead in the concept of a portfolio of risks. This is in contrast to silo or discrete risk management activities limited to parts of the organisation often using disparate and non-comparable methods of analysis, and where the linkage to business objectives is tenuous.

ERM is explicit risk management, in contrast to implicit risk management where risks are being managed but usually under the auspices of other business disciplines or activities. Historically the implicit and discrete approach predominated. Recently corporations have increasingly turned to the explicit, systematic risk management approach to deliver value to shareholders. Practitioners of effective ERM can have confidence that they are meeting the standards expected by the Turnbull Guidance on Internal Control in the UK and by the Sarbanes-Oxley Act 2002 ("SOX") for US-listed companies in respect of company risk management responsibilities.

The new UK Corporate Governance Code has elevated statements on risk management from Code Provisions to Main Principles. Risk is now even more the concern of the board and executives; a part of mainstream direction and management of the business. The Turnbull Guidance on Internal Control is pointing towards an ERM approach as a prerequisite of an effective internal control system. It is not possible to put in place effective internal control if the risks to be controlled are not known, not sufficiently understood, or not understood in the context of other risks the company faces, or in the context of the company's strategic, financial and operational objectives. To have this level of understanding it is necessary to have effective risk management in place. A siloed or discrete approach would not be sufficient. Risk management performed in isolation is risk management practiced without due regard to the company's strategic, financial or operational goals or the relative importance of one risk against another, this approach might lead to risks in one area being tightly managed, but this might not be the best use of risk management resources and funds for the company as a whole. Other important risks might not be identified or given sufficient attention. This might result in a distorted view of the control environment and controls needed for the business. It is the danger of sub-optimisation for the company as a whole that ERM can help eliminate.

The Turnbull Guidance on Internal Control confirms this approach in the Appendix.

"Risk assessment

- *Does the company have clear objectives and have they been communicated so as to provide effective direction to employees on risk assessment and control issues?*
- *Are significant internal and external operational, financial, compliance and other risks identified and assessed on an ongoing basis?*
- *Is there a clear understanding by management and others within the company of what risks are acceptable to the board?*"

It has to be emphasised that even having carried out the sort of assessment suggested by Turnbull this is not to say that nothing bad will happen or nothing will go wrong or that no breaches of good governance standards will occur. There is no such guarantee. It is not about risk elimination, but it is about having confidence that all reasonable steps have been taken with respect to compliance with governance regulations and good business practice.

Useful sources of knowledge

15.014   The case for ERM is effectively presented in James Lam's book *Enterprise Risk Management—From Incentives to Controls*,[5] together with many practical steps, examples, templates and tools. The accessible and pragmatic advice in this book is of particular relevance to medium and larger companies, and has a slight financial services industry bias.

"*Implementing Turnbull—A Boardroom Briefing*"[6] provided by the Centre for Business Performance of the ICAEW contains practical steps to take, processes to follow, templates to use and is illustrated with example case studies and is particularly relevant to smaller companies.

---

[5] Lam, *Enterprise Risk Management From Incentives to Controls*, 2003, John Wiley & Sons, Inc.
[6] "*Implementing Turnbull—A Boardroom Briefing*", ICAEW, Centre for Business Performance. *http://www.icaew.co.uk/centre.*

"*Risk Appetite—How hungry are you?*"[7] is a white paper produced by Richard Barfield of PwC. This is a good exploration of how to go about defining risk appetite and a discussion of the challenges in undertaking this exercise.

"*Avoiding the Black Swan: Barriers to Improving Risk Management*"[8] is an interesting survey conducted by Crowe Horwath in April 2008 and published in November 2009. CFOs are responding to how they are facing the challenges of improving risk management within their organisation.

Risk management policy

As described later in this chapter it is the board's job to establish policy **15.015** and strategy. The contents of a risk management policy would typically include:

- objective of risk management within the organisation;

- commitment of the board;

- scope of risk management in terms of activities subject to risk policy;

- Statement of responsibilities—covering all levels in the organisation;

- Categorisation of types of risks covered by the policy (e.g. financial, operational, strategic);

- High level description of the methodology adopted.

Risk management's objective is to contribute to the making of informed business decisions when faced with future uncertainty. Consider the following questions:

- What could go wrong (or right)?

- What is the likelihood of it going wrong, and what is the impact if it does?

- What should we do to prevent it from becoming a problem?

- Is what we are doing working?

In some cases the answer to the question "What should we do to prevent it (the risk) from becoming a problem?" is the putting in place of internal

---

[7] "*Risk appetite—How Hungry are you?*", Richard Barfield, Director; Valuation & Strategy, UK, PwC
[8] "*Avoiding the Black Swan: Barriers to Improving Risk Management*", Crowe Horwath, November 2009, *http://www.crowehorwath.com.*

control or increasing the effectiveness of existing internal control. Internal control is essentially a management response to certain risk situations. Often in the past the relationship between risk management and internal control has not been understood in this context. Internal control is a risk response measure, albeit a mandated one by various corporate governance legislation or guidelines. Functions such as internal control, are addressing some particular aspects of a company's need and requirement to manage risk, but not all risks can be controlled in this way and some risks cannot be controlled at all.

Risk management tools at a board's disposal include risk detection through internal audit activity, risk transfer through insurance, risk sharing through partnering, making an economic capital provision, and quality control through improved processes and management techniques and, the management of statutory and regulatory risk through the compliance function. In some cases risks require "active management" or "mitigation" by those in the business and some other types of risk, for example, "Acts of God" may just have to be accepted, although this is not always the case. Clearly there is nothing much to be done to prevent an earthquake happening, but there are steps to take to limit the effects and give a business the best possible chance to recover.

This is an essential feature of risk management—it is not about eliminating risk—it is about giving the business the best possible chance of the most favourable outcome within a certain cost benefit equation that reflects the organisation's risk appetite and risk tolerance levels.

How to structure for effective enterprise risk management

The board

15.016　The board must take an overview of the risk portfolio of the entire company. It is this level of awareness of the company's significant risks, from wherever they originate, that the board needs to have. Furthermore it must be clear, to all, that it is the board's mandate for risk management that the business must adhere to and deliver against. This is not a half hearted adjunct to a system of internal control, it goes to the very core of how the business is being managed and how critical business decisions are being made when faced with future uncertainty. In the past senior executives might have claimed to take a portfolio view of risk, citing this as just business as usual, an intrinsic part of what they do. However, the Code now expects risk management to be an explicit transparent process.

The board should determine the risk appetite of the business, namely, how much risk to take on. It should also articulate the degree of deviation from the target or normal range of risk that it has defined as appropriate for the business and it should define what actions need to take place to bring the risk back to where it should be.

Deviation from normal could be in the direction of too little risk as well as too much for the business to bear. To illustrate with an analogy: on the motorway, there is such a thing as driving too slowly, as well as reckless speeding. If a company takes on too little risk it is as likely to disappoint its shareholders with poor returns and diminished prospects for the business as much as if it takes on too much risk.

In a good risk management culture everyone understands their responsibility to manage risk and when they are performing their risk management activities they do so by the mandate of the board. Tone from the top is vital and that there is "a clear articulation to management and others within the company of what risks are acceptable to the board."[9]

The board should clearly communicate to the whole business:

- the risk management responsibilities of the board, management and all employees, as well as those of the risk management function;

- *their* risk management policy; what activities and circumstances require formal risk assessment;

- *their* risk management model for identification, assessment and monitoring risks;

- *their* criteria for acceptable levels of risk and what to do about unacceptable levels of risk.

Executive management

The reality is that no matter how good senior executives are, as human beings they all have a fatal flaw when making decisions in the face of future uncertainty, namely risk. There are "repeated patterns of irrationality, inconsistency, and incompetence in the way human beings arrive at decisions and choices when faced with uncertainty."[10] Risk management is a mechanism to reduce these tendencies and arrive at more informed and consequently improved decisions. It is for this reason alone that companies should embrace the enterprise risk concept. It is surely in the interests of good corporate governance to be making well informed decisions on behalf of the company's shareholders and stakeholders. It is an opportunity to add value to the business by helping it meet its objectives and fulfil its vision. This is the foundation on which effective and efficient internal control can be built and set. **15.017**

---

[9] The Turnbull Guidance on Internal Control.
[10] Bernstein: *Against the Gods The Remarkable Story of Risk,* p.28.

Risk management culture

15.018   It is important to note that a strong risk management culture is one where the business takes responsibility to manage their risks and risk management does not become the activity performed only by a specialist function. Risks are best managed by those responsible for them. A risk management function is a support function to the business by providing expertise and specialist services to help the business manage risk by acting as a "trusted advisor" to the business. Companies are made up of individuals and individuals generally have a negative image of risk while at the same time reacting irrationally, inconsistently and incompetently in relation to it. The risk manager needs to apply the risk management discipline and steer those in the business along a rational path rather than a subjective one and in a pragmatic and non-burdensome way. It is a tricky mix of "partner to the business" and "conscience of the business". High calibre individuals are needed in the risk management function to be able to work successfully in this environment.

Turnbull is clear on what senior executives need to do and what is the responsibility of the board in setting up and maintaining effective risk management (to meet good governance standards), and reporting on this work through the audit or risk Committee of the main board. Typical of the UK governance approach is to avoid prescription, and the Appendix to the Turnbull Guidance on Internal Control further clarifies what needs to be done. Less clear is *how* risk management should be operationalised.

Reporting lines

15.019   Options for appropriate reporting lines for a risk management function within an organisation include direct to the CEO, the CFO, or to the audit or risk committee of the board or to the main board itself. The requirements that need to be met regardless of the organisational structure adopted are: overview of the business activities; direct access with no "filtering" to the board; independence to challenge and whistleblow without fear of adverse consequences for individuals personally or as a team. Within a smaller organisation or one with a strong sales led culture at the top, aligning risk management to the CFO function is a good fit. This is because, for those companies, the CEO is often heavily involved in the sales efforts or other operational duties and therefore the CFO function is the conscience of the business. For larger organisations and those with an engineering or finance-led culture aligning risk management to the CEO could be more appropriate. For organisations in highly regulated industries, such as financial services or pharmaceuticals, alignment of the risk management function directly to the audit committee or the main board may be the most appropriate model to adopt given the high external profile of risks these companies face.

Reporting lines, and an organisational structure, that would not meet the good governance standards that ERM seeks to foster, would be one where the risk management function lies within a discrete line of business or, one where it is only present in parts of the organisation. Nor would it be met with the risk manager or risk managers buried several layers down in the organisation chart regardless of where the risk management function reports.

Best practice points to the appointment of a Chief Risk Officer ("CRO"), as head of an ERM function, who reports directly to a board member, and where the ERM function could include risk management, internal control or a broader compliance unit. The profile for a CRO should include strong facilitation skills, ability to articulate persuasively the ERM message on behalf of the board, leadership and consulting skills as well as strong technical credentials in the discipline of risk management.

The audit committee

The audit committee has a dual role. Firstly; the risk profile of the company, **15.020** most usually via a Risk Balanced Scorecard prepared by the CRO, would be presented to the audit committee (or the main board in the absence of an audit committee), and the most significant or severe risks discussed. Secondly; it would be in the audit committee where the performance of the risk management unit as a whole would be formally reviewed and assessed. If not done at the main board level the audit committee would approve changes to risk policy.

Internal audit

The internal audit function of a company adds value by providing objective, **15.021** independent assurance on the performance of risk management, internal control and general business activity. Internal audit's work is intermittent and evidence based and reviews and examines the performance and work of management and staff.

It is important to note that internal audit cannot perform an assessment (which has credibility) on its own work and therefore the function of risk management cannot be performed by the internal audit function or department. In the past internal control was very much the domain of the internal audit department, and remains so in many companies. Nowadays, even where there exists an internal control group separate from internal audit, internal audit can still play a role, for example, the testing of the design and effectiveness of internal control; this element—the testing process—is a fairly standard part of the remit of an internal audit unit. Provided that the risk management and internal control units are separate from internal audit, they can be audited by it; and internal audit, in turn, can be risk assessed, thus providing the board with an additional level of assurance that all functions are subject to proper and formal review and scrutiny.

Now that the board has specific internal control responsibilities outlined in the UK Corporate Governance Code and the Turnbull Guidance it makes sense for that function to be separate from internal audit. Smaller companies may find this segregation difficult to achieve.

The coupling of internal control and risk management within the same department is a common one. The danger for risk management in this structural alignment is that risk management becomes viewed as a policing function and the true added value that risk management, and particularly enterprise risk management provides can be diminished or lost. Not only would this be a loss of value to the company but it would also be a weakening of good corporate governance. The danger for internal control is a potential loss of ownership, management may experience, if it is owned organisationally by internal audit. Internal control might be perceived as something internal audit does to them, rather than an integral part of the way management controls the activities of the business.

In a large company or multinational corporation there should be sufficient capacity and resources to make these associated functions sufficiently autonomous. In a smaller organisation the temptation is to blur the lines and treat these areas as one function. In such cases outsourcing of parts of the remit of these groups could help overcome the problem as could establishment of separate reporting lines for each of the three. This is a clear case where the segregation of duties principles needs to be applied. What is clear in the guidance from Turnbull (and SOX) however, is that while internal control can be managed within an ERM framework, and hence function, the reverse is not true: ERM is not a sub-set of an internal control framework.

Where to start

15.022   The most useful first steps for a CEO would be to bring the various units from around the business who conduct risk assessment or related quality assurance or compliance tasks, together into an ERM project team under the leadership of a CRO. Of course the CRO may need to be recruited prior to this happening. This step would start the process of getting the existing risk management efforts aligned and into a common framework. Outside consulting assistance could be used to assist the board, with the help of this project team, to work towards the creation of the board's risk policy, model and overall framework.

It is possible that the ERM function would also be responsible for compliance topics including internal control but separate from the internal audit department. In heavily regulated industries, especially financial services, an alternative model is one where there exists a chief compliance officer ("CCO") and function. In such cases internal controls could be aligned under the umbrella of the CCO. Risk management would remain a separate function.

Typically a compliance department would have both an external compliance remit, for example, in Financial Services, ensuring that the FSA rules and regulations are being met through standard operating practices. A compliance function would also be responsible for the investigation of possible breaches of the guidelines and dealing with customer complaints and investigations by the governing bodies. There is also an internal angle to a compliance function. This is one where although no external breach is relevant, the company has committed itself to certain practices to support efficient and effective operation of the business. Examples of this could be sales commission policies, employee code of conduct, an employee helpline or fraud reporting investigations. A compliance function could take responsibility for the delegation of authority rules, namely, who can commit the company to acquire business and incur expenditure, and at what level; and internal signatories' powers, that are authorised to commit the company by signing contracts and payment instructions.

Risk management model

It is the risk management model that describes the process through which **15.023** risk management will operate and the details of the chosen methodology. Popular risk management standards include COSO ERM Framework[11] and ISO 31000 Risk Management standard.[12] There are considerable similarities between the major and internationally accepted risk management or enterprise risk management standards and frameworks. There is no one single "right way". The important thing is to select and follow one methodology because it enforces discipline and consistency.

Typically, at a high level, process steps would include a continuous cycle of:

- planning,

- identification,

- analysis,

- response,

- monitoring and reporting.

---

[11] *"Enterprise Risk Management—Integrated Framework"*, COSO, 2004: *http://www.coso.org*.
[12] ISO 31000:2009 provides principles and generic guidelines on risk management. *http://www.iso.org*.

Risk planning

15.024   Define the context within which business risks are to be managed, including defining risk-threshold levels and identifying the business activities to be assessed.

Risk identification

15.025   Multiple options exist for identification of risk, such as workshops, checklists, brainstorming, self or peer assessment, external benchmarks or industry research, previous incidents, surveys, reviewing audit findings. A bottom up or top down approach or a combination of the two can be taken.

Risk analysis

15.026   By way of analysis best practice normally includes a ranking or quantification of risk on a probability and impact grid or scale resulting in a magnitude of risk. Where possible, risks would be quantified in monetary terms. Either quantitative or qualitative analysis should enable final categorisation of risks according to a scale such as high, medium or low risk. The size and complexity of an organisation, and the diversity of the business, will dictate the level of sophistication required. For a large complex organisation arriving at a workable quantification and aggregation of risk is no insignificant tasks, but one that results in an improved ability to compare risks across business units and geographic regions because it reduces the subjective elements.

The quantification dimension

15.027   The most extensive application of risk management quantification techniques in the corporate arena has been in the financial services industry applicable to financial risks including credit risk and market risk. However, quantification of operational risk and strategic risk (often referred to as business risk) does not necessarily follow and the board should look long and hard before committing to a complex quantification or risk aggregation model. It is as well to remember for it to be successful any quantification model adopted needs to be understood by a broad spectrum of the company's employees and management. If the majority of those engaged in the process do not understand how the risk results are derived then proper adoption of risk management will not follow. Measurement is not an end in itself. The board should keep its sights on the management of the risks revealed.

Risk response

The most important parts of the risk management model are those that **15.028**
pertain to the response strategy and actions and the monitoring and reporting on what is being done. Evaluate the analysed risks and select the risks
(and opportunities) that should be "treated" by balancing the costs of implementing each option against the benefits derived from it. It is important to be
clear about who has to do what and by when, and to make sure this actually
happens.

Risk monitoring and reporting

Monitoring risks could involve periodic risk reviews by risk owners or a **15.029**
group of affected stakeholders. Risk monitoring includes collecting intelligence about factors that could affect the risk's likelihood of occurring and
the impact of the risk if it was realised. The definition of factors that affect the
risk are usually referred to as key risk indicators and the three letter acronym
KRI is becoming common parlance.

Any good risk monitoring process will include escalation steps. Risk incidents should also be documented and the risk management focus reviewed in
the light of the way the business is currently being affected.

Risk reporting

This is the part of the risk management process that causes the most problems **15.030**
and is the most tricky to get right. Risk reporting is problematic. There is no
standard for reporting. Unlike reporting a financial statement, where the
methodology and content are clear, risk reporting is entirely at a company's
discretion and limited by the tools available and, of course, the content which
may not be complete or accurate, insightful or even timely.

Risk management process and tools

It is the risk management process and tools that hold everyone who is con- **15.031**
ducting risk assessments and reporting together in the same way. Following
clearly defined and properly understood steps will enable all those involved
in the process to be consistent. The aim of the process should also be sustainability, repeatability and consistency. The risk management function is
the custodian of the company's risk management methodology, processes
and tools and its role is to support and partner the business as it conducts
risk management in the manner approved. As far as possible the risk

management process should be embedded into the standard business processes and activities, not to disappear, but to be fully enabled and supported by staff and management. The experiences of those who have a track record operating ERM suggest that accomplishing this is an achievement of epic proportions.

The use of technology

15.032   Businesses would be wise to make use of technology to support the risk management process. The following are some of the ways that a business can gain a return on investment if technology is used well:

(1)   institutionalising the risk management process;

(2)   liberation from risk administration;

(3)   proactive risk monitoring.

Institutionalising the risk management process

15.033   Technology can assist with enforcing consistency and adherence to the process. This is desirable because consistently recorded and analysed risks are comparable. Additionally, a consistent risk culture is encouraged when all employees are engaging in the same manner, through the same medium. A robust and scalable software system will stand up to audit scrutiny.

Liberation from risk administration

15.034   If the risk department is spending all its time recording risks and updating documents or spreadsheet or sending endless risk related emails, then it has less time to focus on the value added side of risk management which is proactive monitoring and drawing inferences and insights from the data. Technology can support the process and improve efficiency and effectiveness, with techniques to speed up data entry and features including workflows, reminders and approvals.

Proactive risk monitoring

15.035   Risk is all about things that might happen but haven't happened yet. If they can be prevented then evidence suggests that costs are contained tenfold. Setting up KRIs and having these tracked and alerts generated to advise in any adverse changes improves the likelihood that early actions can be taken to mitigate the detrimental effects. This is something that technology does very well and cost efficiently, compared to human intervention which is slower, inconsistent and subject to error and omission.

Part 2: Internal control

Would a company have a system of internal control in place even if there were no legal or regulatory requirement to do so? The answer to this hypothetical question is, of course, yes.   15.036

Firstly, internal controls can help conformance to desirable behaviours, such as adoption of "green policies", clear desk policies and other corporate values.

Secondly, internal control sets important parameters within which the company intends to pursue its strategy and help prevent employee and business partner behaviour with potentially damaging consequences for the health of the business. Examples of boundaries being overstepped would be; over enthusiastic sales people concluding deals with customers on disadvantageous terms; rogue traders accumulating trading positions unsupportable by the company's assets; dishonest employees or partners defrauding the company. The need to control financial losses due to fraud and non-financial losses such as damage to brand and reputation is a key concern of boards regardless of any regulatory drivers.

However UK-listed companies must comply with the UK Corporate Governance Code (or explain why they have failed to comply). The Code's Main Principles and Code Provisions are unchanged with respect to internal control and guidance with respect to internal control is found in the Turnbull Guidance.

Practical application of the Turnbull Guidance

The board of directors

The board is ultimately responsible for the system of internal control. Turnbull recommends that the board should start by determining what its policies are with regard to internal control and from them will flow the assessment of what constitutes a "sound system of internal control" in the particular circumstances of the company. As noted previously, Turnbull recommends that the board should consider general risk circumstances of business when doing this, and that having in place an ERM framework considerably facilitates this work. If compliance and internal control are part of the ERM framework this further facilitates the work and avoids duplication of effort and inconsistencies.   15.037

Executive management

15.038   The role of management was reinforced in the Smith Report (see App.15), para.5.7 as follows:

> "Management is responsible for the identification, assessment, management and monitoring the system of internal control and for providing assurance to the board that it has done so. Except where the board or a risk committee is expressly responsible for reviewing the effectiveness of the internal control and risk management systems, the audit committee should receive reports from management on the effectiveness of the systems they have established and the results of any testing carried out by internal and external auditors."

Larger enterprises are likely to standardise their internal control work into a single unit who take the lead in working on behalf of and alongside management in ongoing assessment and improvement to internal control and the internal control environment.

Employees

15.039   Turnbull points out that "all employees have some responsibility for internal control as a part of their accountability for achieving objectives". Accordingly, employees should have the necessary knowledge, skills, information and authority to establish, operate and monitor the system of internal control. This in turn will require an understanding of the company, its objectives, the industries and markets in which it operates, and the risks it faces. For many companies who have established internal and formal appraisal and objective vetting processes, these issues would be relatively easy to put into place. Those companies which have not implemented such processes would find it extremely difficult to harness the loyalty and enthusiasm of employees to the risk control environment without suitable training and education.

The audit committee

15.040   Provision C.3.2 states:

> "The main role and responsibilities of the audit committee should be set out in written terms of reference and should include: (one of several clauses). . .
>
>   To review the company's internal financial control and, unless expressly addressed by a separate board risk committee composed of independent

directors, or by the board itself, *to review the company's internal control and risk management systems;*" (author's italics)

The Code here is saying that it is not enough to set up a system of internal control and then for the board and its committees to say "job done" and get on with other things. The audit committee has an ongoing role in the monitoring and assessment of the system of internal control. The board needs to exercise its judgment, and judgment needs to be based on information and analysis. The board does not rubber stamp; it must hear the evidence before making a judgment.

What is a sound system of internal control?

Paragraphs 21–23 of the revised Turnbull Guidance on Internal Control (set out in App.6) explain these elements. In essence an internal control system includes policies, processes, tasks, and behaviours which taken together: **15.041**

(a) enable a company to respond to significant business risks so as to achieve the company's objectives, including safeguards from loss and fraud and the identification and management of liability;

(b) require maintenance of proper records and processes that generate a flow of timely, relevant and reliable information from inside and outside the organisation;

(c) ensure compliance with applicable laws and regulations and internal policies.

The system therefore includes control activities, information processes and processes for monitoring and it is embedded in the operations and culture of the company.

Nevertheless, error and deliberate fraud will continue to occur as part of the human condition and therefore Turnbull makes the point that a sound system of internal control provides reasonable, but not absolute, assurance that a company will not be hindered in achieving its business objectives:

"A system of internal control cannot provide protection with certainty against a company failing to meet its business objectives or all material errors, losses, fraud or breaches of laws or regulations."

How does a board review the "effectiveness" of internal control?

Paragraphs 24–32 of the revised Turnbull Guidance contains advice on how the board should go about this process. The board itself should define the **15.042** process. The process is likely to involve the setting up of one or more committees of the board on which employees are represented in an appropriate manner, and it is also likely to include the production of reports by these committees or working groups, which will have to be considered by the board on a regular basis.

Any significant control failings or weaknesses identified in the reports should be discussed in the reports, including the impact that they have had, or could have, or may have on the company, and the actions that are being taken to rectify them: "It is essential that there be openness of communication by management with the board on matters relating to risk and control".

The board's annual assessment will also consider the changes since the last annual assessment and the scope and quality of management's ongoing monitoring of risks. In particular, the board will also want to consider the incidence of significant control failings or weaknesses which have been identified at any time during the period preceding the annual review. There needs to be a critical review of the extent to which such failings or weaknesses have resulted in unforeseen outcomes or contingencies that have had, or might have in the future, a material impact on the company's financial performance or condition. Should the board become aware at any time of a significant failing or weakness in internal control, it should of course then determine how the failing or weakness arose and reassess the effectiveness of management processes for monitoring the system of internal control.

In the Appendix to the Turnbull Guidance on Internal Control (pp.13–15), there are set out a number of helpful headings and questions which management and the board will find useful in focusing their thinking. The full text is set out in App.6. See also paras 4.5, 4.6, and 4.7 of the Smith Guidance for audit committees set out in App.15.

Updating the Turnbull Guidance on Internal Control[13]

15.043   In 2004, the FRC conducted a review of the impact of the Guidance with the aim of determining if it needed to be updated. Three issues in particular were examined:

- "The scope and content of the guidance to directors;
- Disclosure of information about the internal control system; and
- The role of the external auditor in relation to the guidance."

The results of the consultation and survey was overwhelmingly that the Combined Code principles and provisions have had a substantially positive

---

[13] The FRC will be starting a further review of the Turnbull Guidance in the second half of 2010: see *http://www.frc.org.uk.*

effect on awareness and operation of internal control and the management of risks in listed companies. It was felt (and evidence was cited) that overall a practical balance has been achieved between compliance obligations and beneficial application of the Code's principles. As a result, the guidance remains unchanged. The exception: that there should be more encouragement of the board's disclosure regarding steps taken or being taken to remedy gaps or failings in internal control or risk management systems. The Revised Guidance was published in October 2005, applicable for accounting periods beginning on or after January 1, 2006 for affected companies.

Standards governing internal control evaluation

In the UK the Turnbull Guidance on Internal Control is the most used **15.044** framework for evaluation of internal control. However, there are other frameworks, and boards of companies whose securities are listed in the United States (including "foreign issuers" such as UK companies) are required by the US Securities and Exchange Commission to base their evaluation of internal control for the purposes of compliance with s.404 of SOX[14] on a "recognised control framework" established by a body or group that has followed due-process procedures. Approved frameworks include the Turnbull Guidance on Internal Control; the Canadian Institute of Chartered Accountants' *"Guidance on assessing control"* ("COCO"); and the US Committee of Sponsoring Organisations of the Treadway Commission's *"Internal Control-Integrated Framework"* ("COSO"). Of these it has to be said that the COSO framework is the most widely used not only in the US but in many other jurisdictions.

COSO

COSO—the Committee of the Sponsoring Organizations of the Treadway **15.045** Commission—was originally formed in 1985 to sponsor the National Commission on Fraudulent Financial Reporting, an independent private sector initiative which looked at the reasons for fraudulent financial reporting and developed recommendations for public companies and their auditors, for the SEC and other regulators, and for educational institutions.

The National Commission was jointly sponsored by five major professional associations in the US, the American Accounting Association, the American Institute of Certified Public Accountants, Financial Executives International, the Institute of Internal Auditors, and the National Association of Accountants (now the Institute of Management Accountants). The Commission was, and

---

[14] See below, Ch.24 (US Corporate Governance: An Overview of Key Requirements for Public Companies).

is, wholly independent of each of the sponsoring organisations, and contained representatives from industry, public accounting, investment firms, and the New York Stock Exchange. The chairman of the National Commission at that time was James Treadway, hence the popular name, Treadway Commission. The current COSO chairman is Larry Rittenburg.

The role and significance of COSO

15.046   In the context of corporate governance, the ERM and internal control as expounded by the COSO organisation is widely accepted as one of the leading, if not *the* leading, de facto good practice framework.

It was in 1992 that COSO issued a report, *"Internal Control—Integrated Framework"* to help businesses and other organisations assess and enhance their internal control system. To quote COSO:

> "The framework has since been incorporated into policy, rule and regulation, and used by thousands of enterprises to better control their activities in moving towards achievement of their established objectives."

The release of such a guiding document was timely; and since release of the framework the corporate landscape has become littered with governance related scandals and corporate failures with the resulting loss to investors which has undermined confidence in the business community. In 2001, COSO initiated a project to expand the internal control framework into a broader ERM framework. This endeavour resulted, in 2004, in the launch by COSO of *"Enterprise Risk Management—Integrated Framework"*. Essentially the broader framework articulates key principles and concepts and provides clear direction and guidance for companies in the full management of risks using definitions already established in the narrower internal control framework. Basically, the internal control framework exists within the context of the ERM one. COSO One states:

> "While it is not intended to and does not replace the internal control framework, but rather incorporates the internal control framework within it, companies may decide to look to this enterprise risk management framework both to satisfy their internal control needs and to move towards a fuller risk management process . . . A strong system of internal control is essential to effective enterprise risk management."

The COSO frameworks for internal control and risk management have become widely accepted as a best practice and adoption of the frameworks is extensive. The Public Company Accounting Oversight Board ("PCAOB"), created under SOX to oversee the activity of the auditors of public companies in the US) expects the majority of public companies to adopt the COSO framework and its Auditing Standard No.2, dealing with audit of internal control over financial reporting, assumes that the COSO framework (or one substantially like it) will have been adopted. All the evidence is that the vast majority of SEC registrants and filers have selected COSO as their framework for risk management and internal control. In February 2003 the Institute of Internal Auditors Research Foundation indicated that 63 per cent of publicly held companies use the COSO framework of internal control.

While the Turnbull Guidance can be used as a framework for SOX internal control work, the requirements of SOX are considerably more specific (some would say over-stringent) than those of the UK Corporate Governance Code. For the Securities and Exchange Commission ("SEC") in the US, comply or explain is not sufficient, and furthermore there are specific standards for process and the documentation of internal control work and external reporting in the annual report. In the UK directors have flexibility over how they conduct their internal control assessment and report on it. The SEC puts a clear responsibility on external auditors to attest to the validity (accuracy and completeness) of management's internal control assessment. No such equivalent requirement exists in the UK regulatory environment.

In a useful document *"The Turnbull guidance as an evaluation framework for the purpose of Section 404(a) of the Sarbanes-Oxley Act "*[15] the FRC—the UK's independent regulator for corporate reporting and governance—has provided an evaluation of the extent to which complying with the Turnbull Guidance on Internal Control meets the needs of complying with the comparable sections of SOX, and in particular, the report on internal control under s.404 and the quarterly certificate required from the CEO and CFO of listed companies on the accuracy of the financial statements and the adequacy (or otherwise) of internal control.

SMEs

As there is a high degree of congruence between the COSO and Turnbull Guidance on internal control, directors of smaller and medium-sized UK companies would benefit from reading a report published by COSO in June 2006, namely, *"Internal Control over Financial Reporting—Guidance for Smaller Public Companies"*.[16] In this document the specific challenges for smaller companies are explored and practical advice given on tackling problems such as: **15.047**

- "obtaining sufficient resources to achieve adequate segregation of duties;

[15] December 2004.
[16] *http://www.coso.org:* "Internal Control over Financial Reporting—Guidance for Smaller Public Companies", June 2006.

- management's ability to dominate activities, with significant opportunities for management to override control;

- recruiting individuals with requisite financial reporting and other expertise to serve effectively on the board of directors and audit committee;

- recruiting and retaining personnel with sufficient experience and skill in accounting and financial reporting;

- taking management attention from running the business in order to provide sufficient focus on accounting and financial reporting;

- maintaining appropriate control over computer information systems with limited technical resources."

The report's focus is clearly and solely on the requirements needed to meet s.404 of SOX which pertains to internal control over financial reporting. However, the advice is sound when looking at the broader controls environment in the Turnbull Guidance:

"for the purposes of this guidance, internal control considered by the board should include all types of controls including those of an operational and compliance nature, as well as internal financial controls (p.5) and, contained in SOX 302."

Certainly, the advice is applicable to many medium and larger companies, which may face some of the above characteristics and therefore the challenges due to the particular profile of their business. Regardless of size, highly decentralised businesses also face issues over sufficient and appropriate resources with the requisite skills because each unit operates as a semi-autonomous business in its own right. They also face issues concerning management's ability to dominate activities and override controls.

Cost versus benefit

15.048   The greatest degree of concern raised with applying the Turnbull guidelines came from smaller companies. Of those surveyed, 23 per cent reported the cost benefit equation being unbalanced (i.e. cost outweighing benefits), compared to only 16 per cent of medium and larger enterprises (see p.12—regulatory impact assessment). Overall the vast majority of all companies surveyed (77 per cent) reported that benefits outweighed cost in relation to internal control and risk management requirements of the Code.[17]

---

[17] As reported in the FRC Regulatory Impact Assessment Review of the Turnbull Guidance on Internal Control. The findings of the MORI surveys are set out in detail in "The Review of the Turnbull Guidance on Internal Control: Evidence Paper", FRC, June 2005.

The cost versus benefit debate has raged more heatedly over the SOX to the point of earnest discussion around foreign registrants de-listing from the New York Stock Exchange, and the postponement or cancellation of intended listings. For those companies who have made an implicit objective of the compliance exercise to obtain business process improvement the response is not all negative.[18]

Disclosure and the business review provisions of the Companies Act 2006

The FRC's review of the Turnbull Guidance concluded that there was no added value in requiring companies to comment extensively and publicly on the outcome of their internal control review, and the steps being taken to address any deficiencies. It was felt that detailed additional disclosure might result in "acting in the spirit of the Code" being subverted by focus on the exact wording on any disclosure and deliberations on its implications. **15.049**

However, the revised Turnbull Guidance does include the following (highlighted below) new wording in para.35 in relation to the board's statement on internal control in Code Provision C.2.1, and it is reasonable for such additional guidance to be included.

"the board should summarise the process it (where applicable, through its committees) has applied in reviewing the effectiveness of the system of internal control *and confirm that necessary actions have been or are being taken to remedy any significant failing or weaknesses identified from that review*" (author's italics).

At the time of the review, it was expected that the OFR would be a statutory requirement, in which principal risks together with a commentary on the director's approach to them would be in mandated. It was therefore deemed sufficient that these two regulatory requirements would complement each other and close the previously identified gap. However, in November 2005, shortly after the publication of the revised Turnbull Guidance on Internal Control, the Government abolished the statutory requirement for quoted companies to publish an OFR and hence the disclosure issue may be revisited in the light of this and any other statutory changes at a UK or EU level. The FRC has made it clear that while the statutory requirement has disappeared, it remains good practice for companies to publish an OFR in accordance with the ASB's Reporting Standard RS1.[19] In addition CA 2006 s.417 requires that the annual directors' report must contain "a business review" which among other things must include "a description of the principal risks and uncertainties facing the company".

---

[18] See Ch.24 (US Corporate Governance) for a more detailed treatment of SOX.
[19] *http://www.frc.org.uk/asb/technical/standards/pub0796.html.*

Conclusion

Risk management and internal control in unified governance

15.050   In the post financial crisis era businesses should be actively linking risks to strategic and operational objectives and monitoring risks using automated key risk indicators that offer improved opportunity to prevent risks from occurring. Automation of the risk process frees up the risk management team to concentrate on the implications of the risks and what to do about them rather than risk documentation and administration. This improved efficiency of the process enables executives and the board to make better decision about how to address risk in the business.

What we have seen happening in the arena of internal control is a broadening of the scope from solely *financial* controls to the general controls environment encompassing all areas of the business. For many organisations the FRC Code is not the only regulatory framework within which they operate. An increased emphasis on encouraging corporate social responsibility and green policies is also pushing towards the need to take a co-ordinated approach for controls management to achieve efficiencies and cut the cost burden. The use of technology supports moving away from periodic retrospective inspections of controls to continuous automatic controls monitoring which better safeguards the assets and integrity of a company.

Risk management and internal control management should reside together in an overall risk and control governance framework.

The principle-based "comply or explain" paradigm is reaffirmed in the new Code. The ongoing challenge remains: to try to reconcile entrepreneurship and innovation with sound risk management and good internal control. Turnbull emphasises that a sound and effective system of internal control is in fact a support to the entrepreneurial spirit, not a hindrance to it:

"Since profits are, in part, the reward for success for risk-taking in business, the purpose of internal control is to help manage and control risk appropriately rather than to eliminate it."

Chapter 16

Reporting to Shareholders—The Directors'/Annual Report[1]

Introduction

Under s.415 of the Companies Act 2006 ("CA 2006"), the directors of a company must prepare a "directors' report" for each financial year of the company,[2] and under Listing Rule 9.8R a Premium[3] listed company must produce an "annual" report. In practice, listed companies produce one report which complies both with the CA 2006 and with the Disclosure and Transparency Rules and the Listing Rules, and that report is called either the "directors' report" or the "annual report".[4]

16.001

The directors' report must also under CA 2006 s.417 contain a "business review"; and the Listing Rules and UK Corporate Governance Code between them prescribe that the full weight of the corporate governance reporting regime is to be carried in the "annual report". Thus the annual directors'/annual report has become a significant document.

In recent years the directors' report has become a surprisingly controversial document. There had been a growing feeling that simple compliance with the regulatory requirements of the Companies Act 1985 and UK GAAP/IFRS requirements did not tell shareholders and other stakeholders enough about the strategic objectives of the company let alone the key performance indicators ("KPIs") and the degree to which the company was succeeding in meeting those objectives and indicators. It was argued that a narrative statement which addressed these and other issues would be more helpful.[5]

With this in mind the DTI embarked on a five year process of consultation

---

[1] See also Ch.13 (Financial Reporting).
[2] Failure to comply is an offence on the part of the directors and any other person (e.g. the company secretary) who failed to take all reasonable steps to secure compliance.
[3] See Ch.2 (The Regulatory Regime) for explanation.
[4] See also App.1 of this book which reproduces Sch.B of the UK Corporate Governance Code and sets out an excellent summary of the disclosure requirements of the DTR and LR.
[5] See *Financial Times* August 4, 2010, p.17.

with a view to producing regulations which would both implement the EU Transparency Directive and would go further in terms of detailed assessment of the KPIs and attitudes to stakeholders and the environment. That work was reflected in the Companies Act 1985 (Operating and Financial Review and Directors' Report etc.) Regulations 2005 ("the OFR Regulations") which were due to come into effect in 2006. The OFR Regulations set out detailed requirements for the contents of the Directors' Report, including assessments of the company's approach to the environment, employees, and other stakeholders, and also performance of the company against KPIs. The OFR Regulations also required, more controversially, indications as to future strategy and performance, or "forward looking" statements as they were called. Despite attempts to exempt directors from liability for negligent misstatement in relation to such forward-looking statements ("safe harbour"), no exemptions were built into the OFR Regulations, and this was a cause of some concern. Nevertheless, the OFR Regulations had received broad, if reluctant, acceptance from industry and were strongly supported by shareholder groups and institutional shareholders.[6]

In the meantime the Accounting Standards Board ("ASB") had drawn up in 2003 a statement of best practice for the OFR, and many of the FTSE 100 companies adopted that statement. When the Government tabled the OFR Regulations in draft form, the ASB drew up and published in May 2005 a Reporting Standard in relation to narrative statements in the annual report, built on the original 2003 statement of best practice, and that Standard was called "Reporting Standard RS1, the Operating and Financial Review" ("OFR").

In January 2006, just before the OFR Regulations were due to take effect, the then Chancellor of Exchequer, Mr Gordon Brown, repealed them, on the questionable grounds that it would save "red tape", and, instead, clauses were introduced into the Company Law Reform Bill, which became s.417 of the CA 2006 (contents of directors' report: business review) which were intended more simply to reflect the requirements of the Transparency Directive. Moreover, s.463 (liability for false or misleading statements in reports) contained "safe harbour" wording which will be discussed in greater detail below.

As a result of the repeal of the OFR Regulations, the ASB withdrew the Reporting Standard RS1 and converted it into a Reporting Statement of best practice on the OFR, which has persuasive but not mandatory force. The Reporting Statement was published on January 26, 2006.[7]

This chapter will describe the basic regulatory regime for the directors' report under the CA 2006, including the provisions of the CA 2006 in relation to the business review; the requirements of the Disclosure and Transparency Rules, the Listing Rules and the UK Corporate Governance Code in relation

---

[6] The 2010 Coalition Government policy agreement calls for the re-introduction of an OFR.
[7] *http://www.frc.org.uk*>ASB>reporting statements.

to the "annual" report; and the ASB's Reporting Statement of best practice on the OFR.

The Companies Act 2006 requirements

Signing, filing, circulation and approval of the directors' report

The formal aspects relating to the signing, etc. of the directors' report are set out in Chs 5 through 12 of Pt 15 (accounts and reports) of CA 2006.   **16.002**

CA 2006 s.419 requires that the directors' report must be approved by the board of directors and signed on behalf of the board by a director or the secretary of the company.

A copy of the directors' report has to be delivered to the Registrar of Companies, in the case of a public company, not later than six months from the end of the relevant accounting reference period.[8]

A "quoted" (i.e. listed) company must also ensure the annual accounts and reports are made available on a website until the annual accounts and reports for the next financial year are made available.[9]

A copy of the company's annual accounts and reports[10] must be sent under CA 2006 s.417 to every member of the company and every person who is entitled to receive notice of general meetings, in the case of a public company, not later than 21 days before the relevant "accounts meeting".[11] It should be noted that UK Corporate Governance Code Provision E.2.4 states that the company must arrange for the notice of the annual meeting "and related papers" (which is taken to mean, amongst other things, the annual reports and accounts) to be sent to shareholders at least 20 *working* days before the meeting.

The directors of a public company must "lay before the company in general meeting", copies of its annual accounts and reports.[12] It should be noted that the CA 2006 does not require that the directors' report and accounts be *approved* by members[13]: however, UK Corporate Governance Code Provision E.2.1 requires that the company should "in particular propose a resolution

---

[8] CA 2006 ss.441 and 442.

[9] CA 2006 s.430.

[10] "Reports" means the directors' remuneration report, the directors' report and the auditor's report.

[11] "Accounts meeting" means the meeting of the company "at which the accounts and reports in question are to be laid" (CA 2006 s.437(3)). Normally, this would mean the company's annual general meeting. Under CA 2006 s.336, "every public company must hold a general meeting as its annual general meeting in each period of six months beginning with the day following its accounting reference date (in addition to any other meetings held during that period)".

[12] CA 2006 s.437.

[13] As distinct from the directors' remuneration report which under s.439 must be approved by members at the "accounts meeting".

at the AGM relating to the report and accounts". Characteristically, that resolution will either "receive" or "note" the directors' report and the annual accounts.

Statement as to disclosure by directors to auditors

16.003   Under CA 2006 s.419 the directors' report must contain a statement to the effect that, in the case of each of the persons who are directors at the time the report was approved:

(a)   so far as the director is aware, there is no relevant audit information of which the company's auditor is unaware, and

(b)   (s)he has taken all the steps that (s)he ought to have taken as a director in order to make him or herself aware of any relevant audit information and to establish that the company's auditor is aware of that information.

"Relevant audit information" means information needed by the company's auditor in connection with preparing his report.

A director is regarded as having taken all the steps that (s)he ought to have taken as a director if (s)he has:

(a)   made such enquiries of his or her fellow directors and the company's auditors for that purpose, and

(b)   taken such other steps (if any) for that purpose,

as are required by his or her duty as a director of the company to exercise reasonable care, skill and intelligence.

Where a directors' report containing the statement required by this section is approved but the statement is false, every director of the company who knew the statement was false, or was reckless as to whether it was, and failed to take reasonable steps to prevent the report from being approved, commits an offence and is liable to imprisonment for up to two years.

To all intents and purposes, this section repeats the corresponding section in the Companies (Audit, Investigations and Community Enterprise) Act 2004, which in turn amended s.234 of the Companies Act 1985. It means that directors need to establish a "paper trail" of enquiries to fellow directors and the company's auditors, and probably to relevant senior accounting personnel within the organisation, to record that they have studied those enquiries and regarded themselves as satisfied or otherwise, and otherwise to pursue other avenues of enquiry until they are satisfied.

Contents of the directors' report

The contents of the directors' report are prescribed by a mix of CA 2006, the **16.004** Disclosure and Transparency Rules, the Listing Rules and the UK Corporate Governance Code.[14]

Companies Act 2006

Names of directors, principal activities and dividend

The report is required[15] to state the names of the persons who, at any time **16.005** during the financial year, were directors of the company; the principal activities of the company and its subsidiary undertakings in the course of the year, and (unless a "small" company[16]) the amount (if any) which the directors recommend should be paid by way of dividend.

Other matters as prescribed by regulations

The report is also required to comply with the Large and Medium-sized **16.006** Companies and Groups (Accounts and Reports) Regulations 2008 (SI 2008/410) and includes such matters as:

(a) directors' interests

(b) asset values;

(c) political and charitable gifts;

(d) particulars of any important events affecting the company which have occurred since the end of the financial year;

(e) an indication of likely future developments in the business of the company;

(f) an indication of the activities of the company in the field of research and development;

---

[14] See also App.1 of this book which reproduces Sch.B of the UK Corporate Governance Code and sets out an excellent summary of the disclosure requirements of the DTR and LR.

[15] CA 2006 s.416.

[16] "Small" does not include public companies. The term is defined in CA 2006 s.382 as amended by the Companies Act 2006 (Amendment) (Accounts and Reports) Regulations 2008 (SI 2008/393) as a company which during the relevant year meets two or more of the following requirements—turnover, not more than £6.5 million, balance sheet total (the aggregate of the amounts shown as assets in the company's balance sheet) not more than £3.26 million, and number of employees, not more than 50.

(g)   an indication of the existence of branches outside the United Kingdom;

(h)   acquisitions of the company's own shares;

(i)   disclosure concerning employment of disabled persons;

(j)   employee involvement (information, consultation, employee share schemes, awareness of the financial factors affecting the performance of the company, etc.);

(k)   policy and practice on payment of creditors.

Business review and the resuscitation of the operating and financial review ("OFR")

16.007   All companies (except those as qualifying as "small"[17]) are required under CA 2006 s.417 to have a business review in the directors' report for periods commencing on or after April 5, 2005. Subsidiaries, whether wholly or partially owned are included in the requirement. The contents of the business review are prescribed by CA 2006 s.417[18] and, in non-mandatory form, by the ASB Reporting Statement "Operating and Financial Review" which is described in paras.16.001 above and 16.014 below, or whichever Reporting Standard (if any) replaces that Reporting Statement.[19] Most if not all FTSE 100 companies already adopt the Reporting Statement as the basis of their business review.

Section 417 is set out in full in App.5. Some headline points, however, are as follows:

(a)   the purpose of the review is said (s.417(2)) to be to inform members of the company "and help them assess how the directors have performed their duty under section 158 (duty to promote the success of the company)".

(b)   a business review should contain a fair review of the business and a description of the principal risks and uncertainties facing the company.

(c)   in the case of a quoted company,[20] the business review must under s.417(5) "to the extent necessary for an understanding of the development, performance or position of the company's business" set out:

---

[17] See fn 14 above.
[18] The business review provisions of the CA 2006 do not apply to "small companies": But s.416 (contents: general) a does apply to small companies. see fn 14 above for definition of small company.
[19] The ASB announced in a review published in January 2007 that it did not propose to produce a Reporting Standard. See *http://www.frc.org.uk.*
[20] "Quoted company" is defined in CA 2006 s.385(2), essentially as a listed company.

- the main trends and factors likely to affect future development, performance on and position of the company's business;
- information about environmental matters;
- information about the company's employees; and
- social and community issues, including information about any policies of the company in relation to these matters and the effectiveness of these policies; and
- information about persons with whom the company has contractual or other arrangements which are essential to the business of the company.[21]

If the review does not contain information of that kind the company must state which of those kinds of information it does not contain. It is presumed that information can only legitimately *not* be included if in good faith the directors take the view that such information is not necessary for "an understanding of the development, performance or position of the company's business". For example, it is unlikely that a software company will have environmental issues.

(c)   The review must, to the extent necessary for an understanding of the development, performance or position of the company's business, include analysis using financial and other KPIs. "Key performance indicators" means factors by reference to which the development, performance or position of the company's business can be measured effectively.[22]

(d)   "Safe harbour". CA 2006 s.463 (liability for false or misleading statements in reports) contains provisions imposing liability on directors in relation to untrue or misleading statements in, or omissions from, the directors' report, the directors' remuneration report, and in summary financial statements in so far as it is derived from either of these two reports.

---

[21] This provision was introduced at a very late stage in the passage of the Bill, without consultation, and was said by commentators to be intended to force quoted companies to disclose details of suppliers essential to the company's business following intense lobbying over the way supermarket chains treat their suppliers. However, clearly its scope will extend far beyond that of suppliers to supermarkets and will include disclosure of not only suppliers but also any third party (e.g. customer) doing business with the company which is regarded (a) as "essential" to the business of the company and (b) "necessary for an understanding", etc. of the company's business. It was said by the minister at the DTI, Margaret Hodge, that the new clause was intended to require the disclosure of information "at a high level". It was not, it was said, intended to require companies to produce long lists of the names of their suppliers, but to illustrate the principal risks and uncertainties facing the company.

[22] CA 2006 s.417(6). For an excellent outline of the meaning of "key performance indicators" see Ch.13 (Financial Reporting) and a guide by Trucost Plc on the meaning of the KPIs in the context of the EU Accounts Modernisation Directive: *http://www.trucost.com*. See also the ASB's Reporting Statement itself for helpful guidance: *http://www.frc.org.uk*.

However, a director is only so liable if:

(a) (s)he knew the statement to be untrue or misleading or was reckless as to whether it was untrue or misleading; or

(b) (s)he knew the omission to be dishonest concealment of a material fact.

In addition, no person is to be subject to any liability to a person *other than the company* resulting from reliance by that person or another on information in a report, including any civil liability, including rescission or repudiation of an agreement. The section does not affect liability for civil or criminal penalties.

16.008 *Resuscitation of the OFR*   It was announced in May 2010 as part of the joint policy report produced by the coalition Government that it proposed to introduce regulations which would reinstate the OFR, the Regulations for which had been dropped at a late stage at the in January 2006 at the behest of the then Chancellor, Mr Gordon Brown. The Introduction to this chapter sets out the history and description of the OFR before it was dropped and it remains to be seen what precise form the Government legislation will take and in particular whether the OFR will be covered by the "safe harbour" wording of CA 2006 s.463 (see above).

Listing Rules requirements

General

16.009 Companies whose shares are admitted to the Official List are required by the Financial Services Authority ("FSA") to comply with the Listing Rules and, in particular, in the context of the annual report, Listing Rule 9.8.
   Listing Rule 9.8.1 and 9.8.2 state as follows:

"LR 9.8.1 Publication of Annual Report and accounts

(1) A listed company must publish its Annual Report[23] and accounts as soon as possible after they have been approved.

(2) A listed company must approve and publish its Annual Report and accounts within six months of the end of the financial period to which they relate.

---

[23] Note that the Listing Rules speak of the "Annual Report" as distinct from the CA 2006 which speaks of the "Directors' Report". Listed companies will of course have to comply with both the Listing Rules and the CA 2006, but the title may well be used interchangeably by different companies.

LR 9.8.2 The Annual Report and accounts must:

(1) have been prepared in accordance with the listed company's national law and, in all material respects, with national accounting standards or IAS[24];

(2) have been independently audited and reported on, in accordance with:
    (a) the auditing standards applicable in an EEA[25] State; or
    (b) an equivalent auditing standard;

(3) be in consolidated form if the company has subsidiary undertakings; and

(4) if they do not give a true and fair view of the state of affairs, profit or loss and cash flows of the group, provide more detailed and additional information."

The Listing Rules requirements for the governance section of the annual report—the "comply or explain" regime[26]

Listing Rules 9.8.6R (for UK incorporated companies) and 9.8.7R (for overseas incorporated companies) state that in the case of a company that has a Premium listing of equity shares, the following items must be included in its annual report and accounts: **16.010**

- a statement of how the listed company has applied the Main Principles set out in the UK Corporate Governance Code, in a manner that would enable shareholders to evaluate how the principles have been applied;

- a statement as to whether the listed company has:

  - complied throughout the accounting period with all relevant provisions set out in the UK Corporate Governance Code; or
  - not complied throughout the accounting period with all relevant provisions set out in the UK Corporate Governance Code, and if so, setting out:
    (i) those provisions, if any, it has not complied with;
    (ii) in the case of provisions whose requirements are of a continuing nature, the period within which, if any, it did not comply with some or all of those provisions; and
    (iii) the company's reasons for non-compliance.

---

[24] International Accounting Standards.
[25] European Economic Area (i.e. the EU and EFTA).
[26] See also App.1 of this book which reproduces Sch.B of the UK Corporate Governance Code and sets out an excellent summary of the disclosure requirements of the DTR and LR.

The UK Corporate Governance Code requirements

Summary of disclosures in the Annual Report required under the UK Corporate Governance Code

16.011   The Financial Reporting Council ("FRC") has published, in Schedule B to the UK Corporate Governance Code and reproduced in full in App.1 of this book, an excellent summary of the disclosures required both by the Disclosure and Transparency Rules and the Listing Rules, and also by the UK Corporate Governance Code to be included in the annual report. An extract is set out below:

"The annual report should include:

- a statement of how the board operates, including a high level statement of which types of decisions are to be taken by the board and which are to be delegated to management (A.1.1);
- the names of the chairman, the deputy chairman (where there is one), the chief executive, the senior independent director and the chairmen and members of the board committees (A.1.2);
- the number of meetings of the board and those committees and individual attendance by directors (A.1.2);
- where a chief executive is appointed chairman, the reasons for their appointment (this only needs to be done in the annual report following the appointment) (A.3.1);
- the names of the non-executive directors whom the board determines to be independent, with reasons where necessary (B.1.1);
- a separate section describing the work of the nomination committee, including the process it has used in relation to board appointments and an explanation if neither external search consultancy nor open advertising has been used in the appointment of a chairman or a non-executive director (B.2.4);
- any changes to the other significant commitments of the chairman during the year (B.3.1);
- a statement of how performance evaluation of the board, its committees and its directors has been conducted (B.6.1);
- an explanation from the directors of their responsibility for preparing the accounts and a statement by the auditors about their reporting responsibilities (C.1.1);
- an explanation from the directors of the basis on which the company generates or preserves value over the longer term (the business model) and the strategy for delivering the objectives of the company (C.1.2);

- a statement from the directors that the business is a going concern, with supporting assumptions or qualifications as necessary (C.1.3);
- a report that the board has conducted a review of the effectiveness of the company's risk management and internal controls systems (C.2.1);
- a separate section describing the work of the audit committee in discharging its responsibilities (C.3.3);
- where there is no internal audit function, the reasons for the absence of such a function (C.3.5);
- where the board does not accept the audit committee's recommendation on the appointment, reappointment or removal of an external auditor, a statement from the audit committee explaining the recommendation and the reasons why the board has taken a different position (C.3.6);
- an explanation of how, if the auditor provides non-audit services, auditor objectivity and independence is safeguarded (C.3.7);
- a description of the work of the remuneration committee as required under the Large and Medium-sized Companies and Groups (Accounts and Reports) Regulations 2008 including, where an executive director serves as a non-executive director elsewhere,
- whether or not the director will retain such earnings and, if so, what the remuneration is (D.1.2);
- the steps the board has taken to ensure that members of the board, in particular the non-executive directors, develop an understanding of the views of major shareholders about their company (E.1.2).

The following information should be made available (which may be met by placing the information on a website that is maintained by or on behalf of the company):

- the terms of reference of the nomination, audit and remuneration committees, explaining their role and the authority delegated to them by the board (B.2.1, C.3.3 and D.2.1);
- the terms and conditions of appointment of non-executive directors (B.3.2)
- where performance evaluation has been externally facilitated, a statement of whether the facilitator has any other connection with the company (B.6.2); and
- where remuneration consultants are appointed, a statement of whether they have any other connection with the company (D.2.1).

The board should set out to shareholders in the papers accompanying a resolution to elect or re-elect directors:

- sufficient biographical details to enable shareholders to take an informed decision on their election or re-election (B.7.1);

- why they believe an individual should be elected to a non-executive role (B.7.2); and
- on re-election of a non-executive director, confirmation from the chairman that, following formal performance evaluation, the individual's performance continues to be effective and to demonstrate commitment to the role (B.7.2).
- The board should set out to shareholders in the papers recommending appointment or reappointment of an external auditor:
- if the board does not accept the audit committee's recommendation, a statement from the audit committee explaining the recommendation and from the board setting out reasons why they have taken a different position (C.3.6).

Additional guidance
The Turnbull Guidance and FRC Guidance on Audit Committees contain further suggestions as to information that might usefully be disclosed in the internal control statement and the report of the audit committee respectively. Both sets of guidance are available on the FRC website at: http://www.frc.org.uk/corporate/ukcgcode.cfm"

Responsibility for drafting parts of the annual governance statement

16.012   In the Preface of the June 2010 edition of the UK Corporate Governance Code by the FRC is an exhortation to the chairman to take an active role in drafting parts of the annual governance statement.

> "Chairmen are encouraged to report personally in their annual statements how the principles relating to the role and effectiveness of the board (in Sections A [Leadership] and B [Effectiveness] of the new Code) have been applied. Not only will this give investors a clearer picture of the steps taken by boards to operate effectively but also, by providing fuller context, it may make investors more willing to accept explanations when a company chooses to explain rather than to comply with one or more provisions. Above all, the personal reporting on governance by chairmen as the leaders of boards might be a turning point in attacking the fungus of 'boiler-plate' which is so often the preferred and easy option in sensitive areas but which is dead communication."

The Reuters approach to reporting governance matters

16.013   In March 2006 at a conference sponsored by the London Stock Exchange, the then company secretary of Reuters Plc, Rosemary Martin, summarised the approach of her company to reporting governance matters as follows:

- "describe what the board did in the year. Give solid examples;

- describe how the board's members' attributes are valuable and appropriate for your company;

- describe what criteria the board applies when assessing directors' independence;

- if you balk at disclosing the outcomes of your board effectiveness review, at least describe the approach you took to the evaluation, what you plan to do next and why that's "right" for your company;

- put "colour", by using examples, in your descriptions of what the board's committees do;

- think about breaking up the text with boxes, charts and diagrams;

- make your information as specific as possible;

- direct readers to your website for more information;

- where there are departures from the Code, state clearly the period, nature of and reason for the departure;

- highlight any positive, distinctive aspects of governance at your company;

- use advisers to give you an objective assessment, for example, PwC's 'best practice corporate governance reporting' booklet."

The ASB Reporting Statement on the (non-statutory) Operating and Financial Review[27]

The Reporting Statement can be read in full on the ASB's website: *http://www.* **16.014** *frc.org.uk/asb*. In all essential respects it repeats the withdrawn Reporting Standard RS1, which many companies in the FTSE 100 had in any case already adopted.[28]

The Reporting Statement involves:

(a) the specification of a number of principles for directors to apply when preparing the OFR; and

(b) the provision of recommended key elements of a disclosure framework to apply in an OFR.

---

[27] See para.16.001 above (Introduction) for the background to this Statement.
[28] See para.16.001 above (Introduction) for the background to this Statement.

The principles in particular make clear that the OFR should reflect the directors' view of the business. Its objective is to assist members of the company (the current shareholders) "with a forward looking orientation" in order to assist members to assess strategies adopted by the entity and the potential for those strategies to succeed. While the ASB takes the view that the OFR should focus on matters that are of interest to members, it points out that the information in the review is intended also be useful to other users.

The Reporting Statement sets out a framework of the main elements that should be disclosed in an OFR. It is for the directors to consider how best to structure their review, in the light of the particular circumstances of the entity. It contains recommendations as to the disclosures that should be made in respect of any KPIs[29] included in an OFR, but it does not specify any particular KPIs that entities should address, nor how many, on the grounds that this is a matter for directors to decide.

The Reporting Statement is accompanied by the Implementation Guidance that the ASB prepared in respect of RS1. The Guidance sets out some illustrations and suggestions of specific content and related KPIs directors might consider including in an OFR.

Examples of directors'/annual reports

16.015   Access to the annual directors' report, including the business review, directors' remuneration report, and UK Corporate Governance Code governance statement and disclosures, of the following sample companies can be obtained from the following websites:

- Thomson Reuters—*http://about.reuters.com/csr/corporategovernance*

- Unilever   *http://www.unilever.com/investorrelations/?WT.GNAV=Investor_centre*

- HSBC—*http://www.hsbc.com/hsbcinvestor_centre*

- BP—*http://www.bp.com* search annual reporting

- Marks & Spencer—*http://corporate.marksandspencer.com/investors*

---

[29] For an excellent outline of the meaning of "key performance indicators" see Ch.13 (Financial Reporting) and the business link page *http://www.businesslink.gov.uk/bdotg/action/layer?topicId=1079681127&r.s=sl&tc=000KWBL203200110545|3820524007*. Also the ASB's Reporting Statement "the Operating and Financial Review" is extremely helpful in spelling out examples of how certain KPIs might be demonstrated. See *http://www.frc.org.uk*.

Chapter 17

The Annual General Meeting

Introduction

Main Principle E.2 of the UK Corporate Governance Code states: "The **17.001** board should use the AGM to communicate with investors and to encourage their participation". In recent years, the annual general meeting ("AGM") of a company has tended to become, at least in the case of the larger public companies, the forum (some would say "cockpit") for shareholders, particularly smaller shareholders, to debate a wide range of governance issues. Activist shareholder groups have used the occasion to question directors on pay and policy, and have become increasingly proficient in using procedural tactics to ensure that their voice is heard and that the debate is conducted in public. Sometimes, as in the case of the notorious 1995 British Gas AGM (directors' pay) and, more recently, the 2003 GlaxoSmithKline (animal rights activists and also directors' pay), disruption occurs. The tendency for disruptive proceedings has, in itself, created the danger of a "siege mentality" in relation to the AGM, whereby companies themselves resort either to changes in the articles of association or other procedural measures so as to enable the board to drive through the business of an annual meeting without disruption.

The Companies Act 2006 requirements

Under s.336 of the Companies Act 2006 ("CA 2006"). **17.002**

> "every public company must hold a general meeting as its AGM in each period of six months beginning with the day following its accounting reference date (in addition to any other meetings held during that period)."

It is to be noted that the CA 2006 does not prescribe the business of an AGM, but it does require that a number of matters are dealt with each year by "members in general meeting", or at an "accounts meeting" and this has led to certain items of business being invariably dealt with at the annual meeting.

The Companies (Shareholders' Rights) Regulations 2009[1]

17.003   As from August 3, 2009 the Companies (Shareholders' Rights) Regulations 2009 came into force, thus implementing the EU Shareholder Rights Directive. The Regulations amend CA 2006 Pt 13 relating to resolutions and meetings.

The regulations apply in part to "traded companies" only, and in part to all companies. "Traded companies" are companies listed on the London Stock Exchange main market, PLUS and EDX but *not* AIM.

Since the Regulations apply to AGM's as well as to other meetings, and some of the regulations apply specifically to AGM's it is appropriate to include a summary here:

Additional contents requirements for notice of meetings

17.004
- address of the website where certain meeting information is available;
- record date;
- procedure to attend and vote;
- details of proxy forms;
- right to ask questions;
- AGM notices (but only where notice is given more than 6 weeks before the meeting): explanation of members' rights to requisition resolution and to include a matter in the business to be dealt with at the meeting.

Website: pre-meeting

- a company must publish certain information on a website in advance of a general meeting:
    - the matters set out in notice of meeting;
    - the total numbers of voting shares;
    - the total voting rights of each class of shares;
- must be available from the first date on which is sent until the end of the meeting;
- add any members' statements or member-requisitioned resolutions or matters of business as soon as reasonably practicable.

---

[1] The Regulations can be ordered in full from OPSI: *http://www.opsi.gov.uk/legislation/about_legislation*.

Website: post meeting: poll results

- requirements for traded companies in addition to current requirements relating to publication of the poll results:

  - the total number of votes avowedly passed;
  - the proportion of the company's issued share capital at the voting record time represented by those votes;
  - the number of abstentions (if counted).

Abolishing chairman's casting vote

- articles giving the chairman a casting vote at shareholders meetings became ineffective from October 1, 2007;

- companies with a casting vote provision in their articles on that date were, broadly, allowed to keep it;

- this saving will no longer apply to traded companies.

Voting record date

- voting record date must be determined by reference to the register not more than 48 hours before the time of holding the meeting, ignoring part of any day it is not a working day;

- Crest Regulations: currently apply 48-hour limit on voting record date:

  - Uncertificated Securities Regulations 2001 (reg.41) to be amended from October 1, 2009 to be consistent with the Regulations (i.e. in determining the 48 hour voting record time for shares held in Crest you ignore all or part of any day that is not a working day);
  - amendment is also consistent with CA 2006 s.327 which limits the deadline a company can set for receipt of proxies to no earlier than 48 hours before the meeting, ignoring part of any day that is not a working day.

Members' right to include a matter in AGM business

- Shareholders have a new right to require the company to include a matter *other than a resolution* in AGM business;

- rules on timing, expense etc same as for requisitioned resolutions i.e.:

  - 5 per cent total voting rights/100 plus members with average of £100 plus paid up share capital;
  - request received not later than;
    - six weeks before meeting;
    - if later, time of giving notice;

- company bears expenses if request received before end of financial year preceding the AGM.

New Rules for all companies

17.005   **Corporate representatives**

- a corporate representative is entitled to exercise same powers as appointor;

- CA 2006 s.323 is being changed to solve the issue faced by nominee companies appointing multiple corporate representatives;

- before this change, only one corporate representative effectively could vote on a show of hands or a poll. If multiple corporate representatives purported to vote in different ways, votes were invalid;

- under the new s.323 if a corporation authorises more than one representative, representatives can vote in different ways on a show of hands or a poll, as long as they each vote in respect of different shares;

Proxies' vote on a show of hands

- a proxy appointed by one member has one vote;

- if proxy appointed by more than one member:

  - has one vote if instructed to vote in the same way by all those members;
  - if the proxy is instructed to vote in different ways, he or she has one vote for and one vote against;

- resolves conflicting provisions in CA 2006 about how many votes a proxy appointed by more than one member has on show of hands.

Requiring directors to call a meeting

- regulations reduce to 5 per cent the minimum paid-up voting share capital that members must hold to require the directors to call a general meeting;

- currently the thresholds are:

  - 10 per cent for public companies;
  - 10 per cent from private companies;
  - or 5 per cent for private companies in certain circumstances;

- Treasury shares excluded from the denominator.

Key points

- multiple corporate representatives issue solved;

- show of hands: proxy appointed by more than one member can have a vote for and a vote against;

- requiring directors to call meeting: threshold reduced to 5 per cent.

Matters normally dealt with at AGMs

Company accounts and reports

CA 2006 s.423 requires that copies of the annual accounts and reports for **17.006** each financial year must be circulated to members.

CA 2006 s.437 requires that "the directors of a public company must lay before the company in general meeting copies of its annual accounts and reports".[2]

That meeting is described in the CA 2006 as an "accounts meeting"[3] but in practice will comprise part of the AGM. The accounts and reports must be laid before the company[4] not later than the end of the period for filing the company's annual accounts and reports with the registrar pursuant to ss.441 and 442.

It is to be noted that CA 2006 s.437(1) simply requires that the directors "lay before the company in general meeting" the accounts and reports, not that those accounts and reports should be approved by members. Nevertheless, the UK Corporate Governance Code Provision E.2.1 requires that the company "should in particular propose a resolution at the AGM relating to the report and accounts". It is conventional, therefore, for notices of AGMs to contain, as the first item of "ordinary" business, a resolution which "receives" or "notes" the accounts, and in the case of the Directors' Remuneration Report the approval of that report as required by the CA 2006.[5] It is the resolution to note or receive the directors' report and accounts which characteristically gives rise to the greatest questioning, and the chairman and other relevant directors, namely the respective chairmen of the board committees, the chief executive and finance director will need to brief themselves in detail on all aspects of the company's affairs and should be expected to speak to their particular areas of responsibility.

Directors' retirements and appointments

Most articles of association of public companies require that at every AGM **17.007** of the company, one third of the directors who are subject to retirement by rotation "shall retire from office".

Main Principle B.7, of the UK Corporate Governance Code states: "All directors should submit themselves for re-election at regular intervals subject

---

[2] "Reports" means the directors' report which will contain the "business review" required by s.417 (see Ch.16 (Reporting to Shareholders—The Directors'/Annual Report)), and the directors' remuneration report (CA 2006 ss.420 to 422).

[3] CA 2006 s.437(3).

[4] CA 2006 s.437(2).

[5] CA 2006 s.439.

to continued satisfactory performance". Provision B.7.1 re-enforces that Principle by requiring that:

> "all directors of FTSE 350 companies should be subject to annual election by shareholders. All other directors should be subject to election by share-holders at the first annual general meeting after their appointment, and to re-election thereafter at intervals of no more than three years."

Accordingly, the AGM is the occasion when the required numbers of directors have to retire immediately prior to the meeting and, if eligible for reappointment, are proposed for re-election. It is to be noted that under s.160 of the 2006 Act, unless the meeting unanimously agrees otherwise, resolutions for appointments must be put in respect of each individual director.

Directors' remuneration report

17.008   CA 2006 s.439 requires that "quoted companies"[6] must "prior to the accounts meeting",[7] circulate as an ordinary resolution, a resolution approving the directors' remuneration report required by s.420.

Dividends

17.009   Provisions are invariably included in the articles of the company, to the effect that a company may by ordinary resolution declare dividends in accordance with the respective rights of the members, but no dividend shall exceed the amount recommended by the directors. Directors may actually pay interim dividends, but it is for the members in general meeting to declare the final dividend in respect of a financial year, and therefore the AGM is usually the occasion on which the annual dividend is declared.

Auditor

17.010   Under CA 2006 s.489 an auditor of a public company must be appointed before the end of each "accounts meeting"[8] of the company. Accordingly, since the annual accounts are almost invariably approved at the AGM, the reappointment of auditors and (pursuant to s.492) their remuneration are also dealt with on that occasion.

---

[6] See CA 2006 s.385(2) for definition of "quoted company".
[7] i.e. the meeting at which the annual accounts and reports are laid before members in general meeting (CA 2006 s.437(3)). In practice this will be the AGM.
[8] CA 2006 s.437(3).

Auditor's report and auditor's right to speak

Under the CA 2006 the "auditor's report" comprises three elements: **17.011**

- report on the company's accounts (s.495);
- report on directors' report (s.496);
- report on auditable[9] part of directors' remuneration report (s.497).

Unless the articles (unusually) so require, the auditor's report does not have to be read at the annual meeting. However, under CA 2006 s.502 the auditor is entitled amongst other things to be heard at any general meeting which (s)he attends "on any part of the business of the meeting which concerns him as auditor".

Right of members to raise audit concerns at accounts meeting[10]

Under CA 2006 s.527 members of a "quoted"[11] company holding at least **17.012** 5 per cent of the total voting rights or at least 100 members holding voting rights and who propose to raise a related question at the next meeting at which accounts are to be discussed, can require a company to publish on a website a statement setting out any matter relating to the annual audit of the company's accounts, including the audit report, or any circumstances connected with an auditor of the company ceasing to hold office. A copy of any statement must be sent to the auditor.

Notice of meeting

Not less than 21 clear days' notice in writing must be given of the AGM[12] **17.013** of a public company. However, Provision E.2.4 of the UK Corporate Governance Code states that: "Companies should arrange for the notice of AGM and related papers to be sent to shareholders at least 20 *working days* [author's emphasis] before the meeting". The company secretary should be careful to ensure that the notice of meeting is sent to all directors and to the auditors,[13] and to other third parties as and if required by contracts or securities documents to which the company is a party.

---

[9] See Ch.11 (Directors' Remuneration).
[10] See CA 2006 s.437(3) for definition of "accounts meeting". In terms it is the meeting at which the annual accounts and reports are laid before the company in general meeting, which, in practice, means the annual meeting.
[11] CA 2006 s.531.
[12] CA 2006 s.307(2)(a).
[13] CA 2006 s.310(1) and s.502(2).

Other provisions in relation to the formalities of meetings (e.g. proxies and the right to demand a poll) are set out in CA 2006 Pt 14 Ch.3.

The items comprising the laying of the annual accounts and reports, the declaration of the dividend and the reappointment of directors and auditors are known as "ordinary" business which do not require the resolutions to be set out in full, but simply the general nature of the business to be conducted.

Other items of business at an annual meeting are termed "special" (for example, the disapplication of pre-emption rights) and resolutions comprising "special" business should be set out in full. Best practice recommends that all items of special business be explained in the directors' report. The Listing Rules should also be consulted to ensure that no pre-clearance is required by the UK Listing Authority.

Electronic notice

17.014   CA 2006 ss.333, 1144 to 1148 and Schs 4 and 5 set out in detail how documents or information should be sent by a company and of particular interest are the provisions relating to the electronic communication.

    (a)   Notices of meeting can under s.308 be given in electronic form or by means of a website.

    (b)   Documents or information to be sent or supplied electronically by a company must comply with CA 2006 Sch.5.

    (c)   A company may only send or supply documents or information in electronic form if members have resolved to do so; or the articles contain provisions to that effect (CA 2006 Sch.5 para.7).

    (d)   Websites: a company may only send or supply documents or information through a website to persons who have agreed; or are deemed to have agreed. A person is deemed to have agreed if (s)he has been asked individually to agree, and (s)he has not responded within 28 days (CA 2006 Sch.5 para.8).

    (e)   Result of a poll: A "quoted" company must under s.341 publish the result of any poll on its website. Note that Provision E.2.2 of the UK Corporate Governance Code requires as follows:

> "E.2.2 The company should ensure that all valid proxy appointments received for general meetings are properly recorded and counted. For each resolution, where a vote has been taken on a show of hands, the company should ensure that the following information is given at the meeting and made available as soon as reasonably practicable on a website which is maintained by or on behalf of the company:

- the number of shares in respect of which proxy appointments have been validly made;
- the number of votes for the resolution;
- the number of votes against the resolution; and
- the number of shares in respect of which the vote was directed to be withheld."

It is to be expected that electronic communication will gather momentum as members agree to this method over time in greater numbers.

"Best practice" at the annual meeting, both generally and by reference to the UK Corporate Governance Code

Presentation and communication

Main Principle E.2 of the Code states: "the board should use the AGM to communicate with investors and to encourage their participation". **17.015**

In the 1996 report of the joint City/Industry working group, chaired by Mr Paul Myners, entitled "Developing a Winning Partnership", it was suggested that the "model" company should ensure "efforts to make the annual general meeting an interesting and rewarding occasion for participants". These include:

(a)   encouraging shareholders to submit questions in advance;

(b)   referring minority interest questions for later written response;

(c)   arranging presentations by operational management.

The Hampel Report also recommended that "a full business presentation" should be made to shareholders, which should match, so far as possible, the information given privately to "institutional investors"; chairmen should, of course, beware of disclosing "insider" information in giving answers, unless that information is simultaneously published in the Company Announcements Office of the London Stock Exchange.

For guidance notes on aspects of best practice at general meetings, see the guidance notes on the website of the Institute of Chartered Secretaries and Administrators ("ICSA").[14] See also Provisions E.2.1 to E.2.4 of the UK Corporate Governance Code.

---

[14] *http://www.icsa.org.uk.*

Venue

17.016   The venue of the meeting must be large enough to hold all members who attend. It is not necessary that all members should be physically proximate to the platform, but they must be able to see and be seen and speak, if necessary, by means of television and microphones in rooms adjoining the platform room.[15] If so many shareholders attend as to make this impossible, the meeting will have to be adjourned to a suitable alternative site but in such a way that those who attended the original meeting may have the opportunity to get to the adjourned meeting.[16]

Chairman

17.017   It is usual for the person who holds the title of "chairman of the company" to chair the AGM. Most articles of association make provision to that effect. In the absence of such a provision the meeting can resolve to appoint any member present as chairman, and under CA 2006 s.319, subject to the articles, a proxy may be elected to be the chairman by ordinary resolution.

Script

17.018   The secretary should prepare for the chairman's benefit a "script" containing word for word what requires to be formally said in relation to each resolution so as to ensure that the business of the meeting at a formal level is dealt with correctly. A script is also invaluable to a chairman as a beacon point of reference if the meeting gets heated.

Notice does not need to be read

17.019   The notice of meeting should not be read out in full nor "taken as read". In accordance with Provision E.2.4 of the UK Corporate Governance Code, the notices will have been sent to shareholders at least 20 *working* days before the meeting, and any further notice is ineffectual.

   The chairman should simply introduce each resolution by referring to the number of the item in the notice of meeting itself, and describing it in general terms.

---

[15] *Byng v London Life Association Ltd* [1990] Ch. 170.
[16] *Byng v London Life Association Ltd* [1990] Ch. 170.

Resolutions

The chairman should either propose each individual resolution from the   **17.020**
chair or arrange for other members of the board to propose the relevant
resolution. It is not necessary for the resolution to be "seconded". Many
companies do that as a method of including other shareholders, but it is
not necessary. There should be no "composite" resolutions. The practice of
"bundling" composite resolutions is contrary to Provision E.2.1 of the UK
Corporate Governance Code:

> "Companies should propose a separate resolution at the AGM on each
> substantially separate issue, and should in particular propose a resolution
> at the AGM relating to the report and accounts."

Remuneration report

Under CA 2006 s.420 the directors of every "quoted" company[17] are   **17.021**
required to prepare a directors' remuneration report (see Ch.11 (Directors'
Remuneration) for details) which must be submitted to shareholders for
approval by ordinary resolution at the general meeting of shareholders at
which the annual accounts are laid before members (usually the AGM).[18]
The vote is advisory only, and as such, it does not require directors to
amend contractual entitlements, nor to amend their remuneration policy,
but the result of the vote will send a very strong signal to directors about the
level of support among shareholders for the board's remuneration policy.
In practice, directors will wish to take notice of the views of the company's
members, and to respond appropriately.

In the example of GlaxoSmithKline's 2003 AGM where the remuneration
report was not approved the board undertook to appoint an independent
firm of consultants to look at the remuneration packages again, and the
revised remuneration report was approved at the following AGM.

All "existing directors" (that is, every person who, immediately before the
general meeting, is a director of the company) have a responsibility under
s.447(4) to ensure that the resolution is put to the vote of the meeting. The
requirement does not apply to past directors (even if they served on the board
or as members of the remuneration committee in the current financial year)
but it does apply to "existing directors" who were, for whatever reason, not
present at the general meeting.

---

[17] CA 2006 s.385(2) defines "quoted".
[18] CA 2006 s.439.

Questions and freedom of speech

17.022   It is customary, before putting a resolution to shareholders for approval, to invite questions on the subject matter of the resolution. It is not a requirement of company law or Stock Exchange rules that questions be permitted, and a chairman who is determined to drive the business of the meeting through need not invite questions, unless the deliberate intention is to stifle debate.

Shareholders do have a right at common law to debate the business of a meeting, and therefore a chairman will sensibly use the mechanism of asking for questions in order to allow a debate to take place.

Provision E.2.3 of the UK Corporate Governance Code requires that:

"The chairman should arrange for the chairmen of the audit, remuneration and nomination committees to be available to answer questions at the AGM and for all directors to attend."

The chairman should allow adequate time for questions to be asked and the issues debated, but (s)he has the right to determine the method of the questioning and debate, and to call a halt to these if (s)he thinks that the issues have been aired. It is often good practice to give notice that (s)he will "take one more question" or something similar, so that the meeting is warned in advance that (s)he intends to close questioning.

As indicated earlier, there is a common law right to debate issues raised at an AGM, and this is commonly done through the mechanism of the request by the chairman for questions which precedes the putting of the resolution relating to the report and accounts. There is a clear need to restrict repetitive questions and limit the amount of debate permitted on each resolution. Part of the answer is the need to establish the right balance between encouraging shareholders to raise questions and discuss issues raised by the report and/or accounts, the board and other shareholders; and the need to maintain control of the meeting in the face of many questions on the same subject.

The board should encourage shareholders to submit questions in advance. This facility is already provided by a number of large companies and claims to work to a degree, but it is also suggested that the answers to the most common questions (which may be worded in many different ways, and thus need careful analysis in advance of the meeting) could be circulated at the AGM and used as the point of reference when similar questions are raised.

Such additional material could include graphs and charts to aid the communication of information which it might be difficult to get across orally. This approach has merit for particularly difficult questions, at the same time it is not wise to use advance questions as a justification for restricting the ability of shareholders to raise questions at the AGM or as an alternative to a properly formulated shareholder communications policy.

Voting

After questions have been dealt with, the chairman must then put the resolu- **17.023**
tion to the meeting, inviting those in favour of the resolution to raise their
hands and those against the resolution to raise their hands, and then to
declare the result of the meeting. There should, of course, be "tellers" (usually
provided by the company's registrars) able to count the numbers of hands,
unless it is clear that "on a show of hands" the resolution is either passed or
defeated by an overwhelming majority. It may be necessary for the chairman
to adjourn the meeting whilst a poll is conducted, and the chairman must
then declare the result of the poll. A poll may be demanded[19] by:

(a)   not less than five members;

(b)   holders of not less than 10 per cent of the voting rights;

(c)   holders of 10 per cent of the paid-up capital.

The chairman has an inherent right to require a poll and should do so where
(s)he has reason to believe that the result of a show of hands does not reflect
the proxy votes relating to the resolution.

Under CA 2006 s.332, all notices of meeting must state that a member
entitled to attend and vote may appoint a proxy vote on his or her behalf and
that the proxy need not be a member of the company. Proxies now have the
right to demand a poll[20] and to speak at company meetings[21] and can even be
appointed chair of the meetings by ordinary resolution.[22]

Moreover, where a company gives an electronic address in a notice of
meeting is deemed to have agreed, amongst other things, that proxies can be
lodged electronically.

Articles of association of public companies have detailed articles dealing
with the procedure on a poll, but good practice suggests that every AGM
should be prepared on the basis that a poll may be demanded, and poll cards
duly prepared. It is important to look at the articles of association in relation
to the right to demand a poll, because the articles may have a lesser numeri-
cal standard in terms of members or numbers of shares giving the right to
demand a poll than under the CA 2006.

In recent years, shareholder activist groups have resorted to the use of the
poll with increasing frequency. In the great majority of cases, the support of
the board gives the institutions an overwhelming advantage on a poll. The
intention of the activists is not so much winning a poll, but concentrating

---

[19] CA 2006 s.321.
[20] CA 2006 s.321.
[21] CA 2006 s.324(1).
[22] CA 2006 s.319.

the minds of the institutions when considering the issue on which a poll is being demanded. For that reason, boards of directors are well advised to communicate with their institutional shareholders in relation to items of controversial business, with a view to encouraging them to support the board when it comes to a poll and giving them the information forming the basis of that support. The NAPF has offered its services as an intermediary in that connection.

Finally it is to be noted that implementation of CA 2006 ss.145 to 153 (exercise of members' rights) which will allow the beneficial owners of shares held in the names of nominees the same rights as registered shareholders of information and to attend and speak and vote at meetings will add a dimension to shareholder democracy and activism which has yet to be fully realised.

Disclosing proxy votes and the "vote withheld" requirement

17.024   Provisions E.2.1 and E.2.2 of the UK Corporate Governance Code now read as follows:

> "E.2.1 At any general meeting, the company should propose a separate resolution on each substantially separate issue, and should in particular propose a resolution at the AGM relating to the report and accounts. For each resolution, proxy appointment forms should provide shareholders with the option to direct their proxy to vote either for or against the resolution or to withhold their vote. The proxy form and any announcement of the results of a vote should make it clear that a 'vote withheld' is not a vote in law and will not be counted in the calculation of the proportion of the votes for and against the resolution.
>
> E.2.2 The company should ensure that all valid proxy appointments received for general meetings are properly recorded and counted. For each resolution, after a vote has been taken on a show of hands, the company should ensure that the following information is given at the meeting and made available as soon as reasonably practicable on a website which is maintained by or on behalf of the company;
>
> - the number of shares in respect of which proxy appointments have been validly made;
> - the number of votes for the resolution;
> - the number of votes against the resolution; and
> - the number of shares in respect of which the vote was directed to be withheld."

Under CA 2006 s.341 a quoted company must publish the results of a poll on a website.

Members' powers to require an independent report on a poll

Under CA 2006 s.342 the members of a quoted company may require the **17.025** directors to obtain an independent report on a poll which either already has been taken or is to be taken as a general meeting. The directors are required to obtain such an independent report if they receive requests to do so from members representing not less than 5 per cent of the total voting rights, or not less than 100 members who have voting rights.

If duly requested to obtain an independent report, the directors must appoint an independent assessor to prepare the report. "Independence" is defined in s.344.

The report must state the assessor's opinion as to whether the polling procedures were adequate, the votes cast were fairly and accurately recorded and counted, the validity of the proxies was fairly assessed and the notice of meeting complied with s.324 (statement of rights to appoint proxy).

CA 2006 ss.342 to 351 give wide powers to the assessor to attend meetings and to obtain rights to company records and other information.

Amendments to resolutions

Amendments to resolutions should always be put to the meeting before the **17.026** resolution itself. It should be noted that there are a number of amendments that are not admissible at the meeting itself, unless preceded by proper notice of the resolution constituting the amendment, notice of which is given in accordance with the 2006 Act to shareholders.[23] These inadmissible amendments include the following:

(a)   increasing the dividend above the directors' recommendation;

(b)   varying the terms of service of a director;

(c)   changing the auditors;

(d)   appointing different directors;

(e)   changing the substance of a resolution;

(f)   raising matters outside the scope of the business of the meeting;

(g)   addressing a subject already covered by the meeting or incompatible with a decision already made by the meeting;

---

[23] See *Re Moorgate Mercantile Holdings* [1980] 1 All E.R. 40 for a full statement of the principles governing amendments; and *Shackleton on the Law and Practice of Meetings* (10th edn, 2006, Sweet & Maxwell).

(h)   placing a greater burden on the company than the original resolution;

(i)   amending special or extraordinary resolutions save for typographical errors;

(j)   requiring the board to take actions which are incompatible with its duties under the articles—even so, ordinary resolutions are not binding on the board, because, under most companies' articles of association, the business of the company is delegated to the board and only a special resolution can amend that delegation of authority.

The articles of association may require that notice of amendments must be received at least 48 hours before the meeting. An amendment which is "admissible" must be put by the chairman. The company must vote on the amendment first, and if passed, the original substantive resolution is not then put to the meeting, unless the amendment as passed was not sufficiently comprehensive to allow the original substantive resolution to be, as it were, subsumed in the amendment. In that event, the original resolution, as amended, must then be put to the meeting. If the amendment is not carried, then the original resolution as unamended must be put to the meeting.

Shareholder resolutions

17.027   In recent years there has been a small but increasing tendency for shareholders to require that resolutions drafted by them should be included in the business of a general meeting, usually the AGM.

Some institutional shareholders encourage the use of shareholder resolutions.

> "Shareholders resolutions are an integral part of the corporate governance process. They enable shareholders to take the initiative on issues which directors may be unwilling to address or where directors may face a conflict of interest . . . Shareholders' resolutions are not seen as a no-confidence vote on the board (unless that is specified) but should be judged on the merits of the specific issue addressed. Resolutions will be supported that are evaluated as being in the medium to long-term interests of the fund."[24]

The CA 2006 both preserves and enhances the ability of shareholders under certain circumstances to propose resolutions at the AGM. Under s.338 the members of a public company may require the company to give to

---

[24] West Midlands Metropolitan Authorities' Pension Fund Company Voting Guidelines 2004.

members of the company entitled to receive notice of the next AGM (including nominated beneficial owners under CA 2006 Pt 9) notice of a resolution which "may properly be moved and is intended to be moved at that meeting". The company is required to give notice of such a resolution once it has received requests from members representing at least 5 per cent of the total voting rights or at least 100 members entitled to vote on which there has been paid up an average sum, per member, of at least £100.[25] The request may be in hard copy form or in electronic form, must identify the resolution of which notices to be given, must be authenticated by the persons making it and must be received by the company not later than six weeks before the AGM or, if later, the time at which notice is given of that meeting.

The costs of the requisition must be borne by the requisitionists *unless* the requests sufficient to require the company to circulate the resolution are received before the end of the financial year preceding the meeting.[26]

A company that is required under CA 2006 s.338 to give notice of a resolution must under s.339 send it to all members entitled to receive notice of the AGM.

Statements

CA 2006 ss.314 and 315 provides that members (including nominated **17.028** beneficial owners under Pt 9) have the power to require circulation of statements of not more than a thousand words in relation to the proposed resolution or any other business to be dealt with at the meeting. The same 5 per cent of voting rights or 100 members provision applies to the power to require circulation of statements. The expenses of the statement must be paid for by the members requesting it *unless* (as will normally be the case) the statement relates to the annual meeting and the requisite number of members file their requests before the end of the financial year to which the meeting relates.

The new and additional powers of the private investor to requisition resolutions, etc. arising from the Companies Act 2006[27]

At a relatively late stage clauses were inserted in July 2006 into the Companies **17.029** Bill, after a rather remarkable campaign by the Shareholders Alliance. The clauses are now contained in CA 2006 Pt 9 ss.145 to 153.

In terms, these sections are concerned with the situation where shares

---

[25] In the case of companies where the nominal value is very small, for example, 1p, but the market price is very high, this may be a considerable hurdle to jump.
[26] CA 2006 s.340.
[27] See also Ch.19 (Communication and Engagement with Shareholders) for a fuller treatment.

("traded shares") in companies whose shares are traded on a regulated market (e.g. the London Stock Exchange but not AIM) are registered in the name of a nominee. Nearly one half of shareholdings in the UK are registered in the names of nominees, including PEPs and ISAs, for example, on behalf of the real or, as they are more technically named, "beneficial owners".

Nomination rights

17.030 Section 145 gives rights to the beneficial owner of the traded shares, once nominated for that purpose by the nominee, as if the beneficial owner were himself the registered member. The beneficial owner can now require companies, for example, to be sent resolutions, to notice of meetings, circulate statements or requisition meetings, or appoint proxies. However, the articles of association of a company need to contain a provision enabling a member to nominate another person as entitled to enjoy or exercise all or any of the specified rights of a member in relation to the company.

Information rights

17.031 Under ss.146 to 151 the beneficial owners of shares whose shares are registered in the name of nominees (e.g. ISAs or PEPs or trusts) can, if the articles permit[28] nomination by the registered holder, require companies to send them, as distinct from the nominee, information about the company, including the annual report and accounts, all other communications and the right to hard copies of these documents.

The implications of these provisions may over time be immense, and listed companies will need to gear up to meet the requirements of the beneficial owners who are not registered. If a significant number of individual beneficial owners start to exert their rights under the CA 2006 the result could be an interesting extension of activism as powerful, if not more powerful, than the institutions.

The role of the chairman

17.032 Common law and articles of association of companies give the chairman extensive powers to conduct AGMs. The chairman should ensure that there is good preparation for AGMs by ensuring that each relevant director of the company is fully briefed and able to speak, if called upon, in relation

---

[28] See Model art.79 of the Model Articles of public companies in the Companies (Model Articles) Regulations 2008 Sch.3.

to the items of business at the annual meeting. It is important to discuss or "rehearse" these issues in advance, so that both the chairman and the board give an air of confidence and appear to know what they are about. The good chairman will try to use a mixture of common sense, good humour, patience and personal judgment to keep the meeting on his or her side and to ensure that the business of the meeting is conducted in accordance with the notice and agenda.

One point of control which is sometimes overlooked relates to the use of the microphone. It is important that the microphone is under the control of officials of the company and that the chairman has the ability to "switch off" the microphone if (s)he considers that the use of the microphone is being abused. The chairman should also be prepared to "listen" and not, unless compelled to do so to maintain order, to "talk over" a shareholder who is trying to make a point.

The powers of a chairman to adjourn the meeting are inherent to the extent that a meeting may become out of control or the chairman is reasonably of the view that the views of the majority cannot be validly ascertained (e.g. lack of space). Otherwise, the chairman should not adjourn a meeting unless the meeting so consents, and provisions to that effect are usually incorporated in the articles of association.

The chairman can decide how a debate can be conducted so as to give a fair representation to all shapes of opinion. In practice, it may be difficult to identify in advance who is going speak in what way, but the chairman is entitled to ask for different views to a previous speaker to be expressed (see below: "Keeping order and disruptive behaviour").

Keeping order and disruptive behaviour

Experience has shown that the ability of the chairman to keep control of **17.033** a difficult annual meeting is the key to a successful meeting.[29] The chairman sometimes has to tread a difficult path between, on the one hand, getting the business of the meeting conducted in an efficient manner and, on the other hand, allowing freedom of debate on matters of substance. If the drive for efficiency and expedition comes across as "heavy handed", it is likely to result in disruptive tactics in order to attract the attention of the chair and the meeting; however, if control is not maintained, there is the danger of continuous questioning and comment, often of an irrelevant nature.

The chairman has power to exclude persons in order to maintain order[30]

---

[29] See also an excellent article (AGMs: are you ready?) on this topic by Michelle Wheeler in "PLC" (January 2003 *http://corporate.practicallaw.com/7-102-2559*: for subscribers, *http://www. practicallaw.com*).
[30] *Carruth v ICI* [1937] A.C. 707.

and, with the consent of the meeting, can exclude or include non-members such as the press. Meticulous preparation, security cards and adequate registration and security facilities, impartiality, lack of defensiveness, a sense of humour and control of the microphone are the essential features which a chairman with a light touch can use to manage a meeting effectively.

In the early 1990s, disruptive action inside the AGM had become commonplace in larger utilities and other companies with "sensitive" commercial activities (for example, in South Africa or in environmentally sensitive areas). Guidance was being circulated by protest groups as to how to gain access to the AGM and, once inside the meeting, they could then use that occasion generally to disrupt it. Common tactics were the smuggling in of amplification equipment (this has now been checked by the use of "air-port style" security x-ray machines); heckling, standing on chairs and waving banners, marching around the room, and chaining protesters to chairs or pipes.

If a meeting gets out of control, then the chairman can adjourn the meeting as well as excluding the disruptive element. Any adjournment should be short, in order to cause minimum disruption to shareholders (for example, 15 minutes), should be made with the consent of the meeting, and should otherwise be in accordance with the company's articles of association. The chairman does have a common law[31] limited power to adjourn the meeting, but it is desirable to consult the articles of association for specific provisions (if any) relating to adjournments.

If it is likely that disruptive tactics may be used, then steps must be taken in advance to prepare for that disruptive action. Commercial security organisations can advise on the number of stewards who may be necessary in order to eject any protester who has gone "beyond control", but ejection should be a last resort and should be preceded by switching off the microphone (if the protester has the microphone), by warning the protester and the meeting in advance that s(he) will be removed, and then, in a calm manner, requesting the stewards to remove the protester and continuing with the meeting. Calmness is essential; trying to trade insult for insult or allowing tempers to be raised can often be extremely counter-productive in winning the support of the meeting.

The great majority of persons who attend annual meetings do so in a law-abiding fashion to hear a debate, and if the chairman can succeed in turning the meeting against unreasonable protesters, then (s)he will be able to keep control of the meeting. Stewards should be kept in the background until required, and should be equipped with the necessary equipment to release protesters who have chained themselves. Many protest groups now have as good a knowledge of procedural tactics as the chairman and his or her advis-

---

[31] See *Byng v London Life Association* [1989] 1 All E.R. 560 where the power was held to have been used incorrectly.

ers themselves, and therefore, preparation and awareness of the procedures available to the chairman are essential.

Having said that, not all "protest" groups become disruptive. The chairman must be able to spot the presence of shareholders who may have a determined point of view and an uncomfortable line in questioning, but who are not to be categorised as "protesters". Their voice needs to be heard and the answers to them should be calm and reasoned. Sometimes, the chairman may gain the respect of the meeting by confessing that (s)he does not know the answer, and asking the questioner either to discuss the issue with him or her afterwards or to give him or her time to prepare a full answer in writing. Indeed, it has been suggested that, in that event, the chairman should send copies of the answer to all those who attended the annual meeting, and should say (s)he will do so at the time when (s)he asks the questioner if (s)he may deal with the matter in that way.

Conclusion

There has been a call for the annual meeting to be regarded by companies as a major event, rather than a formality. Anecdotal evidence indicates that many company chairmen and chief executives regard the annual meeting as a waste of time and money and expensive. **17.034**

In addition, a major criticism which is made of institutional shareholders is that they do not attend or vote at AGMs, and it was suggested by one shareholder pressure group (Pension Investment Research Consultants) that all shareholders above a certain percentage should be required to vote by proxy. In 2003 Unilever wrote to the 10 largest shareholders asking them to explain in writing why they had not voted at the AGM.

The National Association of Pension Funds, in its report entitled "Good Corporate Governance", stated that the NAPF:

"is anxious to see company AGMs become more worthwhile occasions. Both boards of directors and shareholders should be encouraged to participate more constructively. Boards of directors should make considerably more effort to explain to shareholders both the company's past performance and future prospects and the strategically corporate objectives.

The amount of effort and preparation made for AGMs by some boards does not compare favourably with that afforded to investment analysts attending the announcement of annual results. This imbalance should be corrected."

It appears that the annual meeting is here to stay, and that its importance is going to be recognised increasingly in the future as the primary means by which private shareholders express their views. As always, however, a balance needs to be struck between the requirement that shareholders should have a forum in which they can express views, forcibly and critically if necessary, but which does not hold the board of directors hostage for weeks during which their undivided attention has to be given to the preparation of an annual meeting.

Chapter 18

Institutional Shareholder Activism—Part 1

Introduction and definitions

In view of the accelerated development in recent years of active interven-   **18.001**
tion by institutional shareholders in the affairs of listed companies, and
particularly intervention on issues of corporate governance, this chapter
will describe the nature of the movement. Part 1 of this chapter will deal
with the historical background and some of the main characteristics; and
Part 2 will describe the particular approach adopted by Hermes Investment
Management Limited ("Hermes" which also includes fund management
companies within the Hermes group), which has been written by Paul Lee of
Hermes together with a case study.

"Activism" may be defined for the purposes of this chapter as the policy by
institutional investors of using or threatening to use or withhold their voting
powers to take direct action (in varying degrees and forms) in relation to an
investee company so as to achieve the goal of enhanced shareholder value
within a framework of good governance.

Different expressions are used in this chapter describing this topic: "activism" or "intervention" have tended to be used by journalists, American
governance writers, some institutional shareholders and institutional shareholder bodies such as the Institutional Shareholders Committee ("ISC"):
"engagement" is the preferred term for the Financial Reporting Council
("FRC") and thus the UK Corporate Governance Code.[1]

The International Corporate Governance Network ("ICGN") interestingly uses none of these expressions in its "Statement on Institutional
Shareholder Responsibilities" preferring to speak throughout of the concept
of the "implementation of fiduciary responsibilities".

The term "institutions" means, for the purpose of this chapter, pension
funds, insurance companies, investment companies, and other collective

---

[1] See Sch.C of the Code: "Engagement principles for institutional shareholders". This schedule
ceased to apply on publication of the UK Stewardship Code in July 2010. See also therefore the
UK Stewardship Code which also uses the word "engagement". *http://www.frc.org.uk.*

investment vehicles, and also includes, where the context requires, the fund managers appointed by these institutions as agents to manage their funds.

Part 1: Background and outline of the nature and characteristics of activism

The regulatory regime

The Companies Act 2006—Power to require information about exercise of voting rights

18.002   CA 2006 ss.1277 to 1280 in terms give the Secretary of State power by regulation to require "institutions"[2] to provide information about the exercise of voting rights. This followed a long debate between the Government and the institutional shareholder bodies such as the ABI and NAPF in which the Government had for some time urged institutions both to cast their votes and to be transparent about how they had voted. Institutions had generally responded actively to this call, but there was still some reluctance to say how they had voted, and they urged the Government not to introduce legislation to compel disclosure. It remains to be seen whether regulations will in fact be introduced or whether institutions will now re-double efforts to demonstrate both that they have used their votes and how they have used their votes.

The UK Corporate Governance Code and the UK Code

18.003   Schedule C of the UK Corporate Governance Code published in June 2010 contained a number of Principles and Supporting Principles, but these ceased to apply when the UK Stewardship Code came into effect in July 2010. Further details of the UK Stewardship Code are outlined in para.18.016 below.

Historical development of activism

18.004   Approximately 85 per cent of UK equities are held by "institutional" investors and the vast majority of those equities are held by insurance companies and pension funds.[3] In practice, most of the funds held by institutions such

---

[2] Defined in s.1278, but broadly speaking meaning institutions as commonly understood, e.g. pension funds, unit trusts, insurance companies, but does not appear to include fund managers themselves who in practice do the voting.
[3] See table below.

as insurance companies and pension funds are managed on behalf of those institutions by "fund managers" such as Hermes Pension Management which, for example, manages the Royal Mail and BT pension funds. In other words, the institutions are clients of the fund managers who owe their living to the institutions.

Until 1990, it was unusual for UK institutional shareholders to exert any direct influence on the conduct of the running of companies in which they invested. Institutions either tended to "vote with their feet" and dispose of shares in companies they considered to be under-performing, or simply held on to their investments hoping that improvements would occur. In recent years, however, this approach has changed markedly as the proportion of shares which institutions own in companies has increased, as have the consequent difficulties in selling large numbers of shares without distorting the market.

The activist movement started in the US, and in particular through the influence of the California Public Employees Retirement System ("CalPERS"). In 1987 CalPERS published a detailed statement in which it indicated its use of a two-tiered approach. In the first tier, 10 companies were identified among the relatively poorest performers in the CalPERS domestic equity portfolio over the long term, and those companies were identified as "focus companies" of CalPERS corporate governance activism. The companies identified in the first tier were the subject of intensive dialogue between CalPERS and the directors of the companies concerned, with the understanding that failure to comply with improvements in governance practice would result in shareholder action against the incumbent board. A second tier of companies was identified as 26 other "poorly performing" companies that might be included in the first tier in the following financial year. Those companies were then subjected to what was described as "heightened monitoring".

It was claimed by CalPERS that the performance of companies targeted by the fund over a five-year period gave rise to a significant improvement in share value performance by reference to the Standard & Poor's 500 Index. Some observers doubted the causal link and others claimed that the improvement in share price was not sustained. Nonetheless the CalPERS approach was highly influential and was followed by a number of large US fund managers such as TIAA-Creff and the Teachers Fund.

In the UK, the first "activist" fund was started by Hermes Investment Management Limited in 1990 and Hermes is currently the largest independent pension fund manager in the United Kingdom, managing over £65 billion worth of investments. Hermes has, over time, extended its activist role by forming "Hermes Focus Asset Management", which, as the name suggests, concentrates on a selected number of investments in fundamentally sound but under performing companies which are then made the focus of active "engagement".[4] Other

---

[4] See Pt 2 of this chapter for a Hermes case study in engagement.

fund managers, such as Morley Fund Management, ISIS asset management, PIRC and GO European Focus Fund are also regarded as activist funds.

Some examples of activism in practice

18.005

Date	Event
May 2003	**GlaxoSmithKline** shareholders vote against the directors' remuneration policy and demand a complete revision to the remuneration package of the CEO.
October 2003	Michael Green, chairman of **Carlton Television**, abandons his bid to be chairman of **ITV** (created from a merger between Carlton and Granada television) after shareholders objected.
January 2004	**Royal Dutch/Shell,** two public companies run in parallel as a "virtual" group announce a reduction of 20 per cent in its previously published statement of "proven" oil and gas reserves sending the share price sharply lower. Shareholders demand that management is made accountable, and the chairman resigns. The two parallel companies are then merged into one group with a single board.
February 2004	Mr Ian Prosser, former chairman of **Bass Group Plc**, abandons his candidacy to be chairman of **Sainsbury** after a number of shareholders complain that he lacks the necessary skills to revive the performance of Sainsbury. It was said that many institutional shareholders remembered that at Bass, Mr Prosser had presided over the $2.9 billion acquisition of Inter-Continental hotels and Resorts in 1998, followed by a reduction in the share price of 50 per cent over the next five years.
May 2004	Shareholders of UK advertising and market research firm **Aegis** reject a two year contract for the CEO which would have paid him as much as £2.4 million if the company were sold.
May 2005	Lord Hollick, chairman of **United Business Media** retired and was awarded a bonus of £250,000 for "services" in ensuring a smooth handover to successor. Institutions lodged objections but Lord Hollick

	refused to give way. The remuneration report was rejected by 76 per cent of votes at the May AGM. Hollick and the board at that point agreed to waive the bonus.
May 2003	In 1995 **Wm Morrisons supermarkets** had no non-executive directors, no audit committee or remuneration committee and an excellent financial and trading record. Sir Kenneth Morrison, was 75 and chairman and CEO. In 2003 it acquired part of Safeway supermarkets. In 2005 Morrisons issued three profit warnings. In May 2005 Rrev, the NAPF/ISC activist fund issued a report which called Morrisons' governance "substandard". Independent non-executive directors have now been appointed and a conventional UK Corporate Governance Code committee structure has been put in place.
April 2006	Hermes and some German institutional shareholders exert pressure on the supervisory board of **Volkswagen** to appoint independent directors to represent shareholders other than Porsche and Lower Saxony, which entered into a shareholders' agreement with each other and to control 40 per cent of **VW**, and to require those independent directors to examine the shareholders' agreement to see whether it constituted a "concert party" which would require a bid to be made for the whole company.

The concept of "ownership" responsibilities in activism and allegations of institutional "short-termism"[5]

A significant aspect of the debate about the value or otherwise of shareholder **18.006** activism focuses on, firstly, the issue of "ownership", that is to say, the assertion by activists that boards should be mindful at all times of the interests of the "owners", and that shareholders should "think like an owner"[6]; and, secondly, the issue of "short-termism".

---

[5] See definition below: "short-termism".
[6] Attributed to the American billionaire and controlling shareholder of the Berkshire Hathaway investment company, Mr Warren Buffet.

Share ownership

18.007 It is useful to make a brief overview of the structure of share ownership of UK companies.

Beneficial ownership of UK shares as at December 31, 2008

Investor category	% holding
Rest of the world	41.5%
Insurance companies	13.4%
Pensions funds	12.8%
Individuals	10.2%
Unit trusts	1.8%
Investment trusts	1.9%
Other financial institutions	10.0%
Charities	0.8%
Private non-financial companies	3.0%
Public sector	1.1%
Banks	3.5%
Total	100%

Source: *Share Ownership: a report on ownership of shares as at December 31, 2008*, Office of National Statistics.[7]

As can be seen from the table, 41.5 per cent of the shares of UK companies are now held by overseas investors. These are typically institutional investors including large public sector pension funds in North America and Europe, and mutual funds. The two big classes of institutional investors, the insurance companies and pension funds, own a little over one quarter of shares, and other domestic institutions account for 29 per cent. 10 per cent is held by individuals. This contrasts with the earliest available comparable figures from 1963 when individuals held over half of UK shares. "The important insight to draw from this is that the significant majority of shares are held by large collective investment vehicles representing the capital of millions of working people. Thus, 'the public' are in large part the owners of British business,"[8] and most institutional investors hold their investments in a fiduciary capacity.

Two further comments are also appropriate: firstly, a high proportion of institutional shareholdings is managed by fund managers on behalf of the institutions. The voting power of those institutions is therefore exercised in many cases by the fund managers.

---

[7] A longer analysis of changes in share-ownership, and its implications, is available in the paper, "*Trading places: Changes in the share-ownership of UK companies*", TUC, September 2005.
[8] "*Investment Chains: Addressing corporate and investor short-termism*", TUC, March 15, 2006.

Secondly, the activities of hedge funds, which are themselves invested in on an increasingly large scale by pension funds, the liquidity mechanism of "stock lending"[9] and the holding of shares through derivative instruments such as "contracts for difference" ("CFD")[10] where the voting rights can be separated from the economic interest, mean that at any one point in time it is difficult for a company to know exactly what the nature of its shareholders—its owners—is:

"Eyewitness accounts from the battlefield of international business tell of a situation that is much less neat and orderly. Demands for action and results have speeded up. What is worse, these demands are made by 'owners' who are elusive, unpredictable and almost anonymous."[11]

In 2005, Mr John Sunderland, President of the CBI and chairman of Cadbury Schweppes, said in a speech:

"The pressure on the sell side has, in my view, made analysts very focused on the near term, and in some instances their understanding of our business fundamentals is less than it used to be . . . The research tends to be more sensational, and on road shows[12] there is increasing pressure to put us in front of hedge funds rather than traditional long funds. It may be old fashioned but I view a shareholder as a shareholder—someone whose interests in the success and prospects of the company lasts more than three weeks . . . I have real concerns about promoting the use of my company's stock as hedge fund plays—just as I would if they were chips in a casino".

Conclusion

It is increasingly difficult to pin down the exact nature of the ownership and voting structure of companies in the UK at any given point in time, and consequently increasingly difficult for managers to understand clearly the nature of the interests whom they are supposed to serve. **18.008**

---

[9] The practice whereby one owner of stock will "lend" that stock to another in order to enable that other to cover a short-term investment position, and with it, often, the voting rights attached to the stock.

[10] A CFD is an agreement to exchange the difference in value of a particular share or index between the time at which a contract is opened and the time at which it is closed. The contract is effectively renewed at the close of each trading day and rolled forward if desired—a position can be kept open indefinitely, providing there is enough margin in the account to support the position.

[11] Stefan Stern, *Financial Times*, March 28, 2006.

[12] "Road shows"—the term used to describe presentations by companies to investment analysts and investment funds.

"Short-termism"

18.009   "Short-termism" may be defined for the purposes of this chapter as the management of portfolios and the judgment of portfolio performance based on short-term (e.g. quarterly) performance, failing which the appointments of fund managers are at risk of termination; and the perceived consequence, asserted by corporate management, that long-term business investment by the corporate sector is made difficult by the demands of fund managers which are required by the institutions and funds which employ them to produce short-term portfolio performance.

In 2004 the National Association of Pension Funds ("NAPF") and the Investment Management Association ("IMA") surveyed their members to ascertain pension fund practice in relation to mandates, and the views of pension funds and fund managers on short-termism.[13] The NAPF's commentary on the results was that they proved that there was no evidence that managers were sacked on the basis of short-term performance. Indeed, this was confirmed by Christine Farnish, chief executive of the NAPF in 2006 when she wrote[14] that:

> "research for the NAPF by MORI shows that 39 per cent of pension funds have retained their manager for more than 10 years. While the trustees will, of course, hold their fund managers accountable for investment performance, nearly all the schemes choose to do this by measuring performance on a rolling basis, year on year or longer. Most pension funds seek to build long term relationships with their investment managers. They should not be accused of short-termism simply because they review fund investment issues every quarter."

However, some of the findings do suggest[15] that pension funds, at the least, give the impression to fund managers that they take short-term performance very seriously. As indicated above by Christine Farnish, the research found that 70 per cent of NAPF members review fund manager performance either quarterly or monthly (although the overwhelming majority of this 70 per cent have reviews on a quarterly basis). Trustees also put performance at the top of the list of issues they monitor fund managers on.

Some of the research carried out in support of the implementation of the Myners Review reinforces the message that there are performance pressures on fund managers coming from their pension funds clients. A Department of Work and Pensions study found that almost of third of schemes gave investment managers 12 months or less to achieve performance targets.

---

[13] *NAPF/IMA Short-termism Study Report*, September 2004.
[14] Letter to *Financial Times*, April 5, 2006.
[15] TUC report: "*Investment Chains*": see fn 8 above.

Shortest time-scale set for investment managers to achieve performance targets when appointment contract(s) were issued

Shortest time-scale	All	Small schemes	Large schemes	
12 months or less	29	32	20	**18.010**
13–24 months	8	9	6	
3 years	37	29	58	
4 years or more	3	4	0	
Don't know	23	25	15	

Source: The Myners Principles and occupational pension schemes, Volume 2 of 2, DWP Research Report 213, p.114, 2004.

Perceptions of the potential for short-termism resulting from such arrangements were significantly different between pension funds and their appointed fund managers. In the NAPF/IMA study[16] most NAPF members disagreed with the assertion that the way mandates were structured promoted an unduly short-termist approach. In contrast most IMA members agreed with the statement.

This suggests that whilst fund managers' clients may not believe that they are exerting short-term pressure, the signals they send through regular reviews of performance and the primary importance of performance in such reviews are significant:

"If one adds to this the reality that the most common reason for the termination of a mandate is poor performance then it is easy to appreciate the views expressed by fund managers. Trustees may be sending far stronger short-term signals than they realise."[17]

Conclusion

There is some persuasive evidence, despite denials, that "activism" may **18.011** to some extent be born out of an atmosphere of short-termism in terms of performance imperatives imposed on fund managers by their institutional clients, which may have the unintended consequence of short-term investment planning by the managers of investee companies.[18]

[16] *NAPF/IMA Short-termism Study Report*, September 2004.
[17] TUC report: "*Investment chains*": see fn 8 above.
[18] See also para.18.027 below for an analysis of research into the share price effects of Hermes activism carried out by Becht and others.

Voting power—the duty to vote or publicly "withhold" a vote

18.012   The point has been made earlier in this chapter that institutional investment comprises by far the greater proportion of the long-term investment funding in the UK and that pension funds, in particular, are trustees for the fund beneficiaries and therefore have a fiduciary duty to invest in an appropriate manner. It is argued that these fiduciary duties go further and require the fund to regard the votes that arise from the investment holding as an asset of the trust that must be utilised in a manner to enhance the overall management and value of that asset.

The UK Corporate Governance Code[19] makes it clear that institutional shareholders have a responsibility to vote. Most institutions have developed "voting policies" on issues such as remuneration of directors, director appointments, social responsibility and pre-emption rights, in accordance with which their fund managers are required to comply, and many of the fund managers also have "voting policies", for example, Henderson Fund Management and PIRC. Hermes Investment Management, which manages the Royal Mail pension fund and the BT pension fund votes in accordance with the Hermes Corporate Governance Principles.[20]

The "vote withheld" option

18.013   In January 2004 Mr Paul Myners produced a report for the Shareholding Voting Working Group on the impediments to voting UK shares. In that report he recommended that companies should include a "vote withheld" box on proxy voting forms and publish the total number of votes withheld as well as votes for and against when declaring the results, and that the FRC should review Provision D.2.1 of the Code in the light of this recommendation. It was argued that the facility to indicate a conscious withholding of votes was a valuable mechanism enabling shareholders to communicate reservations about a particular resolution whilst not going as far as voting against the resolution.

In the same report, Paul Myners stated that where a shareholder decides to withhold their vote. "It is essential that the reasons for the decision are clearly explained to the company if the full impact of the decision is to be apparent". This is consistent with the guidance to investors in the Institutional Shareholders Committee's Statement of Principles.[21] Indeed, the FRC in

---

[19] See the first paragraph in the Guidance to Principle 6 of the 2010 UK Stewardship Code: "Institutional investors should seek to vote all shares held. They should not automatically support the board". *http://www.frc.org*>UK Stewardship Code.

[20] See the corporate governance section of the Hermes website: *http://www.hermes.co.uk*.

[21] *http://www.ivis.co.uk*.

its consultation exercise in January 2006 on proposed changes to the then Combined Code stated that it would "encourage investors to advise the company in advance of their intention to withhold their vote and to explain the reasons for doing so".[22]

The report also recommended that "companies should disclose on their websites and in summary in annual reports, the results of polls at general meetings and, where a poll is not called, the level of proxies lodged on each resolution".[23]

These recommendations were implemented by amendments by the FRC to the then Combined Code and are now largely repeated in the 2010 UK Corporate Governance Code and the relevant Provisions E.2.1 and E.2.2 of the UK Corporate Governance Code now read as follows:

"E.2.1 At any general meeting, the company should propose a separate resolution on each substantially separate issue, and should in particular propose a resolution at the AGM relating to the report and accounts. For each resolution, proxy appointment forms should provide shareholders with the option to direct their proxy to vote either for or against the resolution or to withhold their vote. The proxy form and any announcement of the results of a vote should make it clear that a 'vote withheld' is not a vote in law and will not be counted in the calculation of the proportion of the votes for and against the resolution.

E.2.2. The company should ensure that all valid proxy appointments received for general meetings are properly recorded and counted. For each resolution, after a vote has been taken on a show of hands, the company should ensure that the following information is given at the meeting and made available as soon as reasonably practicable on a website which is maintained by or on behalf of the company:

- the number of shares in respect of which proxy appointments have been validly made;
- the number of votes for the resolution;
- the number of votes against the resolution; and
- the number of shares in respect of which the vote was directed to be withheld.

---

[22] It should be emphasised that the provision of a "vote withheld" option will not affect the current legal position where only "for" and "against" votes are taken into account when deciding whether or not a resolution is carried.
[23] Where a poll *is* called the result must be shown on the company website under CA 2006 s.324.

The banking crisis 2007/2009—political pressure to "behave like owners": the development of a co-ordinated institutional policy on intervention by institutions

18.014 The banking crisis of 2007/2009 provoked a storm of outrage not only against the boards of banks but also against the lack of engagement by institutional investors in the banks, especially on the issue of bonuses and other financial rewards for bankers at all levels from the board downwards. The institutions were accused of abrogating their responsibilities as owners.

In a major article published in the *Financial Times* on October 11, 2009 the Treasury Minister Lord Myners reflected the mood of the time and drew together a number of grievances against the share-owning community.

> "Property rights are supposed to be at the centre of capitalist economies. Ownership encourages responsibility and initiative. But many of the most important capitalist entities, listed corporations, are bordering on the ownerless.
>
> Of course, companies have legal owners: shareholders, whose interests are represented by boards of directors. But in practice, shareholders do not act like owners in terms of exercising control consistent with the maximum long-term benefit of companies.
>
> Ownership has become divorced from control. The problems this generates have been realised since Adam Smith wrote in 1776: 'Directors ... being the managers rather of other peoples' money than of their own, it cannot well be expected that they would watch over it with the same anxious vigilance.'
>
> Another barrier to responsible ownership is that active governance takes time, effort and expertise. It is a public good—if one investor expends the time to act as a responsible owner, all investors benefit. It is too easy for other investors to free-ride on the efforts of the few. This is why I strongly support the announcement from the Financial Services Authority that collective action by shareholders will not be considered market abuse.
>
> Active, responsible ownership requires investors to demand that fund managers make use of the levers available to them and do more to engage with companies. Investors must demand that fund managers develop the skills needed to engage as owners and improve companies.
>
> It is vital to the economy that corporations generate long-term value. To achieve it, we need a new enlightenment in governance. Investors must now rise to this challenge and take up the mantle of responsible ownership."

Lord Myners has also advocated that it is vital to think of radical ways of encouraging investment institutions—who manage money on behalf of pensioners, savers and insurance policyholders—to engage with boards, vanquishing what he called "the ownerless corporation".

He told the BBC:

"We need to look at ways in which we can offer a carrot to some financial institutions to take the issue of ownership more seriously ... things like differential voting rights.

In many cases hedge funds might only be shareholder for a few weeks. Should they be treated in the same way as a long-term shareholder or should we be doing more to reward and engage the long-term shareholder?"[24]

ISC Code 2009, the Walker Review 2009 and the UK Stewardship Code of 2010

ISC Code[25]

A committee comprising representatives from the major institutional investors in the UK and called the Institutional Shareholders' Committee ("ISC")[26] responded in November 2009 to the concerns expressed by Lord Myners and others with a new "code on the conduct of institutional investors"[27] which set out seven principles of best practice for investors on how to engage with the companies to hold boards to account. It also encouraged investors to collaborate.

18.015

The new structure was hoped to result in a standing committee of influential investors whose tasks might include monitoring adherence to the code and facilitating shareholder collaboration.

The ISC also sought international support, from pension funds and sovereign wealth funds. A spokesman said at the time of publication of the code: "We need the presence of senior people in the market who will stand behind the code and give it clout".

The ISC proposed that the voluntary code be on a "comply or explain" basis.

In the form current in May 2010, the code required institutional investors to commit to the following general propositions:

- publicly disclose their policies on how they will discharge stewardship responsibilities (e.g. how they will monitor companies; how monitoring affects investment decisions);

---

[24] *Financial Times* August 3, 2009.
[25] *http://institutionalshareholderscommittee.org.uk.*
[26] ISC members are: the Association of British Insurers; the Association of Investment Trust Companies; the National Association of Pension Funds; and the Investment Management Association.
[27] See *http://www.institutionalshareholderscommittee.org.uk.*

- actively monitor investee companies;

- establish guidelines regarding when they will actively intervene with the company to "protect and enhance" shareholder value. This concept envisions both private discussions but, if necessary, escalating public actions from statements to resolutions to requests for board changes;

- act collectively with other investors where appropriate (and disclose policy on when such collective action is warranted);

- report periodically on their stewardship and voting activities.

The stated purpose of the code was to "enhance the quality of the dialogue" with companies, "reduce the risk of catastrophic outcomes", and aid "efficient exercise of governance responsibilities". Although the code set out a "best practice" for investors that choose to engage with investee companies, the ISC made clear: it "does not constitute an obligation to micro-manage . . . or preclude a decision to sell a holding where this is considered the most effective response to concerns".

However, as described below the ISC Code was subsumed into the UK "Stewardship Code", proposed by Sir David Walker in his bank governance review in 2009 and published by the FRC in July 2010.

The Walker Review and the Stewardship Code[28]

18.016   The final report of the Walker Review recommended that institutional investors should abide by a new Stewardship Code, developed from the principles outlined in the previous paragraph as set out by the ISC.

The review noted that while recommendations relating to engagement by institutional investors and fund managers was prepared "with particular regard to shareholdings in banks and other financial institutions (BOFIs)", they also have wider relevance for holdings in other UK companies.

The UK Stewardship Code—which addresses arrangements for managing conflicts of interest, monitoring and reporting on the monitoring of investee companies, intervention strategies and voting policies—was drafted by the FRC and sits alongside the UK Corporate Governance Code in substitution for what was originally Section D of the Combined Code (Relations with shareholders) and as at June 2010 was Schedule C of the UK Corporate Governance Code (Engagement Principles for Institutional Shareholders).

Following consultation the Stewardship Code was published by the FRC

---

[28] *A review of corporate governance in UK banks and other financial industry entities*, November 26, 2009, chaired by Sir Peter Walker, and the *UK Stewardship Code, http://www.frc.org.uk*.

in July 2010[29] and Schedule C of the UK Corporate Governance Code therefore ceased to apply.

In addition, the Financial Services Authority ("FSA") has said it intends to consult on a "requirement for relevant authorised firms who manage assets on behalf of others to disclose on a 'comply or explain' basis the nature of their commitment to the Stewardship Code".

The Walker Review noted a common problem for long-only shareholders and the boards of their investee companies is that historically:

> "close engagement has often begun only in event-driven problem situations where specific differences of view may be pronounced and which have tended to focus in particular on remuneration rather than wider strategic issues."[30]

The report admitted the recommendations are "UK-centric"[31] in the sense that they relate to the FRC, the FSA and UK-domiciled fund management entities authorised by the FSA. However, it noted that because there is substantial investment in BOFIs from sovereign wealth funds, non-UK pension and endowment funds and non-UK fund managers, these investors should be encouraged to participate in the code voluntarily. The review argued that "this is likely to be in their own interest and in that of their clients as ultimate beneficiaries".

The report also stated[32]:

> "Interest in promoting greater fund manager and investor attentiveness to longer-time scales in portfolio management decisions is most unlikely to be confined to the UK and, hopefully, the enhanced arrangements put in place in this country will come to be seen to have wider relevance internationally, particularly given the continued cross-border diversification of the portfolios of major investors."

The Institutional Investors Council

The Institutional Investor Council ("IIC") was launched in May 2010 under **18.017** the auspices of the ISC, which claimed that the IIC would look into day-to-day issues and government policies affecting the institutional investor sector.

"When there is a profound disagreement between shareholders and board and it is quite clear we are heading for a 'no' vote, this body will provide

---

[29] See *http://www.frc.org.uk*>UK Stewardship Code.
[30] para.5.20.
[31] para.5.41.
[32] para.5.41.

a means by which senior people in the funds industry. . . can find a way forward," said Keith Skeoch, chief executive of Standard Life Investments and acting head of the new body when the body was launched.

"What we are trying to do is when we have a difficult issue to put more power behind the elbow for those responsible for day-to-day engagement," he said, citing remuneration, capital raising, strategy and succession as key issues.

"Sometimes, it's very important for a company to know that the investment community is very joined up and feels strongly about these issues," Skeoch said.

One of the first tasks of the IIC will be to examine the underwriting fees paid to investment banks on rights issues.

The ISC said at the time of launch of the IIC that it would be working on formalising a constitution for the new council which will involve the creation of a nominations committee, representative membership and election of a chair.

It is not at all clear as at the date of publication of this book where the responsibilities of the ISC end and the IIC begin and which body will drive the engagement agenda and in particular the Stewardship Code.

Principal aspects of the UK Stewardship Code

18.018
- the Stewardship Code is published and will be monitored and reviewed from time to time by the FRC[33];

- it is addressed "in the first instance" to firms who manage assets on behalf of institutional shareholders such as pension funds, insurance companies, investment trusts and other collective investment vehicles;

- institutions are free to choose whether or not to adopt the Code, but if they do then the FRC expects those firms to disclose on their websites how they have applied the Code. The FRC will keep a list of institutions which have adopted the Code;

- the Code comprises seven Principles (largely repeating the ISC principles referred to in para.18.015 above) each one of which is supplemented by "Guidance" notes;

- the seven Principles require institutional investors to:
  - publicly disclose their policy on how they will discharge their stewardship responsibilities;
  - have a robust policy on managing conflicts of interest in relation to stewardship and this policy should be publicly disclosed;
  - monitor their investee companies;

---

[33] See *http://www.frc.org.uk*.

- establish clear guidelines on when and how they will escalate their activities as a method of protecting and enhancing shareholder value;
- be willing to act collectively with other investors where appropriate;
- have a clear policy on voting and disclosure of voting activity;
- report periodically on their stewardship and voting activities;

- the FRC will work with the newly established, but as at the date of writing this book unconstituted, IIC to promote the Code, and the IMA will[34] continue to publish its annual survey of compliance by investment managers but in relation to the UK Stewardship Code;

- the first review of the Code is not expected until the second half of 2011 since the FRC rightly takes the view that there are a number of unanswered questions as to how the Code will be taken up by UK and overseas investors and time is needed to assess the situation.

ABI "red top alerts"

The Association of British Insurers ("ABI") whose members control approximately £1,140 billion of investments amounting to 20 per cent of the UK equity market[35] issues so-called "red top alerts" to its members if it has "serious unmet concerns" about the corporate governance of a company—lesser concerns attract "amber alerts". Its voting service is called IVIS[36] and the purpose of issuing alerts is to encourage members either to take direct vote action or to appoint IVIS to vote on their behalf. The alerts also, of course, are a signal to the board of the company concerned that it needs to consider seriously the concern and respond accordingly.   **18.019**

Examples[37] of relatively recent "red top alerts" are:

Company	Event
Berkeley Homes 2005	Executive remuneration scheme. Approved after talks with board.
Reckitt Benckiser 2005	Share scheme which would have diluted equity by more than 10 per cent. Scheme withdrawn.

[34] *http://www.investmentuk.org.*
[35] NAPF members controls approximately £600 billion of funds and PIRC manages funds worth approximately £500 billion.
[36] The NAPF's is called "Rrev".
[37] Notoriously, Collier Stewart Tullitt Plc were about to adopt a pay scheme for the CEO, Mr Terry Smith, despite falling profits. The scheme was voted down by members but not before Mr Smith had reportedly expressed the view that "the ABI is as thick as s*** and should f*** themselves".

Institutional voting policies—specific examples

18.020   A significant number of fund management companies and other institutional shareholders now publish their voting guidelines on their respective websites. This is in accordance with the Pensions Act 1995 as amended in July 2000, the spirit of what is now the UK Stewardship Code, and the general policy of the ISC that companies should be able to understand the background upon which investors are deciding how to vote. What follows is a small sample of voting policies by way of examples.

West Midlands Metropolitan Authorities' Pension Fund Company Voting Guidelines 2004

18.021   The WMMA Pension Fund is one of the largest metropolitan pension funds in the UK and its policy is therefore of interest. In the introduction to its voting guidelines, it makes it clear that it is in no doubt that active interest in senior management brings a recognisable financial benefit:

> "it has a legitimate interest in the senior management arrangements for a company in which it invests and through its voting policy can seek to add value to its investments together with improving the behaviour of the corporate world in terms of business, social and environmental ethics. It generally recognises that some basic features can be identified for the structure and running of a company at a senior level that should create a setting for a company to succeed in its business and in which shareholders have a duty to take an interest."

It also points out that "proxy voting is a key to maintaining effective shareholder oversight of directors and company policies, a process on which the current system of UK corporate governance depends".

It points out that in the amendment to the Pensions Act, effective in July 2000, pension funds are required to disclose "their policy (if any) in relation to the exercise of the rights (including voting rights) attaching to investments". The introduction to the voting policy document also makes it clear that the fund expects companies to make a commitment to achieving environmental excellence.

Under the heading "voting guidelines" the fund makes it clear that it will vote for or oppose a resolution on the following basis:

> *For:* Where the proposal is judged to be in the fund's interests and meets best practice guidelines.
> *Opposed:* Where the proposal:

(a) is judged not to be in the interests of the fund; or
(b) the directors have failed to provide sufficient information to support the proposal; or
(c) is significantly short of best practice.

It explains that the fund will not normally abstain but may do so if the proposal raises issues which do not meet best practice guidelines but either the concern is not regarded as sufficient material to warrant opposition, or an "oppose" vote could have a detrimental impact on corporate structures.

The policy guidelines then set out in a number of headings the expectations of the fund in relation to specific issues, for example:

The report and accounts: The guidelines state that the fund will oppose the report and accounts if there are serious breaches of corporate governance or the accounts have been qualified, or, for example, where there have been party political donations.

Dividend policy: The fund makes it clear that it will vote for a proposed dividend which is adequately covered by earnings or is otherwise justified in the long-term interests of the company, but in a somewhat ambiguous statement it points out that information on dividend policy "in relation to consumer, community or employee benefits is important in assessing whether the company has discharged its responsibilities to all stakeholders in order to maintain long-term relationships".

The directors: There are no surprises in this section of the voting policy but it is comprehensive and covers some six pages. The voting policy makes it clear that it will vote against a proposal in relation to directors which is, in effect, less rigorous than the revised UK Corporate Governance Code. The definition of "independence" in relation to non-executive directors is, however, wider than that contained in the revised UK Corporate Governance Code. In relation to executive directors' contracts it makes the point that it expects terms to not exceed one year, and endorses the principle of "mitigation and the phased payment of compensation". In any event contracts should not pay for liquidated damages in excess of one year. The provisions relating to directors' remuneration covers some four pages and in general have nothing which is out of line with the approach adopted by the UK Corporate Governance Code and the ABI Guidelines of executive remuneration.

Auditors: The fund requires a rotation of audit firms "at least every five years". This is beyond the recommendations of the Smith Report (January 2003), which simply recommended that the lead audit partner should be rotated every three years. The fund says that it might oppose the appointment of auditors "if there are concerns over the status and role of the audit committee or failure to disclose fully all non-audit fees paid in the audit fee".

Shareholders resolutions:

"are an integral part of the corporate governance process. They enable shareholders to take the initiative on issues which directors may be unwilling to address or where directors may face a conflict of interest . . . Shareholders' resolutions are not seen as a no-confidence vote on the board (unless that is specified) but should be judged on the merits of the specific issue addressed. Resolutions will be supported that are evaluated as being in the medium to long-term interests of the fund".

CIS

18.022 CIS is the business name for the Cooperative Insurance Society ("CIS"). CIS does not appear to publish its voting policy, although it has published on its website its detailed and impressive ethical investment policy, but instead it keeps a record of votes cast at all annual and extraordinary general meetings of the UK companies in which it invests. That record is available on its website.[38] It is of interest in showing in relation to the companies listed how it has voted, and the reasons for voting against or abstaining from certain resolutions.

For example, in relation to Matalan Plc it records that on June 4, 2003 at the annual general meeting ("AGM") it voted against the reappointment of a director giving as its reason:

"Given the concerns regarding contract and compensation arrangements outlined in Resolution 8, it is appropriate to vote against the senior independent director and member of the remuneration committee."

Resolution 8 was to approve the board report on directors' remuneration, and CIS cast its vote against that resolution giving as its reason:

"The company has experienced a rapid changeover in executive directors. There is no evidence of mitigation having been applied to severance payments, in spite of the companies' reference to a duty of mitigation in the remuneration report. Executive share options were issued with a performance condition of only one year, which does nothing to align directors' interest with the interests of long-term shareholders. There are no maximum awards disclosed for the Key Management Scheme and the Share Incentive Scheme."

In September 2005 in relation to the AGM resolutions proposed by Berkeley Group Holdings Plc. CIS cast its vote against the standard resolution to

[38] *http://www.cis.co.uk.*

disapply pre-emption rights in relation to the company's long-term incentive plan and also the resolution to approve the directors' remuneration report on the grounds that:

> "the following areas are of concern: the vesting of share options without reference to the satisfaction of performance conditions; the open ended nature of the long term incentive plan, and the fact that shareholders are unable to charge the stringency of the threshold of performance targets; and the potential for excessive remuneration."

In March 2006 CIS voted against the Chemring Group Plc annual report and accounts on the following grounds:

> "CIS takes account of a company's disclosure in its report and accounts of significant social, ethical and environmental risks and opportunities, according to the ABI Disclosure Guidelines. In this case, the company's reporting has been assessed by the ABI and found to be limited. Given the level of exposure to SEE[39] risks in the sector in which this company operates, CIS considered it appropriate to abstain on receiving the report and accounts in 2005. As no progress appears to have been made, CIS intends to vote against this resolution in 2006."

Keeping the score—disclosure of voting by institutions

Increasingly research is being done and publicised which draws attention to the voting record of the institutions.   **18.023**

NAPF/ISS

In May 2003 the NAPF announced that it was forming a new UK company,   **18.024**
Rrev (Research, Recommendations and Electronic Voting), formed jointly and owned equally by the NAPF and the American proxy voting and corporate governance service organisation called Institutional Shareholder Services ("ISS"). This was a significant development and has enabled UK investors to access corporate governance analysis and electronic voting capability on a significantly wider range of companies both in the UK and in some other 80 countries. The service includes:

(a)   corporate governance analysis and recommendations based on NAPF policy, extended to all FTSE all-share companies;

---

[39] Social, Environmental and Ethical—see further Ch.20 (Corporate Social Responsibility).

(b) global access to analyses of, and voting recommendations on, some 22,000 companies both in the UK the Continent and US;

(c) electronic voting capability;

(d) access to corporate governance policy and research services offered by the NAPF and ISS.

At the time of the launch of the new venture, the chief executive of NAPF, Christine Farnish, said:

"There has been a noticeable and welcome upswing in shareholder activism in recent months. Today's announcement highlights the NAPF's determination to build on its position at the cutting edge of corporate governance debate, and to deliver enhanced governance services both to shareholders and to the companies in which they invest."

The Georgeson Shareholder and Hermes Investment Management Voting Policy Survey

18.025 In September 2003 it was announced that Georgeson Shareholder and Hermes had commissioned Lintstock, the London-based corporate advisory consultancy which provides independent corporate governance advice, to make a study of the UK's leading investment institutions by voting policies. The principal findings of the study revealed that:

(a) In their corporate governance policies, three-quarters of the institutions surveyed support the principle that a senior independent director should be appointed irrespective of whether the roles of chairman and CEO are combined. However, less than a quarter of these institutions state their view on the equally controversial question of whether CEOs should be allowed to succeed to the chairmanship of the companies from which they retire.

(b) On the topic of "rewards for failure", the institutions showed a uniform opposition to directors' contracts which allow for notice periods in excess of one year. However, it was said by the survey that the policies also point to a growing divergence of opinion as to whether the compensation paid to departing directors should be based on a pre-determined formula rather than a negotiated process.

(c) Most of the institutions subscribed to the view that listed companies should make annual disclosure of their performance on social, ethical and environmental matters and a small number had also been keen to recommend the Sustainability Reporting Guidelines developed by the Global Reporting Initiative.

TUC

The TUC Fund Manager Survey[40] provides pension fund trustees with **18.026** information about how managers are addressing governance issues at the companies they invest in. The survey claims to be the only resource for trustees which details comparative records of investor engagement because fund managers do not have to disclose publicly how they exercise their voting rights on behalf of pension funds.

Twenty two fund managers responded voluntarily to the 2009 Fund Manager Voting Survey.

In the introduction to the 2009 survey it was stated:

"There is a clear divide amongst investors in their willingness to challenge management. At one end of the spectrum, eight respondents supported over 90 per cent of management proposals on which voting decisions were sought. At the other end six respondents supported less than 50 per cent of management proposals.

Almost three quarters (16 out of 22) of survey respondents now make at least some voting data publicly available. Managers which do not disclose do not appear to given a public explanation of their policy on this matter.

Investors say that remuneration is the issue over which it is most likely that they will oppose management. This is confirmed in the voting data supplied to the survey.

Respondents do not appear to have had a particular issue with remuneration arrangements at UK banks, as votes on the banks' remuneration reports are not out of line with those at other companies. Only a single investor in the sample—Co-operative Insurance Society—opposed the RBS acquisition of ABN Amro. All other respondents voted in favour."

Does activism "work"?

Many commentators have been sceptical about the value of shareholder **18.027** activism, believing it to be disruptive and short-termist. Evidence about its effectiveness has been inconclusive or found activism to generate no net-returns, in particular pension fund activism in the United States. Observers have pointed to the US legal and institutional environment as a possible explanation for the missing link, but have also argued that the UK provides the ideal setting for shareholder activism to work, given the legal and cultural environment, making the UK an ideal "laboratory" for activism research.[41]

On February 9, 2006 the first results of an ongoing independent study

[40] *http://www.tuc.org.uk.*
[41] Karpoff, 2001.

of shareholder activism in the UK found some evidence that activism can produce outcomes that generate significant returns for shareholders. The work was co-authored by Professor Marco Becht, ECARES, Université Libre de Bruxelles; Professor Julian Franks, Centre for Corporate Governance, London Business School; Professor Colin Mayer, Said Business School; and Professor Stefano Rossi, Stockholm School of Economics. The results of the study were presented at a conference at the London Business School on February 9 that was organised jointly by the London Business School Centre for Corporate Governance, the ECGI and the Journal of Applied Corporate Finance.[42]

The team focused on the Hermes UK Focus Fund ("the Fund"), which invests in companies that are fundamentally sound but whose shares have underperformed the market as a result of strategic, governance or financial structuring weaknesses and where Hermes believes shareholder involvement can be the catalyst for change and result in improved performance.

On a confidential basis the team was given access to Hermes' own records including letters, memos, minutes, presentations, transcripts/recordings of telephone conversations, client reports and staff's personal notes and recollections. The Fund in the study was invested in 41 stocks with an average holding period of 691 days (785 for 30 closed positions and 11 stocks still held). The stakes held by all Hermes funds ranged from one to 15 per cent.

The team found that the Fund had engaged with 30 of the stocks held, had decided not to engage with eight (in some cases because change was brought about by means outside Hermes influence) and had yet to engage with three of the stocks. Of the 30 stocks engaged with, the engagement was characterised as collaborative in 10 cases, confrontational in 10, very confrontational in two, and mixed in the remainder of cases. The average holding periods in the stocks where there was engagement, and in particular, where that engagement was confrontational, were the longest of all stocks held (894 days and 1,063 days respectively).

The objectives of the engagement fell broadly under three headings, namely: restructuring, financial policies and board changes. Engagement with the companies was conducted most frequently by behind the scenes methods of contact with the management and the board and contact with other shareholders, and far less often at public shareholder meetings or through other public channels.

The Fund succeeded in securing its desired outcomes in the majority of cases. For example, board changes at the top (chairman and chief executive) followed the Fund intervention as well as changes in cash payouts, rights issue plans and capital expenditure plans. The Fund was perhaps less successful in influencing restructuring where more focus on the core business was achieved in just over half the stocks.

---

[42] See the *Journal of Applied Corporate Finance* [summer edition] 2006.

The study will go on to examine the performance of stocks held around the time of public announcements of events, such as restructuring, board changes and payout announcements, both in the run up to the event and in its aftermath. On average there was a significant increase in the performance by the stocks in question around the event and contributed significantly to the Fund's overall performance.

Conclusion

This research, while interesting, does not in itself validate activism unless the only test of validity is a share-value enhancing "event": a more convincing outcome of activism would surely be an all round and sustained improvement over a period of time not only in share price but also in a number of other key performance indicators.

18.028

The future role of the private investor as activist arising from the Companies Act 2006—early signs of indifference

This chapter would not be complete without referring to some interesting legislation, the clauses for which were inserted at a relatively late stage into the Companies Bill in July 2006, after a rather remarkable campaign by the Shareholders Alliance. The clauses are now reflected in CA 2006 Pt 9 ss.145 to 153.

18.029

In terms, the clauses are concerned with the situation where shares are registered in the name of a nominee. The clauses give rights to the beneficial owner of the shares, once nominated for that purpose by the nominee, as if the beneficial owner were him or herself the registered member. However, the articles of association of a company need to contain a provision enabling a member to nominate another person as entitled to enjoy or exercise all or any specified rights of a member in relation to the company.

If the articles of association do so permit, then in effect the beneficial owner will have the same rights to vote, speak at, appoint proxies, receive information, receive the annual report and accounts, circulate shareholder resolutions and have all other rights as if (s)he were a registered member.

The implications of these provisions may over time be immense but it has to be said that as at 2009 registrars reported (anecdotally) a total indifference to the new rights.

Approximately half of those shareholdings in the UK which are held by private individuals are held through nominees such as ISAs or PEPs or trusts. If a significant number of these individuals start to exert their rights under the CA 2006 the result could be a powerful extension of activism. However, early signs are not encouraging.

Some conclusions on the role of activism

18.030   Although the evidence of any causal link between activism and share price is still unconvincing despite the interesting results of the research described in para.18.027, and there is the danger that an unintended consequence of activism is short-term decision-making by management, it seems clear that institutions believe that activism adds value to their funds under management, and also that activism has in recent years had an impact on boards of directors as the small sample of examples given in para.18.005 shows.

    Certainly at a political level there is great pressure on institutions to "act like owners" and the production in July 2010 by the FRC of the UK Stewardship Code was a rapid response to that pressure.

    Most of the publicity surrounding activism in recent times has related to executive pay, and especially the bonus culture of the banks, where it has been said that the institutions failed dismally in their role to impose controls. As the case study described in Pt 2 of this chapter shows, a great deal of activism is pursued quietly by institutions in one on one discussions with chairmen and CEOs. The then deputy chief executive of Hermes, Mr Charlie Metcalfe, was quoted in the *Financial Times* (March 2006) as saying: "Speak softly and carry a big stick is our way".

    However, the UK Stewardship Code with its emphasis on publicly reporting engagement by institutions may well have changed that approach for ever.

Institutional Shareholder Activism—Part 2

Paul Lee[1]

The Hermes approach and a case study

A couple of years ago I was faced with the ever-difficult task of explaining **18.031** my job at a drinks party. After some moments of attempted explanation, my listener suddenly said, as if she had at that moment seen through my confusing words: "Oh, so you don't invest in shares like others, you invest in companies". While she was betraying an unhappy ignorance of what shares are, there was a good deal of truth in the comment. Hermes regards equity investment on our clients' behalf as long-term ownership of companies rather than short-term trading in shares.

Being a long-term owner of a company brings with it responsibilities as well as the privileges of a share in the financial outcomes. For example, a good long-term owner will pay attention to its investee companies, keep track of developments, stay in touch with directors, and intervene where that is called for. This is not an altruistic activity: just as everyone would rather be the tenant of a property that its owner pays attention to and cares for, so a company which enjoys the benefit of involved and engaged long-term owners will in the long run be worth more than one without. In contrast, too many investment institutions act as then minister Lord Myners repeatedly complained, as "absentee landlords".

Shareholder engagement means different things to different people. Even the guidelines on the Responsibilities of Institutional Investors created by the Institutional Shareholders Committee ("ISC")—most recently updated in 2009 and at the time of writing in 2010 the subject of a consultation by the Financial Reporting Council ("FRC") with a view to it endorsing it as a "Stewardship Code" for investment institutions—seems to be subject to a range of different interpretations. Indeed, some have suggested that some of

---

[1] See Ch.21 (Pension Funds) for the profile of Paul Lee.

its language does seem almost deliberately open to varied interpretations. For example, some institutions believe the ISC paper extends only to requiring active and intelligent voting. We are hopeful that the FRC's consultation will lead to less scope for misinterpretation of the Code, but this ambiguity is one of the reasons we at Hermes favour more explicit statements on the duties of institutions to intervene at investee companies such as that produced by the International Corporate Governance Network ("ICGN") in its "Statement on Institutional Shareholder Responsibilities", which were updated in 2006.

Just as the Erisa law in the US made plain with regards to voting—that votes are an asset belonging to beneficiaries just like any other, and institutions need to fulfil their fiduciary duty to maximise the value of that asset—the ICGN Statement makes clear that all other legal and cultural rights attaching to the ownership of shares are client assets and their value must also be maximised by fiduciaries. Thus, where they can enhance or preserve the value of investee companies by intervention, institutional investors should do so.

As the ICGN does, Hermes sees intervention as an escalating continuum from simply exercising voting rights at general meetings, through discussions with the board on governance and/or strategic matters, and on perhaps to requisitioning EGM or AGM resolutions, and even beyond. In most cases we will engage only having tested our thinking with other investors, to ensure we are acting to the benefit of all, and where possible we seek explicitly to work with others to encourage change more effectively. The UK Takeover Code is clear that shareholders are free to work together in this way provided their intentions fall short of replacing significant portions of the board. We are encouraging the regulators in other markets to offer investors similar clarity.

The ICGN's discursive list of the responsibilities of a long-term owner may be abbreviated to:

- encouraging investee companies to pursue high standards of corporate governance;
- incorporating corporate governance considerations in the investment process;
- exercising ownership rights in a way that is tailored to the specific circumstances of the individual investee company;
- developing a constructive dialogue to increase mutual understanding rather than seeking to interfere in day-to-day management;
- exercising ownership rights responsibly, including by developing consistent corporate governance policies which are communicated to investee companies, fully participating as owners in governance processes and considered voting;
- engagement with investee companies that goes beyond voting and encompasses active dialogue with boards on governance and other matters; and

- developing an approach to escalating engagement through, potentially: expressing concern in private or at an AGM or EGM; making a public statement; submitting shareholder resolutions; nominating directors to the board; calling an EGM; and (though this appears to be frowned on) using legal actions.

At the vast majority of companies, this engagement (we far prefer the term to the often misunderstood, more aggressive-sounding "activism") need go no further than voting, and the communications with the company which always accompany it. But at a minority of companies, we believe that further engagement with the board members can assist them to reach decisions which move the company on to the benefit of all shareholders.

We believe that it is wholly inappropriate for investors to intervene at companies to the extent of micromanagement. And there are other ways in which the activities of some investors might be inappropriate. The ICGN Statement notes that government-sponsored institutional investors need to take care not to be an arm of government policy-making, but must instead focus only on activities which are in the interests of their fiduciaries. The pension funds of unions and other organisations with a campaigning aspect need to apply a similar caution (not least in a UK context, in the light of the famous *Cowan v Scargill* case—though in our view that case should not be read too broadly).

We at Hermes have identified a number of areas which fall far short of such micromanagement where it is wholly appropriate for shareowners to seek to have their input into company decision-making processes. Indeed, not only is it appropriate, we find that by having such input we help the companies become stronger and more highly valued by the stock market. These are high-level issues of major significance to current performance and future success.

We will thus engage with companies on the following high-level issues:

(a)   communications and disclosure;

(b)   strategy;

(c)   capital structure and investment;

(d)   board and sub-committee structures;

(e)   remuneration structures;

(f)   risk management and social, environmental and ethical ("SEE") concerns.

Our views on these issues have been clearly set out in the "Hermes Responsible Ownership Principles", a document first created in 2002 and most recently updated in 2010.

Often, we find that our engagements are most successful and add most value when we are discussing a combination of these issues with companies. Perhaps this is not surprising, given that companies which are in need of assistance in order better to manage more than one of these areas are likely to have greatest scope for transformation.

Theory into practice—a case study

18.032   A good example of a company where we engaged across the full range of these issues was Premier Oil. By 2000, this company had become a cause celebre amongst those concerned with governance and more particularly with the social, ethical and environmental responsibilities of business. Its share price was languishing, and it appeared unable to deliver on its stated strategy. Working with the company, with other shareholders, and with NGOs, Hermes helped the company to resolve these issues.

Hermes accelerated its engagement with Premier Oil in mid-2000. For several years previously Hermes had communicated its concerns over the company's board structure and had voted against the re-election of several of the non-executive directors whom we did not regard as being independent. On the governance side, the fundamental issue was that the company was dominated by two major shareholders, Amerada Hess, a US company, and Petronas, the Malaysian National Oil Company, each of which held 25 per cent of the shares. Not content with the control and influence they wielded as such major shareholders, each of them also had two non-executive directors on the board. Two further non-executives were also deemed non-independent.

These board problems were reflected in a failure by the company to address some of the severe problems that Premier was facing. The strategy was not clear to us as shareholders: it appeared that the strategy proposed in November 1999 when Petronas invested in the company (and on the basis of which independent shareholders had approved that investment) was not being followed, and it was not apparent to investors that an alternative had been developed. The company was in a strategic hole: it was not large enough to compete in production and downstream work with the emerging super-major oil companies, but it was also not as lightweight and fleet-of-foot as it needed to be if it were to be able fully to exploit the exploration opportunities opened up by the super-majors' focus on larger-scale fields. Its freedom of action was also limited by the company's high level of gearing.

In addition, the company had allowed itself to become exposed to major ethical and reputational risks as a result of being the lead investor in the Yetagun gas field in Myanmar. Myanmar, formerly known as Burma, was a country ruled by a military dictatorship which had refused to accept the results of democratic elections in 1990, where summary arrest, forced labour, and torture were widely reported, and which had therefore become a pariah state. Premier's involvement in the country had brought public criticism of the company from a range of sources including Burmese campaigners, Amnesty International, trade union groups and, not least, the UK Government. It was not clear to us as shareholders that the company was effectively managing the reputational and ethical risks it faced as a result of its involvement in Myanmar.

To begin exploring these concerns, we held a meeting in mid-2000 with Premier's then corporate responsibility director, and the company's then finance director. This was an opportunity for us to understand Premier's considerable positive work on the ground in Myanmar—which included building schools, funding teachers, AIDS education and environmental remediation. While we recognised that positive work, we had continuing concerns. The board had not publicly stated that it believed it was effectively managing all the risks that were associated with its presence in Myanmar, and nor did we have the confidence that the board as currently constituted could give shareholders the reassurance that they needed in that regard.

When we had analysed all these issues, it came as no surprise to us that, in the absence of a clear strategy and with a restrictive capital structure, with the lightning rod of its involvement in Myanmar not clearly being managed and a board which did not seem designed to address these issues in the interests of all shareholders, that Premier's share price had dramatically under-performed the market for several years.

Why we chose Premier Oil

With the combination of these issues, governance, strategic, capital structure, **18.033** ethical and share price under-performance, Premier Oil was a natural choice for our first year's selection of companies for a Core Shareholder Programme ("CSP"). As a fund manager with predominantly index-tracking mandates, Hermes believes it is in our clients' interest to become closely involved with companies where we perceive there to be problems. In a sense, these actions are simply putting into effect the stewardship which our clients, as partial owners, should exercise over investee companies. Hermes has a tradition of intervention at under-performing companies but the 2000 CSP was our first attempt to establish a more formal and structured basis for determining where we should intervene. In the 10 years since that time, this programme has developed into a broader, international programme of engagement and intervention, the central value proposition of our Equity Ownership Service—which now sees us engage globally with around 500 companies a year across a range of critical issues. Those companies where we had consistently voted against re-elections of directors but had not seen any sign of reform, and where share price performance remained poor, formed the basis of the 10 stocks chosen for the first year of the CSP. Premier Oil was among these.

As we did with the other CSP companies, we wrote to the chairman of Premier, requesting a meeting to discuss the full range of our concerns.

While we were awaiting that meeting, Hermes was approached by two separate groups asking it to engage on the SEE issues raised by Premier. The first group was our clients, principally led by trade union pension fund trustees. The second was from other NGOs who were focusing on disinvestment from Myanmar/Burma. It is worth considering Hermes' position relative to these two groups.

As regards the trade unions, Hermes believes it is appropriate that they, as client trustee representatives, should take a keen interest in the stewardship of their investment, including investee companies' response to SEE issues. We were invited by the TUC to address the international body which co-ordinates trade union/shareholder campaigns. At that meeting we explained that Hermes could not support trade union campaigns based on a "special interest". We would however be happy to engage where failure to address SEE issues was as the result of poor governance, and threatened long-term shareholder value. Premier was one such case.

The second group which encouraged us to take action were the NGOs. We were invited to a meeting organised by other fund managers with representatives from the Burma Campaign UK and Amnesty International. Alongside the UK fund managers with strong ethical investment mandates, a US-based investor with a reputation for activism on social, environmental and ethical matters was represented at this meeting.

We were somewhat surprised to find that the purpose of the meeting was to discuss proposing a shareholder resolution criticising Premier for its involvement in Myanmar, something which most at the meeting seemed willing to countenance, despite the fact that they had yet to meet the directors of the company to discuss this proposed plan of action. In any case, Hermes (by reason of our passive, index-tracking mandates) was the only fund manager around the table that held a substantial stake in Premier Oil; indeed, most held no shares at all.

At the meeting we took what we felt was the responsible attitude of a part-owner of the Premier Oil business. We argued against the proposing of any immediate shareholder resolution, pointing out that there were much better ways to raise issues with the board which would not of themselves inspire confrontation. We volunteered to lead the engagement.

The meeting did provide us with the opportunity to make contact with some of the NGOs active in Myanmar and among the Burmese people. Notably, we began regular discussions with the Burma Campaign UK, explaining to them the different courses of action which the company might take. We also continued to hold regular discussions with other interested institutional investors. As part of our due diligence, we also accessed publicly and privately other sources of insight, such as the UK Government, academics, consultants, brokers and journalists. This gave us as rounded a view as possible.

Our engagement

Our meeting with the chairman took place in January 2001, and was a frank **18.034**
and honest one. It was rapidly apparent to us that the chairman understood our concerns. In December, the firm had already added a new, fully
independent non-executive director. The chairman assured us that further
developments on the governance side were in train. We approved of these
developments, but said that we doubted that they would ultimately be
adequate to address concerns. The chairman was also willing to discuss our
strategic and ethical concerns. Importantly, he agreed to our request personally to meet representatives of the Burma Campaign UK.

We followed up this meeting with a detailed and direct letter outlining our
concerns and asking the chairman to begin addressing them in the interests
of all shareholders. The chairman's prompt response assured us that the
board would continue to work for a solution to "enable the true value of
the company to be reflected in the share price". In March 2001, Premier Oil
added another fully independent non-executive.

At the May AGM, the chairman made a very important public statement
with regard to the shareholding structure of the company. It was an acknowledgement that the presence of two 25 per cent shareholders was a burden on
the company's share price—a point we had clearly made in our meeting with
him—and a statement of intent about seeking a resolution to this problem.
He said:

> "We believe that the current share price remains low relative to the under-
> lying value of the business partly as a result of the concentration of share
> ownership. The board is continuing to seek ways to reduce the discount on
> assets for the benefit of all shareholders."

Further positive steps occurred in October 2001. The company began to
clarify its strategic position by selling assets in Indonesia and restructuring its
position in Pakistan, having gained shareholder authority at an EGM.

Throughout this time we were in close contact with pension funds in
the United States who were engaged with Amerada Hess over their shareholding in Premier, and hence their involvement in Myanmar/Burma. We
pointed out to them that Amerada's statements—that its investment in
Premier was somehow ring-fenced from Myanmar and that its directors
did not participate in any discussions on the company's involvement in that
country—appeared to be at odds with our understanding of UK law, and
with statements made at the time of Premier Oil's shareholders' circular at the
time of its re-financing. Separate discussions were thus begun privately with
Amerada to progress these issues.

Over 2001, we worked with other institutional investors on their proposal
for a statement on how our investee companies should deal with any involve-

ment in Myanmar. We argued that this document should follow the language of the guidelines we had developed with other institutional investors, which were later published by the ABI in October 2001. We felt that Myanmar should not be singled out as an issue above all others—while the risks of involvement there are significant, there are other countries and other issues where risks are at a similarly high level—and we were not keen to see companies overburdened with a variety of different disclosure requests on a range of issues. Furthermore, we believed that had we signed up to the sort of document that was being proposed it would have been harder for us to achieve the level of access and open conversations we had achieved at Premier Oil. We therefore dropped out of the discussions on this document. The other institutions persevered and eventually published their statement in December.

Moving matters on

18.035   The first year of our engagement had brought some progress but had failed fully to address Premier's fundamental problems. We met the chairman and the then CEO, in early 2002. This was an impressively frank meeting, where they were willing to be more open with us about the work they had been undertaking to resolve Premier's problems. Over the years since 1999, they had proposed a number of solutions to the company's strategic impasse, but each had been in some way barred by one or other of the major shareholders. They were, however, confident that both shareholders now had a different attitude and that a resolution in the interests of all investors could now be achieved—though it might take a number of months.

Following this meeting we sent the chairman a further forthright letter expressing our concerns at the actions of the major shareholders and putting in writing our offer to lend him our support in the negotiations, should that prove valuable. We formally offered to call on our contacts at global institutions and share with them our concerns that certain of the directors of Premier had not proved themselves to be the friends of minority investors. We hoped that the implication of potential difficulties this might cause for fundraising by companies with which those directors were involved could bolster the chairman's hand in negotiations. We also raised again our concerns that public statements by Amerada seemed to us out of line with UK company law and the fiduciary duties of directors to all their shareholders.

The company's preliminary results announcement on March 13 highlighted the positive progress the business was making operationally, but more importantly it detailed the progress being made in relation to the company's fundamental problems. It made clear the roadmap the company was using to solve its problems, talking about shedding mature assets in return for the exit of the major shareholders, and turning itself into a focused, fleet-of-foot exploration company once again. The statement read:

"We are in specific discussions with our alliance partners on creating a new Premier, better balanced to achieve our objectives. While the restructuring process is complex and involves careful balancing of the interests of all shareholders, we are committed to finding a solution before the end of this year and I am hopeful this will be achieved."

As part of our usual series of financial analysis meetings following preliminary or final announcements, we next met representatives of the company on March 27. This meeting gave us further encouragement that genuine progress was being made, as they suggested to us that the major shareholders both now clearly understood that any deal that they agreed would have to be approved by independent shareholders without them having the right to vote. Therefore, any deal would have to offer minorities full value to be allowed to proceed. The implication that we took away from this meeting was that negotiations were now on track to reach a resolution.

That resolution was announced in September 2002. Premier Oil said that it was to "swap assets for shares", with Petronas taking the Myanmar operation and a share of Premier's Indonesian activities, and Amerada a further segment of the Indonesian interest (in which Premier retained a stake). This was in return for cancelling their 25 per cent shareholdings, and losing their right to appoint non-executive directors—as well as a substantial cash payment from Petronas. Thus the shareholding and governance issues were resolved in one step, and the cash was to be used dramatically to cut Premier's debt burden. By the same action, Premier reduced its oil and gas production activities and focused on "fleet-of-foot" exploration. And finally it had withdrawn from Myanmar in a way which was fully acceptable to the Burma Campaign Group, other NGOs, and to the UK Government.

But most critically, the share price of Premier Oil rose 10 per cent on the announcement. Indeed, news of Premier's change in direction had been anticipated by the market for many months. As a result, Premier Oil's share price doubled (relative to the oil and gas sector) during the period of our engagement, netting an excess return to Hermes clients of over £1 million, and more than 50 times that sum to other minority shareholders.

The price continued to rise thereafter until September 12, 2003 when the reconstruction was completed with the exit of the major shareholders and a 10:1 share consolidation. Its shareholders have continued to enjoy significant share price appreciation over the years since the reconstruction. Premier Oil is now established as a strong independent E&P company with a real opportunity to continue to add value.

Achieving success through co-operation

It should be clear from this example that engagement is not done in a spirit **18.036** of confrontation. We seek to work quietly behind the scenes, supporting boards in taking the right decisions. Indeed, by far the bulk of our activities occur under the surface and never become public. We do not seek media scrutiny—and will not talk to the press except in support of the board unless relations have irretrievably broken down. We believe that such publicity does not help boards to take the right decisions in the interests of all shareowners. Many directors of companies with which we have engaged are grateful for our interventions in helping to unlock difficult and possibly deadlocked situations. Importantly, we recognise that Hermes only ever plays a limited role in corporate change. It is the company directors who take the decisions and deserve the credit for creating shareholder value.

In the same way, well-run companies have nothing to fear from engagement. We do not believe that the "Hermes Responsible Ownership Principles", our manifesto for companies run in the long-term interests of their shareowners, discusses anything which good companies do not already do. The principal reason that we believe that the Principles are a valuable contribution to the debate is that their publication marked the first time that long-term public shareowners have made a statement of what they wish for from companies in which they invest, and they remain the clearest and fullest statement of those wishes. The Principles cut through the noise of the trading on the stock markets to highlight how companies can genuinely create value over the long term. In many ways, we have offered the Principles to the corporate community as a defence against any short-termist urges they receive from market participants.

Chapter 19

Communicating and Engagement with Shareholders

Introduction

The Cadbury Report[1] (Report, 6.15) observed that it was important that **19.001** companies should communicate their strategies to their major shareholders and that their shareholders should understand them. Cadbury also pointed out (Report, 6.11) that:

"institutional shareholders should encourage regular, systematic contact at senior executive level to exchange views and information on strategy, performance, board membership and quality of management."

Hampel[2] also recognised (Report, 5.24) that, since private individuals own about 20 per cent of the shares in listed companies directly, private individuals should have access to the same information from companies as institutional shareholders. Both Cadbury and Hampel pointed out, however, that there were dangers in imparting price sensitive information, making people "insiders" and treating one group of shareholders differently from another group.

The 2003 Higgs Review[3] (15.4) stated:

"According to my telephone survey, three-quarters of chairman discuss company business with some of their investors at least once a year. Through such meetings, these members of the board gain a clear insight into the views, and on occasion concerns, of the company's major shareholders. For their part, shareholders develop a better understanding of a wide range of issues from the point of view of management. These

[1] *http://www.ecgi.org/codes/code.php?code_id=132.*
[2] *http://www.ecgi.org/codes/code.php?code_id=130.*
[3] *http://www.ecgi.org/codes/code.php?code_id=121.*

channels of communication are now widely accepted as both desirable and useful.

In contrast, only rarely do non-executive directors hear at first hand the views of major shareholders. The majority of non-executive directors (52 per cent) surveyed for the Review never discuss company business with their investors. Within the FTSE 100, contact is rarer still: only about one in five FTSE 100 non-executive directors discuss company business with investors once a year or more often."

The UK Corporate Governance Code contains positive encouragement to directors to communicate with shareholders (see below).

This chapter will therefore:

(1)   outline the regulatory framework, and in particular the provisions of the Companies Act 2006 ("CA 2006") relating to methods of communication by electronic means; enfranchisement powers of beneficial owners; proxy rights, the power to circulate statements; and the power to raise audit concerns at company meetings;

(2)   outline the potential pitfalls in relation to the giving of information by companies and those associated with them; and

(3)   describe some of the current thinking in relation to communication with shareholders and offer some practical suggestions.

Part 1: The regulatory framework

Companies Act 2006

Electronic communication

19.002   (1)   Notices of meeting can under and subject to CA 2006 s.333 and Sch.5 and other communications can under CA 2006 ss.1144 to 1148 and Schs 4 and 5 be given electronically or on a website.

(2)   A document or information may only be sent in electronic form to a person who has agreed or to a company that is deemed to have so agreed (CA 2006 Sch.5 para.6).

(3)   Websites: a company may only send or supply documents or information through a website to persons who have agreed; or are deemed to have agreed. A person is deemed to have agreed if (s)he has been asked individually to agree; and has not responded within 28 days (CA 2006 Sch.5).

(4)   Result of a poll: A "quoted" company must under CA 2006 s.341 publish the result of any poll on its website. Note that the UK Corporate Governance Code now requires that where a poll is not taken, a company must nevertheless as soon as practicable after the meeting (in addition to announcing it at the meeting) publish on its website the numbers of proxy votes for and against and "withheld" in relation to a given resolution.[4]

Enfranchisement

CA 2006 Pt 9 has significantly increased the rights of beneficial owners whose **19.003** shares are registered in the names of nominees to exercise powers as if they themselves were the registered owners.

Nomination rights (CA 2006 s.145): a company may make provision in its articles[5] enabling a member to nominate another person to enjoy or exercise all or any specified rights of the member.

The provision applies in particular to the right to:

- be sent proposed written resolution;
- require circulation of written resolution;
- require directors to call a general meeting;
- notice of general meeting;
- circulation of a statement;
- appoint proxy to act as a meeting;
- require circulation of a resolution for the annual general meeting ("AGM") of a public company;
- be sent a copy of annual accounts and reports.

Information rights (CA 2006 s.146):

- applies to companies whose shareholders are admitted to trading on a regulated market;
- a member who holds shares of behalf of another person may nominate the person to enjoy information rights;
- "information rights" means:
  - the right to receive a copy of all communications;
  - the right to require copies of reports and accounts.

---

[4] Code Provision E.2.2.
[5] See for example Model art.79 in the Model Articles for public companies in Companies (Model Articles) Regulations 2007 Sch.3 expected to be implemented in October 2008.

The above rights are in addition to the rights of the registered member himself (s.150(5)). The Act includes provisions as to the form in which information should be supplied: the default position is the company's website (s.147). A notice of meeting must warn a beneficial owner that (s)he may have rights in relation to voting (s.149(2)).

Most nominees hold shares on behalf of more than one person. The CA 2006 provides that a nominee holding shares of a half of more than one person need not exercise the rights in the same way; but if (s)he exercises some only of the rights, or exercises them in different ways, (s)he must inform the company (CA 2006 s.152).

Members' requests

19.004 CA 2006 s.153, extends the range of things which companies are required to do if requested by the requisite number of members. These are:

- the power to require circulation of a statement from members;

- the power to require circulation of an AGM resolution for public company;

- the power to require an independent report on a poll;

- the power to require website publication of "audit concerns" (see below).

The company must act on the request of at least 100 persons, including beneficial owners, subject to proof of ownership.

Proxy rights

19.005 CA 2006 ss.324 to 331, enhances the powers of proxy holders including as follows:

- a member may appoint a proxy to exercise all any of his or her rights to attend, speak and vote;

- a member may appoint more than one proxy to exercise rights attached to different shares;

- in calculating the 48-hour period before a meeting (proxies must be lodged no later than 48 hours before a meeting) weekends and bank holidays are to be ignored in counting the time;

- chairing meetings.

Power to circulate statements

The regime prior to implementation of the CA 2006 continues under CA 2006 **19.006**
s.338 whereby a shareholder or shareholders in a public company holding at
least 5 per cent of voting rights, or 100 shareholders on which there has been
paid up an average sum of £100 can requisition a company to give notice of
a resolution to be proposed at the AGM; and to circulate a written statement
relating to the business at an AGM.[6]

The cost must be met by the requisitionists unless the request relates to an
AGM and is received before the end of the financial year in question (s.340).

Audit questions

Members may under CA 2006 s.527 request a quoted company to publish **19.007**
a statement on its website relating to the audit of the company's accounts
(including auditors reports and conduct of the audit) to be laid before the
next "accounts meeting"[7]; or any circumstances connected with an auditor
ceasing to hold office since the previous accounts meeting.

This power applies to members representing at least 5 per cent of the total
voting rights or at least 100 members on which there has been paid up an
average sum of £100 per member (s.541); the request must be received at
least one week before the meeting, and the company must inform members
of the possibility of a statement being placed on the website in the notice of
meeting.

The Companies (Shareholders' Rights) Regulations 2009

These Regulations which implement the European Directive on Shareholders **19.008**
Rights and especially affect shareholders rights in relation to meetings are
fully dealt with at para.17.003 in Ch.17 (the Annual General Meeting).

The UK Corporate Governance Code

"SECTION E: RELATIONS WITH SHAREHOLDERS **19.009**

E.1 Dialogue with Shareholders

---

[6] CA 2006 ss.338 and 314 and 315.
[7] Defined in CA 2006 s.437(3) as the general meeting at which the public company's annual
accounts and reports are laid.

Main Principle
There should be a dialogue with shareholders based on the mutual under-standing of objectives. The board as a whole has responsibility for ensuring that a satisfactory dialogue with shareholders takes place.

Supporting Principles
Whilst recognising that most shareholder contact is with the chief execu-tive and finance director, the chairman should ensure that all directors are made aware of their major shareholders' issues and concerns.

The board should keep in touch with shareholder opinion in whatever ways are most practical and efficient.

Code Provisions
E.1.1 The chairman should ensure that the views of shareholders are communicated to the board as a whole. The chairman should discuss governance and strategy with major shareholders. Non-executive direc-tors should be offered the opportunity to attend scheduled meetings with major shareholders and should expect to attend meetings if requested by major shareholders. The senior independent director should attend suffi-cient meetings with a range of major shareholders to listen to their views in order to help develop a balanced understanding of the issues and concerns of major shareholders.
E.1.2 The board should state in the annual report the steps they have taken to ensure that the members of the board, and, in particular, the non-executive directors, develop an understanding of the views of major shareholders about the company, for example through direct face-to-face contact, analysts' or brokers' briefings and surveys of shareholder opinion.

Nothing in these principles or provisions should be taken to override the general requirements of law to treat shareholders equally in access to information.

E.2 Constructive Use of the AGM

Main Principle
The board should use the AGM to communicate with investors and to encourage their participation.

Code Provisions
E.2.1 At any general meeting, the company should propose a separate resolution on each substantially separate issue, and should, in particular, propose a resolution at the AGM relating to the report and accounts. For each resolution, proxy appointment forms should provide shareholders with the option to direct their proxy to vote either for or against the resolu-tion or to withhold their vote. The proxy form and any announcement of

the results of a vote should make it clear that a 'vote withheld' is not a vote in law and will not be counted in the calculation of the proportion of the votes for and against the resolution.

E.2.2 The company should ensure that all valid proxy appointments received for general meetings are properly recorded and counted. For each resolution, where a vote has been taken on a show of hands, the company should ensure that the following information is given at the meeting and made available as soon as reasonably practicable on a website which is maintained by or on behalf of the company:

- the number of shares in respect of which proxy appointments have been validly made;
- the number of votes for the resolution;
- the number of votes against the resolution; and
- the number of shares in respect of which the vote was directed to be withheld.

E.2.3 The chairman should arrange for the chairmen of the audit, remuneration and nomination committees to be available to answer questions at the AGM and for all directors to attend.
E.2.4 The company should arrange for the Notice of the AGM and related papers to be sent to shareholders at least 20 working days before the meeting."

The Listing Rules—Circulars to shareholders

The Listing Rules set out various requirements which apply to all circulars **19.010** sent by the Company to holders of its listed securities (Ch.13 of the Listing Rules). Any circular sent by the company to holders of its listed securities must amongst other requirements:

(1) provide a clear and adequate explanation of its subject matter giving due prominence to its essential characteristics, benefits and risks;

(2) state why the security holder is being asked to vote or, if no vote is required, why the circular is being sent;

(3) if voting or other action is required, contain all information necessary to allow the security holders to make a properly informed decision;

(4) if voting or other action is required, contain a heading drawing attention to the document's importance and advising security holders who

are in any doubt as to what action to take to consult appropriate independent advisers;

(5) if voting is required, contain a recommendation from the board as to the voting action security holders should take for all resolutions proposed, indicating whether or not the proposal described in the circular is, in the board's opinion, in the best interests of security holders as a whole;

(6) state that if all the securities have been sold or transferred by the addressee the circular and any other relevant documents should be passed to the person through whom the sale or transfer was effected for transmission to the purchaser or transferee;

(7) if new securities are being issued in substitution for existing securities, explain what will happen to existing documents of title;

(8) not include any reference to a specific date on which listed securities will be marked "ex" any benefit or entitlement which has not been agreed in advance with the Recognised Investment Exchanges on which the company's securities are or are to be traded;

(9) if it relates to a transaction in connection with which securities are proposed to be listed, include a statement that application has been or will be made for the securities to be admitted and, if known, a statement of the following matters:

   (a) the dates on which the securities are expected to be admitted and on which dealings are expected to commence;
   (b) how the new securities rank for dividend or interest;
   (c) whether the new securities rank equally with any existing listed securities;
   (d) the nature of the document of title;
   (e) the proposed date of issue;
   (f) the treatment of any fractions;
   (g) whether or not the security may be held in uncertificated form; and
   (g) the names of the Recognised Investment Exchanges on which securities are to be traded;

(10) if a person is named in the circular as having advised the listed company or its directors, a statement that the adviser has given and has not withdrawn its written consent to the inclusion of the reference to the adviser's name in the form and context in which it is included.

Insider dealing, Financial Services and Markets Act 2000 ("FSMA") section 21 and "market abuse"

If directors of companies are to communicate information about the company to analysts and other shareholders, there are a number of potential pitfalls. Directors will need to ensure that they do not unwittingly breach Pt V of the Criminal Justice Act 1993, which deals with insider dealing; the Traded Securities (Disclosure) Regulations 1994, FSMA s.21 (invitations to engage in investment activity) and FSMA (Market Abuse) Pt VIII; and that "inside information" is disclosed at once to the whole market, not just a selected few.   **19.011**

Insider dealing—Criminal Justice Act 1993 Part V

Put simply, a director may be guilty of an offence under the Act if, amongst other things, (s)he discloses "inside information" otherwise than in the proper performance of the functions of his or her employment.   **19.012**
"Inside information" is information which:

(a)   relates to particular securities, or to a particular issuer or issuers;

(b)   is specific or precise;

(b)   has not been made public;

(c)   if it were made public, would have a significant effect on the price of any securities.

This definition encompasses information given to analysts or to major shareholders, even if given to shareholders pursuant to the encouragement given to them by the extracts from the UK Corporate Governance Code quoted above.
Moreover, since the director also commits an offence under the Act if (s)he "encourages" another person to deal, knowing or having reasonable cause to believe the dealing would take place, it may be difficult for a director to prove that, in the act of giving the information, (s)he did not expect the shareholder or analyst to deal or procure others to deal in the shares.

The Financial Services and Markets Act 2000 (as amended by the Financial Services and Markets Act 2000 (Market Abuse) Regulations 2005)

Section 21 of the Act provides in terms that a person must not, in the course of business, communicate an invitation or inducement to engage in an "investment activity" unless such a person is an "authorised person" or the communication contents have been approved by such a person. The section has a very broad application.   **19.013**

Part VIII introduced the unlawful activity of "market abuse" and in s.397, the criminal offence of market manipulation.

Market abuse is defined (s.118) in terms as behaviour "likely to give a regular user of the market a false or misleading impression as to the supply of, or demand for, or as to the price of value of, investments of the kind in question".

Those who commit market abuse can be punished by an unlimited fine or public censure, ordered to make restitution and restrained by injunction. Section 123 states that it is a defence to argue that the person believed on reasonable grounds that his or her behaviour did not amount to market abuse, or that (s)he took all reasonable precautions and exercised all due diligence to avoid market abuse.

Non-exhaustive list of inside information

19.014 (a) Any major new development in the company's sphere of activity.

(b) Any proposed change in capital structure, including that of the company's listed debt securities (if any) approved by the board of directors.

(c) Details of acquisitions or realisations of assets as from time to time required to be notified to the company's Regulatory Information Service or in accordance with the regulations set out in the Rules of the Alternative Investment Market.

(d) Any information notified to the company under CA 2006 Pt 22.

(e) The grant to or by, or acceptance by, a director or a connected person of any option, other right or obligation to acquire or dispose of any securities which are or are to be listed, or any interest of whatsoever nature in such securities and the acquisition, disposal, exercise or discharge or any dealing with any such option, right or obligations by such person which is notified to the company.

(f) Any board decision to submit to the company's shareholders a proposal that the company be authorised to purchase its own shares and any purchase by the company of its own shares.

(g) Any board decision to change the general character or nature of the business of the group.

(h) Any change in the status of the company for taxation purposes under statutory provisions relating to close companies or to approved investments trusts.

(i) The announcement of the interim and final results of the group and any related dividends.

Public information

Since information that has been made public cannot constitute "inside information" and, therefore, no offence can be committed in respect of it, it is important for directors to understand whether or not information has been made public. The Criminal Justice Act 1993 gives some guidance on the circumstances in which information is treated as made public, although the categories are not exhaustive.   **19.015**

Information which will be treated as made public comprises information which:

(a)   is published in accordance with the rules of the Financial Services Authority ("FSA") in order to inform investors and their advisers;

(b)   is included in a record required by any Act of Parliament to be open to public inspection;

(c)   can readily be acquired by anyone likely to deal in any securities;

(d)   is derived from public information;

(e)   is information which may, depending on the facts, be treated as public even if it can be acquired only by the exercise of diligence or expertise, or is communicated only to a section of the public, or can be acquired only by observation, or is communicated only on payment of a fee or outside the UK.

One of the points of the above exemptions is that recommendations of analysts based on research into publicly available material (as distinct from a tip from a director or secretary) will not be inside information.

Defences

There are a number of defences available. In relation to the dealing or encouraging of dealing, it will be a defence if an individual can show: **19.016**

(a)   (s)he did not expect the dealing to result in a profit or the avoidance of loss attributable to the inside information;

(b)   (s)he reasonably believed that the information had been disclosed widely enough and that no party to the dealing would be prejudiced by not having the information; or

(c)   (s)he would have done what (s)he did even if (s)he had not had the information.

In relation to disclosing information, it will be a defence if the discloser shows that (s)he did not expect anyone to deal as a result or, if (s)he did, that (s)he did not expect the dealing to result in a profit attributable to the inside information.

In relation to dealing or encouraging dealing where an individual has "market information" (that is to say, information that certain shares are, or are not to be, or have been, issued, acquired or disposed of, that the acquisition or disposal is under consideration or negotiation, or information regarding the numbers and prices of the shares concerned and/or the identity of buyers and sellers), it will be a defence if either:

(a)   it is reasonable for him or her to deal (in judging which should be taken into account the content of the information, the circumstances in which (s)he first had the information and the capacity in which (s)he now acts); or

(b)   (s)he acts in connection with an acquisition or disposal under consideration or negotiation and with a view to facilitating the accomplishment of such acquisition or disposal.

Obligation to disclose "inside information"

19.017   Prior to the implementation by the FSA/UK Listing Authority of the EU Market Abuse Directive in July 2005 listed companies were expected to observe a code of conduct in relation to what was termed "price sensitive" information—that is to say, a code which required companies to publish "price sensitive" information quickly, and required individuals not to disclose or deal in securities on the basis of undisclosed "price sensitive" information.

The implementation of the Market Abuse Directive[8] did not change the principle but changed the terminology so as to refer to "inside" information instead of "price sensitive" information. The Rules are set out in the "Disclosure Rules and Transparency Rules" ("DTR") section of the FSA Handbook of Listing Rules.[9]

The relevant Disclosure Rules are set out below:

Requirement to disclose inside information
DTR 2.2.1
An *issuer* must notify a *RIS*[10] as soon as possible of any *inside information* which directly concerns the *issuer* unless DTR 2.5.1 R applies. [**Note:** Article 6(1) *Market Abuse Directive.*]

---

[8] Market Abuse Directive Instrument 2005.
[9] *http://fsahandbook.info/FSA/html/handbook/DTR.*
[10] Regulated Information Service.

DTR 2.2.2R
An *issuer* will be deemed to have complied with DTR 2.2.1 R where, upon the coming into existence of a set of circumstances or the occurrence of an event, albeit not yet formalised, the *issuer* notified a *RIS* as soon as was possible. [**Note:** Article 2(2) 2003/124/EC.]

Identifying inside information
DTR 2.2.3G
Information is *inside information* if each of the criteria in the definition of *inside information* is met.

DTR 2.2.4G

(1) In determining the likely price significance of the information an *issuer* should assess whether the information in question would be likely to be used by a reasonable investor as part of the basis of his investment decisions and would therefore be likely to have a significant effect on the price of the *issuer's financial instruments* (the reasonable investor test). [**Note:** Article 1(2) 2003/124/EC.]

(2) In determining whether information would be likely to have a significant effect on the price of *financial instruments*, an *issuer* should be mindful that there is no figure (percentage change or otherwise) that can be set for any *issuer* when determining what constitutes a significant effect on the price of the *financial instruments* as this will vary from *issuer* to *issuer*.

The reasonable investor test requires an *issuer*:

(1) to take into account that the significance of the information in question will vary widely from *issuer* to *issuer*, depending on a variety of factors such as the *issuer's* size, recent developments and the market sentiment about the *issuer* and the sector in which it operates; and

(2) to assume that a reasonable investor will make investment decisions relating to the relevant *financial instrument* to maximise his economic self interest.

DTR 2.2.6G
It is not possible to prescribe how the reasonable investor test will apply in all possible situations. Any assessment should take into consideration the anticipated impact of the information in light of the totality of the *issuer's* activities, the reliability of the source of the information and other market variables likely to affect the relevant *financial instrument* in the given circumstances. However, information which is likely to be considered relevant to a reasonable investor's decision includes information which affects:

(1) the assets and liabilities of the *issuer*;

(2) the performance, or the expectation of the performance, of the *issuer's* business;

(3)   the financial condition of the *issuer*;

(4)   the course of the *issuer's* business;

(5)   major new developments in the business of the *issuer*; or

(6)   information previously disclosed to the market. [**Note:** Recital 1 2003/124/EC.]

DTR 2.2.7G

An *issuer* and its advisers are best placed to make an initial assessment of whether particular information amounts to *inside information*. The decision as to whether a piece of information is *inside information* may be finely balanced and the *issuer* (with the help of its advisers) will need to exercise its judgment.

Note: DTR 2.7 provides additional guidance on dealing with market rumour.

DTR 2.2.8G

The *directors* of the *issuer* should carefully and continuously monitor whether changes in the circumstances of the *issuer* are such that an announcement obligation has arisen under this chapter.

When to disclose inside information
DTR 2.2.9

(1)   Subject to the limited ability to delay release of *inside information* to the public provided by DTR 2.5.1 R, an *issuer* is required to notify, via a *RIS*, all *inside information* in its possession as soon as possible.

(2)   If an *issuer* is faced with an unexpected and significant event, a short delay may be acceptable if it is necessary to clarify the situation. In such situations a holding announcement should be used where an *issuer* believes that there is a danger of *inside information* leaking before the facts and their impact can be confirmed. The holding announcement should:

    (a) detail as much of the subject matter as possible;

    (b) set out the reasons why a fuller announcement cannot be made; and

    (c) include an undertaking to announce further details as soon as possible.

(3)   If an *issuer* is unable, or unwilling to make a holding announcement it may be appropriate for the trading of its *financial instruments* to be suspended until the *issuer* is in a position to make an announcement.

(4)   An *issuer* that is in any doubt as to the timing of announcements required by this chapter should consult the *FSA* at the earliest opportunity.

Communication with third parties

The *FSA* is aware that many *issuers* provide unpublished information to third parties such as analysts, employees, credit rating agencies, finance providers and major shareholders, often in response to queries from such parties. The fact that information is unpublished does not in itself make it *inside information*. However, unpublished information which amounts to *inside information* is only permitted to be disclosed in accordance with the *disclosure rules* and an *issuer* must ensure that at all times it acts in compliance with this chapter."

Practical guide to dealing with inside information—the opportunities for clear communication

General   In the light of the foregoing restrictions and exposure, it must   **19.018** be a concern that the ability of directors of listed companies to communicate with their shareholders and with analysts is risky: there is a certain tension between the encouragement given by the UK Corporate Governance Code to directors to communicate as against the prohibitions of the regulatory regime described above.

Those who wrote the Hampel and Cadbury Reports and Higgs Review were well aware of the difficulties of disclosing price sensitive or "inside information" as it is now termed, but nevertheless the encouragement to communicate persists. Accordingly, companies are bound to attempt to react to that encouragement in a positive matter.

Practical suggestions include the following:

(a)   ensure that inside information is published as rapidly as possible, thus making it public (and therefore enabling more detailed dialogue to take place thereafter);

(b)   insofar as the inside information cannot be published for reasons of security, then that information should be identified and should be "off limits" in any discussion with shareholders or analysts;

(c)   try to agree in advance an agenda of items to be discussed with shareholders (this is almost impossible with analysts);

(d)   reduce to a minimum level the amount of contact with shareholders, analysts and media during the "close periods" of two months prior to the publication of the interim results and the preliminary financial results;

(e)   start a programme of meetings with analysts and shareholders immediately after the publication of the interim and preliminary financial results.

19.019   *"Making" parties an insider?*   The DTR Rules (see above) make it clear that the old practice of making people "insiders" is incompatible with the Disclosure Rules if it is not publicly published at the same time as disclosure to any third party-the "escape" clause however, being a reference to the fact that a lot of information disclosed to third parties might not be "inside information" as defined. Nevertheless, great caution should be exercised if imparting information to analysts or institutions which is not disclosed publicly so that it is clear that such information is not "inside information".

19.020   *Practical guidance*   The following practical measures are suggested for companies to consider in relation to the dissemination of "inside information":

    (a)   identify a restricted number of directors and senior employees permitted to talk to the press and market analysts;

    (b)   determine a consistent policy for communicating information considered likely to be inside information and make such policy publicly known;

    (c)   ensure that inside information is announced promptly;

    (d)   seek the assistance of advisers in order to determine whether information is potentially "inside";

    (e)   prevent disclosure of key financial information—profits, turnover, product sales figures, asset valuations, borrowing levels or anything else likely to move the market except through formal announcements to the company's Regulatory Information Service;

    (f)   consider providing regular updates on trading position including unaudited formal quarterly trading statements;

    (g)   monitor market expectations built into the share price and, if the market appears to be seriously out of line, consider an immediate announcement to correct misunderstandings, but without making a profit forecast;

    (h)   make a formal announcement of information inadvertently disclosed, or ensure the wider availability of information which is the subject of rumours or other broadly correct information which may be known to a limited group;

    (i)   when inside information has to be given to advisers or other parties to a transaction, inform them that they are to become insiders and that they may not deal until the information is publicly disclosed, and obtain their consent to this;

    (j)   make all required disclosures of inside information, even if in the "close period" prior to announcement of results.

Part 2: Investor relationships—some practical suggestions

General approach

Having described the regulatory background to communications with inves- **19.021**
tors and offered guidance as to the ways in which price sensitive information
can be managed, it is appropriate to describe how relationships with investors
may be developed so as to reflect the encouragement to dialogue in the UK
Corporate Governance Code.

In order to avoid the risk of leaking inside information during the "close"
periods of the financial year, namely the two months prior to the interim
(half year) and preliminary (full year) financial results respectively, most
companies reduce to a minimum level the amount of contact they have with
shareholders, analysts and the media during such close periods. However,
immediately upon the publication of the interim and preliminary results
respectively, it is usual for shareholder and analysts meetings to be organised
in order that a greater analysis can take place of the results.

Understanding objectives

Main Principle E.1 of the UK Corporate Governance states: "There should **19.022**
be a dialogue with shareholders based on the mutual understanding of objectives".

The following objectives may be helpful in designing investor relations
("IR") programmes:

(a)   no "surprises" ever;

(b)   set up an IR website (see more in para.19.023 below) and join the
      Investor Relations Society[11];

(c)   generate interest among analysts in the company, accompanied by
      public independent research;

(d)   develop links with financial journalists or from the trade press and
      appoint press advisers to advise on how best to tailor information so
      that it fits the special interest of the journalist or paper in question;

(e)   impart information on what the company actually does now and its
      strategy for what it intends to do in the future. If there are aspects
      of the past performance which need to be explained in terms of the

---

[11]   *http://www.ir-soc.org.uk.*

present position and future objectives of the company, then that should be done as well;

(f)   give an opportunity to meet some of the directors and senior executives in order to assess for themselves the quality of senior management;

(g)   deal with any specific items arising from the recently published information.

Often, the opportunity is taken of meetings with shareholders and analysts to invite along fund managers who may not at that point be investing significantly in the company. In the National Association of Pension Funds ("NAPF") 1998 publication entitled "Good Corporate Governance", it states that it regards regular dialogue between shareholders and a company's management as a fundamental part of good corporate governance, and particularly on strategy and the company's position in the markets:

"Continual and direct communication is part of this process, with many institutional investors having regular, systematic contact at the most senior levels. Policy makers should not underestimate the value of this informal approach. Whilst the formality could be regarded with suspicion by some, pension funds are managed in the best fiduciary interests of scheme members. All shareholders should benefit from institutional encouragement of company management."

Furthermore, say the NAPF:

"institutional investors do not feel that in the first instance public recriminations serve the best interests of shareholders. Such public demonstrations are one of the last routes used by investors."

In meeting members of management, shareholders, analysts and fund managers will be assessing over a period of time (a relationship is not something that can be established on a one meeting only basis) the following matters:

(a)   Do they know their business?

(b)   Are they clear about the strategic direction of the company?

(c)   Are they clear about the principal risks facing the company and how to manage them?

(d)   Are remuneration packages genuinely aligned with shareholders' interests and otherwise comply with the UK Corporate Governance Code?

(e) Is the annual report a genuine attempt to describe the company's financial position/achievements/mistakes/failures to match forecasts and aspirations in a comprehensible and transparent way?

(f) Do they understand the aspirations of shareholders?

(g) Can they point to a solid record of achievement of objectives already set, so as to give confidence to the likely achievement of future objectives?

(h) Does the company offer convincing explanations for any non-compliance with the UK Corporate Governance Code?

Institutional investors are becoming better informed (usually through the issue of detailed analysts' circulars) about the market place in which companies operate, both as to the competition and their customers. Managers should not underestimate that knowledge and should come to meetings at least as well prepared as the institutions not only about the company itself, but about all the external factors and the market place in which the company operates.

Setting up an IR website and the Companies Act 2006

Most companies now have their own website. The website is very often the **19.023** first point of reference for enquiries about the company, and resources spent in an informed way on the website give an invaluable insight into all aspects of the company's operations, and financial position. The Investor Relations Society has set out on its website[12] recommendations for the main headings which investors will expect to see including:

- financial data (annual report, interim, preliminary and quarterly statements, archived financial information for a minimum of three years; five to ten years history of key P&L data; key financial ratios; information on the main intangibles of the businesses, for example, brands and human capital);
- corporate governance and corporate social responsibility;
- shareholder information;
- relevant current news.

Now the CA 2006 has recognised the key role of the website by requiring quoted companies to make available on a website the annual directors' report

---

[12] *http://www.ir-soc.org.uk.*

and accounts and the preliminary statement of results[13] and the results of polls.[14] There are extensive provisions permitting communications with and from shareholders in electronic form.[15]

Prize-winning annual reports

19.024   In November 2009 the Investor Relations Society announced the shortlisted companies in a number of categories as follows:

(1)   Best communication of strategy, performance and KPIs in the annual report

- Capita Group
- Centrica
- Morrisons

(2)   Best communication of governance and risk in the annual report

- Capita Group
- Ferrexpo
- Marks and Spencer
- SEGRO

(3)   Best communication of corporate responsibility in the annual report

- Aviva
- BASF
- Rolls Royce

(4)   Most improved annual report

- Dragon Oil
- Powerflute
- Xstrata

(5)   Best-practice corporate website 2009

FTSE 100
- Anglo American
- Imperial Tobacco
- RSA Insurance Group
FTSE 250
- Cookson
- Go-Ahead Group
- Provident Financial

---

[13]   CA 2006 s.430—see also Ch.17 (The Annual General Meeting).
[14]   CA 2006 s.341.
[15]   CA 2006 ss.333, 1143–1148 and Schs 4 and 5.

Small Cap & AIM
- Advent Capital
- Holidaybreak
- Laird

International
- Aegon
- BASF
- Swedish Match

(6)   Award for the most effective overall annual report (printed and online)

FTSE 100
- 3i Group
- Centrica
- Marks and Spencer
- Tullow Oil

FTSE 250
- Great Portland Estates
- Premier Farnell
- Provident Financial

Small Cap and AIM
- Lancashire Holdings
- May Gurney
- Next Fifteen Communications

International
- BASF
- Daimler
- Hannover Re

The Higgs Review's assessment of relationships of non-executive directors with shareholders

Paragraph 15.1 of the Review states: "The role of the non-executive direc-   **19.025**
tor includes an important and inescapable relationship with shareholders". He pointed out that research undertaken for the Review showed
that in normal circumstances non-executive directors and shareholders
have only minimal direct contact. Interviews with investors revealed that
rarely do they speak directly with non-executive directors, and only then
when there is a serious problem. Even in these circumstances, discussion
often centred on director remuneration rather than wider strategy or
governance issues.

Moreover, the research indicated a widespread view among non-executive
directors that investors are distant and disengaged. Executive directors, by
contrast, were found to have reservations about more direct contact between

non-executive directors and shareholders on the grounds that non-executive directors would not have enough detail available to them to present an accurate picture of company performance. However, the overall view was that relationships between non-executive directors and shareholders could and should be closer.

However, the Higgs Review did not accept the argument that the AGM should be the main or indeed only mechanism through which major shareholders and non-executive directors have direct contact.

To this end a Supporting Principle to Main Principle E.1 (Dialogue with shareholders) states:

"Whilst recognising that most shareholder contact is with the chief executive and finance director, the chairman should ensure that all directors understand their major shareholders' issues and concerns."

The corresponding Code Provision E.1.1 includes the provision that:

"Non-executive directors should be offered the opportunity to attend existing [*inserted in 2010*] meetings with major shareholders and should expect to attend them if requested by major shareholders. The senior independent director should attend sufficient meetings with a range of major shareholders to listen to their views in order to develop a better understanding of the issues and concerns of major shareholders."

The "Winning Partnership Report"

19.026   In 1996, a joint City/Industry working group established under the chairmanship of the then Mr Paul Myners issued a report called "Developing a Winning Partnership" ("the Winning Partnership Report") which was widely praised and referred to with approval by Margaret Beckett, then President of the Board of Trade, in a speech in March 1998. Fifteen years later the report still has much validity, especially since the withdrawal of the Operating and Financial Review Regulations by the Government in 2005/2006, which in many ways reflected the "Winning Partnership" recommendations.

The terms of reference were to suggest practical ways in which the relationship between UK industry and institutional shareholders could be improved "as a stimulus for long-term investment and development". The report developed the concept of a "model" listed company and a "model" institutional investor to demonstrate how the partnership might work.

In responding to criticism that the quality of the relationships between companies and their institutional shareholders is not high enough, the report suggests that the response of management in the "model" company should include:

(a) an annual strategic presentation to institutional investors and stock-brokers analysts—this should include a clear statement of management's vision for the company, corporate objectives and financing policies, and details of capital and revenue investment plans;

(b) improved meetings with shareholders focused on long-term issues, followed by feedback on performance;

(c) recognition of the importance of the annual report and accounts as a means of communication and the need to keep abreast of best practice in disclosure;

(d) regular communications throughout the year, including brief quarterly trading updates;

(e) efforts to make the annual general meeting an interesting and rewarding occasion for participants. These include encouraging shareholders to submit questions in advance, referring minority interest questions for later response and arranging presentations by operational management;

(f) a comprehensive training programme for managers involved in investor relations;

(g) a clearly defined and articulated policy for management remuneration, discussed openly with shareholders.

On the other side of the debate, the "model" institutional investor should act by:

(a) being more open in discussions with company management about corporate strategy and objectives, including a candid assessment of management's performance;

(b) articulating its investment objectives to corporate management so that there is mutual understanding of expectations;

(c) playing an active role in corporate governance including, for example, voting at AGMs;

(d) improving training for individual fund managers, to promote better industry knowledge and commercial awareness setting;

(e) an agenda for meetings with companies and ensuring adequate preparation by its representatives.

The Winning Partnership Report found that institutional investors want company managers to articulate more clearly their long-term corporate objectives and financing policies, of which dividend policy is an important part, and to emphasise in the discussion "their vision for the company and the corporate values". Institutional investors, the report found, want managers to be consistent in their communications with investors and the press "and to be open about bad news as well as good", "'no surprises' was a phrase we heard more than once". More regular communication would be welcome, apparently, in the form, for example, of operational updates in the second and fourth quarters, "these being less detailed than interim and preliminary statements".

The share register

19.027   One interesting point made by the Winning Partnership Report relates to the share register of a listed company. The report suggests that the model company "seeks to understand why particular investors have bought or sold stock". In its analysis, the company establishes which institutions are under, or over, "weight" in the company shares and, through discussion, finds out why. This is not an attempt either to "sell" the company, or necessarily to bring new investors onto the register; "rather, the company is ensuring that an institution's weighting is based on an accurate understanding of the facts".

Meetings with shareholders and analysts

19.028   In terms of meeting with shareholders, the Winning Partnership Report suggests that the model company should give an annual presentation to institutional investors and brokers analysts, and that that presentation will form the backdrop to other meetings between the company and its investors. The meeting will cover management's vision, longer-term corporate objectives, and the company's strategy and operations in each important market and business segment. It will include the rationale for decisions to diversify into new products or markets and a discussion of capital and revenue investment plans: "It specifically does not focus on trading results and is not timed to coincide with any trading or transactional announcement."

The Report also suggests that "one to one" meetings are a "key opportunity for managers to explain further their strategy and objectives for the business and to answer questions from the company's owners and potential investors". Such a meeting requires preparation by agreeing an agenda with the investor and producing an information pack for investors which include copy slides and the main points from the presentation. The focus of the meeting should remain medium to long-term and, within that context, "there is a frank discussion of all aspects of company performance, both good and bad, and management probes and addresses that concerns the investor".

It is suggested that after such a meeting, the company should provide feedback to the investor either directly or through a third party such as the company's broker or investor relations consultant: "The aim is to assess the usefulness of the meeting and to provide indications of how future meetings can be improved".

However, the Winning Partnership Report recognised that "neither smaller companies nor smaller institutions have the resources to conduct a large number of one-to-one meetings, their needs might best be met by meetings with small groups of investors together".

Investment plans

The Winning Partnership Report recognised the commercial sensitivities of **19.029** communicating investment plans to analysts, lest competitors pick them up. Nevertheless:

> "The model company uses all appropriate opportunities to tell investors about investment plans. Management understands that investors cannot be expected to finance long-term investment without knowing how it will impact on the business. In formal presentations, and in discussions in one-to-one meetings, managers focus on both capital and revenue investment plans. The latter covers, amongst other things, research and development, marketing, product development and investment in human resources. Investments are justified in terms of their short and long-term impact on results and corporate cash flow. The challenge of good communication is greater for high-tech companies which need to ensure they achieve the correct balance between strategic and financial benefits, and technical characteristics. The [model] company also takes the opportunity provided by the Operating and Financial Review sections of the Annual Report and Accounts to give details of future strategic investments."

Private individuals own only about 10 per cent of the shares in listed companies directly, and only a minority of private shareholders take an active interest in the companies in which they invest. The Hampel Report concluded that the impact of private shareholders on corporate governance could not be great. A similar implication was made in the Cadbury Report.

Moreover, by far the greater number of shares "held" by individuals are registered in the names of nominees, who are the only entities recognised by companies as entitled to receive information, notices of meetings, appoint proxies, speak at or vote at meetings.

However, the position of private individuals might change dramatically as a result of CA 2006 ss.145 to 153. In terms, these sections are concerned with the situation where shares are registered in the name of a nominee. The sections give rights to the beneficial owner of the shares, once nominated for that purpose by the nominee, as if the beneficial owner were herself or himself the registered member. However, the articles of association of a company need to contain a provision enabling a member to nominate another person as entitled to enjoy or exercise all or any specified rights of a member in relation to the company.[16]

If the articles of association do so permit, then in effect the beneficial owner will have the same rights to vote, speak at, appoint proxies, receive information, receive the annual report and accounts, circulate shareholder resolutions and have all other rights as if (s)he were a registered member.

It has to be said that on the basis of anecdotal evidence from registrars there is as at 2010 complete indifference to these enfranchisement measures by private individuals! The implications of these provisions may over time be immense and will require companies to completely re-think their approach to communications with members who are not registered members.

Conclusion

19.030   It is no coincidence that, along with the growth in understanding of corporate governance and the rise of "shareholder activism" there has been a rising level of consciousness among companies of the need to develop a more constructive dialogue with their shareholders, leading to better understanding. As the Winning Partnership Report pointed out:

> "They [companies] want more openness from investors, candour about objectives and expectations, and a professional approach to the relationship. They expect better shareholder preparation, better sector and industry knowledge and better use of time at meetings."

---

[16] See para.19.003 above.

Chapter 20

Corporate Social Responsibility

Terminology

There are a number of acronyms or initials commonly used in the context of **20.001** corporate social responsibility:

- **"CSR"**: corporate social responsibility, defined by the Institute of Business Ethics as "the voluntary actions taken by a company to address the social and environmental impacts of its business operations and the concerns of its stakeholders".[1]

- **"CR"**: corporate responsibility: said by some commentators to embrace a broader view of corporate activity which includes "corporate citizenship" and corporate aspects of sustainable development or sustainability.[2]

- **"ESG"**: environmental, social, and corporate governance issues.[3]

---

[1] A Government view was that of Mr Malcolm Wicks, the "Minister for CSR" in 2005: "to see every business take account of its economic, social and environmental impact: maximising areas that are beneficial and minimising areas where they are causing harm".

[2] *"Risk returns and responsibility"*, ABI, 2004, Roger Cowe; for an example, see the 2008/2009 British Airways Corporate Responsibility report: *http://www.britishairways.com/cms/global/pdfs/environment/ba_corporate_responsibility_report_2008-2009.pdf* in which the headings are:

- environment;
- community;
- market place;
- work place.

As will be seen from the case studies later in this chapter, these headings are not startlingly different from the "conventional" CSR report, but if there is really a difference it might be said to be that "corporate responsibility" places a slightly heavier emphasis on the sustainability and development of the business itself. On the other hand it might just be semantics.

[3] UN Principles for Responsible Investment.

- **"SEE"**: social, environmental and ethical matters: used by the Association of British Insurers ("ABI") in the Association of British Insurers Disclosure Guidelines on Socially Responsible Investment.[4]

- **"SRI"**: socially responsible investment: investment policies which develop a portfolio of investments in companies which engage actively in CSR and have SEE values.

The fundamental change in attitude between 2000 and 2010

20.002   In March 2006, CIS (the business name of the Co-operative Insurance Society) voted against the annual report and accounts of the Chemring Group Plc on the following grounds:

> "CIS takes account of a company's disclosure in its report and accounts of significant social, ethical and environmental risks and opportunities according to the ABI Disclosure Guidelines. In this case, the company's reporting has been assessed by the ABI and found to be limited. Given the level of exposure to SEE risks in the sector in which this company operates, CIS considered it appropriate to abstain on receiving the report and accounts in 2005. As no progress appears to have been made, CIS intends to vote against this resolution in 2006."

Ten years ago it was very doubtful whether an institutional shareholder would have voted against an annual report resolution on the grounds that the company concerned had failed to address the social, ethical and environmental issues created by the company's operations.

It was reported in the Financial Times on March 29, 2010 that:

> "dissident BP shareholders [about 150] have attacked the global oil company's justification for possible investments in Canada's controversial oil sands by arguing it is based on projections that entail catastrophic consequences for the climate".

The point is that the debate has moved on from the position 10 or so years ago when, as a generalisation, companies and their investors were ambivalent as to whether investment in social and environmental projects was justified in terms of shareholder value, to a position where there is a much greater understanding by a significant proportion (but not by any means all) of investors and companies of the necessity for a business model which puts sustainability as a high priority, followed closely by ethical practices and a significant social contribution: all are seen as simply "good business".

How have these developments come about?

---

[4] ABI, 2001and see further para.20.024 below.

The key drivers for change

There are several factors which explain the change: **20.003**

- **A change in the attitude of society**. There is no doubt that in recent years there has been a considerable change in the awareness of society in general towards issues of sustainability and the part which business should be playing to ensure sustainability. Some commentators[5] have warned quite bluntly that the combination of the continued emission of carbon dioxide at current levels to say nothing of the inevitable increase arising from the industrialisation of China and India, and the use of non-renewable resources on a global scale will result in an extremely problematic economic environment within 50 years: resources which are currently taken for granted will quite simply become scarce if not unavailable. Fresh water is becoming increasingly vulnerable to pollution, diversion of supplies by "upstream" nations from "downstream" nations and drying up altogether due to excessive and wasteful use; fish stocks are reducing rapidly throughout the world due to over fishing, and organisations such as the Marine Stewardship Council and the Sustainable Agricultural Initiative are persuading the UK's biggest food retailers to move towards sustainable supplies of fish. These initiatives alone will not save fish stocks on a global basis. Climate change will result in a highly unstable environment. One side effect which has not escaped the attention of the giant insurance syndicates is that covering the risks arising from these sources of instability will become ruinously expensive both for the insured and the insurers, and therefore self-interest alone requires that in their capacity as investors they exert pressure on businesses as a matter of urgency to do "their bit" to save the planet.[6]

  Unhealthy food has also become a major business concern. One of the key issues in the developed world is obesity, among children in particular, and the extraordinary rise in type 2 diabetes. Food manufacturers are under critical review because of the amount of fat, sugar and salt in their products. Treating obesity related conditions such as heart disease, strokes and diabetes takes an estimated 7 per cent of the European Union health budget.[7] Companies such as the Compass

---

[5] For example, Jared Diamond's *Collapse*, Viking books, 2005; *Capitalism as if the world matters* by Jonathon Porritt, Earthscan, 2005.

[6] "My starting point is extremely pragmatic: we have to make huge changes within the next twenty years. We just don't have any more time than that, and the likelihood of another ideological system emerging to replace [capitalism] is close to zero. We have to deliver improvements to social justice and environmental sustainability through capitalism. This is the reality we are living with, and I don't think it helps when environmentalists ignore that reality", Jonathan Porritt, *The Big Issue*, May 29, 2006.

[7] *Financial Times*, May 29, 2006.

catering group and Britvic have in their histories had their share prices significantly dented and profits significantly reduced following television programmes exposing the poor quality of school foods and the unhealthy nature of sweet drinks. On the other hand, companies dealing in healthy foods are becoming attractive investments.[8]

- **A change in the attitude of senior executives towards CSR.** In 2006 McKinsey conducted a survey among business executives which found that an overwhelming majority of the respondents acknowledged a wider role for corporations than just maximising investor returns, "though this finding is remarkable in itself".[9] In addition, respondents saw environmental concerns, the offshoring debate, and other sensitive matters as potential threats to the creation of value and frankly conceded that their companies handled these issues poorly. 81 per cent of FTSE 100 companies now produce a standalone CSR report.[10]

- **The Companies Act 2006.** This Act reflects a change in the attitude of society towards corporate responsibility in the sense that directors are given the responsibility for, in effect, ensuring that their companies behave like "good citizens". In terms, s.172 of the Companies Act 2006 ("CA 2006") provides that whilst imposing a primary duty on directors to promote the success of the company for the benefit of members as a whole ("enlightened shareholder value") directors must, in arriving at decisions (for the benefit of members as a whole), "have regard to" a number of "pluralist" factors with a distinctly CSR flavour, such as "the impact of the company's operations on the community and the environment"; "the interests of the company's employees" and "the need to foster the company's business relationships with suppliers, customers and others".[11]

- **The ABI Disclosure Guidelines (revised) on socially responsible investment issued in 2007.**[12] The new guidelines have not changed substantially since they were first published in 2001. They focus on encouraging companies to include discussion in their narrative reporting of the environmental, social and governance ("ESG") risks they face, but set in the context of the full range of risks and opportunities the company faces. They also encourage companies to explain what steps they are taking to mitigate and address these risks. The guidelines apply to all companies, including small and medium-sized companies.

---

[8] The US company, United Natural Foods, is the largest distributor of organic foods in the US and is experiencing 15 per cent growth year on year over the past three years reflecting a demand from food retailers such as Wal-Mart for their products.

[9] "When social issues become strategic": The McKinsey quarterly, 2006 No.2.

[10] Corporate register 2005.

[11] See Ch.4 (Directors—Duties and Liabilities) for a more detailed commentary on the section, which poses significant problems for directors.

[12] *http://www.ivis.co.uk* search social responsibility.

There then follows guidelines to the members of the ABI to assist the members in engaging with their investee companies in telling them what they expect to see in the annual report on social, environmental and ethical issues. These are described in greater detail below in para.20.024.

The effect of these Guidelines is difficult to gauge but as can be seen from the quotation from CIS earlier in this chapter opposing the adoption of an annual report and accounts, there is no doubt that members of the ABI have been able to use the Guidelines to articulate their approach to corporate responsibility, and in the case of companies which are indifferent to that approach, as a justification for voting against the annual report.

• **Financial Reporting requirements: The business review/operating and financial review**. For some years there had been a strong feeling among policy makers that it would be desirable for quoted companies to set out in the annual report more "narrative" forward-looking reporting about the strategic direction in which the company wished to go, together with an indication of the key performance indicators ("KPIs") against which performance was being measured. In 2003 the EU adopted the Accounts Modernisation Directive ("AMD")[13] which amongst other things required that quoted companies should include a "business review" in their annual reports. The Accounting Standards Board in May 2005 designed a Reporting Standard, ASB RS1, which has been adopted by most FTSE 100 companies, which also required companies to contain narrative reporting in the annual report of a forward-looking nature including KPIs.[14]

The intention was that the UK would implement the Accounts Modernisation Directive in Regulations[15] which were due to come into effect in November 2005. These regulations included the basic requirement for the AMD business review, but in addition included detailed provisions for an operating and financial review ("OFR") which would, for the purposes of this chapter, have required that companies state in their annual reports, amongst other things, information about environmental matters (including the impact of the business on the environment), information about employees and information about social and community issues. However, the Regulations were withdrawn by the Government in November 2005 without consultation on the grounds that it was trying to lift the burden of regulation on companies.

---

[13] EU Directive 2003/51/EC of 18 June, 2003.
[14] For an excellent guide to KPIs see the ASB's Reporting Statement on the Operating Financial Review; also Ch.16 (Reporting to Shareholders—the Directors/Annual Report) also, Ch.13 (Financial Reporting) and also a paper by Trucost Plc: see *http://www.trucost.com.*
[15] Companies Act 1985 (Operating and Financial Review and Directors' Report, etc.) Regulations 2005 (SI 2005/1011).

Nevertheless it was recognised that the minimum requirements of the AMD plus institutional pressure and activists generally on companies to observe ASB RS1 would create the need for what has been called "an enhanced business review", and thus two events occurred in 2006:

- CA 2006 s.417 implemented the AMD requirement for a business review in the annual report but also required quoted companies "to the extent necessary for an understanding of the development, performance or position of the company's business" to include not only narrative reporting on the main trends and factors likely to affect development but also, and of especial interest to this chapter, information about environmental matters, the company's employees and social and community issues including information about any policies of the company in relation to those matters and the effectiveness of those policies; and contracts or arrangements "essential" to the business. Section 423(5) provides that if the review does not contain that information it must say so, but presumably that information can only legitimately *not* be included if the directors take the good faith view that it is not necessary for an "understanding of the development", etc. of the company's business.

- ASB RS1 has been converted into a Reporting Statement[16] called "The Operating and Financial Review" and this has become the benchmark guidance on best practice. The Reporting Statement contains most of the features of the intended statutory OFR including forward-looking and CSR-type information.[17] The activist fund manager PIRC has said[18]:

  > "we propose for the forthcoming proxy season to use [the Reporting Statement] as the basis for evaluating either voluntary OFR's or 'enhanced' business reviews of listed companies for financial years ending on or after March 31, 2006. In particular, we would wish to see evidence of whether a company is adopting a forward looking orientation and addressing CSR issues 'to the extent necessary' in order to provide a balanced and comprehensive analysis of the development and performance of its business."

In November 2009 the Institute of Chartered Accountants and Environment Agency published new guidance on reporting environmental issues in annual financial reports.[19]

The guidance was aimed at those preparing, auditing and using annual financial statements. Written in a question and answer style, the guid-

---

[16] See *http://www.frc.org.uk.*
[17] See Ch.16 (Reporting to Shareholders—The Directors'/Annual Report).
[18] PIRC shareholder voting guidelines 2006, p.28.
[19] *http://www.environment-agency.gov.uk/static/documents/Business/TECPLN8045_env_report_aw.pdf* (as at November 2009).

ance included examples of good practice from existing annual reports and accounts to assist readers.

Whilst changes to company law made the situation on reporting environmental performance clearer for large and listed companies, the guide sought to help all organisations in reporting these issues.

Some key areas in the guidance include:

- EU Environmental Directives, their implementation in UK law, and their importance and significance to business.

- Accounting standards, interpretations and exposure drafts with UK significance and their environmental implications.

- Clear examples of existing good practice from recent annual reports and accounts.

- Specific sections for report preparers and auditors to address their separate needs.

"Individuals, investors and other stakeholders are increasingly focussing on the environmental performance of organisations" stated the report. With this report, the Institute of Chartered Accountants in England and Wales ("ICAEW") and Environment Agency stated that they were aiming to help companies address the need for greater transparency in their mainstream statutory annual financial reporting.

The ICAEW and Environment Agency also stated in the report that they believe that measuring, managing and reporting on the impacts a company has on the environment would help "to drive internal change and improvement, delivering real benefits to the organisation itself, to the environment and in turn to wider society".

The main point, therefore, is that CSR issues are now going to be required both as a matter of law and best financial reporting practice to be reported on by quoted companies in their annual reports.

What does it mean in practice?

In the ABI's 2001 report entitled "*Investing in Social Responsibility: Risks and*   **20.004**
Opportunities",[20] the ABI explained that CSR is about "how profits are made rather than how much profit there is or how much is given away".

It pointed out that the subject embraces a diverse range of issues, which may change rapidly and will differ from company to company but the key areas are:

---

[20] *http://www.abi.org.uk/Publications/Investing_in_Social_Responsibility_-_Risks_and_Opportunities1.aspx*, ABI, 2001, Roger Cowe.

(a) Employment—ensuring diversity in the workforce, and providing suitable conditions, including subcontractors' and suppliers' labour.

(b) Environment—minimising the impact of products and processes on the quality of land, air, water and ecosystems that make up the environment.

(c) Human rights—working to uphold basic human rights wherever the company operates; including issues such as child labour, sexual harassment, discrimination and abuse, genetic testing, monitoring emails.

(d) Communities—maximising the positive impact of the company's operations through support for and involvement in the communities where it operates.

(e) Business relationships—operating fairly as regards suppliers and customers.

A key element of CSR is the notion that businesses need to meet the expectations of groups other than shareholders, even though directors remain formally accountable only to the investors who own the company. The term "stakeholder" has been coined to describe such groups. It covers employees, suppliers, customers, communities and proxies for the environment such as campaign groups or non-government organisations ("NGOs"). The essence of CSR is about understanding the responsibility to, interests of and risks concerned with, different stakeholder groups. The ABI report points out that it is therefore in that sense "much broader than what is usually described as 'business ethics', which is concerned with moral dilemmas such as bribery and corruption".

The business case for CSR

20.005 The business case may be described as two-fold, the narrow and the broad. The narrow is concerned with the management of risk (effective CSR policies, it is said, assist in the management of risk) and the broad is concerned with assertions of a positive financial benefit to the business.

The management of risk[21]

20.006 In September 1999 the ICAEW published a report which was chaired by Mr Nigel Turnbull entitled "Internal Control: Guidance for Directors on the

---

[21] See also Ch.15 (Risk Management and Internal Control).

Combined Code".[22] The Turnbull Guidance is now annexed to the 2010 UK Corporate Governance Code to assist companies in reporting how they apply Principle C.2 of the Combined Code (risk management and internal control) and if they comply with the corresponding Provisions. The Appendix to the Guidance sets out some questions for directors to consider when conducting an assessment of the effectiveness of the company's risk and control processes. One of the questions asks whether "the significant internal and external ... risks have been identified" and suggests that "significant risks may, for example, include those related to . . . health, safety and environmental, reputation, and business probity issues".

A further question in the Guidance asks whether the company communicates to its employees what is expected of them in areas such as environmental protection.

Thus, there is a strong alignment of risk management and CSR issues at the heart of the business case.

Reputational risk as a sub-set of overall risk management

Organisations have been broken or severely damaged by damage to their reputation: for example, the break-up of the former accounting firm, Arthur Andersen, as a result of shredding papers relating to its Enron work; also, Shell in relation to statements made in the 2003 accounts about provable oil reserves which turned out to be significantly incorrect, as a result, it was said, of management pressure on senior executives to exaggerate the reserves. The exposure of this aspect of the incorrect accounts gave rise to significant adverse publicity as to the probity of the board of Shell and its then chairman. This in turn resulted in a reduction in share price and higher cost of borrowing as well as the resignation of the chairman. The allegedly slow recall in 2010 by Toyota of thousands of cars which had safety problems had a dreadful impact on the reputation of Toyota for quality. Reputation has been seen as a critical asset which can be easily broken or damaged in the context of an invasive media and better informed investors, consumers and employees. Accordingly, the management of reputation is becoming a central risk management issue for companies to consider. It can transform an organisation's fortune, and become a key differentiator affording protection against the occasional ill wind.

Reputation has been defined as "the historic and cultural dimension of a

20.007

---

[22] *http://www.frc.org.uk/corporate/internalcontrol.cfm.* That copy contains the amendments made in October 2005 following a review conducted by the FRC. See also Ch.15 (Risk Management and Internal Control). The Combined Code has been replaced with the UK Corporate Governance Code, and as at the latest date prior to publication of this book, Turnbull was being reviewed by the FRC and a revised Turnbull expected late in 2010 or early 2011.

company—a stakeholder community's "social memory" of the sum total of the company and its activities".[23]

Risks to reputation can arise from a variety of sources. Examples include:

(a) product quality concerns (e.g. Perrier water found to have benzene traces in 2002; Cadbury's chocolate found in 2006 to have minute quantities of salmonella—the damage being a double dose, unsafe product, but more seriously perhaps, the failure to tell the UK Food Standards Agency for some days; the 2010 recall by Toyota of thousands of cars with mechanical problems which had safety implications);

(b) pressure group action (for example, Oxfam's campaign against "big pharmas" patent policies or the "saynototesco" campaign against a proposed store in Norwich in 2006);

(c) failure to comply with laws, regulations or reasonable expectations of integrity and professionalism (for example, Arthur Andersen; Shell; BP (deaths in Texas; unsafe oil pipelines in Alaska) and Cadbury).

Sometimes mere association with a market sector can contribute to reputational damage, for example the banking industry following the 2000 Cruickshank Report.

The broader business case

20.008 The case that effective CSR can win positive benefits to the bottom line is less easy to demonstrate than the narrow case for risk management, because the benefits can be difficult to quantify and causal connection may be difficult to establish.[24] In 2001, the Ashridge Business School published research entitled "Exploring the Boundaries of Corporate Social Responsibility" in partnership with the Copenhagen Centre. The research explored the views of senior executives from four countries who had developed CSR projects, often in partnership with Government. They were clear that the most important impact of CSR was on business performance.

A recent World Economic Forum survey[25] of business leaders concluded that there is broad agreement on the principal business reasons for supporting CSR. Among these claims for the broader business case are as follows:

---

[23] Michael Sherman, Chief Operating Officer, AIG Europe (UK) Ltd, 2003.

[24] See also "*Risk returns and responsibility*", ABI, February 2004, Roger Cowe.

[25] World Economic Forum, Values and Value, findings of a 2003 CEO survey of the World Economic Forum Global Corporate Citizenship Initiative in partnership with the Prince of Wales International Business Leaders Forum, 2004.

Share price performance

Business and investment communities have long debated whether there is a   **20.009**
real connection between socially responsible business practices and positive
share price performance. The conclusions are mildly encouraging. Lower
share price volatility was found in studies by the Institute of Business Ethics
and by Cass Business School for Business in the Environment ("BiE") examining companies from the environmental index, the study correlated the
rankings in the index with share price performance. It found there was slight
(but not statistically significant) underperformance by the high scorers in
the environmental index. But there was apparently a significant difference in
share price volatility between the environmental leaders and the low scoring
companies. A comprehensive review of research over four decades conducted
by the UK's Centre for Sustainable Investment concluded[26]:

> "the evidence reviewed here suggests that the use of SEE screens[27] does not
> impact negatively on the share performance. At best, the evidence appears
> to be moving towards a 'SEE effect' that contributes to portfolio out per-
> formance. At worst, the evidence suggests that an investment policy using
> SEE screens is unlikely to harm financial returns."

A study conducted by UBS investment bank in 2001 concluded:

> "we find no evidence that socially responsible investing confers any sus-
> tainable performance advantage in the long run ... Having said that,
> however, we do not believe that investing responsibly necessarily entails
> financial sacrifices."[28]

Similar findings arose from research conducted by the investment bank
WestLB Panmure in 2002 and by the Swiss private bank Pictet.[29]

Reduced operating costs

Many initiatives aimed at improving environmental performance—such   **20.010**
as reducing emissions of gases that contribute to global climate change or
reducing use of agrochemicals—are said also to lower costs. Many recycling

---

[26] *"Sustainability pays"*, published by CIS, 2002; also *"Does business ethics pay?"* by Simon
Webley and Elise More. April 2003. *http://www.ibe.org.uk.*
[27] The practice by analysts of "screening" companies for particular features.
[28] *The merits of socially responsible investing*, UBS 2001; *"Risk returns and responsibility"*, ABI
February 2004, Roger Cowe.
[29] *More Gain than Pain*, Garz, Volk and Gilles, WestLB Panmure 2002; *Decomposing SRI
Performance*, Pictet, 2003.

initiatives cut waste-disposal costs and generate income by selling recycled materials. In the human resources arena, flexible scheduling and other work-life programmes that result in reduced absenteeism and increased retention of employees are thought to save companies money through increased productivity and reduction of hiring and training costs.

Enhanced brand image and reputation

20.011   It is claimed that customers are often drawn to brands and companies with good reputations in CSR-related areas, for example, Bodyshop. A company considered socially responsible can benefit both from its enhanced reputation with the public as well as its reputation within the business community, increasing a company's ability to attract capital and trading partners. A 2001 Environics International CSR Monitor survey apparently showed that the factors most influencing public impressions of companies were social responsibility (49 per cent); brand quality/reputation (40 per cent); and business fundamentals (32 per cent).

Increased sales and customer loyalty

20.012   A number of studies have claimed to suggest a large and growing market for the products and services of companies perceived to be socially responsible. While businesses must first satisfy customers' key buying criteria—such as price, quality, availability, safety and convenience—studies also purport to show a growing desire to buy (or not buy) because of other values-based criteria, such as "sweatshop-free" and "child-labour-free" clothing, lower environmental impact, and absence of genetically-modified materials or ingredients.

Increased productivity and quality

20.013   Company efforts to improve working conditions, lessen environmental impacts or increase employee involvement in decision making are said to lead to increased productivity and reduced error rate.

Increased ability to attract and retain employees

20.014   Companies perceived to have strong CSR commitments are said to find it easier to recruit and retain employees, resulting in a reduction in turnover and associated recruitment and training costs. As a specific example, the mining group Anglo-American Plc has invested heavily in HIV/AIDS treatment and healthcare in their South African operations which has claimed a dramatically improved level of employee retention and productivity.[30]

Reduced regulatory oversight

Companies that demonstrably satisfy or go beyond regulatory compliance requirements may be given more free reign by both national and local government entities. In the US, for example, federal and state agencies overseeing environmental and workplace regulations have formal programmes that recognise and reward companies that have taken proactive measures to reduce adverse environmental, health and safety impacts. In many cases, such companies are subject to fewer inspections and paperwork, and may be given preference or "fast-track" treatment when applying for operating permits, zoning variances or other forms of governmental permission. The US Federal Sentencing Guidelines allow penalties and fines against corporations to be reduced or even eliminated if a company can show it has taken "good corporate citizenship" actions and has an effective ethics programme in place. **20.015**

Access to capital

It is claimed that the growth of SRI means companies with strong CSR performance have increased access to capital that might not otherwise have been available. **20.016**

SRI assets grew faster than the entire universe of managed assets in the US during the last 10 years, according to the Social Investment Forum's fifth biennial report on SRI trends published in January 2006. Total socially responsible investment assets rose more than 258 per cent from $639 billion in 1995 to $2.29 trillion in 2005, while the broader universe of assets under professional management increased less than 249 per cent from $7 trillion to $24.4 trillion over the same period.

What are companies actually doing about CSR?

General—the sceptical view

Set out below are a limited number of case studies taken from the online annual reports of the FTSE companies concerned. Critics of companies' CSR reports make the following observations: **20.017**

---

[30] *http://www.angloamerican.co.uk*; but it should also be noted that Anglo-American's Ghana operations have been heavily criticised on environmental grounds.

- some of the reports have no independent audit. In para.20.033 below there is a list of some of the independent standards against which CSR reports can be verified;

- some of the reports have too little substantive information and performance data to be considered legitimate CSR reports[31];

- some of the reports are said to contain little more than "environmental spin" or "green wash";

- some companies can indeed point to legitimate achievements in CSR, but nevertheless fall significantly short of the standards expected of them by the community in major areas. For example, **BP** which has a comprehensive CSR report nevertheless suffered a major fire at its Texas refinery doing 2005 killing several employees, which gave rise to questions of safety standards which are now the subject of US Court proceedings; BP has also suffered major oil spills at its Alaska oil fields, when, again, questions were raised about the standard of maintenance of oil pipelines in its Alaska operations leading in July 2006 to a shutdown of its Alaskan pipeline for repairs. It was also accused in 2006 of manipulating the propane gas market in the US so as to raise prices. **Tesco** also has an admirable CSR report and clearly believes in the CSR agenda at many levels, but has land purchase and development policies which are said to drive out truly local retailers and reduce retailing diversity in a community. In 2006, **Cadbury Schweppes**, which, again, has an excellent CSR report, was forced to recall chocolate bars on a large scale after discovering tiny amounts of salmonella. The complaint was as much about the Group's alleged failure to notify the Food Standards Agency in a timely manner, thus giving rise to an appearance of a "cover-up". The defence contractor **BAE Systems** has been at the centre of corruption allegations in relation to its Middle East business which has resulted in the payment of a fine of $400 million to the US Department of Justice;

- mainstream investment decisions by investors are, it is said, not taken on the basis of a company's CSR record.[32]

Accordingly the case studies below should be read with an appropriate degree of caution. However, there is no doubt that in some of the cases studied below the level of community activity is substantial and impressive. Moreover institutional pressure in relation to CSR issues is on the increase

---

[31] The corporate branding and corporate communications design consultancy, Salter Baxter, published a report in February 2006 called "directions 5" which examined the disclosures made by FTSE 100 companies during 2005; the judging panel found that 14 of these companies offered too little information, *http://www.salterbaxter.com.*

[32] *Independent on Sunday*, February 19, 2006.

(see paras 20.024 et seq.) and it is reasonable to suppose that over time the "key drivers for change" described in the introduction to this chapter will impose on companies verifiable action which matches the words.

CSR case studies

Marks & Spencer Plc (general retailer—"How we do business" report 2009)	20.018

Key features

- Report 42 pages in length.

- Ernst & Young provided an independent audit and assurance report on the accuracy of the statements in relation to the CR report.

- Explained its CR policy in terms of a number of "pillars" e.g. climate change, waste, sustainable raw materials

- £9.8 million donated to community programmes.

- Named in the Dow Jones Sustainability Index as the leading retailer for the third year running.

- Launched a "naturally inspired" range of products using only natural or unnaturally-derived cleaning ingredients and free of all artificial colours.

- Replaced a number of chemicals used in children's clothing products believed to be harmful to the environment.

- Introduced a method of buying milk from farmers which guarantees the price level.

- Introduced over 2,635 people into the stores as part of the "marks and start" community programme of work experience for homeless people, people with disabilities, the young unemployed, parents returning to work.

- Started a chain of in-store coffee shops which will sell 100 per cent fair trade coffee.

- Participated in a project with its fishing suppliers to cut down the numbers of cod fish inadvertently caught when fishing for haddock.

- Greenpeace confirmed that Marks & Spencer were one of the most improved retailers at wood sourcing for garden furniture.

- Completed the second year of post-graduate "food miles" research with three studies to identify the environmental impacts of the production and transportation of beans, apples and watercress.

- Approximately 40 tonnes of organic cotton fibre were blended into Marks & Spencer clothing during 2004. The company says that it remains "active participants in the Global Organic Cotton Exchange supporting the growth of the organic cotton market".

- Pesticides: in 2004 the company recorded an overall score of 73 per cent residue-free foods against 72 per cent in 2003. "We have continued to publish our monthly independent pesticide residue testing results every quarter on our website. We are still working with our suppliers to replace 19 pesticides in addition to the 60 we have already banned".

- Global Sourcing Principles: the company reviewed and updated its Global Sourcing Principles to reflect its adoption of the Ethical Trading Initiative Base Code as international best practice.

- Gangmasters: the company worked with government, industry and trade unions to develop the UK Code of Practice for Labour Providers in preparation for the introduction of a licensing system in April 2006.

- SEDEX: having helped found the Supplier Ethical Data Exchange ("SEDEX"), which allows supplier assessments to be collated and shared cost effectively online, the company continued to extend its use to 23 food suppliers.

- Salt: the company reduced the average salt content across products such as ready meals, breakfast cereals, bread and sandwiches. This was said to have achieved the British Retail Consortium's 2009 targets for maximum amounts of salt per serving four years early. "The results of this work and our commitment to continued reductions have been publicly recognised by the Food Standards Agency and the Department of Health".

BAE Systems Plc (Aerospace and defence—2005 Annual report[33])	**20.019**

Key features

- CSR report 42 pages in length.

- Independent assurance report from the Corporate Citizenship Company[34].

- Maintained its position in both the Dow Jones Sustainability World Index and the in the European Dow Jones STOXX sustainability index. "Our total score for 2005 was 81%. This was the highest score reached by a company in our specific industry sector and considerably higher than the average within the sector group of 50%".

- Sets out the governance structure for CSR matters.

- Published a selection of questions from shareholders on aspects of CSR and answers.

- Explained its CSR policy for 2005 in terms of five objectives (for example, developing a formal stakeholder engagement plan, improving health and safety and environment performance, improving the company's rating against Accountability Standard AA1000) and stated its strategic objectives for 2006.

- Set out a number of "stakeholder position" statements and responses by the company some of which are described below.

- Thus, invited the Institute of Business Ethics to set out a statement of ethics for the defence industry and reported response.

- Invited a trades union leader to set out a statement of best approach in relation to employee relations and set out response.

- Invited an institutional shareholder to set out a stakeholder position in relation to lobbying and the company's response.

---

[33] As noted above, BAE Systems in 2010 paid a fine of $400m to the US Department of Justice arising out of allegations of bribery in relation to its Middle East business, *http://www.bae systems/corporateresponsibility/index.htm.*

[34] It may be useful to quote the introductory paragraph of this report:

"In our opinion, the report provides a fair and balanced representation of the progress BAE Systems is making in living out its commitments to corporate responsibility (CR). Where gaps in available performance data and stakeholder views on material issues exist, they are identified below. In forming our opinion and making our comments, we have had regard to the principles underlying the international assurance standard AA1000 (*http://www.account-ability.org.uk*) notably concerning materiality, completeness and responsiveness. We have also had regard to the 11 reporting principles judged essential by the June 2002 GRI sustainability reporting guidelines (*http://www.globalreporting.org*)."

- Set out a stakeholder position in relation to education programmes provided by the company (technology competition is fulfilled children and roadshows to encourage taking science and technology subjects) and the company's response.

- In 2005, the company's total global community investment was £10,525,731. Split between education and young people 65.27 per cent; social welfare 15.14 per cent; emergency relief 9.88 per cent; armed forces 4.94 per cent; health 2.25 per cent; arts and culture 1.58 per cent; economic development 0.50 per cent; other 0.25 per cent; environment 0.19 per cent.

- Published a statement of performance in relation to employee diversity.

- Published a statement of ethics.

- Published a table of performance (or lack of it) in relation to environmental matters: energy use, CO_2 emissions, waste, water use.

- Published graphs in relation to accidents and reportable illnesses over three years.

20.020 | **Daily Mail and General Trust Plc (Media—annual report, 2005[35])**

Key features

- CSR report 15 pages in length.

- Entered the FTSE4Good index in 2004.

- The Group's corporate website, *http://www.dmgt.co.uk*, was stated to have achieved an "AAA" accessibility rating in recent independent tests, "the highest level achievable". "It is independently regarded as one of the best-programmed sites in the FTSE 100 index".

- Charity appeals run by the group in the past five years have raised £29 million.

- In 2003/2004 donated £904,000 to charities.

- 98 per cent of "virgin fibre products" are sourced from managed forests.

[35] *http://www.dmgt.co.uk/corporate-responsibility.*

- Requires that the forests are certified either by the Forest Stewardship Council or the Pan European Forestry Commission.

- All production paper waste is recycled. More than half of office paper waste at headquarters is recycled.

- Risk Management Solutions, a division of DMG Information was said to be "the world's leading provider of products and services for the management of catastrophe risks".

- Has cut its water requirements by 18 per cent since 2003.

- Eighty-five per cent of the group's printing presses use Computer to Plate ("CTP") processes. The environmental benefits of this system are improvements in the use of ink, plates and paper and a reduction in the chemicals used during photographic processes. Digital photography is used in an increasing number of the printing centres. In addition, the IT equipment at Northcliffe Newspapers printing centres is either collected and recycled if reusable, or is collected and disposed of by licensed waste management companies.

- All paper used internally for printers and photocopiers at our headquarters "is sourced under strict quality, environmental and ethical codes applied to products and suppliers. No products are sourced from countries where there is a lack of environmental control or poor labour practices".

- *Bristol Evening Post* named Newspaper Society Campaigning Newspaper of the Year for 2002, 2003 and 2004.

- The *Leicester Mercury* was stated to be "the driving force" behind establishing the city's Multicultural Advisory Group, the first of its kind in the country. This informal talking shop brings together up to 20 groups within the city to discuss promotion of racial understanding at times of tension. The *Mercury*'s editor, Nick Carter, has travelled internationally to advise on the media's role in promoting community cohesion, and community representatives from several European nations have visited the paper to see its initiatives in action.

- "Daily Mail Schools Rugby" was stated to be the largest rugby tournament of its kind in the world with more than 800 schools taking part.

- Each of the group's divisions is stated to have complaints mechanisms, many of them through external bodies such as the Press Complaints Commission. "Performance in relation to complaints and breaches of editorial standards over recent years has been good and the number of complaints upheld has been negligible".

> • The Kabiro Primary School in Nairobi, Kenya, is being rebuilt with the help of Hobsons' Aid Plan, a charity that helps children in developing countries. Hobsons, an education information provider and student recruitment specialist owned by DMG Information, focuses fundraising on education initiatives and has developed a group-wide charity plan. The scheme, now in its fifth year, has raised nearly £100,000 and has helped to build five schools. As part of Hobsons' commitment to the project, an employee from each office in the UK, US, Australia, Germany and France will spend a week at Kabiro in 2005 to help with the reconstruction effort, and report back to colleagues. Chris Letcher, Hobsons' Managing Director, said: "Employees want to work for a company that is operating responsibly. They notice if an organisation is taking that extra step. We explain our charity work to potential employees at interviews because it is part of the fabric of the business".

Governance structures for CSR

20.021   Inevitably governance structures will differ from company to company, and individual companies no doubt change those structures from time to time. However, taking HSBC as but one example of a possible model which is replicated more or less in other companies:

- The Corporate Sustainability Committee is responsible for advising the HSBC board, committees of the board and executive management on corporate sustainability policies, including environmental, social and ethical issues. At an operational level, these issues are managed on a day-to-day basis primarily by Group Human Resources, Group Risk and Group Corporate Sustainability. The terms of reference of the Committee are available on the downloads section on the CR page of the company's website. The members of the Committee in 2008 were W K L Fung (Chairman), Sir Mark Moody-Stuart and N R N Murthy, each of whom is a non-executive Director, G V I Davis, Dame Mary Marsh and Lord May, who are non-director members of the Committee.

- It meets at least four times yearly.

- There is also a CR Executive Steering Group. The objective of the Executive Steering Group is to oversee the implementation of the CR policies, performance evaluation and communications. Comprising executives from business functions that influence the overall CR performance, the steering group also acts as a conduit for keeping the CR Committee of the board informed.

- The department of "Group Corporate Affairs" co-ordinates external and internal communications, and stakeholder engagement. Working groups have also been formed in France, Brazil, Hong Kong and the Middle East to co-ordinate CR at national and regional levels.

The views of institutional investors

As indicated by the passage quoted at the beginning of this chapter from the CIS giving reasons why it was voting against the annual report of the Chemring Group Plc, institutions are becoming increasingly proactive in using their voting powers to influence the corporate social responsibility behaviour of investee companies.   **20.022**

The ABI 2007 revised Guidelines on responsible investment

The guidelines take the form of disclosures, which institutions would expect to see included in the annual reports of listed companies.   **20.023**

Specifically, they refer to disclosures relating to board responsibilities and to policies, procedures and verification.

"With regard to the Board, the company should state in its annual report whether:

1.1 As part of its regular risk assessment procedures, the Board takes account of the significance of environmental, social and governance (ESG) matters to the business of the company.
1.2 The Board has identified and assessed the significant ESG risks to the company's short- and long-term value, as well as the opportunities to enhance value that may arise from an appropriate response.
1.3 The Board has received adequate information to make this assessment and that account is taken of ESG matters in the training of directors.
1.4 The Board has ensured that the company has in place effective systems for managing and mitigating significant risks, which, where relevant, incorporate performance management systems and appropriate remuneration incentives.

With regard to policies, procedures and verification, the annual report should:

2.1 Include information on ESG-related risks and opportunities that may significantly affect the company's short- and long-term value, and how they might impact on the future of the business.
2.2 Include in the description of the company's policies and procedures for managing risks, the possible impact on short and long term value arising from ESG matters. If the annual report and accounts states that the

company has no such policies and procedures, the Board should provide reasons for their absence.

2.3 Include information, where appropriate using key performance indicators (KPIs), about the extent to which the company has complied with its policies and procedures for managing material risks arising from ESG matters and about the role of the Board in providing oversight.

2.4 Where performance falls short of the objectives, describe the measures the Board has taken to put it back on track.

2.5 Describe the procedures for verification of ESG disclosures. The verification procedure should be such as to achieve a reasonable level of credibility.

With regard to the Board, the company should state in its remuneration report:

3.1 Whether the remuneration committee is able to consider corporate performance on ESG issues when setting remuneration of executive directors. If the report states that the committee has no such discretion, then a reason should be provided for its absence.

3.2 Whether the remuneration committee has ensured that the incentive structure for senior management does not raise ESG risks by inadvertently motivating irresponsible behaviour."

The ABI argues that there are two business cases for CSR:

(a)   the control and elimination of business risks associated with the environmental impact, poor labour relations, human rights abuses and bad management of stakeholders;

(b)   competitive advantage—or rather features which in the minds of investors distinguish in a positive fashion the socially responsible organisation.

To these one might add the argument of share price advantage as gradually investors take positions in socially acceptable companies under increasing public pressure to do so.[36]

Examples of individual institutional policies

Aviva Investors (formerly known as Morley Fund Management)

20.024   Aviva Investors ("AI") is a wholly-owned subsidiary of Aviva Plc, whose previous name was Norwich Union Insurance Group. AI owns over 1 per cent

---

[36] See para.20.009 above.

of the UK stock market and manages in the region of £235 billion globally. AI not only manages the Sustainable Future fund for Aviva but also manages a number of other investment funds in respect of which it operates a proactive policy on social and environmental and ethical issues. The Sustainable Future funds offer clients the opportunity to invest in companies that are at the forefront of promoting and supporting sustainable development, either through the products and services they offer, all their leading social, environmental and ethical practices.

AI takes the view that analysis of SEE it is an effective tool in the investment evaluation:

> "Economies and businesses do not operate in isolation from society nor outside the limitations posed by their physical or political environment, so these factors need to be incorporated into predictions about longer-term economic growth and corporate profitability."

With this in mind the Morley policy on SEE disclosure is as follows:

- Morley expects all FTSE 350 index companies to disclose information on their exposure to and management of key social, environmental and ethical risks.

- Where companies do not publish any SEE information, Morley may vote against the resolution to adopt the report and accounts.

- Where companies publish insufficient information on SEE issues, Morley may withhold support on the resolution to adopt the report and accounts.

CIS[37]

CIS is the business name for the Co-operative Insurance Society which has **20.025** approximately £20 billion of funds under its management.

It states as its policy that: "acting responsibly, honestly and with integrity is a key part of our tradition as a co-operative society".

The Co-operative Group in 2008 was voted the UK's most ethical brand. In the area of investments, "ethics similarly plays a part in everything we do".

CIS states that it is the only UK fund manager to analyse social, ethical, environmental and other company management issues (e.g. "fat cat" pay) across all the funds we manage, as well as conventional investment analysis.

They apply this approach to its UK Growth, UK Income with Growth, Sustainable Leaders and Corporate Bond Income Trusts.

---

[37] *http://www.cis.co.uk.*

In addition, their "Sustainable Leaders Trust" takes this one step further by avoiding companies involved in areas such as nuclear power generation, tobacco, armaments and pornography, "among others that do not meet our strict criteria."

Hermes[38]

20.026 Hermes is the largest pension fund investment manager in the UK, independent of any broader financial services organisation. Hermes invests over £21.6 billion (as at March 31, 2009) on behalf of around 240 clients including pension funds, insurance companies, Government entities and financial institutions, as well as charities and endowments. Hermes' largest client is the BT pension scheme.

Hermes is at the forefront of the "activist" corporate governance movement in the UK. Despite this, it does not publish its voting record and has no separate CSR/SEE policy. Instead, its corporate governance philosophy is set out in the "Hermes Corporate Governance Principles", first published in 2001, but republished in 2008.[39] The relevant principle is Principle 9.

> "Behaving ethically
> Principle 9 'Companies should manage effectively relationships with their employees, suppliers and customers and with others who have a legitimate interest in the company's activities. Companies should behave ethically and have regard for the environment and society as a whole.'
>
> Well managed companies cannot ignore the impact of their activities on the wider society. Company activity should be subservient to the law. Basic economic efficiency would argue it is appropriate that companies are open about the impact of their activities. Doing well economically and behaving responsibly are not mutually exclusive.
>
> This does not mean that businesses have limitless social obligations. It is the responsibility of businesses to generate a capital surplus. But it is not appropriate to generate such a surplus without regard to wider obligations.
>
> Of course, to require companies to behave ethically raises many questions, both theoretical and practical. We live in a society where it is appropriate for legislators to pass laws which govern company activities. These do not necessarily set a minimum requirement. It is not our role to act as moral philosophers, still less do we wish to micromanage companies' responses to ethical issues, any more than we would wish to micromanage their commercial operations."

---

[38] Hermes Corporate Governance Global Principles, 2005.
[39] *http://www.hermes.co.uk/pdf/corporate_governance/Hermes_Principles.pdf.*

The UK Government, the UN and OECD policies

The UK Government[40]

The approach of the UK Government is a mix of the role of facilitator in **20.027**
the context of general sustainability policy initiatives; second, in imposing
specific reporting requirements, for example, the reporting by trustees of their
CSR policy in investment decisions under the Pensions Act 2004, and also the
"enhanced" business review[41] in the annual directors' report which CA 2006
s.417 requires; and, thirdly, through the use of public procurement policies
which favour environmentally sensitive companies.

General policy initiatives

The best place to start on Government sustainable development policy is **20.028**
the Government website: *http://www.sustainable-development.gov.uk* coupled
with that of the website of the Department for Energy and Climate Change:
http://www.decc.gov.uk>the Renewable Energy Strategy. Policy initiatives
are also being developed by the UK Sustainability Commission and other
bodies, all of whose websites are set out in the footnote below.[42]

Reporting requirements

Under the business review provisions of the CA 2006,[43] in terms, every quoted **20.029**
company must produce an annual business review which must, to the extent
necessary for an understanding of the development, performance and operation of the business of the company, include analysis using KPIs which include
information relating, amongst other things,[44] to environmental matters.

In order to provide assistance in relation to this analysis Defra[45] has produced a set of "Environmental Reporting Guidelines—Key Performance

---

[40] The author is indebted to Tamar Bourne who while at the UK Sustainable Commission
kindly provided the author with a number of references on UK Government policy on CSR
and sustainability, and also introduced the author to Jonathon Porritt's outstanding book:
Capitalism as if the World Matters, Earthscan, 2005.
[41] See para.20.029 below.
[42] e.g. *http://www.sd-commission.org.uk* (UK Sustainability Commission); *http://www.forum-
forthefuture.org.uk/aboutus/EWB_page1517.aspx* (Forum For the Future); *http://www.bitc.org.
uk* (Business in the Community).
[43] CA 2006 s.417.
[44] See fn 14 above.
[45] The Department for Environment Food and Rural Affairs.

Indicators".[46]

The Guidelines outline how environmental impacts can be measured through KPIs (for example KPI 1 is Greenhouse Gases) and intended to enable companies to make use of standard business data already collected, as well as provide guidance on how data should be reported.[47]

The purpose of these Guidelines asserted by Defra is to help businesses to:

- measure and aggregate the emissions produced from energy use, industrial processes and transport—they include factors to convert electricity and gas or other fuels used into their equivalents in carbon dioxide, and convert transport fuel usage or distances travelled, by road, rail, air or sea, into carbon dioxide equivalents. plus factors to convert emissions of other greenhouse gases into carbon dioxide equivalents;

- set targets to reduce emissions—having established the environmental impact of the business's activities, it can look at any relevant benchmarks and check the scope for improvements in both the short and longer terms;

- achieve savings—better management of greenhouse gas emissions can cut energy and transport costs and reduce environmental risks. In future, domestic and international markets for emissions trading will allow businesses also to benefit directly from their carbon dioxide savings;

- report on performance—publishing information on greenhouse gas emissions and plans for the future "can demonstrate to shareholders, consumers, investors and other stakeholders that yours is a well-run, environmentally responsible business".

Public procurement

20.030   The Government appointed "sustainable[48] procurement task force" announced on June 12, 2006 recommendations for public sector procurement standards in relation to sustainability, covering energy efficiency, carbon dioxide emissions, the efficient use of natural resources and raw materials, transport, measures to avoid pollution and at ways of ensuring environmentally sensitive goods such as timber are obtained from well-managed sources. The Government is expected to incorporate new sustainability guidelines into an easily communicated set of instructions for procurement managers.

---

[46] *http://www.defra.gov.uk/environment/business/index.htm* and see also fn 14 above.
[47] For an excellent guide by Trucost Plc on the meaning of the KPIs in the context of the EU Accounts Modernisation Directive see *http://www.trucost.com.*
[48] *http://www.defra.gov.uk/sustainable/government.*

The United Nations

On April 27, 2006 the then Secretary-General of the United Nations, Mr   **20.031**
Kofi Annan, launched the United Nations Principles For Responsible
Investment,[49] which were sponsored by investment banks and institutional
funds managing funds worth over $6 trillion. They comprise six Principles
which in essence require institutional investors to engage in and report on
investment policies which encourage the development of sound practices on
ESG matters by investee companies:

> "There is a growing view among investment professionals that environ-
> mental, social and corporate governance issues can affect the performance
> of investment portfolios. Investors fulfilling their fiduciary (or equivalent)
> duty therefore need to give appropriate consideration to these issues, but to
> date have lacked a framework for doing so. The 'Principles for Responsible
> Investment' provide this framework."[50]

The Principles are voluntary and aspirational. They are not prescriptive, but
instead provide a menu of possible actions for incorporating ESG issues into
mainstream investment decision-making and ownership practices.

The United Nations Global Compact[51] is an initiative to encourage businesses worldwide to adopt sustainable and socially responsible policies, and
to report on them. Under the Compact, companies are brought together with
UN agencies, labour groups and civil society.

The Global Compact was officially launched in New York on July 26,
2000. As at June 2009, it included more than 5,300 businesses from all regions
of the world.

The OECD

The OECD Guidelines for Multinational Enterprises[52] are an international   **20.032**
benchmark for corporate responsibility. They contain voluntary principles
and standards for responsible business conduct in such areas as human
rights, supply chain management, disclosure of information, anti-corruption,
taxation, labour relations, environment, competition and consumer welfare.
They aim to promote the positive contributions multinational enterprises can
make to economic, environmental and social progress.

The Guidelines are stated to express the shared values of the 39 countries

---

[49] *http://www.unpri.org.*
[50] *http://www.unpri.org.*
[51] *http://www.unglobalcompact.org.*
[52] *http://www.oecd.org.*

that have adhered to them (the 30 OECD members and nine non-member countries). The adhering countries are said to be the source of almost 90 per cent of the world's foreign direct investment and are home to most major multinational enterprises. Although many business codes of conduct are now publicly available, the Guidelines are the only multilaterally-endorsed and comprehensive code that governments are committed to promoting. The Guidelines are part of a broader package of instruments, most of which address government responsibility—they promote open and transparent policy frameworks for international investment.

Independent verification

20.033 Some companies are choosing to have their reports on CSR policy implementation audited or verified by external third parties to assess the quality of information presented by the corporation and the integrity of management reporting systems.

The following are the more widely recognised organisations for measurement of CSR:

(a) **AccountAbility 1000 Series ("AA1000")**. AA1000 is a framework developed by the Institute of Social and Ethical Accountability which companies can use to understand and improve their ethical performance. It focuses on providing a framework through which quality social and ethical accounting, auditing and reporting can be achieved. It comprises principles and a set of process standards. The Standard is currently being revised with five specialised modules: calibration and communication of quality of stakeholder engagement; integration with existing management and metrics systems; quality assurance and external verification; governance and risk management; and for small and medium enterprises.

(b) **Global Reporting Initiative ("GRI")**.[53] The GRI issues guidelines covering three areas: economic, (e.g. wages and benefits), environmental (e.g. impacts on bio-diversity) and social (e.g. labour rights); and has also developed Sustainability Reporting Guidelines.

(c) **Social Accountability 8000 ("SA8000")**. SA8000 was developed in conjunction with representatives from trade unions, businesses and NGOs. The standard is based on a number of existing international human rights and labour standards; including ILO conventions relating to employment as well as the Universal Declaration of Human Rights and the United Nations Convention on the Rights of the Child. The standard aims to provide "transparent, measurable,

---

[53] *http://www.globalreporting.org.*

verifiable" standards for certifying the performance of organisations in nine areas: child labour, forced labour, health and safety compensation, working hours, discrimination, discipline, free association and collective bargaining and management systems.

(d) **ECO-Management and Audit Scheme ("EMAS").** EMAS is a voluntary scheme for organisations willing to commit themselves to evaluate and improve their environmental performance. The scheme requires certification from an accredited body, an environmental policy to be in existence within a company and to be fully supported by senior management.

(e) **The Corporate Citizenship Company.**[54] The Corporate Citizenship Company has developed a comprehensive methodology to help companies self-assess and manage their economic, social and environmental impacts, based on a stakeholder approach. It has been engaged in social audits for several multi-national companies, across a range of businesses and countries. They include: Ford India; Vodafone; Unilever; South African Breweries; Guinness UDV. The team has experience in writing social reports both for publication and for internal communication.

As a development of social auditing the company has undertaken several projects to "define and manage social responsibility in the value chain", for example with Cadbury Schweppes.

(f) **The London Benchmarking Group.**[55] The London Benchmarking Group consists of leading international corporations who have come together to manage, measure and report their involvement in the community. To do this measurement and reporting it has developed a model identifying three categories into which different forms of community involvement can be classified: charity donations, social or community investment and commercial initiatives. These are contributions made over and above those that result from the basic business operations.

(g) **The Association of British Insurers ("ABI").** It is clear (as the opening full paragraph of this chapter demonstrates) that the ABI scrutinises the reports and accounts of selected listed companies to monitor the extent to which the ABI's Disclosure Guidelines on socially responsible investment are being observed, but there is no public access to the criteria used by the ABI in making its assessments.

In addition, there are a number of membership or signatory based organisations and indices to which companies and others may belong in order to

---

[54] *http://www.corporate-citizenship.co.uk.*
[55] *http://www.lbg-online.net.*

measure performance, establish networks and best practice or receive recognition. The better known ones are as follows:

(a) **Ceres Principles**. The Ceres Principles were created by a coalition of environmental groups, socially responsible investors and public pension administrators. The coalition uses shareholder resolutions to initiate discussions on environmental responsibility with companies with the goal of getting companies to endorse the Ceres Principles.

(b) **The Goodcorporation**. The Goodcorporation is a global standard of corporate social responsibility which has been designed to address the needs of all types and sizes of organisation. It covers an organisation's fairness to its employees, suppliers, customers, providers of finance, community and environment. Verification tests the "charter principles" of the organisation on four levels from the existence of policies to evidence of these being implemented effectively.

(c) **Trucost Plc.** Trucost Plc is an independent environmental research organisation that was established to help companies and investors understand the environmental impacts of business activities. Trucost provides data and analysis on company emissions and natural resource usage and presents these in financial as well as quantity terms.

The external cost methodology employed by Trucost outlines a company's environmental impacts in order of significance, enabling directors and auditors to focus their efforts on those impacts that are likely to be material to the business. This also forms part of a process by which a company and its auditors can assess whether it should make a public disclosure, for example under the EU Accounts Modernisation Directive—implemented in the UK by CA 2006 s.417.[56]

"Fund managers and analysts increasingly need to know how environmental issues may have a financially material impact on companies' future earnings and make comparisons between companies in a given sector. Yet their ability to accurately assess this is currently constrained by the lack of consistent or comprehensive environmental data disclosure by companies". Trucost provides data and analysis on over 3,200 companies worldwide, including coverage of the FTSE All-Share, S&P 500, Nikkei 225, DJ EuroSTOXX and MSCI indices.

(d) **Ethical Trading Initiative Base Code ("ETI")**. The ETI is an alliance of companies, NGOs and trade union organisations committed to working together to identify and promote ethical trade good practice

---

[56] See para.20.029 above.

by the implementation of a code of conduct of good labour standards. It covers employment, the ending of child labour, forced labour and sweatshops, health and safety, labour conditions and labour rights.

(e) **FTSE4Good.** A financial index called FTSE4Good was published in July 2001. The FTSE4Good is an index for socially responsible investment and is made up of a series of benchmarks and tradable indices facilitating investment in companies with good records of corporate social responsibilities. The selection criteria cover three areas: working towards environmental sustainability, developing positive relationships with stakeholders and upholding and supporting universal human rights. An independent advisory committee is responsible for the design of the selection criteria and for deletions from the index, the management of the index and the ongoing review process to strengthen the selection criteria. A number of sectors are at present excluded, including tobacco producers and nuclear weapons manufacturers.

(f) **The Dow Jones Sustainability Indexes ("DJSI").** Launched in 1999, the Dow Jones Sustainability Indexes were the first global indexes tracking the financial performance of the leading sustainability-driven companies worldwide. Based on the co-operation of Dow Jones Indexes, STOXX Limited and SAM they provide asset managers with reliable and objective benchmarks to manage sustainability portfolios. As at June 2006 56 DJSI licenses were held by asset managers in 14 countries to manage a variety of financial products including active and passive funds, certificates and segregated accounts. In total, these licensees managed €3.6 billion of funds.

(g) **Business in the Community Corporate Responsibility Index.** The Index is based on a framework that Business in the Community developed with business through a series of consultations and workshops with over 80 companies and engagement with a number of other stakeholders during 2002.

Following the launch of the first year's results in March 2003 BITC continued this process throughout 2003, during which time it engaged with representatives from over 110 companies and made a number of modifications to the survey.

To allow continuity and comparison the Index survey has not been changed since 2004. The Index enables companies to assess the extent to which corporate strategy is integrated or translated into responsible practice throughout the organisation, in the management of four key areas: community, environment, marketplace and workplace and finally performance in a range of social and environmental performance and impact areas. Through the confidential

509

feedback reports that BITC provides to participating companies, the Index helps companies to identify gaps in performance, and establish where improvements can be made. The Index also allows companies to demonstrate to their various stakeholders that business is taking the lead in promoting awareness on public reporting, thus increasing trust in business and transparency in business performance.

Key features of the Index:

- FTSE 100, FTSE 250, DJSI sector leaders and equivalent internationally listed groups are invited to participate, based on operations within their management control worldwide. Selected Business in the Community member companies are also encouraged to participate in the benchmarking process as part of their commitment to continual improvement.
- The Corporate Responsibility Index survey is issued to companies as a web based electronic tool and is password protected for each individual company.
- The Environment section of the Corporate Responsibility Index comprises the Business in the Environment Index of Corporate Environmental Engagement. Companies completing the Corporate Responsibility Index can automatically receive a separate listing in the Environment Index.
- There are comprehensive guidance notes provided with the survey in the form of drop down menus within the online survey tool. These provide definitions and help notes to support the understanding of why a particular aspect is important and how this may be applied within a business. Together with the survey this provides a roadmap for integrating corporate responsibility within the business.
- The Corporate Responsibility Index remains a business led initiative which is inclusive of all sectors.

The Institute of Business Ethics

20.034   The Institute of Business Ethics is a non-profit organisation established to emphasise the essentially ethical nature of wealth creation, to encourage the higher standards of behaviour by companies and to help develop and publicise the best ethical practices. The Institute holds consultations and conferences, publishes research and identifies effective actions which business organisations can take, offering practical advice to companies wishing to establish and implement effective ethics policies. Its website is *http://www. ibe.org.uk*. Amongst its many valuable publications, is a publication entitled "Demonstrating Corporate Values", which gives the relative merits of some the standards testing organisations referred to above.

Pressure Groups

On June 2, 2006 a full page advertisement appeared in the *Guardian* so as to **20.035**
coincide with the first day of the debate in the House of Commons on the
Company Law Reform Bill. The advertisement was promoted by a number
of pressure groups amongst which were two groups calling themselves the
Trade Justice Movement[57] and the Corporate Responsibility Coalition[58]
"representing charities, human rights, environment and development groups,
trade unions and faith groups" in which they called for "changes in the law
to ensure:

- companies report on their social and environmental impacts;

- directors take steps to minimise the harm their company may cause to
  local communities and the environment;

- people overseas who are harmed by a UK company and are denied
  justice in their own country have the right to take legal action in a UK
  court."

Conclusion

There are still many sceptics as to the value or even propriety of companies **20.036**
using resources on CSR activity. In the *Financial Times* of May 30, 2006 the
correspondent Stefan Stern expressed the view that "true believers in free
markets and rigorous competition find the warm words of public relations
driven CSR ridiculous . . . The emergence and growth of CSR betrays the
deep crisis of confidence that afflicts too many business leaders".

At the opposite end of the spectrum there are pressure groups and others
which believe that the response of the corporate sector to issues of sustainability has so far been inadequate. They point to the apparent disconnection
between the words of the CSR reports and the actions in recent years of
companies such as BP, Shell and Cadbury Schweppes, as evidence that the
corporate sector regards CSR with indifference.

However, both are wrong. Anyone who studies the corporate social
responsibility reports of many public companies (and the key features of
some of them appear earlier in this chapter) would surely find it impossible
to characterise the many truly outstanding initiatives by many of the FTSE
350 companies as indicating a "deep crisis of confidence" or an inadequate
response.

Rather it is surely the case that public company boards have now decided

---

[57] *http://www.tjm.org.uk.*
[58] *http://www.corporate-responsibility.org.*

that the business case for an active social responsibility strategy has been convincingly made, and that a growing body of investment opinion at grass roots level as well as institutional level is demanding such a strategy. Having made that decision, the energy which companies apply in developing their commercial objectives has been applied with equal vigour to socially responsible objectives. Demands by boards of their executives for outstanding *commercial* performance are being matched by demands for equally outstanding CSR performance, and the evidence is that executives respond to these demands with extraordinary imagination and commitment. They are motivated, surely, not by feelings of a "crisis of confidence", or cynical indifference, but the conviction that it makes very good business sense in terms of sustaining the long-term future of the company concerned, and also happens to be morally inspiring and motivating.

Chapter 21

Pension Funds

Paul Lee[1]

Introduction

Seven years ago, when I first wrote a chapter on the governance of pension **21.001**
funds for the second edition of this book, there was little material to work

[1] Paul Lee is a Director at Hermes Equity Ownership Services, with overall responsibility for EOS' engagement internationally on public policy and best practice. His work involves discussing issues of concern with board members of companies in client portfolios, with the aim of helping the companies to change and develop in ways which will add long-term value for shareholders, as well as engaging with regulators and policy-makers to ensure the financial system works in the interests of long-term investors. Paul is also seconded for part of his time into BTPS Management, which provides the executive investment oversight of the BT Pension Scheme, the UK's largest. His remit for BTPS Management is to help ensure that environmental, social and governance matters are integrated into investment decision-making and fund manager mandates.

Paul is a member of the UK's Auditing Practices Board and a non-executive director of Australian engagement firm Regnan. He is a member of the executive committee (board) of the Quoted Companies Alliance, having been a member of its corporate governance committee from 2002 to 2008. He is a participant in the Corporate Reporting Users' Forum, which tries to influence the development of accounting standards, as well as a member of the Financial Standards and Analysis Committee of the CFA Society of the UK, and also participates in the Audit Quality Forum and various of its working groups. He sits on the Financial Reporting Faculty Advisory Group at the Institute of Chartered Accountants of England and Wales and is a member of the Private Sector Advisory Group of the IFC's Global Corporate Governance Forum.

Paul chaired the working group which rewrote the overarching Principles of the International Corporate Governance Network in 2009, and also chaired the consultative group which developed *Guidance on Good Practice in Corporate Governance Disclosure* in developing economies for the UN Conference on Trade and Development (Unctad). He was a member of the FRC's working party on Auditor Liability Limitation Agreements, and of the Consultative Committee for the FSA's review of the listing regime. Furthermore, he sat on the advisory board of South Africa's Frater Asset Management from 2004 to 2008.

Paul joined Hermes in 2000. Having graduated with a first in law from Oxford University, he spent a decade as a journalist on various specialist legal and financial journals at Euromoney – including five years as editor of *International Financial Law Review*—and the Economist Group, most recently as managing editor of *CFO Europe*. He continues to write, including chapters for various corporate governance and strategy books and winning the PricewaterhouseCoopers European Shareholder Value Award for his article *Not badly paid but paid badly*.

with. While the governance of companies had developed over years of thought and with the aid in the UK of a series of best practice guidelines over more than a decade, the governance of pension schemes was an issue then little thought of. Still less was it an issue where a substantial body of good practice had developed. To a large extent, this is still the case today. The Pensions Regulator has produced a slew of guidance and rules, but it is still possible for leading industry figures to state baldly "The Pension Governance Deficit: Still With Us" (the title of an article by North American doyen of pension fund issues Keith Ambachtsheer together with Ronald Capelle and Hubert Lum in the first issue of the *Rotman International Journal of Pension Management*—see *http://www.rotman.utoronto.ca/icpm/details.aspx?ContentID=223*).

While there is now more regulation and soft law, we are still all too likely to be faced by directors worrying about the potential for conflicts of interest in board meetings which include directors who are also pension fund trustees, saying: "Who are and who should be trustees? Do they have the necessary skills for the job? It's a nightmare". While that comment was made privately to me four years ago, it seems little in practice has moved on. We are still working to develop the answers to such basic and fundamental questions.

Thus this chapter considers the current and developing framework, both of legislation and of soft law, for pension fund governance. Regulation, and more importantly practice, are developing rapidly at the moment, but the body of best practice is only slowly developing. This chapter reflects the current situation and identifies some tentative pointers for the future.

Legislative and Regulatory Framework: the law

21.002   The two key pieces of legislation in relation to pension scheme governance were both inspired, as is so often the case, by external crises. The Pensions Act 1995 was a response to the Maxwell affair when Robert Maxwell was found to have first abused his corporate pension scheme and in the end simply stolen from it. The Act grew out of the conclusions of the Goode Committee, which considered ways to reform pensions law to ensure that no such scandal could recur.

The Pensions Act 2004 was a response to a more generic crisis: the significant deficits in defined benefit ("DB") pension schemes following the bursting of the dotcom bubble, as revealed by the new accounting standards which placed those deficits for the first time explicitly on corporate balance sheets. These combined events sparked a loss of confidence in pension schemes and a shift away from DB to defined contribution ("DC") schemes. The Pensions Act 2008 introduced some further limited developments to the powers of the Pensions Regulator but was mainly focused on creating a national system of personal pension accounts—a national DC system, with auto-enrolment into it for those without other pension provision.

Nevertheless, these DB schemes will continue to be the dominant form of scheme—in terms of financial responsibilities to beneficiaries and investment scale—for the next several years. In addition, the DC or similar schemes which are being introduced to replace them are largely modelling their governance on that of the DB schemes. At least, this is true with regards to those DC schemes which have a formal governance structure at all; increasing numbers of DC schemes are what's known as "contract-based", meaning that there is in effect no governance, only a contract between the individual and the pension provider (typically an insurance firm). Whether such contract-based structures provide sufficient and appropriate protection for individual beneficiaries in the absence of the disciplines of fiduciary duty is a question raised but not answered later in this chapter. The governance structures for DB schemes described in the rest of this chapter are also generally applied by those government-sponsored schemes which are funded, albeit with a significant oversight role played by politicians at the relevant level of government. For these reasons, it is this model on which most of this chapter focuses.

In this chapter these Acts are known as the 1995 Act, the 2004 Act and the 2008 Act. The 2004 Act gave additional powers and responsibilities to trustees. In particular, these include requirements to have sufficient knowledge and understanding. The powers include those to seek additional funding from sponsors and in relation to deficits and winding up. These additional powers and responsibilities are discussed in the relevant sections below.

The 2004 Act established the Pension Protection Fund ("PPF"), a pension fund industry-funded safety net which intends to catch the beneficiaries of failing pension schemes and seek to ensure that their benefits are not lost entirely. It is funded by contributions from the remaining DB pension schemes, in theory according to their riskiness to reduce the problems of moral hazard which is associated with this sort of structure—under which the schemes with the weakest funding would otherwise be incentivised to take further investment risk because of the availability of the PPF as a safety net funded by other more risk-averse schemes.

The 2004 Act also established the Pensions Regulator to oversee pension schemes, encourage best practice and develop soft law. The Pensions Regulator replaced OPRA, the Occupational Pensions Regulatory Authority, which was seen by some as too unresponsive and too slow to improve best practice; in any case, it proved politically sensible to create a new Regulator in its place. While OPRA's focus was, belying its creation in response to Maxwell, fraud prevention, the new Regulator has a far wider remit. Formally, the functions of the regulator are established as: protecting the interests of scheme members; reducing the risk of situations arising which might require compensation from the PPF; and promoting and improving the understanding of good administration of pension schemes.

Legislative and Regulatory Framework: the Regulator

21.003   The Regulator's powers include:

- providing information, education and assistance to schemes and advisers;

- serving improvement notices on those in breach of legislative requirements;

- appointing independent trustees where needed to protect beneficiary interests;

- issuing third party notices to anyone that has caused a breach of legislative requirements;

- providing clearances, which means approving corporate transactions in advance as not being against the interests of pension scheme beneficiaries;

- requiring a scheme to be wound up where an application has been made to the PPF;

- issuing a freezing order preventing winding up or further benefits accruing in a scheme while the regulator considers other actions.

There have been some 150 corporate transactions which the Regulator has approved since its creation. In practice, where a pension scheme is in deficit, the Regulator will only give approval to a return of capital to shareholders, or a takeover or disposal which might affect the company's ability to fund that deficit, if the transaction is accompanied by a significant additional contribution to the pension scheme which substantially reduces the deficit. These approvals are known as Clearance Procedures, and the Regulator's guidance on clearance was revised in early 2008.

One company that has given us a window onto this process is Sherwood Group, a small lingerie manufacturer. As Sherwood is listed, its plans and how they changed under the influence of the Regulator have been subject to some limited public disclosure. The company planned to return cash to shareholders, but with a significant deficit on the pension scheme the Regulator insisted that a significant portion went to reduce the deficit before any funds were returned to shareholders. The Regulator's initial stance was that all the cash should go to limit the deficit, but Sherwood brought in Deloitte to show that the company had a future and so would be capable of funding pensions into the future. The result has been a payment of £8 million into the scheme over 2006, more than double the funding in the prior year, and sharply reduced payouts to shareholders.

The deficit does not need to be wholly funded: the aim of the clearance procedure is to ensure that the scheme does not later become a burden on the PPF. Thus the level of funding must ensure benefits are available to be paid to the level which would be paid by the PPF, which will typically mean a lower deficit calculation than would arise from a full buy-out analysis. And it is worth noting that the protection offered by clearance does not operate to the benefit of the sponsor company itself, but rather to that of the sponsor's directors who otherwise might be personally liable to make the beneficiaries whole if the company fails and the pension scheme is unable to pay out benefits. But directors need to use their judgment as to whether a clearance may be useful, as the cost in terms of additional funding can be high; the Type A events which can trigger clearance situations are "all events that are materially detrimental to the ability of the scheme to meet its pension liabilities", and these events can be in relation to either the sponsor or the scheme itself.

Beyond these clearances, the bulk of the Regulator's work that has been publicly visible thus far lies in the first area, through the publication of Codes of Practice. Formally, these Codes do not themselves have the status of law and there is no penalty for any failure to comply. However, they do have some highly significant legal effects. They will be—indeed they must be—taken into account by the regulator, court or tribunal if they are relevant to what is being decided. It is hard to see them not being considered in, for example, a negligence case. Nevertheless, trustees and others are not required to follow the Codes—indeed, each makes very clear that trustees need not follow every provision in every circumstance—they are required to meet the underlying legal requirements. Yet it seems highly unlikely that trustees will actively seek alternative approaches to particular issues, given the evidential burden that this might pose to demonstrate that the alternative approach is sufficient to meet the legal requirements. That's especially true given the generally commonsensical nature of what the Regulator has thus far produced, all of which has been subject to open consultation.

Since 2006, governance has been an increasing focus for the Regulator. Its medium-term strategy published in April 2006 uses highly forceful language to highlight this. The key performance indicator ("KPI") in the area is "There will be year-on-year improvement in the extent to which trustees demonstrate knowledge and understanding of the governance requirements for their schemes", but it is in other parts of its medium-term plan document that the extent of the Regulator's ambitions are clear. For example, the section on scheme governance raises concerns about "the often low standards of governance, particularly within smaller schemes". The Regulator believes that better governance will lead to better administration, better awareness of financial risk and better representation of the interests of scheme members. It's worth noting that the Regulator's interest extends beyond the governance just of DB schemes:

"Meeting the challenge of improving governance should also therefore contribute to our challenges of improving scheme funding and, in particular, addressing risks to members of DC schemes".

The governance outcome the Regulator is seeking is "to have in place well informed, capable trustees acting in the best interests of their members". This does not sound overly ambitious, but the Regulator clearly does not believe that this is universally the case at the moment, and indeed has set it as a long-term aim, not even a medium-term one.

In October 2007, following consultation, it laid out a clear plan for itself in relation to governance. Its principal route is education and guidance, including working with the industry to develop guidance. Only after educating and enabling will the regulator focus on intervention to drive change. Its focuses in education are: developing trustee knowledge and understanding; issuing guidance on managing conflicts of interest; guidance on clearance procedures and on monitoring and assessing the employer covenant; and advising on calling advisers to account. These are discussed further below. The Regulator asserted:

"We are not planning to increase the burden on trustees, employers and advisers but to provide education and support to enable a similar understanding on running work-based pension schemes, and to encourage good practice resulting in raised standards where appropriate."

This focus was further accelerated in November 2009 with the launch of a full campaign to foster good governance. The Regulator promised a range of updated guidance on governance issues. CEO Tony Hobman put it simply: "Good governance underpins secure pensions". The campaign's theme is Keeping Pensions Safe—find it at *http://www.thepensionsregulator.gov.uk/safe/index.aspx.*

The launch of this campaign was accompanied by the publication of the Regulator's now annual survey of fund governance. This revealed good progress but significant remaining work needed in the areas of clearance, conflicts of interest, risk management and communication. We should expect these to be particular focuses of the campaign as it develops.

Research and indirect influence will not always be enough, though, according to the Regulator's 2006 Business Plan:

"Scheme specific intervention will, nonetheless, be necessary in schemes where we find that education and support activities are proving to be insufficient, for instance where there has been a significant breakdown in governance, or we have identified risks that are sufficiently serious in the context of the number of members concerned or the gravity of the consequences should the risk materialise."

Intervention might include the use of powers to remove trustees and to appoint independents; suspending and prohibiting trustees; and issuing improvement notices and seeking reports from a skilled person. The Regulators' powers of intervention are substantial. Under s.7(3)(c) of the 1995 Act it can appoint independent trustees to the board of a pension scheme. A rare example of this was the appointment of trustees at Telent in late 2007, discussed further below. These powers were further extended under the 2008 Act so that the appointment no longer needs to be "necessary" but can be reasonable "to protect the interests of the generality of the members of the scheme". This change will presumably make the imposition of trustees easier to accomplish.

Legislative and Regulatory Framework: the Ombudsman

The Pensions Ombudsman was a creation of the mid-1990s, though its posi- **21.004**
tion has advanced in recent years. Its role is to resolve disputes and deal with individuals' complaints about pension providers, managers and administrators. As a result, it also acts to promote best practice.

The best guide to the role and work of the Ombudsman is the document "How to avoid the Pensions Ombudsman", a title guaranteed to catch the eye of every trustee (find it at *http://www.pensions-ombudsman.org.uk*). This covers the following key areas: communicating with members, providing information to individuals, running the scheme, duties and standards for making decisions, administrative principles in making decisions, ill-health retirement, death benefits, complaints handling and winding up a scheme. I will consider only a few of these areas here.

A section of communicating with members is headed "Responsibility remains with the Trustees" and, particularly through the case study which forms part of the section, seems to indicate that trustees are likely to find themselves bound by communications from those to whom they have delegated functions. While the role may be delegated, it is not good enough for trustees to excuse errors by saying that they relied on the delegatee to get things right. Any failure by a delegatee should not have a negative impact on beneficiaries' entitlements, the Ombudsman asserts.

In duties and standards on making decisions, the Ombudsman provides a helpful checklist for action—one that may not be surprising for students of the law of judicial review. For a decision to be proper, trustees will need to:

- ask themselves the correct questions;
- direct themselves correctly in law, in particular by adopting a correct construction of the scheme rules;
- take account of all relevant factors and ignore irrelevant ones, thereby avoiding arriving at a perverse decision;
- consider what is fair and equitable in the circumstances;
- make decisions or exercise discretions so as to use powers only for their proper purpose and not to achieve some other purpose.

The Ombudsman's role in promoting best practice is very clearly seen in the fact that the Ombudsman added to the pre-existing principles of acting fairly, providing accurate information and acting in accordance with the general law and rules of the particular scheme a further principle that pension providers "need to take account of the Codes of Practice issued by the Pensions Regulator". The Ombudsman asserts in "How to avoid the Pension Ombudsman" that:

> "While I will not automatically be critical of a decision not to follow the provisions of such a code I will be expecting Trustees to take account of such provisions and to have reasons for any decision to depart from the guidance."

Just as with the assertion by the Pensions Regulator that its Codes of Practice are not cast iron requirements, this statement that the Ombudsman will not be "automatically critical" seems unlikely to carry full weight. For right or wrong, it seems likely that most trustees will act and take decisions in line with the guidance of the Codes of Practice. Any trustee board which takes a decision not to follow a Code will feel obliged to document and justify that decision so fully that they are likely to take a line of lesser resistance and simply follow the Code. It seems likely that any legal advice taken would push in that same direction. Much of what follows therefore considers the Regulator's guidance closely.

Overall structures of pension scheme governance

21.005 Within the context of this overarching regime, the nature of pension scheme governance is actually driven rather more by scheme-specific factors. Every significant occupational pension scheme is established by a trust deed, which sets out the governance structures and the responsibilities of the various parties. Typically, the board of trustees will be established with roughly equal numbers of sponsor-nominated and member-nominated trustees. Though decisions in practice very rarely split along these lines, many trust deeds seek to avoid deadlock, often by giving the sponsor a slight dominance of the trustee body. Other schemes include an independent chair. The member-nominated trustees are usually appointed by staff and pensioners in rough proportion to the break-down of beneficiary numbers. Very often now there is a corporate trustee but its board follows closely this same breakdown. In later discussions the term trustee is used to refer to trustees proper and also to the directors of a corporate trustee board.

Defined benefit schemes are backed by an employers' guarantee, even if the value of that guarantee has been called into doubt by recent corporate failures where the pension fund has been found insufficient to cover its liabilities. Given this, it is not surprising that employers have significant rights to appoint many if not most of the trustees. As the (at least theoretical) source of funding should the pot of money prove insufficient, the company has the strongest interest in assuring good returns from the pension fund.

Oversight by its appointed trustees is its best means of ensuring that returns are as good as possible, so that the company will not be forced to put its hand deeper into its pockets than currently. Few finance directors (or other sponsor board members) will relish the prospect of the share price fall which would no doubt accompany an announcement that the dividend is to be cut to fund a pension scheme deficit. Eliza Tinsley Plc, the first public company to make such an announcement in recent times, found it a costly experience. Its statement that its dividend would be cut by a two-thirds to safeguard cash for pension fund contributions led to a 30 per cent fall in the company's share price.

Since the Pensions Act 1995, the trustees appointed by members of the pension scheme must form at least a third of the trustee board, though there was formerly a right to derogate from this. As of April 2006, pension schemes can no longer opt out of this standard so at least one-third of trustees of all schemes now need to be member-nominated. The Government seems on occasions to favour an even greater level, 50 per cent, but has indicated that it will not require this until it has more confidence in the capabilities of such trustees. These what might be called lay trustees perform two important roles: ensuring that pension fund decisions are taken with the fullest possible understanding of members' interests and concerns; and giving members the confidence that pension fund matters are being run with their best interests at heart. Although the original requirement was introduced following the Maxwell affair, the Goode Committee ("Pension Law Reform: the Report of the Pension Law Review Committee", HMSO 1993) made clear that it did not intend the lay trustees to play the role of watchdogs on behalf of the members. Nevertheless, many member-representative trustees do act as if they had a formal representative capacity.

The requirement that member-nominated trustees form at least one-third of trustees means that the number must be rounded up; if there are 10 trustees in all, 4 must be member-nominated, if 13, 5 must be. The sponsor's consent is required to exceed this number unless a higher requirement is set in the scheme rules.

The Regulator's 2006 Code of Practice on member-nominated trustees establishes the standard that the process must involve all active members and pensioner members (it is accepted that it may be too onerous to include the rather more dispersed deferred members, though the Regulator expects trustees to consider whether they should be included in the process), though this can be done through the medium of representative bodies if appropriate and if these are properly representative. Other than these standards, the Regulator is keen to allow trustees to use appropriate discretion, requiring only that the arrangements are proportionate, fair and transparent. "We want trustees to have flexibility and so we do not want to specify the design of arrangements", it said in reporting the outcome of its consultation.

As well as member-nominated and sponsor-appointed trustees, there may also be independent professional trustees, or corporate trustees. "Independent" in this context means appointed neither by the sponsor nor by the members; corporate trustees are provided by specialist companies and again provide independent professional insights. There are limited numbers of them, though numbers are steadily increasing. It is something which the Myners Review (as to which see below) strongly commended and so it is not surprising that there is some increase over time, even if only slowly. The Regulator maintains a register of independent trustees. It is not compulsory for independent trustees to be registered but the clear intent is that funds should tend to hire registered trustees and of course the Regulator will only itself appoint independent trustees to schemes under its powers if they are on the register. At the time of writing, the Regulator is consulting on tightening the criteria for trustees to be included on the register.

Conflicts of interest

21.006   The position of sponsor-appointed trustees remains controversial. Most commentators clearly believe that like most conflicts, once recognised these can be managed. Some academic evidence raises some question-marks about this, however: a 2005 paper called "The Corporate Governance of Defined Benefit Pension Plans, Evidence from the United Kingdom" by Joao Cocco and Paolo Volpin of the London Business School suggests that sponsor-appointed trustees may favour the sponsoring company in some of their decision-making. Using, it should be noted, data which preceded the recent increase in trustees' powers and introduction of the Pension Regulator, their research found that pension schemes of indebted companies with a high proportion of sponsor-appointed trustees have a higher proportion of assets invested in equities and that they also allow the indebted companies to make lower contributions and higher dividend payments.

Some would no doubt argue that these findings provide evidence of a willingness and perhaps ability to look through short-term difficulties to the longer-term. In any case, it seems highly doubtful that these findings would be replicated under the current regime. Nonetheless, as the comments of the company director quoted in the introduction to this chapter indicate, conflicts remain between some of the trustees' duties to the pension scheme beneficiaries and their duties as directors (or otherwise) of the sponsoring company, and all parties will need to continue to take care to manage those conflicts effectively.

Typically, this management is simply done by the sponsor-nominated trustees abstaining on decisions or not being included in trustee decisions on particular points. This was, for example, what occurred in relation to WH Smith, the high street newsagent, when it faced a private equity bid. In that case, the private equity firm Permira eventually walked away from a possible deal because its sums did not make the deal attractive given the then unusually strong powers in the hands of the independent trustees. These powers, to seek increased contributions depending on the risks (particularly debt burden) taken on by the sponsor or indeed to seek an immediate closing of the deficit, have in effect now been replicated across all pension schemes through the establishment of the Pension Regulator and the new powers granted to all trustees under the 2004 Act. Martin Taylor, chair of the WHS trustee board, told the *Financial Times* in 2004:

> "The independence of pension trustees has not been great enough and trustees have not felt themselves independent enough of the company. Trustees need to be encouraged to put members' interests first."

The regulatory bodies have shown no willingness to generate a mechanical approach to the issue of conflicts of interest. The Ombudsman says of conflicts:

> "A Trustee who feels that his position with the employer might present him with an unavoidable conflict of interests should consider resigning his trusteeship."

But, when invited to say whether the sponsor's finance director should step down from a role as trustee—more than half have done so, according to reports—Tony Hobman, Pensions Regulator CEO, declines to take a view either way. It is, he says, a question of managing the conflict.

Having noted this comment, the Regulator makes a striking statement in its April 2006 medium-term plan: "Trustee conflicts of interest are also a concern, especially in DB schemes with funding difficulties". In the context of such public comments it will be increasingly hard for trustees who perceive themselves to face conflicts of interest to continue with their role: it may be that the position is gradually hardening. This certainly became apparent in 2008 when the Regulator in new guidance on conflicts urged conflicted trustees—with directors of the sponsoring company clearly at the front of mind—to withdraw from relevant discussions, or indeed to resign from the board. The Occupational Pensioners' Alliance made a call at the end of 2009 that finance directors should be banned from being pension scheme trustees.

There are extreme cases where the concern about conflicts is particularly acute. One of these was the situation at Telent, where in 2007 the Pensions Regulator imposed independent trustees to ensure that the scheme's investment strategy continued to be run in the interests of its beneficiaries rather than that of its new owner, Pension Corporation, which had bought the company particularly because of its outsized pension scheme in relation to the scale of the ongoing company. It is hard to read too much across from this unusual case, given that the Regulator's actions were driven by the specific circumstances of Pension Corporation's business model and the way in which it had spoken about the scheme. Nonetheless, this extreme case re-emphasises the need which applies to all pension schemes that they must be run in the interests of the beneficiaries rather than in the interests of the sponsoring company.

There are also more personal conflicts: again in 2007 the Regulator banned the former chair of trustees at the Ericsson Employee Benefits Scheme from ever serving as a trustee again. David John Foster had failed to make clear his own personal conflict in seeking fuller benefits than were rightly due under the executive section of the scheme. Foster was the first individual to be banned in this way but this is one of the Regulator's powers which seems likely to gain further use over future years.

Having said all that, however, it would seem a shame to lose wholly the skills and knowledge of sponsor-nominated trustees, and it seems unlikely that this is what the regulatory regime intends. It is also worth noting one of Cocco and Volpin's conclusions:

> "the optimal number of insider-trustees [their term for sponsor-appointed trustees] may not necessarily be zero. The presence of a small minority of insider trustees may help information flow between the firm and the pension plan, and be beneficial for both shareholders and pension plan members."

This is clearly the view of the Government, which has acted to enable companies to indemnify their directors and officers who act as pension fund trustees. One of the last amendments to the Companies Act 2006 was the introduction of s.235 which permits this. Lord Sainsbury, explaining the amendment in the House of Lords, stated the policy case very clearly:

> "The point was made that such directors perform a vital role, often for very little direct financial reward, and that directors' and officers' liability insurance policies currently available afford limited protection. We made clear that the Government attach great importance to the work of such directors, and that we are aware it can sometimes be difficult to recruit high-quality directors for companies acting as a trustee of an occupational pension scheme. In view of that, and following consultation with key stakeholders, we tabled amendments to permit companies to indemnify the directors of associated companies acting as trustees of occupational pension schemes."

So, in spite of the ongoing debate, it is clearly well accepted that pension schemes need the skills of such individuals among their trustees. The availability of indemnification should at least assist directors in feeling able to deal appropriately with the inevitable conflicts of interest.

Duties of the pension fund trustee

This leads us naturally to consider what the duties of the individual trustee **21.007** are. In the narrow legal sense, the duty of care expected of trustees now goes beyond the duty of any other trustee, which is to act with the same care as an ordinary man of business would extend to his own affairs (the common law formulation in *Bartlett v Barclays Bank*). The 2004 Act requires pension fund trustees to take decisions with the skill and care of someone *familiar with the issues concerned.* If trustees do not themselves possess the necessary skill and care, they must acquire it or delegate the relevant decisions to someone who does possess it. And this requirement is not restricted, as originally proposed, just to investment issues: it extends across the full range of the trustee's relevant duties. These issues are developed further below.

In a wider sense, a brief document produced by PricewaterhouseCoopers in June 2003 sets out with absolute clarity what ultimately the duties of pension fund trustees are. Called simply "Pension Fund Governance" the four-page overview states bluntly:

"The trustees' business is simply put: to pay the promised pensions, of the right amount, on time. Running this business is no different from running any other. Appropriate structures and processes are needed to ensure proper governance and suitable risk management."

It goes on to suggest a basic checklist of necessary actions to ensure that these fundamental aims are fulfilled:

(a)   having a business plan;

(b)   establishing a clear governance structure;

(c)   identifying the skills and resources needed;

(d)   ensuring sufficient time and resources are committed;

(e)   ensuring proposals are adequately assessed and properly challenged;

(f)   monitoring performance against agreed goals;

(g)   seeking continuous improvement.

This role—deliberately—sounds very like that of a non-executive member of the board of a company. In the same way that the role of the non-executive is being professionalised, expectations of pension fund trustees are being updated. This was a core recommendation of March 2001's "Institutional Investment in the United Kingdom: a Review", a document known in the industry (and this chapter) as the Myners Report, after its principal author, the then Paul Myners, former head of Gartmore Investment Management, and more recently Lord Myners, City minister in the last days of the erstwhile Labour Government. The Myners Report (*http://webarchive.nationalarchives. gov.uk/20100407010852/http://www.hm-treasury.gov.uk/fin_sec_mynfinal.htm*) has set stiff new standards for pension funds and trustees in particular, and is causing some significant changes to governance practice.

While there are many technical aspects of the issues, such as strategic asset allocation, benchmark choice, selection of fund management mandates and then of fund managers themselves, risk allocation, and performance moni-toring, at its heart the core duty of the pension scheme trustee is relatively simple. It is to work out the liabilities of the scheme, and to allocate the funds available (including the ongoing income from the sponsor and from benefici-aries) to a range of investments over the necessary timescales such that those liabilities will be met. Where there is no ready prospect of that being the case, trustees must negotiate for increased contributions. As with any trustee, the duty is the fiduciary one, to act always in the best interests of the beneficiaries.

Advisers report that the best pension scheme boards do indeed start from this foundation-level assessment of their responsibilities and how they are to be fulfilled. These are the funds most willing to take long-term decisions and to seek out unusual asset-classes which are not the current flavour-of-the-month. This willingness to consider the contrarian means that these funds have a far greater opportunity for supernormal gains, as the rail schemes found with their famous investments in fine art. It might also perhaps open the door to the increased investment in private equity and start-ups which was the limited aim of the original remit given to Myners at the start of his review.

As stated above, English law—not least in the strict statements of Megarry J. in the classic 1984 decision *Cowan v Scargill*—lays down that trustees' duties are exclusively to the beneficiaries of the pension fund, and should not encompass any other considerations. There is a discussion later in this chapter on whether this strict understanding of fiduciary duties has hampered discussions between pension funds and sponsors about the best way to share risks, in a way which has tended to exacerbate the current pensions crisis.

It is worth noting that the standard of care for an independent professional trustee will be higher than that for a—for lack of a better term—lay trustee. The Ombudsman will be unforgiving of errors by professional trustees:

> "The professional Trustee, or Trustee Company, effectively hold them-selves out to have special skills and expertise, and often charges not incon-siderable fees for their services. The Ombudsman is therefore likely to accept few excuses from Professional Trustees who do not understand or carry out their duties properly."

The penalties for any trustee of not acting in their beneficiaries' interests can be severe. The general principles of trust law mean that any party to a breach of trust are jointly and severally liable. So in 2008 the Ombudsman found the trustees liable to make good a hole in the pension scheme of a company in liquidation because it found that the hole arose from an unsecured loan from the scheme to the sponsor. The Ombudsman found that there was no reasonable prospect that the loan would ever be repaid, so those trustees who agreed it were faced with a very significant bill.

The skills of individual trustees and the need for training

There are few specific limitations on who may be a trustee and what skills are required. Legislation bars anyone under 18, undischarged bankrupts, anyone disqualified from being a director and anyone convicted of an offence involving dishonesty or deception. However, the positive requirements for the role are few. **21.008**

Though the OECD's guidelines for pension fund governance were rewritten and bolstered in 2005, it is still only the area of suitability—"The governing body should be subject to minimum suitability standards in order to ensure a high level of integrity and professionalism in the administration of the pension fund"—where UK standards fall short of its structural recommendations. The requirements for trustee knowledge are gradually being increased, as is the availability of training to enhance it, but at the moment they remain a relatively low bar which is only slowly being raised.

The 2004 Act requires trustees and directors of trustee companies to be familiar with:

- the scheme trust deed and rules;

- their statement of investment principles;

- the statement of funding principles (see below);

- any other documentation laying out administration policy in relation to the scheme;

- the law relating to pensions and trusts;

- the principles relating to the funding and investment of occupational pension schemes.

The last two are required to the extent needed to enable them to exercise properly their functions as trustees. It is accepted that different trustees may need different levels of knowledge depending on their roles on committees and so on.

Trustees must have appropriate knowledge and understanding of trusts and pensions law and of the principles of funding and investment. The extent of knowledge required is appropriate to the trustee's functions. The Pension Regulator updated its Code of Practice on Trustee Knowledge and Understanding in 2009 (it can be found at *http://www.thepensionsregulator.*

gov.uk/docs/code-07-trustee-knowledge-understanding.pdf). This extends the knowledge expectations in the areas of good administration, personal records, investment oversight and the employer covenant and provides practical guidance for trustees on how they can comply with these requirements.

The Code makes clear that its whole checklist of required knowledge will not apply to all trustees—and it is up to the trustees to decide which elements do apply to them. Trustees are expected to use this as a checklist for their personal learning requirements:

> "Trustees may eliminate items from that list because of their own expertise or experience. They may delete other items because they do not apply to their functions as a trustee of their particular scheme."

Training is definitely needed, believes former chair of the Financial Reporting Council ("FRC"), Sir Bryan Nicholson. In January 2006 he expressed concerns about the ability of trustees to carry out their role in full. "In no sense am I denigrating the work of trustees, but simply pointing out the risks that are inherent in such complicated matters being dealt with by people on a part-time basis", he told BBC Radio 4's *Money Box*. "I would like to see the bringing in of more external advice, the opening up of the trustee community, perhaps by paid trustees to a wide group of people, and the further strengthening of the training requirements".

Trustees themselves seem to agree that more needs to be done. Given the new requirements of the 2004 Act, it is perhaps surprising that a third of trustees told a December 2005 survey by Merrill Lynch Investment Managers and *Engaged Investor Magazine* that they understood pensions law only slightly or not at all. Only 22 per cent rated their understanding of trust and pensions law highly. Less than a third of trustees believed they have a very good understanding of investment principles. One in seven trustees did not know what benchmarking they apply at their scheme.

Training is expected to be an ongoing process—trustees must maintain their knowledge and understanding at the required level—so regular refreshment is needed. If the trustee's role and responsibilities change, so may the requirement for knowledge and understanding. The Regulator recommends an annual review of needs. It also recommends a system of record-keeping of training undergone and levels of knowledge and understanding, though it states that this is more likely to be demonstrated by the minutes of trustee discussions than by anything else. It is to be hoped that this does not lead to excessively detailed minutes nor to trustees feeling obliged to say something—worse still, to say something especially clever—to demonstrate their knowledge and understanding. In some cases there may be a challenge for chairs of trustees to manage such situations effectively so that the tail of demonstrating knowledge does not wag the dog of effective and efficient decision-making.

The Regulator provides its own learning programme—the Trustee Toolkit—on its website, which looks increasingly set to become the default mechanism for training (find it at *http://www.trusteetoolkit.com/arena/index. cfm*), not least because the Regulator has gradually upped the importance of the Toolkit; formerly it merely required that trustees fulfil the 2004 Act requirement that they have knowledge and understanding. But the 2009 knowledge and understanding Code states that:

> "The regulator is of the view that this is required study for new trustees unless they can find an alternative learning programme which covers all the items in the scope guidance at a level relevant for them and within the timescale allowed."

The NAPF has suggested that the training was somewhat at the simple end of the spectrum, but then it has its own online training scheme which it is keen to promote. Its Trustee Development Programme can be found at *http://www. trusteeknowhow.com*.

We might assume that training matters because it helps trustees take better decisions, but it is welcome to find some direct empirical evidence that this is indeed the case. In "Consistency of decision-making: the effect of education, professional qualifications, and task-specific training on the probability judgements of pension fund trustee decision-making", Gordon Clark of the Labor and Worklife Program and Emiko Caerlewy-Smith and John Marshall of Oxford University tested trustees against a control group of Oxford undergraduates. Some might find it unsurprising against such a dubious control, but the research indicated that trustees tend to take decisions that are more consistent and tend to exercise their judgment more effectively. More significantly perhaps, those trustees who held professional qualifications or had undergone training performed better than those who had not. It is to be hoped that this is because the training has proved effective and not because those trustees who have already undergone training are a self-selecting higher quality group.

The academics suggest their research has the following implications for pension scheme governance:

- trustee selection according to education and professional qualifications is something that should be actively considered by trustee boards and sponsors;

- tasks need to be allocated appropriately within trustee boards;

- the use of independent experts should be considered, especially where skill in applying statistics is required;

- the Regulator should consider adding requirements for expertise and not just competence on trustee boards.

Despite the ongoing criticism, lay trustees who lack specialist knowledge and skills remain extremely popular, particularly for their ability to legitimise decisions to the beneficiaries. And there are various forms of support for such trustees. The TUC has a Member Trustee Network, offering advice and knowledge-sharing (see *http://www.tuc.org.uk/pensions*). A similar group of lay trustees is supported by the Pensions Management Institute ("PMI"). The PMI offers various courses and qualifications, including Awards in Pension Trusteeship (see *http://www.pensions-pmi.org. uk/index.php?option=com_content&view=article&id=96&itemid=18*).

And it is clear that the Regulator has no appetite to professionalise trustees at this stage. The aim appears to be to build the capacity through the current trustee base rather than impose an alternative model. Tony Hobman, CEO of the Regulator, told the author in July 2005 that he sees strength from the amateur tradition of trustees, and the mix of different skills it brings. Of particular importance, he said, was the "need to maintain confidence among the beneficiaries" by ensuring that the trustees are not seen as divorced from them. The regulator allowed a six-month window from April 2006 for trustees to complete their learning requirements. In a similar way, each individual trustee newly appointed after April 2006 will have a personal six-month window to acquire the necessary knowledge and understanding—though the Regulator expects every trustee to be equipped to take any decision with which (s)he is faced, and notes that each trustee will be accountable in law for decisions that are taken.

The Regulator accepts that increasing the demands placed on trustees by way of knowledge and understanding might discourage well-informed and capable individuals from becoming or continuing as trustees. But it says, in the April 2006 medium-term plan, that "we have yet to see any significant evidence of this".

One way to square this circle of the need for knowledge and understanding—and indeed, specific skills—among a deliberately amateur base of individuals is to establish devolved governance structures and to delegate decisions to appropriately qualified individuals. Alternatively, or alongside this approach, trustees could seek the advice of specialists, and look to follow that advice having tested its quality.

It is accepted widely by the industry, and also by the Regulator, that different individuals will have differing levels of knowledge and understanding. Indeed, the Code of Practice on trustee knowledge and understanding is explicit that there will be additional burdens for certain individuals:

"Particular responsibilities fall on the chair of the board of trustees and the chair of the investment subcommittee if there is one. Members of those bodies will look to the chair for guidance and it must equip itself to be able to accept the particular responsibilities of its role. This may mean learning at a deeper level than that required at the basic level for the vast majority of trustees, particularly for chairs of large and complex schemes and chairs of investment subcommittees."

Thus there is a drive through the regulation towards a more formal demarcation of duties between the trustees, and a division of the trustee board's roles through the mechanism of board sub-committees. Each of these would include those trustees with skills and expertise in particular areas so that their recommendations when taken to the board would typically be given significant weight.

Decision making and the use of advisers

Even with improved governance structures, trustees will not be able to take **21.009** all decisions themselves. At the NAPF trustee conference in October 2004, Alan Pickering, former chair of that organisation, author of a government report on pensions and now a senior consultant with Watson Wyatt, discussed the need for delegation. Rather than seeking to become experts across the piece, trustee boards "need to understand the "what" and the "why", but not the how", he said. This "how" should be delegated to advisers and fund managers.

The Ombudsman is supportive of this view. It says of seeking specialist advice:

"Trustees and employers should take advice on technical or legal matters where appropriate. They will usually be entitled to rely on that advice, provided it is properly sought and given and they have no reason to believe that it might be correct."

Despite these endorsements of the role of specialist advisers, it is clear from the Myners Report and in guidance from the Regulator that trustees need to take care in their use of the advice available to them.

Reference to the expertise of professional advisers—particularly the dominant four actuarial firms, Hewitt Bacon & Woodrow, Hymans Robertson, Towers Watson and William Mercer—is an important part of the pension fund decision-making process. Indeed, it is often seen as a vital way for trustees to show that they are exercising their fiduciary responsibilities properly. If anything were to go wrong and trustees had not taken professional advice on all significant matters, many individuals feel that they might well be personally exposed to a risk of litigation.

The Myners Report, however, identified the risks of over-dependence on the small group of firms employed as investment consultants:

"Although concentration of the consulting industry and the undue influence of a small handful of individuals on the investment policy of the industry is undesirable, worse is the generic 'one size fits all' advice which the consultants provide."

The Myners Report agreed that significant change was needed in trustee decision making. It proposed a series of simple principles which it believed codified best practice and would improve standards across the board. These were:

(a) decisions should be taken only by persons or organisations with the right skills, information and resources needed to take them effectively;

(b) trustees should set out an overall investment objective for the fund, in terms which relate directly to the circumstances of the fund and not some other objective such as the performance of other pension funds;

(c) the attention devoted to asset allocation decisions should fully reflect the contribution they can make to achieving the fund's investment objective;

(d) decision-makers should consider a full range of investment opportunities across all major asset classes, including private equity;

(e) the fund should be prepared to pay sufficient fees for actuarial and investment advice to attract a broad range of kinds of potential providers;

(f) trustees should give fund managers an explicit written mandate setting out the agreement between them on issues such as the investment objective, and a clear timescale for measurement and evaluation;

(g) in consultation with their investment manager, funds should explicitly consider whether the index benchmarks that they have selected are appropriate. Where they believe active management to have the potential to achieve higher returns, they should set both targets and risk controls to reflect this, allowing sufficient freedom for genuinely active management to occur;

(h) trustees should arrange to measure the performance of the fund and the effectiveness of their own decision making, and formally to assess the performance and decision making delegated to advisers and managers.

Myners also identified some specific principles for decision-making at DC schemes:

(a) in selecting funds to offer as options to scheme members, trustees should consider the investment objectives, expected returns, risks and other relevant characteristics of each such fund;

(b) where a fund is offering a default option to members through a customised combination of funds, trustees should ensure that an objective is set for the option, including expected risks and returns.

The principles are written in simple language—the report itself suggests they appear "basic"—"but the review believes that they call for considerable change in pension fund practice". When the survey which accompanied the review revealed that 23 per cent of trustees of funds with a scheme-specific benchmark did not know what that benchmark was, it is not surprising that simple standards could change behaviours dramatically. Few investment decisions can competently be taken by trustees without such basic knowledge as the benchmark they are targeting. The Myners Report calls on pension funds to comply with these principles or explain why they have not done so on an annual basis in their reports to members.

The Myners Principles were subject to a further consultation in 2008 and this process led to a radical focusing of the document. There are now just six high-level principles: effective decision-making; clear objectives; risk and liabilities; performance assessment; responsible ownership; and transparency and reporting. Each of these has a handful of bullet point explanations, but the tone and approach of the document is very much high-level and principle based, which means that trustees are required to exercise a good deal of judgment as to what is right for them and their beneficiaries. The Government as part of its consultation conclusions set up the Investment Governance Group ("IGG") to develop some of the best practice and more detailed guidance that certain funds will be keen to see and reflect in their practices.

The Regulator also produced guidance, in the form of "Relations with advisers", published in 2008. The term in the document is intended to include other service providers and suppliers as well as those with pure advisory relationships. The guidance provides simple outlines of best practice both at the point of appointing or reviewing performance and in relation to getting better service from existing providers. The guidance—to be found at *http://www.thepensionsregulator.gov.uk/guidance/guidance-relations-with-advisers.aspx*—offers simple pointers to assessing the service provided and to winning an improved service.

These strictures will require some change in approach, as the degree of pension fund reliance on the advice of their actuaries is revealed by the FRC's 2007 Actuarial Stakeholder Group Survey of the needs of Principal Users of Actuarial Services. This said that:

"The actuarial profession is seen by some as pretty impenetrable, with the concepts and workings underpinning the advice regarded as extremely complex. Most trustees appear to lack the confidence to scrutinise or challenge actuarial advice."

The FRC is now rising to the survey's urging to try to improve the clarity of actuarial information and advice, largely through the mechanism of setting actuarial standards.

It may be wise to be cynical about some pension consultants. At least in the US, there is official evidence of failures to manage and communicate conflicts of interest. A Securities and Exchange Commission report released in May 2005 was scathing of the consultants and advisers, highlighting their conflicts and particularly their failure to be open about them to their clients. The report concluded that:

> "the business alliances among pension consultants and money managers can give rise to serious potential conflicts of interest under the Advisers Act that need to be monitored and disclosed to plan fiduciaries."

As an assistance to better transparency, the SEC released a set of tips for pension scheme trustees in selecting and monitoring their consultants. This document, published at the start of June 2005 (*http://www.sec.gov/investor/ pubs/sponsortips.htm*), consists of a set of questions which trustees might ask of their advisers to highlight capacity and any possible conflicts of interest. Perhaps the most interesting is question 8:

> "If you are hired, will you acknowledge in writing that you have a fiduciary obligation as an investment adviser to the plan while providing the consulting services we are seeking?"

One cannot help but think that a great number of problems would be avoided if all service providers to pension schemes always kept in mind this central fiduciary nature of their responsibility to the pension beneficiaries. It is worth keeping this in mind when we consider the governance of fund managers at the end of this chapter.

Risk management and controls

21.010   The principal additions in the 2005 revision of the OECD pension fund governance guidelines were in the area of governance mechanisms, which highlight the need for "appropriate control, communication, and incentive mechanisms that encourage good decision making, proper and timely execution, transparency, and regular review and assessment". The guidance notes four areas for action under this theme: internal controls, reporting, disclosure and redress.

Much of this is now fully covered under the UK regime. The Regulator's Internal Controls Code of Practice, which went into effect in November 2006, is a high level framework and expects trustees themselves to make a judgment as to what is appropriate in the circumstances of their pension scheme. Trustees are required to establish and operate internal controls which are "adequate" for the scheme to be run in accordance with its own rules and with relevant law and regulation.

It reads:

"The extent to which schemes are exposed to risk will vary from one scheme to another. In order to decide what internal controls are appropriate, a risk assessment may be considered appropriate, indeed, the Pensions Regulator would recommend this approach." It expects this risk assessment to be a continual process. The controls regime needs to focus on "key" risks, the Code states, and the controls should be "proportionate to the level of risk identified."

The Code lists the following as likely risks, though it does highlight that the list is not intended to be exhaustive:

- risk that existing controls are not effective;

- risk of fraud;

- risk of failure of the sponsor, or deterioration in its covenant;

- investment risk;

- compliance or regulatory risk;

- non-compliance or maladministration by administrative team or third party advisers;

- computer systems and database failures;

- poor scheme management.

At the end of 2009, the Regulator pushed risk further up the agenda, releasing draft guidance on internal controls for consultation and offering brief training on risk management. In releasing the consultation the Regulator noted that:

"The implementation of robust internal controls is a legal requirement for trustees and the failure to put processes in place now can result in scheme members being exposed to the risks associated with poor record-keeping, inappropriate investment allocation and conflicts of interest in trustee boards."

This broad scope of the risk management standard is shown even in the two-minute safety check which essentially highlights the importance of considering what are the scheme's key risks and putting in place a risk register. The 12-minute overview version considers risk and internal controls using a case study format. Both training courses can be found at *http://www.pensions regulator.gov.uk/safe/index.aspx*.

Funding, deficits and winding up

21.011   The 2004 Act replaced the Minimum Funding Requirement ("MFR") with a scheme-specific funding approach. The Government's reasoning was laid out in its December 2002 Green Paper. The MFR, it said:

> "has proved inflexible and unable fully to reflect the specific circumstances of individual schemes. The need to satisfy the MFR test has also led some schemes to focus too much attention on the impact of short-term market conditions instead of an appropriate strategy for meeting their specific pension commitments."

The result of this substitution of scheme-specific calculations for the blanket provisions of the MFR standard has been a significant added burden of responsibility on trustees. It is they who, with appropriate advice, need to develop the assessment of the scheme-specific liability structure. It is made harder given the range of different ways of calculating funding levels—from the most liability conscious buy-out level, through the FRS 17 level, to various actuarial calculations of the funding on an ongoing business basis. Use of the language of sufficient and appropriate assets challenges trustees to consider and set tolerance levels to dips in the funding level. In some cases these will be made explicit in their statements of investment principles.

These requirements are explicitly drafted to enact the terms of the 2003 Pensions Directive and require schemes to have sufficient assets to cover their specific liabilities. The aim is that there should be a process of negotiation between sponsors and trustees, with the assistance of actuaries, to agree on what is necessary to provide for the scheme's liabilities. This will include a statement of funding principles laying out how funding will be achieved, the assumptions used in arriving at these assessments and the period over which any shortfall will be made up.

Only if this negotiation fails would the Pensions Regulator become involved. Experience suggests that this will only happen with the greatest reluctance and after the regulator has strongly encouraged further discussion between the parties. There is no evidence of eagerness at the Pensions Regulator for substituting its views for those of parties nearer and more appropriately involved in the situation. The most public case where this has happened was when in 2008 the EMI scheme trustees failed to reach agreement with the company's new owners, private equity house Terra Firma and the Regulator stepped in to assist the parties in reaching a resolution. The area where the regulator has become involved much more frequently is in its strong encouragement for relatively short-term horizons for filling deficits—generally in the past this has been no more than 10 years but in recent times (at least during the credit crisis) the Regulator has indicated that a longer period might be appropriate; the June 2009 paper "Scheme funding and the employer covenant" is particularly keen to encourage flexibility and vision through the economic cycle, though at the same time it emphasised the scale of the cost of pension promises.

The courts also have a role weighing in on deficits. In *Alitalia v Rotumo* [2008] EWHC 185 the High Court held that an employer duty to "secure the benefits under the Scheme" did not require that the scheme be funded to a buy-out level of certainty. This, the court held, "made no commercial sense" and it went on to find that the employer contribution rule needed to be interpreted in a way which did make commercial sense both when operating on an ongoing basis and—perhaps more surprisingly—when winding-up seemed possible or likely. Deficits also come to the forefront of attention in cases where the Regulator invokes its material detriment powers (originally called its moral hazard powers). These—extended under the 2008 Act—enable the Regulator to require payments into pension schemes from parties associated with employers to prevent a change in corporate structure or ownership having the effect of significantly reducing the protection for beneficiaries. The Regulator's guidance (finalised in early 2009) indicates that this power may be triggered where: the scheme transfers out of the UK; its sponsor transfers out and this cuts protections for fund members; sponsor support is removed or reduced; the scheme liabilities are transferred to another scheme with insufficient support; or the operation of the scheme appears designed to favour the sponsor and provides inadequate protection for member interests. In 2006 the Regulator required Sea Containers Ltd, a Bermudan company, to provide financial support to—in effect guaranteeing to make good any deficits in—two DB schemes attached to its UK subsidiary. After taking the dispute to the Regulator's Determinations Panel and considering a further appeal, Sea Containers finally bowed to the financial support directions in January 2008. In late 2008 these powers were used to reach a settlement which saw Duke Street Capital, a private equity investor, reportedly agree to inject £8 million into the Focus DIY Pension Scheme fully a year after selling the company to Cerberus. Despite these hard examples, the Regulator remains keen to make clear that normal commercial activities should not be affected by its powers.

Aside from material detriment situations, the pension fund deficit is only a theoretical number until the sponsor goes bust or the scheme is wound up for other reasons. Thus, the wise trustee will have an eye to the solvency of the sponsor company, and is likely to lose a good deal of sleep where its future is in doubt. No trustee would relish the prospect of getting involved with the PPF. The PPF was introduced as a safety net for the pension schemes of failing companies following cases such as that of the pension scheme of the ASW Plc which went bust in 2002. As the 1995 Act required that in such circumstances funds be used first to protect the income of those who had already retired, the burden of the deficit fell on those who had not retired. These therefore found their benefits scaled back substantially—by 70 per cent or perhaps even more.

Now the PPF will step in. Under the new regime, any solvent sponsor choosing to wind up a DB pension scheme will need to buy out in full the accrued rights of members, meaning that it would at a stroke be required to fill the deficit. Trustees are expected to enforce this. It must be noted though that trustees must not place too much reliance on the existence of the PPF. In November 2009 the High Court handed down judgement in *ITS v Hope*, finding it inappropriate to use disproportionate elements of the fund to buy out some liabilities, relying on the PPF to fill the resulting hole for the other beneficiaries. The judge was reasonably scathing about the trustees' proposal, suggesting it used "the availability of PPF compensation as though it were an advantage to be exploited for the Scheme's benefit, whereas Parliament clearly intended the PPF to be a funder of last resort".

March 2006 saw the first company forced into administration by the trustees of its pension scheme. Berkeley Berry Birch was a financial advisory firm which had been loss-making and forced by the Financial Services Authority to cease most activities due to lack of capital. When the company failed to raise new capital itself the pension fund trustees felt they had no option but to apply to the High Court to wind the company up and seek the sale of assets for the benefit of the scheme.

It followed the case of Armstrong, a manufacturer, which earlier the same month went into receivership after the pension scheme trustees rejected the company's proposals for filling the deficit. In this instance, the company directors themselves pulled the plug rather than the trustees having to go to the High Court, but it was clear from the comments of all involved that the driving force behind the step was the pension trustee board.

While these cases are unlikely to be the last, the tone of comments from the Regulator suggest the need for some flexibility and circumspection. Writing in the *Financial Times* in October 2005 Tony Hobman said:

> "We would not expect trustees to take actions that would place a company in jeopardy unless this really would be the only way of securing members' benefits—a viable employer will usually be the best way of providing such benefits."

The Ombudsman has a good deal of advice on how properly to wind up a scheme, but it must be noted that its role in a winding-up situation is not to make good individuals who feel poorly done by because the winding-up means they have received less than they were expecting. Consistent with its general role, the Ombudsman only becomes involved where there has been maladministration or winding-up has not been carried out lawfully.

The Ombudsman's general principles in relation to winding up provide a helpful checklist for trustees as to their appropriate actions in considering and carrying through a wind-up. These are (as laid out in "How to avoid the Pensions Ombudsman"):

- take account of the interests of the whole scheme membership, and avoid conflict with their own personal interest;

- consider whether to resolve to wind up the scheme, if the Trustees have the power to do so, and to crystallise any deficit before it grows, if this is in the members' best interests;

- where there is a doubt about solvency, early retirements and full transfer values should not be granted until the financial position of the scheme has been determined;

- exercise extreme caution in considering whether to grant early retirement benefits just prior to the wind-up;

- benefits should be provided in accordance with statutory provisions and scheme Rules, the former taking precedence;

- pay as high a proportion of benefits as possible when the benefits become due for payment, without jeopardising the benefits of other members;

- keep members regularly informed of progress, or the lack of it, during the winding-up;

- keep the costs of the winding-up to a minimum.

It is hard to better the Ombudsman's brief exposition of the challenge facing trustees in deciding whether to seek to wind up a scheme in deficit. This lays out the various issues that must be considered, but as ever leaves the necessary judgments wholly in the hands of the trustees. The Ombudsman explains:

"The employer might have refused, or have been unable, to pay contribution rates recommended by the actuary. In such circumstances, the Trustees might be advised to wind up the scheme, if they have the power to do so, in order to crystallise the deficit and prevent the risk of employee contributions not being paid over to the investment manager; a failure of the Trustees to wind up the scheme at the appropriate time might constitute maladministration. Winding-up might, however, force a solvent employer into administrative receivership or liquidation, with the loss of the jobs of active members of the scheme. A decision to defer winding-up may be appropriate in some circumstances. The decision of the Trustees, acting in the members' best interests, to wind up the scheme, would need to balance the interests of active members against those of pensioners and deferred members, who would have a less direct stake in the company's continuing existence."

Investment returns and fund management

21.012   No sponsor has an endless pot of money. While a portion of the current pension fund deficits can be addressed by seeking additional contributions from the sponsor, there is a limit, and pension funds need to seek enhanced investment returns to fulfil this need. Indeed, actuaries assume long-term fund returns of between around 5 and 8 per cent a year when calculating the future contributions required of sponsors. Thus, to free sponsors from the burden of increasing contributions still further (for most, any actual *reduction* in contributions is an unlikely dream), trustees need to allocate their resources to enable returns of around that level, and hope for still better performance.

This means that pension fund trustees need to focus still more than usual on ensuring the best possible long-term performance of their fund. This will involve assessing the best asset allocation for the current climate and the specific characteristics of the scheme, setting the right framework for investment decisions, agreeing investment mandates, selecting the right fund manager, and then monitoring its performance against the fund's targets. If this is done effectively, funds should be well diversified and though there will inevitably be periods when performance is poor, over the long run the fund should achieve its financial aims, and fulfil or exceed the growth which actuaries have built into their forecasts.

None of these aspects of the duty is straightforward. They are all those on which most trustees tend to feel the need for independent professional advice (and in many instances they are obliged to seek it), and therefore they are those areas where the investment consultants play their most active role. In a brutal piece in the *Financial Times* in September 2003, Paul Myners said:

> "The job of the investment consultant is to advise pension fund trustees on the best fund managers to run the retirement money. Traditionally, they have resisted taking full responsibility for the final decision. That, they say, is the role of the trustees. Yet, there are few who doubt the extraordinary power of the consultants."

Myners suggests that this power has not always been used entirely wisely, and that trustees need to feel freer to take a contrarian stance.

It is perhaps not surprising that it is in the area of investment management that trustees seek the most detailed advice. Not only is this an area where few trustees will have relevant professional experience, but also it is the area where poor decisions can have the clearest financial impact on beneficiaries. In some cases this can engender a safety-first attitude: taking the advice of a leading firm of consultants, using the standard asset allocation modelling process and picking a current well-performing fund manager are the natural steps.

The same safety-first-attitude can drive some trustees to an over-emphasis on the latest quarterly performance figures from their fund manager. A few "bad" quarters may be tolerable, but underperformance that is prolonged over even just two or three quarters in succession may lead some trustees to consider changing managers. Even though this may be an expensive, even wrong, decision in the long-run, safety-first attitudes may drive some trustees to take such actions. The knowledge that quarterly figures are studied in some detail again feeds into the thinking of the fund management firms, which may be tempted also to focus on short-term performance and hugging the benchmark. Safety first encourages a race to mediocrity.

This process appears to work for none of the parties. A January 2006 Watson Wyatt study confirmed that pension funds have a tendency to change fund managers at exactly the wrong time. Managers are typically hired shortly before their performance deteriorates and existing ones removed ahead of performance improving. Studying recent performance appears to be deeply misleading. Not only that, analysis by the Pension Fund Partnership together with Gissings in the same year indicated also that pension funds are reviewing their managers more frequently. This seems unfortunate and not to reflect the long time horizons over which schemes ought to be investing.

This focus on short-term performance relative to the same benchmark encourages herd-like behaviour by fund managers and does not fit the long-term timescales of pension funds. Breaking out of the cycle which encourages all participants, trustees, advisers and fund managers, to focus on the short term is extremely difficult. Most of the major consultants have active programmes to try to develop more long-term investment mandates which may encourage more long-term thinking—which may just possibly engender the sort of long-term performance which pension funds actually need. The "Marathon Club" of pension scheme trustees and others is also trying to break this unhappy cycle and find ways to direct pension fund investment as if it were the 20-year-plus marathon that it is rather than the current focus on short-term sprints. Whether concrete contracts are signed for mandates of even a fraction of that 20-year horizon we will have to wait and see.

There are things which wise trustees can—and do—do to address the short-termist issue without going to the extent of offering 20-year mandates. Most critical is ensuring that the fund manager is clear on what basis—and over what time-period—performance will be judged. Trustees can carry out their duties to their beneficiaries where there is short-term underperformance by seeking reassurance about the processes and expertise of the fund managers. Setting clear risk parameters for the fund managers to abide by is key: though the case was settled and did not reach a formal judgment, the Unilever suit against Merrill Lynch Investment Management made clear the value to the pension fund of having set strict risk parameters so that the level of underperformance seen in that case should have been highly unlikely.

Wise trustees will focus more on asset allocation than on fund management per se. All the evidence is that asset allocation has a far greater impact on performance than any other aspect of fund management. Having the right exposures to the right asset classes at the right time is thus of far greater value than picking individual stocks from time to time. This is one of the key arguments in favour of passive, index-tracking funds, which in UK equities will match the performance of the FTSE All-Share. Given that this is the benchmark used for most active managers, and it is argued that active fund management is a zero sum game with the index performance mirroring the average active manager, trustees will often find that they get equal performance from cheap passive management as they do from expensive active management. Studies tend to show that after fees and over the long run, active managers underperform the index.

Wise trustees will also ask for details on how their individual fund managers are remunerated. If trustees are expecting their funds to be managed on a 3 year, 5 year or 10-year timescale (or, indeed, more), then they will not be best served by fund managers whose sole financial incentive is relative outperformance of the index on a quarterly basis. Only by understanding what are the likely underlying drivers of individual fund managers' performance will the trustees be able properly to avoid conflicts of interest and judge what sort of performance they can expect to see for their fund.

Another form of conflict arises at the level of the fund management firm. There is the basic conflict arising from the need to maintain profitability, and so do the minimum possible to earn the fees payable; investment in services such as corporate governance, voting and engagement is thus kept to a minimum by many firms. There may also be a desire not to upset current or potential clients. There follows a discussion on the role of pension funds in the corporate governance debate, and the positive impact such "pressure-insensitive" investors can have on investee companies.

In January 2010 the Regulator called on trustees to take a close interest in stock-lending activities, and to have full knowledge of the terms on which scheme stock is lent, as well as the associated risks. Reportedly, this statement was spurred by the Regulator learning that pension schemes' stock had been out on loan without the trustees having been aware. It is another example of the trustees' need to manage the potential conflicts of interest among their agents.

Good advice on many areas of managing the investment process is to be found in a recent book by the former director of pension investments worldwide for Eastman Kodak, Russell Olson. Called "The Handbook for Investment Committee Members", it provides a brief introductory guide to the investment system for non-experts and begins to lead them through the processes and backgrounds to the key decisions of an investment committee. Though it often displays a remarkable degree of US parochialism, even when considering "foreign" investment, I am not aware of a better simple guide written from a more UK perspective. There is though a wider body of developing guidance from other places. For example, the International

Organisation of Pension Supervisors has published a set of Good Practices in Risk Management of Alternative Investments by Pension Funds. This covers the extent to which responsibility can be delegated, advice on portfolio policy, investment strategy and due diligence.

Pension funds and the wider governance debate

Pension funds own nearly 20 per cent of the UK stock market. Even after **21.013** recent declines, when combined with the insurance companies, UK institutions are the dominant shareholder class. This marks a dramatic change from 50, even 30 years ago when individuals holding shares directly were more significant. Because of their scale, and because of the heightened awareness of the value which good ownership activities can add to investee companies, more are now taking a close interest in corporate governance and engagement matters.

Services such as those provided by proxy advisers Glass Lewis and ISS (ISS formerly through a joint venture, Rrev, with the NAPF; even having bought out its partner, ISS still bases its UK decisions on the standards set by the NAPF), make it easier for pension funds to carry out their fiduciary responsibility to vote the shares they hold. This reflects the argument in the Myners Report that a vote is an asset like any other the fund controls, and that therefore the trustees have a duty to make best use of that asset for the good of their beneficiaries.

GlaxoSmithKline Plc's defeat over its remuneration report at its 2003 annual meeting is the best known example, but there have been several occasions where companies have been defeated on resolutions—or indeed heavily influenced by significant adverse votes. This might be seen by trustees as further justification to make best use of the voting asset.

Voting, however, is only part of the story. As the Code on the Responsibilities of Institutional Investors created by the Institutional Shareholders Committee ("ISC")—most recently updated in 2009 and at the time of writing in 2010 the subject of a consultation by the FRC with a view to it endorsing it as a "Stewardship Code" for investment institutions—makes clear, pension funds (and other institutions) have a much greater responsibility to become involved in the affairs of troubled investee companies. The ISC Code emphasises the need for intervention and discussion with companies at an early stage to make clear any concerns which responsible long-term owners have about their activities and their ability to create shareholder returns over the long-term. Most pension funds are taking action now to ensure that they can either take on this role directly, or delegate the duty to specialists who can carry it out on their behalf. The NAPF has assisted with its "first steps" guide, which will be followed in due course by other advice and guidance (find "Pension Funds and the ISC Code—A Practical Guide" at *http://www.napf.co.uk/Policy/Governance.cfm*).

This UK initiative reflects developing thinking around the world. In 2006 the International Corporate Governance Network ("ICGN") updated its "Statement on Institutional Shareholder Responsibilities" (*http://www. icgn.org/files/icgn_main/pdfs/best_practice/inst_share_responsibilities/2007_ principles_on_institutional_shareholder_responsibilities.pdf*), originally promulgated in 2003. In the same way as the ISC paper does, this also makes clear the obligations of institutional investors to their beneficiaries. To maintain value for beneficiaries, institutions need to intervene at companies where value may be being dissipated. Intervention certainly involves voting, but goes further to include active discussion on matters of concern and actively encouraging change, whether informally or through formal ownership mechanisms. It also extends to linking up with other investors if that will be the most likely method of ensuring change happens. These comments were re-emphasised by the ICGN in its commentary on the credit crisis, comments which in turn were reflected in the organisation's redrafted Corporate Governance Principles, published in 2009.

It is particularly important that pension funds play their full ownership role at companies in which they invest, because there is strong evidence of the benefits to companies of being owned by pension funds over and above ownership by other investment institutions.

There are two studies which contrast the influence of pension funds and insurance companies. The first is "Institutional Investors and Firm Innovation: a test of Competing Hypotheses", by Kochhar and Parthiban, published in the *Strategic Management Journal* No.17 (1996) pp.73–84. This study seems to have created the concepts of "pressure-sensitive" institutions (insurers and banks) and "pressure-resistant" institutions (largely, public pension funds) and to have looked at the differential impacts on companies which have a shareholder base dominated either by the pressure-sensitive or the pressure-resistant.

Companies with predominantly pressure-resistant shareholders, the study found, tend to be more innovative than those with pressure-sensitive ones, and therefore perform better in the long-term.

These results were largely replicated in "Entrepreneurship in Medium-Size Companies: Exploring the Effects of Ownership and Governance Systems" by Zahra, Neubaum and Huse, published in the *Journal of Management* 2000 pp.26(5), 947–976. This again discusses the differential effect of dominance by pressure-resistant and pressure-sensitive shareholders and shows that companies with more pressure-resistant owners outperform.

A further study compares the influences of pension funds with those of investment funds. This is "Institutional Ownership Differences and International Diversification: the Effects of Boards of Directors and Technological Opportunity" by Tihanyi, Johnson, Hoskisson and Hitt, in the *Academy of Management Journal* 2003 Vol.46 No.2 pp.195–211. The study, among other things, shows that companies where pension fund holders predominate (rather than investment funds), the long-term attitudes of pension fund owners enable R&D-based companies the time to make investments, and expand overseas, so that they can exploit the value of their R&D for the long term. Without international expansion, many of these firms could not be profitable in the long run, the study suggests.

Interestingly, the impact of funded pensions plays out not just at the investee company level but also across whole economies. In "Is there a link between Pension-Fund Assets and Economic Growth?—A Cross-Country Study", E Philip Davis and Yuwei Hu of Brunel University identify a correlation between funded pension schemes and economic growth, across both developed and emerging economies. Whether this is the macro impact of the micro effects on individual companies is not clear.

A further pressure on pension funds to exercise their ownership rights arises out of developments to the UK's corporate governance system in 2003 and since. The strident debate over these changes have often focused on the lack of confidence that many company directors have in the ability and willingness of institutions to move away from the tick-the-box mentality that many have been prey to. The debate has become focused on the phrase "comply or explain", with many suggesting that this will become a "comply or else" (or some other play on words) model. Detractors fear that institutions do not wish to invest in the resources to listen to and understand explanations and so enter into debate with companies on why it is that they are not compliant with specific terms of the UK Corporate Governance Code.

Through these debates, there seems to have been a very deliberate attempt to throw the spotlight onto institutions and their own governance. This will mean that pension funds should expect to face greater scrutiny of themselves, and particularly the directions that they give to their fund managers. Further questions will be asked about the resources given to considering governance matters and the incentives that individual fund managers have to take a long-term view.

This is all the more likely because those same directors who so castigate institutional investors have the levers of change in their own hands. Each of them, through his or her influence on their own company's pension fund(s), will be able to encourage changes to investment policies and attitudes to the governance debate. They are likely to do so. We can expect significant developments in this area over the next few years, building on the comments of John Sunderland, as discussed below in the section on the governance of fund managers.

The future of pension scheme governance and the challenge of DC

A discussion of a need for different legal structures for pension schemes is not new. The 1977 Wilson Report called for an overhaul: **21.014**

> "The framework within which schemes operate has grown piecemeal and now needs to be systematised and strengthened. It is unsatisfactory that

so much of it should depend on a body of trust law developed for other purposes".

But the clamour has grown in recent years. Alan Pickering, the former chair of the NAPF, has argued explicitly that the trust law system may have outlived its usefulness. "I refuse to defend any longer the Anglo-Saxon trust-based system. I really don't think it has a future", he told the NAPF trustee conference in October 2004. In particular, he noted the challenge posed to the status quo by the increasing numbers of DC or pure contract-based pension arrangements. "I really do question the role of a trustee in this environment", he said. "I think trustees have outlived their usefulness".

A debate about these issues has begun in a small way in the US. In July 2003, the Council of Institutional Investors, an association of North America's major investment institutions, sent to all its members a think piece written by its then chair, Gary Findlay, in his capacity as executive director of the Missouri State Employees' Retirement System. Called "Glass Houses", the piece notes that pension funds must accept some share in the responsibility for the stock market boom and bust of those years, and for the spectacular corporate failures which came in its wake: "If we truly want to know whom to blame," says Findlay, "maybe we should begin by taking a long hard look in the mirror".

Many of Findlay's recommendations will sound familiar to UK ears. He suggests:

(a) that the governance model needs clearly to demarcate the roles and responsibilities of the different parties. Pension fund boards, Findlay argues, should focus on setting policy and monitoring performance of employees and service providers, but should make sure that they avoid micromanagement;

(b) the governance system must make it clear that the focus of all activity is to be in the exclusive interests of plan participants;

(c) pension fund boards should have exclusive authority to determine the fund's operating budget;

(d) pension fund boards should have unilateral authority in establishing actuarial assumptions and methods;

(e) pension fund boards should have exclusive authority to retain any necessary outside service providers.

Many of these calls arise from the limits placed in different state laws in the US, restricting the scope for action particularly of pension funds for state employees—among the most important investment institutions in the US.

Findlay strongly recommends the adoption of the "Best Practices for Trust Independence and Board Governance" identified in two standardised forms of legislation drawn up by the National Conference of Commissioners on Uniform State Laws: the Uniform Management of Public Employee Retirement Systems Act and the Uniform Prudent Investor Act (both to be found at *http://www.law.upenn.edu/bll/ulc/ulc_final.htm*). These set out standards very much akin to those established in the English system, allocating responsibilities, requiring the use of prudence in delegating any duties and in monitoring how those duties are carried out, and ensuring that beneficiaries' interests are held paramount at all times.

Another US initiative led to the publication of "Best Practice Principles" by the Stanford Institutional Investors' Forum's Committee on Fund Governance in 2007. Intended to apply across the spectrum of institutional investors, it includes much that is familiar to UK pension funds, including having clear governance structures and competent and skilled trustees. The document is most instructive in the areas of conflicts of interest and in the delegation of duties and allocation of responsibilities. There is a strong focus on the need for trustees and staff to take personal responsibility for conflicts, with a duty periodically to affirm and verify compliance with conflict rules. In a similar way, the Principles assert that any consultants or staff in material roles must comply with conflicts of interest policies. Given the committee members' significant experience at a number of the largest pension funds in the US, it seems clear that these strictures respond to concerns which they saw the need to manage very directly.

Even though much of what is now proposed in the US is already best practice in the UK, the same pressures to reconsider existing roles and governance standards are being felt among our pension funds. Some radical reconsideration is going on in certain sectors.

For example, in 2008 a report commissioned from veteran fund trustee Brian Holden by magazine *Investment & Pensions Europe* and Pioneer Investments was published. "Ensuring Pension Fund Governance is Fit for Purpose" proposes a shift to a two-tier board structure. Arguing that lay trustees are unable to cope with the requirements of fast-moving markets, the report suggests that these lay individuals take a supervisory, oversight role, and the active decisions are taken by professionals alone—the equivalent of the management board in a corporate two-tier structure. Holden also proposes that a code of pension fund governance be established to provide a form of guidance and to encourage better practice across the industry.

Other thinking is still more radical. While the English understanding of trust law and trusteeship is widely acknowledged as a crucial foundation of our legal and commercial systems, there are those who question whether the strong independence implied by the trustee role is the right form for occupational schemes. In particular, some advisers have found themselves discussing with companies and their pension funds some form of risk-sharing and flexibility such that companies can be enabled to introduce new forms of pensions which fit better with their general benefits profile. It should not be forgotten, after all, that pensions are and will always be an employee benefit, negotiated between the company and its staff. The trustee structure is useful in providing confidence of independent oversight (not least for HMRC's purposes), but it is there just as much because it is a convenient method for sponsors and employees to arrange their affairs.

Yet those advisers trying to arrange some risk-sharing and flexibility have on some occasions found that the fiduciary duties of the pension fund trustees to their underlying beneficiaries and the undertakings that have already been made form a barrier. Such discussions, these advisers report, can be severely limited: trustees may find themselves duty bound not to have the free and frank conversation which might create the best pensions profile for the long run, and for the good of the company, and perhaps its employees. Trustees in such circumstances might be wise to consider seeking to alter the trust deed so that realistic negotiations can happen.

Where such open and frank discussions are impossible, some trustees have already found themselves presented with something decidedly more unpalatable: *faits accomplis* announcements from companies that the existing scheme will be closed to new contributions, or will indeed be wound up at once. Thus it is possible that a strict understanding of the trustees' fiduciary duties is leading to an inability to develop alternative, imaginative structures which might offer beneficiaries the best possible security in the long-run in the context of a company with inevitably limited resources. This concern was to an extent recognised by the Myners review's exhortation to sponsors to provide pension trustees with a greater investment and assessment infrastructure. The Regulator also appears to favour a common sense approach.

Instead of a flexible discussion, the choice becomes stark: continue with DB or switch (for new employees at least, sometimes also for existing ones) to DC. As only 17 per cent of major companies now offer new staff a DB scheme, it is clear which way this trend is driving us, whether or not that creates the right allocation of risk across the economy as a whole.

The Association of Consulting Actuaries in 2007 railed at the inflexibility of the law, which essentially requires schemes to be either DB, or DC. They called for a third way of schemes with an element of shared risk, using average salary structures to manage the cost for the sponsor and relieving individuals of the full investment volatility risks. Such schemes might require new governance structures to give beneficiaries the confidence they will receive the pensions they expect from the slightly equivocal promises implied in a shared risk structure. But short of such radical change, there are those that argue that the general shift from DB to DC schemes requires a reconsideration of what the best pension fund governance structures might be. Timothy Besley and Andrea Prat of the London School of Economics are among them. In a major paper for the Centre for Economic Policy Research (CEPR Discussion Paper No.3955, 2003, *http://www.cepr.org/pubs/dps/DP3955.asp*) called "Pension Fund Governance and the Choice between Defined Benefit and Defined Contribution Plans", they formulate an intellectual framework to understand pension fund governance structures and then suggest that those structures which suit DB schemes may not be best suited to the DC world: "If we see a major shift from defined benefit to defined contribution schemes, we ought to see a shift in pension fund governance", says Besley.

The core of Besley and Prat's argument revolves around who faces residual liability if the fund is insufficient. In the DB world, there is an explicit promise from the sponsor that a certain level of pensions will be paid; if the fund is not capable of making such payments, the sponsor has an obligation to do so. This means that the sponsor will be most vigilant and argues for strong sponsor representation at the trustee level, usually in the form of professionals of some sort or other.

In the DC world, in contrast, there is no such explicit promise and the individual must find additional sources of support if the pension itself proves insufficient. The duty of vigilance clearly therefore falls on the beneficiaries themselves rather than the sponsor, and what is more, there is a greater need for trust among the individuals that the right thing is being done on their behalf. That, Besley and Prat argue, suggests a reduced role for professionals and representatives of the sponsor, and a much greater role for "caring laymen": individuals who are themselves beneficiaries and are trusted to stand in the place of their fellows to take the necessary decisions for the good of all.

In 2007, the NAPF's consideration of pension scheme governance worried about the governance vacuum for some DC schemes. This is clearly also an area of concern for the Regulator. Its February 2010 guidance on DC growled at trustees that they are paying too much attention to legacy DB schemes and neglecting their DC cousins, to the schemes' detriment. This reflects a July 2009 survey by Watson Wyatt, "The future of DC governance", which found that DC scheme governance was suffering because of the burden of legacy DB schemes. In a similar way, the OECD indicated in a 2008 report "Pension Fund Governance: Challenges and Potential Solutions":

"The absence of governance arrangements for defined contribution style pension plans also needs to be addressed, potentially via management committees, increased fiduciary responsibility for relevant parties or via a strengthened role for pension supervisory authorities."

But this vacuum is gradually being filled. The Investment Governance Group is slowly producing guidance. For example, its consultation on how DC schemes might govern the investment process closed in May 2010. This makes several commonsense recommendations which essentially carry over the Myners principles into the DC world. There is also effective guidance in the discussion paper from the Personal Accounts Delivery Authority ("PADA"), "Building Personal Accounts—Designing an Investment Approach". At least one leading consultant, Simon Pearse of Mercer, has indicated the value and general application of this document. In a September 2009 article in *Investment and Pensions Europe* he said:

"It is a must-read for all current (and potential) DC trustees and sponsors, and others working in pensions . . . The research and discussion provides a framework against which other schemes could be compared."

Trustee skills and training have been dealt with above extensively, so we will deal here with the other areas. Many DC schemes model their governance on the DB structures on which we have been concentrating. However, many do not and certainly this governance structure is not seen as relevant to more contract-based structures. The NAPF therefore proposes alternative structures to ensure that the interests of beneficiaries are fully protected, with some of the thinking apparently influenced by the work of Besley and Prat. PricewaterhouseCoopers pensions partner Andrew Evans has argued that there should in practice be no difference in the governance protections in place between contract and trust-based schemes. In a November 2009 article for *Professional Pensions*, Evans raises concerns that contract-based schemes, without proper governance, may disadvantage members. As a minimum he calls for the establishment of staff pensions committees.

For the small-scale schemes, the NAPF in effect proposes a pooling of governance responsibilities through some multi-employer form of structure. The OECD (again in "Pension Fund Governance: Challenges and Potential Solutions") also indicates that some pooling of resources may be of value: "Consolidation of the pension industry . . . may also be required to achieve economies of scale and reduce costs, which in turn would allow pension funds to dedicate more resources to strengthening their internal governance." It notes that "it is unlikely that a small fund will be able to achieve a comparable level of performance, even before fees, to a large fund". One suggested route to achieving the desired better performance that is short of the drastic step of full consolidation of schemes, the OECD suggests, is to adopt some form of the increasingly popular fiduciary management under which day-to-day investment decisions are delegated to a third party management team.

The NAPF's proposed code of governance covers the duties of the trustee board, its structure and appointments and removals of individual trustees, skills and competence, risk management, conflicts, internal controls and dialogue with the sponsor. This is thoughtful and generally good commonsense, and unsurprising to any reader with knowledge of the Corporate Governance Code, but whether the NAPF code gains any traction remains to be seen. This may be a challenge at a time when trustees must assimilate the recommendations of the Regulator's Codes of Practice and other developments, many of which coincide with areas covered in the NAPF Code and so are likely to take precedence in trustee thought patterns.

The Regulator has produced a best practice guide to how DC schemes should produce literature and communicate with their members. Find it at *http://www.thepensionsregulator.gov.uk/pdf/RetirementInfoDCMembers.pdf.*

Postscript

In all of this, it is worth noting the real significance of pension schemes in **21.015**
our modern post-industrial landscape, where we set such store by employee
relations and human capital. Pensions are increasingly seen by companies
and investors as a financial issue, Andrew Higginson, Finance Director of
Tesco, said in the CIMA Anthony Howitt Lecture 2005. "It's not", he added.
Rather, it defines a company's relationship with its staff. That is why Tesco
has maintained its DB scheme, a career average one.

In a world increasingly competing for talented staff, perhaps there is
an opportunity for companies to differentiate themselves effectively in
the market for talent by having a quality pension scheme with exemplary
governance.

The Governance of Fund Managers

21.016   In a well-publicised speech to the Investor Relations Society in April 2005, then Cadbury Schweppes chair John Sunderland laid down a challenge:

> "The corporate sector is now far better governed and audited and transparent. If we want our capital markets to be effective and efficient we should seek the same standards from those who own our companies."

Sunderland suggests that fund managers should be open and transparent in their intentions and policies, they should publicly disclose remuneration structures and payments, that they should subject themselves to the same governance checks and balances which they argue for at investee companies. The subtext of his speech is the hope that this will ensure more long-term investment behaviour.

Sunderland's call is gradually being answered, in the UK and around the world, with a developing set of governance guidelines for fund management organisations. For example, a German working group published a "Corporate Governance Code for Asset Management Companies" in April 2005. This calls for the supervisory board overseeing every fund manager's operations to ensure the protection of investors' interests, and should provide for this through sufficient independent board members, and a sufficiently independent audit committee. Each company should make a public disclosure of its governance structures and how it manages conflicts of interest (in particular those "resulting from the company's ownership structure"). One specific recommendation is very similar to Sunderland's call for remuneration which matches beneficial owners' long-term time horizons:

> "In setting remuneration for the managing directors and employees it shall be ensured that no incentives are given for any investment behaviour that is not aligned with investors' interests."

In 2009, the US-based but in theory global CFA Institute updated its Asset Manager Code of Professional Conduct. This aims to extend its existing code of ethical conduct for individual Chartered Financial Analysts to the firm level. On the face of it, these standards might appear bland, but if they are properly implemented, their effect is likely to be profound. Among the disclosure requirements are:

> "Managers must:
>
> 3.   . . . Include any material facts when making disclosures or providing information to clients regarding themselves, their personnel, investments, or the investment process.

4. Disclose the following:
   (a) Conflicts of interests generated by any relationships with brokers or other entities, other client accounts, fee structures, or other matters.
   . . .
   (d) Management fees and other investment costs charged to investors, including what costs are included in the fees and the methodologies for determining fees and costs.
   (e) The amount of any soft or bundled commissions, the goods and/or services received in return, and how those goods and/or services benefit the client.
   . . .
   (h) Shareholder voting policies.
   . . .
   (k) Significant personnel or organizational changes that have occurred at the Manager.
   (l) Risk management processes."

These disclosure requirements mirror similarly high standards for behaviour in each of these areas.

The updated ICGN's "Statement of Principles on Institutional Shareholder Responsibilities", agreed in 2006, also deals extensively with the issue of the internal governance of fiduciary organisations, including fund managers. "Each intermediary [in the investment chain] should have internal governance arrangements that reflect the particular nature of their own role and responsibilities. The over-arching obligation of each of the intermediaries is to safeguard the interests of beneficiaries", the Statement asserts.

The four central elements of the internal governance standards are:

- transparency, such that beneficiaries can have confidence their assets are handled appropriately;

- disclosure and management of conflicts of interest;

- expertise in relevant areas;

- oversight structures which ensure decisions are taken in beneficiaries' interests.

One particularly contentious issue is pay. The central point is to ensure alignment of interests; in particular, there is a need for something approaching an alignment of timescales.

These issues of transparency, of the need to manage conflicts, of having expertise, training and high standards, and of acting always in the interests of the beneficiaries, are embedded in the ISC Code and seem likely to be central to the Stewardship Code which will be developed from it and on which the FRC is consulting at the time of writing. In 2010 John Sunderland was appointed chair of the FRC's Corporate Governance Committee and so will have oversight responsibility for the Stewardship Code as well as the UK Corporate Governance Code.

While each of these initiatives has involved the active participation of members of the fund management community, others from that industry have kicked against the idea that they should face any general transparency and governance obligations. The argument goes that listed companies must be transparent to their owners, and that the fund managers who represent those owners and act on their behalf should not have to be transparent simply from some mistaken (perhaps jealous, some suggest) sense of reciprocity. The fund managers' duty is to their clients, pure and simple, and it is to the clients that openness and accountability is owed.

There is a good deal of sense in this argument, but perhaps it is not a full answer. Let's deal with the extent to which this argument is right first. It is clear that the sole and simple duty which institutional investors bear is to their underlying beneficiaries. That is the very nature of the fiduciary duties owed by all such institutions, and it's why managing conflicts of interest is so important. It's good business sense too: history is littered with fund management firms which neglected their duty to their clients and thereby over time failed their owners too.

In a sense, the proposed codes of governance and conduct are just a codification of the specific responsibilities which underlie the concept of fiduciary duty. Any fiduciary must put the interests of its beneficiaries ahead of its own. In the fund management industry, this requires for example: certainty that any conflicts of interest are disclosed and managed; transparency of management structures and disclosure of any significant changes in personnel; and that pay structures drive value for the client rather than just for the firm and its individual staff members.

Governance standards for fund managers are also developing because of the need for an open and honest dialogue with investee companies. Such openness and honesty is a prerequisite for investee company management and non-executives to be open in discussions about issues which matter for the long-term; issues such as strategy and the development of future strategy, discipline on capital structure and financial efficiency, board structure and governance matters, employee relations and leadership succession planning, remuneration policy and structures, and risk management.

Fund managers are most likely to generate good long-term returns for their clients by:

- being clear about their requirements and the time-frames over which they expect companies to perform;

- maintaining an open and honest relationship with investee companies, for example by being clear and transparent about their shareholdings, and explaining any changes if requested;

- ensuring long-term thinking by executives and in the boardroom;
- approving incentive pay structures which work for the long-term;
- being consistent in their interactions with companies;
- being discreet in those interactions and not seeking publicity which damages the companies in which their clients invest.

In many ways these are the standards of transparency which John Sunderland was calling for. But importantly, they are the duties of fund managers because they are in their clients' interests, rather than through any reciprocity for the transparency now demanded of listed companies. Those in the fund management industry who fight disclosure and transparency therefore do so in the mistaken belief that these things are not in their clients' interests.

So it is natural for the fund managers' clients—including pension funds— as the best already do, to require disclosure from their fund managers of such things as management structure and culture, remuneration frameworks and timescales, and on their willingness to act as good owners. In other words, hold them to the governance codes which are now being developed for their industry. As their clients increasingly make them accountable in this way, it seems likely that the nature of the discussions between fund managers and investee companies will change. It should ensure a more long-term focus in those discussions and so the more long-term investment behaviour which Sunderland was seeking.

Chapter 22

The Voluntary and Community Sector

Douglas Cracknell[1]

Introduction

As in the wider world, within the voluntary and community sector the **22.001** whole question of governance (see para.22.017 below) has given rise to some concern, careful consideration by many people and the issue of much guidance and information. Of particular significance is *Good Governance: A Code for the Voluntary and Community Sector* which was published by the National Council for Voluntary Organisations ("NCVO") on behalf of the National Hub of Expertise on Governance (the Governance Hub) in July 2005. Indeed, *Good Governance* (as the guidance will here be called) will form the framework, and provide not a little of the substance, for this chapter. How could it be otherwise? *Good Governance* was produced by Charity Trustee Networks, the Association of Chief Executives of Voluntary Organisations, the Institute of Chartered Secretaries and Administrators, NCVO and the Charity Commission and endorsed by the Governance Hub.

The Governance Hub

The Governance Hub was a partnership of organisations which pro- **22.002** vided support to the voluntary and community sector. It arose out of a

---

[1] Since Douglas Cracknell's call to the Bar in May 1957, unexpectedly, much of his life has been, and continues to be, involved with charities, in one way or another. At present a trustee of several charities and Honorary Secretary of the Royal London Society for the Blind, in earlier times he has been General Secretary of NCH, the children's charity, now Action for Children, a member of the Executive of the National Council for Voluntary Organisations and a member of the Goodman Committee on Charity Law and Voluntary Organisations. Author of *Cracknell on Charities* (Sweet and Maxwell) and General Editor of the loose-leaf work *Charities: The Law and Practice* (Sweet and Maxwell), for many years he also covered charity law issues for the *Solicitors Journal*.

recommendation in the Home Office Active Community Unit's *Changeup* report, and the Home Office funded it for two years. Its aim was to deliver a range of services and ideas via its website, as well as through its partnership programme, commissioning research, publishing new resources and organising events.

Its successor

22.003   The Governance Hub completed its programme of work by March 31, 2008. The Leadership and Governance National Support Service, a three-year programme funded by Capacitybuilders and led by NCVO, is building upon, and developing where appropriate, the resources and work of the Government Hub. See further *http://www.improvingsupport.org.uk/leader shipandgovernance*.

Good Governance

22.004   *Good Governance* sets out principles, tailored for the voluntary and community sector. It acknowledges the significance of the "Nolan Principles" (see *Good Governance*, App.5) and recognises that the way organisations "govern" will be different depending on the circumstances. These circumstances can include the size of an organisation, how long it has been in existence, and the culture and values it possesses. *Good Governance* is intended to be applicable in all circumstances, but each organisation must interpret and apply it according to its particular needs and situation.

Where an organisation is already covered by an existing code of governance, prepared by its representative body or regulator, the existing code should take precedence: see further para.22.013 below. Where more than one such code might apply, the organisation should seek advice as to which one should take precedence.

Good Governance has been prepared primarily to meet the needs of organisations working in England: organisations working in other parts of the United Kingdom may make use of it as they see fit. Where an organisation's governing document does not allow the organisation to adopt one or more of the *Good Governance* recommendations, the governing document takes precedence. Organisations seeking to follow the *Good Governance* recommendations are advised to review their governing document, standing orders and other documentation, and consider amending them as may be necessary.

The *Good Governance* principles are not mandatory, but organisations that comply with them are invited to state this in their annual report and other relevant published material. Where an organisation does not comply with a specific recommendation, it is invited to record this fact and to set out the reasons for non-compliance. Smaller organisations with limited resources should focus on the principles rather than the detail of *Good Governance* and make clear that they have adopted this approach.

Availability

Copies of *Good Governance*, in whole or in summary form, may be obtained **22.005** from NCVO, and it is also available on the NCVO and Charity Trustee Networks websites.

Toolkit

A toolkit or practical guide has been produced to assist in the use of *Good* **22.006** *Governance*: it is also published by NCVO and it may be downloaded from its website free of charge.

New edition

With a view to making the high level principles of *Good Governance* easier to **22.007** understand and applicable to all organisations in the sector, those principles have been refashioned and they will form the basis of a new edition of *Good Governance* to be published in the summer of 2010. Meanwhile, the refashioned principles may be seen on the Charity Commission's website (*Key Principles of Good Governance—consultation draft*).

Other publications

Charity Commission

The Commission's key guidance *The Hallmarks of an Effective Charity* **22.008** (CC10) is intended to be complementary to *Good Governance* and sets out six standards to help trustees improve the effectiveness of their charity, and uphold the principles that the Commission's regulatory framework exists to support. *Good Governance for charities* sets out, on the Commission's website, the Commission's guidance and other resources to help trustees translate these principles into good practice in governance.

In June 2009 the Charity Commission issued on its website (although printed copies are available) a checklist reflecting a good practice approach that charities should use when regularly reviewing the way they operate including their governance, an approach which had become especially important during the economic downturn. The Commission strongly encouraged all trustee boards to use it.

NCVO

22.009 Attention is drawn to *The Good Governance Action Plan Workbook* (2005) which is published by and available from NCVO and it costs £7.50 (£5.25 NCVO members). NCVO lists many other relevant publications on its website under the heading *Publications—Leadership, governance and trustee-ship* and these include *Good Trustee Guide* (£25, members £17) and *Developing Trustee Boards* (£25).

National Occupational Standards

22.010 In April 2006 NCVO published the National Occupational Standards for Trustees and Management Committee Members ("NOS") which had first been approved by the Qualifications and Curriculum Authority. NOS complement *Good Governance* and comprise four units:

- Unit 1: Safeguard and promote the values and mission of the organisation.

- Unit 2: Determine the strategy and structure of the organisation.

- Unit 3: Ensure the organisation operates in an effective, responsible and accountable manner.

- Unit 4: Ensure the effective functioning of the board.

NOS and a toolkit, produced by the Governance Hub and published by NCVO, may be downloaded from the NCVO website. Printed copies of NOS cost £10 (NCVO members £7) but a pocket-sized edition is available free of charge.

Charity Trustee Networks ("CTN")

22.011 In November 2008 CTN launched *Codes of Conduct for Trustees* which offers trustee boards practical help in strengthening their governance arrangements. This publication may be downloaded free from the CTN website.

European Union

22.012The European Commission has been addressing concerns as to the vulnerability of not-for-profit organisations to terrorist funding and other criminal abuse: see particularly its Communication dated November 29, 2005. It was acknowledged that measures taken to protect the not-for-profit sector against abuse should not disrupt or discourage legitimate charitable activities, but rather promote transparency, integrity and public confidence in its administration and management. See also Council Framework Decision 2002/475/JHA on combating terrorism, as amended.

Governance in particular situations

22.013While the broad *Good Governance* principles apply to all voluntary and community sector organisations, guidance as to their application in particular situations is often available, including the following:

- Almshouses—Charity Commission Operational Guidance *Almshouse Charities*.

- Arts charities—see below.

- Charity shops—Association of Charity Shops *Code of Charity Retailing 2010–11*.

- Common investment funds—Charity Commission guidance *Common Investment Funds*.

- Corporate charities—Charity Commission Operational Guidance *Corporate Trustees* and *Incorporation of Charity Trustees Companies Act 2006*.

- Faith-based charities—*Faith in Good Governance*, guidance published by the Charity Commission in November 2009.

- National Health Service charities—Charity Commission Operational Guidance *Charity Accounts and Reports* and *Incorporation of Charity Trustees NHS charities: independence, guidance and governance*.

- Registered social landlords—Charity Commission *Guidance for Charitable Registered Social Landlords*.

- Village halls and community centres—Charity Commission Operational Guidance *Management of Village Halls* and Regulatory Study RS9 (*Village Halls and Community Centres*).

As to best practice in relation to the governance of membership charities, see Charity Commission Regulatory Study RS7 (*Membership Charities*), Pt B.

Following a review of The Tate's policies and procedures, on July 19, 2006 the Charity Commission said that, in co-operation with the Department for Culture, Media and Sport and the Arts Council, it hoped to develop specific advice and guidance on good governance practice for charities in the arts sector. See now Charity Commission guidance *Conflicts of interest for arts charities.*

Work in other lands

22.014   While the Charity Commission recognises that charities operating internationally will often be working under very difficult conditions which will require them to work with imagination and flexibility, their governance and operational systems should achieve a proper balance between what is necessary to deliver their charitable benefits on the ground and meeting the requirement for accountability and transparency: see further guidance *Charities Working Internationally* on the Commission's website. See also para.22.008.

Charity Commission publications

22.015   All Charity Commission publications may be downloaded from its website (*http://www.charitycommission.gov.uk*) or, mostly and with the certain exception of SORP 2005, obtained from it in printed form free of charge. Copies of SORP 2005 (£15) may be obtained by calling 0844 561 8199 or visiting *http://www.cch.co.uk*. See also para.22.008.

Other literature

22.016   For a list of other literature concerning governance in the voluntary and community sector, and for the principles of good governance from the Good Governance Standard for Public Services and the National Housing Federation Code of Governance, see *Good Governance*, Apps 4, and 6 and 7 respectively. Reference should also be made to Volresource: *http://www.volresource.org.uk*.

Definitions

22.017   "*Board*"   The organisation's governing body of which every trustee is a member. It may have another title such as Committee, Council or Governors.

"*Charity Commission*"   Established (now) under the Charities Act 1993, as amended by the Charities Act 2006, the Charity Commission registers and regulates charities in England and Wales. It offers them advice and provides a wide range of services and guidance to help them run as effectively as possible. It also keeps the online Register of Charities, which provides information about each of the registered charities in England and Wales. See further *About the Charity Commission* on the Commission's website.

"*Chief executive*"   The organisation's most senior employee and bridge between trustees and staff. Again, persons in this position have a range of descriptions including Director, Principal and General Secretary. Here, "chief executive" covers all of them.

"*Governance*"   In *Good Governance*, Professor Chris Cornforth's definition is cited as follows: "[Governance is] the systems and processes concerned with ensuring the overall direction, effectiveness, supervision and accountability of an organisation". Governance may also be described colloquially along these lines: Since all trustees (or whatever they may be called: see definition "*Trustees*", below) are equally responsible for all of their organisation's assets and every aspect of its activities, governance is the means by which they are all kept sufficiently informed and involved to enable them to make strategic decisions and monitor, guide and question the organisation's performance.

"*Governing document*"   The organisation's main constitutional document, setting out the organisation's objectives and the trustees' powers and duties. It may be called, for example, the organisation's constitution, charter, trust deed, rules or memorandum and articles.

"*Membership organisation*"   An organisation where, in accordance with its governing document, members have the ability to attend and vote at its annual general meeting ("AGM"). Members may be individuals or corporate bodies such as companies and local authorities.

"*Permanent endowment*"   In the Charities Act 1993 "permanent endowment" means, in relation to any charity, property held subject to a restriction on its being expended for the purposes of the charity: s.96(3). A charity is deemed for the purposes of that Act to have a permanent endowment unless all property held for the purposes of the charity may be expended for those purposes without distinction between capital and income: s.96(3).

"*Stakeholders*"   Persons with a legitimate interest in an organisation's work. These might include users of its services, beneficiaries, members, media, partners, staff, volunteers, regulators and other government bodies and funders.

"*Trustees*"   By virtue of Charities Act 1993 s.97(1), in that Act, unless the context otherwise requires, "charity trustees" means the persons having the general control and management of the administration of a charity. Persons having such ultimate and equal responsibility in relation to organisations within the voluntary and community sector have a variety of titles apart from trustee—governor, director and board, council or committee member are just some of them. In this chapter, "trustees" includes them all. See, too, SORP 2005, App.1, para.7.

Key principles of good governance

Board leadership

22.018   Every organisation should be led and controlled by an effective board of trustees which collectively ensures delivery of its objects, sets its strategic direction and upholds its values: see generally booklet CC10 (*The Hallmarks of an Effective Charity*), and section D3 in particular where it says that the structure, policies and procedures of an effective charity enable it to achieve its mission and aims and deliver its services efficiently. While leadership includes ensuring that the organisation is solvent and well run, trustees should avoid becoming involved in day-to-day operational decisions and matters, except in the case of small organisations with few or no staff. Where trustees do need to become involved in operational matters, they should separate their strategic and operational roles.

Statement of essential roles

22.019   The board should have a statement of its strategic and leadership roles, and of key functions which cannot be delegated. These should include as a minimum:

- ensuring compliance with the objects, purposes and values of the organisation, and with its governing document (see para.22.023 below: see also para.22.037 below);

- setting or approving policies, plans and budgets, to achieve those objectives and monitoring performance against them;

- ensuring the solvency, financial strength and good performance of the organisation (see para.22.026 below);

- ensuring that the organisation complies with all relevant laws, regulations and requirements of its regulators (see para.22.023 below);

- dealing with the appointment (and if necessary the dismissal) of the organisation's chief executive (see also para.22.050 below);

- setting and monitoring a framework of delegation and internal control (see paras 22.025, 22.041 and 22.063 below); and

- agreeing or ratifying all policies and decisions on matters which might create significant risk to the organisation, financial or otherwise.

Trustees' overriding duty

Trustees are bound by an overriding duty, individually and as a board, **22.020** to act reasonably at all times in the interests of the organisation and of its present and future beneficiaries or (in the case of a membership organisation) members. They must act personally, and not as the representative of any group or organisation, regardless of how they were elected or selected to become a trustee: see Charity Commission booklet CC29 (*Charities and Local Authorities*) and Operational Guidance *Local authorities and trustees* on the Charity Commission website.

Chief executive's responsibilities

Where an organisation employs staff, the chief executive is responsible for **22.021** maintaining a clear division of responsibilities between the board and the staff team. (S)he should provide an effective link between board and staff, informing and implementing the strategic decisions of the board. Trustees should not seek to become directly involved in decisions which have been properly delegated to staff. Instead, they should hold staff to account through the chief executive. As to the delegation of the chief executive's responsibilities, see para.22.065 below.

Particular points

Accounts and reports   See particularly Charity Commission booklet **22.022** CC15b (*Charity Reporting and Accounting: The essentials*) (April 2009) which applies to both company and non-company charities for financial years ending on or after April 1, 2009. Organisations complying with the *Good Governance* approach could state this in their annual reports: smaller organisations could say that they comply with its principles rather than its detail. See also, on the Commission's website, Operational Guidance *Accounts and Reports* and *Reporting and linked charities—registration, reporting and accounting*).

22.023 *Compliance* Charity Commission booklet CC3 (*The Essential Trustee: what you need to know*) provides guidance for charity trustees and persons about to take up trustee responsibilities. It covers a range of key areas, but acknowledges that further information and advice is sometimes required. Its principal sections of general application are:

- trustee duties at a glance;

- trustees and their responsibilities;

- compliance;

- duty of prudence;

- duty of care;

- if things go wrong.

As to compliance, booklet CC3, section F, states that trustees must:

- Ensure that the charity complies with charity law, and with the requirements of the Charity Commission as regulator, in particular ensuring that the charity prepares reports, annual returns and accounts as required by law: see para.22.022 above.

- Ensure that the charity does not breach any of the requirements or rules set out in its governing document and that it remains true to the charitable purpose and objects set out there.

- Comply with the requirements of other legislation and regulators (if any) which govern the activities of the charity. As to data protection, on the Charity Commission's website see Operational Guidance *Data Protection Act 1998* and *Open Government and Human Rights* which provides information on the Human Rights Act 1998 as well as the Data Protection Act 1998. With regard to fundraising, see *Good Governance*, App.2 (self-regulation), Charity Commission booklets CC20 *(Charities and fundraising)*, CC35 *(Trustees, trading and tax: How charities may lawfully trade*, Regulatory Study RS2 (*Charities and Commercial Partners*) and, on the Commission's website, *Fundraising through partnerships with companies.*

- Act with integrity, and avoid any personal conflicts of interest (see further para.22.071 below) or misuse of charity funds or assets.

As to the ability of charities to engage in political activity, see Charity Commission booklet CC9 (*Speaking out—Campaigning and Political Activity by Charities*).

For guidance as to the content of a trustees' annual report concerning objectives and activities and achievements and performance, see SORP 2005, paras 47–52 and 53–54 respectively. As to a review of a charity's financial position and future plans, see SORP 2005, paras 55–56 and 57–58 respectively. Paragraph 59 sets out the SORP 2005 requirements where a charity, or its trustees, acts as custodian trustees.

Cross-border charities   See, on the Charity Commission's website: **22.024**

- *English and Welsh charities registering with the Office of the Scottish Charity Regulator.*

- *Guidance for English and Welsh Charities that have been asked to amend their governing documents before they can register in Scotland.*

See also, on the website of the Office of the Scottish Charity Regulator (*http://www.oscr.org.uk*):

- *Cross border charity regulation in Scotland.*

- *Seeking charitable status for cross-border charities.*

Delegation   Charity Commission booklet CC3, sections E7 and E8, states   **22.025** that trustees can generally delegate certain powers to agents or employees, but always retain ultimate responsibility for running the charity. A person acting as a delegate or agent of the trustees should always make clear in dealings with third parties that they are acting in that capacity (particularly if they are not an employee of the charity) and should always record in writing what was agreed in the conversation.

Trustees can invite some of their number to look into particular matters and make recommendations, but the decision whether or not to act on the recommendations is for the trustees to take together. The governing document of a charity may permit the trustees to set up committees with delegated powers to carry out particular functions.

Trustees will often need to delegate decisions on day-to-day management matters to employees. In these cases the scope of the authority should be clearly laid down in writing and instructions given for decisions on important matters to be reported to the trustees. Trustees should establish proper reporting procedures and clear lines of accountability.

Financial duties   See generally booklet CC3, section G. The trustees must   **22.026** ensure that their charity's finances are used appropriately, prudently, lawfully and in accordance with its objects. More particularly:

Income and expenditure   Trustees must ensure that all income due to the   **22.027** charity is received and that all tax and rating relief due is claimed. The charity's expenditure must be applied fairly among people who are properly qualified to benefit from it. As to the making of ex gratia payments, see Charity Commission booklet CC7 (*Ex gratia Payments by Charities*) and Operational Guidance *Ex gratia payments* on the Charity Commission's website. The income of a charity must be applied for its purposes within a reasonable period of receipt, unless the trustees have explicit power to accumulate it. Without such a power, the trustees should not allow the charity's income to accumulate unless they have a specific use for it in mind. See further Charity Commission booklet CC19 (*Charities' Reserves*) and para.22.079 below.

22.028　*Permanent endowment*　Trustees of charities with permanent endowment (see para.22.017 above) must maintain a fair balance between the interests of present and future beneficiaries, not least when selecting investments: see further Charity Commission Operational Guidance *Permanent endowment* and *Endowed charities: a total return approach to investment.*

22.029　*Duty of care*　Trustees must exercise an appropriate degree of care in administering their charity: see booklet CC3, section H, on the Charity Commission's website guidance *How to be an effective trustee* and s.1 of the Trustee Act 2000. Amongst much else, trustees must ensure that the way the charity is administered is not open to abuse by unscrupulous associates or employees and that their systems of control are rigorous and constantly maintained: see further Charity Commission booklet CC8 (*Internal Financial Controls for Charities*).

22.030　*Investment*　Money not needed for immediate expenditure should be invested: if expenditure is expected in the near future, surplus cash should be placed on deposit. See further Charity Commission booklets CC14 (*Investment of Charitable Funds: Basic Principles*) and CC19 (*Charities' Reserves*), Regulatory Studies RS3 (*Charity Reserves*) and RS5 (*Small Charities and Reserves*) and, on the Commission's website, *Investment of charitable funds: detailed guidance*, *Charities and social investment*, *Charity reserves and defined benefit pension schemes*, *Charity income reserves* and *Endowed charities: a total return approach to investment.* For the court's approach to ethical investment, see, e.g. *Harries v Church Commissioners for England.*[2]

22.031　*Cheques*　Trustees must follow any relevant clause in the charity's governing document that specifies who is authorised to sign cheques. If there is no provision in the governing document which relates to the operation of bank accounts, the bank mandate must specify at least two trustees as signatories, unless the trustees can reasonably claim that it is necessary for employees to

---

[2] [1993] 2 All E.R. 300.

sign cheques to allow the charity to operate. See further booklet CC8, above and *Guidance on electronic banking* on the Commission's website.

Land or buildings   Where a charity owns land or buildings, trustees need to know on a continuing basis what condition the property is in, that it is being properly used and that adequate insurance is in place. See further Charity Commission booklet CC49 (*Charities and Insurance*).   **22.032**

Trustees' age   People under 18 can be trustees of an incorporated charity, but cannot be trustees of an unincorporated charity. While unincorporated associations and trusts cannot appoint under 18s as trustees, the Charity Commission stresses that young people under that age can still be involved in the decision-making process by, e.g. asking them to look into specific issues and make recommendations to the trustee body: see generally on the Commission's website *Involving young people in running a charity*. By virtue of the Companies Act 2006 ("CA 2006") s.157, a person may not be appointed a director of a company unless (s)he has attained the age of 16 years. However, this does not affect the validity of an appointment that is not to take effect until the person appointed attains that age and, by virtue of CA 2006 s.158, the Secretary of State has power to make provision by regulations for cases in which a person who has not attained the age of 16 years may be appointed a director of a company.   **22.033**

Recruitment and selection   See generally Charity Commission booklets CC24 (*Users on Board: Beneficiaries Who Become Trustees*) and CC30 (*Finding New Trustees: What Charities Need to Know*), Charity Commission Regulatory Studies RS1 (*Trustee Recruitment, Selection and Induction*) and RS10 (*Start as you mean to go on: Trustee Recruitment and Induction*) and, on the Charity Commission's website, guidance as follows: **22.034**

- charitable registered social landlords (includes tenants as members of governing bodies);

- corporate trustees;

- custodian trustees;

- declaration of eligibility for newly appointed trustees;

- disqualification for acting as a charity trustee;

- how to be an effective trustee;

- incorporation of charity trustees;

- safeguarding children;

- waiver of disqualification for acting as a charity trustee.

See also Charity Commission booklet CC42 (*Appointing Nominees and Custodians: Guidance under section 19(4) of the Trustee Act 2000*) and CC43 (*Incorporation of Charity Trustees*).

22.035   *Liability*   As to trustee liability, on the Commission's website see guidance:

- trustee indemnity insurance;
- trustee responsibilities;
- vicarious liability of a charity or its trustees.

See also Charity Commission booklet CC49 (*Charities and Insurance*) and, for the liability of corporate trustees, Operational Guidance *Incorporation of charity trustees* on the Commission's website. See, too, para.22.079 below, and, on the Commission's website, *Company director indemnities*.

The board in control

22.036   The trustees as a board should effectively be responsible and accountable for ensuring and monitoring that the organisation is performing well, is solvent, and complies with all of its obligations. In particular, the board:

- must ensure that the organisation complies with its own governing document and has policies, procedures and reporting mechanisms in place to ensure compliance with relevant laws and the requirements of any regulatory bodies (see para.22.037 below: see also para.22.023, above);

- should maintain and regularly review the organisation's system of internal controls (see para.22.041 below and Charity Commission booklet CC8 (*Internal Financial Controls for Charities*)) and performance reporting, policies and procedures;

- must act prudently to protect the assets and property of the organisation, and ensure that they are used to deliver the organisation's objectives;

- must regularly review the risks to which the organisation is subject and take action to mitigate risks identified (see para.22.042 below);

- should ensure that the organisation upholds and applies the principles of equality and diversity (see, para.22.040 below) and that the organisation is fair and open to all sections of the community in all of its activities.

Particular points

22.037   *Compliance with legislative and regulatory requirements: Charities*   As to charities, the principal legislative requirements are to be found in the

Charities Act 1993 Pt VI (ss.41–49A) (charity accounts, reports and returns), as amended, and the Charities (Accounts and Reports) Regulations 2008 (SI 2008/629). Charitable companies should have regard to the requirements of the CA 2006 and relevant regulations. See, too, SORP 2005, para.60 et seq., para.5 et seq. for the trustees' annual report.

See, too, Charity Commission Regulatory Study RS7 (*Transparency and Accountability*) and, on the Commission's website, *Public Benefit Reporting, SORP 2005 documents* and Operational Guidance *Accounts and reports*.

Community interest companies   As to community interest companies, see   **22.038**
the Companies (Audit, Investigations and Community Enterprise) Act 2004 Pt 2 (ss.26–63), as amended, and the Community Interest Company Regulations 2005 (SI 2005/1788), as amended.

Charitable incorporated organisations   See para.22.080 below.   **22.039**

Equality and diversity   With regard to equality and diversity, the board   **22.040**
should ensure that the organisation upholds and promotes equal opportunities and diversity in all areas of its work, not least in relation to membership of the board and of any sub-committees. The board should set strategies for, and receive regular reports on, the organisation's work to achieve equality and diversity against clear targets where practicable. These reports should be used to help develop the organisation's overall strategies.

Internal controls   As to internal controls, larger and more complex organi-   **22.041**
sations should set up an audit committee, and should also consider the use of an internal audit service. Organisations providing services to users should consider the adoption of an appropriate quality assurance system, or of other forms of accreditation: for a list of organisations offering some or all of these services, see *Good Governance*, App.1.

Risk management   In relation to the management of risks, the board must   **22.042**
not undertake activities which might place at undue risk the organisation's service users, beneficiaries, volunteers, staff, property assets or reputation. Special care, and compliance with the organisation's governing document or any other legal requirements, is called for when investing the organisation's funds or borrowing funds for it to use. A full risk assessment (either periodically or on a rolling basis) should be undertaken and trustees should take appropriate steps to manage the organisation's exposure to significant risks. Appropriate advice should be obtained on all matters where there may be material risk or where the trustees may be in breach of their duties. The board should take ultimate responsibility for dealing with and managing conflicts that may arise within the organisation and it should have a whistleblowing policy and procedures (see further para.22.043 below) to allow confidential reporting of matters of concern, such as misconduct, misuse of funds,

mismanagement and risks to the organisation or to people connected with it. See also *Managing risk* and *Charities and risk management* on the Charity Commission's website.

22.043   *Whistleblowing*   The Public Interest Disclosure Act 1998 protects workers from detrimental treatment or victimisation from their employer if, in the public interest, they blow the whistle on wrongdoing. The Act protects most workers (and former workers: *Woodward v Abbey National Plc (No.1)*[3]) in the public, private and voluntary sectors, including charities. However, it does not apply to genuinely self-employed professionals (other than in the NHS), voluntary workers (including charity trustees and charity volunteers), police officers or workers in the intelligence services. See further Charity Commission guidance *The Public Interest Disclosure Act 1998* on the Commission's website and booklet CC47 (*Complaints about Charities*).

The high performance board

22.044   The board should have clear responsibilities and functions, and should compose and organise itself to discharge them effectively. This key principle embraces supporting principles as follows.

Statement of duties and responsibilities

22.045   Trustees should understand their duties and responsibilities and should be sent a statement (which they should sign and return) defining them. As a minimum, this statement should include obligations to uphold the values and objectives of the organisation, give adequate time and energy to the duties of being a trustee and act with integrity, avoiding or declaring personal conflicts of interest. Individual trustees must not act on their own on behalf of the board, or on the business of the organisation, without proper authority from the board.

Organisation of work

22.046   The board should organise its work to ensure that it makes the most effective use of the time, skills and knowledge of trustees. The board should meet regularly (see further para.22.051 below) and ensure that its work is focused on delivering its strategic role. Within the terms of its governing document, the board should ensure that it has enough trustees to provide the skills and

---

[3] *The Times*, July 11, 2006.

experience needed, without becoming so large that decision-making becomes unwieldy. The chair of the board should ensure that all trustees can contribute at meetings (see further para.22.051 below) and that the proceedings are not dominated by particular trustees. Charity Commission booklet CC10, section D2, observes:

"An effective charity is run by a clearly identifiable board or trustee body that has the right balance of skills and experience, acts in the best interests of the charity and its beneficiaries, understands its responsibilities and has systems in place to exercise them properly".

Trustee decisions

Trustees should ensure that they receive the advice and information they **22.047** need in order to make good decisions. The board should conduct its work efficiently. Board papers should be timely, well presented, circulated well in advance of board meetings, and should make clear recommendations to the board. The board should take professional advice where necessary before making important decisions and should not rely excessively or exclusively on a single source. In *Scott v National Trust for Places of Historic Interest or Natural Beauty*,[4] Walker J. summed up the position as follows:

"Trustees must act in good faith, responsibly and reasonably. They must inform themselves, before making a decision, of matters which are relevant to the decision. These matters may not be limited to simple matters of fact but will, on occasion (indeed, quite often) include taking advice from appropriate experts, whether the experts are lawyers, accountants, actuaries, surveyors, scientists or whomsoever. It is however for advisers to advise and for trustees to decide: trustees may not (except in so far as they are authorised to do so) delegate the exercise of their discretions, even to experts."

For a list of organisations offering assistance to trustees, see *Good Governance*, App.3.

Board membership

The trustee should have the diverse range of skills, experience and knowledge, **22.048** broadly representative of the community and appropriate to the organisation and its beneficiaries' needs, required to run the organisation effectively.

---

[4] [1998] 2 All E.R. 705.

Depending on the organisation's size and the nature of its activities, the experience of trustees should, as appropriate, cover:

- providing effective strategic leadership, and working as a team;

- direct knowledge of the organisation's beneficiaries and users, and of their needs and aspirations, whether gained through life or work experience;

- governance, general finance, business and management;

- human resources and diversity;

- the operating environment and risks that exist for the organisation; and

- other specific knowledge required, such as fundraising, health, social services, property or legal.

The boards of organisations providing services to beneficiaries or users should be open to trustee membership from these groups unless there are clear legal or other reasons why this is not practicable. See generally Charity Commission booklet CC24 (*Users on Board: Beneficiaries who become Trustees*).

Staff of the organisation may only become trustees where this is permitted by law and by the organisation's governing document. It should also be agreed by the board as being demonstrably in the interests of the organisation, and as not creating unacceptable conflicts of interest. A staff trustee should not chair the organisation: staff trustees should be in a minority on the board. See further para.22.055 below.

Induction, training and support

22.049   Trustees should ensure that they receive the necessary induction, training and ongoing support needed to discharge their duties. The board should have a strategy for the support and personal development of all trustees, so that each trustee can keep up to date with the knowledge and skills they need to carry out their role. All new trustees should undergo a full induction, in which they receive all the information and support they need to carry out their role, and can meet key staff, users and beneficiaries, and other stakeholders. Implementation of these strategies may be delegated by the board to the organisation's chief executive or secretary. See also Charity Commission booklet CC30 (*Finding New Trustees: What charities need to know*) and para.22.025 above.

Chief executive—support and remuneration

The board should make formal arrangements for the supervision, support, **22.050** appraisal, personal development and remuneration of the organisation's chief executive. These matters may be entrusted to the chair, another trustee or to a small group of trustees, but, whatever arrangements are made, the remuneration of the chief executive should be ratified by the board.

The remuneration package for the chief executive should be adequate to attract and retain the quality of person required but no more; openly disclosed in the organisation's accounts, including pension and other benefits; and, where there is a performance-related element, be linked to the achievement of measurable targets. The board should seek independent expert or professional advice when required concerning sensitive matters relating to the chief executive's employment. See generally *Governance and leadership—Chief executives* on the NCVO website.

Particular points

Meetings

Frequency   Trustees must meet as often as needed to do justice to the affairs **22.051** of the charity, and make well-informed decisions: subject to any requirement in a charity's governing document, the Charity Commission believes full meetings of trustees should be held at least twice each year. Trustees who do not meet often enough risk breaching their duty of care. See generally Charity Commission booklet CC3, section H2; for detailed guidance, see Charity Commission booklet CC48 (*Charities and Meetings*) and, on the Charity Commission's website, Operational Guidance *Postponement and adjournment of general meetings*. As to charitable companies, see now CA 2006 Pt 13 (resolutions and meetings).

Quorum   Where a charity's governing document stipulates a quorum, the **22.052** trustees must ensure that their number does not fall below it or, if it does, that it does not stay below that number. If there are no such requirements in the governing document, the number of trustees needs to be kept at an effective working strength. This number will depend on the charity's administrative requirements and the rule (if the governing document does not specify otherwise) that no decision can be taken except by the agreement of all or a majority of the trustees. While trustees may invite other persons to attend their meetings, only trustees can vote at them. Trustees cannot delegate their responsibilities in this regard or ask someone else to vote on their behalf.

22.053   *Electronic means*   To constitute a valid meeting, all members of it must be able to see and hear what is going on: *Byng v London Life Association Ltd.*[5] It follows that trustees may conduct meetings by, say, video conferencing or internet video facilities, unless the governing document specifically prohibits it. Where such meetings take place, the Charity Commission recommends that at least one physical meeting of all the charity trustees takes place each year. On the other hand, since telephone conferencing only permits the participants to hear but not see each other, this means cannot be used (save for discussion) unless there is a specific provision in the governing document to this effect.

22.054   *Minutes*   Minutes of trustees' meetings are not open documents and do not have to be made available for public inspection, unless this is required by the governing document. However, the Charity Commission recommends that charities make the minutes of any AGM available to the public on request, charging a reasonable fee should they so wish. The minutes of all meetings, especially trustees' meetings, should be preserved throughout the existence of the charity and, after its dissolution, arrangements should be made for their safekeeping. In the case of charitable companies, records must be kept for at least 10 years: CA 2006 s.248(2).

22.055   *Staff trustees*   In booklet CC3, section F3, the Charity Commission explains that a trustee who becomes an employee of the charity, or an employee of the charity who becomes a trustee, in breach of the general rule, may have to repay to the charity any benefits (s)he has received, such as salary. See further Charity Commission booklet CC11 (*Trustee expenses and payments*).

Board review and renewal

22.056   The board should periodically review its own and the organisation's effectiveness (see para.22.062 below) and take any necessary steps to ensure that both continue to work well. As Charity Commission booklet CC10, section D4, puts it:

> "An effective charity is always seeking to improve its performance and efficiency, and to learn new and better ways of delivering its purposes. A charity's assessment of its performance, and of the impact and outcomes of its work, will inform its planning processes and will influence its future direction."

[5] [1989] 1 All E.R. 560.

Within this broad principle:

Board review and assessment

22.057 The board should regularly review and assess its own performance, that of individual trustees, and of sub-committees, standing groups and other bodies. More particularly, the board should ensure that:

- at least every two years, it sets aside time to reflect on its own perform-ance and functioning as a team;

- the performance of individual trustees is regularly assessed and appraised either by the chair or another trustee, or by using external assistance;

- the performance of the chair is likewise assessed and appraised, either by another trustee, the board as a whole, or using external assistance; and

- the performance of the sub-committees, standing groups and other bodies is similarly appraised and reviewed.

The results of these appraisals should be used to make necessary changes and improvements, to inform the creation of appropriate training programmes and to guide trustee renewal and recruitment.

By virtue of the Charities Act 1993 s.19A, the Charity Commission may direct a charity's trustees to carry out a review of the charity's governance and to keep the Commission informed of the progress being made.

Board renewal

22.058 The board should have a strategy, the implementation of which may be del-egated to a sub-committee or panel, for its own renewal. Recruitment of new trustees should be open and focused on creating a diverse and effective board. Particular attention should be given to succession planning for replacement of the chair and other honorary officers and trustees must be recruited and appointed in accordance with the organisation's governing document, and relevant legislation.

The board should consider setting maximum terms of office to ensure a steady renewal of trustees: these may be set out in standing orders or in the organisation's governing document. Before new trustees are appointed, the board should determine the attributes and knowledge that are needed, and write them down in the form of a role description or role profile. It should also ensure that the recruitment process is open to all sections of the community and should consider open advertising and a range of other recruitment methods to attract a wide range of candidates. Where the organisation's governing document permits, candidates should be interviewed formally and appointed on merit. In the case of organisations where the trustees are nominated by an external body or elected by a wider membership, the board should work in partnership with the organisations or people concerned to ensure that they are aware of the specific skills and experience required from new trustees. The board should ensure that the procedures for joining and leaving the board are clearly understood by all trustees and others involved. See also para.22.034 above.

Co-option

22.059   Where permitted by the organisation's governing document, co-option should be used where necessary to recruit individuals with particular skills, experience and qualities that are not fully provided by existing trustees.

Strategic reviews

22.060   The board should periodically carry out strategic reviews of all aspects of the organisation's work, governance and procedures and use the results to inform positive change and innovation. In particular, the board should ensure that the needs for which the organisation was set up still exist, and its objects as set out in the governing document remain relevant to those needs, and that the organisation is continuing to meet those needs, remains fit for purpose and the needs are being met in the most effective way: see further para.22.061 below. Where possible the board should be open with stakeholders about the results of such reviews, indicate clearly what steps they intend to take in response, and give explanations concerning actions they have decided not to take. In the words of booklet CC10, section D6, an effective charity is accountable to the public and other stakeholders in a way that is transparent and understandable.

Particular points

22.061   *Amending objects*   In the light of the terms of the charity's governing document, whether or not the Charity Commission is required to authorise an amendment of the charity's objects, trustees intending to make or propose an alteration are strongly advised to seek the Commission's views before taking any action. If the charity's governing document has no amendment provision, or one that does not allow the objects to be amended, trustees should contact the Commission for help.

As to incorporated charities, s.64 of the Charities Act 1993, as amended, requires a charitable company to seek the Commission's prior consent to, inter alia, any regulated alterations which include any amendment of the company's objects. See generally booklet CC3, section F10; see also Charity Commission booklets CC36 (*Changing your Charity's Governing Document*) and, on the Charity Commission's website, Operational Guidance *Alterations to governing documents: charitable companies.*

Whether or not the Commission's prior authorisation was needed, trustees must give the Commission details of any change to the objects of the charity.

Flexibility   Booklet CC10, section B1, says: **22.062**

"Adopting good practice can help charities keep pace with changes and make them more effective where it really counts—in providing the best possible service to the people they were set up to benefit."

Such a flexible approach includes:

- having systems in place to gather and analyse information about emerging trends in the environment in which the charity operates, and their likely impact on the charity and partner organisations;

- investigating and making appropriate use of new technologies to carry out the charity's activities more effectively;

- considering different methods of carrying out its administrative work, e.g. buying-in external services or collaborative working such as sharing staff, office or transport resources: see further Charity Commission booklet CC34 (*Collaborative working and mergers*) and Regulatory Study RS4 (*Collaborative Working and Mergers*), on the Commission's website Operational Guidance *Register of charity mergers* and para.22.079 below.

See also Regulatory Study RS6 (*Milestones: Managing key events in the life of a charity*), particularly the section devoted to the management of change.

Board delegation

The board should set out the functions of sub-committees, officers, the chief   **22.063**
executive, other staff and agents in clear delegated authorities, and should monitor their performance: see also para.22.025 above.

Honorary officers

22.064   The board should define and write down the roles and responsibilities of the chair and other honorary officers such as vice-chair, treasurer and the secretary to the board: see further para.22.068 below. For companies, the role of secretary is partly defined by the relevant legislation. The role of the chair should include, as a minimum, ensuring:

- the efficient conduct of business at the organisation's board and general meetings;

- that the organisation's business is efficiently and accountably conducted between board meetings;

- that the organisation complies generally with the *Good Governance* principles;

- specifically, that the appraisal and remuneration of the organisation's chief executive is duly conducted and fixed (see para.22.050 above);

- that the employment of the chief executive complies with employment legislation and good practice; and

- that the appraisal of board and trustee performance is duly conducted: see para.22.056 above.

Where the board has delegated specific roles to honorary officers or to other trustees, ultimate responsibility rests with the board as a whole. In such situations the trustee(s) concerned should separate the specific roles from their wider trustee role.

Staff, volunteers and agents

22.065   The board should ensure that staff, volunteers and agents have sufficient delegated authority to discharge their duties. All delegated authorities must have clear limits relating to budgetary and other matters. In all but the smallest organisations, the board needs to delegate parts of its work to others in a clear, practical and legal manner. Delegations may be made to individual trustees, sub-committees (see below), the chief executive, other staff, volunteers or agents and consultants. Delegations must comply with the terms of the organisation's governing document and any relevant legislation. Where there is a chief executive, delegations to other staff and volunteers should normally be through that individual. Delegations should always be in writing, and should set clear limits on matters such as expenditure, authority and decisions that can be made. Delegations may be written in board minutes, terms of reference for sub-committees, staff job descriptions, or in a separate list.

Sub-committees

The board should set clear terms of reference for sub-committees, standing groups, advisory panels, etc. Such bodies should have clear written terms of reference in addition to any delegated authority. **22.066**

Monitoring of delegated authorities

All delegated authorities must be subject to regular monitoring by the board. The board must remain in ultimate control of all delegations. Honorary officers and other trustees should report back to the board promptly on any use of delegated authority, the board should receive regular reports and minutes from all sub-committees, etc. and the mechanisms established for internal control and performance reporting should be used to monitor use of delegated authority by the chief executive, or other staff or volunteers: see also para.22.036, above. **22.067**

Particular point

Honorary officers As is explained in booklet CC3, section E9, the treasurer and the chair of the charity will often have responsibilities wider than those of other trustees. For instance, the treasurer may ensure that proper accounts are kept, and help set financial and investment policies. The chair, as well as helping to plan and chair trustee meetings, may also be the link between the trustees and the charity's employees and represent the charity at appropriate events. However, when it comes to making decisions, the trustees must make them together. A number of organisations, including the Institute of Chartered Secretaries and Administrators, provide model job descriptions for honorary officers—chairs, secretaries and treasurers—and, indeed, for charity trustees. **22.068**

Board and trustee integrity

The board and individual trustees should act according to high ethical standards and ensure that conflicts of interest are properly dealt with. **22.069**

Trustee benefits and expenses

22.070   Trustees must not benefit, financially or otherwise, from their position beyond what is allowed by the law and the organisation's governing document and is demonstrably in the interests of the organisation. Where the payment of trustees is permitted, no trustee should be involved in setting their own remuneration: mechanisms for setting the level of payment to trustees should be set up to avoid conflicts of interests, including where appropriate making use of independent advice. For some organisations, full disclosure of any payments made to trustees is required by law in the organisation's annual accounts and report. All organisations should follow this course, even where not required by law. See further para.22.074 below.

   The organisation should have procedures for trustees to claim legitimate travel and other expenses incurred while carrying out the organisation's business: trustees should not be out of pocket for the work they carry out for the organisation.

Conflicts of interest

22.071   Trustees should identify and promptly declare any actual or potential conflicts of interest affecting them. The organisation must have procedures for trustees to declare actual or potential conflicts of interest to the board; such declarations should be made at the earliest opportunity. They should be recorded in board minutes or in a register kept for the purpose. Where a material conflict of interest arises at a board meeting the trustee concerned should not vote on the matter or participate in discussions. (S)he should also offer to withdraw from the meeting, and the other trustees should decide if this is required: see further para.22.073 below. Where a trustee has a major or ongoing conflict of interest, (s)he should offer to resign from the board. Boards should have special procedures or standing orders to deal with conflicts of interest for trustees who are the organisation's service users, beneficiaries or members of staff.

Gifts and hospitality

22.072   There should be clear guidelines for the receipt of gifts or hospitality by trustees. Trustees should declare all personal gifts received and hospitality accepted while on the organisation's business, or from people or organisations connected with the organisation: such declarations should be recorded in board minutes or in a register kept for that purpose. Trustees should not accept gifts with a significant monetary value or lavish hospitality; where this may be a frequent issue, the organisation should set a policy to define what is and is not acceptable. Under no circumstances should trustees accept gifts or hospitality where this could be seen as being likely to influence the decisions of the board.

Particular points

Conflicts of interest   In booklet CC3, section G2, it is said that where   **22.073**
trustees are required to make a decision that affects the personal interests of one of their number, the charity's governing document may require that that person should not be present at any discussion or vote on the matter. It is suggested that, even if the organising document does not require this, trustees should follow this procedure as a matter of good practice: see further, on the Charity Commission's website, *A guide to conflicts of interest for charity trustees* and para 22.013 (arts charities).

Payment of trustees   Further information and guidance may be found   **22.074**
in Charity Commission booklets CC3 and CC11 (*Trustee expenses and payments*) and, on the Commission's website, Operational Guidance—*Payment of Trustees* and *Gifts to retiring charity trustees* See also para.22.079 below.

Board openness

The board should be open, responsive and accountable to its users, ben-   **22.075**
eficiaries, members, partners and others with an interest in its work. More particularly:

Communication with stakeholders

Each organisation should identify its stakeholders, and ensure that there is a   **22.076**
strategy for regular and effective communication with them about the organisation's achievements and work. The board should ensure that the whole organisation, and its stakeholders, have a clear understanding of the board's role and of the organisation's objects and values. There should be regular and appropriate communication and consultation with stakeholders to ensure that:

- their views are taken into account in the organisation's decision-making;

- they are informed and consulted on the organisation's plans and proposed developments which may affect them;

- there is a procedure for dealing with feedback and complaints from stakeholders, staff, volunteers and the public; and

- the organisation's performance, impacts and outcomes are reported to stakeholders.

The board must ensure that the organisation produces an annual report and accounts that comply with relevant legislation: see further para.22.023 above. Communication should be offered in formats accessible to the stakeholder audiences, in other words, in plain language, translated into languages commonly spoken among the communities served, or in Braille, as may be necessary.

Annual general meetings

22.077   The organisation must hold an AGM if required by the governing document or by law and this may be an opportunity to invite stakeholders. Of course, in the case of membership organisations, the governing document may provide that members are entitled to attend and vote at AGMs, but trustees are bound by such a vote only to the extent that the governing document may specify. A charity may exclude from membership persons whose membership could be contrary to its best interests, but it must not do this arbitrarily or in a way which is damaging to its good name: *Royal Society for the Prevention of Cruelty to Animals v Att-Gen.*[6] See also para.22.079 below.

Openness and accountability

22.078   The board should be open and accountable to stakeholders about its own work, and the governance of the organisation. The board should ensure that the organisation upholds a commitment to openness and accountability at all levels. This involves:

- being clear about what information is available, and what must remain confidential to protect personal privacy or commercial confidentiality;

- complying with reasonable outside requests for information about the organisation and its work;

- being open about the organisation's governance work and its strategic reviews;

- ensuring that the stakeholders have the opportunity to hold trustees to account and know how to do it; and

---

[6] [2001] 3 All E.R. 530.

- ensuring that the principles of equality and diversity are applied, and that information and meetings are accessible to all sections of the community as may be appropriate.

The board should encourage and enable the engagement of key stakeholders, such as users and beneficiaries, in the organisation's planning, decision-making and strategic reviews. Trustees must ensure that users, beneficiaries members and other stakeholders are involved in the most appropriate way, and that involvement is open to all sections of the community (see further para.22.036 above).

In organisations where the trustees are elected by a wider membership, the board should ensure that it has clear and declared understanding as to who is, and who is not, eligible for membership of the organisation, including users, beneficiaries and staff; keep the members informed about the organisation's work; and use the membership as a way of involving stakeholders in the organisation's governance. See also para.22.079 below.

Charities Act 2006

The Act was given Royal Assent on November 8, 2006 and it has or will come into force in stages: see the Charities Act 2006 (Commencement No.7, Transitional and Transitory Provisions and Savings) Order 2010 (SI 2010/503), including its note as to earlier commencement orders. See, too, the updated implementation plan (March 2010) issued by the Cabinet Office. The Act's long title states that it will: **22.079**

"Provide for the establishment and functions of the Charity Commission for England and Wales and the Charity Tribunal . . . make other amendments of the law about charities, including provision about charitable incorporated organisations . . . make further provision about public charitable collections and other fund-raising carried on in connection with charities and other institutions . . . make other provision about the funding of such institutions; and for connected purposes."

While the Act does not affect the principles of good governance which trustees should apply as they discharge their responsibilities, it does alter significantly some of their powers and duties and the regime and constraints within which they work. In this context, provisions of particular significance include:

- s.25—power of Charity Commission to determine membership of charity;

- s.31 and Sch.8 paras 96, 151—relaxation of restriction on altering memorandum, etc. of charitable company;

- s.34 and Sch.7—charitable incorporated organisations (see below);

- s.36—remuneration of trustees, etc. providing services to charity;

- s.38—power of Charity Commission to relieve trustees, auditors, etc. from liability from breach of trust or duty;

- ss.40–42—power to transfer all property, replace purposes and modify powers or procedures;

- s.43—power to spend capital;

- s.44—merger of charities.

Charitable incorporated organisations ("CIO")

22.080   The CIO is a new legal form and the first to be created specifically to meet the needs of charities. Its purpose is to avoid the need for charities, wishing to benefit from incorporation, to register as companies, rendering them liable to dual regulation by Companies House as well as the Charity Commission. It is not expected that the CIO will be an available option before the end of 2010.

Chapter 23

The EU

Dr David Doyle[1]

Introduction

This chapter summarises the principal elements of the current governance   **23.001**
("CG") regimes in the European Union. In Pt 1 the background to EU institutional policy development in CG institutions are discussed in detail; in Pt 2
developments since the banking crisis of 2007/2009 are outlined including the
Green paper on Corporate Governance issued by the European Commission
in June 2010.

Part 1: Background and institutions

Corporate governance in the European Union

Introduction

Corporate governance is intimately connected with the financial services   **23.002**
environment in Europe, and has thus been an integral part of the 1999 EU
Financial Services Action Plan ("FSAP"), and various post-FSAP initiatives,

---

[1] Dr David P. Doyle is an EU policy expert specialising in financial services. A former diplomat
based in mainland Europe in both multilateral and bilateral posts, he is a member of the board
of the joint MEP-EU industry body, The Kangaroo Group, and a board member of joint UK
cross-parliamentary/SME-owner body, The Genesis Initiative, focused on SME policy development. Dr Doyle is also actively involved in the Transatlantic Business Dialogue (TABD), the
European Council on Corporate Governance/Conference Board and the joint City of London
Corporation/Paris Europlace Accounting Working Group. His authored works include *Cost
Control—A Strategic Guide* (CIMA/Elsevier: London, 1994 and 2002) which was translated into
16 foreign languages. His alumni include the Dublin Institute of Technology, Trinity College,
University of Dublin, and Kingston University (UK).

launched by the European Commission and aimed at creating a single market for risk capital and all financial markets.

The EU quest to create a common approach to corporate governance has faced many daunting challenges since 1999, not least was the existence of divergent corporate governance systems and practices across the EU. These differences impact significantly in the development of a unified pan-EU strategy and codes of conduct. Cross-national differences stem, for the large part, from the differences inherent in the nature of responsibilities and influence exercised by governments, boards of directors, employees and shareholders in each Member State.

The legal systems across Europe also contributed to the fragmentation of corporate governance practices. Academic studies showed that those countries functioning under the civil law tradition, i.e. France, Germany, Italy, Spain, and the countries of the Scandinavian region, tend to rely for a significant part on debt financing via banks to fund corporate growth. Such civil laws countries have traditionally had small stock markets, with creditors and employees enjoying a key influence on boards, thus more risk-averse. From a corporate governance perspective, these economies have also, until recently, been characterised by insider-controlled companies, company cross-shareholdings with voting stock and ownership structures which allow families to maintain control.

The European Commission's role

23.003   As the sole EU legislator and guardian of the EU Treaties, the European Commission identified the contribution of corporate governance as a means of improving the general conditions for an efficient EU financial market in its Communication of 1999 (*Financial Services: Implementing the framework for financial markets—Action Plan* (COM(1999) 232). The Action Plan announced that a "review of existing national codes of corporate governance" would be launched with a view to "identifying any legal or administrative barriers which could frustrate the development of a single EU financial market".

In September 2001, the European Commission set up a group of high-level company law experts (known as the Winter Group) after the name of the chairman, Jaap Winter, and their report.

The Winter's Group was mandated to:

- develop independent recommendations on how to eliminate obstacles for cross-border mergers and acquisitions, by ensuring a level playing field in Europe, and

- produce a blueprint for modernising corporate law and governance in Europe.

From the beginning, the Group was doubtful on the value of creating a common CG code in Europe because of the divergence of company law systems across the EU. The report stopped short of proposing a harmonised CG code, stating that a growing trend towards convergence of national codes in the EU should be encouraged instead.

The preferred approach was greater co-ordination of practices in the EU with a strong emphasis on improved shareholder democracy. Jaap Winter declared his preference for allowing "best practice" to spread naturally, and incrementally, driven by increased investor pressure from shareholders, who are prepared to pay a premium for shares in companies that are well run. Furthermore, legislation was viewed as being inappropriate in a business environment that was constantly evolving.

A revised regulatory framework for company law in Europe was presented to the Commission in November 2002.[2] The Group focused its recommendations on a number of distinct improvements in reforming the EU CG landscape:

- A more transparent regime of corporate disclosure, especially with regard to pyramid structures used in a number of companies to control large groups via a cascade of often obscure privately and publicly-owned holding companies.

- A clearer regime for shareholders to enable them to exercise their voting rights across borders, especially in the case of non-resident shareholders, and establishing the right to proxy votes.

- A clearer statement by large institutional, pension fund investors as to how they use their voting rights.

- The need to instil more professionalism and transparency in board governance structures.

The two key recommendations to arise from the Winter Report were thus:

- All EU-listed companies should include a "coherent and descriptive" statement of their corporate governance practice in their annual report and accounts as well on their websites.

- All EU-listed companies:

  "be required to ensure that the nomination and remuneration of directors and the audit of the accounting for the company's performance within the Board are decided upon by exclusively non-executive or supervisory directors who are in the majority independent."

---

[2] *http://ec.europa.eu/internal_market/company/modern/index_en.htm#background.*

On May 21, 2003, the European Commission published two Communications to the Council of Europe and the European Parliament which reflected in large measure the conclusions of the Winter Report, setting out the Commission's Action Plan for modernising company law and enhancing corporate governance[3]; and for reinforcing the statutory audit in the European Union.[4] Commission recommendations on directors' remuneration[5] and independent directors[6] followed in 2004 along with revised amendments to the Fourth and Seventh Council Directives (the Accounting directives)[7] and the Eighth Council Directive (the Statutory Audit Directive)[8] in 2005/2006.

Enhancing corporate governance within the EU

23.004   The Commission's "Action Plan" for enhancing corporate governance—Modernising Company Law and Enhancing Corporate Governance in the European Union—A Plan to Move Forward (COM(2003) 0284)—has as its main objectives to:

   (a)   strengthen shareholders' rights and protection for employees, creditors and other parties with which companies deal, while adapting company law and corporate governance rules appropriately for different categories of company; and

   (b)   foster the efficiency and competitiveness of business, with special attention to some specific cross border issues.

Whilst concluding that the EU should not devote time and effort to the development of a single European CG code, the Action Plan does outline a common governance framework to be implemented through a mixture of legislative and non-legislative proposals—each prioritised over the short-term

[3] Communication from the Commission to the Council and the European Parliament—Modernising Company Law and Enhancing Corporate Governance in the European Union—A Plan to Move Forward (COM(2003) 0284) *http://ec.europa.eu/internal_market/company/modern/index_en.htm#background.*
[4] Communication from the Commission to the Council and the European Parliament—Reinforcing the statutory audit in the EU (COM(2003) 0286) *http://ec.europa.eu/internal_market/auditing/communications/index_en.htm.*
[5] Commission Recommendation of 14 December 2004 fostering an appropriate regime for the remuneration of directors of listed companies (2004/913/EC)—*http://ec.europa.eu/internal_market/company/directors-remun/index_en.htm.*
[6] Commission Recommendation of 15 February 2005 on the role of non-executive or supervisory directors of listed companies and on the committees of the (supervisory) board (2005/162/EC) *http://ec.europa.eu/internal_market/company/independence/index_en.htm.*
[7] Directive of the European Parliament and of the Council amending Council Directives 78/660/EEC and 83/349/EEC concerning the annual accounts of certain types of companies and consolidated accounts.
[8] Directive 2006/43/EC of the European Parliament and of the Council of 17 May 2006 on statutory audits of annual accounts and consolidated accounts, amending Council Directives 78/660/EEC and 83/349/EEC and repealing Council Directive 84/253/EEC.

(2003/2005), medium-term (2006/2008) and long-term (2009 onwards). The initiatives categorised as the most important and urgent were:

(a) *an annual corporate governance statement* whereby listed companies would be required to include in their annual accounts and reports a coherent and descriptive statement covering the key elements of their corporate governance structures and practices;

(b) *strengthening shareholders' rights* by enhanced access to information prior to general meetings and the exercise of such rights in relation to the asking of questions, the tabling of resolutions, voting by proxy, participating in general meetings via electronic means;

(c) *modernising the board of directors.* The role of independent non-executive directors would be promoted and they would comprise the remuneration and audit committees although executive directors remain best placed to comprise the nominations committee supported by non-executive directors to prevent conflicts of interest. These requirements would be defined at EU level in a Regulation and enforced by Member States at least on a "comply or explain" basis, with further study on the concept of one tier and two tier boards in the medium term;

(d) *directors' remuneration* to be better disclosed by disclosure of remuneration policy in the annual statements, disclosure of individual remuneration, prior approval by shareholders of directors' share option schemes and proper recognition in the accounts of the cost of such schemes;

(e) *encouraging the co-ordination and convergence* of national corporate governance codes and of the way they are enforced and monitored, by the creation of a European CG forum made up of representatives from Member States, regulators, issuers and investors and others, the forum to be chaired by the Commission.

Other corporate governance initiatives proposed in the Action Plan covered: achieving better information on the role played by institutional investors in CG; giving further effect to the principle of proportionality between capital and control; offering to listed companies the choice between the one-tier and two-tier board structures; and enhancing directors' responsibilities for financial and key non-financial statements. The Action Plan further proposed that there is a strong medium to long-term case for aiming to establish a real shareholder democracy and that the Commission intends to undertake a study on the consequences of such an approach.

In October 2004, the European Commission adopted its first two key CG Recommendations, dealing with two specific aspects raised in its Action Plan of 2003, namely,

- ensuring greater transparency of directors' remuneration; and
- building a stronger role for independent non-executive board members of listed companies in Europe.

Directors' remuneration

23.005   The main thrust of the Commission's Recommendation on directors' remuneration—Fostering an Appropriate Regime for the Remuneration of Directors of Listed companies (2004/913/EC)—was that listed companies disclose their policy on directors' remuneration and tell shareholders how much individual directors are earning and in what form, and ensure shareholders are given adequate control over these matters and over share-based remuneration schemes. The Recommendation is non-binding in nature and has had little impact in the UK as most of the recommendations are matched, or surpassed, by the UK Corporate Governance Code, and the Directors' Remuneration Report Regulations 2002 (SI 2002/1986) which are now incorporated in CA 2006 Ch.6.

The key recommendations are:

(a)   *Remuneration policy.* All listed companies should release a statement of their policy on directors' remuneration for the following year which should include information on the breakdown of fixed and variable remuneration, on performance criteria and on the parameters for annual bonus schemes and non-cash benefits.

(b)   *Shareholders' meeting.* To increase accountability, the remuneration policy for directors should be submitted to a vote (either binding or advisory) at the annual general meeting ("AGM"). An advisory vote would require neither directors' contractual entitlement nor remuneration policy to be amended.

(c)   *Disclosure of directors' remuneration* should include detailed information about: the remuneration of individual directors; the shares or rights to share options granted to them; pension entitlements; and any loans, advances or guarantees to each director.

(d)   *Approval of share and share option schemes.* Variable remuneration schemes under which directors are paid in shares, share options or any other right to acquire shares should be subject to prior approval of the AGM of shareholders.

Independent directors

23.006   The Commission's recommendation on independent directors—The Role of Non-executive or Supervisory Directors of Listed Companies and on the

Committees of the (Supervisory) Board (2005/162/EC)—reinforced the presence and role of independent non-executive directors on listed companies' boards. Again, the non-binding Recommendation has had little impact in the UK as most of the recommendations are matched, or surpassed, by the recommendations within the UK Corporate Governance Code.[9] The main principles in the Recommendation are:

(a) boards should include an appropriate balance of executive and non-executive/supervisory directors so that no individual or small group can dominate decision-making;

(b) nomination, remuneration and audit committees should be established. The Recommendation defines minimum standards for the creation, composition and role of such committees;

(c) directors are considered independent if they are free from any business, family or other relationship—with the company, its controlling shareholder or the management—which might jeopardise their judgment;

(d) the (supervisory) board should be composed of members who, taken together, have the diversity of knowledge, judgment and experience to complete their tasks properly;

(e) all directors should devote the necessary time and attention to their duties.

Fourth and Seventh Council Directives

To enhance confidence in the financial statements and annual reports published by European companies, the Fourth and Seventh Directives have been amended to require companies whose securities are traded on a regulated market to include a new corporate governance statement in their annual reports. This statement will have to refer to the CG code applied by the company and explain whether and to what extent the company complies with that code. Also, it will have to include a description of the company's internal control and risk management system and information on the composition and operation of the board and its committees.[10]   **23.007**

In its June 2006 Statement on Risk Management and Internal Control,[11] the European Corporate Governance Forum (see below), the Forum confirmed

---

[9] The UK Corporate Governance Code *http://www.frc.org.uk*.
[10] All the measures in the Directive amending the 4th and 7th Directives are incorporated into UK law under the CA 2006 and relevant accounting standards.
[11] Statement of the European Corporate Governance Forum on Risk Management and Internal Control *http://ec.europa.eu/internal_market/company/ecgforum/index_en.htm*.

that companies' boards are responsible for monitoring the effectiveness of internal control systems. However, the Forum considered that there is no need to impose an EU obligation on boards to certify the effectiveness of internal control as required in the US by the Sarbanes-Oxley Act 2002. Rather, the Forum recognised that the general purpose of risk management and internal control is to manage the risks associated with the successful conduct of business, not to eliminate them and, more specifically, to enhance the quality of financial reporting. It considered that measures to further these aims, whether in law, regulation or corporate governance codes, should be proportionate and an adequate balance should be struck between the benefits of any additional requirements and the costs and other burdens for companies.

Other issues addressed by the amendments to the Fourth and Seventh Directives (all of which are already part of UK law or Generally Accepted Accounting Principles ("GAAP") in the UK) include:

(a) *Responsibility of board members.* Confirmation that board members are collectively responsible to the company for the financial and other key information that they publish and that Member States must have appropriate sanctions and liability rules where board members do not comply with accounting rules.

(b) *The related party disclosures* contained in International Accounting Standard 24 (IAS 24) are extended to unlisted companies. The disclosures, however, apply only to significant transactions with related parties not carried out under normal commercial conditions.

(c) *Disclosure of off-balance sheet arrangements*, including their financial impact, in the notes to the annual and consolidated accounts of both listed and unlisted companies.

Statutory audit

23.008   The EC also turned its attention to ensuring that investors and other interested parties can rely fully on the accuracy of audited accounts and to enhancing the EU's protection against the type of scandals that occurred at the beginning of the millennium. A revised Statutory Audit Directive, which was required to be implemented in the UK by 2008, imposes rigorous audit process for company accounts across the European Union, was issued. It set out to clarify the duties of statutory auditors and certain ethical principles to ensure their objectivity and independence, for example where audit firms are also providing their clients with other services The Directive introduces a requirement for external quality assurance as well as seeking to ensure robust public oversight over the audit profession and improve co-operation between regulatory authorities in the EU. Importantly, the Directive also requires the use of international standards on auditing for all statutory audits conducted in the EU and provides a basis for balanced and effective international regulatory co-operation with third country regulators such as the US Public Company Accounting Oversight Board ("PCAOB").

Some of the provisions in the Directive are intended to help auditors to resist inappropriate pressure from managers of the company they are auditing—in particular—public-interest entities are required to have an audit committee composed of non-executive directors or supervisory directors and/or members appointed by the shareholders in general meeting. At least one member of the audit committee must be independent and have competence in accounting and/or auditing. The role of the audit committee, as set out in the Directive, is to:

(a) monitor the financial reporting process;

(b) monitor the effectiveness of the company's internal control, internal audit where applicable, and risk management systems;

(c) monitor the statutory audit of the annual and consolidated accounts;

(d) review and monitor the independence of the statutory auditor or audit firm, and in particular the provision of additional services to the audited entity.

Furthermore, the board's proposal for the appointment of the statutory auditor must be based on a recommendation made by the audit committee.

Member States may permit the functions assigned to the audit committee to be performed by the board or, where appropriate, the supervisory board as a whole, provided that when the chairman of such a body is an executive member, he or she is not the chairman of the audit committee.

Public-interest entities are essentially entities whose transferable securities are admitted to trading on a regulated market of any Member State. However, Member States may also designate other entities as public interest entities, for instance entities that are of significant public relevance because of the nature of their business, their size or the number of their employees.

European Corporate Governance Forum and Advisory Group

In October 2004, the Commission set up the European Corporate Governance Forum[12] to examine best practices in Member States with a view to enhancing the convergence of national corporate governance codes and providing advice to the Commission. The Forum comprises 15 senior experts (two of whom are currently from the UK) from various professional backgrounds (issuers, investors, academics, regulators, auditors, etc.) whose experience and knowledge of corporate governance are widely recognised at European level.

23.009

---

[12] *http://ec.europa.eu/internal_market/company/advisory/index_en.htm.*

The Commission has also set up an expert Advisory Group[13] (again, two of whom are from the UK) to provide detailed technical advice on preparing corporate governance and company law measures. The group comprises 20 non-governmental experts from various professional backgrounds including issuers, investors, employees' representatives, academics and regulated professions with particular experience and knowledge of the subject.

It is intended that the technical work carried out by the Advisory Group be complementary to the more strategic role in the convergence of corporate governance in Europe undertaken by the European Corporate Governance Forum.

In 2005, the EU Commission launched a public consultation into shareholders rights across the EU. Improvements in such rights was one of the key priorities to emerge from the EC's Action Plan issued in 2003 on modernising company law and enhancing corporate governance in the European Union. Issues to be covered embraced the right to ask questions, the right to table resolutions, the right to vote in absentia and the right to participate in general meetings via electronic means. These facilities were seen as being a fundamental right that should be offered to shareholders in listed companies across the EU. Specific problems relating to cross-border voting was one particular challenge to be addressed in this exercise.

The EU Commission believed that the necessary framework should be developed in a proposed Directive, requiring a statutory instrument to ensure that these rights were backed by cross-Community law applicable in each Member State.

The main issues on which the Commission sought a response were:

- the transparency of stock-lending agreements and the status of depositary receipt holders;

- the dissemination of relevant information before general meetings, notably to ensure that all shareholders, irrespective of their residence, obtain information in time and are able to cast an informed vote;

- the removal of share blocking as a prerequisite to vote and its replacement by a record date;

- the rights to ask questions and table resolutions, taking into account the fact that many shareholders are non-residents;

- various methods of voting at a distance (by post, electronically, or by proxy);

- the availability to all shareholders of voting results following general meetings.

---

[13] *http://ec.europa.eu/internal_market/company/advisory/index_en.htm.*

In January 2005, shortly after his nomination, EU Internal Market Commissioner, Charlie McCreevy, underlined the fundamental importance of sound corporate governance for the European Union, as an element in boosting market confidence, encouraging investment and therefore in contributing to the EU goal enshrined in the Lisbon Strategy of enhanced competitiveness. More significantly, he dismissed the notion of a pan-EU code of CG, on the basis that it would end up being a less than productive political compromise. In his public statement, Commissioner McCreevy stated:

> "That role is to co-ordinate where possible Member States' efforts to improve corporate governance practices, through changes in their national company law, securities law or in corporate governance codes. There are different traditions in different Member States and those should be respected, but we must avoid unnecessary divergences which distort the single market and make life difficult for investors. Member States want and need to learn from each other's experience."

It was envisaged that this process would be facilitated by the newly-created European Corporate Governance Forum, comprising high-level experts from across the EU.

In 2005 the EC issued a Green Paper on Financial Services Policy 2005–2010—text with EEA-relevance Ref: SEC(2005) 1574, in which Commissioner McCreevy appeared to be determined to slow down the pace of legislative initiatives and conduct "economic impact analysis" of existing rules, i.e. are they working? Does the quality of the legislation need further refining? All new draft legislation would also be subject to the same discipline. The short-term needs would be driven by the quest to complete the FSAP programme and finalise legislation under negotiation in the EP and Council. Existing legislation would be judged on the basis of:

- effective transposition of EU rules into national law;
- more rigorous enforcement by supervisory authorities;
- continuous ex-post evaluation.

The Green Paper, subsequently integrated in the White Paper on Financial Services Policy 2005/2010, refers to the Commission's future work on horizontal and complementary policy areas (corporate governance, company law reform, accounting, statutory auditing), which were considered to be of "immense importance in building confidence and transparency in European financial markets". Although outside the scope of the Green Paper, work in these areas would focus on companies, accountants, auditors and other market participants being empowered to "apply the highest ethical standards in their work . . . national supervisors must ensure they are effectively applied".

The future

Policy[14]

23.010   *Possible and probable legislation*   Internal Market Minister at the European Commission, Charlie McGreevy, on November 21, 2006, gave a speech on company law and corporate governance to a European Parliament Committee on Legal Affairs. His comments included the following:

"I am determined to give European firms a flexible regulatory framework that serves their needs, rather than imposing unnecessary regulatory burdens on them. And I am committed to making company law a test case of how we apply Better Regulation principles. All initiatives on company law and corporate governance will build on public consultations and be subject to in-depth regulatory impact assessments. Firstly, we need to make sure that companies can fully reap the benefits of the Internal Market. Companies should enjoy full mobility within the EU—which is not the case today. For that reason, I have asked my services to start assessing the impact of a Directive enabling companies to move their registered office from one Member State to another. On that basis, I envisage submitting a proposal for a 14th Company Law Directive next spring. Secondly, many stakeholders expressed strong support for a Statute for the European Private Company. Your Committee has just voted on a report which also supports this idea. I have asked my services to start work on a study of the feasibility of a European Private Company Statute. We will examine all options for a simple, user-friendly statute which will also meet the needs of small firms. However, I am very cautious about introducing a multiplicity of European corporate forms. And I am not yet convinced about the ability of a European Foundation Statute to respond to the specific needs of foundations. Nonetheless, we will pursue our reflection.

Beyond these individual initiatives, we will launch a simplification scheme to make life easier for companies. We need to simplify the environment in which they operate. We know there still exist unnecessary administrative burdens. We will measure the costs imposed by such burdens and then make proposals on how to remove them. I intend to present a communication on this crucial issue before next summer. As you are already aware, I also intend to continue to provoke a lively debate on the issue of proportionality between capital and control of companies.

Last but not least, there is the separate but linked question of auditor liability. This subject came up last year when we agreed a new 8th Company Law Directive, thanks in large part to the excellent work of Bert

---

[14] Reference is recommended to the website dealing with a wide number of issues in relation to corporate governance in the EU on the Sheffield University website: *http://papers.ssrn.com/sol3/cf_dev/AbsByAuth.cfm?per_id=29035.*

Doorn. The Commission agreed to analyse insurability of audit firms and the risk of losing one of the so-called Big Four audit firms. I hope I can rely on your support in work on this issue."

Shareholder rights   The Companies (Shareholders' Rights) Regulations **23.011** 2009 (SI 2009/1632) ("2009 Regulations") came into effect on August 3, 2009 and implemented the Shareholder Rights Directive (2007/36/EC) ("the Directive") in the UK.

The Directive's aim was to improve shareholder information and participation rights in company meetings, and the 2009 Regulations amended the provisions on company meetings in the CA 2006 accordingly.[15]

Current European corporate governance codes[16]

There are currently in existence a number of pan-European codes, principles **23.012** and guidelines and a number of national codes, principles and guidelines in relation to corporate governance. The principal ones are set out below.

By way of introductory observation, however, it should be remembered that whilst several continental European countries adopt the "unitary" board model (i.e. single board of directors, as in the UK) several adopt a "two-tier" system of a supervisory board and a management board. The supervisory board, as the title suggests, supervises and monitors the management board. It characteristically comprises solely non-executive directors whose explicit role is to represent the stakeholding interests of banks, institutional shareholders and employees. In a two-tier board, principal responsibility for governance rests with the supervisory board. In the unitary system it has been an interesting feature over the past 10 years to see the mechanics being put in place to establish a supervisory function within the board.

It is also a common characteristic of continental European companies to find corporate control vested in a relatively small number of shareholders, often with quite complex interlocking cross-shareholdings. This contrasts with Anglo-American model of large numbers of diverse shareholdings with no common links. One consequence of this is the relative difficulty as compared with Anglo-American companies of launching successful "hostile" takeover bids.

Those countries with mandatory two-tier systems include Austria, Germany and the Netherlands. Those countries where unitary and two-tier boards co-exist but where the unitary board is generally preferred include Belgium, Luxembourg, France, Finland, Greece, Sweden and Denmark. Those countries where the unitary board is mandatory include the United Kingdom, Ireland, Spain, Italy and Portugal.

---

[15] The effect of these Regulations on the AGM is summarised in Ch.17 of this book.
[16] For a full list of European corporate governance codes and their texts see *www.ecgi.org* >codes and principles.

Part 2: Corporate governance developments after the banking crisis 2007/2009

23.013   The financial crisis of 2008/2009 galvanised the European Commission to lay out its views on an EU-wide reform agenda on corporate governance, with particular reference to financial institutions. The result was an EC Communication "Driving European Recovery" issued on March 4, 2010, setting out a commitment to produce a report on corporate governance practices in financial institutions.

The Commission signalled that it would propose measures encompassing:

- directors' remuneration packages;
- director qualifications/competence;
- composition of the board;
- director's liability/responsibilities;
- performance evaluation—link to remuneration;
- independence of internal control/risk management;
- reporting lines to the board—the role of non-executive directors;
- investor responsibilities—including the future of comply or explain as a principle for corporate governance;
- investors' relations with company boards—including disclosure to investors;
- relationship between supervisors and boards—including possible reporting by non-execs to supervisors;
- role of external audit in vetting and supporting corporate governance.

In the banking sector per se, the Committee of European Banking Supervisors ("CEBS"), who give advice to the European Commission on policy and regulatory issues related to banking supervision) published its own risk management guidelines on February 16, 2010. This followed a request by the EU's Economic and Financial Committee ("EFC"), who prepare the work for, and provide policy expertise, to the Council) for CEBS to develop enhanced guidance to strengthen banks' risk management practices. In its analysis of existing risk management guidelines, the body concluded that, in general, the EU and international supervisory bodies had developed a comprehensive set of guidelines for the sector. CEBS also revealed, however, a number of areas where the coverage of risk management practises remained fragmented:

- governance and risk culture;
- risk appetite and risk tolerance;

- the role of the chief risk officer and risk management functions;

- risk models and integration of risk management areas;

- new product approval policy and process.

In a statement to the European Parliament's Legal Affairs Committee on March 22, 2010, newly appointed European Internal Market Commissioner, Michel Barmier, reinforced this notion by stating that:

"we have to incite or even oblige banks and insurance companies and other people in the financial sector to act more responsibly. This responsibility falls on the directors of these companies and their shareholders, who are the first line of defence."

EC corporate governance study

The EC's analytical study into corporate governance practices before and after the financial crisis drew the following key conclusions: **23.014**

- Boards often lacked independent judgment, did not have sufficient involvement in risk management and lacked accountability and oversight of the complexity of the bank's operation and liabilities.

- Shareholders were often passive, holding diversified portfolios and therefore lacking sufficient interest and/or oversight over the businesses in which they held shares. Short-term orientation was endemic and there was less monitoring and challenging of company strategy than required.

- Supervisory authorities are thought to have engaged in a "race to the bottom" and lagged behind the industry curve in terms of developments in business and liabilities.

- External auditors did not raise the alert regarding banks' excessive risk.

BIS Basel Committee on Banking Supervision consultation

On March 16, 2010, the Basel Committee on Banking Supervision issued a consultation paper in which it set out proposed principles for enhancing sound corporate governance practices at banking organisations. Drawn from experiences arising during the financial crisis, the Basel Committee's document, *Principles for enhancing corporate governance*, proposed a series of "best practices for banking organisations". The principles covered the following: **23.015**

- the role of the board, which includes approving and overseeing the implementation of the bank's risk strategy taking account of the bank's long-term financial interests and safety;

- the board's qualifications, for example, the board should have adequate knowledge and experience relevant to each of the material financial activities the bank intends to pursue to enable effective governance and oversight of the bank;

- the importance of an independent risk management function, including a chief risk officer or equivalent with sufficient authority, stature, independence, resources and access to the board; the need to identify, monitor and manage risks on an ongoing firm-wide and individual entity basis. This should be based on risk management systems and internal control infrastructures that are appropriate for the external risk landscape and the bank's risk profile;

- the board's active oversight of the compensation system's design and operation, including careful alignment of employee compensation with prudent risk-taking, consistent with the Financial Stability Board's principles.

The principles also underlined other factors in contributing to robust corporate governance in banks:

- the critical importance of board and senior management having a "clear knowledge and understanding of the bank's operational structure and risks". This should include risks arising from special purpose entities or related structures;

- the role of financial supervisors in ensuring that banks practice good corporate governance. In conformity with the Basel Committee on Banking Supervision's principles, supervisors should establish "guidance or rules requiring banks to have robust corporate governance strategies, policies and procedures". Financial supervisors are recommended to regularly evaluate the bank's corporate governance policies and practices as well as its implementation of the Committee's principles. Such evaluations should, however, be commensurate with a bank's size, complexity, structure and risk profile.

Responsibilities of the board feature highly in the Basel Committee on Banking Supervision's principles. The Committee, for instance, recommends that the board has ultimate responsibility for the bank's business, risk strategy and financial soundness, as well as for how the bank organises and governs itself. Thus the board should:

- approve the overall business strategy of the bank, taking into account the bank's long-term financial interests and safety; and

- approve and oversee the implementation of the bank's:
    - overall risk strategy, including its risk tolerance/appetite;
    - risk policy, risk management and internal control systems, including compliance policy; and
    - corporate governance principles and corporate values, including a code of conduct or comparable document.

- in discharging these responsibilities, the board should take into account the legitimate interests of shareholders, depositors and other relevant stakeholders. It should also ensure that the bank maintains an effective relationship with its supervisors;

- the members of the board should exercise their "duty of care" and "duty of loyalty" to the bank under applicable national laws and supervisory standards. This includes engaging actively in the major matters of the bank and keeping up with material changes in the bank's business and the external environment, as well as acting to protect the interests of the bank;

- the board should give particular attention to ensuring that transactions with related parties are reviewed to assess risk and are subject to appropriate restrictions (e.g. by requiring that such transactions be conducted at arm's-length terms) and that corporate or business resources of the bank are not misappropriated.

The Commission Green Paper on Corporate Governance

On June 3, 2010, the European Commission issued its Green Paper on **23.016** *Corporate governance in financial institutions and remuneration policies.*

The paper sets out to a programme for examining corporate governance rules and practices within financial institutions and where appropriate, makes recommendations discusses options, including possible regulatory measures.

At the time of writing (June 2010), the Commission has launched a public consultation on the basis of the Green Paper until September 1, 2010, focused on possible ways forward to deal with the following issues:

- improving the role, duties, functioning and composition of boards of financial institutions in order to enhance their supervision of senior management decisions;

- cultivating a risk assessment mechanism at senior level within financial institutions in order to ensure that long-term interests of the entity are taken into account;

- enhancing the involvement of shareholders, financial supervisors and external auditors in corporate governance matters;

- reforming remuneration policies in companies to discourage excessive risk taking.

General context[17]

23.017   The EC asserts that improved corporate governance in the financial services sector merited particular attention because of the need to protect the wider stakeholder constituency involved. Corporate governance should thus be broad and robust enough to take account of the interests of financial services creditors (i.e. depositors, savers, life insurance policy-holders, or beneficiaries of pension schemes and, to a certain extent, employees), who may be "potentially at odds with those of their shareholders". Policy measures should go beyond the traditional definition of corporate governance, typically referring to relations between a company's senior management, its board of directors, its shareholders and other stakeholders, such as employees and their representatives.

The Green Paper focuses on this limited definition of corporate governance and, at its own admission, does not deal with some other important aspects, such as separation of functions within a financial institution, internal controls and accounting independence. The EC intends to launch a broader review (scheduled between late 2010 and early 2011) on corporate governance within listed companies in general and, in particular, on the place and role of shareholders, the distribution of duties between shareholders and boards of directors with regard to supervising senior management teams, the composition of boards of directors, and corporate social responsibility.

Identification of current weaknesses and deficiencies in corporate governance in financial institutions

Conflicts of interest

23.018   Potential conflicts of interest can arise due to incompatible roles or activities, i.e. providing advice on investments while managing an investment fund or managing for one's own account, incompatibility of mandates held on behalf of different clients/financial institutions. This problem can also arise because of cross-shareholdings between a financial institution and its shareholders/ investors, in situations where there is a business link between an institutional investor via a parent company structure.

---

[17] Adapted from the European Commission Green Paper entitled "Corporate governance in financial institutions and remuneration policies" COM(2010) 284/3.

The problem of effective implementation by financial institutions of corporate governance principles

In spite of the existence of principles of CG, such as the OECD principles, the **23.019** recommendations of the Basel Committee and other inter-community rules, the financial crisis underlined the lack of effectiveness of existing measures, both at national and pan-EU level. Contributing factors cited in the Green Paper included:

- existing principles are too broad in scope and are not sufficiently precise, resulting in too much scope for interpretation by financial institutions;
- lack of a clear allocation of roles and responsibilities with regard to implementing the principles, both within the financial institution and the supervisory authority;
- the non-legally binding nature of corporate governance principles.

Boards of directors

As principal decision-making body, boards did not exercise effective control **23.020** over senior management and to challenge the measures and strategic guidelines that were submitted to them for approval. Several reasons or factors contributed to this failure on the part of boards and non-executive directors:

- insufficient resources and time in the exercise of their duties;
- lack of diversity of expertise and balance in terms of gender, social, cultural and educational background;
- absence of serious performance appraisal systems for individual members or of the board of directors as a whole;
- unable or unwilling to ensure that an appropriate risk management framework was in place;
- failure to recognise the systemic nature of certain risks and thus to provide sufficient information upstream to their supervisory authorities.

Risk management

Rules on risk management and control failed to be adhered to, because of a **23.021** lack of:

- understanding of the risks on the part of those involved in the risk management chain and insufficient training for those employees responsible for distributing risk products;

- authority on the part of the risk management function to be able to curb the activities of risk-takers and traders;

- expertise or insufficiently wide-ranging experience in risk management and did not cover the entire range of risks to be monitored;

- real-time information on risks.

The role of shareholders

23.022 The growth in new categories of shareholders, some who show little interest in the long-term governance objectives of the businesses/financial institution in which they invest and may have contributed to encouraging excessive risk-taking with relatively short investment horizons.

Several factors can help to explain the uninterest or passivity of shareholders with regard to their financial institutions:

- the costs for institutional investors to engage actively in governance of the financial institution;

- conflicts of interest;

- absence of effective rights allowing shareholders to exercise control, i.e. voting rights on director remuneration in certain jurisdictions, obstacles to the exercise of cross-border voting rights;

- complicated and unreadable information disclosed to shareholders.

The role of supervisory authorities

23.023 Some national and pan-EU level regulators were unable to carry out effective supervision in the face of rapid financial innovation and change in the business models pursued by financial institutions, and ensure that financial institutions' risk management systems and internal organisation were adapted to these developments.

Strict territorial and substantive competencies of supervisory authorities no longer matched the geographical and sectoral spread of financial institutions' activities.

Key options ahead

Key options arising from the Green Paper, summarised below, will be the object of further discussion and review between the European Commission and industry[18] over 2010 and beyond.

23.024

Supervisory authorities

- Establishing a statutory duty for supervisory authorities to check the correct functioning and effectiveness of the board of directors, and to regularly inspect the risk management function to ensure its effectiveness.

  23.025

- Strengthened co-operation between supervisory authorities on CG of cross-border financial institutions, particularly within colleges of supervisors but also in the context of future European supervisory authorities.

- Powers extended to check that the eligibility criteria ("fit and proper test") of prospective directors cover the technical and professional skills, as well as the individual qualities.

Boards

- Introducing the requirement that recruitment policies specify the duties and profile of directors, including the chairman, that directors must possess adequate skills, and that the composition of the board of directors is suitably diverse.

  23.026

- Setting a maximum of boards that directors can sit on, i.e. no more than three at any one time.

- Imposing restrictions on stock options or golden parachutes to board members to prevent them focusing on short-term gain at the expense of the company's future.

- Separating the posts of chairman and CEO to prevent them from being held by the same person.

- Introducing compulsory evaluation of the functioning of the board of directors, conducted by an external evaluator, and the results of this evaluation be made available to supervisory authorities and shareholders.

---

[18] Points adapted from the European Commission Green Paper entitled "Corporate governance in financial institutions and remuneration policies" COM(2010) 284/3.

- Establish a review procedure for the board of directors to approve new financial products.

- Make it an obligation that the board of directors inform the supervisory authorities of any material risks they are aware of.

- Establish a specific duty for the board of directors to take into account the interests of depositors and other stakeholders during the decision-making procedure ("duty of care").

Risk-related functions

23.027
- Creating a risk committee within the board of directors and establish rules regarding the composition and functioning of this committee.

- Appointing one or more members of the audit committee to be part of the risk committee and vice versa.

- Creating the role of chief risk officer:
  - (i)   with equal status to chief financial officer;
  - (ii) directly reporting any risk-related problem to the board of directors including the risk committee; and
  - (iii) backed by a resolution procedure for referring conflicts/problems to the hierarchy.

- Requiring executives to approve a report on the adequacy of internal control systems.

The role of external auditor

23.028
- The desirability of strengthening cooperation between external auditors and the supervisory authorities, whilst taking into account constraints relating to professional secrecy.

- Increase the auditors duty of information towards the board of directors and/or supervisory authorities on possible serious matters discovered in the performance of their duties.

- Extend the auditors control to risk-related financial information of relevance to shareholders.

Shareholder engagement

23.029 As regards shareholder engagement, a range of incentives could be envisaged by financial institutions:

- disclosure by institutional investors of their voting practices at share-holders' meetings;

- the use of discussion platforms to strengthen shareholder co-operation;

- adherence to stewardship codes of best practice by institutional investors;

- potential conflicts of interest identified and disclosed by institutional investors;

- disclosure by institutional investors of the remuneration policy for intermediaries, particularly the managers of asset management companies;

- providing shareholders with better information on risk;

- requiring institutional investors to adhere to a code of best practice (national or international), i.e. the code of the ICGN;

- facilitate the identification of shareholders in order to encourage dialogue between companies and their shareholders and reduce the risk of abuse connected to "empty voting", i.e. a voting shareholder with no corresponding financial interest in the company.

The EC suggest that the other measures that could encourage shareholders to engage in financial institutions' CG might include a more effective and efficient sanctions regime against senior management for failure to assume legal accountability for the correct implementation of these principles (bearing in mind that the rules governing criminal proceedings are not harmonised at European level).

Remuneration

Notwithstanding EU legislative proposals for credit institutions and **23.030** investment firms in the context of the modification of the revised Capital Requirements Directive ("CRD"), specific EC recommendations on remuneration for financial services and the Alternative Investment Fund Managers Directive, the Commission considers in the Green Paper possible additional measures at EU level on remuneration for directors of listed companies in terms of content and form, and whether it should be binding or non-binding:

- Should directors' stock options be regulated at Community level, or even prohibited the granting of stock options?

- Does the favourable tax treatment of stock options and other similar remuneration existing in certain Member States contribute to encourage excessive risk-taking and if so, does it merit discussion at EU level?

- Should the role of shareholders, and also that of employees and their representatives, be strengthened in establishing remuneration policy?

- Are severance packages, i.e. "golden parachutes" to be regulated at Community level, or even prohibit the granting of such packages?

- Should they be awarded only to remunerate effective performance of directors?

European Union Member States—principal codes, guidelines and principles[19]

Austria

23.031 Austrian Code of Corporate Governance, Austrian Working Group for Corporate Governance.

Belgium

23.032 The Belgium Code on Corporate Governance (Lippens' Code), Corporate Governance Committee.

Corporate Governance Recommendations for non-listed Enterprise (Buysse Code), Commission Corporate Governance pour entreprises non cotées.

Cyprus

23.033 Cyprus Corporate Governance Code, Cyprus Stock Exchange.

Czech Republic

23.034 Corporate Governance Code based on the OECD Principles, Czech Securities Commission.

---

[19] See fn 4.

Denmark

Revised Recommendations for Corporate Governance in Denmark, **23.035**
Copenhagen Stock Exchange Committee on Corporate Governance.

Estonia

Corporate Governance Recommendations, Tallinn Stock Exchange. **23.036**

Finland

Corporate Governance Recommendations for listed Companies, The Central **23.037**
Chamber of Commerce of Finland.

France

The Corporate Governance of Listed Corporations, Mouvement des **23.038**
Entreprises de France (MEDEF) and the Association Française des
Entreprises Privées (AFEP).

Germany

German Corporate Governance Code (Cromme Code) as amended, **23.039**
Government Commission German Corporate Governance Code.

Greece

Principles of Corporate Governance, Federation of Greek Industries. **23.040**

Hungary

Corporate Governance Recommendations, Budapest Stock Exchange. **23.041**

Ireland

Listing Rules make reference to the UK's Combined Code on Corporate **23.042**
Governance.

Italy

23.043   Corporate Governance Code (Codice di Autodisciplina), Comitato per la Corporate Governance, Borsa Italiana SpA.

Latvia

23.044   Principles of Corporate Governance and Recommendations on their Implementation, Riga Stock Exchange.

Lithuania

23.045   Corporate Governance Code for the Companies Listed on the National Stock Exchange of Lithuania, National Stock Exchange of Lithuania.

Luxembourg

23.046   The Luxembourg Code of Corporate Governance.

Malta

23.047   Principles of Good Corporate Governance: Revised Code for Issuers of Listed Securities, Malta Financial Services Authority.

Poland

23.048   Best Practices in Public Companies 2005, Best Practices Committee of the Warsaw Stock Exchange in association with the Corporate Governance Forum.

Portugal

23.049   Recommendations on Corporate Governance, Comissão do Mercado de Valores Mobiliários.

White Book on Corporate Governance in Portugal, Instituto Português de Corporate Governance.

Slovakia

Corporate Governance Code, Bratislava Stock Exchange. **23.050**

Slovenia

Corporate Governance Code, Ljubljana Stock Exchange, the Association of **23.051** Supervisory Board Members of Slovenia, and the Managers' Association of Slovenia.

Spain

IC-A Principles of Good Corporate Governance, Instituto de Consejeros- **23.052** Administradores.

Unified Code of Recommendations for Good Governance (Draft), Comision Nacional del Mercado de Valores.

Sweden

Swedish Code of Corporate Governance, Report of the Code Group. **23.053**

The Netherlands

Dutch Corporate Governance Code (Tabaksblat Code), Corporate **23.054** Governance Committee.

United Kingdom

The UK Corporate Governance Code, Financial Reporting Council. **23.055**

Pan-European and other codes[20]

    (a)   Organisation for Economic Cooperation and Development **23.056** ("OECD") Principles of Corporate Governance;

---

[20] See fn 3.

(b)   International Corporate Governance Network ("ICGN"), Statement on Global Corporate Governance Principles;

(c)   The European Association of Securities Dealers ("EASD"), Corporate Governance: Principles and Recommendations.

Chapter 24

US Corporate Governance: An Overview of Key Requirements for Public Companies

Alexander F Cohen, Latham & Watkins LLP[1]

Introduction

This chapter summarises key corporate governance requirements under US law that apply to "foreign private issuers" (a term that covers most non-US issuers, other than foreign governments) that offer securities for sale to the public in the United States or list their securities for trading or quotation on the US stock markets.[2]   **24.001**

Corporate governance in the United States is in a period of significant change. In July 2010, the Dodd-Frank Wall Street Reform and Consumer Protection Act was signed into law. The Act changes corporate governance for US public companies in several key areas. It appears that most of the Act's provisions do not apply to foreign private issuers that are public in the United States, since they modify portions of the securities laws from which foreign private issuers have traditionally been exempted. (One exception to this is the Act's requirements for "clawback" policies to allow companies to recover certain executive compensation in the case of financial restatements.)

[1] Alexander F Cohen is a partner in the Washington, DC office of Latham & Watkins LLP, and is co-Chair of the firm's Capital Markets practice group. He is a former senior official of the US Securities and Exchange Commission.
[2] We do not discuss the Multijurisdictional Disclosure System applicable to Canadian foreign private issuers in this chapter, or the special requirements applicable to registered "investment companies."

Key statutes and concepts

US Securities Act of 1933; US Securities Exchange Act of 1934

24.002　As far as most foreign private issuers are concerned, the two principal federal securities statutes in the United States are the US Securities Act of 1933 (the "Securities Act" or "1933 Act") and the US Securities Exchange Act of 1934 (the "Exchange Act" or "1934 Act"). To simplify considerably, the Securities Act governs the offer and sale of securities in the United States, while the Exchange Act regulates the trading of securities on a US national securities exchange such as the New York Stock Exchange (the "NYSE") or the Nasdaq Stock Market ("Nasdaq"), on-going periodic and annual reporting, and tender and exchange offers.

The US Securities and Exchange Commission (the "SEC") has issued a comprehensive body of rules and regulations under the Securities Act and the Exchange Act. These rules have the force of law. The SEC and its staff have also provided interpretive guidance on a wide range of questions under the securities laws.

Registration under the Securities Act and the Exchange Act

24.003　Registration is a core concept in the US federal securities laws. The Securities Act requires issuers to register transactions. By contrast, the Exchange Act requires issuers to register classes of securities.

Securities Act registration

24.004　The Securities Act requires registration with the SEC of any transaction involving the offer or sale of a security, unless the security is of a type that is exempt from registration or the transaction is structured to take advantage of an available exemption from registration. The terms "offer and sale" and "security" are very broadly defined.

Registered transactions involve filing a registration statement with the SEC and meeting detailed and specific disclosure and financial statement requirements. In addition, registered transactions trigger the wide-ranging provisions of the US Sarbanes-Oxley Act of 2002 (the "Sarbanes-Oxley Act" or "Sarbanes-Oxley") and a comprehensive liability scheme.

By contrast, the requirements of unregistered transactions are generally—but not invariably—less demanding. A foreign private issuer will not typically become subject to Sarbanes-Oxley merely by issuing securities in an unregistered transaction, and the liability regime governing unregistered transactions is more circumscribed. Foreign private issuers contemplating an unregistered transaction typically look to exemptions such as:

- *Offshore transactions*: offers and sales made outside of the United States pursuant to Regulation S under the Securities Act;

- *Private placements*: offers and sales not involving a public offering pursuant to s.4(2) of the Securities Act or Regulation D under the Securities Act; and

- *Rule 144A transactions*: private placements involving resales to "qualified institutional buyers" pursuant to Securities Act r.144A.

Exchange Act registration; rule 12g3-2(b) exemption

A foreign private issuer must register a class of securities under the Exchange **24.005** Act if that class will be listed on a US national securities exchange (such as the NYSE or Nasdaq).[3] In addition, if a foreign private issuer has assets in excess of $10 million and a class of equity securities held by at least 500 shareholders (of whom at least 300 are residents in the United States) it must also register those securities under the Exchange Act,[4] unless it can claim the exemption from registration provided by Exchange Act r.12g3-2(b).

Under the amendments to r.12g3-2(b) that took effect on October 10, 2008,[5] foreign private issuers are no longer required to submit initial written applications or submit their material "non-US disclosure documents"[6] to the SEC in order to qualify for the r.12g3-2(b) exemption. Foreign private issuers are now automatically eligible to claim the exemption if they satisfy the following conditions:

- *Electronic publication of non-US disclosure documents.*[7] The foreign private issuer must publish in English, either via its website or through

---

[3] Exchange Act s.12(a) prohibits transactions on US national securities exchanges with respect to unregistered securities, while s.12(b) sets out the requirement for that registration.

[4] Exchange Act s.12(g)(1); Exchange Act rr.12g-1, 12g3-2(a).

[5] *Final Rule: Exemption from Registration Under Section 12(g) of the Securities Exchange Act of 1934 for Foreign Private Issuers*, Release 34-58465 (September 5, 2008), [*Rule 12g3-2(b) Amendments Adopting Release*].

[6] See Exchange Act r.12g3-2(b)(1)(iii)(A)–(C). Non-US disclosure documents include information that a foreign private issuer: (1) has made public or is required to make public pursuant to the laws of the country of its incorporation, organisation or domicile; (2) has filed or been required to file with the principal stock exchange in its primary trading market on which its securities are traded and which has been made public by that exchange; and (3) has distributed or been required to distribute to its security holders.

[7] In conjunction with the amendments to Exchange Act r.12g3-2(b), the SEC adopted conforming amendments to the Exchange Act r.15c2-11. These amendments enable broker-dealers to satisfy their obligation to make reasonably available upon request information that a foreign private issuer has published pursuant to Exchange Act r.12g3-2(b) by providing instructions on how to obtain this information electronically.

an electronic information delivery system,[8] all material non-US disclosure documents that it has released since the first day of its most recently completed fiscal year.[9] Non-US disclosure documents only need to be published in English if they are material to an investment decision in the issuer's securities. The rule includes a non-exhaustive list of disclosures that can be considered material for these purposes[10] and, at a minimum, English translations of the following documents must be published electronically:

- the foreign private issuer's annual report and annual financial statements;
- its interim reports that include financial statements;
- press releases; and
- all other communications and documents distributed directly to holders of the subject class of securities to which the exemption relates.[11]

- *Foreign listing.* The foreign private issuer must maintain a listing on one or more markets constituting the primary trading market outside of the United States of the subject class of securities. For these purposes, *primary trading market* means:

  - a foreign market that, either alone or together with another foreign market, accounted for at least 55 per cent of the trading in the relevant securities on a worldwide basis in the foreign private issuer's last fiscal year; and
  - if trading in the relevant securities in two foreign markets is combined to meet the 55 per cent threshold, the trading on at least one of them was greater than the trading in the United States.[12]

- *No existing SEC reporting.* The foreign private issuer must not be required to file or furnish reports under ss.13(a) or 15(d) of the Exchange Act (this generally means that the foreign private issuer does not have securities publicly offered or listed in the United States

---

[8] Exchange Act r.12g3-2(b)(1)(iii).

[9] See Exchange Act r.12g3-2(b)(1), Note 2 to para.(b)(1). This provision does not apply to issuers who are claiming the exception based on their termination of registration or report obligations for a class of securities under ss.12(g) or 15(d) of the Exchange Act.

[10] Exchange Act r.12g3-2(b)(3)(i). The issuer is only required to disclose such information to the extent that it is material to an investment decision regarding the subject securities, such as (1) results of operations or financial condition; (2) changes in business; (3) acquisitions or dispositions of assets; (4) the issuance, redemption or acquisition of securities; (5) changes in management or control; (6) the granting of options or the payment of other remuneration to director or officers; and (7) transactions with directors, officers or principal security holders.

[11] See *Rule 12g3-2(b) Amendments Adopting Release*, ¶ 88,268, at 87,107. The SEC specifically declined to permit "English versions" or summaries. However, an issuer may submit English summaries of documents if they would be permitted to do so under Form 6-K or Exchange Act r.12b-12(d)(3).

[12] Exchange Act r.12g3-2(b)(1), Note 1 to para.(b)(1).

and it has not otherwise voluntarily registered its securities under the Exchange Act).

Once established, a foreign private issuer can maintain the r.12g3-2(b) exemption by continuing to publish electronically its disclosure documents in English promptly after the information has been made public in the foreign private issuer's primary trading market.[13] Whether disclosure has been made "promptly" depends on the type of document and the amount of time required to prepare the English translation. Material press releases generally should be published electronically in English on or around the same business day as their original publication.[14]

If a foreign private issuer no longer complies with the provisions of r.12g3-2(b), the foreign private issuer will have to either register the subject class of securities under the Exchange Act within 120 days after the foreign private issuer's fiscal year end, qualify for the exemption under r.12g3-2(a) by concluding that it has fewer than 300 shareholders resident in the United States or, if possible, re-establish compliance with the rule's conditions within a "reasonably prompt manner".[15]

The SEC established a three-year transitional period to provide foreign private issuers who were exempt under r.12g3-2(b) as in effect prior to October 10, 2008, but who do not satisfy the requirements of the amended rule, an opportunity to either register under the Exchange Act or establish compliance with amended r.12g3-2(b). The SEC ceased accepting and processing paper submissions for r.12g3-2(b) ongoing compliance at the end of a three-month transitional period that expired on January 10, 2009.

Exchange Act reporting

Once a foreign private issuer has registered a transaction with the SEC under the Securities Act or a class of securities under the Exchange Act (a "reporting foreign private issuer"), it must make certain filings with the SEC under the Exchange Act.[16] Reporting foreign private issuers also become subject to various other provisions of the US federal securities laws. **24.006**

Annual report on Form 20-F

A reporting foreign private issuer must file an annual report on Form 20-F with the SEC. For fiscal years ending before December 15, 2011, a reporting **24.007**

---

[13] *Rule 12g3-2(b) Amendments Adopting Release,* ¶ 88,268, at 87,113–14.
[14] *Rule 12g3-2(b) Amendments Adopting Release,* ¶ 88,268, at 87,114.
[15] *Rule 12g3-2(b) Amendments Adopting Release,* ¶ 88,268, at 87,115.
[16] 1934 Act ss.13(a), 15(d).

foreign private issuer must file its annual report on Form 20-F within six months after its fiscal year-end. Beginning with fiscal years ending on or after December 15, 2011, the due date for filing annual reports on Form 20-F will be four months after the foreign private issuer's fiscal year-end.[17] While the new accelerated filing due date may approximate the annual report filing due date required by the home securities regulators of foreign private issuers in many jurisdictions,[18] the revised deadline will still provide a substantial accommodation to foreign private issuers as compared to domestic US issuers.[19] Form 20-F contains detailed financial and non-financial disclosure requirements.

Current reports on Form 6-K

24.008   A reporting foreign private issuer must submit current reports to the SEC on Form 6-K.[20] Form 6-K reports must contain all material information that the issuer[21]:

- makes or is required to make public pursuant to the laws of its country of incorporation or organisation;

- files or is required to file with a stock exchange on which its securities are traded and which was made public by that exchange; or

- distributes or is required to distribute to its security holders.

Note that Form 6-K submissions do not need to be certified by an issuer's CEO and CFO under ss.302 and 906 of Sarbanes-Oxley.[22]

---

[17] Form 20-F, General Instructions A(b). See also Exchange Act r.13a-1 (each issuer with s.12 registered securities must file an annual report within the time period specified in the relevant form). The acceleration of the filing due date for annual reports on Form 20-F from six months to four months after the foreign private issuer's fiscal year-end was part of the amendments to reporting requirements applicable to foreign reporting issuers adopted pursuant to recent SEC amendments. The adopting release noted that the SEC staff will consider what accommodations with regards to Industry Guide 3, which relate to bank holding companies, would be appropriate in light of the potential burdens placed on foreign private issuers that provide disclosures under Industry Guide 3. *See Foreign Issuer Reporting Enhancements*, Securities Act Release 8959, Exchange Act Release 58620, International Series Release 1310, [2008 Transfer Binder] Fed. Sec. L. Rep. (CCH) ¶ 88,287 (September 23, 2008) [*Foreign Issuer Reporting Enhancements Release*].

[18] See Directive 2004/109/EC of the European Parliament and of the Council (December 15, 2004). For example, companies listed on a market that is subject to the European Union's Transparency Directive are required to file their annual financial reports within four months of their fiscal year-end.

[19] Large accelerated and accelerated domestic US issuers are required to file their annual reports on Form 10-K within 60 days and 75 days, respectively, of their fiscal year-ends. All other domestic US issuers are required to file their annual reports on Form 10-K within 90 days after their fiscal year-end.

[20] 1934 Act r.13a-16(a); Form 6-K, General Instruction A.

[21] Form 6-K, General Instruction B.

[22] *Certification of Disclosure in Companies' Quarterly and Annual Reports*, Securities Act Release

Other consequences of Exchange Act reporting

A reporting foreign private issuer becomes subject to a variety of other provi- **24.009**
sions under the US federal securities laws including:

- *Books and records; internal accounting controls.*[23] A reporting issuer
  must maintain and keep books, records and accounts that "accurately and fairly reflect" the transactions and dispositions of assets
  of the issuer, and design and maintain a system of adequate "internal
  accounting controls".

- *Limitations on payments to foreign officials.*[24] A reporting issuer may
  not make corrupt payments to foreign officials, foreign political parties
  or their intermediaries.

- *Audit requirements.*[25] A reporting issuer's audit must include procedures
  for the detection of illegal acts, and the issuer's auditors are required to
  take certain steps if illegal acts are found. Those steps include informing
  the issuer's management and audit committee, and potentially include
  a requirement to resign from the engagement or notify the SEC (if the
  issuer's board fails to take appropriate remedial action).

- *Sarbanes-Oxley.*[26] A reporting issuer is subject to the provisions of the
  Sarbanes-Oxley Act.

Other relevant statutes

In addition to the Securities Act and the Exchange Act, a foreign private **24.010**
issuer may trigger a number of other statutes when it issues securities in the
United States, including:

8124, Exchange Act Release 46427, Investment Company Act Release 25722, [2002 Transfer
Binder] Fed. Sec. L. Rep. (CCH) ¶ 86,720 at 86,125, 86,130 (August 28, 2002) [hereinafter
Certification Adopting Release] (s.302 certification not required for Form 6-K submissions);
Securities Act Release 8400, Exchange Act Release 49424, [2003–2004 Transfer Binder] Fed. Sec.
L. Rep. (CCH) ¶ 87,158, at 89,493 n.146 (March 16, 2004) (s.906 certification not required for
form 6-K submissions) [hereinafter *Additional Form 8-K Disclosure Adopting Release*].
[23] 1934 Act s.13(b)(2)-(7); 1934 Act reg.13B-2. See also 1934 Act rr.13a-15(a) and 15d-15(a)
(reporting issuer must maintain "internal control over financial reporting").
[24] 1934 Act s.30A. In addition, any "domestic concern"—whether or not registered with the
SEC—is subject to substantially identical anti-bribery provisions. 15 U.S.C. § 78dd-2(a). A
"domestic concern" for these purposes means any US citizen, national or resident, or any entity
(such as a corporation or a partnership) that has its principal place of business in the United
States or which is organized under the laws of a US State or territory. 15 U.S.C. § 78dd-2(h)(1).
[25] 1934 Act s.10A.
[26] Sarbanes-Oxley Act s.2(a)(7) (definition of "issuer" subject to Sarbanes-Oxley).

- The Sarbanes-Oxley Act, wide-ranging in scope, the Sarbanes-Oxley Act is intended to provide a permanent framework that improves the quality of financial reporting, independent audits and accounting services, strengthens the independence of accounting firms and increases the responsibility of management for corporate disclosures and financial statements.

- The US Investment Company Act of 1940, which regulates offers and sales of securities by investment companies. Some foreign private issuers may be "investment companies" within the meaning of the 1940 Act even though their primary activities are not investment related.

- The US federal tax laws, which impose particular tax treatment on securities of "passive foreign investment companies" ("PFICs") within the meaning of the US Internal Revenue Code (the "Code"). Certain foreign private issuers may be PFICs despite their operational activities.

- The US Trust Indenture Act of 1939, which requires that indentures used for public offerings of debt securities in the United States meet various substantive and procedural requirements.

What is a "foreign private issuer?"

Definition

24.011 A "foreign private issuer" means any issuer (other than a foreign government) incorporated or organised under the laws of a jurisdiction outside of the United States unless[27]:

- more than 50 per cent of its outstanding voting securities are directly or indirectly owned of record by US residents; and

- any of the following applies:
  - the majority of its executive officers or directors are US citizens or residents;
  - more than 50 per cent of its assets are located in the United States; *or*
  - its business is administered principally in the United States.

How is ownership determined?

24.012 In order to determine the percentage of outstanding voting securities held "of record" by US residents, an issuer should start with a review of the addresses

---

[27] 1933 Act r.405; 1934 Act r.3b-4.

of its security holders in its records.[28] But the inquiry does not end there. Instead, an issuer must perform a "look-through" analysis in respect of securities held of record by a broker, dealer, bank or other nominee located in[29]:

- the United States;

- the issuer's jurisdiction of incorporation; and

- the jurisdiction that is the issuer's primary trading market for its voting securities (if different than the jurisdiction of incorporation).

In the case of these securities, the number of separate accounts for which the securities are held should be counted.[30] The issuer may rely in good faith on information as to the number of these separate accounts supplied by the broker, dealer, bank or nominee.[31] If, after reasonable inquiry, the issuer is unable to obtain information about the amount of securities represented by accounts of customers resident in the United States, it may assume that these customers are residents of the jurisdiction in which the nominee has its principal place of business.[32]

When is foreign private issuer status determined?

For new registrants, the determination of whether an issuer qualifies as a foreign private issuer is made as of a date within 30 days prior to the filing of the initial registration statement.[33]   **24.013**

Once an issuer qualifies as a foreign private issuer, it is immediately able to use the forms and rules designated for foreign private issuers.[34] Thereafter, it must test its status annually, at the end of its most recently completed second fiscal quarter.[35]

For example, an issuer that reports as a domestic US issuer but subsequently determines that it qualifies as a foreign private issuer as of the end of

---

[28] Instruction to para.(c)(1) of Exchange Act r.3b-4; Instructions to para.(1) of the definition of "foreign private issuer" in Securities Act r.405. Note that these instructions send the reader to Exchange Act r.12g3-2(a), which in turn refers to Exchange Act r.12g5-1.

[29] Instruction to para.(c)(1) of Exchange Act r.3b-4; Instructions to para.(1) of the definition of "foreign private issuer" in Securities Act r.405.

[30] Exchange Act r.12g3-2(a)(1).

[31] Exchange Act r.12g3-2(a)(1).

[32] Instruction B to para.(c)(1) of Exchange Act r.3b-4; Instruction B to para.(1) of the definition of "foreign private issuer" in Securities Act r.405. The SEC has acknowledged that the information may not be available, if, for example, the nominee is not able to provide the information, refuses to do so, or imposes an unreasonable charge for providing the information.

[33] Exchange Act r.3b-4(d).

[34] Exchange Act r.3b-4(d).

[35] Exchange Act r.3b-4(e). This is the same date used to determine accelerated filer status under Exchange Act 12b-2 and smaller reporting company status in Item 10(f)(2)(i) of Regulation S-K under the Securities Act.

its second fiscal quarter would no longer need to continue reporting on Form 8-K and Form 10-Q for the remainder of that fiscal year. Instead, it could immediately begin furnishing reports on Form 6-K and would file an annual report on Form 20-F (rather than Form 10-K).

Losing foreign private issuer status

24.014   If an issuer does not qualify as a foreign private issuer at the end of its second fiscal quarter, it nonetheless remains eligible to use the forms and rules for foreign private issuers until the end of that fiscal year (in other words, it does not lose its status as a foreign private issuer until the first day of the next fiscal year).[36] Once an issuer fails to qualify as a foreign private issuer, it will be treated as a domestic US issuer unless and until it requalifies as a foreign private issuer as of the last business day of its second fiscal quarter.[37]

By way of example, a calendar year issuer that does not qualify as a foreign private issuer as of the end of its second fiscal quarter in 2009 would still be able to file an annual report on Form 20-F in 2009 in respect of its 2008 fiscal year. It would also not become subject quarterly reporting on Form 10-Q during 2009. However, it would be required to file its annual report on Form 10-K in 2010 in respect of its 2009 fiscal year on the same timetable as a domestic US issuers. It would also become subject to the proxy rules, reporting of beneficial ownership of securities by the officers, directors and beneficial owners of more than 10 per cent of a class of equity securities of the issuer, and reporting on Form 8-K and Form 10-Q as of the first day of 2010.

There is no requirement for a foreign issuer to notify the market if it has switched its status from domestic US issuer to foreign private issuer, or vice versa. However, such an issuer, by changing its applicable reporting forms, will effectively be providing notice that it has switched status.

Key ways in which foreign private issuers are treated differently than domestic US issuers

24.015   Under the US federal securities laws and the SEC's rules and practice, foreign private issuers are not regulated in precisely the same was as domestic US issuers. In particular, foreign private issuers are allowed a number of key benefits not available to domestic US issuers. These include the following.

24.016   *Quarterly reporting not required*   Unlike domestic US issuers, foreign private issuers are not required to file quarterly reports (including quarterly

---

[36] Exchange Act r.3b-4(e).
[37] Exchange Act r.3b-4(e).

financial information) with the SEC.[38] Some foreign private issuers, however, choose (or are required by contract) to file the same forms with the SEC that domestic US issuers use. In that case, they must report quarterly as if they were a domestic US issuer.[39]

Ability to make confidential submissions of first-time registration state- **24.017**
ments Foreign private issuers that are registering for the first time with the SEC may generally submit registration statements on a confidential basis to the SEC staff. By contrast, domestic US issuers must file their registration statements publicly. Confidential submissions can be a significant advantage because the procedure allows the complicated issues often encountered in an initial SEC review to be resolved behind closed doors. A foreign private issuer will still be required to file its registration statement publicly prior to going on a road show or selling its securities. Absent unusual circumstances, once an issuer becomes a reporting foreign private issuer, the staff will not review its registration statements confidentially and so it will have to file these registration statements publicly.[40]

Ability to use US GAAP, IFRS or local GAAP Domestic US issuers must **24.018**
prepare financial statements in accordance with US Generally Accepted Accounting Principles ("US GAAP"). The financial statements of foreign private issuers, however, may be prepared using US GAAP, International Financial Reporting Standards ("IFRS"), or local home-country GAAP ("local GAAP"). In the case of foreign private issuers that use the English-language version of IFRS as issued by the International Accounting Standards Board ("IASB IFRS"), no reconciliation to US GAAP is needed.[41] By contrast, if local GAAP or non-IASB IFRS is used, the consolidated financial statements (both annual and interim) must include a footnote reconciliation to US GAAP.[42]

Exemption from the proxy rules The US proxy rules—which specify the **24.019**
procedures and required documentation for soliciting shareholder votes—are not applicable to foreign private issuers.[43]

---

[38] 1934 Act r.13a-13(b)(2).
[39] 1934 Act r.13a-16(a)(3).
[40] SEC Division of Corporation Finance, Current Issues and Rulemaking Projects Quarterly Update, March 31, 2001, available at *http://www.sec.gov/divisions/corpfin/cfcrq032001.htm#secv*.
[41] *Acceptance from Foreign Private Issuers of Financial Statements Prepared in Accordance with International Financial Accounting Standards Without Reconciliation to US GAAP*, Securities Act Release 8879, Exchange Act Release 57026, International Series Release 1306, [2007–2008 Transfer Binder] Fed. Sec. L. Rep. (CCH) ¶ 88,032, at 85,756 (December 21, 2007) [*Use of IFRS Without GAAP Reconciliation Release*].
[42] See Form 20-F, Items 17(c), 18.
[43] 1934 Act r.3a12-3(b).

24.020 *Exemption from regulation FD*   Regulation FD requires issuers to make public disclosure of any "material non-public information" that has been selectively disclosed to securities industry professionals (for example, analysts) or shareholders.[44] Foreign private issuers are expressly exempt from Regulation FD.[45] The Regulation provides that when a domestic US issuer, or someone acting on its behalf, discloses material non-public information to certain persons (including analysts, other securities market professionals and holders of the issuer's securities who could reasonably be expected to trade on the basis of the information), it must make simultaneous public disclosure of that information (in the case of intentional disclosure) or prompt public disclosure (in the case of non-intentional disclosure).[46]

24.021 *Exemption from beneficial ownership reporting and short-swing profit recapture rules*   Under s.16(a) of the Exchange Act, anyone who owns more than 10 per cent of any class of equity security registered under the Exchange Act, or who is an officer or director of an issuer of such a security, must file a statement of beneficial ownership with, and report changes in beneficial ownership to, the SEC. Similarly, s.16(b) requires any such shareholder, officer or director to disgorge to the issuer profits realised on purchases and sales within any period of less than six months. Securities of foreign private issuers are exempt from s.16.[47]

24.022 *Not subject to accelerated filing*   Under the accelerated filing rules[48] adopted by the SEC in 2002, seasoned domestic US issuers are required to file annual reports 60 days after the end of their fiscal year.[49] Foreign private issuers are not subject to accelerated filing, and may currently file annual reports within six months after the end of their fiscal year.[50] However, this deadline will shorten to four months after a foreign private issuer's fiscal year end (instead of six months), starting with fiscal years ending on or after

---

[44] Regulation FD r.100.
[45] Regulation FD r.101(b)(ii).
[46] Regulation FD r.101(b)(ii).
[47] Exchange Act r.3a12-3(b). These securities remain subject to the beneficial ownership reporting requirements of ss.13(d) and 13(g).
[48] Under Exchange Act r.3b-2, an accelerated filer is any issuer (including a foreign private issuer) that:

   • has an aggregate market value of voting and non-voting common equity held by its non-affiliates is $75 million or more;
   • has been subject to SEC reporting for at least 12 calendar months;
   • has filed at least one annual report with the SEC; and
   • is not a domestic US small business issuer.

[49] *Acceleration of Periodic Report Filing Dates and Disclosure Concerning Website Access to Reports*, Securities Act Release 8128, Exchange Act Release 46464, Financial Reporting Release 63, [2002 Transfer Binder] Fed. Sec. L. Rep. (CCH) ¶ 86,724, at 86,188 (September 5, 2002) [*Acceleration Release*].
[50] *Acceleration Release*, ¶ 86,724, at 86,199.

December 15, 2011.[51] A foreign private issuer that chooses to file the same forms with the SEC that are required for domestic US issuers will be subject to accelerated filing in the same manner as domestic US issuers.[52]

Sarbanes-Oxley Act exemptions   Although the Sarbanes-Oxley Act generally does not distinguish between domestic US issuers and foreign private issuers, the SEC has adopted a number of significant exemptions for the benefit of foreign private issuers in its rules under the Sarbanes-Oxley Act. These exemptions cover areas such as: **24.023**

- audit committee independence;

- black-out trading restrictions (Regulation BTR); and

- use of non-GAAP financial measures (Regulation G).

In addition, foreign private issuers that become public in the United States for the first time, whether through an IPO, a registered exchange offer or a secondary listing on a US securities exchange, or that are non-accelerated filers are not required to immediately comply with s.404(b) of the Sarbanes-Oxley Act (requiring auditor attestation of management's internal control assessment).[53]

More limited executive compensation disclosure   Foreign private issuers are subject to more limited executive compensation disclosure requirements than domestic US issuers.[54]   **24.024**

ADRs and ADSs

Many foreign private issuers that sell equity securities into the United States do so through the use of ADRs. ADRs are issued by a depositary, usually a large multinational bank, and represent a specified number of the issuer's underlying equity securities held by the depositary or its custodian. Although   **24.025**

---

[51] *Foreign Issuer Reporting Enhancements*, ¶ 88,287, at 87,225.

[52] Exchange Act r.13a-13(b)(2).

[53] Newly registered foreign private issuers would be able to take advantage of a transition period and would only have to file the s.404 management assessments of internal controls and the auditor attestation to such internal controls as part of the second 20-F that such foreign private issuer would file with the SEC after becoming a registrant. *See Internal Control Over Financial Reporting in Exchange Act Periodic Reports of Non-Accelerated Filers and Newly Public Companies*, Securities Act Release 8760, Exchange Act Release 54942, [2006–2007 Transfer Binder] Fed. Sec. L. Rep. (CCH) ¶ 87,721, at 83,858 (December 15, 2006) [*2006 Delay Release*]; *Internal Control Over Financial Reporting in Exchange Act Periodic Reports of Non-Accelerated Filers*, Securities Act Release 8934, Exchange Act Release 58028, [2008 Transfer Binder] Fed. Sec. L. Rep. (CCH) ¶ 88,232, at 86,690 (June 26, 2008) [*2008 Delay Release*].

[54] Foreign private issuers provide executive compensation disclosure on an aggregate basis if the information is reported on such a basis in the issuer's home country. See Form 20-F, Item 6B.

ADR holders have essentially the same ultimate rights as holders of the underlying securities and can, with limited exceptions, exchange their ADRs for the underlying securities at any time, ADRs are denominated in US dollars and their terms are negotiated between the issuer and the depositary bank. The depositary typically receives fees for transactions in the underlying shares, such as withdrawals from or deposits into the ADR facility and currency exchanges in connection with the payment of dividends, as well as ongoing annual depositary service fees.

The SEC considers ADRs to be separate securities from the underlying shares they represent. The issuer must register the offering of the underlying shares on the applicable form. Issuances of ADRs in connection with a US public offering by the issuer are known as "Level III ADR programs"; issuances of ADRs in connection with listing or quoting existing shares in the United States are known as "Level II ADR programs"; and issuances of ADRs representing existing shares that are traded only over-the-counter in the United States are known as "Level I ADR programs". ADR depositaries may establish a Level I ADR program to facilitate secondary trading in a foreign private issuer's previously issued shares either with the issuer's participation (a "sponsored program") or without the issuer's participation (an "unsponsored program"). In either case, the issuer must either register the underlying class of shares with the SEC under the Exchange Act or claim the benefit of the r.12g3-2(b) exemption. If, however, the issuer desires to have its ADRs listed on a US national securities exchange (e.g. the NYSE or Nasdaq), r.12g3-2(b) is not available and accordingly the issuer must register the shares under the Exchange Act.

The US Sarbanes-Oxley Act of 2002—overview and key corporate governance topics

Background

Who is subject to Sarbanes-Oxley?

24.026 The Sarbanes-Oxley Act applies to all issuers—including foreign private issuers—that:

- have registered securities under the 1934 Act;
- are required to file reports under s.15(d) of the 1934 Act; or
- have filed a registration statement under the 1933 Act that has not yet become effective.[55]

---

[55] Sarbanes-Oxley Act s.2(a)(7).

This means, for example, that any foreign private issuer that has listed its securities in the United States, or issued securities to the public in the United States whether or not listed (such as in a registered exchange offer for high-yield bonds) is subject to the Sarbanes-Oxley Act. A foreign private issuer that has not sold securities to the public in the United States, or that is exempt from Exchange Act registration by virtue of Exchange Act r.12g3-2(b) is not subject to the requirements of the Sarbanes-Oxley Act. Accordingly, in this section of the Overview when we refer below to "issuers" and "foreign private issuers" we mean those companies that are subject to Sarbanes-Oxley.

Although the Sarbanes-Oxley Act does not generally distinguish between US domestic and foreign private issuers, the SEC has, in its implementing rules, made various exceptions for the benefit of foreign private issuers.

When does Sarbanes-Oxley take effect?

The Sarbanes-Oxley Act's provisions have taken effect at different times, ranging from immediately upon enactment to later dates specified in the Act or on which the required SEC implementing regulations came into force. Currently, all of the Act's provisions have taken effect with the exception, as discussed in detail below, of certain auditor attestation requirements for issuers that qualify as non-accelerated filers (as defined below). **24.027**

Section 404—internal control over financial reporting

Internal control requirements

Section 404 of Sarbanes-Oxley contains two related requirements. First, under s.404(a), the SEC must adopt rules require an issuer's annual report filed with the SEC to contain an internal control report: (1) stating management's responsibility for establishing and maintaining an adequate internal control structure and procedures for financial reporting; and (2) containing an assessment, as of the end of the issuer's most recent fiscal year, of the effectiveness of the issuer's internal control structure and procedures for financial reporting. **24.028**

In addition, s.404(b) requires an issuer's independent auditor to attest to, and report on, management's s.404(a) assessment, in accordance with standards adopted by the US Public Company Accounting Oversight Board (the "PCAOB"). (Section 404(b) provides, however, that the attestation cannot be a separate engagement of the auditor.) The PCAOB has adopted

Auditing Standard No.5 as the current standard for s.404(b) attestation engagements.[56]

24.029   *Section 404(a)—management's assessment*   As required by s.404(a), the SEC has adopted rules under which an issuer must:

- maintain internal control over financial reporting[57];

- evaluate (with the participation of the CEO and CFO) the effectiveness of internal control as of the end of each fiscal year[58]; and

- evaluate (with the participation of the CEO and CFO) any change in its internal control that occurred during the fiscal year that has materially affected, or is reasonably likely to materially affect, the issuer's internal control over financial reporting.[59]

In addition, in its annual report on Form 20-F, the issuer must provide a report on the issuer's internal control over financial reporting that contains, among other things[60]:

- a statement of management's responsibility for establishing and maintaining adequate internal control over financial reporting;

- a statement identifying the framework used by management to evaluate the effectiveness of the issuer's internal control over financial reporting;

- management's assessment of the effectiveness of the issuer's internal control over financial reporting as of the end of the most recent fiscal year, including a statement as to whether or not the issuer's internal control over financial reporting is effective. The statement must also include disclosure of any material weakness in the issuer's internal control over financial reporting identified by management. Management is not permitted to conclude that the issuer's internal control over financial reporting is effective if there are one or more material weaknesses in internal control; and

---

[56] *Public Company Accounting Oversight Board, Auditing Standard No.5—An Audit of Internal Control Over Financial Reporting That Is Integrated with An Audit of Financial Statements*, PCAOB Release 2007-005A, PCAOB Rulemaking Docket Matter 021, (June 12, 2007) at *http://www.pcaobus.org/Rules/Rulemaking/Docket%20021/2007-06-12_Release_No_2007-005A. pdf* [*Auditing Standard No.5 Release*]. (Auditing Standard No.5 is the current standard on attestation engagements referred to in s.404(b), having superseded the prior *Auditing Standard No.2: Public Company Accounting Oversight Board, An Audit of Internal Control Over Financial Reporting Performed in Conjunction with an Audit of Financial Statements*, PCAOB Release 2004-001, PCAOB Rulemaking Docket Matter 008, [2003–2004 Transfer Binder] Fed. Sec. L. Rep. (CCH) ¶ 87,151, at 89,327 (March 9, 2004) [*Auditing Standard No.2 Release*]).
[57] 1934 Act rr.13a-15(a); 15d-15(a).
[58] 1934 Act rr.13a-15(c); 15d-15(c).
[59] 1934 Act rr.13a-15(d); 15d-15(d).
[60] See Form 20-F, Items 15(b) and 15T(b).

- a statement that the independent auditor that audited the financial statements included in the annual report has issued an attestation report on management's assessment of the issuer's internal control over financial reporting (the independent auditor's attestation report must also be provided in the annual report).

Section 404(b)—auditor's attestation   Under the SEC's rules, a foreign **24.030** private issuer's annual report on Form 20-F must include:

- an attestation report of the independent auditor on management's assessment of the issuer's internal control over financial reporting; and

- disclosure of any change in its internal control that occurred during the fiscal year that has materially affected, or is reasonably likely to materially affect, the issuer's internal control over financial reporting.[61]

However, s.989G of the Dodd-Frank Act adds a new s.404(c) to Sarbanes-Oxley, exempting non-accelerated filers from the requirement to provide a s.404(b) auditor's attestation. For these purposes:

- A *large accelerated filer* is an issuer that, as of the end of its fiscal year[62]:
    - has an aggregate worldwide market value of voting and non-voting common equity held by non-affiliates (market capitalisation) of $700 million or more (measured as of the last business day of its most recently completed second fiscal quarter);
    - has been subject to SEC reporting under the 1934 Act for a period of at least 12 calendar months;
    - has filed at least one annual report under the 1934 Act with the SEC; and
    - is not eligible to use the requirements for smaller reporting companies in Regulation S-K.[63]

- An *accelerated filer* is an issuer meeting the same conditions, except that it has a market capitalisation of $75 million or more but less than

---

[61] See Form 20-F, Items 15(c), (d) and Item 15T(d).
[62] See Exchange Act Rule 12b-2.
[63] See Exchange Act r.12b-2. In general, the primary determinant for "smaller reporting company" eligibility is whether the company has less than $75 million in public float or, in the case of issuers with a public float of zero (e.g. companies with no common equity outstanding or no market price for their outstanding common equity), revenue of less than $50 million in the last fiscal year. *Smaller Company Regulatory Relief Release,* Fed. Sec. L. Rep. (CCH) ¶ 88,029, at 85,724. Note that foreign private issuers would never be eligible to file as smaller reporting companies, unless they prepare their financial statements in accordance with US GAAP and file all forms with the SEC using domestic US issuer forms (e.g. Form 10-K, Form 10-Q, Form 8-K, etc.). *Smaller Company Regulatory Relief Release,* Fed. Sec. L. Rep. (CCH) ¶ 88,029, at 85,724, at 85,729-10.

$700 million (measured as of the last business day of its most recently completed second fiscal quarter).[64]

- Although the term *non-accelerated filer* is not defined in the SEC's rules, the SEC uses it to mean an issuer that, as of the end of its fiscal year:

  - has a market capitalisation of under $75 million, or
  - does not otherwise meet the requirements of the accelerated filer or large accelerated filer definitions above.

Transition relief for new reporting companies (such as IPO issuers)

24.031   A foreign private issuer need not comply with s.404(a) or 404(b) requirements until it either: (1) has been required to file an annual report for the prior fiscal year; or (2) has filed an annual report for the prior fiscal year.[65] This means, for example, that IPO issuers do not need to include a s.404(a) management assessment or s.404(b) auditor's attestation in the first Form 20-F they file after their IPO. These issuers are required, however, to include a statement in their first annual report that the annual report does not include either management's assessment on the company's internal control over financial reporting or the auditor's attestation report.[66]

Definition of internal control over financial reporting

24.032   "Internal control over financial reporting" is defined as a process designed by, or under the supervision of, the issuer's CEO and CFO, and effected by the issuer's board of directors, management and other personnel, to provide reasonable assurance regarding the reliability of financial reporting and the preparation of financial statements for external purposes in accordance with generally accepted accounting principles and includes those policies and procedures that:

- pertain to the maintenance of records that in reasonable detail accurately and fairly reflect the transactions and dispositions of the assets of the issuer;

- provide reasonable assurance that transactions are recorded as necessary to permit preparation of financial statements in accordance with generally accepted accounting principles, and that receipts and expenditures of the issuer are being made only in accordance with authorisations of management and directors of the issuer; and

---

[64] See Exchange Act r.12b-2.
[65] See Form 20-F, Instructions to Item 15.
[66] See Form 20-F, Instructions to Item 15.

- provide reasonable assurance regarding prevention or timely detection of unauthorised acquisition, use or disposition of the issuer's assets that could have a material effect on the financial statements.[67]

Evaluation of internal control

Framework for evaluation   The SEC does not require that an issuer use a   **24.033**
particular framework in undertaking an evaluation of internal control over financial reporting. In fact, the SEC has affirmed that the framework for evaluating internal controls over financial reporting will vary from company to company.[68] The SEC has, however, published an interpretative release to provide guidance for management in evaluating and assessing internal controls over financial reporting (the *Interpretive Guidance*).[69] Although not the only permissible framework, the SEC has stated that an evaluation of internal controls over financial reporting that complies with the Interpretive Guidance will satisfy the evaluation requirements of its rules.[70]

Auditor independence[71]   Although management may coordinate its evalu-   **24.034**
ation of internal controls with that of its auditors, it cannot compromise the auditors' independence. Auditors may assist management in documenting internal controls, but management must be actively involved in the documentation process. In addition, management cannot delegate its responsibilities to assess internal control to the auditor.

Material weaknesses   Management may not determine that an issuer's   **24.035**
internal control over financial reporting is effective if it identifies one or more material weaknesses in the issuer's internal control.[72] The term "material weaknesses" for these purposes has the same meaning as under the auditing standards of the PCAOB.[73]

---

[67] 1934 Act rr.13a-15(f); 15d-15(f).
[68] See *Commission Guidance Regarding Management's Report on Internal Control Over Financial Reporting Under Section 13(a) or 15(d) of the Securities Exchange Act of 1934*, Securities Act Release 8810, Exchange Act Release 55929, [2007 Transfer Binder] Fed. Sec. L. Rep. (CCH) ¶ 87,913, at 84,835, 84,838 (June 20, 2007) [*Interpretative Guidance Release*].
[69] See *Interpretative Guidance Release* ¶ 87,913, at 84,835, 84,838.
[70] See *Interpretative Guidance Release* ¶ 87,913, at 84,835, 84,838; see also *Amendments to Rules Regarding Management's Report on Internal Control Over Financial Reporting*, Securities Act Release 8809, Exchange Act Release 55928, [2007 Transfer Binder] Fed. Sec. L. Rep. (CCH) ¶ 87,912, at 84,819 and 84,821-823 (June 20, 2007) [*2007 Amendments to Rules on Management's Report on Internal Control*].
[71] *Management's Reports on Internal Control Adopting Release* ¶ 86,923, at 87,685-87,686.
[72] Form 20-F, Item 15(b)(3).
[73] *Management's Reports on Internal Control Adopting Release,* ¶ 86,923, at 87,686.

24.036 *Method of evaluation*   The SEC has not specified a method or procedures to be followed in the evaluation.[74] An issuer must, however, maintain "evidential matter, including documentation" to provide reasonable support for management's assessment of the issuer's internal control over financial reporting.[75]

The assessment must be based on procedures sufficient both to evaluate design and to test operating effectiveness.[76] Controls that are subject to assessment include[77]:

- controls over initiating, recording, processing and reconciling account balances, classes of transactions and disclosure and related assertions included in the financial statements;

- controls related to the initiation and processing of non-routine and non-systematic transactions;

- controls related to the selection and application of appropriate accounting policies; and

- controls related to the prevention, identification and detection of fraud.

The SEC has cautioned that inquiry alone generally will not provide an adequate basis for management's assessment.[78]

Certain internal control issues

24.037 *September 2007 FAQ*   The SEC has issued and subsequently revised (most recently in September 2007) answers to certain frequently asked questions regarding management's report over internal control (the "September 2007 FAQ").[79] Under the September 2007 FAQ:

- *Equity investees:* an issuer must have controls over the recording of amounts related to its investment that are recorded in its consolidated

[74] *Management's Reports on Internal Control Adopting Release,* ¶ 86,923, at 87,686.
[75] Form 20-F, Instruction 1 to Item 15. The SEC has stated that it believes it is important for the internal control report to be located near the auditor's attestation report, and that it expects issuers will place the report and attestation near MD&A disclosure or immediately preceding the financial statements. *Management's Reports on Internal Control Adopting Release,* ¶ 86,923, at 87,687.
[76] *Management's Reports on Internal Control Adopting Release,* ¶ 86,923, at 87,687.
[77] *Management's Reports on Internal Control Adopting Release,* ¶ 86,923, at 87,687.
[78] *Management's Reports on Internal Control Adopting Release,* ¶ 86,923, at 87,687.
[79] See generally Office of the Chief Accountant, Division of Corporation Finance, *Management's Report on Internal Control Over Financial Reporting and Certification of Disclosure in Exchange Act Periodic Reports: Frequently Asked Questions* (September 24, 2007) available at *http://www.sec.gov/info/accountants/controlfaq.htm* [*September 2007 FAQ*].

financial statements, although it need not evaluate the recording of transactions into the investee's accounts.[80]

- *Material business combinations:* if an issuer consummates a material business combination during a fiscal year and is unable to conduct an assessment of the acquired business's internal control during the period between the consummation date and the date of management's assessment, it may omit an assessment of the acquired business's internal control for not more than one year from the date of acquisition (and must make certain disclosures about the acquired business and the effect of the acquisition on the issuer's internal control).[81]

- *Initial internal control report:* management need not disclose changes or improvements made in preparation for the first internal control report, although the SEC cautioned that if the issuer were to identify a material weakness it should carefully consider whether that fact should be disclosed, as well as any changes made in response to the material weakness.[82]

- *Subsequent internal control reports:* after an issuer's first management report on internal control, it is required to identify and disclose material changes in internal control in its annual report on Form 20-F. This would include discussing a material change (including an improvement) even if that change was not in response to an identified significant deficiency or material weakness.[83]

- *Internal control of supplementary information in financial statements:* management is required to perform and regularly assess adequate internal controls over the preparation of its financial statements, including the supplementary information thereto (e.g. the financial statement schedules required by Regulation S-X as well as any supplementary disclosures required by the relevant accounting standards board). However, the SEC is currently evaluating whether an issuer's internal control over such supplementary information in its financial statement should form part of management's report on their assessment of internal control over financial reporting. Until such time as the SEC has

[80] See Office of the Chief Accountant, Division of Corporation Finance, *Management's Report on Internal Control Over Financial Reporting and Certification of Disclosure in Exchange Act Periodic Reports: Frequently Asked Questions* at Question 2.

[81] See Office of the Chief Accountant, Division of Corporation Finance, *Management's Report on Internal Control Over Financial Reporting and Certification of Disclosure in Exchange Act Periodic Reports: Frequently Asked Questions* at Question 3.

[82] See Office of the Chief Accountant, Division of Corporation Finance, *Management's Report on Internal Control Over Financial Reporting and Certification of Disclosure in Exchange Act Periodic Reports: Frequently Asked Questions* at Question 7.

[83] See Office of the Chief Accountant, Division of Corporation Finance, *Management's Report on Internal Control Over Financial Reporting and Certification of Disclosure in Exchange Act Periodic Reports: Frequently Asked Questions* at Question 7.

completed its evaluation of this area, internal control over the preparation of this supplementary information need not be encompassed in management's assessment of internal control over financial reporting.[84]

- *Reference to "interim financial statements" in definition of "material weakness":* the reference to interim financial statements in the definition of material weakness is not applicable to foreign private issuers because home country requirements regarding the preparation of interim financial information vary significantly and there are no uniform requirements under the Exchange Act. However, foreign private issuers filing on domestic US forms are subject to the same requirements with respect to interim information as domestic US issuers.[85]

- *Consolidated entities on a proportionate basis*: typically, management's report on internal control over financial reporting should include all consolidated entities, even if those entities are consolidated on a proportionate basis. However, there may be circumstances where the issuer does not have the right or authority to evaluate the internal controls of the entity consolidated on a proportionate basis and also lacks the access necessary to make the evaluation. In such cases, management should evaluate its controls over the recording of the amounts related to the proportionately consolidated entity recorded in the consolidated financial statements.[86]

---

[84] See Office of the Chief Accountant, Division of Corporation Finance, *Management's Report on Internal Control Over Financial Reporting and Certification of Disclosure in Exchange Act Periodic Reports: Frequently Asked Questions* at Question 11

[85] See Office of the Chief Accountant, Division of Corporation Finance, *Management's Report on Internal Control Over Financial Reporting and Certification of Disclosure in Exchange Act Periodic Reports: Frequently Asked Questions* at Question 13.

[86] See Office of the Chief Accountant, Division of Corporation Finance, *Management's Report on Internal Control Over Financial Reporting and Certification of Disclosure in Exchange Act Periodic Reports: Frequently Asked Questions* at Question 15. Note that the *September 2007 FAQ* also discuss issues relating to foreign private issuers that file financial statements prepared in accordance with home country generally accepted accounting principles or IFRS, with a reconciliation to US GAAP (see Questions 12 and 14). The SEC notes that foreign private issuers should always plan and conduct their evaluation process based on their primary financial statements and not the US GAAP reconciliation. The issues presented by these questions have, to a certain extent for issuers who prepare their financials under IASB IFRS, been superseded in that the SEC now accepts financial statements from foreign private issuers without reconciliation to US GAAP if prepared under IFRS as issued by IASB. See *Use of IFRS Without GAAP Reconciliation Release*, ¶ 88,032, at 85,756. See also Latham & Watkins Client Alert No.667, *SEC Accepts Financial Statements From Foreign Private Issuers Without Reconciliation to US GAAP If Prepared Under International Financial Reporting Standards* (January 16, 2008), available at *http://www.lw.com/upload/pubContent/_pdf/pub2082_1.pdf*. In addition to permitting foreign private issuers to file financial statements prepared under IASB IFRS, the SEC has also proposed a "Roadmap" that could lead to the mandatory use of IASB IFRS by US issuers beginning in 2014 if the Commission believes it to be in the public interest and consistent with the protection of investors. See Securities and Exchange Commission, Speech by SEC Chairman: Proposing a Roadmap Toward IFRS by Chairman Christopher Cox (August 27, 2008) available at *http://www.sec.gov/news/speech/2008/spch082708cc_ifrs.htm*. See also Securities and Exchange Commission, Speech by SEC Commissioner: Roadmap for the Potential Use of Financial

May 2005 SEC Staff Statement   On May 16, 2005, the SEC issued a "Staff **24.038** Statement on Management's Report on Internal Control Over Financial Reporting" (the "*SEC Staff Statement*").[87] The SEC Staff Statement focuses on management's report on internal control required by s.404.

The SEC Staff Statement (which reflects the views of the staff of the SEC's Division of Corporation Finance) provides that:

- *Overall focus of reporting:* while identifying control deficiencies and significant deficiencies represents an important component of management's internal control assessment, the "overall focus" of internal control reporting should be on those items that could result in material errors in a company's financial statements.

- *Reasonable assurance:* management is required to assess whether internal control is effective to provide "reasonable assurance" about the reliability of financial reporting. This is a high standard, but does not mean absolute assurance. Exchange Act s.13(b)(7) defines reasonable assurance as a level of assurance that "would satisfy prudent officials in the conduct of their own affairs".

- *Preferred approaches:* in place of a "check-the-box" approach, management should focus on controls related to those processes and classes of transactions for financial statement accounts and disclosures that are most likely to have a material impact on an issuer's financial statements. In addition, management should use a top-down, risk-based approach in determining the controls to be tested. The use of a percentage as a minimum threshold can be a reasonable starting place, but management must also exercise judgment (including qualitative factors) to determine if amounts above or below the threshold should be evaluated.

- *Annual and company measures versus interim measures:* companies should generally focus on annual and company measures rather than interim or segment measures. If management identifies a deficiency when it tests a control, however, at that point it must measure the significance of the deficiency by using both quarterly and annual measures and must also consider segment measures where applicable. In addition, although management's assessment is stated as of year end, this does not mean that controls must only be tested during the period leading up to the year-end close. It is instead preferable to test over a longer period of time.

Statements Prepared in Accordance with International Financial Reporting Standards from US Issuers by Commissioner Elisse B Walter (August 27, 2008) available at *http://www.sec.gov/news/speech/2008/spch082708ebw.htm*.
[87] Office of the Chief Accountant, Division of Corporation Finance, *Staff Statement on Management's Report on Internal Control Over Financial Reporting* (May 16, 2005) (*http://www.sec.gov/info/accountants/stafficreporting.htm*).

- *Restatements:* Section 404 does not require that a material weakness must be found in every case of restatement resulting from an error. Instead, management and the auditors should "use their judgment in assessing the reasons why a restatement was necessary and whether the need for restatement resulted from a material weakness in controls".

- *Disclosure:* companies should consider including in material weakness disclosure a discussion of:

  - the nature of the material weakness;
  - its impact on financial reporting and the control environment; and
  - management's current plans, if any, for remediating the weakness.

- *Impact of material weaknesses:* issuers are strongly encouraged to provide disclosure that allows investors to assess the potential impact of each material weakness, and that distinguishes those material weaknesses that have a "pervasive impact" on internal control from those that do not.

- *IT issues:* the SEC staff would not expect testing of general information technology ("IT") controls that do not pertain to financial reporting. New IT systems and upgrades may not be excluded by management from the scope of its assessment of internal control.

- *Auditor independence:* with respect to auditor independence:

  - discussing internal control issues with a company's auditors and exchanging views with them does not compromise auditor independence;
  - so long as management, and not the auditor, makes the final determination as to the accounting used, and the auditor does not design or implement accounting policies, involving auditors in a consideration of the proper application of accounting standards is appropriate and does not indicate an internal control deficiency;
  - management should not be discouraged from providing draft financial statements to auditors, even those that may be incomplete or contain errors. Errors in draft financial statements by themselves should not be the basis for determining that a deficiency in internal control exists.

Internal control audits—Auditing Standard No.5[88]

As part of its enhanced regulation of the accounting profession, the Sarbanes-Oxley Act established the PCAOB (in s.101 of the Act) and charged the PCAOB with, among other things, supervising public accounting firms that prepare the attestation reports issuers must file with their annual reports[89] and establishing the standards governing the preparation of such reports.   **24.039**

Auditing Standard No.5 sets out the PCAOB's rules for internal control audits (the PCAOB chose to refer to an "audit" rather than an "attestation").[90] As an update and replacement of the prior Auditing Standard No.2, Auditing Standard No.5 is effective for audits of fiscal years ending on or after November 15, 2007.[91] The PCAOB stated that Auditing Standard No.5 reflects a refinement of the prior standard, rather than a significant shift in approach.[92] In particular, the main goals of the PCAOB in creating Auditing Standard No.5 were: (1) to align the PCAOB's standard with the SEC's Interpretive Guidance and focus the internal control audit on the most important matters; (2) to scale the 404 audit to account for the particular facts and circumstances of individual companies, particularly smaller companies; (3) to allow auditors to use their professional judgment, particularly with regard to risk assessment; and (4) to follow a principled approach at determining when and to what extent auditors can rely on the work of others.[93] The new standard is meant to eliminate unnecessary procedures and generally simplify the internal control audit process.[94]

The PCAOB stated that the objective of the internal control audit is to enable auditors of an issuer to express an opinion on the effectiveness of the issuer's internal control over financial reporting.[95] In practice, therefore, the auditor must plan and perform the audit to compile competent evidence supporting a reasonable assurance that no material weakness exists.[96] Using the same framework that management uses for its evaluation of internal controls, the auditor must bring to bear technical training, proficiency as an

---

[88] See *Auditing Standard No.5 Release.*
[89] See Form 20-F, Item 15(c).
[90] See *Auditing Standard No.2 Release,* ¶ 87,151, at 89,329. The PCAOB believed that "attestation" was "insufficient to describe the process of assessing management's report on internal controls."
[91] See *Auditing Standard No.5 Release* at 15.
[92] See *Auditing Standard No.5 Release* at 5.
[93] See *Auditing Standard No.5 Release* at 4; *see also* Public Company Accounting Oversight Board, *News Release: Board Approves New Audit Standard For Internal Control Over Financial Reporting and, Separately, Recommendations on Inspection Frequency Rule* (May 24, 2007) available at *http://www.pcaobus.org/News_and_Events/News/2007/05-24.aspx* [*PCAOB News Release*].
[94] See *PCAOB News Release.*
[95] See *Auditing Standard No.5 Release* at A1-4, ¶ 3.
[96] See *Auditing Standard No.5 Release* at A1-4, ¶ 3.

auditor, independence, due professional care and due professional scepticism to the audit of internal controls.[97]

24.040   *Significant deficiencies and material weaknesses*   Auditing Standard No.5 defines the concepts of "deficiency,"[98] "significant deficiency",[99] and, as noted above, "material weakness." Each of these terms describes faults in internal controls of varying levels of severity, with "deficiency" being the least severe and "material weakness" being the most severe: internal controls cannot be considered effective if one or more material weakness exists.[100] Auditors must evaluate the severity of each control deficiency and determine whether such deficiencies, individually or in the aggregate, rise to the level of material weaknesses in an issuer's internal controls.[101] This will depend on whether there is a reasonable possibility that the controls could fail (even if they have not actually failed) to detect or prevent a misstatement or disclosure and the magnitude of such potential failure.[102]

Auditing Standard No.5 requires auditors to communicate in writing to the management and the audit committee all material weaknesses identified during the audit. Further, if the auditor concludes that the audit committee's oversight of the issuer's financial reporting and internal controls is ineffective, the auditor must communicate this conclusion in writing the issuer's board of directors.[103] The auditor must also communicate in writing to the audit committee all significant deficiencies identified during the audit and should communicate in writing to the management (and notify the audit committee when such communication has been made) all deficiencies identified during the audit that have not previously been communicated in writing to management.[104]

---

[97] See *Auditing Standard No.5 Release* at A1-5, ¶¶ 3-4.

[98] See *Auditing Standard No.5 Release* at A1-41, ¶ A2 ("A deficiency in internal control over financial reporting exists when the design or operation of a control does not allow management or employees, in the normal course of performing their assigned functions, to prevent or detect misstatements on a timely basis. A deficiency in design exists when: (1) a control necessary to meet the control objective is missing; or (2) an existing control is not properly designed so that, even if the control operates as designed, the control objective would not be met. A deficiency in operation exists when a properly designed control does not operate as designed, or when the person performing the control does not possess the necessary authority or competence to perform the control effectively.").

[99] See *Auditing Standard No.5 Release* at A1-44, ¶ A11 ("A significant deficiency is a deficiency, or a combination of deficiencies, in internal control over financial reporting that is less severe than a material weakness, yet important enough to merit attention by those responsible for oversight of the company's financial reporting.").

[100] See *Auditing Standard No.5 Release* at A1-44, ¶ 2; *see also Interpretive Guidance Release*, ¶ 87,913, at 84,837, n.11.

[101] See *Auditing Standard No.5 Release* at A1-26, ¶ 62.

[102] See *Auditing Standard No.5 Release* at A1-26, ¶¶ 63-64.

[103] See *Auditing Standard No.5 Release* at A1-31, ¶¶ 78-79.

[104] See *Auditing Standard No.5 Release* at A1-32, ¶¶ 80-81.

Identifying significant deficiencies and material weaknesses   Auditing   **24.041**
Standard No.5 identifies a number of risk factors that "affect whether there
is a reasonable possibility that a deficiency, or a combination of deficiencies,
will result in a misstatement of an account balance or disclosure".[105] These
include:

- the nature of the financial statement accounts, disclosures, and assertions involved;

- the susceptibility of the related asset or liability to loss or fraud;

- the subjectivity, complexity, or extent of judgment required to determine the amount involved;

- the interaction or relationship of the control with other controls,
  including whether they are interdependent or redundant;

- the interaction of the deficiencies; and

- the possible future consequences of the deficiency.

The PCAOB notes that multiple deficiencies affecting the same account
balance or disclosure increase the probability of misstatement and could, in
combination, constitute a material weakness, even though such deficiencies
may be less severe alone.[106]

In addition, Auditing Standard No.5 identifies a number of indicators of
material weaknesses in internal control over financial reporting.[107] These
include:

- identification of fraud, whether or not material, on the part of senior
  management;

- restatement of previously issued financial statements to reflect the cor-
  rection of a material misstatement;

- identification by the auditor of a material misstatement of financial
  statements in the current period in circumstances that indicate that the
  misstatement would not have been detected by the company's internal
  control over financial reporting; and

- ineffective oversight of the company's external financial reporting
  and internal control over financial reporting by the company's audit
  committee.

---

[105] See *Auditing Standard No.5 Release* at A1-26, ¶ 65.
[106] See *Auditing Standard No.5 Release* at A1-26, ¶ 65.
[107] See *Auditing Standard No.5 Release* at A1-28, ¶ 69.

24.042 *Auditor's report*   Under Auditing Standard No.5, the auditor's report includes the auditor's opinion on whether the company maintained, in all material respects, effective internal control over financial reporting as of the specified date, based on the control criteria.[108]

An auditor may not conclude that an issuer's internal control over financial reporting is effective if it has identified one or more material weaknesses.[109] If the auditor cannot perform all of the necessary procedures, the auditor may either withdraw from the engagement or disclaim an opinion.[110] If an overall opinion cannot be expressed, Auditing Standard No.5 requires the auditor to explain why.[111]

Auditing Standard No.5 provides that if there are deficiencies that, individually or together, result in one or more material weaknesses, the auditor must express an adverse opinion on the issuer's internal control over financial reporting, unless there is a restriction on the scope of the engagement.[112] When expressing an adverse opinion on internal control over financial reporting, the auditor's report must include a statement that a material weakness has been identified and identify the material weakness described in management's assessment.[113] If the material weakness has not been included in management's assessment, the report should be modified to state that a material weakness has been identified but not included in management's assessment.[114]

Disclosure controls and procedures

Definition

24.043 In addition to internal control, the SEC's implementing rules under the Act have introduced the concept of "disclosure controls and procedures".[115] For these purposes (as well as for the s.302 certification discussed below), disclosure controls and procedures means controls and other procedures of an issuer that are designed to ensure that information required to be disclosed by the issuer in the reports that it files or submits under the Exchange Act is: (i)

---

[108] See *Auditing Standard No.5 Release* at A1-34, ¶ 85(k); *see also* the *PCAOB News Release* (discussing changes from Auditing Standard No.2 to Auditing Standard No.5, the PCAOB said "the new standard does not include the previous standard's detailed requirements to evaluate management's own evaluation process and clarifies that an internal control audit does not require an opinion on the adequacy of management's process").

[109] See *Auditing Standard No.5 Release* at A1-4, ¶ 2, A1-34, ¶ 87.

[110] See *Auditing Standard No.5 Release* at A1-55, ¶ C3.

[111] See *Auditing Standard No.5 Release* at A1-55—A1-56, ¶¶ C3—C6.

[112] See *Auditing Standard No.5 Release* at A1-37, ¶ 90.

[113] See *Auditing Standard No.5 Release* at A1-38, ¶ 91.

[114] See *Auditing Standard No.5 Release* at A1-38, ¶ 91.

[115] 1934 Act rr.13a-15(a), 15d-15(a).

timely recorded, processed, summarised and reported; and (ii) accumulated and communicated to the issuer's management, to allow for timely decisions about disclosure.[116]

Interaction between disclosure controls and procedures and internal control

There is substantial overlap between the concepts of disclosure controls and **24.044** procedures and internal control over financial reporting, although there are some elements of each term that are not subsumed within the other. In particular, "disclosure controls and procedures will include those components of internal control over financial reporting that provide reasonable assurances that transactions are recorded as necessary to permit preparation of financial statements in accordance with generally accepted accounting principles."[117] By contrast, disclosure controls and procedures would not necessarily include accurate recording of transactions and disposition or safeguarding of assets, which would remain components of internal control.[118]

Accordingly, the effectiveness of an issuer's disclosure controls and procedures is directly linked to the effectiveness of its internal control over financial reporting. Recall that management may not determine that an issuer's internal control over financial reporting is effective if it identifies one or more material weaknesses in the issuer's internal control over financial reporting. While the SEC has not established that existence of a material weakness prevents management from concluding that an issuer's disclosure controls and procedures are effective, statements by senior SEC officials make clear that an issuer with a material weakness in internal control must overcome a high hurdle in order to conclude that its disclosure controls and procedures are nevertheless effective. The SEC has noted specifically that when an issuer restates previously issued financial statements to correct a material misstatement, management should consider whether its original disclosures concerning the effectiveness of its internal control over financial reporting are still appropriate and:

"[s]imilarly, while there is no requirement that management reassess or revise its conclusion related to the effectiveness of its disclosure controls and procedures, management should consider whether its original disclosures regarding effectiveness of disclosure controls and procedures need to be modified or supplemented to include any other material information that is necessary for such disclosures not to be misleading."[119]

---

[116] 1934 Act rr.13a-15(e), 15d-15(e).
[117] See *Management's Reports on Internal Control Adopting Release*, ¶ 86,923, at 87,689.
[118] See *Management's Reports on Internal Control Adopting Release*, ¶ 86,923, at 87,689.
[119] See *Interpretive Guidance Release*, ¶ 87,913, at 84,848.

Requirements

24.045 The regime governing disclosure controls and procedures is similar to that for internal control. Accordingly:

- an issuer must maintain disclosure controls and procedures[120];

- an issuer's management must evaluate, with the participation of the CEO and CFO, the effectiveness of the issuer's disclosure controls and procedures, as of the end of its fiscal year[121]; and

- the issuer must disclose the conclusions of its CEO and CFO regarding the effectiveness of the disclosure controls and procedures based on their review as of the end of the period to which the report relates.[122]

There is, however, no required audit of disclosure controls and procedures.

Certification requirements

24.046 Sarbanes-Oxley contains two overlapping certifications that must be provided by an issuer's CEO and CFO (or persons performing similar functions): the s.302 certification and the s.906 certification. Section 302 amends the Exchange Act, whereas s.906 amends the US federal criminal code.

Section 302

24.047 Section 302(a) of the Sarbanes-Oxley Act directs the SEC to adopt rules requiring CEO and CFO certification of each "annual or quarterly report" filed by issuers. In response, the SEC has adopted new 1934 Act rr.13a-14 and 15d-14 and the text of a certification for Form 20-F.[123]

24.048 *Section 302 certification text*   Rules 13a-14 and 15d-14 require a foreign private issuer's annual report on Form 20-F (but not its current reports

---

[120] 1934 Act rr.13a-15(a), 15d-15(a).
[121] 1934 Act rr.13a-15(b), 15d-15(b).
[122] Form 20-F, Item 15(a).
[123] *Certification of Disclosure in Companies' Quarterly and Annual Reports,* Securities Act Release 8124, Exchange Act Release 46427, Investment Company Act Release 25722, [2002 Transfer Binder] Fed. Sec. L. Rep. (CCH) ¶ 86,720, at 86,132, 86,152 (August 28, 2002) [hereinafter *Certification Adopting Release*].

on Form 6-K)[124] to include separate certifications by the issuer's CEO and CFO.[125] The certifications must state that[126]:

- the officer has reviewed the annual report;

- based on the officer's knowledge, the annual report does not contain any untrue statement of a material fact or omit to state a material fact necessary to make the statements made, in light of the circumstances under which such statements were made, not misleading with respect to the period covered by the report;

- based on the officer's knowledge, the financial statements, and other financial information included in the annual report, fairly present in all material respects the financial condition, results of operations and cash flows of the issuer;

- the CEO and CFO are responsible for establishing and maintaining "disclosure controls and procedures" and "internal control over financial reporting" for the issuer and have:

    - designed such disclosure controls and procedures, or caused such disclosure controls and procedures to be designed under their supervision, to ensure that material information relating to the issuer, including its consolidated subsidiaries, is made known to them by others within those entities, particularly during the period in which the annual report is being prepared;
    - designed such internal control over financial reporting, or caused such internal control over financial reporting to be designed under their supervision, to provide reasonable assurance regarding the reliability of financial reporting and the preparation of financial statements for external purposes in accordance with generally accepted accounting principles;
    - evaluated the effectiveness of the issuer's disclosure controls and procedures and presented in the annual report their conclusions about the effectiveness of the disclosure controls and procedures, as of the end of the period covered by the report based on such evaluation[127]; and
    - disclosed in the report any change in the issuer's internal control over financial reporting that occurred during the period covered by the report that has materially affected, or is reasonably likely to

---

[124] The SEC has stated that *current* reports such as those on Forms 6-K and 8-K, as opposed to *periodic* reports (i.e. quarterly and annual reports), are not covered by s.302's certification requirements.

[125] 1934 Act rr.13a-14(a), 15d-14(a).

[126] Form 20-F, Instructions as to Exhibits, Instruction 12.

[127] Note, however, that no specific date for the evaluation is specified. *Management's Reports on Internal Control Adopting Release*, ¶ 86,923, at 87,706.

materially affect, the issuer's internal control over financial reporting; and

- the CEO and CFO have disclosed, based on their most recent evaluation of internal control over financial reporting, to the issuer's auditors and the audit committee:

  - all significant deficiencies and material weaknesses in the design or operation of internal control over financial reporting which are reasonably likely to adversely affect the issuer's ability to record, process, summarise and report financial information; and
  - any fraud, whether or not material, that involves management or other employees who have a significant role in the issuer's internal control over financial reporting.

The certifications must be included as an exhibit to the issuer's annual report on Form 20-F.[128] The wording of the certification may not be changed in any respect, even if the changes would appear to be inconsequential.[129]

24.049   *Violations of section 302*   While s.302 carries no criminal sanctions, false certifications are subject to SEC enforcement action for violating the Exchange Act and also possibly to both SEC and private litigation alleging violations of the anti-fraud provisions of the Exchange Act (e.g. s.10(b) of the Exchange Act and Exchange Act r.10b-5). A false certification also may have liability consequences under ss.11 and 12(a)(2) of the Securities Act if the accompanying report is incorporated by reference into a registration statement (e.g. on Form F-3) or into a prospectus.

Section 906

24.050   *Section 906 certification text*   Section 906 added new Section 1350 to the US federal criminal code. Section 906 requires that each "periodic report containing financial statements" filed by an issuer must "be accompanied by" a certification by the issuer's CEO and CFO that:

- the periodic report fully complies with the requirements of s.13(a) or s.15(d) of the Exchange Act; and

- the information contained in the periodic report fairly presents, in all material respects, the financial condition and results of operations of the issuer.

---

[128] 1934 Act rr.13a-14(a), 15d-14(a) and Form 20-F, Instructions as to Exhibits, Instruction 12.
[129] *Certification Adopting Release*, ¶ 86,720, at 86,132. However, "a company's certifying officers may temporarily modify the content of their Section 302 certification to eliminate certain references to internal control over financial reporting until the compliance date". *Management's Reports on Internal Control Adopting Release*, ¶ 86,923, at 87,701.

Although s.906 is self-implementing, the SEC has adopted 1934 Act rr.13a-14(b) and 15d-14(b) to require that the s.906 certification (which may be a joint certification of the CEO and CFO) must be provided, and must be furnished as an exhibit to the relevant periodic report. Because the Section 906 certification is not considered "filed" as a technical matter, it would not attract liability under s.18 of the Exchange Act or be incorporated by reference into the issuer's subsequent Securities Act registration statements (unless specifically incorporated by the issuer).[130] As with the s.302 certification, s.906 certification is not required for current reports on Form 6-K.[131]

Violations of section 906   Under s.906, an officer who certifies a statement **24.051** "knowing that the periodic report accompanying the statement" does not meet the certification can be fined not more than $1 million or imprisoned for not more than 10 years, or both. By contrast, an officer who "willfully" certifies his or her written statement while "knowing" that the annual report does not "comport with all the requirements" of s.906 can be fined not more than $5 million or imprisoned not more than 20 years, or both. The distinction between "knowing" and "willful" certification is not set out in the Sarbanes-Oxley Act, but in other contexts "willfully" normally requires a showing that the person had specific knowledge of the law he or she was violating, whereas "knowingly" does not.[132]

Differences between section 302 and section 906 certifications

Although the text of the two required certifications overlap, there are some **24.052** important differences between them. In contrast to the s.302 certification, the text of the s.906 certification does not explicitly provide for the officer to certify as to his or her knowledge. However, the US Department of Justice has confirmed that an officer may qualify a s.906 certification to his or her knowledge because knowledge would, in any event, be a necessary element of criminal prosecution.[133] Furthermore, whereas the s.302 certification is required for any amendment to an annual report on Form 20-F containing financial statements, Form 20-F amendments do not require a new s.906 certification.[134]

---

[130] *Management's Reports on Internal Control Adopting Release*, ¶ 86,923, at 87,699. Not "filing" will also limit enforcement of the certificate to criminal proceedings rather than civil litigation. John J Huber and Julie K Hoffman, *The Sarbanes-Oxley Act of 2002 and SEC Rulemaking*, ¶ II.B.1.c, at 20 (April 2, 2004) [hereinafter *Huber Outline*].
[131] *Additional Form 8-K Disclosure Adopting Release*, ¶ 87,158, at 86,923, fn.146.
[132] *Huber Outline*, ¶ II.B.3.b(1), at 23.
[133] *Huber Outline*, ¶ II.B.2.b(3), at 21.
[134] *Management's Reports on Internal Control Adopting Release*, ¶ 86,923, at 87,699.

Standards relating to listed company audit committees

24.053   Section 301 of the Sarbanes-Oxley Act adds new s.10A(m) of the Exchange Act. Section 10A(m) charges the SEC with creating rules to prohibit the listing of any security in the United States of an issuer that is not in compliance with certain substantive standards for audit committees. The SEC has adopted final rules under s.301 as 1934 Act r.10A-3.[135]

Under r.10A-3, audit committee members each have to be a member of the board of directors and otherwise independent.[136] To be "independent," an audit committee member is barred from accepting any compensatory fees other than in that member's capacity as a member of the board[137] and may not be an "affiliated person" of the issuer.[138] The definition of affiliated person includes a person that, directly, or indirectly through one or more intermediaries, controls, or is controlled by, or is under common control with the specified person.[139] There is, however, a safe harbor for certain non-executive officers and other persons that are 10 per cent or less shareholders of the issuer.[140]

Foreign private issuers are entitled to certain exemptions from the independence prong of r.10A-3. For example, the inclusion of a non-management employee representative,[141] a non-management affiliated person with only observer status,[142] or a non-management governmental representative on the audit committee will not violate the affiliated person prong of the independence test.[143] In addition, issuers involved in an IPO are entitled to certain exemptions during a transitional period following their public offering.[144]

Rule 10A-3 also requires that:

- the audit committee must be "directly responsible" for the appointment, compensation, oversight and retention of the external auditors, who must report directly to the audit committee[145];

- the audit committee must establish procedures for the receipt, retention and treatment of complaints regarding accounting, internal controls or

---

[135] Listed foreign private issuers were required to be in compliance with r.10A-3 by July 31, 2005. 1934 Act r.10A-3(a)(5)(i)(A); see also *Standards Relating to Listed Company Audit Committees*, Securities Act Release 8220, Exchange Act Release 47654, Investment Company Act Release 26001, [2003 Transfer Binder] Fed. Sec. L. Rep. (CCH) (April 9, 2003) [hereinafter *Listed Company Audit Committee Adopting Release*].
[136] 1934 Act r.10A-3(b)(1)(i).
[137] 1934 Act r.10A-3(b)(1)(ii)(A).
[138] 1934 Act r.10A-3(b)(1)(ii)(B).
[139] 1934 Act r.10A-3(e)(1)(i).
[140] 1934 Act r.10A-3(e)(1)(ii)(A).
[141] 1934 Act r.10A-3(b)(1)(iv)(C).
[142] 1934 Act r.10A-3(b)(1)(iv)(D).
[143] 1934 Act r.10A-3(b)(1)(iv)(E).
[144] 1934 Act r.10A-3(b)(1)(iv)(A).
[145] 1934 Act r.10A-3(b)(2).

auditing matters, and for the confidential, anonymous submission by employees of concerns regarding questionable accounting or auditing matters[146];

- the audit committee must have the authority to engage independent counsel and other advisors as it deems necessary to carry out its duties[147]; and

- the issuer must provide the audit committee with appropriate funding for payment of external auditors, advisors employed by the audit committee and ordinary administrative expenses of the audit committee.[148]

These requirements are not intended to conflict with local legal or listing provisions (or requirements under the foreign private issuer's organisational documents), and instead relate to the allocation of responsibility between the audit committee and the issuer's management.[149] Accordingly, the audit committee may recommend or nominate the appointment or compensation of the external auditor to shareholders if these matters are within shareholder competence under local law,[150] and it must be granted those responsibilities that the board of directors can legally delegate.[151]

Rule 10A-3 contains a general exemption for foreign private issuers that have a statutory board of auditors or statutory auditors established pursuant to home country law or listing requirements, which in turn meet various requirements.[152]

A foreign private issuer relying on r.10A-3's exemption from independence, or the general exemption noted above, will need to disclose in its annual report its reliance on the exemptions and an assessment of whether this reliance will materially adversely affect the audit committee's ability to act independently and to satisfy any of the other requirements of r.10A-3.[153]

Audit committee financial expert

Section 407(a) of the Sarbanes-Oxley Act directs the SEC to issue rules requiring an issuer to disclose in its periodic reports whether its audit committee has at least one "financial expert" or if not, why not.   **24.054**

The SEC's final rules implementing s.407(a) use the term "audit committee

---

[146] 1934 Act r.10A-3(b)(3).
[147] 1934 Act r.10A-3(b)(4).
[148] 1934 Act r.10A-3(b)(5).
[149] Instruction 1 to 1934 Act r.10A-3.
[150] Instruction 1 to 1934 Act r.10A-3.
[151] Instruction 2 to 1934 Act r.10A-3.
[152] 1934 Act r.10A-3(c)(3).
[153] 1934 Act r.10A-3(d) and Form 20-F, Item 16D.

financial expert" instead of "financial expert". The SEC has implemented these rules as new Item 16A of Form 20-F.

Under Item 16A, a foreign private issuer must disclose in its annual report that the issuer's board of directors has determined whether or not it has one audit committee financial expert serving on its audit committee, or if not, why not.[154] If the issuer has a two-tier board of directors, the supervisory or non-management board would make this determination.[155] The issuer must also disclose the name of the audit committee financial expert (if any)[156] and whether that person is "independent" from management.[157] An issuer's board of directors must make an affirmative determination whether or not it has at least one audit committee financial expert, and may not simply fail to reach a conclusion.[158]

In order to qualify as an audit committee financial expert, the audit committee member must have the following "attributes"[159]:

- an understanding of GAAP;

- the ability to assess the general application of GAAP in connection with the accounting for estimates, accruals and reserves;

- experience preparing, auditing or analysing financial statements similar to those of the issuer, or actively supervising others engaged in these activities;

- an understanding of internal controls and procedures for financial reporting; and

- an understanding of audit committee functions.

In addition, an audit committee financial expert must have gained those attributes through[160]:

- education and experience as a principal financial officer, principal accounting officer, controller, public accountant or auditor, or experience in similar positions;

- experience actively supervising these functions;

---

[154] Form 20-F, Items 16A(a)(1) and (3).
[155] Form 20-F, Instruction 3 to Item 16A.
[156] Form 20-F, Item 16A(a)(2).
[157] Form 20-F; see also *Listed Company Audit Committee Adopting Release*, ¶ 86,902, at 87,433.
[158] *Disclosure Required by Sections 406 and 407 of the Sarbanes-Oxley Act of 2002*, Securities Act Release 8177, Exchange Act Release 47234, [2002-2003 Transfer Binder] Fed. Sec. L. Rep. (CCH) ¶ 86,818, at 86,885 (as corrected, January 24, 2003 and March 31, 2003) [hereinafter *Sections 406 and 407 Adopting Release*].
[159] Form 20-F, Item 16A(b).
[160] Form 20-F, Item 16A(c).

- experience overseeing or assessing the performance of companies or public accountants with respect to the preparation, auditing or evaluation of financial statements; or

- other relevant experience.

The term "GAAP" as used in Item 16A refers to the body of GAAP used by the issuer in its primary financial statements.[161] Accordingly, the audit committee financial expert of a foreign private issuer need only be versed in local GAAP, and not in US GAAP or in reconciliation to US GAAP (although that experience would, of course, be useful).[162]

Item 16A also contains a liability "safe harbor" for the audit committee financial expert, under which:

- a person who is determined to be an audit committee financial expert is not deemed to be an "expert" for any purpose, such as s.11 of the Securities Act;[163] and

- the designation of a person as an audit committee financial expert does not impose greater duties, obligations or liabilities on the person than on other audit committee and board members, and does not affect the duties, obligations or liabilities of other audit committee and board members.[164]

NYSE and Nasdaq corporate governance requirements

NYSE corporate governance requirements

In addition to certain quantitative listing and maintenance standards, a foreign private issuer must meet certain corporate governance standards for initial listing and maintenance of a listing on the NYSE. As described below, foreign private issuers are permitted to follow home country practice in lieu of most of the NYSE corporate governance requirements.   **24.055**

Majority of independent directors

A majority of the issuer's board of directors must consist of independent directors.[165] A director will qualify as independent only if the board   **24.056**

---

[161] Form 20-F, Instruction 3 to Item 16A.
[162] *Sections 406 and 407 Adopting Release*, ¶ 86,818, at 86,883.
[163] Form 20-F, Item 16A(d)(1).
[164] Form 20-F, Items 16A(d)(2)-(3).
[165] See *New York Stock Exchange Listed Company Manual*, § 303A.01 [*NYSE Manual*].

affirmatively determines that the director has no material relationship with the company (either directly or as a partner, shareholder or officer of an organisation that has a relationship with the company).[166] Material relationships can include commercial, industrial, banking, consulting, legal, accounting, charitable and familial relationships. However, ownership of even a significant amount of stock (that is, 10 per cent), by itself, is not a bar to an independence finding.[167]

A company must disclose these determinations in its annual proxy statement or, if the company does not file an annual proxy statement, in its annual report filed with the SEC. A board may adopt and disclose categorical standards to assist it in making determinations of independence and may make only general disclosure if a director meets these standards.[168]

In addition, a director cannot be independent unless at least three years (except as provided in the transition rule below) have passed since:

- the director (or an immediate family member) was an employee or executive officer of the company[169];
- the director (or an immediate family member) received more than $100,000 per year in direct compensation from the company, other than director and committee fees and pension or other forms of deferred compensation for prior service not contingent on continued service[170];
- the director was affiliated with or employed by (or any immediate family member was affiliated with or employed in a professional capacity by) a present or former external auditor[171];
- the director (or any immediate family member) was employed as an executive officer of another company whose compensation committee includes an executive of the company[172]; and
- any single fiscal year when a company of which the director is an executive officer or an employee (or of which the director's immediate family member is an executive officer) made payments to, or received payments from, the listed company for property or services in an amount exceeding the greater of $1 million or 2 per cent of such other company's consolidated gross revenues.[173]

An *immediate family member* is defined to include a person's spouse, parents, children, siblings, mothers and fathers-in-law, sons and daughters-in-law,

[166] See *NYSE Manual* at § 303A.02.
[167] See Commentary to *NYSE Manual* § 303A.02.
[168] See Commentary to *NYSE Manual* § 303A.02.
[169] See *NYSE Manual* at § 303A.02(b)(i).
[170] See *NYSE Manual* at § 303A.02(b)(ii).
[171] See *NYSE Manual* at § 303A.02(b)(iii).
[172] See *NYSE Manual* at § 303A.02(b)(iv).
[173] See *NYSE Manual* at § 303A.02(b)(v).

brothers and sisters-in-law, and anyone (other than a domestic employee) who shares that person's home. References to the *company* would include any parent or subsidiary in a consolidated group with the company.[174]

Executive session

Non-management directors must meet at regularly scheduled executive sessions without management and, if any such directors are not independent under the standards described above, an executive session of solely independent directors must be scheduled at least once a year.[175]   **24.057**

Nominating/corporate governance committee

Companies must have a nominating/corporate governance committee composed entirely of independent directors.[176] That committee must have a written charter that: **24.058**

- addresses the committee's purpose and responsibilities, which must include identifying and selecting or recommending director nominees, developing and recommending corporate governance principles and overseeing the evaluation of the board and management[177]; and

- provides for an annual performance evaluation of the committee.[178]

The nominating/corporate governance committee charter should also address:

- committee member qualifications;

- committee member appointment and removal;

- committee structure and operations (including the authority to delegate to subcommittees); and

- committee reporting to the board.[179]

If a company is legally required by contract or otherwise to provide third parties with the ability to nominate directors, the selection and nomination of such directors need not be subject to the nominating committee process.

---

[174] See Commentary to *NYSE Manual* § 303A.02(b).
[175] See Commentary to *NYSE Manual* at § 303A.03.
[176] See Commentary to *NYSE Manual* at § 303A.04(a).
[177] See Commentary to *NYSE Manual* at § 303A.04(b)(i).
[178] See *NYSE Manual* at § 303A.04(b)(ii).
[179] See Commentary to *NYSE Manual* § 303A.04.

Compensation committee

24.059 Companies must have a compensation committee composed entirely of independent directors.[180] That committee must have a written charter that:

- addresses the committee's purpose and responsibilities, which at a minimum must include the direct responsibility to:
    - review and approve corporate goals and objectives relevant to CEO compensation, evaluate the CEO's performance, and to determine and approve (either as a committee or together with other independent directors) the CEO's compensation level based on this evaluation[181];
    - make recommendations to the board with respect to non-CEO compensation, incentive-compensation plans and equity-based plans that are subject to board approval[182]; and
- produce a compensation committee report on executive compensation as required by the SEC to be included in the company's annual proxy statement or annual report filed with the SEC[183]; and
- provides for an annual performance evaluation of the compensation committee.[184]

The compensation committee charter should also address committee member qualifications, committee member appointment and removal, committee structure and operations (including authority to delegate to subcommittees) and committee reporting to the board.[185]

Audit committee

24.060 *Sarbanes-Oxley*   Companies must have an audit committee that satisfies the independence and other requirements of Exchange Act r.10A-3 (implementing s.301 of Sarbanes-Oxley).[186]

24.061 *Charter*   The audit committee must have a written charter that addresses:

- the committee's purpose, which at a minimum must be to:

---

[180] See *NYSE Manual* § 303A.05(a).
[181] See *NYSE Manual* at § 303A.05(b)(i)(A).
[182] See *NYSE Manual* at § 303A.05(b)(i)(B).
[183] See *NYSE Manual* at § 303A.05(b)(i)(C).
[184] See *NYSE Manual* at § 303A.05(b)(ii).
[185] See Commentary to *NYSE Manual* § 303A.05.
[186] See *NYSE Manual* §§ 303A.06, 303A.07(b).

- assist board with oversight of: (1) the integrity of the company's financial statements; (2) the company's compliance with legal and regulatory requirements; (3) the independent auditor's qualifications and independence; and (4) the performance of the company's internal audit function and independent auditors[187]; and
- prepare an audit committee report as required by the SEC to be included in the company's annual proxy statement[188];

- an annual performance evaluation of the audit committee[189]; and

- the duties and responsibilities of the audit committee, which at a minimum must include those set out in Exchange Act r.10A-3(b)(2), (3), (4) and (5) (concerning responsibilities relating to: (1) registered public accounting firms; (2) complaints relating to accounting, internal accounting controls or auditing matters; (3) authority to engage advisers; and (4) funding as determined by the audit committee),[190] as well as to:

  - at least annually, obtain and review a report by the independent auditor describing: (1) the firm's internal quality-control procedures; (2) any material issues raised by the most recent internal quality-control review, or peer review, of the firm, or by any inquiry or investigation by government or professional bodies, within the preceding five years respecting one or more independent audits carried out by the firm, and any steps taken to deal with any such issues; and (3) all relationships between the independent auditor and the company (to assess the auditor's independence)[191];
  - discuss the company's annual audited financial statement[192]; quarterly unaudited financial statements with management and the independent auditor, including the company's MD&A disclosures[193]; earnings press releases[194]; financial information and earnings guidance provided to analysts and rating agencies[195]; and policies with respect to risk assessment and risk management[196];
  - meet separately, periodically, with management, with internal auditors and with independent auditors[197];

---

[187] See *NYSE Manual* at § 303A.07(c)(i)(A).
[188] See *NYSE Manual* at § 303A.07(c)(i)(B).
[189] See *NYSE Manual* at § 303A.07(c)(ii).
[190] See *NYSE Manual* at § 303A.07(c)(iii).
[191] See *NYSE Manual* at § 303A.07(c)(iii)(A).
[192] See *NYSE Manual* at § 303A.07(c)(iii)(B).
[193] See *NYSE Manual* at § 303A.07(c)(iii)(B).
[194] See *NYSE Manual* at § 303A.07(c)(iii)(C).
[195] See *NYSE Manual* at § 303A.07(c)(iii)(C).
[196] See *NYSE Manual* at § 303A.07(c)(iii)(D).
[197] See *NYSE Manual* at § 303A.07(c)(iii)(E).

- review with the independent auditors any audit problems or difficulties and management's response[198];
- set clear hiring policies for employees or former employees of the independent auditors[199]; and
- report regularly to the board.[200]

24.062 *Composition* The audit committee must have a minimum of three members, each of whom is *independent* and *financially literate* and at least one of whom has accounting or financial management expertise. Such qualifications are left to the company's board to determine based on its business judgment. If an audit committee member simultaneously serves on the audit committees of more than three public companies, and the company does not limit the number of audit committees on which its audit committee members serve, then in each case the board must determine that the simultaneous service would not impair the ability of such member to serve effectively on its audit committee. The company must also disclose that determination in the company's annual proxy statement or, if the company does not file an annual proxy statement, in its annual report filed with the SEC.[201]

Audit committee members must meet both the NYSE's independence rules applicable to directors, and also the independence requirements of Exchange Act r.10A-3.[202]

Internal audit

24.063 Companies must have an internal audit function to provide management and the audit committee with ongoing assessments of the company's risk management processes and system of internal control. This function may be outsourced to a third-party service provider other than the company's independent auditor.[203]

Shareholder approval of certain transactions

24.064 Shareholder approval is required for each of the following material transactions, with certain exceptions:

---

[198] See *NYSE Manual* at § 303A.07(c)(iii)(F).
[199] See *NYSE Manual* at § 303A.07(c)(iii)(G).
[200] See *NYSE Manual* at § 303A.07(c)(iii)(H).
[201] See *NYSE Manual* at § 303A.07(a); see also Commentary to *NYSE Manual* § 303A.07(a). While the NYSE does not require that an audit committee include a person who satisfies the definition of audit committee financial expert as set out in Item 401(h) of Regulation S-K, a board may presume that such a person has accounting or related financial management expertise.
[202] See *NYSE Manual* § 303A.07(b).
[203] See *NYSE Manual* at § 303A.07(d); see also Commentary to *NYSE Manual* § 303A.07(d).

- the implementation of equity-compensation plans and material revisions thereto[204];

- an issuance of more than 1 per cent of the outstanding common stock or 1 per cent of the voting power outstanding of the issuer (measured either by amount of shares or voting power) to a related party (that is, directors, officers or substantial security holders of the issuer) or to a subsidiary, affiliate or company owned by the related party[205];

- an issuance of more than 20 per cent of the outstanding common stock of the issuer (measured either by amount of shares or voting power)[206]; and

- an issuance that will result in a change of control of the issuer.[207]

Corporate governance guidelines

Companies must adopt and disclose corporate governance guidelines. Areas that must be addressed include: **24.065**

- director qualification standards;

- director responsibilities;

- director access to management and, as necessary and appropriate, independent advisers;

- director compensation;

- director orientation and continuing education;

- management succession; and

- annual performance evaluation of the board.

The company must state in its annual proxy statement or, if the company does not file an annual proxy statement, in its annual report filed with the SEC that this information is available on its website, and is available in print to any shareholder who requests it.[208]

---

[204] See *NYSE Manual* § 312.03(a); see also Commentary to *NYSE Manual* at § 303A.08.
[205] See *NYSE Manual* § 312.03(b).
[206] See *NYSE Manual* at § 312.03(c). Shareholder approval will not be required for any issuance involving: (1) any public offering for cash; (2) any bona fide private financing, if it involves a sale of common stock, for cash, at a price at least as great as each of the book and market value of the issuer's common stock; or (3) securities convertible into or exercisable for common stock, for cash, if the conversion or exercise price is at least as great as each of the book and market value of the issuer's common stock.
[207] See *NYSE Manual* at § 312.03(d).
[208] See *NYSE Manual* at § 303A.09; see also Commentary to *NYSE Manual* § 303A.09.

Code of business conduct and ethics

24.066 Companies must adopt and disclose a code of business conduct and ethics for directors, officers and employees and promptly disclose any waivers of the code for directors or executive officers.

This code should address, among other things:

- conflicts of interest;
- corporate opportunities;
- confidentiality;
- fair dealing;
- protection and use of company assets;
- compliance with laws, rules and regulations (including insider trading laws); and
- encouraging the reporting of illegal or unethical behaviour.

The code must contain compliance standards and procedures to facilitate its effective operation and must require that any waiver of the code for executive officers or directors be made only by the board or a board committee and must be promptly disclosed to shareholders.

The company must state in its annual proxy statement or, if the company does not file an annual proxy statement, in its annual report filed with the SEC that this information is available on its website, and is available in print to any shareholder who requests it.[209]

Certification requirements

24.067 Each year the CEO must certify to the NYSE that they are not aware of any violation by the company of NYSE corporate governance listing standards. In addition, the CEO must promptly notify the NYSE in writing after any executive officer of the company becomes aware of any material non-compliance with any NYSE corporate governance listing standard.[210]

Written affirmation

24.068 In addition to the CEO certification mentioned above, an officer of the company must provide to the NYSE, within about 30 days after the annual

---

[209] See *NYSE Manual* § 303A.10; see also Commentary to *NYSE Manual* § 303A.10.
[210] See *NYSE Manual* §§ 303A.12(a), 303A.12(b).

shareholders' meeting, a wide-ranging *written affirmation* with exhibits that describes the company's compliance or non-compliance with the NYSE's corporate governance requirements.[211] Besides the annual written affirmation, an interim written affirmation will be required:

- each time a director is added to or removed from the board;

- if any change is made to the composition of the audit, nominating or compensation committee; and

- if the required responsibilities of the nominating/corporate governance committee and/or the compensation committee have been reallocated to any other board committees, and any changes to the composition of those committees occurs.[212]

NYSE communication and notification requirements

The NYSE expects any listed company to release quickly any information that might reasonably be expected to materially affect the market for its securities. In addition, a listed company should act promptly to dispel any unfounded rumours that produce unusual market activity or price variations.[213]   **24.069**

When announcement of a material event or a statement dealing with a rumour is made shortly before or during market hours (9:30am to 5:00pm, New York City time), the issuer's NYSE representative should be notified by telephone at least 10 minutes before the announcement is released to the news media. This will allow the NYSE to determine if a trading halt should be imposed.[214]

Corporate governance requirements for foreign private issuers

Foreign private issuers are permitted to follow home country practice in lieu of the NYSE's corporate governance standards, other than the NYSE's requirements that it must: (1) have an audit committee that meets the requirements of Exchange Act r.10A-3; and (2) provide prompt notification from its CEO of material non-compliance with the applicable provisions of the   **24.070**

---

[211] See *NYSE Manual* at § 303A.12(c).
[212] See *NYSE Listed Company Manual Section 303A Corporate Governance Listing Standards: Frequently Asked Questions*, Question B.4 (February 13, 2004).
[213] See *NYSE Manual* § 202.05.
[214] See *NYSE Manual* at § 202.06(B).

NYSE's corporate governance rules.[215] A foreign private issuer must also provide an annual written affirmation to the NYSE.[216]

Whether a listed foreign private issuer follows the NYSE corporate governance standards or its home country practice, it must disclose any ways in which its corporate governance practices differ from those followed by domestic US issuers under NYSE listing standards.[217] A detailed and cumbersome analysis is not required, and instead a brief, general summary of differences is enough. An issuer may provide this disclosure either on its website (provided it is in English and accessible from the United States) and/or in its annual report distributed to shareholders in the United States. If the disclosure is only made available on the company's website, its annual report must state this fact and must provide the web address at which the information can be obtained.[218]

Nasdaq corporate governance standards

24.071   There are three distinct markets within Nasdaq: the Nasdaq Global Market ("NGM"), the Nasdaq Global Select Market ("NGSM")[219] and the Nasdaq Capital Market ("NCM"). The NGSM mandates the highest initial listing requirements of any market in the world, while its maintenance requirements are identical to those of the NGM. The NGM, in turn, has more stringent quantitative listing and maintenance requirements than the NCM. Except as noted below, the quantitative listing and maintenance criteria applicable to non-Canadian foreign private issuers for the NGM, NGSM and NCM are identical to those of domestic US issuers and Canadian issuers. Foreign private issuers (including Canadian issuers) may, however, elect to follow home country practice in lieu of compliance with the Nasdaq corporate governance requirements (other than as described below).

Majority of independent directors

24.072   A majority of the issuer's board of directors must consist of independent directors.[220] The board of directors must affirmatively determine that the director has no relationship with the issuer that would impair their

---

[215] See *NYSE Manual* at § 303A.00.
[216] See *NYSE Listed Company Manual Section 303A Corporate Governance Listing Standards: Frequently Asked Questions*, Question B.7 (February 13, 2004).
[217] See *NYSE Manual* § 303A.11.
[218] See Commentary to *NYSE Manual* § 303A.11.
[219] The NGSM was implemented on July 1, 2006.
[220] See Nasdaq rr.5605(b)(1), 5615(c)(1). "Controlled companies," which are companies of which more than 50% of the voting power is held by an individual, a group or another company, are exempt from the requirements relating to having a majority of independent directors, executive compensation and director nominees.

independence,[221] and the issuer must disclose in its annual proxy (or, if it does not file a proxy, on its annual report on Form 10-K (or Form 20-F for foreign private issuers) filed with the SEC, those directors that the board of directors has determined to be independent.[222]

Ownership of an issuer's stock, by itself, is not a bar to an independence finding.[223] The Nasdaq rules define an independent director to mean a person other than an officer or employee of the company or its subsidiaries or any other individual having a relationship that, in the opinion of the company's board of directors, would interfere with the exercise of independent judgment in carrying out the responsibilities of a director.[224]

A director cannot be independent who:

- is, or at any time in the past three years was, employed by the issuer or any parent or subsidiary (as defined below) of the issuer;[225]

- has accepted, or who has a family member (as defined below) who has accepted, any payments from the issuer or any parent or subsidiary of the issuer in excess of $120,000 during any period of 12 consecutive months within the three years preceding the determination of independence,[226] other than:

  - compensation for director or board committee service[227];
  - compensation paid to a family member who is a non-executive employee of the issuer or a parent or subsidiary of the issuer[228]; or
  - benefits under a tax-qualified retirement plan, or non-discretionary compensation[229];

- is a family member of an individual who is, or at any time during the past three years was, employed by the issuer or any parent or subsidiary of the issuer as an executive[230];

- is, or has a family member who is, a partner in, or controlling shareholder or executive officer of, any organisation to which the issuer made, or from which the issuer received, payments for property or services in the current or any of the past three fiscal years that exceed 5 per cent of the recipient's consolidated gross revenues for that year, or $200,000, whichever is more,[231] other than:

---

[221] See Nasdaq Interpretive Material 5605 [*Nasdaq IM*].
[222] See Nasdaq r.5605(b)(1).
[223] See *Nasdaq IM* 5605.
[224] See Nasdaq r.5000(a)(19), 5605(a)(2).
[225] See Nasdaq r.5000(a)(19), 5605(a)(2)(A).
[226] See Nasdaq rr.5000(a)(19), 5605(a)(2)(B).
[227] See Nasdaq rr.5000(a)(19), 5605(a)(2)(B)(i).
[228] See Nasdaq rr.5000(a)(19), 5605(a)(2)(B)(ii).
[229] See Nasdaq rr.5000(a)(19), 5605(a)(2)(B)(iii).
[230] See Nasdaq rr.5000(a)(19), 5605(a)(2)(C).
[231] See Nasdaq rr.5000(a)(19), 5605(a)(2)(D).

- payments arising solely from investments in the issuer's securities[232]; or
- payments under non-discretionary charitable contribution matching programs[233];

- is, or has a family member who is, employed as an executive officer of another entity where at any time during the past three years any of the executive officers of the issuer serves on the compensation committee of such other entity[234]; or

- is, or has a family member who is, a current partner of the issuer's outside auditor, or was a partner or employee of the issuer's outside auditor who worked on the issuer's audit at any time during any of the past three years.[235]

For these purposes, a *parent or subsidiary* covers entities that the issuer controls and consolidates with its financial statements as filed with the SEC (but not if the issuer reflects such entity solely as an investment in its financial statements).[236] A family member is defined to include a person's spouse, parents, children, siblings, whether by blood, marriage or adoption, or anyone residing in such person's home.[237]

Meetings of independent directors

24.073   Independent directors must have regularly scheduled meetings at which only independent directors are present.[238] Those meetings should occur not less than twice a year.[239]

Director nominees

24.074   Director nominees must be selected, or recommended for the board of director's selection, either by a majority of the independent directors or by a nominations committee comprised solely of independent directors.[240] Each issuer must certify that it has adopted a formal written charter or board resolution

---

[232] See Nasdaq rr.5000(a)(19), 5605(a)(2)(D)(i).
[233] See Nasdaq rr.5000(a)(19), 5605(a)(2)(D)(ii).
[234] See Nasdaq rr.5000(a)(19), 5605(a)(2)(E).
[235] See Nasdaq at rr.5000(a)(19), 5605(a)(2)(F).
[236] See *Nasdaq IM 5605*.
[237] See Nasdaq rr.5000(a)(17), 5605(a)(2) Excerpt.
[238] See Nasdaq r.5605(b)(2) (the rule refers to these meetings as *executive sessions*).
[239] See *Nasdaq IM 5605-2*.
[240] See Nasdaq r.5605(e)(1)(A-B).

addressing the nominations process (and such related matters as may be required under the federal securities laws).[241] In certain circumstances a single non-independent director, who is not a current officer or employee (or family member of an officer or employee), may serve for up to two years on an independent nominations committee comprised of at least three members.[242] Independent director oversight of director nominations does not apply in cases where the right to nominate a director belongs legally to a third party (although the requirement that the nominations committee be composed entirely of independent directors remains).[243] This rule also does not apply if the issuer is subject to a binding obligation inconsistent with the rule, and such obligation predates November 2003.[244]

Executive compensation

Compensation of the CEO and all other executive officers must be deter- **24.075**
mined either by a majority of the independent directors or by a compensation committee comprised solely of independent directors. The CEO may not be present during voting or deliberations concerning their compensation.[245] In certain circumstances a single non-independent director, who is not a current officer or employee (or family member of an officer or employee), may serve for up to two years on an independent compensation committee comprised of at least three members.[246]

Audit committees

Sarbanes-Oxley   An issuer's audit committee must satisfy the independ- **24.076**
ence and other requirements of Exchange Act r.10A-3 (implementing s.301 of Sarbanes-Oxley).[247]

Charter   Each issuer must certify that it has a written audit committee **24.077**
charter and that the audit committee has reviewed and assessed the adequacy of the audit committee charter on an annual basis.[248] The charter must specify:

---

[241] See Nasdaq r.5605(e)(2).
[242] See Nasdaq r.5605(e)(3).
[243] See Nasdaq r.5605(e)(4).
[244] See Nasdaq r.5605(e)(5).
[245] See Nasdaq rr.5605(d)(1)(A-B), 5605(d)(2)(A-B).
[246] See Nasdaq r.5605(d)(3).
[247] See *Nasdaq IM* 5605-1, 5605-2, 5605-3, 5605-4, 5605-5, 5605-6 and 5605-7.
[248] See Nasdaq r.5605(c)(1).

- the scope of the audit committee's responsibilities, and how it carries out those responsibilities, including structure, processes, and membership requirements[249];

- the audit committee's responsibility for ensuring its receipt from the outside auditors of a formal written statement delineating all relationships between the auditor and the issuer, and the audit committee's responsibility for engaging in a dialogue with the auditor with respect to any disclosed relationships or services that might impact the objectivity and independence of the auditor and for taking, or recommending that the full board take, appropriate action to oversee the independence of the outside auditor[250];

- the committee's purpose of overseeing the accounting and financial reporting processes of the issuer and the audits of the financial statements of the issuer[251]; and

- the specific audit committee responsibilities and authority necessary to comply with the audit committee requirements of Sarbanes-Oxley and Nasdaq r.4350(d)(3) concerning responsibilities relating to: (1) registered public accounting firms; (2) complaints relating to accounting, internal accounting controls or auditing matters; (3) authority to engage advisers; and (4) funding as determined by the audit committee.[252]

24.078 *Composition*   The issuer must have, and certify that it has and will continue to have, an audit committee of at least three members, each of whom must:

- be independent, within the meaning of the Nasdaq director independence rules discussed above;

- meet the requirements for audit committee independence, set out in Exchange Act r.10A-3(b)(1), that, subject to certain limited exceptions: (1) such member be a member of the board of directors of the issuer; (2) such member not (other than in his or her capacity as a member of the board of directors, the audit committee or another board committee) accept directly or indirectly any consulting, advisory, or other compensatory fee from the issuer or any subsidiary thereof; and (3) such member not be an affiliated person[253] of the issuer or any subsidiary thereof;

---

[249] See Nasdaq r.5605(c)(1)(A).
[250] See Nasdaq r.5605(c)(1)(B).
[251] See Nasdaq r.5605(c)(1)(C).
[252] See Nasdaq r.5605(c)(1)(D).
[253] In the case of investment company issuers, the term *affiliated person* is replaced with *interested person*, as defined in s.2(a)(19) of the Investment Company Act of 1940.

- not have participated in the preparation of the financial statements of the issuer or any current subsidiary of the issuer at any time during the past three years; and

- be able to read and understand fundamental financial statements, including an issuer's balance sheet, income statement and cash flow statement, at the time of appointment.[254]

In addition, each issuer must certify that it has, and will continue to have, one member of the audit committee who has past employment experience in finance or accounting or other comparable experience or background which results in financial sophistication.[255] Note a director who qualifies as an audit committee financial expert under Item 407(d)(5) of Regulation S-K or Item 407(d)(5) of Regulation S-B will be deemed to meet this financial sophistication requirement.[256] Under certain circumstances a single director who meets the independence requirements of Exchange Act r.10A-3(b)(1) but not the independence requirements of the Nasdaq rules, who is not a current officer or employee (or family member of an officer or employee), may serve for up to two years on an audit committee. Such a person may not, however, chair the audit committee.[257]

Responsibility and authority

The audit committee must have the specific responsibilities and authority **24.079** needed to satisfy Exchange Act r.10A-3(b)(2), (3), (4) and (5) (concerning responsibilities relating to: (1) registered public accounting firms; (2) complaints relating to accounting, internal accounting controls or auditing matters; (3) authority to engage advisers; and (4) funding as determined by the audit committee).[258]

Cure periods   The Nasdaq rules provide for certain cure periods if an **24.080** audit committee member ceases to be independent for reasons outside the member's reasonable control, or if there is a vacancy on the audit committee.[259]

---

[254] See Nasdaq r.5605(c)(2)(A).
[255] See Nasdaq r.5605(c)(2)(A).
[256] See *Nasdaq IM* 5605-4.
[257] See Nasdaq r.5605(c)(2)(B).
[258] See Nasdaq r.5605(c)(3).
[259] See generally Nasdaq rr.5605(c)(4)(A), (c)(4)(B).

Shareholder meetings

24.081   An issuer must hold an annual meeting of shareholders and provide notice of that meeting to Nasdaq.[260]

Quorum

24.082   An issuer must provide for a quorum of at least 33 per cent of the outstanding shares of the issuer's common voting stock, as specified in its by-laws for any meeting of the holders of its common stock.[261]

Proxy solicitation

24.083   An issuer must solicit proxies and provide proxy statements for all meetings of shareholders and must provide copies of such proxy solicitation to Nasdaq.[262] Note, however, that foreign private issuers are not subject to the US proxy rules.

Conflicts of interest

24.084   An issuer must conduct an appropriate review of all related party transactions for potential conflict of interest situations on an ongoing basis, and all such transactions must be approved by the audit committee or another independent committee of the board of directors. A "related-party transaction" for this purpose means those transactions required to be disclosed pursuant to Item 404 of Regulation S-K or Item 404 of Regulation S-B (and includes transactions and loans between management and the issuer for amounts over $120,000) or, in the case of foreign private issuers, pursuant to Item 7.B of Form 20-F (and includes transactions and loans between the issuer and enterprises under common control of the issuer, associates, individuals owning an interest in the voting power of the company that gives them significant influence or key management).[263]

---

[260]   See Nasdaq r.5620(a).
[261]   See Nasdaq r.5620(c).
[262]   See Nasdaq r.5620(b).
[263]   See Nasdaq r.5630(a-b).

Shareholder approval of certain transactions

An issuer must obtain shareholder approval prior to the issuance of **24.085**
securities:

- when a stock option or purchase plan is to be established or materially amended,[264] subject to limited exceptions[265];

- when the issuance or potential issuance will result in a change of control of the issuer[266];

- in connection with the acquisition of the stock or assets of another company: (1) if any director, officer or substantial shareholder of the issuer has a 5 per cent or greater interest (or such persons collectively have a 10 per cent or greater interest), directly or indirectly, in the company or assets to be acquired or in the consideration to be paid in the transaction, and the issuance of securities could result in a 5 per cent or greater increase in outstanding common shares or voting power[267]; or (2) where, other than in a public offering for cash: (a) the common stock to be issued has or will have upon issuance voting power equal to 20 per cent or more of the voting power outstanding before the issuance of the stock or convertible securities; or (b) the number of shares of common stock to be issued is or will be 20 per cent or more of the number of shares of common stock outstanding before the issuance of the stock or convertible securities[268]; and

- in connection with a transaction other than a public offering involving the sale, issuance or potential issuance by the issuer of common stock (or securities convertible into or exercisable for common stock): (1) at a price less than the greater of book or market value which together with

---

[264] See *Nasdaq IM* 5635-1-para.2. "Material amendments" to an equity compensation arrangement include any material increase in the number of shares to be issued under the plan (other than to reflect a reorganisation, stock split, merger, spin-off or similar transaction), any material increase in benefits to participants, any material expansion of the class of participants eligible to participate in the plan and any expansion in the types of options or awards provided under the plan.

[265] See Nasdaq r.5635(c). The exceptions include: (1) warrants or rights issued generally to all security holders of the issuer or stock purchase plans available on equal terms to all security holders; (2) certain tax-qualified non-discriminatory employee benefit and parallel nonqualified excess plans; (3) plans or arrangements involving mergers or acquisitions, either when conversions, replacements or adjustments of outstanding options or other equity compensation awards are necessary to reflect the transaction, or when shares available under certain plans acquired in acquisitions or mergers are to be used for certain post-transaction grants; and (4) employment inducements to new employees. The items described under (2) and (4) above must be approved by the issuer's independent compensation committee or a majority of independent directors. See Nasdaq r.5635(c)(1)-(4).

[266] See Nasdaq r.5635(b).

[267] See Nasdaq r.5635(a)(2).

[268] See Nasdaq r.5635(a)(1)(A-B).

sales by certain affiliates of the issuer equals 20 per cent or more of the common stock or voting power outstanding before the issuance[269]; or (2) equal to 20 per cent or more of the common stock or voting power outstanding before the issuance for less than the greater of book or market value of the stock.[270]

An exception may be made upon application to Nasdaq when a delay in securing stockholder approval would seriously jeopardise the financial viability of the enterprise and the audit committee (or other comparable body) expressly approves reliance on this exception.[271]

Only shares actually issued and outstanding (excluding treasury shares or shares held by a subsidiary) are to be used for any calculation under the shareholder approval requirement. Shareholder approval must be obtained prior to the issuance of certain private financing instruments generally in the form of convertible securities under which the number of shares that will be issued is uncertain until the conversion occurs, unless the instrument contains certain features (potentially a cap on the number of shares that can be issued upon conversion or a floor on the conversion price) and the issuance will not result in a change of control.[272]

Shareholder approval is not required for a public offering. Generally, any securities offering registered with the SEC and which is publicly disclosed and distributed in the same general manner and extent as a firm commitment underwritten securities offering will be considered a public offering for purposes of the shareholder approval rules.[273]

Listing agreement

24.086   An issuer must execute a listing agreement in the form designated by Nasdaq.[274]

Auditor registration

24.087   An issuer must be audited by an independent public accountant that is registered as a public accounting firm with the PCAOB, as provided for in s.102 of the Sarbanes-Oxley Act.[275]

---

[269] See Nasdaq r.5635(d)(1).
[270] See Nasdaq r.5635(d)(2).
[271] See Nasdaq r.5635(f).
[272] See Nasdaq r.5635(e)(1); see also *Nasdaq IM* 5635-1.
[273] See *Nasdaq IM* 5635-3.
[274] See Nasdaq r.5205(a).
[275] See Nasdaq r.5210(b); see also 15 USC § 7212.

Code of conduct

An issuer must adopt a code of conduct applicable to all directors, officers **24.088** and employees and make it publicly available. A code of conduct satisfying this requirement must comply with the definition of a *code of ethics* set out in s.406(c) of the Sarbanes-Oxley Act and any regulations promulgated thereunder. Also, the code must provide for an enforcement mechanism. Any waivers of the code for directors or executive officers must be approved by the issuer's board and must be disclosed on a Form 8-K (or Form 6-K for foreign private issuers).[276]

Notification of non-compliance

An issuer must provide Nasdaq with prompt notification after an executive **24.089** officer of the issuer becomes aware of material non-compliance by the issuer of the corporate governance standards required by the Nasdaq rules.[277]

Annual corporate governance certification

An issuer must make an annual certification regarding various aspects of **24.090** corporate governance, in a form prescribed by Nasdaq.[278]

Nasdaq communication and notification requirements

Except in "unusual circumstances", Nasdaq requires an issuer to make **24.091** prompt disclosure to the public through any Regulation FD-compliant method of disclosure of material information that would reasonably be expected to affect the value of its securities or influence investors' decisions.[279]

The issuer must notify Nasdaq prior to the release of certain types of information (and should make that notification at least 10 minutes prior to the release), including:

- financial-related disclosure (including earnings releases and restatements);

- corporate reorganisations and acquisitions;

---

[276] See Nasdaq r.5610.
[277] See Nasdaq r.5625.
[278] See generally Nasdaq r.5600.
[279] See Nasdaq r.5250(b)(1).

- new products or discoveries, or developments regarding customers or suppliers;

- material senior management changes or a change in control;

- resignation or termination of independent auditors, or withdrawal of a previously issued audit report;

- events regarding its securities (e.g. defaults on senior securities, calls for securities redemption, re-purchase plans, stock splits or changes in dividends, changes to the right of security holders, or public or private sales of additional securities);

- significant legal or regulatory developments; and

- any event requiring the filing of a Form 8-K.[280]

An issuer (other than an issuer of ADRs) must notify Nasdaq on the appropriate form not later than 15 calendar days prior to certain events, including:

- establishing or materially amending a stock option plan, purchase plan or other equity compensation arrangement pursuant to which stock may be acquired by officers, directors, employees or consultants without shareholder approval[281];

- issuing securities that may result in a change of control of the issuer[282];

- issuing any common stock (or security convertible into common stock) in connection with the acquisition of another company, if an officer, director or substantial shareholder of the issuer has a 5 per cent or greater interest in the company to be acquired[283]; or

- entering into a transaction that may result in the potential issuance of common stock (or securities convertible into common stock) greater than 10 per cent of either total shares outstanding or the voting power outstanding on a pre-transaction basis.[284]

An issuer must also file a form prescribed by Nasdaq, within 10 days after any increase or decrease of any class of shares included in Nasdaq that exceeds 5 per cent of the amount of securities of the class outstanding.[285]

---

[280] See *Nasdaq IM* 5250-1.
[281] See Nasdaq r.5250(e)(2)(A).
[282] See Nasdaq r.5250(e)(2)(B).
[283] See Nasdaq r.5250(e)(2)(C).
[284] See Nasdaq r.5250(e)(2)(D).
[285] See Nasdaq r.5250(e)(1).

Corporate governance requirements for foreign private issuers

A listed foreign private issuer is permitted to follow home country practice **24.092** in lieu of Nasdaq's corporate governance standards, other than the Nasdaq's requirements that it must[286]:

- execute a listing agreement in the form designated by Nasdaq[287];

- provide Nasdaq with notification of material non-compliance by the issuer with its Nasdaq corporate governance requirements[288]; and

- have an audit committee that meets the requirements (including independence requirements) of Exchange Act r.10A-3.[289]

A listed foreign private issuer that follows home country practice in lieu of the Nasdaq corporate governance requirements must disclose in its annual report on Form 20-F each requirement which it does not follow and describe the home country practice followed by it in lieu of such requirements.[290] In addition, a foreign private issuer making its initial public offering or first listing on Nasdaq must make the same disclosure in its registration statement.[291]

---

[286] See Nasdaq r.5615(a)(3).
[287] See Nasdaq r.5205(a).
[288] See Nasdaq r.5625.
[289] See Nasdaq rr.5605(c)(3), (c)(2)(A).
[290] See Nasdaq r.5255(c).
[291] See Nasdaq r.5255(c).

Chapter 25

Governance of Banks and Other Financial Industry Entities (BOFIs)

Introduction

The author of this work is not a specialist in the financial sector and at **25.001** the latest practicable time prior to publication issues of governance in the financial sector are still somewhat in flux,[1] but even so it is possible and desirable to summarise briefly the principal features of the likely short to medium-term governance regime in this sector in so far as it differs from the mainstream governance regime for UK Premium listed companies described in this book.

The 2007/2009 banking crisis[2]

The mnemonic "BOFI" was invented by Sir David Walker in 2009 in his **25.002** "review of corporate governance in UK banks and other financial industry entities".[3]

As is by now well known, in the years 2007 to 2009 the US and British banking systems suffered a collective nervous breakdown. In both countries banks had both financed and brought onto their balance sheets hundreds of billions worth of mortgages and derivatives based on so-called "sub-prime" borrowers and houses: that is to say, borrowers of uncertain earnings to whom the banks had lent large multiples of "self-certified" earnings in order to finance mortgages often over 100 per cent of the value of houses whose

---

[1] The FSA's rules relating to the vetting and monitoring of directors of BOFIs.
[2] See also OECD: *The Corporate Governance Lessons from the Financial Crisis*, February 2009 (at *http://www.oecd.org/dataoecd/32/1/42229620.pdf*) and *Corporate Governance and the Financial Crisis: Key Findings and Main Messages*, June 2009 (at *http://www.oecd.org/dataoecd/3/10/43056196.pdf*).
[3] *"A review of corporate governance in UK banks and other financial industry entities"*, November 26, 2009, *http://www.hm-treasury.gov.uk/walker_review_information.htm*.

values had plunged overnight. These derivatives and other financial products based on sub-prime financing were quickly dubbed "toxic assets" because of their poisonous effects on the balance sheets of US and UK banks.

In the UK the Northern Rock Bank was brought into public ownership in February 2008 in order to stop a full scale run on the bank.

In October 2008 the Government effectively took control of a number of large UK banks by injecting £37 billion of new equity capital into Royal Bank of Scotland Group Plc ("RBS"), Lloyds TSB and HBOS Plc, in order to avert the collapse of these banks. The Government stressed, however, that it was not "standard public ownership" and that the banks would return to private investors "at the right time".

The iconic "villain" of those times was Sir Fred Goodwin, chief executive of RBS, who was cast as the architect of the bank's downfall and required to resign shortly before the announcement by RBS in November 2008 of the then largest corporate loss in British history of £24.1 billion. Sir Fred's early retirement on an annual pension of £700,000 (subsequently reduced to £340,000 p.a.) caused a national outcry.

The crisis caused many to think that the governance of financial institutions had failed and that yet again destruction of shareholder value on a huge scale to say nothing of the disastrous impact on the UK economy had occurred as a result of over-powerful chief executives and weak non-executive directors. In addition a "bonus culture" existed whereby employees of financial institutions were paid grotesque bonuses regardless of long-term performance as rewards for unmeasured risk taking. It was also said that the chief regulatory body for the financial sector, the Financial Services Authority ("FSA"), had failed to spot the danger signs and rein in the financial institutions.

The Government therefore in February 2009 asked Sir David Walker to conduct a review into the corporate governance of UK banks and other financial industry entities (using the mnemonic of "BOFIs") and the final recommendations of the review were published in November 2009. At the same time the Financial Reporting Council ("FRC") announced a review of the Combined Code.

The Walker Review found that the necessary element of boardroom challenge to chief executives was absent in many BOFIs: it was a behavioural issue, not something which could be dealt with by more prescription. Moreover, the "bonus culture" had resulted in a complete lack of reference to the long-term measurement of success.

There were also a series of interventions by the Treasury minister Lord Myners during 2009 ranging from boardroom reform (compulsory seminars, greater diversity, professional "devil's advocates" on boards and technical specialists to guide audit committees) to radical ideas to encourage greater shareholder activism including giving long-term shareholders double voting rights; and the proposal that the Takeover Code should be extended to require the bidder company to set out the risks and rewards it expects its own shareholders to be affected by following a proposed takeover.

Other suggestions were that annual general meeting ("AGM") votes approving the annual accounts and the appointment of directors should comprise an actual majority of the total votes able to be cast and not just those voting at the meeting: it being argued that this would really require the engagement of shareholders.

The Walker Review of corporate governance in UK banks and other financial industry entities

The outcomes of the Walker Review were threefold: **25.003**

(1)   The review itself (November 2009) which contained 39 recommendations;

(2)   a revised code of corporate governance for the UK (the UK Corporate Governance Code, June 2010) which was produced by the FRC and substituted for the former Combined Code with effect for financial years beginning on or after June 29, 2010. This book deals with the UK Code in detail throughout;

(3)   a set of proposals from the FSA to be converted into rules and policy statements for the financial sector called "Effective corporate governance".[4]

The Walker Review recommendations

The 39 recommendations may be found in the Walker Review on the HM   **25.004**
Treasury website.[5] The main points are:

• non-executive directors of major banks should commit 30 to 36 days each year to their role;

• the chairman of a major bank should commit two thirds of his or her time to the role;

• the chairman of a BOFI should be elected annually;

• institutional shareholders should sign up to a "stewardship code"[6];

---

[4] This is the title of the Consultation Paper published by the FSA in January 2010 (CP 10/3) *http://www.fsa.gov.uk/pubs/cp/cp10_03.pdf.* The objective was stated of producing final rules in a Policy Statement ("PS") in the third quarter of 2010: too late for inclusion in this edition but of course which may be accessed on the FSA website.
[5] p.14 et seq. *http://www.hm-treasury.gove.uk/d/walker_review_261109.pdf.*
[6] See the July 2010 UK Stewardship Code: *http://www.frc.org.uk.*

- FTSE 100 listed banks and life insurance companies should have a separate board risk committee;

- a chief risk officer should be appointed to report directly to the off the board;

- FTSE 100 listed banks and comparable unlisted entities must disclose, by numbers within bands, the remuneration of employees earning over £1 million; and

- if the remuneration report is approved by fewer than 75 per cent of the votes cast, the chairman of the remuneration committee must stand for re-election the following year.

Above all, however, Sir David Walker pleaded for higher standards from chairmen. It was essential in his view that "behavioural" attitudes in boards be improved so that an atmosphere of constructive challenge to the executives could be fostered:

"It will accordingly be a high priority for a chairman to ensure that there is open debate and challenge within both the executive team and the whole board, which should not be dominated by a single voice."[7]

"The pressure for conformity on boards can be strong, generating corresponding difficulty for an individual board member who wishes to challenge group thinking. Such challenge on substantive policy issues can be seen as disruptive, non-collegial and even as disloyal. Yet, without it, there can be an illusion of unanimity in a board, with silence assumed to be acquiescence. The potential tensions here are likely to be greater the larger the board size, so that an individual who wishes to question or challenge is at greater risk of feeling and, indeed, of being isolated."[8]

Recommendation 9 of the Walker Review states:

"The chairman should facilitate, encourage and expect the informed and critical contribution of the directors in particular in discussion and decision taking on matters of risk and strategy and to promote effective communication between the executive and non-executive directors."

This recommendation appears in modified form in the UK Code as part of Supporting Principle A.3 (the chairman).

[7] para.3.5 Walker Review.
[8] para.4.3 Walker Review.

The UK Corporate Governance Code ("the Code")

The Code was published in June 2009 to take effect in respect of financial years **25.005** commencing on and after June 29, 2010. The Code applies to all "Premium" listed companies in the manner explained in Ch.2 (The Regulatory Regime) of this book. Accordingly, it follows that the Code applies both to BOFIs and non-BOFIs. The view was taken by the FRC that the recommendations in the Walker Review should be reflected in the Code only to the extent that they had general application, and in the context of a wider review and consultation exercise carried out by the FRC in 2009. The FRC further took the view that it was up to the FSA to regulate in respect of the BOFI specific recommendations of the Walker Review.[9]

The principal "Walker" features of the Code are:

- the increased emphasis in the Code on the role of the chairman in ensuring adequate time for discussion on strategic issues and promoting a culture of openness and debate (for example, see Supporting Principle A.3 (the chairman);

- the increased emphasis in the Code on the responsibilities of non-executive directors to "constructively challenge" (see, for example, new Main Principle A.4 (non-executive directors));

- the increased emphasis in the Code on directors having an appropriate balance of skills, experience, independence and knowledge of the company (for example new Main Principle B.1 (the composition of the board));

- external evaluation of the board at least every three years (Provision B.6.2);

- the boards of FTSE 350 companies should be subject to annual election by shareholders (Provision B.7.1);

- the provision that directors should include in the annual report an explanation of the basis on which the company generates revenues and makes a profit from its operations and its overall financial strategy (Provision C.1.2);

- the responsibility of the board, as distinct from individuals or committees, for defining the company's risk appetite and tolerance (Main Principle C.2 (risk management and internal control));

- the removal of Section 2 (institutional shareholders) from the Combined Code in order to reflect the intention that a separate "Stewardship Code" for institutional investors be introduced during 2010 by the FRC.[10]

---

[9] See further para.25.006 below.
[10] See fn 6 above.

The FSA proposals on "Effective Corporate Governance (significant influence controlled functions and the Walker Review)"[11]

25.006 The proposals were set out in a Consultation Paper in January 2010 (see CP 10/03). The paper put forward a necessarily disparate set of proposals to reflect a wide ranging response to the banking crisis. The proposals were to be reflected:

(a) in a revised FSA Handbook;

(b) in a Policy Statement and Rules to be published in the third quarter of 2010;

(c) minor consequential amendments to the Listing Rules Sourcebook mainly to reflect the changed name of the Combined Code.

The scope of the proposals was as follows:

- a new framework of classification of controlled functions (Ch.2);

- other changes to the approved persons regime, including the scope and definition of some controlled functions (Ch.3);

- some guidance on the FSA's expectations in relation to non-executive directors (Ch.5); and

- risk governance guidance and the FSA's plans for other implementing measures in support of the Walker recommendations (Ch.6);

- The FSA also took the opportunity to provide more information on its "Significant Influence Function" ("SIF") process (Ch.4).

In general, the proposals made it clear that the FSA intended to significantly enhance the level of governance supervision and monitoring of companies and directors and senior executives in the financial sector.

"In evaluating the quality of governance, we will look closely at:

- the practical effectiveness of board, management and organisational structures including shareholder relationships, particularly looking for evidence of depth of understanding and effective discussion, challenge and risk-based decision making in practice;

---

[11] CP 10/03, January 2010; *http://www.fsa.gov.uk/pubs/cp/cp10_03.pdf.* It was expected that the proposals in this CP would be converted into a Policy Statement and Rules "in the third quarter of 2010": regrettably too late to be included in this book. The Coalition Government has launched a consultation (closed October 18, 2010) to reform the FSA which will entail many of its functions being transferred under the control of the Bank of England. See *www.hm-treasury. gov.uk* for the up-to-date position.

- the formulation of strategy and determination of risk appetite and the subsequent monitoring of performance against strategy/appetite, including the role of the key control functions;
- the quality of reporting and analysis of management information and reporting to the board and evidence that it is understood and gives rise to feedback and actions; and
- the key factors, such as incentives and culture, which support and enable robust governance, building on the work already taking place to verify compliance with the FSA's new code of remuneration practice."[12]

Risk oversight and management

In CP 10/03, Ch.6 the FSA considered the issues of risk oversight[13]:   **25.007**

"Sir David Walker has placed particular emphasis, as do we, on the central role of the governing body, or board of directors, of a firm in ensuring that risk is properly managed within a financial services firm. We fully agree with his view that boards must take appropriate steps to ensure that, in addition to the necessary review of the quality and effectiveness of internal controls in their firm, the overall risk appetite of the firm is clearly articulated and its future strategy appropriately aligned with that risk appetite. Sir David has described how the scale of work required to deliver the necessary level of active oversight of risk in larger and more complex firms, means that some boards will need to delegate the detail of this work to a sub-committee established for that purpose. This committee would be charged with advising the board on high-level issues about current risk exposures and future risk strategy. We agree with Sir David's analysis and propose to include guidance on the need for firms—in particular FTSE 100-listed banks and insurers—to consider the value of establishing such a committee. As indicated elsewhere in this consultation, we consider the role of chair of this committee to be of such significance to the quality of risk governance in the firm that it merits identification as a specific controlled function.

Similarly, we have long stressed the importance to regulated firms of an effective and independent risk oversight function ('second line of defence'). We agree with Sir David that boards should, where possible, ensure that one individual is appointed within the executive to be accountable to them on risk issues. The board should be able to look to this person for advice on the subject of risk, so we are proposing to give guidance on the need for some firms to appoint a chief risk officer (CRO). This senior executive will

---

[12] para.6.12 CP 10/03.
[13] para.6.24 CP 10/03.

play a pivotal role in ensuring that the board receives balanced and accessible information and advice on high-level risk issues."

Accordingly, the FSA proposed in CP 10/03 to implement the Walker recommendations 23 to 26 regarding the appointment of chief risk officers ("CRO") and board risk committees to FTSE 100 banks and other relevant entities through guidance in the FSA's High Level Systems and Controls Sourcebook (SYSC).

The SYSC guidance on CRO's is said by the FSA to reflect Walker recommendations in relation to:

- the primacy of the CRO's accountability to the board, underpinned by adequate seniority in the executive hierarchy;

- the CRO's need for independence, access and resources;

- the CRO's responsibility for delivering and advice to the board on enterprise-wide risk management issues; and

- the provision of independent challenge to the executive on matters relating to risk, particularly in relation to strategic proposals, and including the risks in the business capital and liquidity strategies.

In addition the FSA identified the need for the CRO to oversee the quality of risk data used within a firm, to ensure that it is reliable and sufficient in the depth and scope, and to validate the firm's external disclosures on risk.

A new framework of classification of significant influence controlled functions

25.008   Under the Financial Services and Markets Act ("FSMA") the FSA have powers to regulate two types of individuals—those who have a significant influence on the conduct of the firm's affairs ("SIFs") and those who deal with customers (or the property of customers).

The FSA created the "significant influence controlled functions" to capture those individuals who in the opinion of the FSA, exercised a "significant influence" on a firm ("SIFs"). Both the governing body and senior management of firms have a crucial role to play in ensuring that effective governance structures, systems and controls are developed and operate well.

"Without the right behaviours and competence on the part of those who govern and manage firms, the establishment of sound governance structures will not succeed fully in ensuring that firms are well run."[14]

---

[14] para.2.2 CP 10/03.

The FSA proposed in CP 10/3 a number of new, more specific, controlled functions capturing key roles in organisations. These are:

- chairman;
- chairman of risk committee;
- chairman of audit committee;
- chairman of remuneration committee;
- senior independent director;
- parent entity SIF;
- finance function;
- risk function;
- internal audit function.

In future the FSA will monitor the appointment and conduct of these individuals more closely.

Non-executive directors-commitment and performance required under threat of sanction

CP 10/03, Ch.5 sets out the FSA's view of the commitment in time and performance required of non-executive directors.   **25.009**

> "5.The commitment of NEDs and Chairpersons
> 5.1 The Walker Review recommended that the overall time commitment of NEDs as a group on a FTSE 100-listed bank or life assurance company board should be greater than has been normal in the past. Sir David Walker recognised that how this is achieved in particular board situations will depend on the composition of the NED group on the board. However, he recommended that for several NEDs, a minimum expected time commitment of 30 to 36 days in a major bank board should be clearly indicated in letters of appointment and will in some cases limit the capacity of an individual NED to retain or assume board responsibilities elsewhere. He also recommended that for any prospective director where so substantial a time commitment is not envisaged, the letter of appointment should specify the time commitment agreed between the individual and the board.
>
> 5.2 We agree that the level of commitment required for the chairmen and NEDs of major firms is substantial, and consider that the capacity to deliver it is relevant to an individual's capability to perform these

controlled functions. We therefore propose to make clear in our guidance on the 'fit and proper' test for approved persons that in assessing an individual's capability, we may have regard to the extent to which they are capable of meeting the level of time commitment that the firm has specified in its contractual terms of appointment for the role. It will be for the firm and individual, as part of the application for approval, to demonstrate they have given due consideration to the amount of time required for the role, and that the individual has the capacity to deliver it. In relation to NEDs and chairpersons, we would expect a firm to have taken into account any time individuals have committed to other roles and activities, including other NED positions held at other companies, when considering whether the individual is capable of undertaking the proposed role.

5.3 Our key message remains that NEDs have a pivotal role to play in the active governance of firms. Where it appears to us that executives have persistently made poor decisions, we will look closely at NEDs' performance if we feel they have not intervened in a timely and sufficient way. Consistent with this message, we propose to delete current guidance in the Handbook that discusses the limits of NED liability.[15] While it is not our intention to take disciplinary action against a NED (or any other approved person) for matters that clearly fall outside the scope of their responsibilities, we believe those responsibilities are broad. We are concerned that the existing guidance could be misinterpreted and taken to mean that we would not hold NEDs responsible for, for example, failing to intervene and challenge the executive. This is not the case, as we see such challenge and intervention as a key part of any NED's responsibilities."

The EU and Basel

25.010   The European Commission issued in June 2010 a Green Paper on corporate governance for financial institutions, and the so-called "Basel Committee" on banking supervision has consulted widely with a view to producing new capital adequacy rules. A fuller discussion on these measures is set out in paras 23.013 et seq. in Ch.23 (The EU).

---

[15] This reference to safe harbours and their removal caused disquiet to be expressed by the ABI that it would discourage non-executive directors from coming forward (See *Financial Times* April 16: Companies and Markets section), and it is not known as at the latest practicable date prior to publication if in fact the FSA's approach has been modified and reference will need to be made to the finally published FSA PS on governance and corresponding Rules.

Conclusion

This summary of the governance regime as it affects the financial sector has **25.011** been merely a brief overview: the topic requires a handbook in order to deal with it adequately.

However, it is hoped that the interested enquirer will have gained an insight into the sources of the rules dealing with the governance of the sector and the general direction of travel of those rules. There is no doubt that the FSA (or its successor) will be expected by Government to play a much more intrusive role in monitoring the quality and performance of directors and senior executives both prior to and during their appointments, and anecdotal evidence suggests that a rigorous approach to these individuals is already being adopted by the FSA.

Appendices Contents

Appendix 1

The UK Corporate Governance Code[1]

The full text as amended from time to time can be found on the FRC website at:
http://www.frc.org.uk> UK Corporate Governance Code

The full text, however, of the excellent Corporate Governance Disclosure arrangements set out in Schedule B of the Code is here reprinted in full as a helpful digest of the relationship between the Disclosure and Transparency Rules and the Listing Rules and the Code itself.

SCHEDULE B: DISCLOSURE OF CORPORATE GOVERNANCE ARRANGEMENTS

Corporate governance disclosure requirements are set out in three places:

- FSA Disclosure and Transparency Rules sub-chapters 7.1 and 7.2 (which set out certain mandatory disclosures);

- FSA Listing Rules 9.8.6 R, 9.8.7 R, and 9.8.7A R (which includes the 'comply or explain' requirement); and

- The UK Corporate Governance Code (in addition to providing an explanation where they choose not to comply with a provision, companies must disclose specified information in order to comply with certain provisions).

These requirements are summarised below. The full text of Disclosure and Transparency Rules 7.1 and 7.2 and Listing Rules 9.8.6 R, 9.8.7 R, 9.8.7A R are contained in the relevant chapters of the FSA Handbook, which can be found at http://fsahandbook.info/FSA/html/handbook/.

The Disclosure and Transparency Rules sub-chapters 7.1 and 7.2 apply to issuers whose securities are admitted to trading on a regulated market (this includes all issuers with a Premium or Standard listing[2]). The Listing Rules 9.8.6 R, 9.8.7 R and 9.8.7A R and UK Corporate Governance Code apply to issuers of Premium listed equity shares only.

---

[1] © Financial Reporting Council (FRC). Adapted and reproduced with the kind permission of the Financial Reporting Council. All rights reserved. For further information please visit *http://www.frc.org.uk* or call +44 (0)20 7492 2300.
[2] See Ch.2 (The Regulatory Regime) of this book for explanation of these terms.

There is some overlap between the mandatory disclosures required under the Disclosure and Transparency Rules and those expected under the UK Corporate Governance Code. Areas of overlap are summarised in the Appendix to this Schedule. In respect of disclosures relating to the audit committee and the composition and operation of the board and its committees, compliance with the relevant provisions of the Code will result in compliance with the relevant Rules.

Disclosure and Transparency Rules

Sub-chapter 7.1 of the Disclosure and Transparency Rules concerns audit committees or bodies carrying out equivalent functions.

DTR 7.1.1 R to 7.1.3 R set out requirements relating to the composition and functions of the committee or equivalent body:

- DTR 7.1.1 R states than an issuer must have a body which is responsible for performing the functions set out in DTR 7.1.3 R, and that at least one member of that body must be independent and at least one member must have competence in accounting and/or auditing.

- DTR 7.1.2 G states that the requirements for independence and competence in accounting and/or auditing may be satisfied by the same member or by different members of the relevant body.

- DTR 7.1.3 R states that an issuer must ensure that, as a minimum, the relevant body must:

  (1) monitor the financial reporting process;

  (2) monitor the effectiveness of the issuer's internal control, internal audit where applicable, and risk management systems;

  (3) monitor the statutory audit of the annual and consolidated accounts;

  (4) review and monitor the independence of the statutory auditor, and in particular the provision of additional services to the issuer.

DTR 7.1.5 R to DTR 7.1.7 G set out what disclosure is required. Specifically:

- DTR 7.1.5 R states that the issuer must make a statement available to the public disclosing which body carries out the functions required by DTR 7.1.3 R and how it is composed.

- DTR 7.1.6 G states that this can be included in the corporate governance statement required under sub-chapter DTR 7.2 (see below).

- DTR 7.1.7 G states that compliance with the relevant provisions of the UK Corporate Governance Code (as set out in the Appendix to this Schedule) will result in compliance with DTR 7.1.1 R to 7.1.5 R.

Sub-chapter 7.2 concerns corporate governance statements. Issuers are required to produce a corporate governance statement that must be either included in the directors' report (DTR 7.2.1 R); or in a separate report published together with the annual report; or on the issuer's website, in which case there must be a cross-reference in the directors' report (DTR 7.2.9 R).

DTR 7.2.2 R requires that the corporate governance statements must contain a reference to the corporate governance code to which the company is subject (for companies with a Premium listing this is the UK Corporate Governance Code). DTR 7.2.3 R requires that, to the extent that it departs from that code, the company must explain which parts of the code it departs from and the reasons for doing so. DTR 7.2.4 G states that compliance with LR 9.8.6 R (6) (the 'comply or explain' rule in relation to the UK Corporate Governance Code) will also satisfy these requirements.

DTR 7.2.5 R to DTR 7.2.10 R set out certain information that must be disclosed in the corporate governance statement:

- DTR 7.2.5 R states that the corporate governance statement must contain a description of the main features of the company's internal control and risk management systems in relation to the financial reporting process. DTR 7.2.10 R states that an issuer which is required to prepare a group directors' report within the meaning of Section 415(2) of the Companies Act 2006 must include in that report a description of the main features of the group's internal control and risk management systems in relation to the process for preparing consolidated accounts.

- DTR 7.2.6 R states that the corporate governance statement must contain the information required by paragraph 13(2)(c), (d), (f), (h) and (i) of Schedule 7 to the Large and Medium-sized Companies and Groups (Accounts and Reports) Regulations 2008 where the issuer is subject to the requirements of that paragraph.

- DTR 7.2.7 R states that the corporate governance statement must contain a description of the composition and operation of the issuer's administrative, management and supervisory bodies and their committees. DTR 7.2.8 G states that compliance with the relevant provisions of the UK Corporate Governance Code (as set out in the Appendix to this Schedule) will satisfy these requirements.

Listing Rules

Listing Rules 9.8.6 R (for UK incorporated companies) and 9.8.7 R (for overseas incorporated companies) state that in the case of a company that has a Premium listing of equity shares, the following items must be included in its annual report and accounts:

- a statement of how the listed company has applied the Main Principles set out in the UK Corporate Governance Code, in a manner that would enable shareholders to evaluate how the principles have been applied;

- a statement as to whether the listed company has:
  - complied throughout the accounting period with all relevant provisions set out in the UK Corporate Governance Code; or
  - not complied throughout the accounting period with all relevant provisions set out in the UK Corporate Governance Code, and if so, setting out:

(i) those provisions, if any, it has not complied with;

(ii) in the case of provisions whose requirements are of a continuing nature, the period within which, if any, it did not comply with some or all of those provisions; and

(iii) the company's reasons for non-compliance.

The UK Corporate Governance Code

In addition to the 'comply or explain' requirement in the Listing Rules, the Code includes specific requirements for disclosure which must be provided in order to comply. These are summarised below.

The annual report should include:

- a statement of how the board operates, including a high level statement of which types of decisions are to be taken by the board and which are to be delegated to management (A.1.1);

- the names of the chairman, the deputy chairman (where there is one), the chief executive, the senior independent director and the chairmen and members of the board committees (A.1.2);

- the number of meetings of the board and those committees and individual attendance by directors (A.1.2);

- where a chief executive is appointed chairman, the reasons for their appointment (this only needs to be done in the annual report following the appointment) (A.3.1);

- the names of the non-executive directors whom the board determines to be independent, with reasons where necessary (B.1.1);

- a separate section describing the work of the nomination committee, including the process it has used in relation to board appointments and an explanation if neither external search consultancy nor open advertising has been used in the appointment of a chairman or a non-executive director (B.2.4);

- any changes to the other significant commitments of the chairman during the year (B.3.1);

- a statement of how performance evaluation of the board, its committees and its directors has been conducted (B.6.1);

- an explanation from the directors of their responsibility for preparing the accounts and a statement by the auditors about their reporting responsibilities (C.1.1);

- an explanation from the directors of the basis on which the company generates or preserves value over the longer term (the business model) and the strategy for delivering the objectives of the company (C.1.2);

- a statement from the directors that the business is a going concern, with supporting assumptions or qualifications as necessary (C.1.3);

- a report that the board has conducted a review of the effectiveness of the company's risk management and internal controls systems (C.2.1);

- a separate section describing the work of the audit committee in discharging its responsibilities (C.3.3);

- where there is no internal audit function, the reasons for the absence of such a function (C.3.5);

- where the board does not accept the audit committee's recommendation on the appointment, reappointment or removal of an external auditor, a statement from the audit committee explaining the recommendation and the reasons why the board has taken a different position (C.3.6);

- an explanation of how, if the auditor provides non-audit services, auditor objectivity and independence is safeguarded (C.3.7);

- a description of the work of the remuneration committee as required under the Large and Medium-Sized Companies and Groups (Accounts and Reports) Regulations 2008 including, where an executive director serves as a non-executive director elsewhere, whether or not the director will retain such earnings and, if so, what the remuneration is (D.1.2);

- the steps the board has taken to ensure that members of the board, in particular the non-executive directors, develop an understanding of the views of major shareholders about their company (E.1.2).

The following information should be made available (which may be met by placing the information on a website that is maintained by or on behalf of the company):

- the terms of reference of the nomination, audit and remuneration committees, explaining their role and the authority delegated to them by the board (B.2.1, C.3.3 and D.2.1);

- the terms and conditions of appointment of non-executive directors (B.3.2) (see footnote 9);

- where performance evaluation has been externally facilitated, a statement of whether the facilitator has any other connection with the company (B.6.2); and

- where remuneration consultants are appointed, a statement of whether they have any other connection with the company (D.2.1).

The board should set out to shareholders in the papers accompanying a resolution to elect or re-elect directors:

- sufficient biographical details to enable shareholders to take an informed decision on their election or re-election (B.7.1);

- why they believe an individual should be elected to a non-executive role (B.7.2); and

- on re-election of a non-executive director, confirmation from the chairman that, following formal performance evaluation, the individual's performance

691

continues to be effective and to demonstrate commitment to the role (B.7.2).

The board should set out to shareholders in the papers recommending appointment or reappointment of an external auditor:

- if the board does not accept the audit committee's recommendation, a statement from the audit committee explaining the recommendation and from the board setting out reasons why they have taken a different position (C.3.6).

Additional guidance

The Turnbull Guidance and FRC Guidance on Audit Committees contain further suggestions as to information that might usefully be disclosed in the internal control statement and the report of the audit committee respectively. Both sets of guidance are available on the FRC website at:
http://www.frc.org.uk/corporate/ukcgcode.cfm

Appendix 2

The Higgs Review[1]

Extracts from the 2003 Higgs Review of the role and effectiveness of non-executive directors

Role of the board

The board is collectively responsible for promoting the success of the company by directing and supervising the company's affairs.

The board's role is to provide entrepreneurial leadership of the company within a framework of prudent and effective controls which enable risk to be assessed and managed.

The board should set the company's strategic aims, ensure that the necessary financial and human resources are in place for the company to meet its objectives, and review management performance.

The board should set the company's values and standards and ensure that its obligations to its shareholders and others are understood and met.

(Suggested Code principle A.1 and provision A.1.1).

4.1   The role and the effectiveness of the non-executive director needs to be considered in the context of the board as a whole.

4.2   In the unitary board structure, executive and non-executive directors share responsibility for both the direction and control of the company. The benefit of the unitary board, strongly supported in consultation responses, is the value of executive knowledge within the board, alongside non-executive directors who can bring wider experience. Increasing the effectiveness of non-executive directors, while preserving the benefits of the unitary board, is a principal objective of the Review.

4.3   In contrast, the European system of corporate governance typically sepa-

---

[1] At the latest date prior to publication of this book the Institute of Chartered Secretaries and Administrators ("ICSA") is engaged in a consultation exercise to review the Higgs Review. Accordingly reference should be made to the ICSA website for up-to-date information and possible amendments to the Review: *http://www.icsa.org.uk*.

rates legal responsibility for running the company between a management and a supervisory board. In the US, the board is composed largely of non-executive ("outside") directors with only a few executives. Evidence collected during the Review has not convinced me of the merits of moving away from the unitary board structure in the UK.

4.4   In the UK, the general legal duties owed to the company by executive and non-executive directors are the same. All directors are required to act in the best interests of the company. Each has a role in ensuring the probity of the business and contributing to sustainable wealth creation by the company as a whole.

4.5   Included in the Companies White Paper[2] is a draft statutory statement of directors' duties to act, subject to the company's constitution, to promote the success of the company for the benefit of its shareholders as a whole. In determining how best to promote the success of the company, directors must where relevant take account of "material factors". As set out in the draft statutory statement, these include long as well as short term consequences of their actions, the need to foster business relationships, including with employees, suppliers and customers, impact on communities and the environment, business reputation and fairness between different shareholders.

4.6   The Code requires every listed company to be headed by an effective board which should lead and control the company. **I recommend that the Code should include more detailed provision on the board's role, building on the principle in the Companies White Paper proposals, as set out in the box at the beginning of this Chapter** (suggested Code provision A.1.1).

4.7   A greater understanding of how a board operates is likely to create greater confidence amongst shareholders and others in the leadership and governance of a company. Information on the number of board and committee meetings held, and on attendance by individual directors, is not routinely published by all companies and would help shareholders judge the extent of directors' participation.

4.8   Recognising that companies differ, both in the detailed role of the board and in the specific circumstances in which they operate, **I recommend that individual boards should publish in the annual report a statement describing how the board operates. This should include a high level statement of which decisions are taken by the board and those which are delegated to management** (suggested Code provision A.1.3). **The number of meetings of the board and of each of its established committees should be stated in the annual report, together with attendance by individual directors** (suggested Code provision A.1.2).

4.9   The board needs to be an effective decision-making body. Its size is an important factor. Several submissions expressed concern about

---

[2] "Modernising Company Law—Draft Clauses" (clause 19, schedule 2) published July 2002 TSO.

the effective functioning of boards that are excessively large or small. Currently, the average size of the board of a UK listed company is seven, comprising three executive and three non-executive directors and a chairman. A FTSE 100 board is generally bigger with an average of 12 members, of whom six are non-executive directors, five are executive directors and one is the chairman. Nearly half FTSE 100 boards have 12 or more members. The trend has been towards smaller boards which I welcome.

4.10 **An effective board should not be so large as to become unwieldy. It should be of sufficient size that the balance of skills and experience is appropriate for the requirement of the business and that changes in the board's composition can be managed without undue disruption** (suggested Code provision A.3.1).

4.11 Board membership and the conditions that help foster an effective board are discussed in Chapter 8.

Role of the chairman

The chairman is responsible for:

- leadership of the board, ensuring its effectiveness on all aspects of its role and setting its agenda;

- ensuring the provision of accurate, timely and clear information to directors;

- ensuring effective communication with shareholders;

- arranging the regular evaluation of the performance of the board, its committees and individual directors; and

- facilitating the effective contribution of non-executive directors and ensuring constructive relations between executive and non-executive directors.

(Suggested Code provisions A.2.5 and A.6.1).

5.1 The chairman is pivotal in creating the conditions for overall board and individual non-executive director effectiveness, both inside and outside the boardroom. I therefore examine the role of the chairman before considering that of the non-executive director. The particular nature of the chairman's role will inevitably be shaped by the challenges facing the company, its scale and complexity and the nature of its business. The role differs significantly from that of other non-executive and executive directors.

5.2 The chairman has the responsibility of leading the board in setting the values and standards of the company and of maintaining a relationship of trust with and between the executive and non-executive members. The Code already recognises the distinction between this role and that of the chief executive, whose task is to run the business under delegated authority from the board and to implement the policies and strategy set by the board. The Code currently requires public justification if the two roles are combined in one person.

5.3 There is already a high level of compliance with the Code's provision to separate the roles of chairman and chief executive, recommended by Cadbury a decade ago. Around 90 per cent of listed companies now split these roles. Separation of the roles of chairman and chief executive is one of the strengths of the UK corporate governance regime. It avoids concentration of authority and power in one individual and differentiates leadership of the board from running of the business. The benefits envisaged by Cadbury are now widely acknowledged. **I therefore propose that the Code contain a straightforward statement that the roles of chairman and chief executive should be separated** (suggested Code provision A.2.1).

5.4 A strong relationship between the chairman and chief executive lies at the heart of an effective board. As set out in the research conducted for the Review, the relationship works best where there is a valuable mix of different skills and experiences which complement each other. The chairman should not seek executive responsibility and should let the chief executive take credit for their achievements. The chairman can be an informed, experienced and trusted partner, the source of counsel and challenge designed to support the chief executive's performance, without becoming an obstacle to questioning of the chief executive by the non-executive directors. The separation of roles can contribute to the greater achievement of the chief executive as well as being important in creating the conditions for effective performance by the non-executive directors.

5.5 **The division of responsibilities between the chairman and chief executive should be set out in writing and agreed by the board** (suggested Code provision A.2.1).

5.6 My research also highlighted the potential difficulties of the chairman being a former chief executive of the same company. Having been responsible for the day-to-day running of the company and with the detailed knowledge of it that this brings, such a chairman can sometimes find it difficult in practice to make room for a new chief executive. In addition, a chairman who was formerly the chief executive of the same company may simply take for granted their inside knowledge and fail as an informational bridge to the non-executive directors.

5.7 For these reasons, it is generally undesirable for the chief executive of a company to become chairman of its board. Over three-quarters of FTSE 100 companies currently have a chairman who was not formerly the chief executive. **I recommend that the Code should provide that a chief executive should not become chairman of the same company** (suggested Code provision A.2.3).

5.8 The chairman needs to foster relationships of trust with both the executive and non-executive directors on the board, whilst at the same time maintaining support for, and partnership with, the chief executive. A degree of detachment from the executive can also be valuable in ensuring objective debate on strategy and other matters. For these reasons my view is that **at the time of appointment the chairman should meet the test of independence** (suggested Code provision A.2.4). Chapter 9 explains in more detail the benefits independence can bring to the board.

5.9   Once appointed, the chairman will have a much greater degree of involvement with the executive team than the non-executive directors. Applying a test of independence at this stage is neither appropriate nor necessary.

5.10   A chairman who is not full-time is sometimes described as being a "non-executive chairman". This description is unhelpful. An effective chairman will spend as much time as needed to fulfil their role and is best described simply as "chairman". The title "executive chairman", on the other hand, connotes additional executive powers and should only be used consciously and in those circumstances, for example of temporary and unexpected transition between chief executives, where it is not possible to meet the relevant provisions of the Code for separation of the roles of chairman and chief executive.

5.11   The board agenda must take full account of the issues and concerns of all board members for the board to be effective. This is the chairman's responsibility. The chairman should also make efficient use of board time by ensuring that board agendas are forward looking and concentrate on strategy, rather than approving proposals which should be decided by management.

5.12   The chairman is responsible for managing the business of the board to ensure that sufficient time is allowed for discussion of complex or contentious issues and, where appropriate, arranging for informal meetings beforehand to enable thorough preparation for the board discussion. It is particularly important that non-executive directors have sufficient time to consider critical issues and are not faced with unrealistic deadlines for decision-making.

5.13   As the role of the chairman is so central to realising the potential of the unitary board, a number of respondents to the consultation requested further guidance on the role of the chairman. Annex D describes some of the attributes and behaviours of an effective chairman.

Role of the non-executive director

Strategy: Non-executive directors should constructively challenge and contribute to the development of strategy.

Performance: Non-executive directors should scrutinise the performance of management in meeting agreed goals and objectives and monitor the reporting of performance.

Risk: Non-executive directors should satisfy themselves that financial information is accurate and that financial controls and systems of risk management are robust and defensible.

People: Non-executive directors are responsible for determining appropriate levels of remuneration of executive directors and have a prime role in appointing, and where necessary removing, senior management and in succession planning.

(Suggested Code provision A.1.4).

6.1   The role of the non-executive director is frequently described as having two principal components: monitoring executive activity and contributing to the development of strategy. Both Cadbury and Hampel identified a tension between these two elements.

6.2   Research commissioned for the Review drew a somewhat different conclusion. Based on 40 in-depth interviews with directors, the research found that while there might be a tension, there was no essential contradiction between the monitoring and strategic aspects of the role of the non-executive director. Polarized conceptions of the role, the research noted, bear little relation to the actual conditions for non-executive effectiveness. An overemphasis on monitoring and control risks non-executive directors seeing themselves, and being seen, as an alien policing influence detached from the rest of the board. An overemphasis on strategy risks non-executive directors becoming too close to executive management, undermining shareholder confidence in the effectiveness of board governance.

6.3   The research concludes that it is important to establish a spirit of partnership and mutual respect on the unitary board. This requires the non-executive director to build recognition by executives of their contribution in order to promote openness and trust. Only then can non-executive directors contribute effectively. The key to non-executive director effectiveness lies as much in behaviours and relationships as in structures and processes.

6.4   The Code currently offers no guidance on the role of the non-executive director. The lack of clarity about the role has been a recurrent theme in submissions to the Review and in the interviews with directors. In part, this may be due to the tensions implicit in the role and uncertainty on how best to manage the various relationships. Companies of course differ, in terms of scale, diversity and complexity and in what they require from their boards. Nonetheless, consultation suggested that clarifying the core elements of the role would be helpful.

6.5   Executive and non-executive directors have the same general legal duties to the company. However, as the non-executive directors do not report to the chief executive and are not involved in the day-to-day running of the business, they can bring fresh perspective and contribute more objectively in supporting, as well as constructively challenging and monitoring, the management team.

6.6   Non-executive directors must constantly seek to establish and maintain their own confidence in the conduct of the company, in the performance of the management team, the development of strategy, the adequacy of financial controls and risk management, the appropriateness of remuneration and the appointment and replacement of key personnel and plans for management development and succession. The role of the non-executive director is therefore both to support executives in their leadership of the business and to monitor and supervise their conduct.

6.7   **I therefore propose that a description of the role of the non-executive director be incorporated into the Code as set out in the box at the beginning of this Chapter** (suggested Code provision A.1.4). This definition brings together the essential elements of the role identified in consultation responses and research.

6.8   In practice, non-executive directors will pursue some of their activities through their role on board committees. In smaller companies, non-executive directors may also often provide specific expertise or experience to complement that of the executive team which may be valuable in coaching and supporting management.

The behaviours and personal attributes of the effective non-executive director

6.9   The non-executive director role is complex and demanding and requires skills, experience, integrity, and particular behaviours and personal attributes.

6.10   Non-executive directors need to be sound in judgement and to have an inquiring mind. They should question intelligently, debate constructively, challenge rigorously and decide dispassionately. And they should listen sensitively to the views of others, inside and outside the board.

6.11   In order to fulfil their role, non-executive directors must acquire the expertise and knowledge necessary properly to discharge their responsibilities. They must be well-informed about the business, the environment in which it operates and the issues it faces. This requires a knowledge of the markets in which the company operates as well as a full understanding of the company itself. Understanding the company is essential to gain credibility and reduce the inevitable disparity in knowledge between executive and non-executive directors. Developing such knowledge cannot be done within the confines of the boardroom alone.

6.12   A number of consultation responses identified the personal attributes required of the effective non-executive director. They are founded on:

- integrity and high ethical standards;
- sound judgement;
- the ability and willingness to challenge and probe; and
- strong interpersonal skills.

6.13   First and foremost, integrity, probity and high ethical standards are a prerequisite for all directors.

6.14   Second, sound judgement is central to the non-executive director's role. This is essential for each of the elements of the non-executive director's role I have set out above.

6.15 Third, all non-executive directors must be able and willing to inquire and probe. They should have sufficient strength of character to seek and obtain full and satisfactory answers within the collegiate environment of the board. The objectivity and fresh perspective acquired through their relative distance from day-to-day matters, combined with experience acquired elsewhere, is the basis for questioning and challenging the accepted thinking of the executive.

6.16 Questioning does not only serve to raise specific concerns, it can also prompt stronger executive performance. Skilful questioning can be penetrating and demanding. The response can both reassure the non-executive director and stimulate reflections and actions that contribute to more effective executive performance. Executive directors especially value informed and constructive debate with non-executive directors.

6.17 Fourth, strong interpersonal skills are an essential characteristic of the effective non-executive director. Much of their effectiveness depends on exercising influence rather than giving orders and requires the establishment of high levels of trust.

6.18 Inevitably, the effectiveness of a non-executive director's contribution will change over time. Non-executive directors should be willing and able to acknowledge when their individual contribution is no longer fresh, and should make way for newcomers in an orderly and managed way.

6.19 The term "non-executive director", focuses on what they are not rather than what they are. Other terms have been suggested. "Outside director" is a term used in the US and elsewhere but it is not widely recognised in the UK. The term "independent director" is given a particular meaning in this Review, and by no means all non-executive directors could, or need to, meet it. I do not suggest a change in the term.

The senior independent director

7.1 Currently, the Code envisages a role for a senior independent non-executive director (senior independent director) whether or not the roles of chairman and chief executive are combined.

7.2 Responses to consultation contained a range of views on the identification of a senior independent director. Some saw the role as unnecessary or divisive. It was pointed out that shareholders may make use of their own connections with non-executive directors, or contact the chairmen of board committees, if they have concerns.

7.3 Most respondents, however, supported the concept of a senior independent director, noting the importance of sensitivity in the conduct of the role. I agree with them.

7.4 **I therefore endorse the Code provision that a senior independent director be identified.** They should of course meet the test of independence set out in this report. Unless it is anticipated that they will become chairman, and provided they meet the test of independence, the role could be assumed by the deputy chairman, if there is one.

7.5   I see the role of the senior independent director as important in the relationship between major shareholders and the board, as set out in paragraphs 15.15 and 15.16. **The senior independent director should be available to shareholders, if they have reason for concern that contact through the normal channels of chairman or chief executive has failed to resolve** (suggested Code provision A.3.6). **The senior independent director should also chair meetings between non-executive directors where the chairman does not attend** (suggested Code provision A.1.5), discussed below.

The effective board

8.1   Many submissions to my consultation identified a set of key characteristics of an effective unitary board. A chairman who has a strong, complementary relationship with the chief executive and the members of the board is a central element of an effective board, as already described. A culture of openness and constructive dialogue in an environment of trust and mutual respect is also a prerequisite for an effective board. The chairman has a central role to play in fostering these conditions through their own actions and through engagement with the members of the board.

8.2   The research I commissioned found that confidence in executive conduct is not achieved once and for all but rather through continuous active engagement of the non-executive directors with the executive in all aspects of the board's work. There is the potential for a virtuous dynamic in which executive perceptions of the value of non-executive directors' experience and contribution encourages greater executive openness that, in turn, allows for greater non-executive engagement. Inappropriate or ill-formed non-executive contributions can quickly break this virtuous dynamic, by leading to executive frustration or defensiveness and attempts to minimise the role of the non-executive directors. In turn this feeds the non-executive directors' suspicion of executive directors.

8.3   The culture of the boardroom can also benefit significantly from a planned programme of recruitment and retirement of board members, discussed in Chapter 10.

8.4   Many submissions emphasised the need for both a proper balance of skills and experience and the need for boards to include both executive and non-executive directors in the boardroom, such that no one group or individual dominates. My research shows that the overwhelming majority of boards exceed the current Code requirement for one-third of the board to be non-executive. One FTSE 100 board and 14 per cent of FTSE 250[3] boards are less than one-third non-executive. A higher proportion of smaller listed boards (34 per cent) do not meet the Code's guidelines.

---

[3] The FTSE 250 comprise the 250 most highly capitalised companies outside the FTSE 100 (i.e. from the 101st largest by market capitalisation to the 350th largest by market capitalisation).

701

8.5   On average, non-executive directors comprise around half a FTSE 100 board. In smaller listed companies, the non-executive directors on average comprise just over a third of the board.

8.6   It is important to ensure that the board as a whole is well informed about the company. At present, most larger company boards have a significant executive representation on the board. Only 12 FTSE 100 companies have fewer than three executive directors on the board. There is a greater risk of distortion or withholding of information, or lack of balance in the management contribution to the boardroom debate, when there is only one or a very small number of executive directors on the board. **For this reason, I recommend that the Code provides that there should be a strong executive representation on the board** (suggested Code provision A.3.2).

8.7   A number of submissions suggested that non-executive directors should meet on their own to increase their effectiveness and to allow for more organised discussion of issues of governance and overall performance. The New York Stock Exchange (NYSE) listing rules published last year require independent directors to meet regularly at scheduled sessions without management present. Their regular scheduling helps prevent any negative inference being drawn from the occurrence of the meetings.

8.8   I agree that it is helpful for non-executive directors to have such meetings without executive directors present, and on occasion without the chairman present. Such discussions are informal and do not replace other discussions between the board as a whole. They should not be seen to signal a problem. But they can allow concerns to be raised and shared on matters such as the provision of information or succession planning. **I therefore propose that the non-executive directors should meet as a group at least once a year without the chairman or executive directors present. There should be a statement in the annual report on whether the non-executive directors have met without the chairman or executives present** (suggested Code provision A.1.5). There may be a case for additional meetings of the non-executive directors together with the chairman.

Independence

9.1   A major contribution of the non-executive director is to bring wider experience and a fresh perspective to the boardroom. Although they need to establish close relationships with the executives and be well-informed, all non-executive directors need to be independent of mind and willing and able to challenge, question and speak up. All non-executive directors, and indeed executive directors, need to be independent in this sense.

9.2   At least a proportion of non-executive directors also need to be independent in a stricter sense. There is natural potential for conflict between the interests of executive management and shareholders in the case of director remuneration, or audit (where decisions on the financial results can have a direct impact on remuneration), or indeed in a range of other instances.

702

9.3   Although there is a legal duty on all directors to act in the best interests of the company, it has long been recognised that in itself this is insufficient to give full assurance that these potential conflicts will not impair objective board decision-making.

9.4   Requiring a greater degree of independence on boards has been a central theme in the recent US corporate governance reform measures. The Sarbanes-Oxley Act requires all members of the audit committee to be independent. Under the new NASDAQ listing rules and the new NYSE listing rules, a majority of the board must be independent. The Bouton report on corporate governance in France also recommended that half the board should be independent.

9.5   I agree with the conclusions of these reports that a board is strengthened significantly by having a strong group of non-executive directors with no other connection with the company. These individuals bring a dispassionate objectivity that directors with a closer relationship to the company cannot provide. In the light of the need to manage conflict of interests, the increasing role of the board committees, and the positive benefits of independence, **I recommend that the Code should provide that at least half of the members of the board, excluding the chairman, should be independent non-executive directors** (suggested Code provision A.3.5). I recognise that practical considerations mean that widespread compliance with this recommendation may take time to achieve.

9.6   The recommendation should not, however, be interpreted as meaning that non-executive directors who have a recent or existing connection of some kind with the company have no place on the board. They may indeed be valuable, but they should be additional to the requisite proportion of independent non-executive directors.

Definition of independence

9.7   The Code currently provides that the majority of non-executive directors should be independent of management and free from any business or other relationship which could materially interfere with the exercise of their independent judgement, leaving it to boards to identify which of its non-executive directors are considered to meet this test.

9.8   This definition gives little guidance to companies as to what the test should entail. Shareholder bodies, in particular, have drawn up their own definitions against which appointments are assessed. There are over a dozen such definitions in the UK, all with different criteria. This proliferation of definitions is, I believe, unhelpful. What is needed is a set of guidelines which can be intelligently and consistently applied.

9.9   I have considered carefully the different definitions which are applied in different jurisdictions and by various bodies in the UK, together with the different approaches provided in response to consultation. I am not convinced by the case, made in some submissions, that independence should be defined in statute.

9.10   On the basis of my work, **I recommend that it should be a provision of the Code that all directors have to take decisions objectively in the interests of the company** (suggested Code provision A.3.3). That is the existing legal position, but it is valuable to state it clearly as it is a fundamental feature of the unitary board. Requiring some board members to be more obviously free from other connections with the company would thus not be seen as reducing the need for independence of mind from all of them.

9.11   **I also recommend including in the Code a definition of independence** (suggested Code provision A.3.4), which I hope will replace the current multitude of definitions which many consultation responses regretted. This proposed new definition addresses not just relationships or circumstances that would affect the director's objectivity, but also those that could appear to do so.

9.12   I very much hope that business and investor bodies will endorse this new definition so that, for the first time, there is a widely accepted definition of director independence.

9.13   When a director is proposed for appointment or re-appointment, the board should state whether they are to be regarded as meeting the test of independence. It is the responsibility of the whole board to produce the statement, and for the individual director to ensure its accuracy.

9.14   The definition makes it clear that receiving additional remuneration beyond the director's fee compromises an individual's independence. In addition, it is important that a non-executive director is not so dependent on the income from their role or shareholding as to prejudice independence of judgement, and I would expect boards to take this into account in determining independence. Remuneration is discussed in Chapter 12.

Independence

A non-executive director is considered independent when the board determines that the director is independent in character and judgement and there are no relationships or circumstances which could affect, or appear to affect, the director's judgement.
    Such relationships or circumstances would include where the director:

- is a former employee of the company or group until five years after employment (or any other material connection) has ended;

- has, or has had within the last three years, a material business relationship with the company either directly, or as a partner, shareholder, director or senior employee of a body that has such a relationship with the company;

- has received or receives additional remuneration from the company apart from a director's fee, participates in the company's share option or a performance-related pay scheme, or is a member of the company's pension scheme;

- has close family ties with any of the company's advisers, directors or senior employees;

704

- holds cross-directorships or has significant links with other directors through involvement in other companies or bodies;

- represents a significant shareholder; or

- has served on the board for more than ten years.

The board should identify in its annual report the non-executive directors it determines to be independent. The board should state its reasons if a director is considered to be independent notwithstanding the existence of relationships or circumstances which may appear relevant to its determination.

(Suggested Code provision A.3.4).

Recruitment and appointment

10.1   Ensuring that the board as a whole has an appropriate mix of skills and experience is essential for it to be an effective decision-making body. There is no "standard" board or "standard" non-executive director, nor can there be. It is the range of skills and attributes acquired through a diversity of experiences and backgrounds that combine to create a cohesive and effective board. The balance of skills and experience required inevitably changes to reflect the changing needs of the business.

10.2   Identifying individuals of suitable quality and background is essential for a high performing board. The nominations and appointments process is crucial to strong corporate performance as well as effective accountability.

The nomination and appointment process

10.3   The Code currently offers guidance on the nomination and appointment process. It provides for a nomination committee to make recommendations to the board on all new board appointments unless the board is small. A majority of the members of this committee should be non-executive directors.

10.4   Almost all FTSE 100 companies have a nomination committee, compared to only 30 per cent of companies outside the FTSE 350. However, interviews conducted for the Review suggested that where the nomination committee does exist it is the least developed of the board's committees, usually meeting irregularly and often without a clear understanding of the extent of its role in the appointment process. In some cases, board members who are not committee members are present at committee discussions, effectively making the committee indistinct from the board as a whole.

10.5   A high level of informality surrounds the process of appointing non-executive directors. Almost half of the non-executive directors surveyed for the Review were recruited to their role through personal contacts or friendships. Only four per cent had had a formal interview, and one per cent had obtained their job through answering an advertisement. This situation was widely criticised in responses to consultation, and I accept that it can lead to an overly familiar atmosphere in the boardroom.

10.6   I have considered whether lessons can be learnt from the appointments and nominations process in the public sector, where there is a clear requirement to appoint on merit set out in the Nolan Principles. Recruiting or nominating committees are typically set up and draw up a comprehensive job or role description. Best practice is that essential and desirable competencies are identified before candidates are approached. Advertising of roles is considered good practice, often alongside other forms of search.

10.7   I was also told that voluntary and charitable organisations are increasingly making use of formal recruitment processes, including the use of advertising, search consultants and external agencies, to appoint trustees. The Association of Chief Executives of National Voluntary Organisations (ACEVO) promotes as good practice the completion of a skills audit prior to any appointment alongside an open recruitment process and a clear statement on term of office.

10.8   I believe that a rigorous, fair and open appointments process is essential to promote meritocracy in the boardroom and that existing best practice for nominating and appointing directors should be universally adopted.

10.9   I recommend that:
- **All listed companies should have a nomination committee which should lead the process for board appointments and make recommendations to the board** (suggested Code provision A.4.1).
- **The nomination committee should consist of a majority of independent non-executive directors. It may include the chairman of the board, but should be chaired by an independent non-executive director** (suggested Code provision A.4.1).
- **The chairman and members of the nomination committee should be identified in the annual report and should make publicly available their terms of reference explaining clearly their role and the authority delegated to them by the board** (suggested Code provisions A.4.1 and A.4.2). Annex F provides specimen terms of reference for the nomination committee developed with the ICSA. I am very pleased that ICSA have agreed to keep the guidance under review in the future to reflect improvements in best practice.
- **Before making an appointment, the nomination committee should evaluate the balance of skills, knowledge and experience on the board and, in the light of this evaluation, should prepare a description of the role and capabilities required for a particular appointment** (suggested Code provision A.4.3).
- **A statement should be made in the annual report detailing the activities of the nomination committee and the process used for appointments. An explanation should be given if external advice or open advertising has not been used** (suggested Code provision A.4.10). **The number of committee meetings and individual attendance over the course of the year should be stated** (suggested Code provision A.1.2).

- **The nomination committee should ensure that on appointment, non-executive directors receive a formal letter of appointment setting out clearly what is expected of them in terms of time commitment, committee membership and involvement outside board meetings** (suggested Code provision A.4.4). A specimen letter of appointment is provided in Annex H.

10.10   As discussed in Chapter 12, **non-executive directors should disclose to the chairman the nature and extent of their other appointments and confirm that they will have available the time required for their role** (suggested Code provision A.4.6). During their period of office, non-executive directors should inform the chairman of any other appointments they take up (including the amount of time they will need to devote to them), and make the chairman aware of any changes to their other commitments which might impact on the time they can devote to the company's affairs. Once reported to the chairman, such matters should be formally recorded by the company secretary at the next board meeting.

10.11   It is important that shareholders have sufficient information on which to base approval of appointments. **I therefore recommend that, when an appointment of a non-executive director is put forward for approval to shareholders, the board should explain why they believe the individual should be appointed and how they meet the requirements of the role set out in Chapter 6** (suggested Code provision A.4.5).

10.12   Taken together, it is my hope that these recommendations will result in a nominations and appointments process that is rigorous, fair and transparent and promotes meritocracy in the boardroom.

Succession planning

10.13   A planned programme of recruitment and retirement amongst board members can be of significant benefit. It is an important part of the board's work to ensure that there is adequate management development and succession planning. An often overlooked role for the nomination committee is to provide support on this. Succession planning should involve an assessment of the challenges and opportunities facing the company, and an evaluation of the skills and expertise that will be needed on the board in the future. Both executive and non-executive requirements should be considered. **The committee should satisfy itself that processes and plans are in place for orderly succession for appointments to the board and to senior management to maintain an appropriate balance of skills on the board. I recommend that the Code include reference to this important role for the nomination committee** (suggested Code provision A.4.9).

10.14   More also needs to be done to develop the directors of the future. **Chairmen and chief executives should consider implementing executive development programmes to train and develop suitable individuals for future director roles.**

The pool of non-executive directors

10.15　It is generally assumed that business experience is important for a non-executive director. I believe, however, that the qualities necessary for an effective contribution to the board can also be acquired from a variety of backgrounds. The interplay of varied and complementary perspectives amongst different members of the board can significantly benefit board performance.

10.16　The composition of a board sends important signals about the values of the company. A commitment to equal opportunities which can be of motivational as well as reputational importance is inevitably undermined if the board itself does not follow the same guiding principles.

10.17　In the research and consultation responses, evidence diverged on the extent to which there is a shortage of good people to take on non-executive roles. Part of the problem seems to be however that the supply of talent that does exist is not being sufficiently drawn upon.

10.18　One explanation is likely to be the attitudes of boards when considering appointments. A number of responses to the consultation identified a self-perpetuating tendency in the appointments process that militates against wider representation in the boardroom. Previous PLC board experience is often seen to be the main, and sometimes only, competence demanded of potential candidates. Too often due consideration is not given to candidates with a broader mix of skills and experience.

10.19　It has been suggested that search consultants have a tendency to identify candidates from a narrow pool of candidates. If that is so, nomination committees can and should insist that their consultants look beyond the "usual suspects" to find candidates who would make good board members.

10.20　It is clearly in the interests of the company to ensure that the best people are recruited to direct and supervise it. It is important that boards recognise their responsibility and appoint on merit.

10.21　My research shows that non-executives are typically white males nearing retirement age with previous PLC director experience. There are less than 20 non-executive directors on FTSE 100 boards under the age of 45. In the telephone survey for the Review, seven per cent of non-executive directors were not British, and one per cent were from black and ethnic minority groups.

10.22　The very low number of female non-executive directors is striking in comparison with other professions and with the population of managers in UK companies overall. Across the corporate sector as a whole, around 30 per cent of managers overall are female[4]. Only six per cent of non-executive posts are held by women, and there are only two female chairmen in the FTSE 350.

---

[4] Labour Force survey (reference, EOC).

10.23   The diversity and mix of experience of public sector appointees is broader than in the private sector boardroom. In the year to 31 March 2002, of the 3,856 appointments and re-appointments to public bodies, 38 per cent were female (for chairmen, the proportion is slightly lower at 34 per cent) and nine per cent were from ethnic minorities.

10.24   Using personal contacts as a main source of candidates will tend to favour those with similar backgrounds to incumbent directors. A rigorous appointments process is important to offset this natural bias. The various criteria used for selection may also implicitly discriminate against women, such as requiring wide senior executive or PLC board experience.

10.25   Part of the reason for the small number of female directors may be that areas where women tend to be more strongly represented are in roles such as human resources, change management and customer care which are not regarded as traditional routes to the board. Yet the issues dealt with in such roles are important ones for the board, and the roles themselves encourage skills and attributes that are highly relevant to the boardroom. **I hope that in future boards will draw more actively from these groups when making appointments, even if the appointees are not yet at board level**.

10.26   Currently, few executive directors or talented individuals just below board level sit as non-executive directors in other companies. Of more than 5,000 executive directors in UK listed companies, currently 282 hold a non-executive director post in a UK listed company. There are many benefits of doing so. The company that employs the individual on a full-time basis will benefit from the individual gaining a broader perspective and developing skills and attributes relevant to any future role as a director. Conversely, the board of the company receiving the individual benefits from executive experience elsewhere. This encourages the sharing and disseminating of best practice.

10.27   **I therefore invite the chairmen of listed companies to encourage and facilitate their executive directors and suitable senior management just below board level to take one non-executive director position on a non-competitor board.**

10.28   Companies are increasingly operating across borders. International experience can bring an important dimension to a boardroom. **All companies operating in international markets could, I believe, benefit from having at least one international non-executive director with relevant skills and experience on their board.** In practice I have been told that candidates from jurisdictions where two-tier boards are prevalent sometimes have difficulty understanding the workings of a unitary board structure. I believe training on the distinctive characteristics of the unitary board structure and the behaviours needed to be effective in this context could play a role here.

10.29   **Lawyers, accountants and consultants are used to working in an advisory capacity to business and to analysing and learning about a business from the outside. As a non-executive director, they can bring a set of skills that are useful to the board.** Such groups contain a relatively high proportion of women. I would encourage these organisations to allow suitable candidates to take on non-executive director roles.

10.30   **Boards should also look to private companies, some of which are of significant scale, as a source of non-executive directors.** I would hope that private
companies would look favourably on the experience that might thereby be
gained by their directors.

10.31   The skills and experience gained through careers in the non-commercial
sector can be highly relevant to a PLC boardroom. **There are individuals in charitable or public sector bodies who have developed strong commercial and market understanding. Including them on a PLC board can
increase the breadth and diversity of experience that can in turn increase its
effectiveness.**

10.32   The challenge is to provide greater opportunities for such individuals to be
appointed. **I am therefore very pleased that a group of business leaders and
others will be formed to help bring to greater prominence candidates from
the non-commercial sector who could have the skills and experience to make
an effective contribution to the boards of listed companies. The group will
describe the profile of relevant skills and experience that make an effective
non-executive director with a non-commercial background. A list will also
be developed of around 100 individuals from the non- commercial sector. As
women are more strongly represented at senior levels in the non-commercial
sector, the expected outcome would be that a significant proportion would
be female. The group will report to the Secretary of State for Trade and
Industry in May.**

10.33   In order to address the perceived need for previous board experience,
an option which some companies have found useful is to bring onto the
boards of subsidiary companies talented individuals from wider and more
diverse backgrounds, to give them exposure to the operation of a board as
a possible stepping-stone to the board of a listed company.

Nominating and appointing chairmen

10.34   An effective chairman, as described above, is critical to fostering a
constructive boardroom environment. A number of respondents to my
consultation expressed concern that it was difficult to find able people for
this demanding and important role. I have no easy answers on how to
widen the pool of potential chairmen, although the recommendations I
have made to encourage a much stronger mix of non-executive directors
should help.

10.35   Ensuring that the process for appointing the chairman is robust is an
essential pre-condition for getting the right person in the role. **Three
principles should be observed when a board is appointing a new chairman:**

  •   **The senior independent director or deputy chairman, if independent,
should normally lead the appointment process.** The incumbent chairman should not assume this role. Clearly, any individual who is
putting themselves forward as a candidate should not be involved in

the appointment process. Although the decision is ultimately for the board as a whole, the group leading the process, if not the nomination committee, should comprise a majority of independent non-executive directors.

- **A systematic approach should be taken to identify the skills and expertise required for the role and a job specification prepared.**
- **A short-list of good candidates should be considered, rather than possible individuals being considered in turn.** The process will almost certainly benefit from external advice.

The well-informed non-executive director

Induction

11.1   To be effective, newly appointed non-executive directors quickly need to build their knowledge of the organisation to the point where they can use the skills and experience they have gained elsewhere for the benefit of the company. **A comprehensive, formal and tailored induction should always be provided to new non-executive directors to ensure an early contribution to the board** (suggested Code provision A.5.6).

11.2   Responses to consultation showed a widespread acceptance of the importance of induction. However, the telephone survey showed that less than one quarter of non-executive directors received a formal briefing or induction after appointment.

11.3   Often it is left to new non-executive directors to take the initiative in seeking an induction programme and to ask the right questions in order to receive the right information. This is not acceptable.

11.4   **As part of running an effective board, companies need to set aside adequate resources and ensure sufficient time is allowed for a thorough induction for directors** (suggested Code provision A.5.7). **The chairman should take the lead in providing a properly constructed induction programme, facilitated by the company secretary.** It can be helpful for existing non-executive directors to give feedback on what they found useful. Induction programmes should be tailored to the company and the individual.

11.5   Non-executive directors interviewed for this Review reported that visiting company locations and attending company events, together with the informal contact with board and management that this brings, has significantly developed their knowledge of the business and its people. Opportunities should also be provided to ensure that non-executive directors see regularly, and at first hand, the performance of the senior management team. As guidance, the checklist at Annex I, developed with ICSA, provides guidance on the core elements of the induction process.

Professional Development

11.6   On appointment, non-executive directors will already have relevant skills, knowledge, experience and abilities. Nonetheless a non-executive director's credibility and effectiveness in the boardroom will depend not just on their existing capability but on their ability to extend and refresh their knowledge and skills.

11.7   The telephone survey revealed that two-thirds of non-executive directors and chairmen had not received any training or development. Of those who said that they had, the training was often in the form of experience of business or being a member of a board, rather than any structured provision. It is questionable the extent to which this experience alone is sufficient to maintain up-to-date knowledge.

11.8   The word "training" in this context is not altogether helpful as it carries rather limited connotations of formal instruction in a classroom setting. Comments to the Review confirm this. By contrast, what I envisage is continued professional development tailored to the individual.

11.9   Potential directors need to understand the role of the board, obligations and entitlements of directors of listed companies and the behaviours needed for effective board performance. For foreign directors, the working of the unitary board could usefully be covered.

11.10   For existing directors, knowledge of issues such as strategy, management of human and financial resources, audit and remuneration can often usefully be updated and expanded. Updates on legal, regulatory and other obligations can also be helpful. In addition, revisiting the effective behaviours of a board director, such as influencing skills (which may be different for different purposes), conflict resolution, chairing skills and board dynamics can often be beneficial (see paragraphs 11.19 to 11.24).

11.11   My research confirmed that some non-executive directors were concerned about the increasing amount of technical knowledge necessary in order to fulfil their roles on board committees such as audit and remuneration. Others noted the value of training on issues such as risk management. There are also instances where mastery of complicated, fast-evolving financial products or technology is necessary for non-executive directors sensibly to appraise the suitability of a company's strategy.

11.12   **I would expect that, as part of the evaluation process, non-executive directors should regularly appraise their individual skills, knowledge and expertise, and determine whether further professional development would help them develop their expertise and fulfil their obligations as members of the unitary board.**

11.13   Demand for formal training is very low. The relatively limited supply of training specifically aimed at non-executive directors by business schools and other providers may be a factor, but some such provision has been reduced because of poor take-up. Another factor may be that provision does not match the needs of non-executive directors. However it is also the case that an entrenched boardroom culture tends to regard non-executive directors as being fully equipped for the role without the need for any further personal development. In some cases this presumption may be justified; in most, it is not.

11.14 **Companies should acknowledge that to run an effective board they need to provide resources for developing and refreshing the knowledge and skills of their directors, including the non-executive directors** (suggested Code provision A.5.7). **The chairman should address the developmental needs of the board as a whole with a view to enhancing its effectiveness as a team.**

11.15 The chairman should also lead in identifying the development needs of individual directors, with the company secretary playing a key role in facilitating provision. Non-executive directors should be prepared to devote time to keeping their skills up-to-date.

11.16 Interviews conducted as part of the Review suggested that a case-study based approach using dynamic, real corporate life situations, such as mergers and acquisitions and risk management, may be as useful as a lecture-based approach. There are also a number of briefing programmes and networking groups through which non-executive directors and chairmen can share best practice information with their peers and refresh their knowledge. These programmes could usefully be developed, and non-executive directors should recognise the benefits of participating in them. Awareness of what is available should also be increased.

11.17 **It is my belief that there should be a step change in training and development provision so that it is suited to the needs of boards.**

11.18 More could also be done to ensure that the non-executive directors of the future are prepared for what is an increasingly complex and demanding role. Providers of MBA courses might consider the benefits of including elements on the behaviours and skills needed in the boardroom, as well as corporate governance and the role of the board, to prepare prospective board members at an earlier stage in their career.

Performance evaluation

11.19 Every board should continually examine ways to improve its effectiveness. Boards can benefit significantly from formally reviewing both individual and collective board performance, including committees. Yet my research shows that over a third of boards never formally evaluate their own performance, while over three-quarters of non-executive directors and over half of chairmen never have a formal personal performance review.

11.20 The Code does not offer guidance on evaluating the performance of individual directors or of the board as a whole. It also has no specific guidance on dealing with under-performance, except for the recommendation that the re-appointment of non-executive directors should not be automatic.

11.21 The majority of submissions were in favour of the Code being modified to include guidance on conducting board and individual performance reviews. This view was supported in interviews with both directors and investors.

11.22 A board performance appraisal gives the chairman the information and confidence to manage the board more effectively. **It helps the chairman to identify and address the strengths and weaknesses of the board and consider whether the board has the right balance of skills for the future.** If not, the chairman should seek the resignation of under-performing directors and make new appointments to the board. **I therefore propose that the Code provides that the performance of the board as a whole, of its committees and of its members, is evaluated at least once a year** (suggested Code provision A.6.1). **It should be stated in the annual report whether such performance evaluation is taking place and how it is conducted** (suggested Code provision A.6.2).

11.23 Sometimes it can become clear either to the board and its chairman or to the director concerned that a new appointment is not working. In these circumstances an early "blame-free" resignation is preferable to continuing an unsatisfactory role.

11.24 The chairman has a key role in arranging the evaluation process for the board and for individual non-executive directors. Conduct of the evaluation by an external third party can bring objectivity to the process and its value should be recognised by chairmen. It is the chairman's own performance is reviewed, an external third party or the senior independent director should act as facilitator. While the results of board evaluation as a whole should be shared with the board, the results of individual assessments should remain confidential between the chairman and the non-executive director concerned. The process of performance evaluation is evolving; suggested guidelines for carrying out performance appraisal, for both the board as a whole and for non-executive directors individually, are set out in Annex J for companies to tailor to meet their own needs.

Information and the Company Secretary

11.25 In order for a non-executive director to be effective, adequate information of the right kind is vital. Information must be provided sufficiently in advance of meetings to enable non-executive directors to give issues thorough consideration and must be relevant, significant and clear. Some who responded to consultation stressed the dangers of data-overload, which could lead to important issues being overlooked. This was confirmed by my telephone survey where 21 per cent of the FTSE 100 non-executive directors interviewed said that they receive too much information.

11.26 Where a board is working effectively there will be a culture of openness. Non-executive directors' contributions will be valued and trusted and the manipulation of information should not be an issue. The emphasis in all information flows should be on clarity and transparency. **The chairman,** supported by the company secretary, should assess what information is required. The executive directors should assemble it and be ready to validate its accuracy, reliability and compliance with laws and standards (suggested Code provision A.2.5).

11.27 **Good non-executive directors will also satisfy themselves that they have appropriate information of sufficient quality to make sound judgements. Non-executive directors should not hesitate in seeking clarification or amplification where necessary** (Code provision A.5.1).

11.28 It is also important that non-executive directors give constructive feedback on the value of material provided and guidance on what is required. Where information is not appropriate this should be clearly signalled through the chairman. It should be part of the annual evaluation of the board's performance to examine whether the information provided to the board meets directors' expectations and requirements.

11.29 The role of the company secretary is important in the provision of information and more widely in supporting the effective performance of non-executive directors. The value of a good company secretary was a recurring theme amongst consultees. Ultimately the value of a company secretary's contribution will be determined by the calibre of the individual concerned. At their best, as a provider of independent impartial guidance and advice, a good company secretary is uniquely well placed to assist a non-executive director and to support the chairman in ensuring good use is made of the non-executive directors.

11.30 The company secretary has a wide range of responsibilities but among those most central to enhancing non-executive director performance are the facilitation of good information flows, provision of impartial information and guidance on board procedures, legal requirements and corporate governance, together with best practice developments. They can also play a key part in facilitating induction and professional development for board members. To ensure good communication within the board and its committees, it is good practice for the company secretary, or their designee, to be secretary to all board committees.

11.31 The effectiveness of the company secretary will hinge on the nature of their working relationship with the chairman. **The company secretary should be accountable to the board through the chairman on all governance matters** (suggested Code provision A.5.2). Though there may be certain matters on which the company secretary reports to the chief executive, this should not undermine their overall responsibility to the board on all matters of corporate governance.

11.32 It is crucial to safeguard the integrity of the position, so that their impartiality is not compromised. All the board also need a clear understanding of the role of the company secretary.

11.33 In some companies, particularly smaller ones, the roles of company secretary and finance director are combined. Around 40 per cent of companies outside FTSE 350 combine the roles. There are obvious tensions in this in the context of impartiality and information provision. It is therefore desirable for larger companies, who are able, to separate the roles and for smaller companies with limited resources to recognise the potential for conflict of interest and to build "Chinese walls" between the roles, by ensuring that information received in one capacity is not used for other purposes.

11.34   At present company law makes appointment of the company secretary a matter for the board. The Code, on the other hand, identifies the removal of the company secretary as a board matter. I recommend, for clarity, that both appointment and removal of the company secretary are a matter for the board and that this is set out in the Code (suggested Code provision A.5.5).

Terms of engagement

Tenure

12.1   A board should regularly re-evaluate the mix of skills and experience it needs and be able and willing to change its membership in an orderly manner over time. According to my research, the current population of non-executive directors have been in their roles to date for an average of 4.6 years. This suggests that on average a non-executive director spends significantly longer in a post.

12.2   Some submissions argued that there is a lengthy learning curve for a non-executive director, and that a long tenure is in the company's interests. I believe it is desirable to do everything possible to enable the non-executive director to accelerate this learning curve, by systematic and thorough due diligence and induction processes, followed up by training and professional development as necessary.

12.3   A balance has to be struck on tenure between all these factors. I do not favour an initial appointment for a non-executive director of less than three years (subject to satisfactory performance) and it is reasonable to expect most non-executive directors also to serve a second term of three years. Beyond six years the possible benefits of a fresh appointee need more careful consideration, although there will be cases where the particular director continues to justify their place on the board over a full nine year period.

12.4   It was put to me that non-executive directors should face annual re-election on the basis that under-performers can more readily be removed. However, I accept the argument that in the UK, where shareholders can vote against the re-election of a director and can call a special general meeting to remove a board, annual re-election of all directors could be potentially damaging to a company. It might encourage short-termism or leave a vacuum at the top of a company if an entire board is voted out in a protest by a minority of shareholders.

12.5 **I consider therefore that a non-executive director should normally be expected to serve two three-year terms with a company. There will be occasions where value will be added by a non-executive director serving for longer, but I would expect this to be the exception and the reasons for it explained to shareholders** (suggested Code provision A.7.3).

12.6 **I consider that after nine years annual re-election is appropriate for non-executive directors** (suggested Code provision A.7.3).

12.7 Taken together, these recommendations should encourage planned and progressive refreshing of listed company boardrooms.

12.8 As part of my research I found that the current population of chairmen of UK listed companies have on average been on the board for about seven years. There is certainly value in continuity and stability in the chairman's role. I do not believe that a standard term for tenure of chairmen is appropriate.

12.9 **However, it is useful to appoint the chairman for three-year terms which may be renewed where appropriate.** As part of its role in succession planning, the nomination committee should review the chairman's position and should take account of the advantage of continuity set against the desirability of a freshness of approach. For their part, chairmen should be sensitive to the need to make way for a successor when this would be in the interests of the company.

Time commitment

12.10 This Review sets out the high standards expected of non-executive directors. To meet these standards and be effective, it is essential that non-executive directors commit the necessary time to the role. Other parts of the Review identify a need to ensure that non-executive directors devote time to induction, professional development, developing a strong base of knowledge of the company's affairs, participating in succession planning and greater involvement in discussions with shareholders.

12.11 Although there are wider extremes, research suggests that a non-executive director role usually involves a time commitment of between 15 and 30 days a year. Practice varies on whether the time commitment is articulated and agreed between the non-executive director and the board. The time involvement of a chairman varies much more widely. Both for the chairman and non-executive directors it is important that they are available at short notice to deal with major issues when they arise. At such times, a non-executive director, and particularly a chairman, may need to commit substantially more time.

12.12 The responses to my consultation showed that there was widespread concern about non-executive directors devoting insufficient time to what is an increasingly demanding role. This was also the most commonly expressed barrier to greater effectiveness of non-executive directors cited in the telephone survey (25 per cent).

12.13   There is value, therefore, in clarity of the expected time commitment of non- executive directors and chairmen. **I propose that the nomination committee should articulate the time and responsibility (including in relation to chairmanship, as the senior independent director, or membership of board committees) envisaged in the appointment of a non-executive director** (suggested Code provision A.4.4). **The non-executive director should undertake that they will have available sufficient time to meet what is expected of them, taking into account their other commitments. These commitments should be disclosed to the company before appointment, with an indication of the time involved** (suggested Code provision A.4.6). In this way, a proper judgement can be made of whether the director is likely to have enough time for the role and would have sufficient flexibility to devote additional time where this was needed. Shareholders would be expected not to support the election (or re-election) of non-executive directors who are not in a position to commit appropriate time to their role.

12.14   **The nomination committee should annually review the time required and performance evaluation should be used to assess whether the non-executive director is spending enough time to fulfil their duties. If the non-executive director is offered appointments elsewhere, the chairman should be informed before any new appointment is accepted and the board should subsequently be informed** (suggested Code provision A.4.7).

12.15   The popular perception is that there are a large number of people holding multiple non-executive directorships and a number of submissions suggested that the number of such posts be subject to a limit. I found that less than one-fifth of non-executive directors hold more than one non-executive directorship in a UK listed company. 13 individuals hold five or more such posts. One in 14 non-executive directors also hold an executive director post. However many non-executive directors may also hold appointments in unlisted or non-UK companies as well as charitable, public sector or other roles.

12.16   The variety of different appointments and individual circumstances means that it is arbitrary and unrealistic to set a prescriptive limit for the number of non-executive directorships any individual not in full time employment may hold, and I do not propose one.

12.17   I consider, however, that the position as regards executive directors and chairmen of major companies is, as a matter of principle, different. There is undoubtedly value in executive directors participating on other boards of non-competing companies as non-executive directors. But shareholders have every reason to expect executive directors of the companies they own to focus effectively all their full time energies on the company which employs them. I propose that there should be a limit on the number of external roles in major companies which executive directors assume.

12.18   The role of the chairman is distinct from that of the non-executive director. In major companies it will be close to a full time engagement. The chairman, moreover, has the ultimate responsibility for the conduct of the board.

12.19   **I believe therefore that best practice should be that:**

- **a full time executive director should not take on more than one non-executive directorship, nor become chairman, of a major company, and**
- **no individual should chair the board of more than one major company** (suggested Code provision A.4.8).

I define a major company in this context as one included, or likely to be included shortly, in the FTSE 100.

Remuneration

12.20   Research showed that the average remuneration of FTSE 100 non-executive directors is £44,000 p.a. Average remuneration for a non-executive director of a company outside the FTSE 350 is £23,000 p.a. For chairmen it is £426,000 p.a. and £78,000 p.a. respectively.

12.21   Views I received in response to consultation generally argued that the risk-reward balance was becoming less favourable and that in principle non-executive directors should be paid more, particularly as the time envisaged for the role is increasing.

12.22   In the telephone survey, ten per cent of chairmen and six per cent of non-executive directors cited insufficient pay as a barrier to greater non-executive effectiveness. This is much lower than barriers such as time, which 22 per cent of non-executive directors cited. It was not however generally argued that pay was a significant constraint on attracting high quality people to be non-executive directors, with the exception of those directors based in the US, where pay is considerably higher. Other views expressed were that if pay was significantly increased, or if the non-executive director was dependent on the pay from a particular company, their independence of mind could be prejudiced.

12.23   A parallel survey of board remuneration[5] showed that a majority felt that non-executive directors' pay was too low. However, when asked to quantify what the level of pay should be, an annual rate of between £40,000 and £60,000 for FTSE 100 (compared to £44,000 in practice) and between £25,000 and £40,000 (compared to £23,000 now) for smaller listed companies was suggested. This suggests that pay is not in practice significantly out of line with expectations for larger companies, but may possibly be out of line with expectations for smaller listed companies.

12.24   Remuneration for directors needs to be sufficient to attract and retain high calibre candidates but no more than is necessary for this purpose. **The level of remuneration appropriate for any particular non-executive director role should reflect the likely workload, the scale and complexity of the business and the responsibility involved.** In practice, it may be helpful in assessing remuneration for non-executive directors to use as a benchmark

---

[5] Institute of Directors' survey, September 2002.

the daily remuneration of a senior representative of the company's professional advisers. The risk of high levels of remuneration (or a large shareholding) prejudicing independence of thought is real and should be avoided. Where a non-executive director has extra responsibilities (such as membership or chairmanship of board committees), the total remuneration should reflect these. I recommend that **non-executive directors' fees should be more clearly built up from an annual fee, meeting attendance fees (to include board committee meetings) and an additional fee for the chairmanship of committees (typically a multiple of the attendance fee) or role as senior independent director**. The level of remuneration for non-executive directors should be a matter for the chairman and the executive directors of the board.

12.25   In addition, companies should expect to pay additional, reasonable expenses in addition to the director's fee to cover related costs incurred by their non- executive directors (such as travel and administrative costs). Any significant support of this kind should be agreed in advance.

12.26   Some responses to consultation opposed the holding of shares by non-executive directors. The more general view was that shares could be helpful in aligning the interests of the director with the long-term interests of shareholders. It is undesirable, however, for any shareholdings to represent a large proportion of the individual non-executive director's financial wealth. **I conclude that there is merit in the current practice of some companies giving their non-executive directors the opportunity to take part of their remuneration in the form of shares in lieu of cash**.

12.27   Most responses to consultation opposed the use of options in non-executive director remuneration because of the risk of undesirable focus on share price rather than underlying company performance. Similarly, participation by non-executive directors in incentive or pension schemes was felt to be undesirable. **I conclude that non-executive directors should not hold options over the shares of their company** (suggested Code provision B.1.7). **If, exceptionally some payment is made by means of options, shareholder approval should be sought in advance and any shares acquired by exercise of the options should be held until one year after the non-executive director leaves the board.**

12.28   I recommend in Chapter 10 that it would be desirable for companies to encourage executive directors and senior executives to take on non-executive posts elsewhere. **Where companies release an executive director to serve as a non-executive director elsewhere, they should include in their remuneration policy reports whether or not the director will retain such earnings and, if so, what the remuneration is.**

12.29   The Company Law Review recommended (as originally suggested by the Law Commission) that non-executive director terms of engagement (both contracts and ancillary provisions) should be disclosed. **It is important that these should be publicly available. I consider that the Code should be clarified to require this** (suggested Code provision A.4.11).

12.30   As regards remuneration of chairmen, concern was expressed in consultation about the shortage of supply of able candidates for the role of chairman. This was not, however, attributed to levels of pay, which already reflect the considerable commitment and time required for the role. There is, nonetheless, scope for the remuneration of chairmen to be more imaginatively structured to provide a greater degree of alignment with shareholders' interests than would be appropriate for non-executive directors.

Resignation

12.31   Some of those who responded to the consultation described the resignation of a non-executive director as being the ultimate sanction at their disposal. I believe that resignation should be regarded very much as a last resort once other efforts to resolve problems have failed. Indeed, non-executive directors may be constrained from resigning by their fiduciary duty to act in the company's best interests. **Where non-executive directors have real concerns about the way in which a company is being run or about a course of action proposed by the board, the first step should be to raise their concerns with the chairman and their fellow directors. Non-executive directors should, as a matter of course, ensure that their concerns are recorded in the minutes of the board meeting if they cannot be resolved.**

12.32   **If the non-executive director feels that resignation is the only course of action left, a written statement should be provided to the chairman, for circulation to the board, setting out the reasons for resignation. I would also recommend that a non-executive director should explain their reasons for resigning when they leave in other circumstances** (suggested Code provision A.1.6). While I would not anticipate the chairman usually making such a statement publicly available, although there may be circumstances when they would wish to do so, I would expect shareholders to make their own enquiries into the reasons for resignation of directors when they are not apparent.

Audit and remuneration committees

13.1   The increased use of board committees on audit, remuneration and nomination has played an important role in raising standards of corporate governance. Although the board retains ultimate responsibility, these committees give assurance that important board duties are being rigorously discharged. The Code provides that non-executive directors, and in particular independent non-executive directors, should play a leading role in these committees to avoid conflicts of interest for executive directors.

13.2   When appointing committee members, boards should draw on the independent non-executive directors with the most relevant skills and experience. Consideration should also be given to rotating committee members. In order not to concentrate too much influence on one individual, **I consider it undesirable for any one individual to be on all three principal board committees at the same time** (suggested Code provision A.3.7).

13.3   The nomination committee was discussed in Chapter 10.

Audit committee

13.4   In the wake of a number of high profile corporate collapses in the US, the audit committee has become the subject of close scrutiny in both the US and the UK.

13.5   As noted earlier, in February 2002, alongside this Review, the Secretary of State for Trade and Industry and the Chancellor set up the CGAA to consider wider issues of accountancy and audit reform. The Group produced an interim report in July. It recommended that the role and membership of audit committees should be strengthened and that the audit committee should approve the purchase of non-audit services and should have the principal responsibility for making recommendations on auditor appointment to shareholders. In her July statement to the House of Commons on the interim report, the Secretary of State for Trade and Industry called for audit committees to consist exclusively of independent non-executive directors.

13.6   The interim report of the CGAA also proposed the creation of a separate group, under the auspices of the FRC, to develop existing Code guidance for audit committees. The group, chaired by Sir Robert Smith, today published detailed recommendations on audit committees.

13.7   **I welcome Sir Robert Smith's recommendations and I believe that they will assist audit committees in increasing their effectiveness.** Where the group makes recommendations for the Code, these have been incorporated into the proposed new draft Code at Annex A.

Summary of recommendations by Sir Robert Smith Group

Composition of the audit committee

*   Committee to include at least three members, all independent non-executive directors.

*   At least one member to have significant, recent and relevant financial experience.

Role of the audit committee

*   To monitor the integrity of the financial statements of the company, reviewing significant financial reporting judgements;

- To review the company's internal financial control system and, unless expressly addressed by a separate risk committee or by the board itself, risk management systems;

- To monitor and review the effectiveness of the company's internal audit function;

- To make recommendations to the board in relation to the appointment of the external auditor and to approve the remuneration and terms of engagement of the external auditor;

- To monitor and review the external auditor's independence, objectivity and effectiveness, taking into consideration relevant UK professional and regulatory requirements; and

- To develop and implement policy on the engagement of the external auditor to supply non-audit services, taking into account relevant ethical guidance regarding the provision of non-audit services by the external audit firm.

Resources

- The committee to be provided with sufficient resources to undertake its duties.

Reporting to shareholders

- The directors' report to contain a separate section that describes the role of the committee and what action it has taken.

- The chairman of the audit committee to be present at the AGM to answer questions, through the chairman of the board.

Code provisions and related guidance

- The recommendations above to be reflected in the revised Code (suggested Code provisions D.2.2 and D.3.1 to D.3.5) and amplified in detailed guidance.

The full report is available at www.frc.org.uk/publications.

Remuneration committee

13.8   The Code provides that a board should have a remuneration committee consisting exclusively of non-executive directors who are independent of management. Most listed companies have a separate remuneration committee. All except two in the FTSE 350 do, as do 85 per cent of companies outside the FTSE 350. The independence of members of the remuneration committee from executive management is necessary in view of the potential for conflicts of interest. This is not to say, however, that the chairman and chief executive may not attend committee meetings when invited to do so. Indeed, I would expect the committee to wish to know their views.

13.9   Judgements on remuneration require sensitivity not just to the expectations of executive directors but also to the perceptions and concerns of investors and wider constituencies. Research confirmed the worries of many directors that compensation consultants were often perceived to be too close to executive management and too ready to encourage companies to position their remuneration policy in the "upper quartile" of their peer group comparators. Such a policy can have a one way ratchet effect which is undesirable for individual companies and inflationary and self-defeating in the market place.

13.10　**The remuneration committee needs to work closely with the nomination committee to ensure that incentives are appropriately structured for directors and for senior executives and that terms in the event of severance are carefully considered. The broad aim should be to avoid rewarding poor performance while dealing fairly with cases where departure is not due to poor performance** (suggested Code provision B.1.10).

13.11　**I recommend that the Code should provide that all members of the remuneration committee should meet the test of independence. The committee should have at least three members. It should have published terms of reference which set out its delegated responsibilities** (suggested Code provisions B.2.1 and B.2.2). A summary of the principal duties of the remuneration committee is provided in Annex E.

13.12　**At a minimum, the committee should have delegated responsibility for setting remuneration for all executive directors and the chairman. The committee should also set the level and structure of compensation for senior executives. The committee should be responsible for appointing remuneration consultants. If executive directors or senior management support the remuneration committee, this role should be clearly separated from their executive role within the business** (suggested Code provision B.2.2). The frequency of and attendance of members at remuneration committee meetings should be disclosed in the annual report (suggested Code provision A.1.2).

...

Liability

14.4　In a range of legislation (such as health and safety, environmental law, competition, as well as companies and insolvency legislation) obligations are imposed on the directors of a company as well as (or instead of) on the company itself. Some of these carry criminal sanctions, others may give rise to civil remedies in the hands of private third parties, insolvency practitioners or regulators.

14.5　General duties owed by directors to their company, which set standards of propriety of conduct and of skill and care, have been established over time through case law. These duties are owed to the company. This means that only the company (or a member by means of a derivative action on the company's behalf) can take action for breach. Scope for speculative shareholder litigation of the kind common in the US is extremely limited because of differences in both law and the procedure for bringing claims.

14.6   The remedy for breach of the duty of skill and care is damages. A director will not be liable unless the company can show that the director is in breach of the duty and that loss resulted. Currently it is possible for a director to ask for relief from liability under section 727 of the Companies Act 1985 if it appears to the Court that the director acted honestly and reasonably and that in all the circumstances ought fairly to be excused. Although the law does not apply different duties to executive and non-executive directors, it has been recognised that the knowledge, skill and experience expected will vary between directors with different roles and responsibilities (for example between the finance director or the sales director and a non-executive director).

14.7   An important problem faced by directors, particularly non-executive directors, has been that of knowing with certainty the extent of these duties. If the proposals of the Company Law Review to set out a statement of duties in statute are adopted, this uncertainty should be considerably reduced. Alongside the duties, it is, I understand, intended that guidance will be provided by the Government for the benefit of directors, which should also help.

14.8   **I suggest that in addition to that general guidance, some further guidance should be provided, by way of provision in the Code. I would expect that the Courts would wish to pay regard to such provision where it might be relevant to the case (for example in the context of determining what would be reasonably expected of a director in the defendant's position).**

14.9   The provisions I suggest are set out in the proposed new schedule to the Code at Annex A. The statement builds on directors' duties in relation to care, skill and diligence, by making clear that although non-executive directors and executive directors have the same legal duties and objectives as board members, their involvement is likely to be different. In particular, the time devoted to the company's affairs is likely to be significantly less for a non-executive director than for an executive director and the detailed knowledge and experience of a company's affairs that could reasonably be expected of a non-executive director will also in most cases be less than for an executive director.

14.10   The statement also reflects the recommendations I make elsewhere in the Review on non-executive directors ensuring that they have adequate knowledge and raise concerns appropriately, and on management providing sufficient, timely and accurate information.

14.11   Improved Court procedures and active case management are also very important. The long drawn out nature of proceedings is very detrimental reputationally as well as financially. This can be of particular importance, for example, where a director is applying for relief under section 727 of the Act. This is an important power for the Court and if such applications could be dealt with promptly it would give considerable reassurance to directors. **I recommend that the Lord Chancellor's Department consider steps to promote active case management in cases applying to directors.**

14.12   The Company Law Review looked at the question of the setting of sanctions which might apply to directors and set out some key principles in Annex D of its final report which should be applied when new legislation is being introduced. **I consider that it would be useful if, when criminal sanctions in relation to directors are being considered by Government, these principles are taken into account**.

14.13   I am also aware that the Law Commission recently reviewed limitation periods (which prevent claims in relation to events more than a certain time ago) and that the rules may be clarified. The benefits of reducing uncertainty about potential litigation for non-executive directors should be taken into account in this.

Insurance and indemnification

14.14   Company law (section 310 of 1985 Act) allows a company to insure its directors against actions by the company or by third parties. It also allows a company to indemnify a director in respect of third party claims where the director is not in breach of duty or obligation to the company, but a commitment in advance to indemnify against legal costs is invalid unless contingent on a successful defence.

14.15   The Company Law Review recommended (in paragraph 6.3 of the Final Report) that companies should be able to indemnify in advance against the cost of defending proceedings, or of a section 727 relief application, provided that the decision was made by the disinterested members of the board on the basis of appropriate legal advice that the prospects of success were good, and that if the outcome was adverse the director would be bound to reimburse the company. It also recommended that it should be lawful for the company to indemnify a director against a bona fide excess of loss requirement on a liability insurance policy, under which the director is bound to pay the first tranche of any liability.

14.16   I support these recommendations. **I also suggest that the Government should go further, and provide that a company should be able to indemnify a director in advance against the reasonable cost of defending proceedings from the company itself, without trying to establish in advance the prospects of success of the case. The director would be bound to repay the costs if they lost**.

14.17   I recognise that the defendant director's ability to defend themselves would be dependent on the plaintiff's money and the company would in effect be paying the director's defence costs in a situation where the company would have decided that it was in its best interests to bring the proceedings. Although the director would be bound to repay the costs if they lost, there might be difficulty in recovering such money in practice. Nonetheless I consider that this proposal would be justified, taking account of the importance of ensuring that directors can rely on being defended with legal support comparable to that available to the company itself, and the wider aspects of safeguarding the pool of non-executive directors from being narrowed because of concerns about potential legal action.

14.18 As regards insurance cover, this is normally purchased by the company, although it can on occasion be purchased by individual directors. There is usually differentiation between executive and non-executive directors, but policies cover all directors and any subsidiary directors worldwide.

14.19 I consider that insurance is a basic protection for non-executive directors against suits by third parties. The benefit for companies is that it avoids the need to indemnify directors against such suits. **The Code should make reference to the need to provide appropriate directors' and officers' insurance** (suggested Code provision A.1.7). **I consider that companies should also supply details of their insurance cover to potential non-executive directors before they are appointed. If and when the law is changed, I consider that companies should also indemnify directors against any excess of loss requirement.**

14.20 It would appear that guidance for companies could be useful on what insurance should be provided for directors. **I am pleased that the City of London Law Society and ICSA, together with the ABI and BIBA, have agreed to draw up such guidance. This could include the risks that should be covered and those that cannot be, together with illustrative specimen policy terms. The guidance could also set out relevant factors that need to be considered, such as aggregate limits and exposure to potential actions outside the UK and the definition of what is a "wrongful act". Companies could then use this guidance as an aid in obtaining appropriate directors' and officers' insurance.**

Relationships with shareholders

15.1 The role of the non-executive director includes an important and inescapable relationship with shareholders.

15.2 The structure of the UK equity market is diverse and has changed significantly over the last thirty years. Individual share ownership has fallen from over 50 per cent of the market in the 1960s to less than one fifth today. Meanwhile the UK market has become increasingly international, with overseas investors owning 30 per cent of the market, compared to below ten per cent three decades ago[6].

15.3 The most significant change has, however, been the institutionalisation of the market. Occupational pension funds, insurance companies, pooled investment vehicles (for example unit and investment trusts) and other financial institutions such as charities, endowments and educational institutions, now hold more than half the equity capital of UK listed companies.

---

[6] "Institutional Investment in the UK: A Review" by Paul Myners, April 2001.

15.4   It is common practice for chief executives to have regular contacts with major shareholders. Chairmen often also participate. According to my telephone survey, three-quarters of chairmen discuss company business with some of their investors at least once a year. Through such meetings, these members of the board gain a clear insight into the views, and on occasion concerns, of the company's major shareholders. For their part, shareholders develop a better understanding of a wide range of issues from the point of view of management. These channels of communication are now widely accepted as both desirable and useful.

15.5   In contrast, only rarely do non-executive directors hear at first hand the views of major shareholders. The majority of non-executive directors (52 per cent) surveyed for the Review never discuss company business with their investors. Within the FTSE 100, contact is rarer still: only about one in five FTSE 100 non-executive directors discuss company business with investors once a year or more often.

15.6   Qualitative research undertaken for the Review showed that in normal circumstances non-executive directors and shareholders have only minimal direct contact. Interviews with investors revealed that rarely do they speak directly with non-executive directors, and only then where there is a serious problem. Even in these circumstances, discussion often centred on director remuneration rather than wider strategy or governance issues.

15.7   Corroborating the evidence from the telephone survey, in-depth interviews revealed a widespread view amongst non-executive directors that investors are distant and disengaged. While expressing concern about the time commitment involved, small company non-executive directors tended to be sympathetic to the value of increased shareholder contact.

15.8   Executive directors, by contrast, were found to have reservations about more direct contact between non-executive directors and shareholders on the grounds that non-executive directors would not have enough detail available to them to present an accurate picture of company performance.

15.9   Despite significant variations in practice, the overall view amongst submissions to the consultation was that relationships between non-executive directors and shareholders could and should be closer.

15.10   Best practice as set out in the Code envisages the AGM as the forum for contact to take place between smaller shareholders and the board. This is important and I believe that, as the current Code provides, **non-executive directors, and in particular the chairmen of committees, should attend the AGM and be prepared to discuss issues that are raised in relation to their role** (suggested Code provision C.2.3).

15.11   I do not however accept the argument made in some submissions that the AGM should be the main or indeed only mechanism through which major shareholders and non-executive directors have direct contact.

15.12   One approach to strengthening relationships which has been mooted is for non-executive directors to meet with some of the company's major shareholders, individually or collectively, on a regular formalised basis without executive management present. The purpose of the meeting would not be for non-executive directors to communicate the company's strategy or to account for its performance. Non-executive directors would attend such meetings to listen to investors' views and to answer questions about governance. There has, however, been resistance to the format proposed on the basis that such meetings could be unduly time consuming for non-executive directors, might not be taken seriously by investors and could cause unhelpful tension between executive and non-executive directors. I understand and share these concerns.

15.13 Nevertheless, there is much merit in the principle that non-executive directors should hear directly the views of their major investors. A number of submissions—the Institute of Directors (IOD), ABI and the National Association of Pension Funds (NAPF) amongst them—suggested that a preferable approach would be for non-executive directors to attend some of the regular meetings that executive directors and the chairman have with key shareholders.

15.14 The chairman, as part of their role in ensuring effective communication with shareholders, needs to keep the board informed of major concerns raised by shareholders.

15.15 **In addition, I propose that the senior independent director should attend sufficient of the regular meetings of management with a range of major shareholders to develop a balanced understanding of the themes, issues and concerns of shareholders. The senior independent director should communicate these views to the non-executive directors and, as appropriate, to the board as a whole** (suggested Code provision C.1.2).

15.16 **Boards should recognise that non-executive directors may also find it instructive to attend meetings with major investors from time to time and should be able to do so if they choose. Moreover, non-executive directors should expect to attend such meetings if requested by major investors in the company. They should, however, rely on the chairman and the senior independent director to ensure a balanced view is taken of the range of shareholder views** (suggested Code provision C.1.2).

15.17 In addition, there are in practice a number of ways in which non-executive directors can inform themselves about the views of investors. Many companies undertake formal, regular investor relations surveys through their advisers or specialist intermediaries. Non-executive directors should encourage this practice and the board as a whole should discuss the results. There is also value in non-executive directors joining formal presentations to analysts and others of interim and final results to listen to questioning of executive management. **On appointment, non-executive directors should meet major investors, as part of the induction process** (suggested Code provision C.1.3).

15.18 The Code does not currently identify non-executive directors as having particular responsibilities towards shareholders, only that companies should be ready to enter into a dialogue with shareholders, based on a mutual understanding of objectives. **I recommend that companies should state in the annual report what steps they have taken to ensure that the members of the board, and in particular the non-executive directors, develop a balanced understanding of the views of major investors** (suggested Code provision C.1.1).

15.19 Several investors have complained of difficulties in making contact with non-executive directors (given that a number have several appointments) and were keen to have better access to discuss issues in a timely manner. To address this, **the company secretary should act as a conduit for contacts from major shareholders to non-executive directors**.

The role of institutional investors

15.20 Investors can, and I believe should, play their part in ensuring that non-executive directors play an effective role on boards by questioning them on corporate governance matters. Such matters would include the functioning of the board, evaluation of the board's performance and how its results have been acted upon, the composition and diversity of experience of the board and the rigour and transparency of the appointments process. Investors should, however, not expect non-executive directors to be the source of information on company performance.

15.21 It is of real concern that many non-executive directors are critical of institutional investors who are often regarded as being too passive in relation to the companies in which they invest. The Government is trying to promote a culture in which institutional investors can and do pursue their beneficiaries' interests.

15.22 A need for more active engagement by institutional shareholders with the companies in which they invest was a central theme of Paul Myners' review of institutional investment, published in April 2001. Myners expressed concern about the value lost to institutional investors through the reluctance of fund managers actively to engage with companies in which they have holdings, even where they have strong reservations about strategy, personnel or other potential causes of underperformance.

15.23 Responding to the Myners Review, the Government has consulted on possible legislation to oblige institutions to promote their beneficiaries' interests through increased activism. In November last year, the ISC published on behalf of the industry a set of principles setting out strengthened responsibilities of institutional investors and agents. The principles outline best practice on the part of institutional investors to promote their members' interests through more active engagement as shareholders. The new principles will be included in industry fund management contracts.

15.24 **I endorse the Government's approach to more active engagement by shareholders and hope that the financial community will make the ISC's code of activism work in practice. For completeness, I therefore propose that the ISC** code of activism be endorsed through reference in section 2 of the Code (suggested Code provision E.2.1).

15.25   **I also recommend that institutional investors should attend AGMs where practicable** (suggested Code provision E.1.4).

Smaller listed companies

Smaller listed companies (outside FTSE 350)

- There are 1,847 listed companies outside the FTSE 350.

- The market capitalisation of these range from a few hundred thousand pounds to hundreds of millions of pounds.

- The average size of the board is six, with two non-executive directors, three executive directors and a chairman.

- Audit and recommendation committees are commonplace. (85 per cent of smaller listed companies have them.) However, less than a third (29 per cent) have a nomination committee.

16.1   In the Review I make recommendations for listed companies in the UK. In doing this, I am mindful that no one size fits all and in particular that listed companies vary significantly in size. I have separately examined what recommendations I should make for smaller listed companies.

16.2   Like Cadbury and Hampel, my starting point is that high standards of corporate governance are as important for smaller listed companies as for larger ones. All public companies, irrespective of size, have obligations to their owners.

16.3   The governance of smaller listed companies has improved over the last decade, but compliance with the Code is less for smaller companies.

16.4   Many of the directors of smaller companies we interviewed recognised the value non-executive directors bring. In addition to the role played in larger companies, mentoring the executive team was a benefit often cited of non-executive directors in smaller companies.

16.5   I recognise that it may be more challenging for smaller listed companies to comply with some of the Review's recommendations and I have given careful consideration to the concerns about the costs of compliance for smaller companies, as expressed in responses to the consultation document and in interviews with directors of smaller listed companies.

16.6   In particular I am conscious that smaller listed companies tend to have fewer non-executive directors, and a number of these may not be independent.

16.7   Many consultation responses were, however, keen for the principles that apply to larger listed companies to apply to smaller listed companies. In addition, none of the directors of smaller listed companies that we inter-viewed argued for different principles for smaller listed companies. The nature of the Code is such that companies can explain to shareholders where there is good reason for complying with the principles in a different way.

16.8   **I propose that the recommendation that no one individual should sit on all three committees should not apply to smaller listed companies** (suggested Code provision A.3.7). I do so acknowledging that even with half the board independent the overall size of the board of smaller listed companies may not make this feasible. **With this exception, I recommend that there should be no differentiation in the Code's provisions for larger and smaller companies. I recognise, however, that it may take more time for smaller listed companies to comply and that some of the Code's provisions may be less relevant or manageable for smaller companies.**

16.9   My recommendations are directed at listed companies, but I hope and expect that many of them will also be of relevance to non-listed companies.

Appendix 3

Listing Rules

Governance related information required by the Financial Services Authority under the Listing Rules to be included in the Annual Report

Please refer to Appendix 1 which contains an excellent outline prepared by the FRC on the requirements of the Disclosure and Transparency Rules and the Listing Rules.

Reference should also be made at any given time to the online text of the DTR and LR contained in the FSA Handbook at fsa.gov.uk. As at the date of publication of this book the online link to the Handbook was *http://fsahandbook.info/FSA/index.jsp*.

Appendix 4

Companies Act 2006, Part 15, Chapter 4—The Annual Accounts Provisions

CHAPTER 4

ANNUAL ACCOUNTS

General

393   Accounts to give true and fair view

(1) The directors of a company must not approve accounts for the purposes of this Chapter unless they are satisfied that they give a true and fair view of the assets, liabilities, financial position and profit or loss—

(a)   in the case of the company's individual accounts, of the company;

(b)   in the case of the company's group accounts, of the undertakings included in the consolidation as a whole, so far as concerns members of the company.

(2) The auditor of a company in carrying out his functions under this Act in relation to the company's annual accounts must have regard to the directors' duty under subsection (1).

Individual accounts

394   Duty to prepare individual accounts

The directors of every company must prepare accounts for the company for each of its financial years.
Those accounts are referred to as the company's "individual accounts".

395   Individual accounts: applicable accounting framework

(1) A company's individual accounts may be prepared—

(a)   in accordance with section 396 ("Companies Act individual accounts"), or

(b)   in accordance with international accounting standards ("IAS individual accounts").

This is subject to the following provisions of this section and to section 407 (consistency of financial reporting within group).

(2) The individual accounts of a company that is a charity must be Companies Act individual accounts.

(3) After the first financial year in which the directors of a company prepare IAS individual accounts ("the first IAS year"), all subsequent individual accounts of the company must be prepared in accordance with international accounting standards unless there is a relevant change of circumstance.

(4) There is a relevant change of circumstance if, at any time during or after the first IAS year—

(a)   the company becomes a subsidiary undertaking of another undertaking that does not prepare IAS individual accounts,

(b)   the company ceases to be a company with securities admitted to trading on a regulated market in an EEA State, or

(c)   a parent undertaking of the company ceases to be an undertaking with securities admitted to trading on a regulated market in an EEA State.

(5) If, having changed to preparing Companies Act individual accounts following a relevant change of circumstance, the directors again prepare IAS individual accounts for the company, subsections (3) and (4) apply again as if the first financial year for which such accounts are again prepared were the first IAS year.

396 Companies Act individual accounts

(1) Companies Act individual accounts must comprise—

(a)   a balance sheet as at the last day of the financial year, and

(b)   a profit and loss account.

(2) The accounts must—

(a)   in the case of the balance sheet, give a true and fair view of the state of affairs of the company as at the end of the financial year, and

(b)   in the case of the profit and loss account, give a true and fair view of the profit or loss of the company for the financial year.

(3) The accounts must comply with provision made by the Secretary of State by regulations as to—

(a)   the form and content of the balance sheet and profit and loss account, and

(b)   additional information to be provided by way of notes to the accounts.

(4) If compliance with the regulations, and any other provision made by or under this Act as to the matters to be included in a company's individual accounts or in notes to those accounts, would not be sufficient to give a true and fair view, the necessary additional information must be given in the accounts or in a note to them.

(5) If in special circumstances compliance with any of those provisions is inconsistent with the requirement to give a true and fair view, the directors must depart from that provision to the extent necessary to give a true and fair view.

Particulars of any such departure, the reasons for it and its effect must be given in a note to the accounts.

397   IAS individual accounts

Where the directors of a company prepare IAS individual accounts, they must state in the notes to the accounts that the accounts have been prepared in accordance with international accounting standards.

Group accounts: small companies

398   Option to prepare group accounts

If at the end of a financial year a company subject to the small companies regime is a parent company the directors, as well as preparing individual accounts for the year, may prepare group accounts for the year.

Group accounts: other companies

399   Duty to prepare group accounts

(1) This section applies to companies that are not subject to the small companies regime.

(2) If at the end of a financial year the company is a parent company the directors, as well as preparing individual accounts for the year, must prepare group accounts for the year unless the company is exempt from that requirement.

(3) There are exemptions under—

> section 400 (company included in EEA accounts of larger group),
>
> section 401 (company included in non-EEA accounts of larger group), and
>
> section 402 (company none of whose subsidiary undertakings need be included in the consolidation).

(4) A company to which this section applies but which is exempt from the requirement to prepare group accounts, may do so.

[Reference should be made to the CA 2006 itself for the text of ss.400 to 411 of the Act containing more detailed provisions in relation to accounts.]

412   Information about directors' benefits: remuneration

(1) The Secretary of State may make provision by regulations requiring information to be given in notes to a company's annual accounts about directors' remuneration.
(2) The matters about which information may be required include—

- (a)   gains made by directors on the exercise of share options;
- (b)   benefits received or receivable by directors under long-term incentive schemes;
- (c)   payments for loss of office (as defined in section 215);
- (d)   benefits receivable, and contributions for the purpose of providing benefits, in respect of past services of a person as director or in any other capacity while director;
- (e)   consideration paid to or receivable by third parties for making available the services of a person as director or in any other capacity while director.

(3) Without prejudice to the generality of subsection (1), regulations under this section may make any such provision as was made immediately before the commencement of this Part by Part 1 of Schedule 6 to the Companies Act 1985 (c. 6).
(4) For the purposes of this section, and regulations made under it, amounts paid to or receivable by—

- (a)   a person connected with a director, or
- (b)   a body corporate controlled by a director,

are treated as paid to or receivable by the director.
The expressions "connected with" and "controlled by" in this subsection have the same meaning as in Part 10 (company directors).
(5) It is the duty of—

- (a)   any director of a company, and
- (b)   any person who is or has at any time in the preceding five years been a director of the company,

to give notice to the company of such matters relating to himself as may be necessary for the purposes of regulations under this section.
(6) A person who makes default in complying with subsection (5) commits an offence and is liable on summary conviction to a fine not exceeding level 3 on the standard scale.

413   Information about directors' benefits: advances, credit and guarantees

(1) In the case of a company that does not prepare group accounts, details of—

- (a)   advances and credits granted by the company to its directors, and
- (b)   guarantees of any kind entered into by the company on behalf of its directors,

must be shown in the notes to its individual accounts.

(2) In the case of a parent company that prepares group accounts, details of—

(a)   advances and credits granted to the directors of the parent company, by that company or by any of its subsidiary undertakings, and

(b)   guarantees of any kind entered into on behalf of the directors of the parent company, by that company or by any of its subsidiary undertakings,

must be shown in the notes to the group accounts.

(3) The details required of an advance or credit are—

(a)   its amount,

(b)   an indication of the interest rate,

(c)   its main conditions, and

(d)   any amounts repaid.

(4) The details required of a guarantee are—

(a)   its main terms,

(b)   the amount of the maximum liability that may be incurred by the company (or its subsidiary), and

(c)   any amount paid and any liability incurred by the company (or its subsidiary) for the purpose of fulfilling the guarantee (including any loss incurred by reason of enforcement of the guarantee).

(5) There must also be stated in the notes to the accounts the totals—

(a)   of amounts stated under subsection (3)(a),

(b)   of amounts stated under subsection (3)(d),

(c)   of amounts stated under subsection (4)(b), and

(d)   of amounts stated under subsection (4)(c).

(6) References in this section to the directors of a company are to the persons who were a director at any time in the financial year to which the accounts relate.

(7) The requirements of this section apply in relation to every advance, credit or guarantee subsisting at any time in the financial year to which the accounts relate—

(a)   whenever it was entered into,

(b)   whether or not the person concerned was a director of the company in question at the time it was entered into, and

(c)   in the case of an advance, credit or guarantee involving a subsidiary undertaking of that company, whether or not that undertaking was such a subsidiary undertaking at the time it was entered into.

(8) Banking companies and the holding companies of credit institutions need only state the details required by subsections (3)(a) and (4)(b).

Approval and signing of accounts

414   Approval and signing of accounts

(1) A company's annual accounts must be approved by the board of directors and signed on behalf of the board by a director of the company.

(2) The signature must be on the company's balance sheet.

(3) If the accounts are prepared in accordance with the provisions applicable to companies subject to the small companies regime, the balance sheet must contain a statement to that effect in a prominent position above the signature.

(4) If annual accounts are approved that do not comply with the requirements of this Act (and, where applicable, of Article 4 of the IAS Regulation), every director of the company who—

   (a)   knew that they did not comply, or was reckless as to whether they complied, and

   (b)   failed to take reasonable steps to secure compliance with those requirements or, as the case may be, to prevent the accounts from being approved,

commits an offence.

(5) A person guilty of an offence under this section is liable—

   (a)   on conviction on indictment, to a fine;

   (b)   on summary conviction, to a fine not exceeding the statutory maximum.

Appendix 5

Companies Act 2006, Part 15, Chapter 5, Section 417: Contents of directors' report: business review

417 Contents of directors' report: business review

(1) Unless the company is subject to the small companies' regime, the directors' report must contain a business review.

(2) The purpose of the business review is to inform members of the company and help them assess how the directors have performed their duty under section 172 (duty to promote the success of the company).

(3) The business review must contain—

(a)   a fair review of the company's business, and

(b)   a description of the principal risks and uncertainties facing the company.

(4) The review required is a balanced and comprehensive analysis of—

(a)   the development and performance of the company's business during the financial year, and

(b)   the position of the company's business at the end of that year,

consistent with the size and complexity of the business.

(5) In the case of a quoted company the business review must, to the extent necessary for an understanding of the development, performance or position of the company's business, include—

(a)   the main trends and factors likely to affect the future development, performance and position of the company's business; and

(b)   information about—

    (i)   environmental matters (including the impact of the company's business on the environment),

    (ii)   the company's employees, and

    (iii) social and community issues,

    including information about any policies of the company in relation to those matters and the effectiveness of those policies; and

(c)   subject to subsection (11), information about persons with whom the company has contractual or other arrangements which are essential to the business of the company.

If the review does not contain information of each kind mentioned in paragraphs (b) (i), (ii) and (iii) and (c), it must state which of those kinds of information it does not contain.

(6) The review must, to the extent necessary for an understanding of the development, performance or position of the company's business, include—

(a)   analysis using financial key performance indicators, and

(b)   where appropriate, analysis using other key performance indicators, including information relating to environmental matters and employee matters.

"Key performance indicators" means factors by reference to which the development, performance or position of the company's business can be measured effectively.

(7) Where a company qualifies as medium-sized in relation to a financial year (see sections 465 to 467), the directors' report for the year need not comply with the requirements of subsection (6) so far as they relate to non-financial information.

(8) The review must, where appropriate, include references to, and additional explanations of, amounts included in the company's annual accounts.

(9) In relation to a group directors' report this section has effect as if the references to the company were references to the undertakings included in the consolidation.

(10) Nothing in this section requires the disclosure of information about impending developments or matters in the course of negotiation if the disclosure would, in the opinion of the directors, be seriously prejudicial to the interests of the company.

(11) Nothing in subsection (5)(c) requires the disclosure of information about a person if the disclosure would, in the opinion of the directors, be seriously prejudicial to that person and contrary to the public interest.

Appendix 6

Financial Reporting Council: Internal Control—Guidance for Directors ("Turnbull Guidance")

In view of the review of this Guidance which was taking place as this book was being published the author has taken the view that it would be more useful to direct readers to the FRC website: *http://www.frc.org.uk* where the then current version of the Turnbull Guidance at any point can be found.

The Higgs Review

Pre-appointment due diligence checklist for new board members

(This checklist was also compiled with the assistance of ICSA which in 2010 was reviewing this and other precedents suggested by Higgs and reference should be made to the ICSA website for the up-to-date position *http://www.icsa.org.uk*.)

Why?

Before accepting an appointment a prospective non-executive director should undertake their own thorough examination of the company to satisfy themselves that it is an organisation in which they can have faith and in which they will be well suited to working.

The following questions are not intended to be exhaustive, but are intended to be a helpful basis of the pre-appointment due diligence process that all non-executive directors should undertake.

Questions to ask

What is the company's current financial position and what has its financial track record been over the last three years?

What are the key dependencies (e.g. regulatory approvals, key licences)?

What record does the company have on corporate governance issues?

If the company is not performing particularly well is there potential to turn it round and do I have the time, desire and capability to make a positive impact?

What are the exact nature and extent of the company's business activities?

Who are the current executive and non-executive directors, what is their background and their record and how long have they served on the board?

What is the size and structure of the board and board committees and what are the relationships between the chairman and the board, the chief executive and the management team?

Who owns the company i.e. who are the company's main shareholders and how has the profile changed over recent years?

What is the company's attitude towards, and relationship with, its shareholders?

Is any material litigation presently being undertaken or threatened, either by the company or against it?

Is the company clear and specific about the qualities, knowledge, skills and experience that it needs to complement the existing board?

What insurance cover is available to directors and what is the company's policy on indemnifying directors?

Do I have the necessary knowledge, skills, experience and time to make a positive contribution to the board of this company?

How closely do I match the job specification and how well will I fulfil the board's expectations?

Is there anything about the nature and extent of the company's business activities that would cause me concern both in terms of risk and any personal ethical considerations?

Am I satisfied that the internal regulation of the company is sound and that I can operate effectively within its stated corporate governance framework?

Am I satisfied that the size, structure and make-up of the board will enable me to make an effective contribution?

Would accepting the non-executive directorship put me in a position of having a conflict of interest?

Sources of information

- Company report and accounts, and/or any listing prospectus, for the recent years.
- Analysts' reports.
- Press reports.
- Company web site.
- Any Corporate Social Responsibility or Environmental Report issued by the company.
- Rating agency reports.
- Voting services reports.

Published material is unlikely to reveal wrong-doing, however a lack of transparency may be a reason to proceed with caution.

This guidance has been compiled with the assistance of ICSA who have kindly agreed to produce updated guidance on their website www.icsa.org.uk in the future.

Appendix 8

The Higgs Review

Guidance on the role of the non-executive director

(This guidance was also compiled with the assistance of ICSA which in 2010 was reviewing this and other precedents suggested by Higgs and reference should be made to the ICSA website for the up-to-date position *http://www.icsa.org.uk*.)

As members of the unitary board, all directors are required to:

- Provide entrepreneurial leadership of the company within a framework of prudent and effective controls which enable risk to be assessed and managed;

- Set the company's strategic aims, ensure that the necessary financial and human resources are in place for the company to meet its objectives, and review management performance; and

- Set the company's values and standards and ensure that its obligations to its shareholders and others are understood and met.

In addition to these requirements for all directors, the role of the non-executive director has the following key elements:

- **Strategy:** Non-executive directors should constructively challenge and contribute to the development of strategy.

- **Performance:** Non-executive directors should scrutinise the performance of management in meeting agreed goals and objectives, and monitor the reporting of performance.

- **Risk:** Non-executive directors should satisfy themselves that financial information is accurate and that financial controls and systems of risk management are robust and defensible.

- **People:** Non-executive directors are responsible for determining appropriate levels of remuneration of executive directors and have a prime role in appointing, and where necessary removing, senior management and in succession planning.

Non-executive directors should constantly seek to establish and maintain confidence in the conduct of the company. They should be independent in judgement and have an enquiring mind. To be effective, non-executive directors need to build a recognition by executives of their contribution in order to promote openness and trust.

To be effective, non-executive directors need to be well-informed about the company and the external environment in which it operates, with a strong command of issues relevant to the business. A non-executive director should insist on a comprehensive, formal and tailored induction. An effective induction need not be restricted to the boardroom, so consideration should be given to visiting sites and meeting senior and middle management. Once in post, an effective non-executive director should seek continually to develop and refresh their knowledge and skills to ensure that their contribution to the board remains informed and relevant.

Best practice dictates that an effective non-executive director will ensure that information is provided sufficiently in advance of meetings to enable thorough consideration of the issues facing the board. The non-executive director should insist that information is sufficient, accurate, clear and timely.

An element of the role of the non-executive director is to understand the views of major investors both directly and through the senior independent director.

The effective non-executive director:

- upholds the highest ethical standards of integrity and probity;

- supports executives in their leadership of the business while monitoring their conduct;

- questions intelligently, debates constructively, challenges rigorously and decides dispassionately;

- listens sensitively to the views of others, inside and outside the board;

- gains the trust and respect of other board members; and

- promotes the highest standards of corporate governance and seeks compliance with the provisions of the Code wherever possible.

Appendix 9

The Higgs Review

Sample letter of non-executive director appointment

(This letter was also compiled with the assistance of ICSA which in 2010 was reviewing this and other precedents suggested by Higgs and reference should be made to the ICSA website for the up-to-date position *http://www.icsa.org.uk*.)

On [date], upon the recommendation of the nomination committee, the board of [company] ("the Company") has appointed you as non-executive director. I am writing to set out the terms of your appointment. It is agreed that this is a contract for services and is not a contract of employment.

Appointment

Your appointment will be for an initial term of three years commencing on [date], unless otherwise terminated earlier by and at the discretion of either party upon [one month's] written notice. Continuation of your contract of appointment is contingent on satisfactory performance and re-election at forthcoming AGMs. Non-executive directors are typically expected to serve two three-year terms, although the board may invite you to serve for an additional period.

Time commitment

Overall we anticipate a time commitment of [number] days per month after the induction phase. This will include attendance at [monthly] board meetings, the AGM, [one] annual board away day, and [at least one] site visit per year. In addition, you will be expected to devote appropriate preparation time ahead of each meeting.

By accepting this appointment, you have confirmed that you are able to allocate sufficient time to meet the expectations of your role. The agreement of the chairman should be sought before accepting additional commitments that might affect the time you are able to devote to your role as a non-executive director of the company.

Role

Non-executive directors have the same general legal responsibilities to the company as any other director. The board as a whole is collectively responsible for promoting the success of the company by directing and supervising the company's affairs. The board:

- Provides entrepreneurial leadership of the company within a framework of prudent and effective controls which enable risk to be assessed and managed;

- Sets the company's strategic aims, ensures that the necessary financial and human resources are in place for the company to meet its objectives, and reviews management performance; and

- Sets the company's values and standards and ensures that its obligations to its shareholders and others are understood and met.

In addition to these requirements of all directors, the role of the non-executive has the following key elements:

- **Strategy.** Non-executive directors should constructively challenge and contribute to the development of strategy;

- **Performance.** Non-executive directors should scrutinise the performance of management in meeting agreed goals and objectives and monitor the reporting of performance;

- **Risk.** Non-executive directors should satisfy themselves that financial information is accurate and that financial controls and systems of risk management are robust and defensible; and

- **People.** Non-executive directors are responsible for determining appropriate levels of remuneration of executive directors and have a prime role in appointing, and where necessary removing, senior management and in succession planning.

Fees

You will be paid a fee of £[amount] gross per annum which will be paid monthly in arrears, [plus [number] ordinary shares of the company per annum, both of] which will be subject to an annual review by the board. The company will reimburse you for all reasonable and properly documented expenses you incur in performing the duties of your office.

Outside interests

It is accepted and acknowledged that you have business interests other than those of the company and have declared any conflicts that are apparent at present. In the event that you become aware of any potential conflicts of interest, these should be disclosed to the chairman and company secretary as soon as apparent.

[The board of the company have determined you to be independent according to the provision of the Combined Code.]

Confidentiality

All information acquired during your appointment is confidential to the Company and should not be released, either during your appointment or following termination (by whatever means), to third parties without prior clearance from the chairman.

Your attention is also drawn to the requirements under both legislation and regulation as to the disclosure of price sensitive information. Consequently you should avoid making any statements that might risk a breach of these requirements without prior clearance from the chairman or company secretary.

Induction

Immediately after appointment, the Company will provide a comprehensive, formal and tailored induction. This will include the information pack recommended by the Institute of Chartered Secretaries and Administrators, available at www.icsa.org.uk. We will also arrange for site visits and meetings with senior and middle management and the Company's auditors. We will also arrange for you to meet major investors in the first twelve months of your appointment.

Review process

The performance of individual directors and the whole board and its committees is evaluated annually. If, in the interim, there are any matters which cause you concern about your role you should discuss them with the chairman as soon as is appropriate.

Insurance

The Company has directors' and officers' liability insurance and it is intended to maintain such cover for the full term of your appointment. The current indemnity limit is £ [amount]; a copy of the policy document is attached.

Independent professional advice

Occasions may arise when you consider that you need professional advice in the furtherance of your duties as a director. Circumstances may occur when it will be appropriate for you to seek advice from independent advisors at the company's expense. A copy of the board's agreed procedure under which directors may obtain such independent advice is attached. The Company will reimburse the full cost of expenditure incurred in accordance with the attached policy.

Committees

This letter refers to your appointment as a non-executive director of the Company. In the event that you are also asked to serve on one or more of the board committees this will be covered in a separate communication setting out the committee(s)'s terms of reference, any specific responsibilities and any additional fees that may be involved.

This sample appointment letter has been compiled with the assistance of ICSA who have kindly agreed to produce updated guidance on their website www.icsa.org.uk in the future.

Appendix 10

The Higgs Review

Induction checklist

(This guidance was also compiled with the assistance of ICSA which in 2010 was reviewing this and other precedents suggested by Higgs and reference should be made to the ICSA website for the up-to-date position *http://www.icsa.org.uk*.)

Guidance on induction

Every company should develop its own comprehensive, formal induction programme that is tailored to the needs of the company and individual directors. The following guidelines might form the core of an induction programme.

As a general rule, a combination of selected written information together with presentations and activities such as meetings and site visits will help to give a new appointee a balanced and real-life overview of the company. Care should be taken not to overload the new director with too much information. The new director should be provided with a list of all the induction information that is being made available to them so that they may call up items if required before otherwise provided.

The induction process should:

1. Build an understanding of the **nature of the company, its business and the markets in which it operates**. For example, induction should cover:

    *   the company's products or services,
    *   group structure / subsidiaries / joint ventures,
    *   the company's constitution, board procedures and matters reserved for the board,
    *   summary details of the company's principal assets, liabilities, significant contracts and major competitors,
    *   the company's major risks and risk management strategy,
    *   key performance indicators, and
    *   regulatory constraints.

2. Build a link with the **company's people** including:

    *   meetings with senior management,

- visits to company sites other than the headquarters, to learn about production or services and meet employees in an informal setting. It is important, not only for the board to get to know the new non-executive director, but also for the non-executive director to build a profile with employees below board level, and
- participating in board strategy development. "Awaydays" enable a new non-executive director to begin to build working relationships away from the formal setting of the boardroom.

3. Build an understanding of the **company's main relationships** including meeting with the auditors and developing a knowledge of in particular:

- who are the major customers,
- who are the major suppliers, and
- who are the major shareholders and what is the shareholder relations policy—participation in meetings with shareholders can help give a first hand feel as well as letting shareholders know who the non-executive directors are.

The induction pack

On appointment, or during the weeks immediately following, a new director should be provided with certain basic information to help ensure their early effective contribution to the company. ICSA has produced, and undertaken to maintain, on their website www.icsa.org.uk a guidance note detailing a full list of such material.

Appendix 11

The Higgs Review

Guidance on the role of the chairman

(This guidance was also compiled with the assistance of ICSA which in 2010 was reviewing this and other precedents suggested by Higgs and reference should be made to the ICSA website for the up-to-date position *http://www.icsa.org.uk*.)

The chairman is pivotal in creating the conditions for overall board and individual director effectiveness, both inside and outside the boardroom. Specifically, it is the responsibility of the chairman to:

- run the board and set its agenda. The agenda should take full account of the issues and the concerns of all board members. Agendas should be forward looking and concentrate on strategic matters rather than formulaic approvals of proposals which can be the subject of appropriate delegated powers to management;

- ensure that the members of the board receive accurate, timely and clear information, in particular about the company's performance, to enable the board to take sound decisions, monitor effectively and provide advice to promote the success of the company;

- ensure effective communication with shareholders and ensure that the members of the board develop an understanding of the views of major investors;

- manage the board to ensure that sufficient time is allowed for discussion of complex or contentious issues, where appropriate arranging for informal meetings beforehand to enable thorough preparation for the board discussion. It is particularly important that non-executive directors have sufficient time to consider critical issues and are not faced with unrealistic deadlines for decision-making;

- take the lead in providing a properly constructed induction programme for new directors that is comprehensive, formal and tailored, facilitated by the company secretary;

- take the lead in identifying and meeting the development needs of individual directors, with the company secretary having a key role in facilitating provision.

It is the responsibility of the chairman to address the development needs of the board as a whole with a view to enhancing the overall effectiveness as a team;

- ensure that the performance of individuals and of the board as a whole and its committees is evaluated at least once a year; and

- encourage active engagement by all the members of the board.

The effective chairman:

- upholds the highest standards of integrity and probity;

- sets the agenda, style and tone of board discussions to promote effective decision-making and constructive debate;

- promotes effective relationships and open communication, both inside and outside the boardroom, between non-executive directors and the executive team;

- builds an effective and complementary board, initiating change and planning succession in board appointments, subject to board and shareholders' approval;

- promotes the highest standards of corporate governance and seeks compliance with the provisions of the Code wherever possible;

- ensures a clear structure for and the effective running of board committees;

- ensures effective implementation of board decisions;

- establishes a close relationship of trust with the chief executive, providing support and advice while respecting executive responsibility; and

- provides coherent leadership of the company, including representing the company and understanding the views of shareholders.

Responsibility for drafting parts of the annual governance statement

Not part of the Higgs appendix but included in the foreword of the June 2010 edition of the UK Corporate Governance Code by the FRC.

"Chairmen are encouraged to report personally in their annual statements how the principles relating to the role and effectiveness of the board (in Sections A and B of the new Code) have been applied. Not only will this give investors a clearer picture of the steps taken by boards to operate effectively but also, by providing fuller context, it may make investors more willing to accept explanations when a company chooses to explain rather than to comply with one or more provisions. Above all, the personal reporting on governance by chairmen as the leaders of boards might be a turning point in attacking the fungus of 'boiler-plate' which is so often the preferred and easy option in sensitive areas but which is dead communication."

Appendix 12

The Higgs Review

Performance evaluation guidance

(This guidance was also compiled with the assistance of ICSA which in 2010 was reviewing this and other precedents suggested by Higgs and reference should be made to the ICSA website for the up-to-date position *http://www.icsa.org.uk*.)

Guidance on performance evaluation

This Review recommends that the Code is updated to reflect best practice that the performance of the board a whole, of its committees, and of its members, is evaluated at least once a year. Companies should disclose in their annual report whether such performance evaluation is taking place.

It is the responsibility of the chairman to select an effective process and to act on its outcome. The use of an external third party to conduct the evaluation will bring objectivity to the process.

The evaluation process will be used constructively as a mechanism to improve board effectiveness, maximise strengths and tackle weaknesses. The results of board evaluation should be shared with the board as a whole, while the results of individual assessments should remain confidential between the chairman and the non-executive director concerned.

The following are some of the questions that should be considered in a performance evaluation. They are, however, by no means definitive or exhaustive and companies will wish to tailor the questions to suit their own needs and circumstances.

The responses to these questions and others should enable boards to assess how they are performing and to identify how certain elements of their performance areas might be improved.

Performance evaluation of the board

- How well has the board performed against any performance objectives that have been set?

- What has been the board's contribution to the testing and development of strategy?

- What has been the board's contribution to ensuring robust and effective risk management?

- Is the composition of the board and its committees appropriate, with the right mix of knowledge and skills to maximise performance in the light of future strategy? Are inside and outside the board relationships working effectively?

- How has the board responded to any problems or crises that have emerged and could or should these have been foreseen?

- Are the matters specifically reserved for the board the right ones?

- How well does the board communicate with the management team, company employees and others? How effectively does it use mechanisms such as the AGM and the annual report?

- Is the board as a whole up to date with latest developments in the regulatory environment and the market?

- How effective are the board's committees? (Specific questions on the performance of each committee should be included such as, for example, their role, their composition and their interaction with the board.)

The processes that help underpin the board's effectiveness should also be evaluated e.g.:

- Is appropriate, timely information of the right length and quality provided to the board and is management responsive to requests for clarification or amplification? Does the board provide helpful feedback to management on its requirements?

- Are sufficient board and committee meetings of appropriate length held to enable proper consideration of issues? Is time used effectively?

- Are board procedures conducive to effective performance and flexible enough to deal with all eventualities?

In addition, there are some specific issues relating to the chairman which should be included as part of an evaluation of the board's performance e.g.:

- Is the chairman demonstrating effective leadership of the board?

- Are relationships and communications with shareholders well managed?

- Are relationships and communications within the board constructive?

- Are the processes for setting the agenda working? Do they enable board members to raise issues and concerns?

- Is the company secretary being used appropriately and to maximum value?

Performance evaluation of the non-executive director

The chairman and other board members should consider the following issues and the individual concerned should also be asked to assess themselves. For each non-executive director:

- How well prepared and informed are they for board meetings and is their meeting attendance satisfactory?

- Do they demonstrate a willingness to devote time and effort to understand the company and its business and a readiness to participate in events outside the boardroom, such as site visits?

- What has been the quality and value of their contributions at board meetings?

- What has been their contribution to development of strategy and to risk management?

- How successfully have they brought their knowledge and experience to bear in the consideration of strategy?

- How effectively have they probed to test information and assumptions? Where necessary, how resolute are they in maintaining their own views and resisting pressure from others?

- How effectively and proactively have they followed up their areas of concern?

- How effective and successful are their relationships with fellow board members, the company secretary and senior management? Does their performance and behaviour engender mutual trust and respect within the board?

- How actively and successfully do they refresh their knowledge and skills and are they up to date with:

  - the latest developments in areas such as corporate governance framework and financial reporting?
  - the industry and market conditions?

- How well do they communicate with fellow board members, senior management and others, for example shareholders. Are they able to present their views convincingly yet diplomatically and do they listen and take on board the views of others?

Appendix 13

Matters Which Should be Presented to the Board

(See Chapter 3 "The Board and its Structure")

1. **Management Structure and Appointment**

   - Senior management responsibilities
   - Board and other senior management appointments and/or removals
   - Board and senior management succession, training and development
   - Appointment or removal of company secretary
   - Remuneration, contracts and grants of options for senior management
   - Delegation of the Board's powers
   - Agreeing membership and terms of reference of Board committees and task forces
   - Establishment of managerial authority limit for smaller transactions
   - Matters referred to the Board by Board Committees

2. **Strategic/Policy Considerations**

   - Business strategy
   - Diversification/retrenchment policy
   - Specific risk management policies including insurance, hedging, borrowing limits, corporate security
   - Agreement of codes of ethics and business controls
   - Annual assessment of significant risks and effectiveness of internal controls
   - Calling of shareholders' meetings
   - Avoidance of wrongful or fraudulent trading

3. **Transactions**

   - Acquisition and disposals of subsidiaries or other assets or liabilities over, say, 5% of net assets/profits
   - Investment and capital projects over a similar level
   - Other transactions over a similar level
   - Substantial commitments including:

     — pension funding
     — contracts in excess of one year's duration

761

— giving security over significant group assets (including mortgages and charges over the company's property)

- Contracts not in the ordinary course of business
- Actions or transactions where there may be doubt over propriety
- Approval of prospectuses and issue documents
- Disclosure of directors' interests
- Transactions with directors or other related parties

4. **Finance**

- Raising new capital and confirmation of major financing facilities
- Treasury policies including foreign currency and interest rate exposure
- Discussion of any proposed qualification to the accounts
- Final approval of annual and interim reports and accounts and accounting policies
- Appointment/proposal of auditors
- Charitable and political donations
- Approval and recommendation of dividends
- Operating budgets

5. **General**

- Governance of company pension schemes and appointment of company nominees to Board of Trustees
- Allotment, calls or forfeiture of shares

Appendix 14

Summary of the Principal Duties of the Nomination Committee

(This guidance was also compiled with the assistance of ICSA which in 2010 was reviewing this and other precedents suggested by Higgs and reference should be made to the ICSA website for the up-to-date position *http://www.icsa.org.uk*.)

There should be a nomination committee which should lead the process for board appointments and make recommendations to the board.

A majority of members of the committee should be independent non-executive directors. The chairman or an independent non-executive director should chair the committee, but the chairman should not chair the nomination committee when it is dealing with the appointment of a successor to the chairmanship.

Duties

The committee should:

- be responsible for identifying and nominating for the approval of the board, candidates to fill board vacancies as and when they arise;

- before making an appointment, the nomination committee should evaluate the balance of skills, knowledge and experience on the board and, in the light of this evaluation, prepare a description of the role and capabilities required for a particular appointment;

- review annually the time required from a non-executive director. Performance evaluation should be used to assess whether the non-executive director is spending enough time to fulfil their duties;

- consider candidates from a wide range of backgrounds and look beyond the "usual suspects";

- give full consideration to succession planning in the course of its work, taking into account the challenges and opportunities facing the company and what skills and expertise are needed on the board in the future;

- regularly review the structure, size and composition (including the skills, knowledge and experience) of the board and make recommendations to the board with regard to any changes;

- keep under review the leadership needs of the organisation, both executive and non-executive, with a view to ensuring the continued ability of the organisation to compete effectively in the marketplace;

- make a statement in the annual report about its activities; the process used for appointments and explain if external advice or open advertising has not been used; the membership of the committee, number of committee meetings and attendance of members over the course of the year;

- make publicly available its terms of reference explaining clearly its role and the authority delegated to it by the board; and

- ensure that on appointment to the board, non-executive directors receive a formal letter of appointment setting out clearly what is expected of them in terms of time commitment, committee service and involvement outside board meetings.

The committee should make recommendations to the board:

- as regards plans for succession for both executive and non-executive directors;

- as regards the re-appointment of any non-executive director at the conclusion of their specified term of office;

- concerning the re-election by shareholders of any director under the retirement by rotation provisions in the company's articles of association;

- concerning any matters relating to the continuation in office of any director at any time; and

- concerning the appointment of any director to executive or other office other than to the positions of chairman and chief executive, the recommendation for which would be considered at a meeting of the board.

This guidance has been compiled with the assistance of ICSA who have kindly agreed to produce updated guidance on their website www.icsa.org.uk in the future.

Appendix 15

The Smith Report

Audit Committees—Combined Code Guidance

(As annexed to the 2003 Combined Code)

1. Introduction

1.1. This guidance is designed to assist company boards in making suitable arrangements for their audit committees, and to assist directors serving on audit committees in carrying out their role.

1.2. The paragraphs in bold are taken from the Combined Code (Section C3). Listed companies that do not comply with those provisions should include an explanation as to why they have not complied in the statement required by the Listing Rules.

1.3. Best practice requires that every board should consider in detail what arrangements for its audit committee are best suited for its particular circumstances. Audit committee arrangements need to be proportionate to the task, and will vary according to the size, complexity and risk profile of the company.

1.4. While all directors have a duty to act in the interests of the company the audit committee has a particular role, acting independently from the executive, to ensure that the interests of shareholders are properly protected in relation to financial reporting and internal control.

1.5. Nothing in the guidance should be interpreted as a departure from the principle of the unitary board. All directors remain equally responsible for the company's affairs as a matter of law. The audit committee, like other committees to which particular responsibilities are delegated (such as the remuneration committee), remains a committee of the board. Any disagreement within the board, including disagreement between the audit committee's members and the rest of the board, should be resolved at board level.

1.6. The Code provides that a separate section of the annual report should describe the work of the committee. This deliberately puts the spotlight on the audit committee and gives it an authority that it might otherwise lack. This is not incompatible with the principle of the unitary board.

1.7.   The guidance contains recommendations about the conduct of the audit committee's relationship with the board, with the executive management and with internal and external auditors. However, the most important features of this relationship cannot be drafted as guidance or put into a code of practice: a frank, open working relationship and a high level of mutual respect are essential, particularly between the audit committee chairman and the board chairman, the chief executive and the finance director. The audit committee must be prepared to take a robust stand, and all parties must be prepared to make information freely available to the audit committee, to listen to their views and to talk through the issues openly.

1.8.   In particular, the management is under an obligation to ensure the audit committee is kept properly informed, and should take the initiative in supplying information rather than waiting to be asked. The board should make it clear to all directors and staff that they must cooperate with the audit committee and provide it with any information it requires. In addition, executive board members will have regard to their common law duty to provide all directors, including those on the audit committee, with all the information they need to discharge their responsibilities as directors of the company.

1.9.   Many of the core functions of audit committees set out in this guidance are expressed in terms of "oversight", "assessment" and "review" of a particular function. It is not the duty of audit committees to carry out functions that properly belong to others, such as the company's management in the preparation of the financial statements or the auditors in the planning or conducting of audits. To do so could undermine the responsibility of management and auditors. Audit committees should, for example, satisfy themselves that there is a proper system and allocation of responsibilities for the day-to-day monitoring of financial controls but they should not seek to do the monitoring themselves.

1.10. However, the high-level oversight function may lead to detailed work. The audit committee must intervene if there are signs that something may be seriously amiss. For example, if the audit committee is uneasy about the explanations of management and auditors about a particular financial reporting policy decision, there may be no alternative but to grapple with the detail and perhaps to seek independent advice.

1.11. Under this guidance, audit committees have wide-ranging, time- consuming and sometimes intensive work to do. Companies need to make the necessary resources available. This includes suitable payment for the members of audit committees themselves. They—and particularly the audit committee chairman—bear a significant responsibility and they need to commit a significant extra amount of time to the job. Companies also need to make provision for induction and training for new audit committee members and continuing training as may be required.

1.12. This guidance applies to all companies to which the Code applies—i.e. UK listed companies. For groups, it will usually be necessary for the audit committee of the parent company to review issues that relate to particular subsidiaries or activities carried on by the group. Consequently, the board of a UK-listed parent company should ensure that there is adequate cooperation within the group (and with internal and external auditors of individual companies within the group) to enable the parent company audit committee to discharge its responsibilities effectively.

2. Establishment and role of the audit committee; membership, procedures and resources

Establishment and role

2.1 The board should establish an audit committee of at least three, or in the case of smaller companies two, members.

2.2 The main role and responsibilities of the audit committee should be set out in written terms of reference and should include:

- to monitor the integrity of the financial statements of the company and any formal announcements relating to the company's financial performance, reviewing significant financial reporting judgements contained in them;
- to review the company's internal financial controls and, unless expressly addressed by a separate board risk committee composed of independent directors or by the board itself, the company's internal control and risk management systems;
- to monitor and review the effectiveness of the company's internal audit function;
- to make recommendations to the board, for it to put to the shareholders for their approval in general meeting, in relation to the appointment of the external auditor and to approve the remuneration and terms of engagement of the external auditor;
- to review and monitor the external auditor's independence and objectivity and the effectiveness of the audit process, taking into consideration relevant UK professional and regulatory requirements;
- to develop and implement policy on the engagement of the external auditor to supply non-audit services, taking into account relevant ethical guidance regarding the provision of non-audit services by the external audit firm;

and to report to the Board, identifying any matters in respect of which it considers that action or improvement is needed, and making recommendations as to the steps to be taken.

Membership and appointment

2.3   All members of the committee should be independent non-executive directors. The board should satisfy itself that at least one member of the audit committee has recent and relevant financial experience.

2.4   The chairman of the company should not be an audit committee member.

2.5   Appointments to the audit committee should be made by the board on the recommendation of the nomination committee (where there is one), in consultation with the audit committee chairman.

2.6   Appointments should be for a period of up to three years, extendable by no more than two additional three-year periods, so long as members continue to be independent.

Meetings of the audit committee

2.7   It is for the audit committee chairman, in consultation with the company secretary, to decide the frequency and timing of its meetings. There should be as many meetings as the audit committee's role and responsibilities require. It is recommended there should be not fewer than three meetings during the year, held to coincide with key dates within the financial reporting and audit cycle[1]. However, most audit committee chairmen will wish to call more frequent meetings.

2.8   No one other than the audit committee's chairman and members is entitled to be present at a meeting of the audit committee. It is for the audit committee to decide if non-members should attend for a particular meeting or a particular agenda item. It is to be expected that the external audit lead partner will be invited regularly to attend meetings as well as the finance director. Others may be invited to attend.

2.9   Sufficient time should be allowed to enable the audit committee to undertake as full a discussion as may be required. A sufficient interval should be allowed between audit committee meetings and main board meetings to allow any work arising from the audit committee meeting to be carried out and reported to the board as appropriate.

2.10   The audit committee should, at least annually, meet the external and internal auditors, without management, to discuss matters relating to its remit and any issues arising from the audit.

2.11   Formal meetings of the audit committee are the heart of its work. However, they will rarely be sufficient. It is expected that the audit committee chairman, and to a lesser extent the other members, will wish to keep in touch on a continuing basis with the key people involved in the company's governance, including the board chairman, the chief executive,

---

[1] For example, when the audit plans (internal and external) are available for review and when interim statements, preliminary announcements and the full annual report are near completion.

the finance director, the external audit lead partner and the head of internal audit.

Resources

2.12 The audit committee should be provided with sufficient resources to undertake its duties.

2.13 The audit committee should have access to the services of the company secretariat on all audit committee matters including: assisting the chairman in planning the audit committee's work, drawing up meeting agendas, maintenance of minutes, drafting of material about its activities for the annual report, collection and distribution of information and provision of any necessary practical support.

2.14 The company secretary should ensure that the audit committee receives information and papers in a timely manner to enable full and proper consideration to be given to the issues.

2.15 The board should make funds available to the audit committee to enable it to take independent legal, accounting or other advice when the audit committee reasonably believes it necessary to do so.

Remuneration

2.16 In addition to the remuneration paid to all non-executive directors, each company should consider the further remuneration that should be paid to members of the audit committee to recompense them for the additional responsibilities of membership. Consideration should be given to the time members are required to give to audit committee business, the skills they bring to bear and the onerous duties they take on, as well as the value of their work to the company. The level of remuneration paid to the members of the audit committee should take into account the level of fees paid to other members of the board. The chairman's responsibilities and time demands will generally be heavier than the other members of the audit committee and this should be reflected in his or her remuneration.

Skills, experience and training

2.17 It is desirable that the committee member whom the board considers to have recent and relevant financial experience should have a professional qualification from one of the professional accountancy bodies. The need for a degree of financial literacy among the other members will vary according to the nature of the company, but experience of corporate financial matters will normally be required. The availability of appropriate financial expertise will be particularly important where the company's activities involve specialised financial activities.

2.18 The company should provide an induction programme for new audit committee members. This should cover the role of the audit committee, including its terms of reference and expected time commitment by members; and an overview of the company's business, identifying the main business and financial dynamics and risks. It could also include meeting some of the company staff.

2.19 Training should also be provided to members of the audit committee on an ongoing and timely basis and should include an understanding of the principles of and developments in financial reporting and related company law. In appropriate cases, it may also include, for example, understanding financial statements, applicable accounting standards and recommended practice; the regulatory framework for the company's business; the role of internal and external auditing and risk management.

2.20 The induction programme and ongoing training may take various forms, including attendance at formal courses and conferences, internal company talks and seminars, and briefings by external advisers.

3. Relationship with the board

3.1 The role of the audit committee is for the board to decide and to the extent that the audit committee undertakes tasks on behalf of the board, the results should be reported to, and considered by, the board. In doing so it should identify any matters in respect of which it considers that action or improvement is needed, and make recommendations as to the steps to be taken.

3.2 The terms of reference should be tailored to the particular circumstances of the company.

3.3 The audit committee should review annually its terms of reference and its own effectiveness and recommend any necessary changes to the board.

3.4 The board should review the audit committee's effectiveness annually.

3.5 Where there is disagreement between the audit committee and the board, adequate time should be made available for discussion of the issue with a view to resolving the disagreement. Where any such disagreements cannot be resolved, the audit committee should have the right to report the issue to the shareholders as part of the report on its activities in the annual report.

4. Role and responsibilities

Financial reporting

4.1 The audit committee should review the significant financial reporting issues and judgements made in connection with the preparation of the company's financial statements, interim reports, preliminary announcements and related formal statements.

4.2　It is management's, not the audit committee's, responsibility to prepare complete and accurate financial statements and disclosures in accordance with financial reporting standards and applicable rules and regulations. However the audit committee should consider significant accounting policies, any changes to them and any significant estimates and judgements. The management should inform the audit committee of the methods used to account for significant or unusual transactions where the accounting treatment is open to different approaches. Taking into account the external auditor's view, the audit committee should consider whether the company has adopted appropriate accounting policies and, where necessary, made appropriate estimates and judgements. The audit committee should review the clarity and completeness of disclosures in the financial statements and consider whether the disclosures made are set properly in context.

4.3　Where, following its review, the audit committee is not satisfied with any aspect of the proposed financial reporting by the company, it shall report its views to the board.

4.4　The audit committee should review related information presented with the financial statements, including the operating and financial review, and corporate governance statements relating to the audit and to risk management. Similarly, where board approval is required for other statements containing financial information (for example, summary financial statements, significant financial returns to regulators and release of price sensitive information), whenever practicable (without being inconsistent with any requirement for prompt reporting under the Listing Rules) the audit committee should review such statements first.

Internal controls and risk management systems

4.5　The audit committee should review the company's internal financial controls (that is, the systems established to identify, assess, manage and monitor financial risks); and unless expressly addressed by a separate board risk committee comprised of independent directors or by the board itself, the company's internal control and risk management systems.

4.6　The company's management is responsible for the identification, assessment, management and monitoring of risk, for developing, operating and monitoring the system of internal control and for providing assurance to the board that it has done so. Except where the board or a risk committee is expressly responsible for reviewing the effectiveness of the internal control and risk management systems, the audit committee should receive reports from management on the effectiveness of the systems they have established and the conclusions of any testing carried out by internal and external auditors.

4.7　Except to the extent that this is expressly dealt with by the board or risk committee, the audit committee should review and approve the statements included in the annual report in relation to internal control and the management of risk.

Whistleblowing

4.8   The audit committee should review arrangements by which staff of the company may, in confidence, raise concerns about possible improprieties in matters of financial reporting or other matters. The audit committee's objective should be to ensure that arrangements are in place for the proportionate and independent investigation of such matters and for appropriate follow-up action.

The internal audit process

4.9   The audit committee should monitor and review the effectiveness of the company's internal audit function. Where there is no internal audit function, the audit committee should consider annually whether there is a need for an internal audit function and make a recommendation to the board, and the reasons for the absence of such a function should be explained in the relevant section of the annual report.

4.10   The audit committee should review and approve the internal audit function's remit, having regard to the complementary roles of the internal and external audit functions. The audit committee should ensure that the function has the necessary resources and access to information to enable it to fulfil its mandate, and is equipped to perform in accordance with appropriate professional standards for internal auditors.[2]

4.11   The audit committee should approve the appointment or termination of appointment of the head of internal audit.

4.12   In its review of the work of the internal audit function, the audit committee should, inter alia:

- ensure that the internal auditor has direct access to the board chairman and to the audit committee and is accountable to the audit committee;
- review and assess the annual internal audit work plan;
- receive a report on the results of the internal auditors' work on a periodic basis;
- review and monitor management's responsiveness to the internal auditor's findings and recommendations;
- meet with the head of internal audit at least once a year without the presence of management; and
- monitor and assess the role and effectiveness of the internal audit function in the overall context of the company's risk management system.

---

[2] Further guidance can be found in the Institute of Internal Auditors' Code of Ethics and the International Standards for the Professional Practice of Internal Auditing Standards.

The external audit process

4.13　The audit committee is the body responsible for overseeing the company's relations with the external auditor.

Appointment

4.14　The audit committee should have primary responsibility for making a recommendation on the appointment, reappointment and removal of the external auditors. If the board does not accept the audit committee's recommendation, it should include in the annual report, and in any papers recommending appointment or reappointment, a statement from the audit committee explaining its recommendation and should set out reasons why the board has taken a different position.

4.15　The audit committee's recommendation to the board should be based on the assessments referred to below. If the audit committee recommends considering the selection of possible new appointees as external auditors, it should oversee the selection process.

4.16　The audit committee should assess annually the qualification, expertise and resources, and independence (see below) of the external auditors and the effectiveness of the audit process. The assessment should cover all aspects of the audit service provided by the audit firm, and include obtaining a report on the audit firm's own internal quality control procedures.

4.17　If the external auditor resigns, the audit committee should investigate the issues giving rise to such resignation and consider whether any action is required.

Terms and remuneration

4.18　The audit committee should approve the terms of engagement and the remuneration to be paid to the external auditor in respect of audit services provided.

4.19　The audit committee should review and agree the engagement letter issued by the external auditor at the start of each audit, ensuring that it has been updated to reflect changes in circumstances arising since the previous year. The scope of the external audit should be reviewed by the audit committee with the auditor. If the audit committee is not satisfied as to its adequacy it should arrange for additional work to be undertaken.

4.20　The audit committee should satisfy itself that the level of fee payable in respect of the audit services provided is appropriate and that an effective audit can be conducted for such a fee.

Independence, including the provision of non-audit services

4.21 The audit committee should have procedures to ensure the independence and objectivity of the external auditor annually, taking into consideration relevant UK professional and regulatory requirements. This assessment should involve a consideration of all relationships between the company and the audit firm (including the provision of non-audit services). The audit committee should consider whether, taken as a whole and having regard to the views, as appropriate, of the external auditor, management and internal audit, those relationships appear to impair the auditor's judgement or independence.

4.22 The audit committee should seek reassurance that the auditors and their staff have no family, financial, employment, investment or business relationship with the company (other than in the normal course of business). The audit committee should seek from the audit firm, on an annual basis, information about policies and processes for maintaining independence and monitoring compliance with relevant requirements, including current requirements regarding the rotation of audit partners and staff.

4.23 The audit committee should agree with the board the company's policy for the employment of former employees of the external auditor, paying particular attention to the policy regarding former employees of the audit firm who were part of the audit team and moved directly to the company. This should be drafted taking into account the relevant ethical guidelines governing the accounting profession. The audit committee should monitor application of the policy, including the number of former employees of the external auditor currently employed in senior positions in the company, and consider whether in the light of this there has been any impairment, or appearance of impairment, of the auditor's judgement or independence in respect of the audit.

4.24 The audit committee should monitor the external audit firm's compliance with applicable United Kingdom ethical guidance relating to the rotation of audit partners, the level of fees that the company pays in proportion to the overall fee income of the firm, office and partner, and other related regulatory requirements.

4.25 The audit committee should develop and recommend to the board the company's policy in relation to the provision of non-audit services by the auditor. The audit committee's objective should be to ensure that the provision of such services does not impair the external auditor's independence or objectivity. In this context, the audit committee should consider:

- whether the skills and experience of the audit firm make it a suitable supplier of the non audit service;
- whether there are safeguards in place to ensure that there is no threat to objectivity and independence in the conduct of the audit resulting from the provision of such services by the external auditor;
- the nature of the non-audit services, the related fee levels and the fee levels individually and in aggregate relative to the audit fee; and
- the criteria which govern the compensation of the individuals performing the audit.

4.26 The audit committee should set and apply a formal policy specifying the types of non-audit work:

- from which the external auditors are excluded;
- for which the external auditors can be engaged without referral to the audit committee; and
- for which a case-by-case decision is necessary.

In addition, the policy may set fee limits generally or for particular classes of work.

4.27 In the third category, if it is not practicable to give approval to individual items in advance, it may be appropriate to give a general pre-approval for certain classes for work, subject to a fee limit determined by the audit committee and ratified by the board. The subsequent provision of any service by the auditor should be ratified at the next meeting of the audit committee.

4.28 In determining the policy, the audit committee should take into account relevant ethical guidance regarding the provision of non-audit services by the external audit firm, and in principle should not agree to the auditor providing a service if, having regard to the ethical guidance, the result is that:

- the external auditor audits its own firm's work;
- the external auditor makes management decisions for the company;
- a mutuality of interest is created; or
- the external auditor is put in the role of advocate for the company.

The audit committee should satisfy itself that any safeguards required by ethical guidance are implemented.

4.29 The annual report should explain to shareholders how, if the auditor provides non-audit services, auditor objectivity and independence is safeguarded.

Annual audit cycle

4.30 At the start of each annual audit cycle, the audit committee should ensure that appropriate plans are in place for the audit.

4.31 The audit committee should consider whether the auditor's overall work plan, including planned levels of materiality, and proposed resources to execute the audit plan appears consistent with the scope of the audit engagement, having regard also to the seniority, expertise and experience of the audit team.

4.32 The audit committee should review, with the external auditors, the findings of their work. In the course of its review, the audit committee should:

- discuss with the external auditor major issues that arose during the course of the audit and have subsequently been resolved and those issues that have been left unresolved;
- review key accounting and audit judgements; and
- review levels of errors identified during the audit, obtaining explanations from management and, where necessary the external auditors, as to why certain errors might remain unadjusted.

4.33 The audit committee should also review the audit representation letters before signature by management and give particular consideration to matters where representation has been requested that relate to non-standard issues[3]. The audit committee should consider whether the information provided is complete and appropriate based on its own knowledge.

4.34 As part of the ongoing monitoring process, the audit committee should review the management letter (or equivalent). The audit committee should review and monitor management's responsiveness to the external auditor's findings and recommendations.

4.35 At the end of the annual audit cycle, the audit committee should assess the effectiveness of the audit process. In the course of doing so, the audit committee should:

- review whether the auditor has met the agreed audit plan and understand the reasons for any changes, including changes in perceived audit risks and the work undertaken by the external auditors to address those risks;
- consider the robustness and perceptiveness of the auditors in their handling of the key accounting and audit judgements identified and in responding to questions from the audit committees, and in their commentary where appropriate on the systems of internal control;
- obtain feedback about the conduct of the audit from key people involved, e.g. the finance director and the head of internal audit; and
- review and monitor the content of the external auditor's management letter, in order to assess whether it is based on a good understanding of the company's business and establish whether recommendations have been acted upon and, if not, the reasons why they have not been acted upon.

5. Communication with shareholders

5.1 The terms of reference of the audit committee, including its role and the authority delegated to it by the board, should be made available. A separate section in the annual report should describe the work of the committee in discharging those responsibilities.

5.2 The audit committee section should include, inter alia:

- a summary of the role of the audit committee;
- the names and qualifications of all members of the audit committee during the period;
- the number of audit committee meetings;
- a report on the way the audit committee has discharged its responsibilities; and
- the explanation provided for in paragraph 4.29 above.

---

[3] Further guidance can be found in the Auditing Practices Board's Statement of Auditing Standard 440 "Management Representations".

5.3   The chairman of the audit committee should be present at the AGM to answer questions, through the chairman of the board, on the report on the audit committee's activities and matters within the scope of audit committee's responsibilities.

Appendix 16

Summary of the Principal Duties of the Remuneration Committee

(This guidance was also compiled with the assistance of ICSA which in 2010 was reviewing this and other precedents suggested by Higgs and reference should be made to the ICSA website for the up-to-date position *http://www.icsa.org.uk*.)

The Code provides that the remuneration committee should consist exclusively of independent non-executive directors and should comprise at least three or, in the case of smaller companies,[1] two such directors.

Duties

The Committee should:

- determine and agree with the board the framework or broad policy for the remuneration of the chief executive, the chairman of the company and such other members of the executive management as it is designated to consider[2]. At a minimum, the committee should have delegated responsibility for setting remuneration for all executive directors, the chairman and, to maintain and assure their independence, the company secretary. The remuneration of non-executive directors should be a matter for the chairman and executive members of the board. No director or manager should be involved in any decisions as to their own remuneration;

- determine targets for any performance-related pay schemes operated by the company;

- determine the policy for and scope of pension arrangements for each executive director;

---

[1] A smaller company is one that is below the FTSE 350 throughout the year immediately prior to the reporting year.
[2] Some companies require the remuneration committee to consider the packages of all executives at or above a specified level such as those reporting to a main board director whilst others require the committee to deal with all packages above a certain figure.

- ensure that contractual terms on termination, and any payments made, are fair to the individual and the company, that failure is not rewarded and that the duty to mitigate loss is fully recognised;[3]

- within the terms of the agreed policy, determine the total individual remuneration package of each executive director including, where appropriate, bonuses, incentive payments and share options;

- in determining such packages and arrangements, give due regard to the comments and recommendations of the Code as well as the UK Listing Authority's Listing Rules and associated guidance;

- be aware of and advise on any major changes in employee benefit structures throughout the company or group;

- agree the policy for authorising claims for expenses from the chief executive and chairman;

- ensure that provisions regarding disclosure of remuneration, including pensions, as set out in the Directors' Remuneration Report Regulations 2002 and the Code, are fulfilled;

- be exclusively responsible for establishing the selection criteria, selecting, appointing and setting the terms of reference for any remuneration consultants who advise the committee;

- report the frequency of, and attendance by members at, remuneration committee meetings in the annual report; and

- make the committee's terms of reference publicly available. These should set out the committee's delegated responsibilities and be reviewed and, where necessary, updated annually.

This guidance has been compiled with the assistance of ICSA who have kindly agreed to produce updated guidance on their website www.icsa.org.uk in the future.

---

[3] Remuneration committees should consider reviewing and agreeing a standard form of contract for its executive directors, and ensure that new appointees are offered and accept terms with the previously agreed level.

Appendix 17

Association of British Insurers—Guidelines on Executive Remuneration

The Guidelines together with the ABI/NAPF Joint Statement on Executive Contracts and Severance can be found on the IVIS website: *http://www.ivis.co.uk.*

Appendix 18

Types of Employee/Executive Schemes

1. All employee Schemes (HMRC approved)
Share save   Employees are granted options to acquire shares in the company at a price which can be set at a discount of up to 20 per cent on the current market value of the shares at that time. In parallel, employees enter into a savings contract of 3, 5 or 7 years which is designed to fund the exercise price at the end of the period, together with a tax-free bonus. The maximum savings amount is £250 per month. Employees are not obliged to exercise their share options at the end of the savings period and may cash-in their savings with interest. Bonus and interest rates are set by HMRC and adjusted from time to time. Provided the options are held for 3 years, or other "good-leaver" reasons exist, no income tax or national insurance contributions are payable on exercise. Any gain made on the subsequent sale of shares will be subject to capital gains tax.
Share incentive plans   These plans were introduced in 2000 to provide companies with flexibility to offer share ownership in a variety of ways. Participants can buy shares out of gross pay in the form of partnership shares (up to an annual maximum of £1,500). The company can provide matching shares for every partnership share purchased up to a maximum ratio of 2:1. The company can also provide free shares to participants (up to £3,000 per year) and these can be awarded subject to the satisfaction of performance conditions. All shares must be held within a UK trust. No income tax or national insurance contributions are payable provided the shares are held within the trust for a period of 5 years. Different tax treatment applies where shares are withdrawn before the 5 year period.

2. Executive Schemes	
Approved options	HMRC approved options may be granted to full time directors and employees. The maximum market value of shares under unexercised approved share options cannot exceed £30,000 (measured at the date of grant of the options). Performance targets may be attached to the exercise of options. The shares in the company must satisfy the legislative requirements, which can cause problems in the context of private companies and venture capital backed entities. Provided the options are held for 3 years, they may be exercised free of income tax and national insurance contributions. Any subsequent gain on the disposal of shares will be subject to capital gains tax.
Enterprise Management Incentive Options	EMI are again are a type of HMRC approved share option arrangement, but have more extensive tax benefits than their approved counter parts. Only companies with gross assets of less than £30 million can offer EMI options, and they must be performing a qualifying trade within the UK. Once again there are certain requirements in relation to the company's share capital which can limit the use of this type of scheme. Only companies (or if relevant a group of companies) with no more than 250 employees (or full time equivalents) are qualifying EMI companies. Participants may be granted options over a market value of shares (measured at the time of grant) of £120,000. For maximum tax efficiency it is necessary to set the exercise price at the market value of the shares at the time of grant. This being the case, any gain made on the exercise of the option is tax free (there are no minimum holding periods for the option prior to exercise). If options are offered at a price which is less than the market value of the options at the time of grant, the discount element is subject to income tax and national insurance contributions at the time of exercise. The market value of the shares can be agreed in advance with Shares and Assets Valuation division of HMRC. Capital gains tax is payable on the eventual disposal of the shares.
Unapproved Share Options	All gains from unapproved options are taxable as income in the hands of participants and are subject to national insurance contributions. As no HMRC approval is required, there are no restrictions on the types of shares which can be offered or on the maximum value that can be awarded to participants. However, as income tax rates have increased, unapproved options are becoming less attractive.

Performance Share Plans	Performance share plans are an alternative to share options and have emerged in response to the volatility of equity markets in recent years and changes to the way share benefits are accounted for. Unlike with share options, which require the payment of an exercise price, shares are usually awarded at no cost to the participant. They can therefore potentially continue to hold value when adverse market conditions prevail. Awards of shares are usually made subject to the satisfaction of performance conditions measurable over a period of 3 years. Participants are taxed to income and national insurance contributions on the value of the shares when they are received.
Deferred Bonus/Investment Plans	These plans are increasingly common in listed companies and are favoured by the institutions as they require the investment by participants of their own cash (often funded from annual bonus) or capital. Such contributions may be matched by the company at the end of a further performance period. Income tax and national insurance contributions will arise on the additional benefits provided by the company.
Joint Ownership Plans ("JOPs")	These plans allow employees to acquire a joint interest in shares in their company, subject to certain terms. The interest is usually jointly held with the trustees of an off-shore employee benefit trust. It is common for JOPs to be structured such that the trustee retains the value of the underlying shares as at the time of the joint interest is acquired, with the employee being entitled to all or a proportion of the growth in value of the shares over a specified period. The intention is that the growth in value of the shares attributable to employees will be charged to capital gains tax. As income tax rates for higher earners have increased, there has been increased interest in using JOP, although HMRC has indicated that it will conduct a review during 2010 of "geared growth" arrangements that deliver capital gains, rather than benefits taxed as income and it is possible that the current favourable tax treatment of JOPs may be challenged.

Employee Benefit Trusts ("EBT")	An EBT, also known as an Employee Share Ownership Trust, is a discretionary trust established by a company for the benefit of its employees. An offshore trust is an EBT with trustees resident outside the UK and where the general administration of the trust is carried on outside the UK. This has the advantage that the trustees are outside the scope of the charge to UK capital gains tax.
	EBTs can be used in support of other employee share schemes, for example to hold shares for distribution to employees on the exercise of options. They are particularly useful for companies operating plans that deliver free shares to employees.
	They can also form the basis of other types of longer-term remuneration planning for executives, particularly in the form of additional pension arrangements or investment programmes.

Appendix 19

The Model Code: Listing Rule 9 Annex 1[1]

Rules set by the Financial Services Authority for dealings by senior managers of and insider employees in Listed companies

Note: references to "the Act" are to the Companies Act 1985 and it is assumed that consequent upon implementation of the Companies Act 2006 the references will be updated,

Reference should be made to all the Listing Rules, which are published by the FSA on its website: *http://fsahandbook.info/FSA/html/handbook/D85*

Introduction

This code imposes restrictions on dealing in the *securities* of a *listed company* beyond those imposed by law. Its purpose is to ensure that *persons discharging managerial responsibilities* and employee insiders do not abuse, and do not place themselves under suspicion of abusing, *inside information* that they may be thought to have, especially in periods leading up to an announcement of the *company's* results.

Nothing in this code sanctions a breach of section 118 of the *Act* (Market abuse), the insider dealing provisions of the Criminal Justice Act or any other relevant legal or regulatory requirements.

Definitions

1   In this code the following definitions, in addition to those contained in the *listing rules*, apply unless the context requires otherwise:

    (a)   "*close period*" means:

        (i)   the period of 60 days immediately preceding the preliminary announcement of the *listed company's* annual results or, if shorter, the period from the end of the relevant financial year up to and including the time of announcement; and

        (ii)   if the *listed company* reports on a half-yearly basis, the period of 60 days immediately preceding the publication of the half-yearly report in accordance with LR 9.9.3 R or, if shorter the period from the end of the relevant financial period up to and including the time of such publication; or

[1] © The Financial Services Authority.

      (iii)   if the *listed company* reports on a quarterly basis, the period of 30 days immediately preceding the announcement of the quarterly results or, if shorter, the period from the end of the relevant financial period up to and including the time of the announcement;

(b)   *"connected person"* has the meaning given in section 96B (2) of the *Act* (Persons discharging managerial responsibilities and connected persons);

(c)   "dealing" includes:

      (i)   any acquisition or disposal of, or agreement to acquire or dispose of any of the *securities* of the *company*;

      (ii)   entering into a contract (including a contract for difference) the purpose of which is to secure a profit or avoid a loss by reference to fluctuations in the price of any of the *securities* of the *company*;

      (iii)   the grant, acceptance, acquisition, disposal, exercise or discharge of any option (whether for the call, or put or both) to acquire or dispose of any of the *securities* of the *company*;

      (iv)   entering into, or terminating, assigning or novating any stock lending agreement in respect of the *securities* of the *company*;

      (v)   using as security, or otherwise granting a charge, lien or other encumbrance over the *securities* of the *company*;

      (vi)   any transaction, including a transfer for nil consideration, or the exercise of any power or discretion effecting a change of ownership of a beneficial interest in the *securities* of the *company*; or

      (vii)   any other right or obligation, present or future, conditional or unconditional, to acquire or dispose of any *securities* of the *company*;

(d)   *"employee insider"* means an employee of the *company*, its parent undertaking or any member of its *group* whose name is required to be placed on an *insider list* in accordance with DR 2.8.1 R;

(e)   *"prohibited period"* means:

      (i)   any *close period*; or

      (ii)   any period when there exists any matter which constitutes *inside information* in relation to the *company*;

(f)   *"restricted person"* means a *person discharging managerial responsibilities* or employee insider; and

(g)   *"securities* of the *company"* means any publicly traded or quoted *securities* of the *company* or any member of its *group* or any securities that are convertible into such *securities*.

Dealings not subject to the provisions of this code

2   The following dealings are not subject to the provisions of this code:

    (a)   undertakings or elections to take up entitlements under a rights issue or other offer (including an offer of *securities* of the *company* in lieu of a cash dividend);

(b)   the take up of entitlements under a rights issue or other offer (including an offer of *securities* of the *company* in lieu of a cash dividend);

(c)   allowing entitlements to lapse under a rights issue or other offer (including an offer of *securities* of the *company* in lieu of a cash dividend);

(d)   the sale of sufficient entitlements nil-paid to take up the balance of the entitlements under a rights issue;

(e)   undertakings to accept, or the acceptance of, a takeover offer;

(f)   dealing where the beneficial interest in the relevant *security* of the *company* does not change;

(g)   transactions conducted between a *person discharging managerial responsibilities* and their spouse, civil partner, [1]child or step-child (as defined in section 346 of the Companies Act 1985);

(h)   transfers of *shares* arising out of the operation of an *employees' share scheme* into a savings scheme investing in *securities* of the *company* following:

    (i)   exercise of an option under a savings related share option scheme; or
    (ii)   release of *shares* from a profit sharing scheme;

(i)   with the exception of a disposal of *securities* of the *company* received by a restricted person as a participant, dealings in connection with an HM Revenue and Customs approved *employees' share scheme*, or any other *employees' share scheme* under which participation is extended on similar terms to those contained in an HM Revenue and Customs approved *employees' share scheme*, to all or most employees of the participating *companies* in that scheme;

(j)   the cancellation or surrender of an option under an *employees' share scheme*;

(k)   transfers of the *securities* of the *company* by an independent trustee of an *employees' share scheme* to a beneficiary who is not a restricted person;

(l)   transfers of *securities* of the *company* already held by means of a matched sale and purchase into a saving scheme or into a pension scheme in which the restricted person is a participant or beneficiary;

(m)   an investment by a restricted person in a scheme or arrangement where the assets of the scheme (other than a scheme investing only in the *securities* of the *company*) or arrangement are invested at the discretion of a third party;

(n)   a dealing by a restricted person in the units of an authorised unit trust or in *shares* in an *open-ended investment company*; and

(o)   bona fide gifts to a restricted person by a third party.

Dealing by restricted persons

3   A restricted person must not deal in any *securities* of the *company* without obtaining clearance to deal in advance in accordance with paragraph 4 of this code.

Clearance to deal

4   (a)   A *director* (other than the chairman or chief executive) or company secretary must not deal in any *securities* of the *company* without first notifying the chairman (or a *director* designated by the board for this purpose) and receiving clearance to deal from him.

     (b)   The chairman must not deal in any *securities* of the *company* without first notifying the chief executive and receiving clearance to deal from him.

     (c)   The chief executive must not deal in any *securities* of the *company* without first notifying the chairman and receiving clearance to deal from him.

     (d)   If the role of chairman and chief executive are combined, that *person* must not deal in any *securities* of the *company* without first notifying the board and receiving clearance to deal from the board.

     (e)   *Persons discharging managerial responsibilities* (who are not *directors*) and employee insiders must not deal in any *securities* of the *company* without first notifying the company secretary or a designated *director* and receiving clearance to deal from him.

5   A response to a request for clearance to deal must be given to the relevant restricted person within five *business days* of the request being made.

6   The *company* must maintain a record of the response to any dealing request made by a restricted person and of any clearance given. A copy of the response and clearance (if any) must be given to the restricted person concerned.

7   A restricted person who is given clearance to deal in accordance with paragraph 4 must deal as soon as possible and in any event within two *business days* of clearance being received.

Circumstances for refusal

8   A restricted person must not be given clearance to deal in any *securities* of the *company*:

     (a)   during a prohibited period; or

     (b)   on considerations of a short term nature. An investment with a maturity of one year or less will always be considered to be of a short term nature.

Dealings permitted during a prohibited period

Dealing in exceptional circumstances

9   A restricted person, who is not in possession of *inside information* in relation to the *company*, may be given clearance to deal if he is in severe

financial difficulty or there are other exceptional circumstances. Clearance may be given for such a *person* to sell (but not purchase) *securities* of the *company* when he would otherwise be prohibited by this code from doing so. The determination of whether the *person* in question is in severe financial difficulty or whether there are other exceptional circumstances can only be made by the *director* designated for this purpose.

10   A *person* may be in severe financial difficulty if he has a pressing financial commitment that cannot be satisfied otherwise than by selling the relevant *securities* of the *company*. A liability of such a *person* to pay tax would not normally constitute severe financial difficulty unless the *person* has no other means of satisfying the liability. A circumstance will be considered exceptional if the *person* in question is required by a court order to transfer or sell the *securities* of the *company* or there is some other overriding legal requirement for him to do so.

11   The *FSA* should be consulted at an early stage regarding any application by a restricted person to deal in exceptional circumstances.

Awards of securities and options

12   The grant of options by the board of *directors* under an *employees' share scheme* to individuals who are not restricted persons may be permitted during a prohibited period if such grant could not reasonably be made at another time and failure to make the grant would be likely to indicate that the *company* was in a prohibited period.

13   The award by the *company* of *securities*, the grant of options and the grant of rights (or other interests) to acquire *securities* of the *company* to restricted persons is permitted in a prohibited period if:

(a)   the award or grant is made under the terms of an *employees' share scheme* and the scheme was not introduced or amended during the relevant prohibited period; and

(b)   either:

    (i)   the terms of such *employees' share scheme* set out the timing of the award or grant and such terms have either previously been approved by shareholders or summarised or described in a document sent to shareholders, or

    (ii)   the timing of the award or grant is in accordance with the timing of previous awards or grants under the scheme; and

(c)   the terms of the *employees' share scheme* set out the amount or value of the award or grant or the basis on which the amount or value of the award or grant is calculated and do not allow the exercise of discretion; and

(d)   the failure to make the award or grant would be likely to indicate that the *company* is in a prohibited period.

Exercise of options

14   Where a *company* has been in an exceptionally long prohibited period or the *company* has had a number of consecutive prohibited periods, clearance may be given to allow the exercise of an option or right under an *employees' share scheme*, or the conversion of a convertible security, where the final date for the exercise of such option or right, or conversion of such security, falls during a prohibited period and the restricted person could not reasonably have been expected to exercise it at a time when he was free to deal.

15   Where the exercise or conversion is permitted pursuant to paragraph 14, clearance may not be given for the sale of the *securities* of the *company* acquired pursuant to such exercise or conversion including the sale of sufficient *securities* of the *company* to fund the costs of the exercise or conversion and/or any tax liability arising from the exercise or conversion unless a binding undertaking to do so was entered into when the *company* was not in a prohibited period.

Qualification shares

16   Clearance may be given to allow a *director* to acquire qualification *shares* where, under the *company's constitution*, the final date for acquiring such *shares* falls during a prohibited period and the *director* could not reasonably have been expected to acquire those shares at another time.

Saving schemes

17   A restricted person may enter into a scheme under which only the *securities* of the *company* are purchased pursuant to a regular standing order or direct debit or by regular deduction from the *person*'s salary, or where such *securities* are acquired by way of a standing election to re-invest dividends or other distributions received, or are acquired as part payment of the *person*'s remuneration without regard to the provisions of this code, if the following provisions are complied with:

(a)   the restricted person does not enter into the scheme during a prohibited period, unless the scheme involves the part payment of remuneration in the form of *securities* of the *company* and is entered into upon the commencement of the *person*'s employment or in the case of a non-executive *director* his appointment to the board;

(b)   the restricted person does not carry out the purchase of the *securities* of the *company* under the scheme during a prohibited period, unless the restricted person entered into the scheme at a time when the *company* was not in a prohibited period and that person is irrevocably bound under the terms of the scheme to carry out a purchase of *securities* of the *company* (which may include the first purchase under the scheme) at a fixed point in time which falls in a prohibited period;

(c)   the restricted person does not cancel or vary the terms of his participation, or carry out sales of *securities* of the *company* within the scheme during a prohibited period; and

(d)   before entering into the scheme, cancelling the scheme or varying the terms of his participation or carrying out sales of the *securities* of the *company* within the scheme, the restricted person obtains clearance in accordance with paragraph 4.

Acting as a trustee

18   Where a restricted person is acting as a trustee, dealing in the *securities* of the *company* by that trust is permitted during a prohibited period where:

(a)   the restricted person is not a beneficiary of the trust; and

(b)   the decision to deal is taken by the other trustees or by investment managers on behalf of the trustees independently of the restricted person.

19   The other trustees or investment managers acting on behalf of the trustees can be assumed to have acted independently where the decision to deal:

(a)   was taken without consultation with, or other involvement of, the restricted person; or

(b)   was delegated to a committee of which the restricted person is not a member.

Dealing by connected persons and investment managers

20   A *person discharging managerial responsibilities* must take reasonable steps to prevent any dealings by or on behalf of any *connected person* of his in any *securities* of the *company* on considerations of a short term nature.

21   A *person discharging managerial responsibilities* must seek to prohibit any dealings in the *securities* of the *company* during a close period:

(a)   by or on behalf of any *connected person* of his; or

(b)   by an investment manager on his behalf or on behalf of any *person* connected with him where either he or any *person* connected has funds under management with that investment fund manager, whether or not discretionary (save as provided by paragraphs 17 and 18).

22   A *person discharging managerial responsibilities* must advise all of his *connected persons* and investment managers acting on his behalf:

(a)   of the name of the *listed company* within which he is a *person discharging managerial responsibilities*;

(b)   of the *close periods* during which they cannot deal in the *securities* of the *company*; and

(c)   that they must advise the *listed company* immediately after they have dealt in *securities* of the *company*.

Appendix 20

Auditors' Liability: The Caparo Case

(Appendix 6 to the Cadbury Report)

Outline of the case

1. Caparo Industries plc owned shares in a public company, Fidelity plc, whose accounts for the year ended March 31, 1984 showed profits far short of the predicted figure which resulted in a dramatic drop in the quoted share price. After receipt of the audited accounts for the year ended March 31, 1984 Caparo purchased more shares in Fidelity and later that year made a successful takeover bid for the company. Following the takeover, Caparo brought an action against the auditors of the company, alleging that Fidelity's accounts were inaccurate and misleading in that they showed a pre-tax profit of {GBP}1.2m when in fact there had been a loss of over {GBP}0.4m, that the auditors had been negligent in auditing the accounts, that Caparo had purchased further shares and made their takeover bid in reliance of the audited accounts, that they had thereby suffered loss, and the auditors owed them a duty of care to prevent that loss either as potential bidders for Fidelity because they ought to have foreseen that the 1984 results made Fidelity vulnerable to a takeover bid from one quarter or another, or as an existing shareholder of Fidelity interested in buying more shares.

2. The case went to the House of Lords which held that the auditors did not owe Caparo a duty of care to prevent the loss suffered in consequence of purchasing additional shares, either as potential investors or as existing shareholders (*Caparo Industries plc v. Dickman and others* [1990] 2 A.C. 605).

Basis for the decision

3. In broad terms, the House of Lords considered the issue on the following basis:

   (a) If A makes a negligent statement, he may (independently of any contractual or fiduciary relationship) be liable to B if B relies on that statement and thereby suffers loss, provided A is under duty of care to B to avoid or prevent that loss.

795

(b)   Such a duty of care will exist where a three-pronged test of foreseeability, proximity, and fairness is satisfied:

      (i)   **foreseeability:** when making the statement, A should reasonably have foreseen that B might suffer that loss if the statement proved to be wrong;

      (ii)   **proximity:** there must, in relation to the statement, be a sufficient relationship between A and B. Such a relationship will exist if, at the time he made the statement, A knew:

- that the statement would be communicated to B, either as an individual or as a member of an identifiable class;
- that the statement would be so communicated specifically in connection with a particular transaction, or transaction of a particular kind; and
- that B would be very likely to rely on it in deciding whether or not to enter into that transaction or a transaction of that kind;

      (iii)   **fairness:** the Court must consider it to be fair, just and reasonable that the law should impose the specified duty of care on A for the benefit of B.

(c)   In suggesting this three-pronged test, the House of Lords nevertheless recognised that there would often be an overlap between the three elements, that the elements, themselves were "labels" rather than precisely applicable definitions, and that there was a necessary element of pragmatism in applying the test to any given set of circumstances.

(d)   So far as concerns audited accounts, whilst it cannot fairly be said that the purpose of the statutory provisions as to publication is solely to assist members and debenture holders to an informed supervision and appraisal of the stewardship of the company's directors, that is nevertheless the original, central and primary purpose of these provisions.

4.   Caparo's case foundered as a matter of law because in the view of the House of Lords the necessary proximity did not exist. A relationship of proximity could not be deduced between an auditor and a member of the public who relied on the accounts to buy shares in the company when to do so would give rise to an unlimited liability on the part of the auditor. Nor could a relationship of proximity be deduced between an auditor and an individual shareholder in the company in relation to further purchases of shares in the company by that shareholder, since an individual shareholder stood in no different position from any other investing member of the public to whom the auditor owed no duty, and the auditors' statutory duty to prepare accounts was owed to the body of shareholders as whole, to enable them as a body to exercise informed control of the company and not to enable individual shareholders to buy shares with a view to profit.

Principles established

5.   The case has established that in the absence of special features, auditors are not regarded as owing a duty of care to prevent loss to anyone relying on their

report except (a) the company, and (b) the shareholders as a body. In the absence of special features, no duty of care is owed in particular to individual shareholders, subscribers to new shares, purchasers or intended purchasers of shares from third parties including those conducting takeover bids, bankers or other lenders to the company, or persons doing business with the company.

Arguments for and against extending auditors' duty of care

6.   Some of the arguments that have been expressed for and against extending auditors' duty of care to individual shareholders, purchasers of shares, and possible other third parties are as follows:

Arguments for extension

(a)   Third parties, to the knowledge of all, in fact rely to a considerable extent on the integrity of the audited accounts—if legal liability is not imposed there is an allegedly justified expectation gap.

(b)   Professional men are paid—they should therefore be accountable in a wide sense.

(c)   The auditors' liability to the company may provide an effective remedy where the auditors have negligently failed to discover fraud or theft from the company—but in general not where, for example, the directors have been overvaluing assets or otherwise inflating profits. In any case, the company's loss may be less than that suffered in aggregate by the shareholders.

(d)   The case is bad publicity for the accounting profession and has prompted the perception that, for example:

    (i)   auditors are answerable to no-one;

    (ii)   the requirement for the auditors to exercise due care and skill has been lessened;

    (iii) having accounts audited is of little or no benefit.

Arguments against extension

(a)   To hold the auditors liable to all and sundry for any purpose for which they may choose to rely on the auditors' statement would result, in the classic words of Cardozo C.J., in "liability in an indeterminate amount for an indeterminate time to an indeterminate class".

(b)   Quite apart from the difficulty of defining the extent of liability, there would be endless problems in determining where liability was due to reliance on audited accounts and where not.

(c)   The principal purpose of the statutory provisions for audit and the publication of the accounts is to assist shareholders and debenture holders collectively in monitoring the stewardship of the directors—there is no basis for assuming that the legislature had a secondary purpose to provide protection for the public at large and investors in particular.

(d) The potential magnitude of the liability is out of all proportion to the size of the audit fee.

(e) The primary responsibility for producing true and fair accounts lies with the directors—and it would be unfair if, in practice, the auditors (and their insurers) had to foot the bill on their own, or substantially on their own.

(f) It is, in practice, difficult for auditors to obtain adequate insurance cover.

(g) The third parties have themselves paid nothing to the auditors—why should they be able to call the auditors to account?

(h) The scope and cost of audit work might rapidly become uneconomic if wide-scope liability to all users of accounts were accepted.

The Committee's view

7. The Committee recognises that the House of Lords judgment involved a careful and complex balancing of interests—not just those of users of accounts and auditors, but more generally the interests of professional people and those who suffer loss as a result of professional negligence, and the public interest in having a viable and fair system. The principal practical concerns which lay behind the conclusions reached by the House of Lords included the size of auditors' potential liabilities, the difficulties in defining wider liability in any fair yet realistic way, and the likely difficulties in establishing whether third party losses were due to reliance on the accounts. Bearing in mind the wide range of users of accounts, the Committee is unable to see a practical and equitable way in which the House of Lords could have broadened the boundaries of auditors' legal duty of care without giving rise to a liability that was indeterminate in scope, time and amount, nor does it consider that the decision should be altered by statutory intervention at the present time.

Possible ways of extending duty of care without creating open-ended liability

8. If, notwithstanding the Committee's recommendation, it were decided to change the principles laid down by *Caparo,* it would be necessary to amend the law by statute to impose a liability on auditors to compensate accounts users in general, or specified classes of user such as investors, who suffer loss by relying on negligently audited accounts. Those proposing such a change have suggested as a *quid pro quo* that auditors' liability should be proportionate only, or that it should be limited. There are, however, serious objections in both cases:

(a) **Proportionate liability only:** it is proposed that the law should be changed so that those who together cause damage should not, as at present, each be liable for the whole of the loss, but should each only assume a reasonable proportion of the loss. However, there are considerable technical difficulties in this proposition, not least because not all the potential defendants may be before the court. The proposition would also need to be considered in relation to the law as a whole, and there is no particular reason for singling out the auditors for special treatment. It should in any event be recognised that even with liability limited to a proportion of the claimant's loss, the amount payable by the auditors could still put them out of business.

(b) **Limited liability:** it is proposed that the law should be changed to permit auditors to limit their liabilities by contract with the relevant company. Apart from any practical problems in reaching agreement with the company, there is a fundamental legal problem in establishing a basis on which an auditor might found a limitation of his liability to those with whom he had no contractual tie. Another possibility would be to impose a statutory "cap" on an auditor's liability, either fixed for all auditors or related to variables such as the size of audit fee or the size of audit firm. However this suggestion would be an unsatisfactory compromise. When the cap operated it would prevent plaintiffs from recovering the full loss suffered, whilst if the auditors faced more claims in relation to one year than their insurance provided cover for, they might still be put out of business and not all the successful plaintiffs would be able to recover the amount of the cap.

Appendix 21

Association of British Insurers: Disclosure Guidelines on Socially-Responsible Investment

See the IVIS website at *www.ivis.co.uk/responsibleinvestmentdisclosure.aspx*.

Appendix 22

Institutional Shareholders' Committee: The Responsibilities of Institutional Shareholders— Statement of Principles—The Stewardship Code

The Stewardship Code replaced in June 2010 the ISC Statement of Principles and also Schedule C (Engagement Principles for Institutional Shareholders) in the UK Corporate Governance Code. The author has taken the view that it is of more help to readers if they are directed to the FRC and ISC websites for the whole document.
FRC website: *http://www.frc.org.uk.*
ISC website: *http://institutionalshareholderscommittee.org.uk.*

Index